*Ciné-Ethnography*

VISIBLE EVIDENCE

Edited by Michael Renov, Faye Ginsburg, and Jane Gaines

VISIBLE EVIDENCE, VOLUME 13

# Ciné-Ethnography

Jean Rouch

Edited and Translated by Steven Feld

 University of Minnesota Press

Minneapolis

London

Publication information for previously published material reprinted in this book is on pages 390–92.

All photographs are courtesy of Jean Rouch and the Comité du Film Ethnographique, Musée de l'Homme, Paris.

Published by the University of Minnesota Press
111 Third Avenue South, Suite 290
Minneapolis, MN 55401-2520
http://www.upress.umn.edu

Library of Congress Cataloging-in-Publication Data

Rouch, Jean.
    Ciné-ethnography / Jean Rouch ; edited and translated by Steven Feld.
        p.    cm. — (Visible evidence ; v. 13)
    Essays and interviews translated from French.
    Includes bibliographical references and index.
    ISBN 0-8166-4103-X (HC : alk. paper) — ISBN 0-8166-4104-8 (PB : alk. paper)
    1. Motion pictures in ethnology.   2. Rouch, Jean.   3. Ethnology—France.
    I. Feld, Steven.   II. Title.   III. Series.
    GN347.R57 2003
    305.8—dc21

                                                              2002013793

Printed in the United States of America on acid-free paper

The University of Minnesota is an equal-opportunity educator and employer.

12 11 10 09 08 07 06 05 04 03            10 9 8 7 6 5 4 3 2 1

# Contents

## Acknowledgments

Since 1972 I've enjoyed a number of conversations about Jean Rouch's work and how and why it matters for cinema and anthropology. For these I'd like to thank Emilie de Brigard, James Clifford, Jean-Paul Colleyn, Manthia Diawara, Barry Dornfeld, Faye Ginsburg, Karl Heider, Jay Ruby, Paul Stoller, Lucien Taylor, the late Annette Weiner, Carroll Williams, Joan S. Willams, and the late Sol Worth.

Jay and Sol deserve a very special thanks for encouraging and enthusiastically publishing my original translations of Rouch's work in the journals they edited, as does Faye, for encouraging publication of this collection in the Visible Evidence series.

I am neither a professional translator nor a fluent French speaker, much less an anthropologist of West Africa. Thus the translations would not have been possible without a great deal of aid. The early ones benefited from the help of Marielle Delorme, and the later ones from the collaboration of Shari Robertson, Anny Ewing, and Catherine Maziére. The historical, ethnographic, and linguistic knowledge of James Clifford, Jean-Paul Colleyn, and Paul Stoller was also invaluable.

For help assembling the collection, I am grateful to Jay Ruby, who prepared the collection of photographs; to Françoise Foucault of the Comité du Film Ethnographique, who coordinated texts, images, and permissions; and especially to Ruti Talmor and Jennifer Soroko, who tackled numerous editorial details with skill and patience.

Over the years, Jean Rouch has always helped unpack his mysteries, even when producing new and bigger ones and acknowledging that he prefers ideas to fall more toward the poetic side of complication than the precise side of determination. In a spirit of warm friendship and solidarity with this mad master and pale fox (or is it mad fox and pale master? All, no doubt), it has been a great pleasure to translate and edit this collection of his work.

S. F.

STEVEN FELD

## *Editor's Introduction*

▶

### Chronicle of a Book

I first encountered Jean Rouch's films in 1972, at a National Science Foundation Summer Institute in Visual Anthropology organized by Jay Ruby, Sol Worth, Karl Heider, and Carroll Williams. I had just finished my first year of graduate school in African studies and anthropology, and I was deeply moved by the complex layers of the Africa I saw represented in *Les maîtres fous, The Lion Hunters,* and *Jaguar.* I wanted to know more. If these were the kinds of films and ethnography Rouch had done in the 1950s and 1960s, what could he possibly be doing in the 1970s? I decided to devote a year to filmic anthropology.

That's how I ultimately arrived at the Musée de l'Homme in January 1974. As promised for the season, the Parisian light was as crisp as the air. By instant contrast, the dark cases and heavy displays I encountered at the Musée de l'Homme seemed of a piece with the ones I knew well from New York's American Museum of Natural History, where I'd spent so much time in the African collection as an undergraduate. There I had learned that museums were places where virtually every corner, closet, and passageway held important things, which must be why I was hardly surprised to find the Comité du Film Ethnographique located on a converted fire escape.

"Yes! Yes! Your passport is stamped!" Punctuated by a grin, those were Rouch's first words to me, overlapping my clumsy attempt to say something formal in French when Marielle Delorme first introduced us on the stairwell. Before I could recover, Rouch disappeared, and Françoise Foucault ushered me away to the editing room down the hall, with cans of film to occupy me for the rest of the afternoon. With that I learned how much Rouch was on the move. Exuberant and enigmatic, he could be quite difficult to pin down for even a few moments. But during the following semester I attended his Saturday morning classes at the Cinémathèque, and the Thursday film séances he convened in the Musée de l'Homme's screening room. And thanks to the familiar generosity of Marielle and Françoise, I got to spend a great many afternoons, whenever the editing table was free, looking shot by shot at numerous films from the Comité's collection.

I came home saturated with French ethnographic film, especially cinema about and occasionally by Africans, and with a notebook crammed with sketches and details about the hundred films I'd seen. These included some thirty films by Rouch. I had studied most of them closely, from his earliest films, made silently with a twenty-five-second-per-shot spring-wound camera, to the later ones made in ten-minute-long sync-sound shot sequences.

I also returned with a rough translation of an essay Rouch had recently written. When I showed it to Sol Worth at the Annenberg School of Communication, he instantly suggested that *Studies in the Anthropology of Visual Communication,* the new journal he was editing with Jay Ruby, would be a perfect venue to publish translations of Rouch's key essays on ethnographic cinema. So "The Camera and Man" appeared in the journal's first issue in 1974, followed by "The Situation and Tendencies of the Cinema in Africa," in two installments in 1975.

Then, by way of detour from Africa and film, I ended up in Papua New Guinea. When I returned home in fall 1977, I hardly had time for culture shock; the real shock that greeted me was the news of Sol Worth's recent death. Within days I met up with Rouch again; he was appearing as the guest of honor at the first Margaret Mead Film Festival at the American Museum of Natural History. At the reunion, it was Jay Ruby who insisted that we continue the plan of publishing Rouch's key essays in the journal, and so "On the Vicissitudes of the Self" appeared in 1978. Jay was also excited by the possibility of publishing *Chronique d'un été (Chronicle of a Summer),* the innovative and provocative book about the film that Rouch produced with Edgar Morin. I drafted translations of several of the sections, but it wasn't until 1985 that the project was finally realized as an entire issue of *Studies in Visual Communication,* the successor journal that Jay edited with Larry Gross.

A few years later, it was again Jay who took the initiative, as editor of the journal *Visual Anthropology,* with the idea of a Festschrift issue in Rouch's honor. When it appeared, in 1989, as both a complete journal issue and a book, it featured my translation from the longest retrospective interview Rouch had given about his work. It also included an expanded edition of the complete filmography, translated from the 1981 catalog *Jean Rouch: Une rétrospective,* still the most comprehensive work on Rouch by Rouch.

During all this time, many of my connections with film and Africa slipped away, overcome by work in music and Papua New Guinea. In fact, I wasn't in much contact with Rouch or his films from the late 1980s through the late 1990s. But in April 2000, Faye Ginsburg, director of New York University's Center for Media, Culture, and History, produced Rouch 2000, a weeklong film retrospective at NYU. I was inspired by a reunion, after twelve years, with Jean Rouch. And the chance to see some of the films again with Françoise Foucault, Jay Ruby, and other friends led to several enjoyable dialogues. But what excited me most was seeing a new generation of film and anthropology students respond so deeply to the stimulus of Rouch's cinema. And with that it seemed obvious that despite the continued annoyance of having so few of Rouch's films in North American distribution, the time was right to publish a Rouch dossier to bring together all of my out-of-print translations with some other key documents.

At the NYU retrospective, Rouch himself was in mourning for his friend and colleague Germaine Dieterlen. In her honor and memory, he devoted the first night of the festival to a screening of *Le Dama d'Ambara,* their 1974 film collaboration about Dogon funerary rituals. That suggested adding an additional essay, the one he had written in 1978 as the introduction to a collection in Dieterlen's honor. Rouch was most pleased by the thought. With the book plan then in place, a translation was drafted, the filmography updated, all the translations reviewed, and the manuscript assembled.

It should be clear now that the idea all along has been for this to be a book in Rouch's voice. The varied dates and contexts of the essays and interviews certainly make it possible for his stories to emerge. From his personal biography to his intellectual history, from his convictions and methods to his politics and aesthetics, the texts map his passion for uniting cinema and ethnography, for linking documentary and drama, for bridging empirical science and surrealist dreams.

Given the breadth and depth of Rouch's works included here, not to mention the existence of several recent studies and films about him—Paul Stoller's *The Cinematic Griot: The Ethnography of Jean Rouch* (1992); the *Cinema of Jean Rouch* Festschrift issue of *Visual Anthropology* (1989); Manthia Diawara's film *Rouch in Reverse* (1995); Steef Meyknecht, Dirk Nijland, and Joost Verhey's film *Rouch's Gang* (1993)—a long introduction may seem quite unnecessary. Nonetheless, I'd like to review some of the basic biographical matters and themes in Rouch's work, and cite some of the relevant historical and parallel texts for the benefit of those approaching this remarkable career and array of films for the first time.

## Jean Rouch's Ciné-Ethnographic Path

Jean Rouch was born in Paris in 1917. After studies in mathematics and engineering, he went to West Africa during the war, in 1941, as a bridge and causeway engineer. He became interested in local cultures during this time and, when he found himself in Dakar, Senegal, began spending time at the library of l'Institut Français d'Afrique Noir (IFAN), where Théodore Monod encouraged him to study African ethnography and write up his observations. When Rouch returned to France, he decided to take a doctorate in anthropology under the supervision of Marcel Griaule. In 1946 Rouch returned to Africa with some friends from his engineering days; they spent nine months descending the Niger River by canoe. Before his return, Rouch purchased a wartime Bell and Howell 16 mm spring-wound camera at a flea market in Paris. During his voyage he shot black-and-white footage and continued taking ethnographic notes (see "The Mad Fox and the Pale Master" and "A Life on the Edge of Film and Anthropology," in this volume, for Rouch's narratives of this early history).

This trip marked the real beginnings of Rouch's intertwined career as an ethnographer and a filmmaker. With his notes, he completed a dissertation in anthropology (Rouch 1953). With his films, he was able to do much less. Sixteen millimeter was still an amateur medium, editing equipment was not available, and there was no way to make prints for distribution. Rouch used his films to experiment with editing and screened them publicly only at lectures where he would speak an on-the-spot commentary for a sound track. Actualités Françaises became interested in the material, and some of it was blown up to 35 mm.

Shortly thereafter Rouch returned to Niger to do more ethnography and film, this time in color. He made three short films in the course of his work: *La circoncision, Les magiciens de Wanzerbé,* and *Initiation a la danse des possédés.* When these films were completed (a term used loosely, as 16 mm editing was still crudely done with a projector and hand splices, and sound tracks were unwedded to film), Rouch got his first break, a showing at the Festival of Biarritz. During the screening to an audience that included directors such as Clement and Cocteau, Rouch was shocked to realize that the films held the attention of sophisticated viewers. Later, the three shorts were reedited into a single film, *Les fils de l'eau;* it was the first color film blown up from 16 mm to 35 mm in France.

During the late 1940s and early 1950s, Rouch continued his ethnographic trips, working with the Sorko and Songhay peoples of Niger. He

began to concentrate on the topics of migration and religion and collaborated with Roger Rosfelder on several short films on these themes.

At the beginning of the 1950s, Rouch became one of the first to experiment extensively with the early "portable" field sound recorders (again, a
loose notion, as they were tremendously heavy and difficult to use compared to technologies from the 1960s onward). He recorded West African
music and also recorded sounds at the same time as images, for pseudo-
synchronous filming, as no method of synchronization existed then for
portable equipment. Also during this period, Rouch made his first film
among the Dogon in Mali (a group he had not studied but who, since 1931,
had been the subject of many periods of research by Marcel Griaule and
his collaborators).

Both the endorsement of Griaule and growing recognition of Rouch's
own ethnographic and film work in Niger helped establish Rouch and
ethnographic film in France. In 1952, with the backing of André Leroi-
Gourhan, the Comité du Film Ethnographique was formed as a department at the Musée de l'Homme, with Rouch as secretary-general. Shortly
afterward, at the Fourth International Congress of Anthropological and
Ethnological Sciences in Vienna, Rouch was instrumental in the formation
of the Comité International du Film Ethnographique et Sociologique
(CIFES), an organization devoted to the production, compilation, conservation, and distribution of ethnographic films on an international scale.

In the mid-1950s, Rouch's continuing research on migrations led him
to follow Songhay men from Niger to large West African cities such as
Accra and Abidjan. In Ghana he made the films *Madame l'eau* and *Les
maîtres fous* and also began filming *Jaguar* about these migrations.

*Les maîtres fous* was his first departure from purely descriptive cinema into a more synthetic approach to event structures. Having observed a
ritual several times, he realized that he could break down the crucial aspects and approach them as theatrical narrative. Using montage to create
contexting boundaries and making the most of the technical limitation of
twenty-five-second shots (he was still using a spring-wound 16 mm camera), Rouch was able to make a short film with more explicative depth and
synthesis than his previous ethnographic studies.

*Les maîtres fous* is about the Hauka, a possession cult among the
Songhay that reached full expression in Ghana, where migrants from Niger
brought it. The film shows cult members working at menial tasks in the
city during the week, then in possession trances during the weekend, then
back in the city context. Hauka members become possessed by colonial
and technological masters. Because the actual ritual depicted in the film is

violent, and is disturbing to many viewers, Rouch was urged by friends to destroy the film; he refused on the grounds that the participants in the film had themselves requested it be made.[1]

During the late 1950s, Rouch devoted the major part of his field-work to research on Songhay religion; this culminated in the completion of his *doctorat d'état,* published as *La religion et la magie Songhay* (Rouch 1960a, 1989). This remains his major ethnographic publication, of enduring value both in relation to the films that he has made about Songhay religion and cosmology and in relation to continuing studies of Songhay society and magic.[2]

While Rouch continued to make shorter film studies of topics close to his research, colonial Africa was increasingly turbulent in the late 1950s. This led him to experiment with more overtly dramatic forms, choosing subject matter that, like *Les maîtres fous,* could have a more direct impact on a wide audience.

The first of these, *Moi, un Noir,* shows a group of Africans in an Ivory Coast slum, Treichville, playing out a psychodrama about themselves. It was filmed silently, and then Rouch asked the principal player, Oumarou Ganda, to improvise a narration as he saw a rough cut of the film. Ganda's commentary consists of referencing his actions to the war in Indochina, from which he returned bitter and sad. This device made the film very dreamlike and confused many audiences. Rouch himself felt that the success of the film was in its deliberate attempt to be subjective and let Africans portray their own imaginary world and their own fantasies while being filmed in the context of their actual situation. The movements back and forth from the immediate reality of the players to their dramatic fantasies were taken by some to indicate that *Moi, un Noir* was the first film that actually gave a voice to Africans and allowed them to present the realities of their world. Indeed, its protagonist, Oumarou Ganda, went on to become a filmmaker. Nonetheless, the film was censored in Ivory Coast, and Rouch's defense that "fiction is the only way to penetrate reality" was slow to gain sympathetic response, either from anthropologists or from African viewers.[3]

The next film that emerged in the context of both Rouch's interest in psychodrama and his desire to chronicle the intercultural politics of African modernities was *La pyramide humaine.* This film was an attempt to develop the method of improvised ethnographic fiction. It was acted out by a group of people who were given a general story line by Rouch, who in turn catalyzed the action by filming and interrupting the filming according to how he felt the group was progressing.

The actors are two sets of high school students from Abidjan, one group white, the other group black. They had previously not socialized. Rouch proposed that they collectively act out a story on the topic of what would happen if they all newly met each other and decided to be friends and overcome racial prejudices. The film was shot silently, like the preceding one, with the plan of using postsynchronization: the players making up a sound track as they saw the edited film. This was done, then supplemented by bringing in blimped 16 mm synchronous-sound equipment and shooting several sync-sound sequences, with Rouch and the players in front of the camera. This makes it possible for Rouch to add to the self-conscious dimension of the film; indeed, the film begins with a sequence where he proposes his idea of a collectively improvised story. There is also a similar sequence in the middle of the film. The action breaks off, and all the actors comment on what they have been trying to do up until that point.[4]

The making of these two films involved major technical obstacles to the kind of improvised spontaneity Rouch sought. At this time there were no noiseless portable 16 mm cameras for shooting synchronized sound; noiseless sync could only be accomplished by housing the camera in an enormous blimp. The films attempted to overcome the technical limitations of the medium at the time in part through experiments with reflexivity and narrative realism.

Continuing reflection on the question of how one films what is subjectively real about and for people and their cultural situation led to what is Rouch's best-known film. Significantly, it was also his first film in his own society, *Chronicle of a Summer,* made in Paris in 1960 in collaboration with sociologist Edgar Morin. Rouch was responsible for organizing the filming, Morin for the fieldwork and organizing the participants. The film is presented as an inquiry into the lives of a group of Parisians in the summer of 1960. It combines the techniques of drama, fiction, provocation, and reflexive critique that Rouch developed from previous films. It was during this film that the prototype Eclair lightweight 16 mm camera was used for the first time with the Nagra recorder to achieve truly portable handheld synchronous sound.

This film is associated with the origins of the term *"cinéma-vérité"* to refer to a process, visual aesthetic, and technology of cinema. Additionally some took it as an ideology of authenticity, as well. But in the context of the experimental gestures in *Chronicle of a Summer, cinéma-vérité* came to mean four things: (1) films composed of first-take, nonstaged, nontheatrical, nonscripted material; (2) nonactors doing what they do in natural, spontaneous settings; (3) use of lightweight, handheld portable synchronous-sound equipment; and (4) handheld on-the-go interactive filming and recording techniques with little if any artificial lighting.[5] Rouch summed it up more directly, simply claiming that *Chronicle* was the first film to show that "you can film anything anywhere" ("Ciné-Anthropology," this volume).

Immediately after *Chronicle of a Summer,* Rouch made *La punition* and *Rose et Landry;* the former appeared on French television and the latter on Canadian television. *La punition* was largely a response to the problem of editing *Chronicle,* for which there were twenty-two hours of rushes. *La punition* was made in two days, with Rouch again, in the fashion of *La pyramide humaine,* provoking a situation (a woman wanders through Paris and meets three different men, a student, an African, a middle-aged engineer, and . . .). It was filmed with single takes, no location setups, and handheld camera. *La punition* and *Rose et Landry* reflect very much of a concern with revisiting issues raised by *Les maîtres fous* and *Moi, un Noir,* namely, the impact of European racism on Africans, as well as African responses to European colonialism. Not surprisingly, these films were made at the height of both African independence movements and political debates about the psychological impact of colonialism, racism, and lingering European anti-Semitism. From this standpoint, the films can be seen as merging filmic experimentalism with engaged antiracist politics.

Rouch's developing interest in filming in his own society and in the interplay of drama and reality led to another production in Paris during this period. In 1966 he participated (along with Eric Rohmer, Jean-Luc Godard, Claude Chabrol, Daniel Pollet, and Jean Douchet) in a film entitled *Paris vu par . . . ,* in which each of the six directors contributed a short sequence on a different section of Paris. Rouch's episode, *Gare du nord,* was a drama about a marital quarrel and suicide. The scene was improvised and simply provoked by Rouch, who told the participants the themes and what he generally had in mind (they were not professional actors). The film further gives the illusion of *cinéma-vérité* by its filmic style. It was done entirely in two shots, each the length of a camera magazine. The film magazine was changed in an elevator, between a shot of the closing and opening of the doors; thus the film presents the illusion that it consists of only one shot, of about twenty minutes' duration. This film was yet another indication of the relevance of Rouch's technical and narrative innovations to the French Nouvelle Vague film movement.

In 1964 *The Lion Hunters* was released. This is a feature-length ethnographic study that Rouch had been working on for eight years in between the series of films in Paris. It was immediately followed by *Un lion nommé "l'Américain,"* which tells the story of the capture of the lion that eluded the hunters in the first film. The two films indicate another synthetic turn in Rouch's approach, combining the older style of ethnographic reportage with a much more developed sense of plot and narrative structure, very much as in more dramatic films. In making these films, and a few shorter ethnographic studies in the early 1960s, Rouch experimented extensively with the new portable sync-sound equipment in Africa.[6]

*Jaguar,* begun in the mid-1950s, was finished in 1965. At the ethnographic level, this film is a distillation of Rouch's research on migrations (Rouch 1956, 1960c). At the narrative level, it was also a distillation of his experiences with drama and fiction. In the film, three men, Lam, Damouré, and Illo, take a trip from Niger to the coast of Ghana (then Gold Coast). The film attempts to capture the spirit of preindependence West Africa, when borders were not difficult to cross, and when considerable adventure and possibility, as well as risk, were associated with going to large cities. The film was shot silently in the 1950s, when Rouch was still using a small 100-foot-load spring-wound camera. In finishing the film, Rouch maintained the continuity of that style and made it like the earlier fiction films. During a screening of the rough cut, the actors improvised a sound track with dialogue.[7]

Also in the mid-1960s, Rouch began working again with the Dogon in Mali, this time in collaboration with the ethnographer Germaine Dieterlen, a member of the original Griaule research team. Between 1966 and 1973, Rouch filmed the Sigui ceremony. In the Dogon ceremonial cycle, Sigui occurs every sixty years for seven years.[8] With ethnomusicologist Gilbert Rouget, also a collaborator on one of the *Sigui* films, Rouch also made *Batteries Dogon,* a study of Dogon drumming (Rouget 1965), and some shorter films among the Dogon, such as *Funérailles du Hogon,* an interesting contrast with his early 1951 Dogon funerary film *Cimetière dans la falaise.* But perhaps the most developed sense of ritual, history, and cinematic poetics comes together in two longer Dogon funeral ritual studies completed in the early 1970s: *Funérailles à Bongo: Le vieil Anaï, 1848–1971* (1972), and *Le Dama d'Ambara* (1974).

Also in the late 1960s and into the 1970s, Rouch continued to film with the Songhay, concentrating on studies of rituals and religion, specifically rainmaking rites, possession dances, and divination (Stoller 1992, 48–62). Many of these rituals are described both in Rouch's book and in earlier films. But here they begin to be filmed in a very different way, due both to the use of direct cinema techniques (handheld sync sound, long takes) and to the depth of sophisticated observing gained from having seen so many of these ceremonies over a period approaching thirty years. Films such as *Horendi, Yenendi de Gangel,* and *Tourou et Bitti* are made in the style of continuous ten-minute shots, filmed while Rouch is walking among the participants in the events. Rouch calls these "shot sequence" *(plan sequence)* films.

In the verbal introduction to the sound track of *Tourou et Bitti,* he describes what is to come as "ethnography in the first person" because he plays the roles of both participant and catalyst as he films. The purpose of these films is not to break down and explicate events into component structures and sequences. Rather, they show how the familiar observer authors a subjectively experiential and interactive account of them at the moment he films. This style of shooting long sequences with a single focal-length lens (frequently wide angle, 10 mm) and extensive walking is also considered by Rouch to be an answer to the problem of editing; namely, to edit everything in the camera as it is being shot and then string the shot sequences together. The film is thus imaged as a way of seeing in the moment. It is at once a temporal index of observational experience and a spacial icon resembling the participatory dialectic of scanning and focusing.[9]

Alongside this evolution in field filming, Rouch concentrated in the late 1960s and onward to the 1990s on producing feature-length ethnographic fiction films that descend directly from *Jaguar,* but also show the influence of *Moi, un Noir,* and *La pyramide humaine.* All are improvised and filmed directly by Rouch and jointly conceived by him, Damouré Zika, and Lam Ibrahim Dia (hence the name Films Dalarou, in some cases Dalarouta, to indicate the participation of Tallou Mouzourane, another longtime collaborator). These men have been in numerous Rouch films and have also worked as close field assistants. In this series of films are *Petit à Petit, Cocorico, Monsieur Poulet,* and *Madame l'eau.* Very broadly, the subject of these films is post- and neocolonialism and its effects on the lives of Africans, and their relations to a changing Africa and a changing Europe. There is a particular emphasis on dramatic storytelling, and on ironies of cross-cultural (mis)communication. In these films, Rouch continually works to refine a way of crossing lines and expectations; fantasy, absurdity, and surrealist scenarios are constantly juxtaposed with, or blended into, mundane everyday experiences of political and economic realities.

In *Petit à Petit,* for example, Rouch was responding directly to the changed political climate in France after May 1968, as well as the complexities of postcolonial African modernities and desires. Damouré, Lam, and Illo play the roles of African businessmen who go to Paris to investigate how people live in high-rise buildings so that they might build one themselves in Niger. In the course of the Parisian visit, Rouch provokes his actors to act out a reverse—some would say perverse—anthropology: measuring heads of Europeans with calipers in front of the Musée de l'Homme, asking to inspect French mouths and count teeth, interviewing passersby on the street about their color categories. Through these absurdities, Rouch directly confronts the power positions of anthropologists and Africans. Decentering stereotypical subject/object relationships is particularly poignant in these fictions, as is the way the story unfolds, when the crew of expatriate Africans and French bohemians return to Africa and things fall apart.[10]

The second film, *Cocorico, Monsieur Poulet,* is much more of an attempt to deal with the subtleties of colonial response, namely, the development of a subculture of African marginals. This collective improvisation on a popular fable from Niger features Damouré, Lam, and Lam's little Citroën 2 CV on a yearlong expedition that shifts from mundane peddling, to supernatural adventures with sorcery, to the allegory of how a car crosses a river (see "Ciné-Anthropology" and "The Politics of Visual Anthropology," in this volume).

These fictions reach their most playfully ironic heights in *Madame l'eau.* Damouré, Lam, and Tallou visit Holland, the land of windmills, in search of a way to irrigate their lands in Niger, which have been ravaged by drought. Encounters with Holland, and friendships with Dutch people, some quite comical, some quite bizarre, lead to the realization that a wooden windmill can be built on the banks of the Niger. And indeed, in time, one is (the Dutch film *Rouch's Gang* chronicles the making of *Madame l'eau*).

Among other central features—particularly a preoccupation with dreams—these films are an attempt to develop a visual poetic of African storytelling. Yet in all cases, Rouch eschews a film structure precisely parallel to African epics, deprivileging any single narrative and often developing an underlying tone that is extremely cynical about the self-serving nature of historical accounts. His concentration on the connection between desires for modernity and marginals, whom he occasionally refers to as a "populist avant-garde," involves a perception of both the injustices and ironies of postcolonial Africa that tends to provoke strong responses from critics and audiences in both Africa and Europe.

Throughout the later 1970s and through the 1980s and 1990s, Rouch continued on several tracks in addition to ethnographic fiction. One involved continuing fieldwork in Niger on Songhay ritual and everyday life and producing new film studies in the "shot sequence" style. An additional series of films begun in the late seventies includes ciné-portraits; subjects include Margaret Mead, Germaine Dieterlen, Taro Okamoto, and Paul Levy.

At the time of this writing there are more than one hundred finished films, and at least another twenty-five in various stages of completion (see annotated filmography, this volume). Of this extraordinary output, it is remarkable—in the extreme negative, that is—that only five films, *Les maîtres fous, The Lion Hunters, Jaguar, Chronicle of a Summer,* and *Paris vu par . . . (Paris Seen by . . .),* are available in the United States. Indeed, until the mid-1970s, Rouch's other films were rarely been seen outside of Europe and Africa, and it was only in the 1970s and 1980s that his basic publications on ethnographic film and African cinema were translated and substantial interviews published in English.

Beginning in the late 1970s, Rouch's appearances at U.S. film festivals, summer seminars, and retrospectives brought considerably more U.S. attention to his work. Around this time as well, anthropologists and filmmakers began to more regularly discuss the specifically theoretical implications of Rouch's film style for a more participatory and reflexive ethnographic cinema.[11] In recent years, however, Rouch's work has been the subject of considerably more attention in different quarters of the anthropological and film communities.[12]

▶

### Thematics of Rouch's Ciné-Ethnography

To further situate this general overview of Rouch's career and films, it is useful to review the four key themes that are revealed in his films and writings. These are an attempt to synthesize and elaborate the key documentary impacts of Robert Flaherty and Dziga Vertov; the refinement of the concepts of cinema verite and direct cinema; the development of the ethnographic fiction genre; and the preoccupation with filmic conventions of reflexivity, authorship, autocritque, and "shared anthropology."

In published interviews and writings, as well as public discussions, Rouch has continually cited his esteem for Robert Flaherty and Dziga Vertov.[13] For Rouch, Flaherty and Vertov "invented" a new discipline of filmmaking by "experimenting with cinema in real life" ("Vicissitudes"). In doing so, they "discovered the essential questions that we still ask ourselves today: must one 'stage' reality (the staging of real life) as did Flaherty, or should one, like Vertov, film 'without awareness' (seizing improvised life)?" ("The Camera and Man"). To understand why Rouch finds these the "essential" questions, one must examine their relation to ethnography.

Rouch sees Flaherty—specifically the Flaherty of *Nanook of the North*—as the unconscious originator of filmic equivalents of the most basic ethnographic field methods, participant observation and feedback. Specifically, Rouch views the film as a celebration of a relationship; it combines the familiarity that accrues from observation with the sense of contact and spontaneity that comes from rapport and participation. By developing and printing rushes on location and screening them with Nanook and other Inuit, Flaherty initiated filmic feedback as a form of stimulation and rapport.

Moreover, Rouch takes it as critical that Flaherty was able to teach Nanook that in order to make a film, actions could not take place as they normally do. Flaherty was not interested in simply recording things as they happened, nor was he technically able to do so. He instead solicited Nanook's help to get people to enact themselves, but with the understanding that such enactments could only take place at the point when he was ready to film them. Citing the phrase of Luc de Heusch (1962, 35), Rouch applauds this achievement of the "participating camera," and its connection to the "staging" of reality.[14]

Rouch's debt to Dziga Vertov seems less romantic and mythologizing, as well as more specifically filmic. It concerns the development of a cinematic realism in which the theory of realism was not confused with "reality." Vertov was concerned with the structures of film realism and the methods of filming real life, as opposed to theatrical enactment. He articulated his theory and method in ways that showed that cinema was different from lived reality and that the camera was not a human eye but a specifically mediated mechanical one. For Vertov, film realism was thematic and structural, built up from tiny units of observation of real people doing real things. These units were always organized by the filmmaker to express his version or statement of the content.

For Rouch, Vertov's importance rests in the break from cinema realism that was confined to isolated observations and the espousal of a cinema realism that had an explicit notion of editing and organizing these "crumbs," as Vertov called them, into a thematic reality. Although Vertov insisted on filming improvised life (no actors, no scripts, no costumes) to seize reality, he both stressed and resorted to extensive montage and metaphoric juxtapositions to "decipher" reality, that is, to elaborate it from the "crumbs" of the footage.

The key factor here is that Vertov described the kino-eye not as a model for seeing the truth but as a new kind of seeing that created its own peculiar truth. Rouch writes that Vertov "called the entirety of this discipline kino-pravda (*cinéma-vérité*, film truth), an ambiguous or self-contradictory expression, since, fundamentally, film truncates, accelerates, and slows down actions, thus distorting the truth. For me, however, 'kinopravda' *(cinéma-vérité)* is a precise term, on the same order as 'kinok' (ciné-eye), and it designates not 'pure truth' but the particular truth of the recorded images and sounds—a filmic truth, *ciné-vérité*" ("Vicissitudes," this volume). Describing Vertov's impact on *Chronicle of a Summer*, years later, he continues, "With the ciné-eye and the ciné-ear we recorded in sound and image a

Sounds Godardian ✓

*ciné-vérité*, Vertov's kinopravda. This does not mean the cinema of truth, but the truth of cinema" ("Ciné-Anthropology," this volume).

In this regard, Rouch's use of Vertov goes beyond his use of Flaherty. This is because with Vertov, the camera gains consciousness, and the mediating work of the filmmaker is itself put on the screen as a way of making a work process explicit. It is this self-consciousness of process, the idea that the truth or the reality of a film is always a socially constructed one, that Rouch derives from Vertov (Sadoul 1971; Sauzier 1985).

Of these concerns raised by Flaherty and Vertov—participant observation, feedback, staging reality, seizing improvised life, editing for thematic subjective truth, *ciné-vérité*, making the camera the principal actor, revealing the process of making and the authorship of the director—Rouch is heir. His claim, all told, is that film and anthropology share the same essential concerns with the nature of intersubjectivity.

From Vertov, Rouch focused on a cinema concerned with exposing its own process of seizing improvised life and simultaneously commenting on its own form of seeing, hearing, and organizing. It was with this in mind that the term *"cinéma-vérité"* was actually first used in an article by Morin reporting on the Florence International Ethnographic Film Festival of 1960 (see Morin's essay, this volume). Morin was on the jury with Rouch and after the festival wrote a newspaper article for *France-Observateur* titled "Pour un nouveau cinéma-vérité." His intention was to pay homage to Vertov. The same phrase was used on the publicity flyer when *Chronicle of a Summer* premiered at Cannes in 1961. At the time, both Morin and Rouch held that the important word in the phrase was "nouveau." They stressed the realization of a combined ciné-eye and ear, the development of portable synchronous sound, the new potential for the role of speech in the cinema, and the closeness and contact of direct filming without the intervention of a large crew. In short, they stressed both the arrival of the technical means that Vertov lacked and its role in realizing, with new sophistication, the self-revelatory and self-critical process kinopravda promised.

Like many other filmmakers, however, Rouch dropped the term *"cinéma-vérité"* as the generic name for the film style in which he was engaged, fearing that it was tainted by the pretension of an absolutist notion of truth. Instead, he adopted the term *"cinéma-direct"* (direct cinema, as it was immediately termed in English), first suggested by Mario Ruspoli (Marsolais 1974, 21–25). Gilles Marsolais presents a consensus definition of *cinéma-direct* as "a cinema that records directly in the field, not the studio, words and gestures through the use of synchronous camera and tape recorder that is lightweight and flexible to handle. This, in other words, is a cinema that establishes direct contact with people, trying to 'paste together reality' as best as possible while always taking into account that the enterprise is mediated" (1974, 22). Since 1963 Rouch has used this term to denote both a set of attitudes and a set of techniques; the two are felt to be mutually interdependent and are not concerned with "truth" in any positivist sense. Karel Reisz and Gavin Millar, in the classic manual on documentary film editing, stress this intersection of the technical and processual in the editing of *Chronicle of a Summer:* "It has as its aim not 'truth' but the many truths out of which some picture of reality can be built" (1968, 303).

Direct cinema brought together the technical breakthroughs that took place at the Canadian Film Board, in France, and in the United States between 1958 and 1960 (Issari 1971; Mamber 1974). These developments centered on portability. The possibility to film with cameras quieted by their own material casing (called "self-blimped") developed simultaneously with techniques of synchronization between the camera and an independent portable recorder. These developments were also accompanied by the manufacture of faster film stocks and laboratory forced processing ("pushing") of film stocks to higher speeds so that heavy lighting equipment could be minimized.

These innovations came together considerably during the making of *Chronicle of a Summer,* during which Coutant developed the prototype Eclair 16 mm self-blimped camera (which became known as the NPR, or "noiseless portable reflex"). With feedback from Rouch on design, this camera was used with a portable Nagra tape recorder with a neopilot system for synchronizing image and sound. At the same time, a new wide-angle lens that had considerably less distortion problems than earlier models was introduced. Simultaneously, two additional aspects of portability were brought from Canada by Michel Brault of the Canadian Film Board. These were the lavaliere microphone and the technique of walking with the handheld camera.[15]

The basic spirit of a new cinema, of a direct cinema, was quickly established. This meant reliance on synchronous sound, avoidance of voice-over and narration associated with classical documentary, and insistence on "live" natural settings and "first takes" with no repetition of what really happened (so that the camera could film it from another angle for match cutting, for example). Rouch insisted that this approach make no abstract claims for truthfulness, only for the necessity of contact, and the hope that it will play a catalytic role in the film process. This is the sense in which Rouch prefers "direct cinema" to either "observational cinema," which he finds embodies a certain distance from his catalytic, intersubjective stance (MacDougall 1998, 125–39), or *"cinéma-vérité,"* which raises the positivist—if not moralistic—specter of "the truth."

For Rouch, the problem with the early phase of the American cinema verite movement was its positivism, particularly the "fly-on-the-wall" principle of nonintervention, as indicated by a number of the early experiments by Richard Leacock and his associates. In these films, Rouch saw a denial of what all ethnographers are forced to learn: that realities are coconstructed and that meanings always change as contexts of interpretation change, continually revealed and modified in numerous ways. Provoking, catalyzing, questioning, and filming are simply strategies for unleashing that revealing process. Rouch insisted that the presence of the camera, like the presence of the ethnographer, stimulates, modifies, accelerates, catalyzes, opens a window (phrases he has used over the years); people respond by revealing themselves, and meanings emerge in that revelation. Drama is inherent in this revealing, and drama is inherent in the act of filming it. Filming in personal, narrative, and authored styles is a choice made about the most direct and explicit way to grasp the drama of "improvised life." Perhaps this is what Louis Marcorelles means when he says, "having gone beyond all truth, Jean Rouch first of all tells us his stories" (1973, 91).

Storytelling is, in fact, maybe the best way to characterize Rouch's concerns on the whole.[16] Rouch indicates that ethnographic cinema can be exciting and liberating (as cinema and as ethnography) precisely because of the capacity to intimately project the richness of local sensibilities. One can go beyond descriptive inventories; one can grasp and show and reveal significances, some of which are only emergent in the actual process of filming and editing. It is this excitement of projecting locally articulated and emergent dramas that is exemplified in David MacDougall's comment that "one sometimes feels that Jean Rouch has tried to make the kinds of films about West Africa that West Africans might have made had they had the means" (1976, 149). Gilles Deleuze expressed the same sentiment in a more polemical voice: "It may be objected that Jean Rouch can only with difficulty be considered a third world author, but no one has done so much to put the West to flight, to flee himself, to break with a cinema of ethnology and say *Moi, un Noir . . .*" (1989, 223; also Brahimi 1997, 19).

Provocation of an empathetic sort contributes substantially to Rouch's attempts to transcend brute cinematic description, to get beyond observational passivity. The classic example is perhaps the scene in *Chronicle of a Summer* during the lunch at the Musée de l'Homme. When the subject turned to anti-Semitism, Rouch asked the African students what they thought of the tattoo on Marceline's arm. Of course they did not realize that this was a number put on Marceline's arm by the Nazis. When they questioned the tattoo as an adornment, given the African context of bodily tattoos, and wondered if it was Marceline's phone number, an extraordinary moment of drama was revealed as interpretive worlds clashed. Is this not "truthful" or "objective" "evidence" of a profound reality because of the clear intervention? Here is Rouch's ethnographic rationale for the notion that when there is participation and provocation in direct cinema, there is the possibility of crystallized expressions of what might otherwise be obtuse, unsaid, or unrevealed. Although such techniques were criticized as "mere psychodrama" by those seeking an authentic, untouched, objective "recording" of reality, Rouch was always clear in his conviction that direct cinema must confront the epistemology of intersubjectivity.

Provocation and storytelling affect the structure and cinematic conventions of *Chronicle of a Summer, La punition, Rose et Landry,* and *Gare du nord* in ways that have stimulated and refined cinema direct filming, but Rouch has actually done more experimenting with these methods in his African films. *Les maîtres fous* and *The Lion Hunters* clearly express both an anthropological view of ritual as dramaturgy and the notion of anthropological film as narrative storytelling. Each essentially resorts to cinematic answers (editing to show the referent of a symbol in *Les maîtres fous,* climactic structure of the hunt editing in *The Lion Hunters*) to deal with explicative needs while retaining the subjective sense of plot. Additionally, the shot sequence films such as *Tourou et Bitti* involve narrative experiments by the linkage of film time to ritual time and to experiential and observational time. As Rouch puts it: "Cinema, the art of the instant and the instantaneous, is, in my opinion, the art of patience, and the art of time" ("Ciné-Anthropology," in this volume).

While anthropologists have used novels and other written fiction, most ethnographic filmmakers have generally only exploited the descriptive realism of film and have seemingly stayed away from fiction. This leads to one of the unique things about Rouch's work in anthropology. This is his extensive use of fiction formats for revealing ethnography, his use of surrealist and dream techniques, and perhaps, most significantly, his blurring of the very cinematic distinction between documentary and fiction film in favor of a more ethnographic and imaginative integration.[17]

In *Moi, un Noir, La pyramide humaine,* and *Jaguar,* Rouch turned the limitations of the time (no sync sound) into an innovative use of the sound track by screening films back to the participants and provoking them to make up their own dialogues and commentaries as an improvised response both to themselves acting and to Rouch's editing. Here storytelling and provocation take on a reflexive dimension; for the viewer, the process of making the film and the relationships in it are explicated at the moment of watching. In *La pyramide humaine,* this is enhanced by Rouch's direct appearances on-screen; the form and manner of provocation from Rouch to the actors becomes part of the story itself. In *Jaguar* this dimension is even more poignant; as one watches and learns about an Africa that no longer existed by the time the film was finished, one hears Damouré and Lam as if they were watching a home movie with their own families.

In *Petit à Petit,* fiction is taken to deeper levels of both fantasy and political statement. Damouré, the director of Petit à Petit Imports, goes to France to have an architect draw up plans for him to build a skyscraper in Niger. While on the streets of Paris, Damouré acts out the role of the curious African anthropologist, performing some spontaneous physical anthropology to some fairly astonished Parisians. Then he brings Lam over to work with him. They buy a Bugatti, bomb around town, meet a Senegalese beauty (the filmmaker Safi Faye) who quotes Baudelaire, a white woman who dances with them in a discotheque, and a Quebecois who is a hobo. Eventually all five go back to Niger, and the building is constructed. Damouré marries both women in village and church ceremonies, Lam and the Quebecois discover each other's strangeness, the women decide to go back to Paris, and Damouré decides he would rather ride a horse and live in a hut by the sea. In the playing out of this collective improvisation there is much pure zaniness. But there is also much mockery of both African and French elites, and a deep sense of the alienation that is produced when either culture is reduced to imitation and parody of the other.

*Cocorico, Monsieur Poulet,* based on a story by Damouré, is an equally trenchant statement on the theme of separate realities. Here Lam, a marginal chicken merchant, goes trading and in the process must get his car back and forth across the Niger River three times. The first time he drives it in the water, the second time he takes it apart, and the third time he floats it on tubes. Rouch uses this process to show that Africans adapt to challenges in ways that are totally different from Europeans. He even contrasts the logic and local sensibility of these marginal schemes with the appearance of European "experts" who have come to do quick and superficial surveys and give development advice in the arrogant voice of social science. Out of this emerges the mix of improvised fun and sarcastic critique that has cultivated both adoring and annoyed audiences.

A final theme linking Rouch's obsession with authorship and his concern with ethnographic reflexivity is what he has called "anthropologie partagée," or "shared anthropology." This term implies several attitudes and is manifested in different ways. The most basic method involved is feedback (which Rouch translates as *contredon audiovisuel,* or audiovisual reciprocity, playing in the French, as well, on *Le Don*, the title of Marcel Mauss's celebrated 1925 classic *The Gift*). For Rouch, a critical difference between the product of visual anthropology and other anthropological documents is the ability to "share" the report (i.e., the analysis) with those it is about, those who appear in it. As a process, this enhances participation and allows the ethnographer-filmmaker to meditate openly and self-critically on his or her own role.

As an example of this kind of feedback, Rouch often cites playing back one of his early films on hippopotamus hunting to the Sorko. With the climax of the chase, Rouch used music on the sound track, namely, a hunter's air (the film was made with preportable sync sound). When the hunters saw the film, they remarked that this was inappropriate; the hunt must be completely silent. Rouch points out that the feedback taught him something specific about hippopotamus hunting and the Sorko notion of drama. Simultaneously, it taught him something about his own cultural predisposition to using music as a theatrical device.

Another kind of "sharing" anthropology is in the notion of fieldwork as "ethnodialogue." Rather than analyzing behaviors as if they were unaffected by the presence of the anthropologist, Rouch has directly confronted how people are changed and modified by his presence. In his study of the "self" and transformations of possession, sorcery, and magic ("Vicissitudes of the Self," in this volume), he broadens the scope of inquiry by comparing these altered states with the altered states of ethnography and filmmaking. This involves analyzing how the people he films interpret the transformation that takes place when he films. He develops the theme that there is a cultural analogue between the filmer and the possession dancer that is played out as the ciné-trance of the one filming the possession trance of the other. Later playback of the film is a strong enough provocation that people will become repossessed. Rouch attempts to state how this kind of participation and reflexivity redefines the roles of observer and observed into ethnodialogue.

Other kinds of sharing anthropology that operate clearly in Rouch's work surround the collaborative style developed in his association with Damouré Zika, Lam Ibrahima Dia, Tallou Mouzourane, and Illo Gaoudel. Additionally Rouch has been active in training African filmmakers so that they can image their own cultures as they see fit (e.g., Oumarou Ganda, Moustapha Alassane)[18] and also image the culture of the anthropologist (e.g., Inoussa Ousseini, whose film *Paris c'est joli*, about the misadventures of a young African who clandestinely arrives in France, shows a very different side of the clash of cultures than does Rouch's work).

In this regard, Manthia Diawara says that Rouch "is to African cinema what Jean-Paul Sartre was to *Négritude*" (1992, 24). But other African scholars and filmmakers are neither as subtle in their phrasing nor as nuanced in their assessment of the complexity of Rouch's subjectivity. The Senegalese director Ousmane Sembène said that Rouch depicts Africans as insects (1982). Other writers insist that Rouch's world of ethnographic film was born of, and can only extend, the ideology of colonial cinema, and thus the colonial project in general—which is to show the colonized as quaint, primitive, and exotic. They insist that Europeans are steeped in personal, cultural, and institutional privilege, easy to deny or camouflage by self-critical or self-aware pronouncements.[19] Ukadike sees a deeper contradiction, namely, the extent to which participants in Rouch's films or associates of his who went on to become filmmakers (Oumarou Ganda, Safi Faye, Moustapha Allasane, Inoussa Ousseini) are ultimately critical both of his praxis and of the real effect of his films (1994, 50–51, 79, 90). These charges surely point out one of the deeper ironies of Rouch's films, namely, that in their reflexivity and risks they both anticipate and participate in the very critique leveled at them by postcolonial studies and African scholars.

While acknowledging the currency of these critical perspectives, it is also unquestionable that by any standard of quality, volume, or sheer vitality, Rouch's impact on the evolution of ethnographic cinema and cinematic ethnography in the second half of the twentieth century has been enormous. His work has simultaneously promoted the value of cinema to ethnography and ethnography to cinema, in both cases at the levels of theory, method, and practice. With each film project, Rouch tried new experiments, took new risks, and mapped new options.

Rouch's films enunciate a dedication to participation, involvement, long-term ethnographic commitment, and interpersonal engagement. They enunciate the processual, revelatory power of cinema to unleash and stimulate new ways of representing scenes both familiar and fantastic, mundane and spectacular. It is a recognition of the parallel intersubjective, improvisatory, and dramaturgical qualities of both everyday life and direct filming that signals the intersection of social and cinematic theory in Rouch's oeuvre. And it is from this recognition that his work so forcefully dissolves and obliterates parochial distinctions between fact and story, documentary and fiction, knowledge and feeling, improvisation and composition, observation and participation. Rouch's own words state it best:

> For me, as an ethnographer and filmmaker, there is almost no boundary between documentary film and films of fiction. The cinema, the art of the double, is already the transition from the real world to the imaginary world, and ethnography, the science of the thought systems of others, is a permanent

crossing point from one conceptual universe to another; acrobatic gymnastics, where losing one's footing is the least of the risks.

## Plan of the Book

The plan of this book responds to both the historical and biographical dimensions of Rouch's career, and the thematics of his fused cinematic and ethnographic work. It opens with four key essays that Rouch wrote in the 1960s and 1970s; each is a key document in the history of visual anthropology. And each, in a different way, brings together aspects of cinematic and social theory. The first, "The Camera and Man," is perhaps Rouch's best-known and most widely cited essay. In it he lays out his overall engagement with ethnographic cinema, his sense of its history, methods, prospects, and problems. Next comes a long essay entitled "The Situation and Tendencies of the Cinema in Africa." In addition to its historical merit, the piece is of significant value as an early work on the filmic representation of Africa and Africans. It is an essay that stands on its own in the context of the state of knowledge in the early 1960s, and one that can profitably be reread in the context of debates about the colonial gaze and representation, matters taken up critically in recent critical postcolonial histories of African film.[20]

The final two essays concern filming in the Songhay and Dogon worlds. "On the Vicissitudes of the Self: The Possessed Dancer, the Magician, the Sorcerer, the Filmmaker, and the Ethnographer" is a lively mix of Rouch's cinematic and ethnographic praxis, revealing how the ethnographic study of West African rituals is intertwined with the epistemology of cinema. "The Mad Fox and the Pale Master" treats Rouch's relation to his Dogon teachers and collaborators Marcel Griaule and Germaine Dieterlen and locates his filming of the Sigui and of Dogon rituals in the dual contexts of the history of postwar French anthropology and the development of ethnographic cinema. This is the most autobiographical of his essays, and also the one that most closely treats the relation of surrealism to ethnography. It is the most distinctly postmodern and experimental of his writings included here.

Four conversations and interviews follow, further embellishing these essays, clarifying their author's intentions, and providing meaningful context for viewing the related films. This quartet begins with a conversation with Lucien Taylor from 1990, where Rouch speaks considerably about his personal background, locating himself not just as an anthropologist and filmmaker but as an artist and intellectual in the broadest historical sense. Then comes a long conversation produced for the most important retrospective of Rouch's work in 1980. Enrico Fulchignoni walks Rouch through his whole career. This conversation is particularly valuable for locating the experiences and experiments of each film in the larger narratives of Rouch's poetics and politics.

This is followed by two shorter interviews, both originally conducted in English at the first Margaret Mead Film Festival, in 1977, where Rouch was the guest of honor. In the first of them, filmmaker John Marshall and anthropologist John W. Adams question Rouch in detail about *Les maîtres fous, The Lion Hunters,* and *Jaguar.* These conversations are particularly valuable because these three films are still Rouch's most widely seen in the United States, particularly in classes in ethnographic film and representations of Africa. In the second interview, with *Cineaste* magazine critics Dan Georgakas, Udayan Gupta, and Judy Janda, Rouch answers questions about the politics of cinema and ethnography not closely covered elsewhere. While the other three conversations were conducted with good friends and colleagues, this one has a different edge. The interviewers bring a mix of Marxist, feminist, and critical postcolonial critiques to the table and are clearly suspicious of Rouch's politics and praxis. His responses reveal additional dimensions of his intertwined politics and aesthetics, touching on matters unspoken in the other conversations and essays.

These four essays and four interviews are followed by the 1962 book documenting one of Rouch's best-known films, *Chronicle of a Summer.* The book begins with an essay on the making of the film and on the question of *cinéma-vérité* by Rouch's collaborator, sociologist Edgar Morin. Rouch's essay on the birth of direct cinema follows. Then there is a complete transcript of the film. Finally Rouch and Morin present their postfilm interviews with the principal participants.

While it is widely acknowledged that 1960's *Chronicle of a Summer* was a tremendously innovative film that inspired many documentary, ethnographic, experimental, and New Wave films to follow, it will become equally clear that this book, too, is a historically innovative text. Far more than the transcript of an unscripted film, Morin's and Rouch's essays, interviews, and restoration of cut dialogue in the film transcript are a deep exercise in intellectual reflexivity and autocritique, and a substantial contribution to discussing issues of intersubjectivity, realism, and deception in documentary cinema.

Closing the collection is an updated filmography. In as many instances as possible, I have included annotations that are wholly or substantially Rouch's own. The filmography is followed by a selective bibliography of Rouch's most available writings.

## NOTES

1. For description and review, including the controversies raised by the film, see Muller 1971; Rouch 1960a; Stoller 1984, 1992, 145–60, 1995; Loizos 1993, 45–66; Ukadike 1994, 50–52; Gabriel 1982, 75–77; Russell 1999, 221–29. Also see "Ciné-Anthropology" and "Les maîtres fous, The Lion Hunters, and Jaguar," in this volume.
2. Stoller and Olkes 1987; Stoller 1989, 1992, 1995.
3. On the complexities of this film, including its critical opposition, see Eaton 1979, 7–11; Loizos 1993, 49–53; Muller 1971; Ukadike 1994, 50–51, 57–58. On the impact of the film on the politics of French film and the New Wave, see Godard 1972; Sadoul 1961. Also see "Ciné-Anthropology," in this volume.
4. See Rouch 1960b for a transcript of the film. Also see Loizos 1993, 53–56; and "Ciné-Anthropology," in this volume.
5. Marsolais 1974; Loizos 1993, 56–64; Dornfeld 1989. Also see the Chronicle of a Summer film book, part 3 of this volume.
6. Stoller 1992, 118–30; also see "Les maîtres fous, The Lion Hunters, and Jaguar," in this volume.
7. See Stoller 1992, 63–79, 131–44, on the history of migrations and the ethnofictional innovations of the film. Also see "Ciné-Anthropology" and "Les maîtres fous, The Lion Hunters, and Jaguar," in this volume.
8. For details see Dieterlen 1971; Stoller 1992, 174–91; also see "The Mad Fox and the Pale Master" and the Dogon section of "Ciné-Anthropology," in this volume.
9. For a detailed discussion, see "On the Vicissitudes of the Self," in this volume. Stoller (1992, 161–73) reviews Tourou et Bitti and the phenomenology of Songhay rituals.
10. See Rouch 1972 for the full text of the film and a gallery of photographs, commentaries, and interviews. Also see "Ciné-Anthropology," in this volume.
11. See especially Eaton 1979; also, for example, Dumont 1978; Heider 1976, 1983; MacDougall 1975, 1976, 1978, 1998; Ruby 1980, 1982; Barnouw 1983, 253–62; Yakir 1978.
12. For example, in anthropology, Ruby 1989, 2000; Loizos 1993; MacDougall 1998; Taussig 1993; and most significantly Stoller 1992, 1995; in film, Barbash and Taylor 1997; Nichols 1991; Russell 1999; Marks 2000.
13. See particularly Rouch 1968; and "The Camera and Man," "On the Vicissitudes of the Self," "The Cinema of the Future," and "Ciné-Anthropology," in this volume.
14. From the French "mettre en scène la réalité" (see "The Camera and Man," this volume).

On the complexities of Flaherty's "participation" idea, see Rotha 1980.
15. See Rouch's and Brault's comments on these developments in Marsolais 1974, 355–58. Also see "The Camera and Man," "The Cinema of the Future," and "Ciné-Anthropology," in this volume.
16. See Stoller 1992 for a development of this metaphor along the lines of both the African oral tradition and the institution of the griot.
17. Fieschi 1979; DeBouzek 1989; Stoller 1992. Also see "Ciné-Anthropology," in this volume.
18. See also Diawara 1992, 93–103, on Rouch's role in the Mozambique project.
19. See, for example, the arguments in Hennebelle 1972, 281–85; Gabriel 1982; Predal 1982; Harrow 1999; Ukadike and Gabriel 2002.
20. For example, Hennebelle 1972; Diawara 1992; Ukadike 1994; Brahimi 1997; Harrow 1999; Ukadike and Gabriel 2002. Also see "The Politics of Visual Anthropology," in this volume.

## REFERENCES

Barbash, Ilisa, and Lucien Taylor. 1997. Cross-Cultural Filmmaking: A Handbook for Making Documentary and Ethnographic Films and Videos. Berkeley: University of California Press.

Barnouw, Erik. 1983. Documentary: A History of the Nonfiction Film. New York: Oxford University Press.

Brahimi, Denise. 1997. Cinémas d'Afrique Francophone et du Maghreb. Paris: Éditions Nathan.

DeBouzek, Jennette. 1989. "The 'Ethnographic Surrealism' of Jean Rouch." Visual Anthropology 2 (3–4): 301–15.

de Heusch, Luc. 1962. The Cinema and Social Science. Paris: UNESCO.

Deleuze, Gilles. 1989. Cinema 2: The Time Image. Trans. Hugh Tomlinson and Robert Galeta. Minneapolis: University of Minnesota Press.

Diawara, Manthia. 1992. African Cinema: Politics and Culture. Bloomington: Indiana University Press.

———. 1995. Rouch in Reverse. Distributed by California Newsreel.

Dieterlen, Germaine. 1971. "Les cérémonies soixantenaires du Sigui chez les Dogon." Africa 41: 1–11.

Dornfeld, Barry. 1989. "Chronicle of a Summer and the Editing of Cinéma-Vérité." Visual Anthropology 2 (3–4): 317–31.

Dumont, Jean-Paul. 1978. "Review: Chronicle of a Summer." American Anthropologist 80 (4): 1020–22.

Eaton, Mick, ed. 1979. *Anthropology-Reality-Cinema: The Films of Jean Rouch*. London: British Film Institute.

Fieschi, Jean-André. 1979. "Slippages of Fiction: Some Notes on the Cinema of Jean Rouch." In *Anthropology-Reality-Cinema: The Films of Jean Rouch*, ed. Mick Eaton. London: British Film Institute.

Gabriel, Teshome. 1982. *Third Cinema in the Third World: The Aesthetics of Liberation*. Ann Arbor: University of Michigan Research Press.

Godard, Jean-Luc. 1972. "L'Afrique vous parle de la fin et des moyens." In *Godard on Godard*, ed. Jean Narboni and Tom Milne. London: Secker and Warburgh.

Harrow, Kenneth W. 1999. *African Cinema: Postcolonial and Feminist Readings*. Trenton: Africa World Press.

Heider, Karl. 1976. *Ethnographic Film*. Austin: University of Texas Press.

———. 1983. "Fieldwork with a Cinema." *Studies in Visual Communication* 9 (1): 2–10.

Hennebelle, Guy. 1972. *Les cinémas Africains en 1972*. Dakar and Paris: Société Africaine d'edition.

Issari, M. Ali. 1971. *Cinema Verite*. East Lansing: Michigan State University Press.

Loizos, Peter. 1993. *Innovation in Ethnographic Film: From Innocence to Self-Consciousness, 1955–1985*. Chicago: University of Chicago Press.

MacDougall, David. 1975. "Beyond Observational Cinema." In *Principles of Visual Anthropology*, ed. Paul Hockings. The Hague: Mouton.

———. 1976. "Prospects of the Ethnographic Film." In *Movies and Methods*, ed. Bill Nichols. Berkeley: University of California Press.

———. 1978. "Ethnographic Film: Failure and Promise." *Annual Review of Anthropology* 7: 405–25.

———. 1998. *Transcultural Cinema*. Princeton: Princeton University Press.

MAE/SERDDAV. 1981. *Jean Rouch: une rétrospective*. Paris: Ministère des Affaires Etrangères.

Mamber, Stephen. 1974. *Cinema Verite in America: Studies in Uncontrolled Documentary*. Cambridge: MIT Press.

Marcorelles, Louis. 1973. *Living Cinema*. New York: Praeger.

Marks, Laura U. 2000. *The Skin of the Film: Intercultural Cinema, Embodiment, and the Senses*. Durham: Duke University Press.

Marsolais, Gilles. 1974. *L'aventure du cinéma-direct*. Paris: Éditions Seghers.

Meyknecht, Steef, Dirk Nijland, and Joost Verhey. 1993. *Rouch's Gang*. Distributed by Documentary Educational Resources.

Muller, Jean-Claude. 1971. "Review of: *Les Maîtres Fous*." *American Anthropologist* 73: 1471–73.

Nichols, Bill. 1991. *Representing Reality: Issues and Concepts in Documentary*. Bloomington: Indiana University Press.

Predal, R., ed. 1982. "Jean Rouch jugé par six cinéastes d'Afrique Noire." *CinémAction* 17: 66–76 (special issue, *Jean Rouch, un griot gaulois*).

Reisz, Karel, and Gavin Millar. 1968. *The Technique of Film Editing*. New York: Focal Press.

Rotha, Paul, with Basil Wright. 1980. "Nanook and the North." *Studies in Visual Communication* 6 (2): 33–60.

Rouch, Jean. 1953. *Contribution à l'histoire des Songhay*. Dakar: Institut Français d'Afrique Noir (Memoire 29).

———. 1956. "Migrations au Ghana." *Journal de la Société des Africanistes* 26 (1–2): 33–196.

———. 1960a. *La religion et la magie Songhay*. Paris: Presses Universitaires de France.

———. 1960b. "*La Pyramide Humaine*: Scenario." *Cahiers du Cinema* 112: 1527.

———. 1960c. "Problèmes relatifs à l'étude des migrations traditionelles et des migrations actuelles en Afrique occidental." *Bulletin de l'Institut Français d'Afrique Noir* (Serie B: Sciences Humaines) 22 (34): 369–78.

———. 1968. "Le film ethnographique." In *Ethnologie générale, Encyclopedie de la Pléiade* Paris: Gallimard.

———. 1972. "Petit à Petit (dossier, scenario)." *L'Avant-Scène* 123: 3–52.

———. 1989. *La religion et la magie Songhay*. 2d ed. Brussels: Université de Brussels.

Rouget, Gilbert. 1965. "Un film expérimental: *Batteries Dogon*, éléments pour une étude des rythmes." *L'Homme* 5 (2): 126–32.

Ruby, Jay. 1980. "Exposing Yourself: Reflexivity, Anthropology, and Film." *Semiotica* 30 (12): 153–79.

———. 2000. *Picturing Culture: Explorations in Film and Anthropology*. Chicago: University of Chicago Press.

———, ed. 1982. *A Crack in the Mirror*. Philadelphia: University of Pennsylvania Press.

———, ed. 1989. "The Cinema of Jean Rouch." *Visual Anthropology* 2 (3–4).

Russell, Catherine. 1999. *Experimental Ethnography: The Work of Film in the Age of Video*. Durham: Duke University Press.

Sadoul, Georges. 1961. "De l'exotisme aux réalitiés africaines." *Les lettres Françaises* 873 (April): 5.

———. 1971. *Dziga Vertov: Préface de Jean Rouch*. Paris: Editions Champ Libre.

Sauzier, Bertrand. 1985. "An Interpretation of *Man with a Movie Camera*." *Studies in Visual Communication* 11 (4): 30–53.

Sembène, Ousmane. 1982. "Jean Rouch–Sèmbene Ousmane: 'Comme des insectes.'" *CinémAction* 17: 77–78 (special issue, *Jean Rouch, un griot gaulois*).

Stoller, Paul. 1984. "Horrific Comedy: Cultural

Resistance and the Hauka Movement in Niger." *Ethos* 12 (2): 165–88.

———. 1989. *Fusion of the Worlds.* Chicago: University of Chicago Press.

———. 1992. *The Cinematic Griot: The Ethnography of Jean Rouch.* Chicago: University of Chicago Press.

———. 1995. *Embodying Colonial Memories: Spirit Possession, Power, and the Hauka in West Africa.* New York: Routledge.

Stoller, Paul, and Cheryl Olkes. 1987. *In Sorcery's Shadow: A Memoir of Apprenticeship among the Songhay of Niger.* Chicago: University of Chicago Press.

Taussig, Michael. 1993. *Mimesis and Alterity: A Particular History of the Senses.* New York: Routledge.

Ukadike, Nwachukwu Frank. 1994. *Black African Cinema.* Los Angeles: University of California Press.

Ukadike, Nwachukwu Frank, and Teshome H. Gabriel. 2002. *Questioning African Cinema: Conversations with Filmmakers.* Minneapolis: University of Minnesota Press.

Yakir, Dan. 1978. "Ciné-transe: The Vision of Jean Rouch." *Film Quarterly* 31 (3): 2–11.

*I   Essays by Jean Rouch*

## The Camera and Man

In 1948, when André Leroi-Gourhan organized the first ethnographic film congress at the Musée de l'Homme, he asked himself, "Does the ethnographic film exist?" He could only respond, "It exists, since we project it."

And in 1962, Luc de Heusch quite justly wrote:

> To brandish the concept of the "sociological film," isolating it within immense world production, is this not a chimerical and academic exercise? The very notion of sociology is fluid, varying by country and local tradition. The term does not apply itself to the same research in Russia, the United States, or Europe. Is it not, on the other hand, the helpless mania of our time to catalogue, to cut up into arbitrary categories, the mixture of confused ideas, of moral values, and aesthetic research on which these artists, who are the creators of films, feed with such extraordinary avidity?

These two statements take on a particular value in 1973. This value derives, on the one hand, from the shameful situation in which anthropologists (and increasingly sociologists, too) find their discipline and, on the other, from the unwillingness of filmmakers to face up to their creative responsibilities. Ethnographic film has never been so contested, and the authored film has never been so questioned. And yet year after year, the number and quality of ethnographic films continues to grow.

It is not my concern here to pursue polemic, but simply to state the paradox: the more these films are attacked from the exterior or the interior (i.e., by the actors and viewers or by the directors and researchers), the more they seem to develop and affirm themselves. It is as if their total marginality was a way of escaping the reassuring orbit of all the daring attempts of today.

For example: since 1969, when ethnographers were compared (rather skillfully) to "salesmen of black culture," and sociologists to "indirect exploiters of the working class" by angry delegates at the Montreal African

Studies Association meetings, or the Pan-African Festival in Algiers, there have never been so many enrollments of new students in university departments of sociology and anthropology.

For example: since young anthropological filmmakers declared that films on rituals and traditional life were out-of-date, there have never been so many films depicting "primitive" cultures, and so few on the problems of development.

For example: since the creation of film collectives, there have never been so many authored films in cinema and human sciences, and, simultaneously, so much decadence on the part of filmmakers participating in these collectives.

In short, if ethnographic film is attacked, it is because it is in good health, and because, from now on, the camera has found its place among man.

▶ _____

## One Hundred Years of Films of Man
### The Pioneers

The arduous route that brought us here began in 1872, when Eadweard Muybridge made the first chronophotograph in San Francisco in order to settle an argument over the manner in which horses trot. Muybridge was able to reconstruct movement by decomposing it with a series of still images, which is to say, to "cinematograph" it.

From the beginning, after animals and horses, it was man: the horseman or horsewoman (nude for reasons of muscular observation), the walker, the crawler, the athlete, or Muybridge himself—all with their hair blowing in the wind, twirling about in front of thirty automatic still cameras. In those furtive images, American West Coast society one hundred years ago exposed more of itself than any Western could. They were horsemen, of course, but white, violent, muscular, harmoniously impudent, ready to give the world the virus of goodwill, and, as a bonus, the "American way of life."

Twelve years later, in 1888, when Marey used Edison's new pliable film and enclosed Muybridge's apparatus in his "chronophotographic rifle," it was again man who was the target. And in 1895, forty years before Marcel Mauss would write his unforgettable essay on body techniques, "Les Techniques du Corps," Doctor Felix Regnault, a young anthropologist, decided to use chronophotography for a comparative study of human behavior, including "ways of walking, squatting, and climbing" of a Peul, a Wolof, a Diola, or a Madagascan.

In 1900 Regnault and his colleague Azouley (who was the first to similarly use Edison cylinders for recording sound) conceived the first audiovisual museum of man: "Ethnographic museums must contain chrono-photographs. It is not enough to have a loom, a wheel, a spear. One must know the way they operate, and the only way to know this precisely is by means of the chronophotograph." Alas, some seventy years later, such an ethnographic museum of films and recordings is still a dream.

After the appearance of the animated image with the cinema of Lumière, it was still man who was the principal subject. As de Heusch wrote:

> Film archives of this century began with naive films. Was the cinema going to be an objective instrument capable of capturing the life and behavior of man? The marvelous ingenuity of Lumière's *Sortie des Usines (Leaving the Factory)*, *Déjeuner de Bébé (Baby's Lunch)*, and *Pêche à la Crevette (Shrimp Fishing)* permitted one to believe that it could.

But from the beginning, the camera was equally revealed to be a "thief of reflections." Perhaps those workers hardly paid attention to Lumière's little cranking box as they left the factory. But some days later, upon seeing the projection of the brief images, they suddenly became conscious of an unknown magical ritual—that old fear of the fatal meeting with one's double.

Then, de Heusch writes, "the illusionists" came along and "uprooted this new type of microscope from scholars and turned it into a toy." And so film viewers preferred Méliès's trick-optical version of the eruption of the Pelée Mountain volcano to the terrifying documents that Lumière's crews brought back from the China wars.

### The First Geniuses

It took the turmoil of the 1914–1918 war, the thorough questioning of values, the Russian Revolution, and the European intellectual revolution for the camera to refine its place among man.

At that point, our discipline was invented by two geniuses. One, Robert Flaherty, was a geographer-explorer who was doing ethnography without knowing it. The other, Dziga Vertov, was a futurist poet who was doing sociology, equally without knowing it. The two never met, but both craved cinema "reality." And ethnographers and sociologists who were inventing their new disciplines in the very midst of these two incredible observers had no contact with either of them. Yet it is to these two men that we owe everything that we are trying to do today.

For Flaherty, in 1920, filming the life of the Northern Eskimos meant filming a particular Eskimo—not filming things, but filming an individual. And the basic honesty of the endeavor meant showing that individual all the footage he had shot. When Flaherty built his developing lab at Hudson Bay and projected his images for Nanook, he had no idea that he was inventing, at that very instant, "participant observation" (a concept still used by ethnographers and sociologists fifty years later) and "feedback" (an idea with which we are just now clumsily experimenting).

If Flaherty and Nanook were able to tell the difficult story of the struggle of man against a thriftless but beneficial nature, it was because there was a third party with them. This small, temperamental, but faithful machine, with an infallible visual memory, let Nanook see his own images in proportion to their birth. It is this camera that Luc de Heusch so perfectly called the "participatory camera."

Undoubtedly, when Flaherty developed those rushes in his cabin, no one realized that he was condemning to death more than 90 percent of film documents that would follow. No one realized that they would have to wait some forty years before someone would follow the still-new example of the old master of 1921.

For Dziga Vertov, at the same period of time, it was a question of filming the revolution. It was no longer an issue of staging, or adventures, but of recording little patches of reality. Vertov the poet thus became Vertov the militant, and perceiving the archaic structure of the newsreel film, he invented the kinok, the "ciné-eye."

> I am the ciné-eye, I am the mechanical eye, I am the machine that shows you the world as only a machine can see it. From now on, I will be liberated from immobility. I am in perpetual movement. I draw near to things, I move myself away from them, I enter into them, I travel toward the snout of a racing horse. I move through crowds at top speed, I precede soldiers on attack, I take off with airplanes, I flip over on my back, I fall down and stand back up as bodies fall down and stand back up.[1]

This pioneering visionary thus foresaw the era of *cinéma-vérité*. "*Cinéma-vérité* is a new type of art; the art of life itself. The ciné-eye includes: all shooting techniques, all moving pictures, all methods—without exception—which will allow us to reach *the truth—the truth* in movement" ("Kinok Manifesto").

Vertov was talking about the "camera in its natural state"—not in its egotism but in its willingness to show people without makeup, to seize the moment. "It is not sufficient to put partial fragments of truth on the screen, as if they were scattered crumbs. These fragments must be elaborated into

an organic collective, which, in turn, constitutes thematic truth" ("Kinok Manifesto").

In these feverish declarations, we find everything of today's cinema: all the problems of ethnographic film, of documentary TV film, of the "living cameras" we use today. And yet no filmmaker in the world has been so poorly received; no seeker so inspired has been so unrecognized. We had to wait until the 1960s for directors and theoreticians to get back on the track of the kinoks, those "ciné-eyes" who made "films which produced films."

In 1920, when Flaherty and Vertov were trying to resolve the same problems that today's filmmakers face, camera equipment and techniques were elementary, and the making of a film required more craft than industry. The camera used for *Nanook,* forerunner of the "eyemo," had no motor, though it did already have a reflex viewer through coupled lenses.[2] The camera of the ciné-eyes that brought us *Man with a Movie Camera* was also hand cranked and continually rested on a tripod. Vertov's "eye in movement" was only able to move about in an open-topped car. Flaherty was alone, as cameraman, director, lab technician, editor, and projectionist. Vertov worked only through another cameraman and had a small family crew, with his brother Mikhail shooting and his wife editing. Later on, Flaherty too had a family crew, with his brother David operating the second camera and his wife Frances as assistant.

Perhaps it was due to such simplicity and naïveté that these pioneers discovered the essential questions that we still ask ourselves today: Must one "stage" reality (the staging of "real life") as did Flaherty, or should one, like Vertov, film "without awareness" ("seizing improvised life")?

■───────────────────────────────

*The Eclipse of the Cinema Industry*

In 1930 technical progress (the change from silent films to "talkies") transformed the cinema art and industry. No one asked anyone else what was happening, and nobody took the time to figure out what was really going on. But it was then that a white, cannibalistic cinema emerged. It was the time of exoticism, Tarzan, and white heroes among the wild savages. Making films then meant crews of ten technicians, tons of camera and sound equipment, and responsibility for thousands of dollars. So it was obviously simpler to bring man to the studio and place him in front of the camera than to take the camera out to man. Johnny Weissmuller, the most famous king of the jungle, never left the sacred Hollywood forest; it was the African beasts and feathered Tubis that were brought onto the camera set.

You had to be crazy, as some ethnographers apparently were, to take such forbidden tools to the field. And today, when one watches the first clumsy attempts of Marcel Griaule (*Au pays du Dogon* and *Sous les masques noirs,* both shot in 1938) or Patrick O'Reilly (*Bougainville,* shot in 1934 and later retitled *Popoko, the Wild Island*), one can easily understand the discouraging results of their efforts. After rather admirable camera documents were brought back, they were "made" into films with insensitive editing, Orientalist music, and a newsreel-style commentary more befitting of a sportscast. It was this betrayal that Margaret Mead and Gregory Bateson managed to avoid at the same point in time (1936–1938) with their "Character Formation" series *(Bathing Babies, Childhood Rivalry in Bali and New Guinea, First Days in the Life of a New Guinea Baby).* Here, thanks to American university financial aid, it was understood (before it was understood by other universities) that it was absurd to try to mix research and commercialism.

■───────────────────────────────────────────

### The Postwar Technical Revolution: Lightweight Cinema

New technical developments brought about by the war—the arrival of the 16 mm format—allowed for the revival of ethnographic film. The American army used lightweight cameras in the field; they were no longer 35 mm monsters but precise and robust tools, born directly of amateur cinema. Thus at the close of the 1940s, young anthropologists, following Marcel Mauss's manual of ethnography to the letter ("You will film all techniques"), brought the camera to man. And although some expeditions continued the dream of 35 mm superproductions (such as the admirable *Pays des pygmées,* brought back in 1947 along with the first authentic sound discs recorded in the equatorial forest), 16 mm would not be far behind in asserting itself.

From then on, things happened quickly. In 1951 the first self-governing tape recorders appeared. Even though they had crank motors and weighed seventy pounds, they replaced a sound truck of several tons. Yet no one except a few anthropologists initiated themselves into the mania of these bizarre tools, which no professional in the film industry would even look at. And so a few ethnographers simultaneously made themselves director, cameraman, sound recordist, editor, and also producer. Curiously, Luc de Heusch, Ivan Polunin, Henri Brandt, John Marshall, and I realized that as a by-product, we were inventing a new language. In the summer of 1955, at the Venice Festival, I was thus led to characterize ethnographic film in the following way for the journal *Positif*:

> What are these films, and by what weird name shall we distinguish them from other films? Do they actually exist? I still don't know, but I do know that there are those rare moments when the spectator can suddenly understand an unknown language without the gimmick of subtitles, moments where he can participate in strange ceremonies, move through a village, and cross places he has never seen before but nonetheless recognizes perfectly well. Only the cinema can produce this miracle, but no particular aesthetic gives it the means to do so, and no special technique uniquely provokes it. Neither the learned counterpoint of a cut nor the use of stereophonic cinerama can cause such a wonder. Often this mysterious contact is established in the middle of the most banal film, in the savage mincemeat of a current events newsreel, or in the meanderings of amateur cinema. Perhaps it is the close-up of an African smile, a Mexican winking his eye for the camera, or a European gesture so common that nobody would imagine filming it; things like these force a bewildering view of reality on us. It is as if there were no cameraman, soundman, or light meter there; no longer that mass of technicians and accessories that make up the great ritual of classical cinema. But today's filmmakers prefer not to adventure on these dangerous paths. It is only masters, fools, or children who dare push these forbidden buttons.

But soon the flashing development of TV gave professional status to our silly tools. And it was then, in working to satisfy our needs (lightweight, durable construction, quality), that manufacturers gave us their first marvelous portable silent sync cameras and automatic tape recorders. The first crews[3] to use the equipment were those of Ricky Leacock (*Primary* and *Indianapolis*) in the United States, and that of Edgar Morin, Michel Brault, and myself *(Chronicle of a Summer)* in France.

▶ ─────────────────────────────────────────

## Ethnographic Cinema Today

Hence today we have extraordinary equipment at our disposal, and the number of ethnographic films has grown each year since 1960 (evidenced by the fact that more than seventy recent films were sent to the selection committee of the first Venezia Genti festival in 1972). Yet ethnographic film has not found its voice. Having solved all of its technical problems, it has yet failed to reinvent for us, as Flaherty and Vertov did in 1920, the rules of a new film language that will permit the opening of frontiers between all civilizations. It is not my aim here to make a statement summarizing all experiments and trends, but simply to report on those that appear to me to be the most pertinent.

### Ethnographic Film and Commercial Cinema

Even though the technical barriers no longer exist, it is rare that an ethnographic film finds commercial distribution. However, the majority of ethnographic films made in recent years share the same format as productions made for commercial release: credits, background music, sophisticated editing, narration addressed to the general public, proper duration, et cetera. For the most part, the result is a hybrid product that neither satisfies scientific rigor nor cinematic art. Of course, some major works or original films escape this inevitable trap (as ethnographers consider film like a book, and an ethnographic book is no different from an ordinary book).

The outcome is a notorious increase in the cost of these films, which makes even more annoying their almost total lack of distribution (except when the cinema market is open to sensational films such as *Mondo Cane*). The solution to the problem is to study the film distribution networks. Only when universities, cultural agencies, and TV networks cease their need to make our documents conform to their other products, and learn to accept the differences, will a new type of ethnographic film, with specific criteria, be able to develop.

### Filmmaker-Ethnographer or Filmmaker and Ethnographer Teams

It is for similar reasons, and in order to make the most of technical possibilities, that ethnographers have recently preferred not to film by themselves but to call on a crew of technicians. (Actually, it is sometimes the production crew, sent out by a TV company, that calls on the anthropologist.)

Personally, unless forced into it, I am violently opposed to crews. The reasons are many. The soundman must absolutely be able to understand the language of the people being recorded; it is thus indispensable that he be a member of the group being filmed, and, of course, be trained in all aspects of his work. Moreover, in today's manner of shooting sync-sound direct cinema, the director can only be the cameraman. It is the ethnographer alone, to my mind, who really knows when, where, and how to film, in other words, to "direct." Finally, and this is without a doubt the decisive factor, the ethnographer must spend a long time in the field before beginning to shoot. This period of reflection, apprenticeship, and mutual awareness might be quite long (Flaherty spent a year in the Solomon Islands before rolling a foot of film) and is thus incompatible with the schedules and salaries of a crew of technicians.

But, of course, there are always a few exceptions: *The Hadza,* shot by the young filmmaker Sean Hudson in close collaboration with anthropologist James Woodburn; or *Emu Ritual at Ruguri* and the rest of director-filmmaker Roger Sandall's Australian series, made in conjunction with anthropologists; or *The Feast,* where Timothy Asch was completely integrated in Napoleon Chagnon's study of the Yanomamo.

Yet the Eskimo films of Asen Balikci and Ian Dunlop's recent series on the New Guinea Baruya are for me examples of what should never happen again—the intrusion of a group of first-rate technicians into a difficult field situation, even with the aid of an anthropologist. Every time a film is made there is a cultural disruption. But when the anthropologist-filmmaker is alone, he cannot push what problems may arise onto his crew, and he must assume responsibility himself. (We must remember that two whites in an African village are enough to constitute a solid foreign body, and hence to risk rejection.) And I've always wondered how that small group of Eskimos reacted to those crazy whites who made them clean out their camp of all that good canned food!

This ambiguity doesn't appear in Dunlop's earlier *Desert People* series, owing no doubt to the "piece of trail" shared by the filmmakers and the Aboriginal family they met. But it naturally manifests itself in the New Guinea film. Here, at a most extraordinary moment at the end of the ceremony, the group responsible for the initiation asks their anthropologist friend to limit the film's distribution so that it will not be shown inside New Guinea (a posteriori rejection). In cases like these, it is the awkwardness of the crew's presence that creates the obstacle to a "participating camera."

This is why it appears to me essential that we teach film and sound recording skills to students of ethnography. And even if their films are technically far inferior to those of professionals, they will nevertheless have that irreplaceable quality of the real contact between those who film and those who are filmed.

■————————————————————————————

### Handheld versus Tripod Shooting, Zoom versus Fixed Focal Lens

After the war, when American TV was searching for films (especially the "Adventure" series of Sol Lesser, and that of CBS), the idea of shooting without a tripod was almost prohibited by the desire for steadiness. Yet most of the 16 mm war footage (including the extraordinary *Memphis Belle,* the adventures of a Flying Fortress and the first film blown up to 35 mm) had been shot handheld. But when we took the example of the old pioneers and filmed without a tripod, it was principally due to economy of means, and to permit rapid movement between two cameras. Most of the time, however, the camera remained fixed, occasionally panning, and only exceptionally moving about (for example, in "crane" effects achieved by crouching, or when traveling in a car).

It took the audacity of a young crew from the Montreal Canadian Film Board to liberate the camera from its immobility. Koenig and Kroiter's *Corral* (1954) opened the way for the traveling shot, more definitively developed in the classic scene in *Bientôt Noël* (1959) where the camera follows the bank guard's revolver.[4] When Michel Brault came from Canada to Paris to shoot *Chronicle of a Summer,* this technique was a revelation to all of us, and for the TV cameramen as well. The classic example of this style is now undoubtedly the shot in *Primary* where Leacock follows the entrance of John F. Kennedy. Since then (1960), camera manufacturers have made considerable efforts to improve the balance and manageability of their products. And today all cameramen who shoot direct cinema know how to walk with their cameras, thus transforming them into "living cameras," the ciné-eyes envisioned by Vertov.

This technique is particularly useful in ethnographic filming, for it allows the cameraman to adapt to the action as a function of the spatial layout. He is thus able to penetrate into the reality, rather than leaving it to unroll itself in front of the observer.

Yet some directors have continued the general use of the tripod, always for the sake of technical rigor. This is to my mind the major fault in the films of Roger Sandall and the last New Guinea film by Ian Dunlop. (Perhaps it is not coincidental that we're talking here of Australian directors, since the best tripods and pan heads are made in Sydney!) The physical immobility of a tripod-fixed camera is thought to be compensated for by the wide use of variable-focal-length lenses (zoom lenses), which create an optical imitation of a dolly shot. But in fact, these lenses don't allow one to forget the unseen rigidity of the camera, because the zooming is always from a single point of view. Although these casual ballets may appear seductive, one must recognize that they only bring the camera and man together optically, because the camera always rests at a distance. Actually, this type of shooting more closely resembles a voyeur looking at something from a faraway perch, and zooming in for the details. This involuntary arrogance on the part of the camera is resented not only a posteriori by the attentive viewer but also by the people who are filmed, because it is like an observation post.

For me then, the only way to film is to walk with the camera, taking it where it is most effective and improvising another type of ballet with it, trying to make it as alive as the people it is filming. I consider this dynamic improvisation to be a first synthesis of Vertov's ciné-eye and Flaherty's participating camera. I often compare it to the improvisation of the bullfighter in front of the bull. Here, as there, nothing is known in advance; the smoothness of a faena is just like the harmony of a traveling shot that articulates perfectly with the movements of those being filmed. In both cases as well, it is a matter of training, mastering reflexes as would a gymnast. Thus instead of using the zoom, the cameraman-director can really get into the subject. Leading or following a dancer, priest, or craftsman, he is no longer himself, but a mechanical eye accompanied by an electronic ear. It is this strange state of transformation that takes place in the filmmaker that I have called, analogously to possession phenomena, "ciné-trance."

■——————————————————————————————

### Editing

The director-cameraman who shoots direct cinema is his own first spectator in the viewfinder of the camera. All of his bodily improvisations (camera movement, framing, shot lengths) finally result in editing while shooting. Here again we are back to Vertov's idea: "The ciné-eye is: I *edit* when I choose my subject (from among millions of possible subjects). I *edit* when I observe (i.e., film) my subject (making a choice among millions of possible observations)" ("A.B.C. of the Kinoks").

It is this aspect of fieldwork that marks the uniqueness of the ethnographic filmmaker: instead of elaborating and editing his notes after returning from the field, he must, under penalty of failure, make his synthesis at the exact moment of observation. In other words, he must create his cinematic report, bending it or stopping it, at the time of the event itself. There is no such thing here as writing cuts in advance, or fixing the order of sequences. Rather, it is a risky game where each shot is determined by the one preceding and determines the one to follow. And obviously this type of shooting requires perfect coordination of the cameraman and soundman, who, I repeat, must perfectly understand the language of the group being filmed, and who plays an essential role in the adventure. If this "ciné-eye-ear" team is well trained, all technical matters (e.g., focus, f-stops) are simply reduced to reflexes, and the two are free to spontaneously create. "Ciné-eye = ciné–I see (I see with the camera) + ciné–I write (I record with the camera on film) + ciné–I organize (I edit)" ("A.B.C. of the Kinoks").

When they are shooting, this team immediately knows, from the simple image in the viewfinder or the sound in the headphones, the quality of what they've recorded. If there is a problem, they can stop and take another course; if things are all right, they can continue, linking together the sentences of a story that creates itself simultaneously with the action. This is what I would call the "participating camera."

The second spectator is the editor. He must never participate in the shooting but must be the second ciné-eye. Knowing nothing of the context, he can only see and hear what has been recorded, that which has intentionally been brought back by the director. Editing, then, is a dialogue between the subjective author and the objective editor; it is a rough and difficult job, but the film depends on it. And here too there is no recipe, but "association (addition, subtraction, multiplication, division, bracketing) of similar film pieces. Uninterrupted permutation of bits of images until the right ones fall together in a rhythmic order where chains of meaning coincide with chains of pictures" ("A.B.C. of the Kinoks").

A supplementary stage, not foreseen by Vertov, appears indispensable. Namely, the presentation of the rough cut, from head to tail, for the people who were filmed. For me, their participation is essential (more on that point later on).

■─────────────────────────────────────

### Narration, Subtitles, Music

It is not possible to decode two sound sources simultaneously, as one will always be heard to the detriment of the other. The ideal, then, would be to make films only with original sync sound. Unfortunately, however, ethnographic films usually present foreign cultures where a language unknown to most viewers is spoken.

Narration, born of silent and lecture-type films, seemed the most simple solution. It is the direct discourse of the director, mediating between the viewer and himself. But this discourse, which should be subjective, is most often objective and makes out to be a sort of scientific exposition, a manual providing the maximum amount of information possible. Thus instead of clarifying the images, the track simply obscures them, masking them until it finally substitutes itself completely for them. And so the film ceases to be a film and becomes a lecture, a demonstration based on visual designs rather than a demonstration actually made by the images themselves. Rare indeed are ethnographic films where the commentary is in direct counterpoint to the images. Two examples come to mind: One is Luis Buñuel's *Las hurdes (Land without Bread)*, where Pierre Unik's violently subjective text brings the necessary oral cruelty to match the unbearably cruel visuals. And the other is John Marshall's *The Hunters*, where the director leads us down the trail of the giraffes and their hunters with a very simple story. In doing so, the film becomes as much the adventure of the filmmaker as that of the hunters themselves.

With the use of sync equipment, ethnographic films (like all direct cinema) became chattery, and narration attempted the impossible operation of dubbing a second language. More and more, actors were called upon to recite the narrations, always in the anxiety of approaching the norms of commercial cinema. With a few rare exceptions, the results were pitiable. Far from translating, transmitting, or reconciling, this type of discourse betrayed the communication, making it even more remote. And personally, after a bad experience with the American version of *The Lion Hunters*, I prefer to recite myself, even in bad English and with a bad accent, the texts of the foreign versions of my films (e.g., *Les maîtres fous*).

It would be interesting to make a study of the style of narration in ethnographic films since the 1930s. One would see how they passed from baroque colonialism to adventurous exoticism to the dryness of scientific statement and, most recently, to ideological discourse in which the filmmaker shares with others the revolt that he can no longer contain within himself. One would thus obtain a series of profiles, characteristic in time and space, of the investigators of our discipline, profiles that no book or lecture could better reveal.

Titling and subtitling appeared the most sensible way to escape the trap of narration. It was John Marshall, if I'm right, who was the first to use this process for his Peabody Museum "Kalahari" series. *The Pond,* a very simple sync film depicting the gossiping and verbal flirting of Bushmen at a water hole, is a model of this genre. Nevertheless, one cannot overlook the problems involved. Besides mutilating the image, the most difficult problem is screen time, for as in commercial cinema, the subtitles cannot condense and cover everything that is said. I tried to use subtitles for a sync film on lion hunting *(Un lion nommé "l'Américain"),*[5] but it was impossible to satisfactorily transcribe the difficult translation of the text (praises to the arrow's poison recited at the moment the lion dies) within the given screen time. I thus made a version where I speak the text (the hearing time is shorter) superimposed over the sync-sound original. But in fact, the result here is also deceiving, for although the text takes on an esoteric and poetic value at the moment it is recited, it actually does not bring any complementary information into the film. So I have gone back to a version with neither narration nor subtitles, feeling that in the long run it would be miraculous indeed if in twenty minutes one could gain access to the complex knowledge and techniques that demand some ten years of apprenticeship from the hunters themselves. In this case, the film can be no more than an open door to this science; those who want to know more can refer to a pamphlet, which, like the exemplary "ethnographic companion to films" (booklets) should henceforth accompany all ethnographic films.

I should mention, to close my discussion of titles and subtitles, the excellent attempt made by Timothy Asch in *The Feast*. The film begins with a preamble of freeze-frame condensations of the principal sequences, and indispensable explanations are given, a priori, on the sound track. The film is then titled in order to tell who is doing what, and discreetly subtitled. Of course, this process demystifies the film from the start, but to my mind it is the most original attempt to deal with the problem that has been made until now.

I will just say a few words about musical accompaniment. Original music was, and still is, the basic stuff of the sound track of most documentary films, as well as pre-sync-sound ethnographic films. This was simply "how films were made." I learned the heresy of doing this early on (1953) when showing my film *Bataille sur le grand fleuve* to hippopotamus hunters in Niger among whom I shot it two years earlier. At the moment of the chase, I put a very moving hunting air, played on a one-stringed bowed lute, on the sound track; I found this theme particularly well suited to the visuals. The result of the playback, however, was deplorable. The chief of the hunters demanded that I remove the music because the hunt must be absolutely silent. Since that adventure, I have paid much attention to the way music is used in my films.

Today I have the conviction that even in commercial cinema, the use of music follows nothing but an outdated theatrical convention. Music envelops, puts us to sleep, helps bad cuts pass unnoticed, and gives an artificial rhythm to pictures that don't have, and never will have, any rhythm of their own. In short, music is the opium of the cinema. Television has now seized the mediocrity of the process as well, and I find the admirable Japanese ethnographic films *Papua New Life* and *Kula, Argonauts of the Pacific* to be spoiled by the musical sauce with which they are served. On the other hand, we should be aided by music that really supports an action, be it ritual, everyday, work rhythm, or dance. And although it is beyond the scope of this paper, I must mention the importance that sync filming will have in the field of ethnomusicology.

Sound editing (background, speech, music) is undoubtedly as complex as picture editing. I believe that we still have enormous progress to make here in order to rid ourselves of prejudices we've come to via radio, prejudices that have led us to treat sound with more respect than image. I find many recent direct cinema films ruined by the incredible amount of attention paid to chattering, as if the oral statement were more important than the visual one. Where a director would never hesitate to cut on a movement, he wouldn't dare cut in the middle of a sentence or even a word, much less cut a musical theme before its final note. I believe that it won't be long before this archaic habit (TV is the current prime offender) will slowly disappear and the image will regain priority.

---

### The Ethnographic Film Public: Research and Distribution of Films

A final notion, which viewed in terms of intention is really the first point, is to my mind essential for ethnographic film today. Because in Africa, in the universities, at the cultural centers, the scientific research centers, or the cinematheques, the first question asked after the projection of an ethnographic film is, "For whom, and why, have you made this film?"

For whom, and why, do I take the camera among mankind? My first response will always, strangely, be the same: "For me." Not because it is some type of drug whose habit must be regularly satisfied, but because I find that in certain places, close to certain people, the camera, and especially the sync camera, seems necessary. Of course it will always be possible to justify this type of filmmaking scientifically (creating archives of changing or disappearing cultures), politically (sharing in the revolt against an intolerable situation), or aesthetically (discovering the fragile mastery of a landscape, of a face, or of a movement that is irresistible). But in fact, what is there is that sudden intuition about the necessity to film, or conversely, the certainty that one should not film.

The frequenting of movie theaters, and the intempestuous use of audiovisual equipment, makes it clear that we are today's Vertovian *kinoki*, ciné-eyes who were formerly the "pen-hands" (Rimbaud) who could not resist writing: "I was there, so many things happened to me . . ." (La Fontaine). And if the ciné-voyeur of his own society will always be able to justify himself by this particular militarism, what reason can we, anthropologists, give when we pin our subjects up against the wall?

This question is obviously addressed to all anthropologists, but anthropological writing has never been contested the way anthropological film has. And that's where I get my second response to "For whom, and why?" Film is the only means I have to show someone else how I see him. For me, after the pleasure of the ciné-trance in shooting and editing, my first public is the other, those whom I've filmed.

The situation is clearly this: the anthropologist has at his disposal the only tool (the participating camera) that offers him the extraordinary possibility of direct communication with the group he studies—the film he has made about them. Of course there are still some technical hang-ups here, and the projection of film in the field is still at an experimental stage. The development of the Super-8 sync-sound projector with a twelve-volt battery will doubtless be serious progress in this area. But my experiences with a 16 mm projector and a small portable 300-watt battery have been conclusive enough. The projection of my film *Sigui 1969* in the village of Bongo where it was shot brought considerable reaction from the Dogon (of the Bandiagara cliffs, in Mali) and the demand for more films; a *Sigui* series is now in progress.[6] And the projection of my film *Horendi* on the initiation of possession dancers in Niger also brought demands for more films. By studying this film on a small moviescope viewer with my informants, I was able to gather more information in two weeks than I could get in three months of direct observation and interview. This type of a posteriori working is just the beginning of what is already a new type of relationship between the anthropologist and the group he studies, the first step in what some of us have labeled "shared anthropology."[7] Finally, then, the observer has left the ivory tower; his camera, tape recorder, and projector have driven him, by a strange road of initiation, to the heart of knowledge itself. And for the first time, the work is judged not by a thesis committee but by the very people the anthropologist went out to observe. This extraordinary technique of "feedback" (which I would translate as "audiovisual reciprocity") has certainly not yet revealed all of its possibilities.[8] But already, thanks to it, the anthropologist has ceased to be a sort of entomologist observing others as if they were insects (thus putting them down) and has become a stimulator of mutual awareness (hence dignity).

This type of totally participatory research, as idealistic as it may seem, appears to me to be the only morally and scientifically feasible anthropological attitude today. And it is to the development of its technical aspects (e.g., Super-8 and video) that today's equipment manufacturers should dedicate maximum effort.

But at the same time, it is obviously absurd to condemn ethnographic film to such a closed information circuit. That is why my third response to the question "For whom, and why?" is "For everyone, for the largest viewing public possible." I believe that if the distribution of ethnographic film is, with rare exceptions, limited to university networks, cultural organizations, and scholarly societies, the fault is more our own than that of commercial cinema. The time has come for ethnographic films to become films.

I don't think that this is impossible, as long as a film's essential quality of being the unique statement of one or two people is preserved. If exploration lectures and TV travelogues are a success, it is, I repeat, due to the fact that behind the clumsy images there is the presence of the person who shot them. If for reasons of science, or ideological shame, anthropological filmmakers insist on hiding behind their comfortable incognito, they will irrevocably castrate their films and doom them to an existence in archives, where they will be reserved only for specialists. The success of pocketbook editions of ethnographies once confined to a small scientific library network is an example that ethnographic film should follow.

And so now we find ourselves awaiting the appearance of true ethnographic films; films that "join scientific rigor and cinematographic language," a definition we gave them nearly twenty years ago. Meanwhile, at the Venezia Genti festival of 1972, the International Committee of Ethnographic and Sociological Films decided to create, with the help of UNESCO, a true network for the conservation, documentation, and distribution of "films of man." Why? Because we are people who believe that the world of tomorrow, the world we are in the process of building, cannot be viable without a regard for cultural differences; the other cannot be denied as his image transforms. For this it is necessary to be aware, and for that knowledge there is no better tool than ethnographic film. This is not just a pious vow, and a similar example comes to us from Japan, where a TV company, in an effort to broaden Japanese perspectives, has decided to broadcast an hour of ethnographic film each week for three years.

▶ ─────────────────────────────────────────

### Conclusion: Shared Ciné-Anthropology

Now we are at the close of our story of the place of the camera among man, yesterday and today. And for the moment, the only conclusion that one can draw is that ethnographic film has not yet passed the experimental stage. Although anthropologists have this fabulous tool at their disposal, they still haven't figured out how to make it best serve their needs.

For the moment, no "schools" of ethnographic film exist; there are only tendencies. Personally, I hope this marginal situation will prolong itself so that our young discipline can avoid sclerosis in an iron collar, or in sterile bureaucracy. It is good that there are differences in American, Canadian, Japanese, Brazilian, Australian, British, Dutch, and French ethnographic films. Within the universality of concepts in the scientific approach, we maintain a multiplicity of orientations: if the ciné-eyes of all countries are ready to unite, it is not simply to have one point of view. Thus film in the human sciences is, in a certain respect, in the avant-garde of film research. And if one finds similar features in the diversity of recent films, such as the multiplication of shot sequences (I have asked a manufacturer of lightweight cameras to make a one-thousand-foot magazine so that shooting can go for half an hour), it is because our experiences have led us to similar conclusions and thus have given birth to a new cinema language.

And tomorrow? . . . Tomorrow will be the time of completely portable color video, video editing, and instant replay ("instant feedback"). Which is to say, the time of the joint dream of Vertov and Flaherty, of a mechanical ciné-eye-ear and of a camera that can so totally participate that it will automatically pass into the hands of those who, until now, have always been in front of the lens. At that point, anthropologists will no longer control the monopoly on observation; their culture and they themselves will be observed and recorded. And it is in that way that ethnographic film will help us to "share" anthropology.

(1973)

## TRANSLATOR'S NOTES

1. An exact reference for this text, and for other Vertov materials quoted later, is not given. French translations of Vertov can be found in *Cahiers du Cinéma*, nos. 144 (June 1963), 146 (August 1963), and 220–21 (May–June 1970).
2. The "eyemo" is the name of the early Bell and Howell handheld camera that was the ethnographer's and newsman's staple camera the world over.
3. The French is *équipe*, literally "team"; Rouch and Morin were not "crew" in the English sense of the term. Rouch credits Michel Brault of the French Unit of the Canadian Film Board as the first cameraman to bring the new shooting techniques to France. Other sections of *Chronicle* were shot by Roger Morillère, Raoul Coutard, and Jean-Jacques Tarbès.
4. The English release of *Bientôt Noël* was titled *The Days until Christmas;* the cameraman was Michel Brault.
5. *Un lion nommé "l'Américain" (A Lion Named the American)* was finished in 1971 and is a sequel to *The Lion Hunters*. It tells the story of the lion who escaped the hunters in the first film.
6. From 1967 to 1974, Rouch filmed the Sigui ceremonies of the Dogon. *Sigui 1969: La caverne du Bongo* and *Sigui 1971* are finished; the other films are being cut. A short description of the ceremonies and a summary of *Sigui 1969* can be found in Germaine Dieterlen's "Les cérémonies soixantenaires du Sigui chez les Dogon," *Africa*, no. 41 (1971): 1–11.
7. The attitude Rouch is speaking of is similar to what is called "self-reflexive" anthropology in the United States.
8. Rouch uses the English word "feedback" in quotes and refers to the way he would translate the notion into French with "contredon audio-visuel."

## REFERENCES

de Heusch, Luc. 1962. *Cinéma et sciences sociales*. Paris: UNESCO.
Leroi-Gourhan, André. 1948. "Cinéma et sciences humaines: Le film ethnologique existe-t-il?" *Revue de Geographie Humaine et d'Ethnologie*, no. 3.

# The Situation and Tendencies of the Cinema in Africa

The cinema began to take hold in Africa from the first years that followed its invention. In South Africa, for example, as early as 1896, cinema was introduced by a vaudeville magician who had stolen a "theatregraph" from the Alhambra Palace in London. And today, the word "bioscope," used from the turn of the century by "Warwick bioscope" projectors, is still the usual word for cinema in South Africa.

In West Africa, the first attempts at cinema projections date from 1905, the year that traveling cinemas projected the first animation strips in Dakar and surrounding areas. At the same time pioneers and explorers began to use the camera, and the French Cinémathèque has several catalogs of Georges Méliès referring to the first films made in Africa.

Since this pioneering period, the cinema has developed considerably, but one must nevertheless note, along with Georges Sadoul, that sub-Saharan Africa remains not only one of the most underdeveloped areas of the world in terms of films shown but moreover the most backward continent in the area of film production.[1] While Asia, South America, and Indonesia have long been making films, sub-Saharan Africa has not yet in 1961 produced a single feature-length film.

In the words of Georges Sadoul, "Sixty-five years after the invention of the cinema, in 1960, there is not to my knowledge a single true feature length African film production—acted, photographed, written, conceived, edited, etc., by Africans and in an African language. Thus two hundred million people are shut out from the most evolved form of the most modern of the arts. I am convinced that before the close of the 1960s this scandal will be but a bad souvenir of the past."[2]

It thus appears particularly opportune today, at a time when African cinema is being born, to take account of current productions in Africa, the possibilities of new productions and distribution, and to analyze the current tendencies in the new African cinema.

The plan of our study will be the following: (1) an account of commercial, educational, and documentary films made in Africa up to today; (2) an analysis of the importance of these types of films from filmic, cultural, and social viewpoints; and (3) an analysis of new tendencies and the conditions for the development of a true African cinema.

As to reference documents: it is important to note here the considerable difficulties of documentation in the field of African cinema. I apologize for many errors and omissions that are inevitable in this type of study, but I think that above all this report is a foundation, which after the necessary corrections and rectifications will give researchers access to information for their studies.

I have gathered these data by using the classic literature, unfortunately very slight, on African cinema (Georges Sadoul, Leprophon, Thévenot); a review of the first and only international conference on "Cinema in Sub-Saharan Africa," organized in Brussels during the World Fair in July 1958; different UNESCO reports (in particular the report of January 1961, concerning the development of information media in underdeveloped countries); different articles on African cinema published in the journal *Présènce Africaine;* and the special issue of *La Vie Africaine* on African cinema (June 1961). I have also made as much use as possible of reports on information services prepared by African republics in response to a questionnaire circulated by the Comité du Film Ethnographique of the Musée de l'Homme in Paris. Finally, I will make much reference to my own experience as a filmmaker and observer during the course of several trips to West Africa since 1941.

▶

### Account of African Films to Present

In this rapid survey we will only distinguish two categories of film: (1) commercial and documentary films, and (2) educational films. In fact, it is not possible to establish neat boundaries between commercial, documentary, scripted, and ethnographic films; these genres have frequently been mixed since the beginning of African film. On the other hand, educational films can neatly be placed to the side, as their appearance has been recent, and their aim and manner of technical production has been completely different.

## Commercial and Documentary Films

The first films shot in Africa by foreign directors (and with rare exceptions, all of the films analyzed in this account are, unfortunately, of this type) were boldly exotic. One sees here a logical continuation from colonial literature, which also, until the last few years, was aimed toward this sense of removal and bewilderment.

We know very little about the first Méliès documentaries or the films made by Pathé before 1925, but what their catalog titles indicate is the capricious foreignness of savagery and cannibalism, showing the African as a peculiar animal whose behavior is rather laughable, when not classed at the very limits of pathology.

The First World War allowed Europeans to discover another aspect of the African: the courage and good humor of the Senegalese sharpshooter favored the creation of the stereotype of the complacent childish black, the "Uncle Tom."[3] It is peculiar to note parallel images of the black stereotype: In the United States, until the Second World War, the black American was reserved for film roles of the smiling domestic, just as at the same time in African cinema the black African was either the incomprehensible savage or the devoted servant, never lacking in a sense of humor.

The first noteworthy film about black Africa is undoubtedly Léon Poirier's *La croisière noire,* made during the first automobile crossing of Africa, from north to south, by Citroën tractors (October 1924–June 1925). The basic subject of this film is auto adventure, but parallel to this real epic, some representative aspects of populations encountered during the trip are shown. The travelers were undoubtedly in a hurry, but it is obvious that they took some time to choose and look at their subjects. The documents have aged but remain as inestimable archival data, in terms of both the discovery of Africa and the evolution of African cultures. Without doubting the sincerity and goodwill of the filmmakers, two orientations are clearly apparent; the incomprehension of a world just glimpsed, and having stopped to look closer, the barbary of what is discovered there (platter-lipped women, circumcision rites, aspects of the daily life of pygmies, etc.). Although they are rendered as objectively as possible, these images remain frozen, if not ironic documents, quite far from the human warmth of the films made previously or at the same time by Robert Flaherty *(Nanook of the North, Moana).* The same feeling was present in all of the written or filmed reports of expeditions of the period; the West discovered the rest of the world with a lens little different in viewpoint from the pen of Marco Polo.

Unfortunately, the situation degenerated, and in succeeding films Africa was but a continent of barbarism and inhumanity. Clearly, Africa was not the only continent subjected to this treatment: Asia, South America, Greenland, and generally all colonized countries were recalled on the screen from meager images of wild dances, guitar players, or primitive hunts. Titles like *Among the Cannibals, Among the People Eaters,* and *Bali, Island of Naked Breasts* sufficiently evoke the spirit, or rather the lack of spirit, of the period.

Raymond Barkan, in a particularly well-documented study, "Vers un cinéma universel" *(Cinéma 61),* describes several typical scenarios:

> An ivory hunter (frequently accompanied by the widow of an explorer) abandoned by his porters, captured by a ferocious and vociferous tribe, is saved at the last minute by the bullets of an emergency squad. Or: In the debilitating climate of the tropics, a white man (generally a plantation owner) and a white woman, in the midst of dreadful love-life complications, are aggravated by an indigenous rebellion, or occasionally by an earthquake or floods. Or: In India, the polo addicted officers of His Majesty's Britain, gain fame at the head of their Sepoys against revolting bands. Or: In the Sahara, foreign legionnaires or Arab troopers (their captain joined the Army in a fit of the blues) victoriously battle against a group of pillagers. These explorers universally dream of civilization penetrating the Dark Continent, vehemently attacking the powers of sorcerers, and blazing the trail for missionaries who would convert the natives to Christianity and doctors who would immunize them against sleeping sickness.

"We are writing with a minimum of humor and dramatization," observes Barkan justly.

> As a completely new means of expression, the cinema neither had the spare time nor the desire to read the works of Lévy-Bruhl and Frazer. Working at the level of newsstand adventure novels, the racism of these films was more stupid than deliberate. If cinema sacrificed itself to all of the commonplace colonialist ideas, it was equally for purposes of commercial conformism as for political conformism. . . . In truth, the Hindus, Africans, Indians, and Arabs were of little more consequence than the lions, tigers, orangutans, cobras, and scorpions among whom they accomplished their missions in the jungle, the tropical forest, or the desert.

And Barkan concludes: "Whatever antipathy comes from this cavalier treatment inflicted on our colored brothers, there is no proof that it added to the racialism upheaving mankind."

From this period, dominated in France by the colonial exposition of 1931, we are reminded of *Trader Horn,* where one of the chief attractions was an African being devoured alive by a crocodile (and from the statement of the filmmakers, it was never really clear whether the sequence was faked or accidental), and above all of *Bozambo* (also known as *Sanders of the River*), a sound film with music, starring the black American singer Paul Robeson. I will dwell upon this latter film at length for two reasons: *Bozambo* was one of the first quality sound films made in Africa, and, chiefly, *Bozambo* was quite an appreciable success in France and is still a considerable success in Africa.

On the musical level, it is interesting to note that thanks to Paul Robeson's extraordinary voice, a low-quality pseudo-African music was successfully imposed on both European and African listeners. For example, I've heard young Africans sing the canoer's tune, *ayoko;* this is a very rare example of musical falsification simultaneously abused by foreigners and indigenes alike.

The African success of this film is even more peculiar, because there has never been a film that so elevates the glories of colonialism. Based on a novel by Edgar Wallace, the film is the story of a British colonial administrator, Sanders (nicknamed "Sandy the strong"), who with his African servant, Bozambo, arrives at a river area in his administrative district to establish traditional authority and maintain colonial order. For the most part, the film takes place in Nigeria; for the needs of certain action, some exteriors were also shot in the Congo among Wagenia fishermen, and in animal reserves in Kenya. These authentic settings served as the basis for the studio sets in Hollywood, where the rest of the film was shot.

One can see, equally on the visual, auditory, and ideological levels, that this is one of the most faked films that has ever been made, and yet the film continues to enjoy quite a success in Africa. Some African friends with whom I've discussed this problem have perhaps given me the key to understanding this success: for the first time in film, a black plays a leading role, and even if it is as a puppet of a British colonial administrator, it is nevertheless sufficient to create considerable sympathy among African audiences.

*Bozambo* opened the way for an African fantasy cinema, and the hero that followed was not black but the white Tarzan of the familiar unending film series. The raceless ape-man and his fantastic adventures against men and beasts became a pastime whose prodigious success touched upon the entire world.

To finish with films of this tradition made between the two wars, we will just note two very interesting films by Léon Poirier: *Cain,* made in Madagascar, and *L'homme du Niger,* made with Henry Baur in the interior Ségou region of the Niger delta. Despite the defects of these two films, the directors deserve credit for not faking anything. For the first time, cameras were set in place and shot natural surroundings and real people. In reviewing these films today, it is strange to discover, because of the time since an earlier viewing, a sort of inversion in the pictures: the environment being the principal object of interest, to the detriment of the actors, who are transformed into secondary accessories.

On the other hand, the first true documentary films began to appear at this time. Previously, Marc Allégret, accompanying André Gide in the Congo, brought back the naive but pretty pictures of *Voyage au Congo* (1928), where most frequently aesthetics took precedence over ethnographic and social documentation. If the film had been the cinematic mirror of Gide's classic book bearing the same title—a violent testimony against the excesses of colonialism—it would certainly have oriented those to follow in the 1930s, thus playing for Africa a comparable role to that played for Asia by Pudovkin's *Storm over Asia* (1928) or, above all, for America by Eisenstein's *Thunder over Mexico*. But it would be necessary to await the images of the Ivory Coast rescued by Vautier *(Afrique 50)* in order for the number one problem of Africa in the twentieth century—its relation with the white world—to be evoked with sincerity, if not impartiality.

In the area of documentary film, the experience of the period between the two wars was already very conclusive. Marcel Mauss, uncontested master of the French school of ethnology, had already professed in his lectures an interest in adding still photography, cinema, and sound recording to traditional ethnographic research. And it is interesting to note that it was infinitely easier then to depart on an exploration with a 35 mm camera and Edison cylinder recorder than it is today to pull together a simple expedition to the Sahara. But in fact, if for most present-day leaders in French ethnology—André Leroi-Gourhan, Claude Lévi-Strauss, Roger Bastide—this teaching of Marcel Mauss remains theoretical, a few pioneers made the first African ethnographic films during the Dakar-Djibouti expedition, which went from the Atlantic to the Indian Ocean, under the leadership of Marcel Griaule, André Schaeffner, and Michel Leiris. The first attempts were made particularly among the Dogon of the Bandiagara cliffs, and in 1938 Marcel Griaule, during a second mission, made two model 35 mm sound ethnographic films.

*Au pays du Dogon* is a short fifteen-minute film illustrating aspects of the daily life, material culture, and religion of the Dogon. *Sous les masques noirs* shows funeral ceremonies of a village in the cliffs and documents the construction, role, and use of large masks, which through ritual dances permit the soul of the deceased to be returned to the dwelling of its ancestors in the next world.

At about the same time, in 1936, Jean d'Esme shot *La grande caravane* (35 mm, sound) in Eastern Niger; it retraces the voyage of a salt caravan from Agadès to Bilma, where the salt mines are found. Unfortunately, despite the passionate images, the author could not escape the manner of the early sound documentaries, namely, the use of a gossipy and exasperating narration, and tedious music in the style of the "Persian March."

It is the same defect that marred a short and completely forgotten film, *Coulibaly à l'aventure,* made in 1936, in Guinea, by G. H. Blanchon. This was the first African sociological film, and its subject is one of the most important phenomena found in West Africa—the migration of young people from the savannah to the cities of the coast. The adventures of Coulibaly, leaving upper Guinea to earn the dowry for his fiancée by working as a docker in Conakry, and then as a miner in Sigiri, could have been an extremely valuable document, if it hadn't been spoiled by the propagandist narration (in the "benefits of our civilization" style).

Outside of the scene in French Colonial Africa, and some spectacular type pseudodocumentaries that I have already said too much about, I would only mention a single valuable ethnographic film, *Pêcheurs Wagenia,* shot by Surbeck, at Stanley Pool, upstream from Stanleyville in Belgian Congo. One had to wait until after the war to finally see the development of the African cinema, both in the realm of fiction film as well as that of documentary film.[4]

Finally, one other aspect of filming between the wars should be noted. It is probable that Africa was the subject for several German filmmakers who were traveling all over the world in the 1930s, making the large series of UFA and Tobias films that included Walter Ruttman's *Melody of the World* (1929). Unfortunately, all of our research in this area has been in vain, and only documents dealing with South America and the Far East are in the film library of the Musée de l'Homme.

The Second World War indirectly favored the development of "cinema on the move" ("cinéma au long cours," in the excellent phrase of Jean Thévenot), because during this period army film units used portable materials rather than the more perfected 35 mm cameras, which were heavy, cumbersome, and could not leave the studio. It was at this time that 16 mm, previously only an amateur format, gained its first stronghold.

Most professional filmmakers at that time were reticent about 16 mm (and many still are today). Yet the first color 35 mm enlargements made from 16 mm films about aircraft carriers and Flying Fortresses in operation had drawn the attention of some filmmakers, as well as some young researchers (like myself) impassioned about the cinema and the wonderful possibilities of the 16 mm medium. These divergent options created in France two opposing currents, which have a tendency to unite today—35mm professional film, and 16 mm exploration and research film.[5]

It was in France chiefly, just after the war, that the new movement had its birth. French youth, leaving the occupation, the liberation movement, the armed forces, or the underground, were desirous of a means of escapism, a feeling that has been accurately portrayed, though through a romantic veil, in Jacques Becker's *Rendez-vous de Juillet*. The Musée de l'Homme effectively became a magnet of attraction for all youth seeking adventure and discovery. Around ethnologists such as Marcel Griaule, André Leroi-Gourhan, Reverend Leenhardt, and Théodore Monod, and great travelers such as Paul-Émile Victor or Bertrand Flornoy, there developed a spontaneous grouping of young, well-disposed people ready to go off to Greenland, the Antarctic, Borneo, Tierra del Fuego, New Guinea, or Africa. Noël Ballif, a young organizer out of the underground, put together a short Musée de l'Homme mission, the 1946 Ogooué-Congo expedition, which was the first collaboration of ethnologists and filmmakers and remains a model of this genre. During this mission the first quality sound recordings in Africa were made; in addition, they allowed for making film sound tracks that would not have to fake exotic music. The three 35 mm black-and-white films made during this trip—*Danses Congolaises, Au pays des pygmées,* and *Pirogues sur l'Ogooué*—remain the first high-quality images and sounds of sub-Saharan Africa, and they constitute first-rate documents on traditional Congo dances, the daily life of the Ba-Binga pygmies, and canoe transportation from the Lastourville falls to Lambaréné, on the Ogooué river.[6]

Concurrently, a young French filmmaker, François Villiers, shot two very different films in equatorial Africa: *Autour de Brazzaville* and *Amitié noire*. The first told the story of how the Middle Congo rallied behind Free France during the war, and the second, narrated by Jean Cocteau, was a poetic essay on the cultures of Chad. It is necessary to say that these films are not of great interest but nevertheless constitute one element of the renewal of African cinema.

The films of Villiers and the Ogooué-Congo mission were shot in 35 mm, in the same way that conventional commercial productions were made; they required the use of heavy equipment and reliance on a camera crew. This was due to the influence of the Institute des Hautes Études Cinématographiques (IDHEC), which advocated the use of 35 mm materials and technical crews for the production of all films, even those shot in the most remote areas. Yet at the same time this institute was also interested in the experiments by young groups of travelers and researchers who were voluntarily oriented toward 16 mm.

For example, at the same time as the Ogooué-Congo mission, the author of this report, with two comrades, Ponty and Sauvy, descended the Niger river by canoe, and made 16 mm black-and-white films during the trip. I must note that we had chosen 16 mm as a last resort, because commercial cinema producers were not interested in our project. If the results were disappointing (in particular, we used a very fast negative film, and we didn't have the money to deal with problems of heat and humidity), a document on hippopotamus hunting by harpoon on the Niger river was nevertheless completed. From these pieces, Actualités Françaises made a 35 mm blowup (the first black-and-white blowup to be made in France) and edited a ten-minute film entitled *Au pays des mages noirs*. From this point on, there was a split in African cinema between two options: 35 mm films with commercial and technical guarantees, and 16 mm films for eventual blowup or use in lectures.[7]

Here we must note a single exception to the general rule of 16 mm's evolution (i.e., shooting in 16 mm and then enlarging to 35 mm). This is the case of Albert Mahuzier, who began by making 35 mm films on hunting in Chad for Actualités Françaises and later created a sort of family enterprise of world travel (including a trip across Africa with his wife and nine children) and directed 16 mm films for lectures. These films have been an enormous popular success in France and Belgium but concern Africa only in a secondary manner, as the principal subject was the life of the Mahuzier family in the course of their expeditions.

After 1948, films made in Africa multiplied; it is not possible to mention them all; I will nevertheless try to group them by types, illustrated by a few titles. The first postwar African fiction film seems to be *Paysans noirs* (titled *Famoro, le tyran* in Africa), by Georges Régnier; the film was shot and produced by the same crew that made the Ogooué-Congo films. Despite the naïveté of the scenario (Voltaic countrymen are terrorized by a black despot, and it is only the intervention of the colonial administration that brings them happiness and prosperity), this film represents an important stage in the development of African cinema. For here, alongside the story, a real Africa—its countrysides, its peoples, and above all its dialogues—appeared for the first time. After *Paysans noirs,* all African films shot on studio sets appeared singularly null. For example, *Le char des dieux,* a film made at about the same time in Cameroon by Alfred Chaumel, and then edited using footage from all over Africa, was outdated before it reached the screen.

Another noteworthy pre-1950 effort was Thorold Dickenson's *Le sorcier noir (The Black Witch Doctor).* This film was shot in a studio near London and was deliberately nondocumentary, in terms of both framework and characters. Nevertheless it was the first treatment of the problem of the confrontation of White and African civilization.

Also before 1950, 16 mm developed further due to the new possibilities of color film and printing 16 mm sound composite copies. Thus I made three films in 1948: *Les magiciens de Wanzerbé, La circoncision,* and *Initiation à la danse des possédés.* These films, like those I made preceding them, were attempts to illustrate systematic ethnographic studies in the loop of Niger. However, in the course of projections limited to professional film people, I realized that with a portable 16 mm camera, an ethnographer-filmmaker could bring back documents whose scope could reach beyond limited specialist audiences. After 1948 it was thus necessary to envision 16 mm to 35 mm color blowups,[8] but this operation was not technically possible in Europe until after 1951. In the United States this experiment had already proved possible using the technicolor process. Unfortunately this process necessitated printing a great number of copies in order to be commercially feasible and was not applicable to films where the maximum demand to be hoped for would not exceed ten copies.

The year 1950 is an important turning point in the evolution of African film. The attempts of the preceding years marked the end of the cheap exoticism so characteristic of the prewar films, and showed the necessity of discovering and understanding African cultures if one wanted to communicate about them to members of other cultures. Moreover, 1950 historically marked the opening of the colonial crisis and the first independence movements in African countries. From this point until the present, one sees the following trends in African films.

●———————————————————————————

## Exotic Africa

Outside of the Tarzan films, for which Africa was but a backdrop, a certain number of filmmakers, chiefly Americans, continued to exploit the "cannibal" and "witch doctor's dance" film genre. Africa, as before the war, was no more than scenery, and the Africans themselves functioned only as the unfortunate extras that one never hesitated to dress up in costumes of materials from the far Atlantic and paint with dreadful tattoos in order to take advantage of "local color."

As an example, one can cite *King Solomon's Mines* (which started the Tutsi dancers of Ruanda-Urundi on their film career), whose first images—a wounded elephant supported by its cows—are the only ones worth the trouble of keeping. Other examples are *Nagana,* a ghastly gangster film made among the Peul of Cameroon, but which could just as well have taken place in Marseilles or Chicago; and finally, a film made in Gabon by the production crew that made *Lost Continent,* for which a plastic skeleton was brought from Rome for the witchcraft scenes. This genre of film is far from exhausted, and today, in Kenya or Chad, someone is still shooting some new production in which Africa will serve as a country of beasts and savages, precisely fitting the white man's standard of adventure.[9]

## Ethnographic Africa

Here we find filmmakers and ethnographers trying, sometimes rather clumsily, to show the most authentic aspects of African cultures. The influence of ethnographic film has not been limited to scientific research and has already modified quite a few commercial films made in Africa.

In the purely ethnographic field, we must first note the films of Luc de Heusch, one illustrating an ethnographic thesis on Tutsi kinship *(Ruanda)*, another concerning the lineage system of the Hamba of the Kasai *(Fête chez les Hamba)*. Here the ethnographer turned filmmaker and tried to use film as a contribution to the techniques of ethnographic research. These two unpretentious but carefully made films remain the only authentic documents on cultures of the Congo before the troubles of independence. And in comparison, the numerous high-budget Belgian films made in the Congo, such as *Congo, splendeur sauvage,* or most of the short films by Gérard de Boe, seem less faithful.

The case of Henri Brandt is different: he was a filmmaker who came to ethnography to make a film in Africa. After a preparatory mission among the Peul Bororo nomads of Niger, Professor Gabus, director of the ethnographic museum at Neuchâtel, sent Brandt out to the field for a year alone with these savannah pastoralists. Working in 16 mm, Brandt brought back an extremely valuable document, accompanied by remarkably well recorded location sound. Brandt's *Les nomades du soleil* remains a classic film, even though it has never been distributed commercially.

From the beginning, all of these efforts were not particularly well greeted in scientific circles, and when the Comité du Film Ethnographique was created at the Musée de l'Homme, and charged with the responsibility of initiating students of ethnography into the techniques of cinema, a certain number of ethnographers reproached us for placing the research of an image before ethnographic research itself.[10] Despite this slight resistance, a true school of Africanist filmmakers has developed, some working alone, others working with the aid of film technicians. We should mention the following.

Among the ethnographers: Capron, who with filmmaker Serge Ricci made *Noces d'eau* (fertility rites of the Bobo and Bambara in the San region of Mali) and *Bobo-Oulé* (daily life of the Bobo-Oulé on the border of Upper Volta and Mali); Igor de Garine, who alone shot *Gourouna, bergers sacrés* and *Les hommes du Loyone* (both concerning daily life and religion of peoples in Chad); Claude Millet, who despite problems with a bad camera made one of the most disturbing films on rites of passage in equatorial Africa, *Rites de la circoncision chez les Mongom;* Monique and Robert Gessain, who illustrated their work on large initiation ceremonies of the Coniagui (Guinea-Senegal border) with the color film *Le temps du Caméléon;* Guy le Moal, ethnographer and director of the Research Institute in Upper Volta, who during the many years of research for his thesis on the Bobo-Fing made a film on the role of children in religious masking traditions, *Les masques des feuilles;* and Dr. Zahan, anthropology professor at the University of Strasbourg, thanks to whom I was able to make a film on the funeral ceremonies of Mossi chieftans in Upper Volta, *Moro-Naba.*

Among the filmmakers: Jacques Darribehaude, who made two 16 mm color films in Mali, *Pays Mandingue* and *Saison seche* (daily life in Malinke country in the goldfields of the Sigiri region); Georges Bourdelon, who made a 16 mm documentary on artisans of the Sahara, *Forgerons du désert;* Pierre Ichac, who while out shooting a film on wild animals brought back a 16 mm synthetic documentary on populations of Chad, *En regardant passer le Tchad.*[11]

Even professional filmmakers began trying to make truly ethnographic films. Jacques Dupont, filmmaker of the 1946 Ogooué-Congo expedition, later made, in 1951, a remarkable film, *La grande case,* concerning Bamiléké, Peul, and Bamoun chieftainships in western Cameroon. Pierre-Dominique Gaisseau (also a former member of the Ogooué-Congo mission) made a series of films in Guinea on the Toma, Bassari, and Nalou peoples, *Forêt sacrée* (first version in 1953), *Pays Bassari,* and *Naloutai.* Following these first documents, Gaisseau went back to Africa with two European friends to be initiated into the secret societies of the Toma. The long version of *Forêt sacrée* is the story of their attempt. Little by little, they are received by members of Toma society, are tattooed, make a retreat into the forest for purification rites, but then, at the last moment, are not allowed to penetrate into the sacred forest. Sick and demoralized, they abandon their attempt. This film, which was contested by a number of ethnologists who felt that being initiated into another society was the surest way to lose the objectivity necessary for scientific study, nevertheless brought an entirely new aspect of ethnography to the screen. For the first time, one is an actual witness to the research, which perhaps was hopeless but nevertheless shows an unbounded respect for African culture. In the end, this defeated attempt is a defense of the forest, which refused to be violated by unknowns, despite the fact that they had made relatively considerable accomplishments.[12]

## Evolving Africa

Here filmmakers tried to show the problems posed by contact between traditional Africa and the modern world. In this instance the cinema is up against the same obstacles as African sociology. In both cases the principal stumbling block appears to me to be an ignorance of traditional cultures in the process of evolution. This fault is particularly serious when manifest in films of a propagandistic tendency, where the filmmakers preferred to mock traditional African cultures, rather than attempt to understand them.

We have already mentioned the first film on acculturation, *Coulibaly à l'aventure,* made in 1936. This topic was not dealt with again until 1950, when a young student at IDHEC (the French Film Institute), Vautier, clandestinely made *Afrique 50.* This film shows the struggle of the young RDA party in the Ivory Coast, which was then under attack from the colonial administration. Shot in 16 mm, black and white, with a makeshift sound track added later, *Afrique 50* was prohibited in Africa and France and limited to cinémathèque showings.

Another banned film was Alain Resnais and Chris Marker's *Les statues meurent aussi,* made in European African museums by means of a remarkable montage of archive documents from Africa. The thesis was that the statues of African art in Western museums are degraded because they have lost the meaning of their representations, and the new African art that has been influenced by the West is already completely decadent. This violent and admirable film was censored and has only been seen by a privileged few.[13]

At the same time, the first African students at IDHEC, unable to obtain administrative permission to film in their own countries, turned the situation around and began making African films in Europe. If Mamani Touré's *Mouramani,* a story based on Guinean folklore, is only of slight interest, *Afrique sur Seine,* by Paulin Soumanou Vieyra, Jacques Melokane, Mamadou Sarr, and cameraman Caristan, is truly the first black film. It is an interesting attempt to show the lives of Africans in Paris; unfortunately it only remained an experiment, since the final editing and the sound track were never carried to completion.

Besides these more or less ill-starred films of the 1950s, a great number of films were shot in all countries throughout Africa on the subject of acculturation. But as already noted, they were made in ignorance—if not in contempt—of traditional cultures in the process of evolving. In these films, as before in *Paysans noirs, L'homme du Niger,* and even *Bozambo,* African cultures were considered as archaic, as unworthy of surviving contact with Western culture. Their existence was simply to be assimilated over time by "progress." In this connection, I should mention *Men of Africa,* made in East Africa by Grierson and his group. This film treats the rivalry of the educated blacks of the savannah and the primitive pygmies of the forest. Also, *C'était le premier chant,* by Carlos Vilardebo, a story of a young French civil servant who tries to improve the situation of a Cameroon bush village that is impoverished by both dryness and the lack of initiative of its inhabitants. Other films are *Bongolo,* made in Belgian Congo by André Cauvin, a story that follows the misadventures of a young Bapende girl who runs away from her village to be reunited with her fiancé, a nursing aide, because her parents want her to marry against her will.[14] Finally, *The Boy Kumasenu,* made by Sean Graham and the Ghana Film Unit in 1952, a story of the difficulties of a young fisherman who runs away from his village in the lagoon and falls into the corrupt city, where he turns from justice to delinquency.

Two films made by Claude Vermorel in Gabon and Guinea, *Les conquérants solitaires,* and *La plus belle des vies,* must be put in a somewhat different category. Here the author has tried to treat the reverse aspect of acculturation: the European who lets himself be taken in by the African cultures that he first set out to discover.

The political struggles for independence have equally inspired a certain number of films, but unfortunately very few seem satisfactory. It was singularly the Mau-Mau struggle in Kenya that inspired the largest number of films. An example is Peter Brooks's *Something of Value* (1953), which tried to show the evolution of a friendship between two young students, one white and one black, who as a result of circumstances find themselves in two opposing camps. This tremendously naive and quite evidently prejudiced film is one more example of the unconscious attack on African dignity. Once again Africans and their civilization are placed on an inferior level. For example, the major scene in the film shows the confession of an African nationalist leader who betrays his compatriots because he was afraid of a calamity.

*Simba,* made by Brias Desmond Huerst in 1955, is an incredibly violent exposé about an African medical doctor whose father is the chief of a Mau-Mau group named Simba; the doctor can find no other solution to this drama than death. *Freedom,* an extremely costly film made by Moral Rearmament, stresses the movement's customary theme of redemption of sin by confession. Properly speaking, and despite its title, this is not a film about political emancipation but a propaganda film for the International Moral Rearmament Organization.

A rather similar category includes films made by African film units on the occasions of their countries' independence. A typical example is *Freedom for Ghana,* by Sean Graham, concerning the independence of Ghana on March 6, 1957. The historical interest of this film helps one forget its slightly irritating propaganda angle.

It is too soon to discuss Joris Ivens's *Demain à Nanguila,* made in Mali during the summer of 1962. This film treats the possible evolution of a peasant community supported by the government party.

●────────────────────────────────────────────

## Outlines of a True African Cinema

All of the films just discussed were attempts by foreigners using film to convey their impressions or their knowledge of certain African problems. Here again the influence of ethnographic film, despite its modesty, is really considerable. Very quickly we have filmmakers wanting to reach below the surface, wanting to transcend the stage of exoticism, wanting to make the spectator enter easily into the African world, be it traditional or modern. And these are the first efforts toward a true African cinema of tomorrow.

The first example comes from South Africa, where in 1948 the Reverend Michael Scott made an extremely violent black-and-white film, *Civilization on Trial in South Africa,* which shows the reactions of black South Africans to problems of racial segregation. Also from South Africa came the first film with a truly African story, even though it is told by a white. The film is Englishman Donald Swanson's *Magic Garden,* based on a ballad by a young black man from Johannesburg (Ralph Trewhela, who plays the role of the lame flutist). The film recounts the amazing adventures of a thief who robs forty pounds from a church, loses it, then recovers it, and so on, with someone helped at every turn along the way, until the money is finally returned to the church. This little masterpiece has unfortunately passed unnoticed in France owing to the fact that its French adaptation was particularly difficult.

In Ghana, Sean Graham followed something of the same idea in *Jaguar (High Life),* a ballet based on the theme of a popular song making fun of "been to" Africans who had studied in Great Britain.

Other films were already in the works. In South Africa an American director, Lionel Rogosin, made *Come Back, Africa* (1959), which presented an even stronger message about the victims of South African racism.

Undoubtedly, one might demand to know whether this film is not more the testimony of Rogosin on apartheid than it is a cry of revolt by the victims of segregation themselves. But letting the role of the filmmaker be what it may, at some moments it is Africa that speaks, and the director is no longer the master of the door he has unlocked.

It is in this same spirit that I, too, have worked over the last several years. As far back as the making of my conventional ethnographic film *Les fils de l'eau,* I tried to avoid the traps of exoticism. Flaherty had already shown me a way of directing the documentary; by organizing and ordering the authentic elements of a culture, the filmmaker takes them out of their alien framework and renders them accessible to a world public. But no one could hope to rival Flaherty's achievement of making Nanook the friend of men who had never seen an Eskimo. I thus tried another path, that of giving a voice to Africans themselves and asking them to comment directly on their behavior, actions, and reactions. In 1955 I used this method in *Jaguar* (not yet edited with a final sound track),[15] giving three young Nigerian migrants the opportunity to tell of an imaginary though plausible voyage to Ghana. In 1957 I had the same experience in the Ivory Coast with *Moi, un Noir.* During the shooting, I projected the silent film footage tracing the life of a poor dockworker from Abidjan to this same docker who had acted his own part, and asked him to improvise a narration. The result was remarkable: the docker, Robinson, stimulated by the projection of his own image, improvised an astounding monologue in which he not only reconstructed the dialogues for the action but explicated and even judged his own actions and those of his fellow actors.[16]

●————————————————————————————————

## African Cinema by Africans for Africans

The attempts that I have just discussed have arrived at their own limits. For when all is said and done, neither Rogosin, Graham, nor I will ever be Africans, and the films that we make will always be African films by Europeans. This shortcoming is not bad in itself, nor does it prevent us from continuing to make African films. But it is time that the statement is made, as it has been by Georges Sadoul, "that Africans make African films using African money." This is starting to happen (I will discuss the technical training of African filmmakers a bit later), and already Paulin Soumanou Vieyra, the earliest of the African students trained at IDHEC, teaching in Dakar for several years, has produced a film, though perhaps still a bit awkward. *Un homme, un idéal, une vie* portrays the misadventures of a fisherman on the Senegal shore who violates tradition by putting a motor on his canoe. But despite the awkwardness, what ingenuity! Here the African tradition is not judged; it is stated and exhibited, and if the forest trees speak and join in with the council of village elders, no one dreams of ridiculing it.

Owing to lack of funds, this film has never been completed. But Paulin Soumanou Vieyra has other projects, and he is no longer alone. Just to mention French-speaking Africa, it is from Vieyra and his comrades, Blaise Senghor, Timité Bassari, Thomas Coulibaly, Jean-Paul N'Gassa, and others, that we must wait for this film that we all hope for above all, we European directors of African films.[17]

### Educational Films

Undoubtedly, some of the films that I have classified as commercial and documentary are equally educational films. Nevertheless, I wish to place in a separate class those films where entertainment is merely a pretext and whose real aim is instructional. As I have already said, the appearance of educational films is relatively recent, occurring around 1950 in both the Congo and the British territories. In former French Equatorial Africa, it is even more recent, having developed at the end of the 1950s. My discussion will deal separately with English-speaking Africa, the former Belgian Congo, and former French Africa.

### English-Speaking Africa

Before the last war, audiovisual media were extremely rare in sub-Saharan Africa, although lantern slides were used to illustrate health lectures in Nigeria as early as 1920. It was in 1929 that the first truly educational film in Africa was produced, to help combat an epidemic of the plague in Lagos, the capital of Nigeria. This film showed Africans how rats spread the disease, and encouraged them to cooperate in a general rat extermination campaign, which was so successful that the government of Nigeria decided to continue using film in the future. Fortunately, however, there were very few similar occasions calling for recourse to this kind of education through films. Yet it was in Nigeria, some years later, that the organization of overseas films was to take shape.

The Colonial Film Unit was founded in 1939 by the British government to secure African participation in the war effort; William Sellers, who was responsible for the first experiments in education through films in

Nigeria, was appointed as director. Although the immediate purpose of the Colonial Film Unit was war propaganda,[18] Sellers's long-run aim was in fact to generalize the use of films for African audiences.

At the outset, the only films produced were European films; these were simply reedited with a new narration for African screenings (and for screenings in other overseas English-speaking countries). To add to their attraction, short sequences shot in Africa were spliced in. This so-called Raw Stock Scheme for producing local sequences served the double purpose of introducing and popularizing 16 mm motion pictures in Africa, and supplying raw stock for local shooting to a few enthusiastic filmmakers. By the end of the war, this operation had allowed for the distribution of 200,000 meters (about 666,000 feet) of 16 mm film, and the equipping of twenty mobile cinema trucks in tropical Africa.

In 1955 the British Colonial Film Unit changed it objectives and began a program of film production to deal with the main social problems of its territories in tropical Africa while continuing to make a few films in Great Britain showing Africans the British way of life (the best of this series is *Mister English at Home*).

Between 1945 and 1950, the Colonial Film Unit established twelve film production sections (each called "Film Units") in eight British territories in East and West Africa. During this same period, the running time of finished films totaled five hours, and distribution rose to over 1,200 prints shown in Africa. These Film Units were manned by first-rate technicians, but although their films always aroused great interest in Europe, it must be admitted that their success with the African public (to whom they were addressed) was relatively slight.

Systematic studies revealed the difficulties inherent in making this type of film and showed that one of the most serious problems was the technicians' ignorance of the local communities in which the films were shot: one could hardly demand that the technicians be equally proficient as ethnographers.

In 1951 a research team consisting of a filmmaker and an anthropologist paid a long visit to Nigeria to study the question of audience reactions to films. Their report showed that the only solution was to make films with a minimum of foreign elements to distract the spectator. This, of course, threw the entire conception of "colonial cinema" into chaos, and for the first time, it appeared that it would be necessary for films to be made for Africans by Africans.

At about this time, the British Colonial Film Unit discontinued almost all it was doing directly for the territorial Film Units. The main reason was financial: the British government considered that it no longer had any obligation to make educational films for countries with independence a near prospect, and that it was up to the treasuries of the territories concerned to provide for the management of their own film services. In 1955 it was concluded that the British Film Unit had served its purpose, and the work was to be taken over by the fourteen African film services.

The Colonial Film Unit then became the Overseas Television and Film Centre, keeping its original staff, still headed by Sellers, who transformed it first into the British agency of all the overseas film production centers (except Ghana), and then into a training school for African technicians. The value of such an organization is obviously tremendous: each African film service had its representative in London to supervise the laboratory work, film shipments, purchase of equipment, and to provide optimum spare parts services. The growth of television is even further increasing the activities of the center.[19]

But in my opinion, the most important part of the center's work is the "film training school," the prime mover of which, George Pearson, is one of William Sellers's oldest colleagues in Nigeria and London. The first school was opened in 1950 in Accra and trained three Ghanaian and three Nigerian students, who were given a seven-month course that enabled them to become familiar with 16 mm and 35 mm film equipment. The school moved to Jamaica, then to Cyprus, and finally to London. In all, about one hundred students were trained during this time. Of course, as Georges Sadoul has pointed out, none of these technicians has thus far produced a real African film, but that was not the aim of William Sellers and his followers; their only goal was to enable Africans to make their own educational films.

What, then, might be said of these films, generally speaking? It is certain that Sellers must in any case be considered one of the true pioneers of African cinema, and if, perhaps soon, a true African filmmaker springs up in Nigeria, Rhodesia, or Kenya, it will certainly be the result of the modest but obstinate effort of this man.

I have had the opportunity of seeing some of the films made by these Film Units. Many are quite disappointing, if one considers them from a purely cinematographic point of view. But their educational value is sometimes considerable, as for instance in a 1950 film by the Central African Film Unit titled *Lusaka Calling*. The purpose of this film was to promote demand for low-cost radio sets; showings of the film produced actual riots among the audiences, who immediately dashed to the shops to buy wireless radio sets, which most could not obtain because the stock had been sold out almost immediately.

On the other hand, all of these films exhibit what I consider to be an extremely serious fault (a fault that is by no means reserved only for the cinema), namely, the paternalism characteristic of even the films made with the best intentions. For example, the film *Leprosy,* shot in Nigeria by an entirely African crew, intends to communicate the necessity of seeking treatment yet brings in some "African witchcraft" scenes rarely equaled for their superficiality. Was it really necessary to denigrate traditional African culture in order to better show the efficacy of foreign medical methods? Was it necessary to once again destroy in order to build? Is it not nauseating to show Africans themselves mocking their own culture, and in precisely one of the fields in which Africa has a few things to teach the rest of the world?[20]

The work of the Ghana Film Unit requires separate treatment. For reasons of which I am ignorant, it split off fairly early from the Colonial Film Unit, in favor of association with groups of independent English producers, or with first-rate producers such as Grierson, one of the masters of the English documentary film. The unit received its initial impetus from one of Grierson's young assistants, Sean Graham, who, with the help of the excellent Canadian cameraman George Noble, got the center started and produced an impressive number of outstanding films between 1950 and 1955.

I have already mentioned the films *Jaguar* and *The Boy Kumasenu.* In fact, both of these films began as educational films, but their quality was such that they were extremely successful both in their own country and abroad. The educational films made by the Ghana Film Unit for strictly African audiences have always been of such high quality, both technically and dramatically, that they are models of their genre. From *Progress in Kodjokrom,* showing why taxes must be paid, to *Mr. Mensah Builds His House,* a propaganda film for building loans, the pictures, music, and dialogue are in the best tradition, with no concession whatsoever to demagogy. But here we reach the limit of this genre of films. The time came for Sean Graham to make a film about the recruitment of nurses. His Irish temperament, a certain romanticism, and his talent combined to make *Theresa,* a shattering document about the difficult life of nurses. The government hesitated for quite a while over releasing this film, fearing that there would not be a young woman in Ghana with enough courage to embark on such a testing career.

After Ghanaian independence, Sean Graham left the Film Unit. Although his influence is still discernible, the quality of films made since his departure is definitely lower.

Thus in Ghana, Nigeria, Sierra Leone, and East Africa, Africans have been trained to take over. Their work is by no means extraordinary, but—and this is the inestimable contribution of the Film Unit's promoters—films are now regarded everywhere as an essential medium of mass communication. This means that the situation is particularly favorable for the flowering of a typically African cinematographic art in the very near future.[21]

●────────────────────────────────────────────────────────

Former Belgian Congo

The Belgian effort in the Congo followed close behind that of the British. Toward the end of the war, the Congo government began to think about the value of cinema for the Congolese masses. As was always the case in the Congo, this action was divided into two distinct forms: government film production, and missionary film production. In both cases, and quite contrary to British Film Unit practice, attention was given to making entertainment as well as educational films.

The initial outcome was the production of special films for the Congolese, distributed together with other films selected in either Belgium or neighboring African countries (Rhodesia supplied a larger number). These films were shown either by permanent cinemas or by mobile film trucks.

The language problem seems to be one of the major obstacles that the Belgians tried to overcome. The multiplicity of vernacular languages, over and above the four major ones of Kikongo, Lingala, Tschiluba, and Kiswahili, made it necessary to use local interpreters, who would deliver a translation of the dialogue into a microphone simultaneously while the sound track played in one of the four major languages. This experiment is perhaps one of the most significant made in Africa in the area of projection techniques, because, as we shall see at the end of this report, it is toward a similar system that the new African educational film industry must move, using double system projection, with the sound track in the local dialect.

Belgian efforts reached their maximum in 1957 with fifteen thousand showings for a total audience of nearly nine million people. But what can we say of these films produced by the Belgians in the Congo before independence?

The government films strike me as incredibly superficial and paternalistic, with the African invariably treated as an overgrown child to whom everything must be explained. The missionary films, on the other hand, seem more advanced, and mention should be given to the Centre Congolais Catholique d'action cinématographique in Leopoldville, where genuinely African productions started to appear through the stimulation provided by Fathers Develoo, van Haelst, van Overschelds, and van den Heuvel. For instance, the missionaries made film versions of Congolese folktales and even cartoons, such as the series *Mboloko, la petite antilope*. I do not know how the missionary film would have developed if it had continued on this course. The existing films stop, both technically and in spirit, at the level of a minor guild production, while still offering promise of improvement, which, unfortunately, has not taken place.

The missionaries themselves were conscious of the shortcomings we have mentioned, and although they held to the view that films for Africans should "exclude all the love scenes, vain dreams, and violence of Westerns," they did support, as far back as 1956, the idea of Africans making African films. (See, for example, the paper read by Father van den Heuvel at the international symposium "The Cinema and Africa South of the Sahara.")

As regards the present state of the film industry in the Congo, in 1960 I met a few young Information Service trainees in Berlin who had come to Europe to learn filmmaking. Judging from what they said, no films had been made in the Congo since independence. Here again we must wait for what the next few years might bring.

●————————————————————————————————————————

## French-Speaking Africa

In the area of educational films, it must frankly be said that French-speaking Africa comes last by a long shot. A few films were produced by individuals, particularly in the area of medicine (on combating malaria and other endemic diseases), but most of them date from before the war. Moreover, I cannot imagine where these films could have been shown at the time, as it is only in the last few years that the former French African territories have had projection equipment.

The quality of these few films is in fact doubtful, to say the least. I have had the occasion to see the antimalaria film at the cultural center in Niamey; no clear explanation was given of the difference in scale between the macroscopic and microscopic shots, and as a result, half of the audience (uneducated, of course) thought they were seeing cartoons, and the rest (still less educated) thought it was a film about mythical animals like Godzilla or other monsters from the deep from the science fiction films being shown at the same time in the Niamey public cinema. When a territory had a young administrator who was a film enthusiast, he would try to arrange a bush film circuit with a generator truck that was borrowed; but the only program available would be documentaries on the castles of the Loire or the fishermen of Brittany. Thus in 1957, while the Ivory Coast was economically comparable to its neighbor, Ghana, all it had to compare with the Ghanaian fleet of twenty mobile film trucks was one beat-up power wagon in almost unusable condition, and an old 16 mm projector belonging to the Cultural Center that was death to any film projected through it.

However, in 1958, the Ministry of French Overseas Territories began to wake up and asked a producer, Pierre Fourré, to make a series of films for African audiences. These films, made ten years after the British Colonial Film Unit's *Mister English at Home,* showed a few simple facets of life in France (this was the period of the French community). Of these few films made—*Bonjour Paris, L'élevage du mouton, Un petit port de pêche français,* and so on—only the memory remains today (and only in France, not in Africa), although they did incorporate an interesting experimental commentary in basic French, using a vocabulary of only 1,500 carefully chosen words. The few showings that these films had in Africa appear to have yielded encouraging results there, but the experiment, like many others, was never pursued.

It is only since independence that genuinely African educational films have begun to be made on former French Africa. As usual, the initial impetus came partly from the enthusiasm of a few individuals for the cinema, but the main factor was the appreciation that the young African nations had for film's possibility as a medium of communication.

Film centers have sprung up quite rapidly, and although their initial efforts may be modestly limited to a few films on current political events, the centers are at least operating, and educational films figure in all of their production programs. I have not been able to collect all of the information hoped for on the organization of these centers; many of them prefer to remain modestly silent about their activities until they have produced some real films. The general pattern, though, is to use 16 mm film for basic production and, for more important films, to call in outside producers who make 35 mm films for general distribution. The centers are equipped with projection trucks either converted locally or received as gifts on the occasion of the country's independence (Togo, for example, received a complete mobile cinema truck as a gift from the United States). Examples of recent productions are the following:

*Mauritania.* A 35 mm film on independence by a good crew from France (unfortunately a high-budget film).

*Senegal.* The Film Section, after likewise having called in foreign producers (e.g., *Dakar a un siècle* made by Actualités Françaises), has since 1958 had its own newsreel crew. Since 1959, it has had, thanks to Paulin Soumanou Vieyra, the first African producer to graduate from IDHEC, a center with 16 mm and 35 mm equipment that makes educational films locally, and is a coproducer (with a Senegalese motion picture company headed by another African filmmaker, Blaise Senghor) of short and feature films.

*Mali.* Since the breakup of the Mali Federation, a Mali Film Center has been set up at Bamako for "the political education of the individual, the citizen, and the worker." It has already made political events films on the visits of foreign heads of state (shot in 16 mm), and has also called in foreign technicians to make purely educational films such as Joris Ivens's excellent *Demain à Nanguila.*

*Ivory Coast.* The Film Center of the Information Service of the Ivory Coast, after making a number of 16 mm information shorts, sometimes with sound, since 1958, called in the French producer, Jean Ravel, to make the first synthetic film about the Ivory Coast, in connection with the opening of the Abidjan Bridge. The Center also cooperated fairly actively in the making of two of my own films, *Moi, un Noir* and *La pyramide humaine.* For the past year, an Ivory Coast motion picture company (associated with the Société de Dakar) has been expanding its activities and is now competing with a French newsreel company for the production of a newsreel program.

*Dahomey.* Despite a relatively restricted budget (15 million francs CFA for the whole Information Service, as compared with 40 million in Upper Volta and 71 million in the Ivory Coast), the film section, spurred on by the energetic minister of information, has since 1959 been producing a *Revue Dahoméenne Trimestrielle* in 16 mm color, which runs for about half an hour. Sixteen-millimeter color film has also been used for some ten educational films since 1960, including *J'étais un Tilapia,* which recently won first prize at the 16 mm film festival at Saint-Cast, France, in 1961. Dahomey has only one mobile cinema truck, but it does remarkable work; 132 shows have been screened in six months to a total of 300,000 spectators.

*Cameroon.* The Cameroon Film Service, run by an enthusiastic group, has installed its own developing and printing laboratories, cutting rooms, and sound synchronization rooms and thus can meet the optimum newsreel criterion of screening topical events within twenty-four hours of their occurrence. It may be expected, with Alain Gheerbrandt's team in charge, to expand its activities still more in the coming months.[22]

*Chad.* In 1959, to mark the republic's independence, the ministry of information asked Serge Ricci to make a 16 mm color film with the title *Le Tchad a un an;* and in 1960, Suzanne Baron, a French producer, and formerly chief editor of many African films, made a 35 mm color film for the Independence Day celebrations.

*Upper Volta.* At the present time, the Republic of Upper Volta is undoubtedly a model in the field of African educational film production. Under Serge Ricci's leadership, a complete 16 mm production and distribution center (without laboratory) has been established at Ouagadougou. Although the first films made were mainly political in character (*A minuit, l'indépendance,* a 16 mm color film on the independence of the four alliance states of Niger, Dahomey, Ivory Coast, and Upper Volta), since 1961 the center has been producing true educational films with an African technical staff trained on the spot.

*Niger.* The Mass Communications Service of Niger so far has no more than an embryonic film center (specializing in political newsreels), but the republic has done a good deal in the area of mass education through films in cooperation with the Niger Museum and the Research Institute (IFAN). On the production end, recourse has been taken to European directors (I have made seven films in Niger, Henri Brandt has made one, etc.). An interesting experiment in production was a Niger-Canadian effort made in 1959–1960 to mark the republic's first birthday and Independence Day. This film, *Le Niger, jeune république,* was directed by Claude Jutra and produced by the National Film Board of Canada. At this time, an initial version has been broadcast over Canadian television, and the National Film Board of Canada is preparing a Djerma and a Hausa language version for distribution within the Republic of Niger. With UNESCO's help, an audiovisual center attached to the Research Institute is now being organized; it plans to build, in 1962, a 4,000-seat open-air theater where plays can be performed and films shown.[23]

To conclude this bird's-eye view of educational films in former French Africa, it may be noted that many avenues toward the cooperation of these efforts are now being explored, either at the government level (the African Mass Communications Services, in France the Ministry of Aid and Cooperation, the Comité du Film Ethnographique of the Musée de l'Homme, and the National Film Center) or on the commercial plane (Actualités Françaises, Pathé, Gaumont, the television branch of SORAFOM). So far, no solution has been agreed upon, but opinion seems to be leaning toward a center in Paris (like the Overseas Film and Television Center in London), which I myself suggested following a meeting on African cinema in Niamey in June 1960. Such a center would provide a permanent liaison at the technical, artistic, and professional levels between Africa and the only readily accessible laboratories, in Paris.[24]

▶
─────────────────────────────────────────────

### The Importance of These Different Types of Film from Cinematographic, Cultural, and Sociological Points of View

In analyzing the cinematographic, cultural, and sociological value of African films, I will again divide them into the two categories already briefly surveyed: (1) commercial and documentary films, (2) education films. The reason again is the impossibility of making a combined study of films so different in object and having developed on such different lines.

## Commercial and Documentary Films
### Cinematographic Value

Although the growth of commercial and documentary filmmaking has obviously been accompanied by an improvement in quality, it must be emphasized from the beginning that the relative worth of the results, cinematographically and socially, remains lower than that of corresponding films from other areas of production. This phenomenon should not be considered in isolation but rather should be viewed in the context of the overall policy of mediocrity, whose effects are still making Africans suffer.

In English-speaking Africa, motion pictures achieved far less healthy growth than trade or education: the British were not interested in African cinema except for use in educational areas (which will be discussed later) and left the field in their African territories to American filmmakers more concerned with exoticism and the box office than with African culture or motion picture art.

In French-speaking Africa, the evolution of quality followed a more complex pattern. Although Léon Poirier and the crew that made *La croisière noire,* Marc Allégret, Marcel Griaule, and more recently the Ogooué-Congo and ethnographic film crews undoubtedly outclassed the Colonial Civil Service filmmakers, all too frequently genteelness or contamination by the surrounding mediocrity made them incapable of aiming at a job that was totally creative. Today it is a peculiar experience to rewatch a film like *Sous les masques noirs,* made in 1938 by Marcel Griaule, a film set in a "Colonial Exposition" context with a commentary and incidental music that seem entirely old-fashioned. Why has a comparable film like *Las hurdes,* made at the same period by Buñuel, not aged similarly? Is it because of Africa's considerable progress, as compared with Spain's post–Civil War stagnation? It is impossible to say, but all old films on Africa are terribly dated, and those who love both the cinema and Africa, and are able to catch from the still-splendid images the message now stifled, feel the urge to reedit the films and add authentic sound effects and a scientific commentary.

The same applied to more recent films. *Au pays des pygmées,* made in 1948 with terrific precautions, was Africa's first ethnographic film. Yet today it has lost the power it had ten years ago to stir artistic emotions or the feeling of scientific discovery. Here again one wants to remake the commentary, reedit the film, or even take the more serious step of starting again from the beginning.[25]

How is it, then, that African films have aged so quickly? I am afraid that the reason is their lack of quality. It is the masterpieces among European and American films that are perennial, but the bulk of their output of ten years back is now just as impossible to sit through as the African films of the same period.

A point that we must grasp is that, in fact, African masterpieces are extremely rare. Admittedly, I have often drawn attention to good qualities in these films in my current report, but even so, the level is pretty low by world standards. We know that after *Louisiana Story* (which has not aged in the slightest), Robert Flaherty intended to go to Africa to make a fifth film and fifth masterpiece. Unfortunately, death was to prevent African film production from achieving a place of honor in the history of cinema through a film by Flaherty.

Should this be taken to mean that in the cinema art, Africa's score is nil? I don't think so: all the films mentioned had some merit to them, and still do, yet not one of them will really find a place in the history of the cinema.[26]

●────────────────────────────────────────

## Cultural and Sociological Value

Is the same to be said for these films on the cultural and sociological level? Sociologically, these films retain their value; even though films grow scientifically sound as ethnographic techniques improve, the fact remains that the intervening stages are of great interest. Films now out of date like *Voyage au Congo* or *La croisière noire,* or aging films like *Au pays des pygmées* or *Masques Dogon,* are of considerable historical value, not only as milestones in the history of African films but also as unique evidence of the outlook and behavior of an epoch, its culture in the scientific sense.

Keeping to the classification in the previous chapter of more recent films made since 1950, we find in each class of film a sociological content area of great importance.

The "exotic Africa" films, like *King Solomon's Mines, Nagana,* or the *Tarzan* films, exhibit screen stereotypes of the continent as seen by outside observers, and however distorted the latter's vision may be, the errors are of absorbing interest in themselves. It is due to this genre of film and above all because it has a public that it becomes easier to explain some manifestations of racism that today seem incongruous. Even when Africa has become just another continent and when men have stopped basing their judgments on the color of their neighbors' skin, the exotic style will survive, just as Westerns survive long after the end of the adventure period on the western prairies of America.

The "ethnographic Africa" films, evolving from superficiality to a steadily increasing degree of penetration, provide world culture with visual and sound records of civilizations either vanishing or becoming completely transformed. For instance, when I was beginning to shoot *Moro Naba* in Upper Volta in 1957, a film of the Mossi chieftain's funeral in the old tradition, I was fully aware that my ramshackle camera and poor tape recorder were capturing data of essential importance, not merely to Upper Volta but to world culture, since this was almost certainly the last observance of a dying custom. The next Moro Naba was definitely going to be Catholic, and without my film, the great traditional funeral rites would have faded away into oral tradition or a few incomplete reports by ethnographers.

The films of "emergent Africa," told in the pictures already discussed, are just as irreplaceable, and even though the technique is often poor and the narrations outdated even before the film is printed, documents such as *Afrique 50, Les statues meurent aussi,* or *Le carnival des dieux* remain, despite the irritation they may arouse, unique testimonies of a history that is a perpetual source of wonder. Indeed, one would be almost tempted to welcome their premature aging as a proof of the vitality of African evolution.

Lastly, films of Africa by Africans, or films of Africa with Europeans providing technical know-how only and leaving action and words as much as possible to Africans, will probably always retain the quality of bold experimentation. It has already been emphasized that European filmmakers, however sympathetic, cannot get inside the skins of Africans, and that over-indulgence toward the first purely African films was a form of racism as sterile as any other. While these films were suspect to begin with, these suspicions have gradually been allayed, projecting an image of Africa that could be related to by people who hitherto had completely ignored the continent. For example, thanks to a film such as *Come Back Africa,* the problem of racial segregation in South Africa has been brought home to many Europeans who before had never known or cared to know anything about it. Another more personal example is found in the unexpected results of the showing of my *Moi, un Noir.* From the African point of view, this film has been repeatedly criticized for presenting a portrayal of a "low-life" African milieu. Yet it also awoke the spontaneous sympathy of the humblest audiences, who discovered a man who looked different, spoke a different language, behaved differently, but after all was quite close to themselves.

It is on this level that some of us impatiently and eagerly await the coming of genuinely African films. They will not, of course, be a series of masterpieces from the start, but they will be a thousand times more moving than any of the films we have been discussing, since for the first time, Africans will be speaking directly with other people. Cinematographically, African films may well be of indeterminable length, in a language that makes subtitles necessary, and using music in ways that would be unthinkable to us. But once the first shock is over, I know that such documents will have an unequalable value. Sociologically, film, a medium whose full scope is still unexplored, will enable men to tell and show the world directly what they are, what they do, and what they think. Culturally, the impact of these films will be still greater, since they will be made for people of a common culture, people to whom the idiom will be understandable from the start, without their being able to read or write.

■──────────────────────────────────────────

## Educational Films

The recent date at which educational films started in Africa, as well as their moderate quality, prohibits my dwelling on their cinematographic, sociological, or cultural value.

From the cinematographic point of view, it must be admitted that with very few exceptions (in particular the Ghana Film Unit), the films are frankly of quite limited artistic value. They are, of course, a particularly difficult type of film to make and for that very reason require absolutely first-rate directors. Unfortunately alike in former French, British, or Belgian Africa, most of the directors (leaving aside exceptions such as Sean Graham) were (and are) amateurs, administrators, or missionaries.

Sociologically, more value can be derived from these films by studying where they failed rather than by seeing where they succeeded. In particular, it would be interesting to make a methodical study of the means employed and actual results obtained in a specific field such as health or housing. If one took films of quality such as *The Boy Kumasenu, Demain à Nanguila,* or *À minuit, l'indépendence,* I think that it would become apparent that they did not have, and will not have, the slightest influence at all on juvenile delinquency, the role of agricultural cooperatives, or the building of a national spirit.

Should one then condemn these films? I think not, since the role they do and should fulfill culturally remains essential in spite of everything. Actually, they are irreplaceable (if awkward) means of communication about a continent where information is precisely what is lacking. (In the capital of an African state, more is known about what is going on everywhere else in the world than about the surrounding community.) Secondly, these education films remain a training school for the African film industry of tomorrow. I have already said that whatever we may think of the films produced by the Colonial Film Unit and by William Sellers and his group, it is through these films that the cinema has reached the smallest villages in Africa and has become a familiar means of education. And it is in making them that the technicians of the African cinema of tomorrow are learning their craft.

▶

## Analysis of New Trends and the Conditions for the Development of African Cinema

In this last section, I shall not separately discuss education, commercial, and documentary films, since all of them, in my view, are equally involved in the future of the new African cinema. The only type of film requiring separate consideration is the newsreel. So far, it has hardly been mentioned, for two reasons. First, apart from a few more or less periodical "screen magazines" that cannot really be thought of as newsreels, the latter is a very recent development in response to the demands of the newly independent African republics. Second, newsreels are mainly irrelevant to our present subject, since despite the fact that they provide excellent training for film technicians, time factor requirements in shooting, editing, adding sound, and distributing make the newsreel a highly specialized area of cinematography.

It is the failure to understand this difference that has led some African nations to harness their promising young filmmakers to the production of this kind of film, condemning them thereby to total frustration in the area of motion picture art itself. Undoubtedly the young African republics urgently need newsreel services, but in fact, the only way of meeting this need is to attend to it independently of all other film activities. Each state should have a team specializing exclusively in this type of filmmaking and should have an arsenal of equipment reserved for this type of work. Even so, there are from the start two conflicting choices: between news films shot and processed entirely in the country and those processed abroad.

Using the methods recommended by UNESCO, it is possible, in 16 mm black and white, to create a complete newsreel system at low cost, including cameras, sound recording equipment, development and printing labs, and projection rooms. A disadvantage of this is the visual mediocrity of the films thus far made, but an important advantage is the ability to show the films (as elsewhere in the world) a few days, if not a few hours, after being shot—the essential quality of newsreels.

However, the example of newsreels made in the developed countries in 35 mm (and then in color) has tempted the young republics to try to make films of the same quality, although they do not have the means to do so locally. Results of this situation are as follows: either as in Senegal or the Ivory Coast, monthly or bimonthly news digests, shot in 35 mm, are processed in Paris by a specialist firm, or as in Mali, newsreels are shot in color and then have a narration or background music added. In both cases, the result is more like a magazine than a true cinematographic journal; the delays in shipping and other adjustments prohibit the films from being projected immediately after being shot.

The problem arises in the same terms for commercial or educational films: in my view, it is the choice of technical method that will set the course of African filmmaking. Financially speaking, African film production is stuck with following the low-budget route, first because of the scarcity of cinemas and second because of the extremely meager budgets of the African republics. These countries therefore need to be able to resort to money-saving methods. We will consider possibilities concerning shooting, sound recording, editing and sound synchronization, distribution via both commercial cinemas and mobile truck units, and finally in terms of television possibilities. It must be emphasized here that a low-budget film need not be a low-grade film. The reduction need not be made at the expense of the story, but simply by changing the operation's financial terms along lines that may need refinement in detail but have already been followed successfully (the so-called Nouvelle Vague school in France is in fact an attempt to liberate cinematographic art from economic constraints).

■────────────────────────────────────────────────

*Shooting*

The choice to be made is between 16 mm and 35 mm. I have already drawn attention, in the first part of this report, to the important influence of the 16 mm camera's appearance in the postwar African film scene. The 16 mm camera was originally only for amateurs. The enormous extension of its use was due to the war, when it became the tool of the combat cameramen. In the United States in particular, the 16 mm format has made considerable progress, and as early as 1945, successful blowups were made from 16 mm to 35 mm. These attempts were so conclusive that Walt Disney, a filmmaker so exacting in his concern with image quality, used blown-up 16 mm for his great *Wonders of Nature* series.

In Europe, 16 mm only came into professional use with the appearance of television, but already, pictorial quality is practically unaffected by the film format.[27] The only outstanding problem until recently was color enlargement (the size of grain made it impossible to use the 16 mm color negative directly, and copies had to be made from dupe negatives with a displeasing increase in contrast). The appearance of soft color original film of the Ektachrome type has solved the problem.

The advantages of shooting in 16 mm are considerable: the cameras are lighter and thus easier to handle. Film costs are a quarter of the costs of 35 mm. Finally, successful tests of a series of prototypes suggest that in the very near future, noiseless portable cameras will be available, permitting synchronous-sound shooting under all conditions with both minimum equipment and crew.

Of course, great progress has also been made in reducing the weight and increasing the flexibility of 35 mm cameras. But why use a technique that may be equaled or surpassed in a few years time and costs four times as much for results of hardly perceptible technical superiority?

■─────────────────────────────────────

### Sound Recording

Sound recording techniques have also made progress toward greater simplification. When the crew of the Ogooué-Congo films was shooting *Au pays des pygmées,* in 1946, its sound recording equipment (a disc recorder) weighed nearly a ton and required a crew of three or four for operation. I have already mentioned that I was among the first to use a battery-powered tape recorder in tropical Africa. Although the original models weighed nearly fifty pounds and yielded rather indifferent results, improvement was fairly rapid. Today these tape recorders are standard motion picture equipment, both on location and in the studio.

Three years ago a number of manufacturers solved the problem of synchronizing unperforated sound tape (which slips, whereas perforated film does not) by recording on the tape a separate signal emitted by the camera motor. This technique is also progressing quickly, and today perfect synchronization is obtainable by using two frequency generators, one regulating the camera speed and the other printing a signal on the unperforated quarter-inch sound tape.

Thus today the noiseless camera and battery-powered tape recorder combination weighs about twenty-five pounds and can be handled by two people, or even one. This technique, which is already revolutionizing a part of cinematographic art, is progressing appreciably each month: miniature microphones eliminate all wires and boom poles, interoperator signals between cameramen allow for the simultaneous use of more than one synchronous camera, and the next step will undoubtedly be to start and stop the camera function by remote control. And we can expect more progress as a result of television.[28]

Once again, at the very moment when these developments are taking place in motion picture technique, it would be a great pity for the emergent African cinema to opt for the conventional methods and thereby be obliged to replace all of its capital equipment within a few years, in order to regain ground that should never have been lost.

### Editing and Sound Tracks

In this area there is less to choose from between 16 mm and 35 mm on financial grounds, since the editing equipment for picture and sound is much the same in cost regardless of the film format. Quality is the same in either case, but once again the cost of 16 mm is lower, owing to the saving of tape, which is a quarter of the price of 35 mm.

The materials for a cutting room are extremely simple and basically require comparatively inexpensive equipment (viewer with synchronizer and magnetic head sound reader and amplifier). It is essential that the filmmaking centers in the African republics each have at least one editing table setup; it must not be forgotten that cutting a film remains the best way for the filmmaker to learn his craft, and it would be a pity not to see this exploited by the African film centers.

A sound recording studio is a bit more complex, but in any case, infinitely less so than the broadcasting studio variety. In practice, a small studio with facilities for mixing four sound tracks appears to be essential. With this, all recording can be done locally, and more particularly, the dubbing of dialogue or narration in the vernacular languages, which is most important for African filmmaking. (I shall return later to this question, which is essential to the showing of films in rural areas.) The most serious difficulty is not building and equipping editing rooms or sound studios but maintaining them: good electronic engineers are rare, and it will be necessary to make a special effort to train some to meet this situation.

### Distribution

The question of distribution in 16 mm versus 35 mm is not a problem in Africa, since most existing commercial cinemas have both types of projector. In projection, too, 16 mm has recently made enormous progress, and with arc projectors, the images are fully up to 35 mm standards. Rural (or "bush") cinema is already exclusively equipped with 16 mm projectors and cannot be supplied with another size. This, then, is not the question; the two important problems seem to me to be the following.

## Projection Technique

Although in Europe the traveling cinemas can make do with small-screen projectors, owing to their limited audiences, the same is not true in Africa, where full-scale commercial cinemas are comparatively rare. In Africa, an open-air film show in a village is attended by the whole population of the village, that is, an audience as large if not larger than that in a normal European commercial theater. Part of this audience consists of young people who have traveled extensively and know the experience of urban film showings, and thus cannot be satisfied by a tiny screen with an image that is of inferior luminosity, or by feeble loudspeakers that are easily drowned out by the noise of the audience.

It is therefore necessary to devise projectors adapted to this kind of problem, namely, relatively portable and easily handled units, giving results up to the standards of town cinemas. It seems that the manufacturers are already on the verge of a solution to this problem, using xenon light sources that give comparable luminosity to that of arc sources, without the inconveniences or dangers. Similarly, these manufacturers have almost solved the problem of designing sound amplifiers that are both powerful enough and portable enough to reach the whole of an audience of several thousand people.

This technical aspect of the distribution problem is extremely important: if we want Africans to go to films, it is essential for projection to be up to normal standards. This was the point that was overlooked until recently by most equipment manufacturers, who were under the impression that educational films could be screened cheaply and draw audiences because admission was usually free.

## Language Question

The question of the language used is also very different in Africa as compared with other places. In European countries, a foreign film is dubbed or subtitled. But as Africa is still largely illiterate, subtitling is out of the question, since it would help only a very small proportion of the audience. Dubbing is therefore one solution, but once again the proposition is not the same as in other countries, and the multilingualism of African republics calls for a fresh approach to the problem. Although the official languages of the modern African nations are French or English, this by no means signifies that they are either understood or spoken by the majority of the population, and it is precisely the uneducated and uninstructed sectors of the African public who should be reached with films. It is thus essential to be able to dub films in the languages spoken in all the different regions of a country.

As we have already seen, the Belgians studied and dealt with the problem by having local people deliver a spoken commentary on the film as it was screened. The French, on the other hand, favored the use of a narration in simplified "basic" French, using an abbreviated vocabulary.

Both of these solutions strike me as being outdated, and here again a technological solution appears to be found in the use of double-system projection, with 16 mm projectors of this type having in fact been developed by some manufacturers, though for quite other purposes (better sound quality for preparation of sound effects and music tracks). These projectors have an ordinary picture reel, plus a 16 mm perforated sound magnetic tape reel. The result is the flexibility of being able to play a composite optical sound film print, or a double-strand sound and picture copy. What could be done might be to use the optical reel for screening the film with the sound and voice track in the official language (English or French) while the magnetic tape would be recorded in the local sound studio, in one or more vernacular translations. In areas where there is a need for dubbing in several languages, a corresponding number of magnetic sound reels could be recorded, and the correct version selected for a particular performance, according to the language spoken by the majority of viewers.

This solution, or something along similar lines, seems to me to be the only one that will make Africa's transition to real films of its own possible, not merely financially but above all artistically, since it is well known that an art can only grow in contact with the people among whom it is born: there will not really be an African cinema until it is made for and by the peoples of Africa themselves.

Incidentally, these remarks apply equally to all of the film genres we have discussed—education, documentary, and feature commercial films. African audiences have learned the language of the cinema at a school that was not always perhaps a good one; now they need to build upon that knowledge, to read in "books" appropriate to their own cultures.[29]

Although television did not originally enter into the purview of this report, it seems to me necessary to say just a few words about it, as it has already appeared in Nigeria. Initially, the government of Nigeria went no further than experiments in television rebroadcasts and broadcast only programs on film. However, local merchants have put television receivers on sale, and their success was so immediate and so huge that in Southern Nigeria, live television has come to stay.

Of course, for the present, the shows are restricted to political news and to original film programs and advertisements of questionable quality, but I feel that it is necessary to go through this stage to settle a number of technical problems, and that the quality of Nigerian television will improve as time goes on.

Following Nigeria's example, Ghana and Ivory Coast are planning to open television networks quite soon, and even in the least-developed countries, the problem is rapidly coming to the fore.

Actually, although African television so far may be thought of as serving somewhat materialistic ends, its development can be viewed in another light. It appears that as techniques improve, the cost price of mounting a television network is likely to be lower than that of establishing a rural film circuit. For example, one film truck per seven villages is required to provide one program per week, and the number of print copies will thus be equal to the number of seven-village circuits in the whole of the particular state. On the other hand, with one television in a village, a program per evening can be shown, perhaps by direct broadcast. But there is also another point: television can be an administrative tool of considerable power, for while improved transportation puts any African capital within a few hours' travel of the other capitals of the world, the difficulties of local travel keep those same capitals several days' journey from some of their own villages. The latter are only in touch with the district administrative center once a year and with the capital only one day every ten years, plus occasional official flying visits.

Although the same situation is also found in industrial countries, essential daily contact with the rest of the world is ensured through the press. Thus African television appears a means of settling the difficult problem of ineffectual administration owing to difficulties of communication. And one might even go further to say that if television does take root, it will give rise to a communication process of unforeseeable possibilities. I have already said that the masses in Africa have grasped the idiom of the cinema screen. They will understand the television medium in the same way and thus, at one bound, without literacy, will be in direct daily contact with the outer world and with other cultures hitherto beyond their reach.[30]

▶

## Conclusion

All of these forecasts may seem a bit like something out of science fiction. But rereading this paper will show how much ground has really been covered from the time when that bioscope was stolen in 1896 by a vaudeville magician and shown in South Africa. This very report is probably already out of date in all the young African republics. Before it reaches them, the full-fledged African cinema will be born. Things are, of course, still in an apprenticeship stage of news film or educational film, but the new nations' young technicians are avid to learn and to follow in the steps of those who have gone before them in the world's schools of cinema art. They are reaching London, Paris, New York, and Moscow little by little, and if their qualifications are not good enough for entry into advanced schools, they attend more modest technical schools or simply find their way to the studios and get taken onto camera crews. Some of them are almost completely non-literate, but they know their cinema by heart; they have already outgrown the Westerns and the gangster films and are turning their attention to more difficult productions. They have found their way to the film libraries and to the art and experimental cinemas. They are jostling to buy 16 mm cameras and whatever film they can scrape up, and they are making their first experiments in cinematography.

Already contact has been made between them and the veterans from the film institutes, and after being separated for a long time, they can meet again speaking the same tongue: a language not to be learned from grammars or dictionaries but before the screens of darkened film theaters, through the eyepiece of the camera, the earphones of the tape recorder; a language whose words and phrases are not printed on paper but recorded on film and tape, an audiovisual language that all people in the world find they can understand without even knowing that they learned it, a true international language.

(Written 1961; published 1967)

1. Europeans go to films on an average of thirty or forty times per year; Indians, Middle Easterners, and North Africans, one time per year; Africans, one time every thirty or forty years, and in some African countries, once per century.

2. See Georges Sadoul, "Le Marché Africain," *Afrique Action*, Tunis, 1 May 1961.

3. ["Le courage et la bonne humeur du tirailleur 'sénégalais' favorisèrent la création du stéréotype du Noir bon enfant, style 'Y'a bon Banania.'" The Senegalese sharpshooter is a common West African stereotype. "Y'a bon" is a publicity slogan for Banania, a commercial breakfast cocoa with bananas. The picture illustrating the product shows a smiling black brandishing bananas and speaking pidgin French. This image of the happy banana-eating African is perhaps most similar to the "Uncle Tom" and "Aunt Jemima" stereotype of African Americans. —*Trans.*]

4. We should note a film shown in Paris in 1935: *Soeurs noires,* a religious propaganda film in which the actors spoke Zulu. It is mentioned by Georges Sadoul in *La Vie Africaine,* 15 June 1961: "Africa has remained, until now, a country of filmic poverty."

5. In the United States, on the other hand, the problem was previously studied by Walt Disney Studios. They decided to shoot in 16 mm and then enlarge to 35 mm; their celebrated series of films that included *The Living Desert* was done in this fashion. Despite their technical ingenuity, these films are of limited scientific interest.

6. These films were made by Jacques Dupont, assisted by an exceptional ethnographic team (Raoul Harweg, Gilbert Rouget, Guy de Beauchêne), as well as an exceptional film crew (Edmond Séchan, Pierre-Dominique Gaisseau, André Didier, Nef, Francis Mazières). All of them have since continued in this work.

7. We cannot speak here about lecture "exploration" films, as most of them have disappeared owing to the absurd lecture circuit system that required projecting the original. These lecture circuits began to be extraordinarily popular in France in 1946 (the "Connaissance du Monde" series held at Salle Pleyel, as well as series in the provinces) and in Belgium in 1950 (the "Exploration du Monde" series). Here we will simply report the format of these lectures: 16 mm color films of about one hour in length, with direct narration by the lecturer-filmmaker. As a matter of fact, from the beginning of these lecture circuits, Africa was one of the weakest attractions. So the loss of African films here is not very serious. The only valuable documents were edited elsewhere, had sound added, and were then marketed; we will discuss these films shortly.

8. The instigator was filmmaker René Clément, who had made a 16 mm color film of a trip to Yemen, around 1939. Titled *L'Arabie interdite,* the film was only shown at lectures.

9. We should also mention Armand Denis's TV films of safaris in Kenya, where one finds some remarkable sequences on wild animals (baboons attacking an antelope who is giving birth), but where Africa and Africans are merely scenery.

10. The Comité du Film Ethnographique was founded by the permanent advisory committee of the International Congress of Anthropological and Ethnological Sciences during the Vienna meetings in 1952. Its creation followed the projection of films by the author, which were presented under the heading of an ethnographic contribution. These films were made with the help of Roger Rosfelder in Niger in 1951 and 1952. They were all 16 mm Kodachrome with original sound tracks: *Bataille sur le grand fleuve* (hippopotamus hunting), *Cimetière dans la falaise* (funeral rites of the Dogon of the Bandiagara cliffs), and *Yenendi: Les hommes qui font la pluie* (rainmaking rites among the Songhay and Zarma). These films were later joined together and blown up to 35 mm—one of the first made in Europe—and retitled *Les fils de l'eau.*

11. We should also mention François Balsan's *L'expédition Panhard-Capricorne* on the Kalahari Desert of South Africa, Fiévet's films on Nigeria, especially Kano, the films now being edited by Father Pairaut on Northern Cameroon, and Civatte's films on Niger. All of these films are 16 mm Kodachrome, unfortunately reserved for limited distribution.

12. Also deserving of mention is *Omaru,* a film made in 1954 in 35 mm Agfacolor by Quendier, an Austrian filmmaker. Shot among the Kirdi and Peul of the Mandara Mountains, its subject is a sort of African epic about the unhappy loves of a young Kipsiki shepherd. Without any scientific pretensions whatsoever, this film offers some interesting views of the life of the Kipsiki and the Peul chiefdom of Rai Bouba.

13. The commercial release of *Statues* was an emasculated version that has been publicly rejected by the authors.

14. André Cauvin has since made a film on the visit of King Badouin to the Congo, and an-

other on Congolese independence. The editing of these two films together with a film on present-day Congo (1961 ) would make Cauvin's collected work into the most important document on the evolution of a single African state.

15. *[Jaguar* was finished in 1967. The catalog to which Rouch's paper is appended lists a French version of 130 minutes. A 90-minute version with English subtitles has been available in the United States since 1972. —*Trans.*]

16. Finally we should mention the American TV films made in Kenya for Time-Life, Inc., by Richard Leacock, formerly Flaherty's assistant on *Louisiana Story*. For the first time in Africa, Leacock and his crew used a portable camera synchronized to a portable tape recorder. I will return to this subject in the third part of this report.

17. I have not cited the films made in South Africa by local companies (particularly the films of Jack and Jamy Ulys) treating typically South African subjects. Although the production of these films is important and liable to increase given the favorable conditions in South Africa, they cannot be considered as African films, since they are almost exclusively films made by Afrikaaners, in Afrikaans, and dealing only with subjects of interest to Afrikaaners.

18. It is interesting to note that the National Film Board of Canada was established by Grierson for similar propaganda purposes. This, incidentally, is how Norman MacLaren's career began.

19. It is interesting to note the annual production and distribution figures for films in English-language African territories, reported by Sellers in 1958. *West Africa* (not including Ghana): The five film units of the Federation of Nigeria plus the Gambia and Sierra Leone units produced about 100 35 mm films and 150 16 mm films. Sixty-eight mobile cinema trucks served a total audience per year of nearly 15 million. *East Africa*: The six film units were producing ten 35 mm and 78 16 mm films per year, had thirty mobile cinema trucks, and reached a million viewers.

20. There was a heated discussion on this point in July 1958 during the international symposium "The Cinema in Africa South of the Sahara" at the Brussels World Fair. The whole team of the Colonial Film Unit took part, and the present writer, carried away by his feelings, argued that in the long run, the effect of this sort of film was even negative.

21. Once again, I have not cited the educational films made in South Africa, as they, too, are mostly Afrikaaner in language and outlook. A few English-speaking films that I was able to see were mainly semipublicity films for the mining industries and in that way were only of secondary interest from the filmic and educational points of view. Nevertheless, now and then, I believe that it is better to have poor films being produced than no films at all. Moreover, it is quite in the cards that in the cinema, we will witness a phenomenon similar to that which has occurred in the sphere of the press, with the rise in South Africa of genuine African journalism (cf. the magazine *Drum*).

22. I was unable to obtain specific information about the other republics of equatorial Africa, except the Congo, which in June 1961 indicated that its Mass Communication Service was trying to start a film section, but that with the meager resources at its disposal, no real filmmaking could be undertaken before 1962 or 1963.

23. At Claude Jutra's instigation, a young designer at the research center, Moustapha Allasane, has already produced a pilot animation, with the shooting being done in Montreal by Claude Jutra, Michel Brault, and Norman McLaren. Since then, this young artist has prepared a medium-length educational film, also animated, and has applied for a UNESCO fellowship for training in Paris and Montreal.

24. I cannot discuss Portuguese-speaking Africa, as I have no information on the subject. The only films I have been able to see, which were of quite good quality, were made by Portuguese anthropologists in Angola, about the Bushmen of the Northern Kalahari.

25. Needless to say, my reaction to the majority of my own earlier films is exactly the same.

26. Going through the chronology of major films between 1892 and 1951 (see *L'art du cinéma des origines à nos jours,* by Georges Sadoul), the following are the few African films that can be found: 1896, France, Pathé, *La dame Malgache;* 1900, Great Britain, William Paul, *Kruger: A Dream of Empire,* and Rosenthal, *Escarmouche avec les Boërs;* United States, James White, *Scènes reconstituées de la guerre du Transvaal;* France, Pathé, *La guerre du Transvaal;* 1930, Germany, Ruttman, *Melody of the World;* 1951, United States, John Huston, *The African Queen*—a total of seven films, only two of which were made later than 1900.

27. A very recent film of my own, *Chronicle of a Summer,* was shot in 16 mm and enlarged to 35 mm. Many professional filmmakers who saw the film did not even notice this.

28. These technical advances are mainly in 16 mm equipment, which is natural enough, considering that television services, using 16 mm exclusively, have to provide shows twenty-four hours a day, or, with two channels, forty-eight hours per day.

29. An experiment along these lines is to be tried shortly at Niamey, where, with UNESCO's help, a community theater-cinema is to be built. The present writer, who is partly responsible, will try out more particularly the double-system projectors discussed earlier, showing not only films from Niger but also film classics with dialogue and narration where necessary, in various local languages.

30. The gulf is partially bridged already by sound broadcasts. Experiments made with "radiovision" (direct projection of filmstrip during a broadcast program) had a degree of success that argues well for that of television.

*On the Vicissitudes of the Self:*
*The Possessed Dancer, the Magician,*
*the Sorcerer, the Filmmaker, and the*
*Ethnographer*

This essay is based, on the one hand, on knowledge about the Songhay-Zarma, at the loop of Niger, which I have gathered over a period of thirty years of ethnographic research. On the other hand, it is based on experimentation with direct cinema, deriving from the theories, under the name *cinéma-vérité*, prophesied in 1927 by the Russian filmmaker Dziga Vertov. I have used direct cinema as a special research tool in doing ethnography among these West African groups.

If the notion of *personne*—the self, person—is effectively one of the key religious factors involved in trance, possession dance, magic, and sorcery, it appears that it would be dishonest to leave the matter there, since the "self" of the observer who attends to these phenomena equally merits critical attention. This is especially so when the observer records and plays back the sounds and visual images for the subjects of these trances; those filmed consider these images to be a reflection of themselves and of their divinities; that is, part of the "self" of both men and gods.

This article is intended as a contribution to "shared anthropology." First, I will try to point out, within the limits of present knowledge, the concepts of the "self" among the Songhay-Zarma in certain critical periods.

| | |
|---|---|
| Possession dance | The character of the possessed person and of the possessing spirit |
| Magic | The character of the magician and of clairvoyant states |
| Sorcery | The character of the *tyarkaw* (eater of souls) and the character of his victim |

After this I will show how the filmmaker-observer, while recording these phenomena, both unconsciously modifies them and is himself changed by them; then how, when he returns and plays back the images, a strange dialogue takes place in which the film's "truth" rejoins its mythic representation. Finally, this demonstration of the active, involuntary role played by the observer will lead me to attempt to get closer to the situation of the ethnographer in his own field.

▶

## The "Self" in Possession Dance

A previous international colloquium of the Centre National de la Recherche Scientifique provided us with an occasion to review research on possession phenomena. It seems that even though we now have a baseline of complete information about different manifestations of possession in the world—and particularly in sub-Saharan Africa—it is still not possible to establish a precise typology or sketch out a satisfactory theory. However, it now appears that the phenomenon of trance (whether wild or controlled) is one of the essential features in the momentum behind great religious movements, and, perhaps, behind great movements in artistic creativity. For example, schools of theater have, for twenty years, used ethnographic information about possession to extract methods applicable for training actors (e.g., Julian Beck and the Living Theatre, Peter Brook, Roger Blin, and Grotowski).

In the present work, I will not go back over the particular mechanics of Songhay possession but rather will deal with the metamorphosis in "the person" or "self" of the possessed subject and of the spirit that possesses him or her. It is enough to note that in this region of the Niger Valley, possession is a means of special reciprocal communication between people and their gods.

The possessed, the "horses of the spirits," are largely women and are specialists who enter into a recognized group after a long and difficult initiation. After that, they are involved in "wild trances," which treat the sick excluded from the society. These trances are run by priests *(zimas)* and take place only during public ceremonies regularly organized by and for the entire society.

Some hundred divinities form the pantheon that reveals itself here. These gods are invisible, but they appear as men. They are of different races, have particular characteristics, and are special "masters" (of water, wind, bush, thunder, rainbow, etc.) from complicated legends that make up a very diverse mythology, one that continually reenriches itself with each new ritual and revelation.

After the initiation, each dancer is a "horse," reserved for one or sometimes several "horsemen," who will mount her (sometimes a male) during the trance and for minutes or hours "operate" the body and speak through the mouth of the horse. For the Songhay-Zarma, contrary to other neighboring systems, it is this dialogue with the gods that is the essential aim of possession ceremonies. There is thus a profound metamorphosis of the self of the horse, who gives up a part of herself to a part of the self of the god who is now incarnated in her body.

While observation of possession phenomena is easy because of the essentially public character of the ceremonies, interpretation is much more delicate because for the Songhay-Zarma, the possessed person does not, at least theoretically, have a single memory of the trance and resists all allusion to the possessing god. Of course, while in a normal state herself, she has seen others possessed, but this does not seem to influence her.

The sources of information are thus limited to the *zimas;* they are responsible for the initiation, become possessed themselves, and have acquired control over the possession of others. (I have sometimes tried to question the gods themselves through the horse during possession, but this technique seemed to be both singularly dangerous and, all things considered, too incoherent.) The most widespread theory propounded by the *zimas* is that during possession the "double" *(bia)* of the god has taken the place of the double of the horse. It is this exchange of doubles that I would like to analyze.

The notion of *bia* itself is very fuzzy, designating at the same time "shadow" (it literally means "somber"), "reflection" (in a mirror or pool of water), and "soul" (spiritual principle of all animate beings). This *bia* is tied to the body throughout life; it can temporarily leave the body during sleep (in dreams) or, occasionally, while awake (in a state of imagination, reflection, or possession). It leaves the body at the moment of death to follow its own course in the hereafter. Curiously, some people locate this double a bit to the rear of the body, on the left side (when dreaming, one must sleep on the right side); it is here that the possessing god temporarily comes to place himself or his double.

Do invisible gods, in effect, merely have a double, or are they themselves a double? The question must rest there, because in certain circumstances (for the important *zimas*), these gods can materialize and show themselves in human form (thus having or not having a *bia,* shadow, reflection, double).

It appears, however, that possession is only the affair of the gods, but even at this level of the double, the phenomena of possession merit careful attention. I have attended several hundred possession ceremonies (I have filmed about twenty) and have been able to observe, under the best conditions, this strange metamorphosis of trance and vertigo. It begins with the apparent loss of consciousness and is followed by the slow appearance of a new character, first trembling and howling, then becoming calm. Then the behavior takes on another manner, manifested by speaking in another voice and sometimes in another language. Once one is accustomed to the repertoire of personages, immediate identification is possible: it is *Dongo,* the spirit of thunder, or *Zatao,* the captive of the Peul people.

In January and February 1971, after making and showing my film *Horendi,* which concerns the seven days of initiation into possession dance, a group of musicians, *zimas,* and *sorko* fishermen brought out some important data about the metamorphosis of "self" in the possession state. These are the principal traits:

It is the left hand of the bowed lute *(godye)* player that is "inspired" or driven by the spirits who are collectively called out at the beginning of the ceremony by "the air of the hunters" *(gawey-gawey).* The drummers, playing on calabashes or skin drums, follow the play of the left hand, and the vibration of bass notes gives "power" to the dancer. It is also in the left hand that the lute player expresses the first sign of the arrival of the spirit in the dancer's body. He kicks the drummer in front of him, who in turn accentuates the rhythm; this accelerates the power of the dancer and "reinforces" the spirit that has begun to straddle him.

What is happening with the dancer? Following numerous indirect accounts (it has already been noted that the dancer is not supposed to remember his state), the dancer "sees" the spirit penetrate into the dance circle and direct himself toward him. Occasionally the important initiates see him, too. The spirit has in his hands the skin of a freshly sacrificed animal, which he holds out with the bloody side toward the dancer. He offers it three times. The first time the dancer's eyes tear. The second time the dancer's nose runs. The third time the dancer howls. If several "horses" of the same spirit appear in the course of the dance, they will all see him, and they can all have the same reaction simultaneously. However, only one selection is made during the three provocations.

After this, the spirit approaches a fourth time and retrieves the bloody skin from the head of the dancer. The dancer chokes—it is the climax of the ceremony. At this point the spirit embodies the double of the dancer and takes the double's place. The dancer is now mounted on his or her horse; that is, the dancer is possessed. During the entire period of the possession, the *bia,* or double, remains enclosed and protected, particularly against witches, by the bloody skin. When the spirit wants to leave, the skin is lifted, liberating the *bia.* When this happens, the horse opens his eyes, is dazzled, coughs as if having been strangled, and snorts to remove the traces of the bloody skin from his face.

The Songhay theory of the person in the possession state thus involves three elements:

1. A temporary substitution of the double of the person by the double of a spirit or *bia* spirit himself.
2. The preservation of the substituted double in a protective fresh skin.
3. The role of music and dance in calling the spirit into incarnation.

▶

## The Self of the Magician

Contrary to the case of possession dance, where through the intermediary of a horse-medium men can communicate directly and publicly with their gods, the case of magic is different. Here it is a question of an indirect and private consultation with invisible forces, in which the magician, all alone, performs a special and difficult role.

The magician *(sohantye)* is a descendant, through his father, of Sonni Ali, the *Si,* founder of the Songhay empire. He is chosen and initiated by his parent or by a more skilled master who is trained in the difficult exercise of permanent contact with invisible forces. He cannot practice his art until after the death of his father (or of his initiator), for it is at this time that he swallows a small initiation chain, which he in turn will vomit up several days before his death. The magician has a solitary and distant personality. He is feared but indispensable. A master of gestures and words, of trees and stones, he is guardian of the spiritual order of the village and capable of reconciling the spirits with men who dare ask it. These permanent "seers" are, without an intermediary, the masters of their doubles. They are sent in the form of vultures to encounter allied spirits and to reconnoiter through space and time the course of certain enterprises.

One consults a magician with a certain reticence, and only under grave conditions, because once his action commences, it is hardly ever possible to reverse it. Misfortune without recourse befalls the imprudent person who goes astray on the dangerous routes of the invisible. The consultation is long and difficult. The magician must take all precautions, study his client, and discover the unacknowledged purpose involved. After several days of consultation, he may stop short and reconsider if an awkward gesture or word has revealed any deceit in the actual transaction.

Whether divination is involved (by either throwing of cowries or direct prophecy) or the preparation of a magical charm *(korte),* the procedure is always the same. By his words and movements, the magician converts his double and sends him to gather the necessary materials for his work. Or he simply projects his double by the side of the double of the client to find out things that the client has not said or may not even be aware of.

The recited texts (which I have discussed at length elsewhere) are extraordinary. The magician first locates himself spatially, in relation to the six cardinal directions, and then situates himself in respect to his initiation chain. The identifying text is said in a loud voice, which both strengthens the magician himself and gives his *bia* the necessary energy to undertake the "path," or voyage.

As Luc de Heusch has correctly noted, it is more important for a shamanistic act than for a possession phenomenon to be disguised. Thus the recited texts are accounts of the dangerous voyage; they convey how the double of the magician confronts the double of both beneficial and evil spirits, confronts the doubles of other magicians who try to destroy his work, and, above all, confronts the double of the demiurge Ndebi, and of god himself. Through his double, the magician must triumph in successive tests, emerging superior to all other forces encountered. Throughout he does not require the assistance of these secret powers; rather, the double should be able to compel them to actualize what the magician has asked. Then, when all has been decided, the double returns, following the reverse route, ending up next to the magician, who has never lost control of it.

This brief but total power sometimes manifests itself in a dramatic public way, during the festival of magicians *(sohantye hori)*. For the occasion of a circumcision, the *gossi* (an ancient initiation of young girls), or, more simply, for the purification of a village, the *sohantye* will all come together for a festival. The magicians dance to the rhythms of the hourglass drums, brandishing in one hand a saber *(lolo)* to lance or pierce the doubles of sorcerers, and in the other a branch from a euphorbia plant.

This dance is a dramatic mime of a fight with the forces of evil. The magicians dance continually until the moment when one who feels himself to be the strongest enters into a trance. This trance has little in common with the state of possession previously described; the magician trembles violently, and then up from his mouth gushes a piece of the metallic chain that he swallowed at the time of his father's (or initiator's) death. This initiation chain is, in fact, his "superior identity," inasmuch as it materialized from his initiated ancestors. During the short time that the chain is visible, the *bia* of the magician, in the form of a vulture, quickly accomplishes its journey to the land of the spirits and their doubles. The purpose of the voyage is to discover and then wipe out the causes of impurity in the village. The risk involved here is considerable: if an enemy or rival has more power than the magician who has spit up his chain, the former can hinder the reswallowing. This would effectively prevent the retreat of the magician's double, who, as a result, would die from the loss of his essential source (the chain).

Based on this description, one can sketch out a Songhay theory of the self of the *sohantye,* or magician:

1. The double leaves the body of the magician, but without substitution by another double (as in possession).
2. This double undertakes a dangerous voyage among spirits and invisible forces.
3. The magician's speech (or the music of the drumming griots) and his special gestures (or ritual dance) are the underlying driving forces behind the shamanistic voyage.
4. Communication with other men is made by the material preparation of charms, by direct prophecy, and by the dramatic exhibition of the chain.
5. The voluntary projection of the double can be accompanied by mortal risk.

▶

## The Self of the *Tyarkaw,* the "Sorcerer/Soul Eater"

The sorcerer *(tyarkaw)* is much like the magician, but instead of using his or her power to defend or guide other men, the sorcerer uses it to work evil, causing the death of victims by stealing doubles.

The power of the sorcerer, like that of the magician, is inherited through mother's milk—an infant nourished by a *tyarkaw* will become a *tyarkaw.* Songhay mythology emphasizes this irremediable character. Once upon a time, a sacred woman, responsible for a community of women as a result of having made a vow of chastity, yielded to a visitor who spent the night with her. The next morning, she changed him into a sheep. Her companions in turn asked permission to eat this mysterious animal; as they did, the woman ate also. Thus she was pregnant by a man whom she helped eat. From this union of a woman and a man she had eaten, a child was born—a female "eater of doubles," a *tyarkaw.* From this *tyarkaw,* all other sorcerers descend.

Since that mythic time, each Songhay village has contained a fairly large number of *tyarkaw.* Of course, everybody knows who they are, but nobody speaks about it. *Tyarkaw* work evil because they are obligated to do so; in actuality they are criminals, but from the Songhay point of view, their criminality is not intentional. This mysterious system can only be comprehended by means of the concept of the self, or *personne,* of the *tyarkaw,* but inquiries about these people are so risky that they are almost impossible.

Like the magician, the sorcerer has the skill to direct his double, and it is the double who is in fact the actual agent of the sorcery. The double performs the task of hunting other doubles. Often at night near certain villages, one perceives from the bush visions of rapidly moving fires, which stop and start up again in successive bounds. These suspicious lights, whose explanation is not clear, are interpreted as *tyarkaw* roaming about. In effect, these sorcerers have the power to propel themselves through the air by means of fire that is emitted from their armpits and anuses. The few inquiries that I have been able to make indicate that the sorcerer's double is responsible for these manifestations; in other words, it is the moving about of the double that is perceived in the form of the fire movements. Meanwhile the body of the sorcerer is at home in the village, "in a state of deep meditation."

The flashing double can self-metamorphose into a calabash, a crying baby, or a donkey with two heads—forms it takes to frighten its future victim. While flying, the *tyarkaw* double sees a delayed traveler; the double successively turns itself into these three forms along the road, and should the traveler pick up the calabash, touch the baby, or strike the donkey with two heads, misfortune befalls him. He lapses into a state of panic and fear, losing his reason and hence the control of his own double. At this point, the *tyarkaw*'s double seizes the double of the victim and eats it. Once his body is empty of its double, the victim returns to the village, stupefied. If after seven days no one has returned his double, he dies.

One of the basic functions of the magicians is to engage in combat with the sorcerers and force them to return stolen doubles before they are eaten. This involves a strange kind of fight—double against double, while each corresponding person has his intact body lying in a corner of his house.

The accounts of these imaginary combats are fabulous. Armed with a *lolo* lance, the magician tries to prick the *tyarkaw,* who defends himself by throwing millet stalks. At dawn, when the doubles rejoin their respective bodies, they are marked with the wounds they received, swollen scars that they proudly exhibit. But never does the fight otherwise prolong itself in reality. The magician never asks about the actual sorcerer (who might very well be a neighbor). The only exception here is when the sorcerer has overstepped his or her bounds, by attacking either the children of the *sohantye* or those taken in by his family. If this happens, the *sohantye* takes a *lolo* and pierces the *tyarkaw,* forcing him or her to defecate the "egg of power."

This fight of doubles does materialize into reality; the sorcerer is deprived of the egg, which the *sohantye* uses to concoct charms for his defense. (This allusion to an "egg of the witch" appears generally throughout the savannah of West Africa and deserves systematic study.)

But all this notwithstanding, what becomes of the double of the victim, his stolen soul? Mysteriously passive and defenseless, the double is "hidden" (or perhaps pierced by a *lolo*) over the course of seven days. At the end of this period, the sorcerer leaves in the form of an owl to share his hunted double with other sorcerers who belong to the same "society." (This concept is analogous to the "diabolical societies" found along the West African coast.) Alternatively, it is given to his protecting spirit, himself a sorcerer. The double is then "eaten" by one or the other, and the victim dies.

While apparently logical, this scheme is nonetheless insufficient. For example, there are several things it does not explain:

1. The personal benefit the sorcerer or the society derives from his risky acts. Is it accumulation of power? How? And for what?
2. The particular role—benevolent or malevolent—of the sorcerer in the society where he or she also acts in a vulnerable manner.
3. The fate of the double (in principle, immortal) of the victim after death. Does the double change into something else? Is the double reincarnated? Or surrendered following some particular use in the world of doubles? Does the double become a spirit? If so, he could become an originator of other myths.
4. The total immunity of certain people from their village *tyarkaw*. The *tyarkaw* are known by all but tacitly ignored. In some villages, for example, where there are many known sorcerers, young men avoid marrying their daughters. These women then either exile themselves or become courtesans.

In-depth studies of these questions are evidently quite difficult, but obviously necessary; a phenomenon so widespread must hold an essential key to systems of thought in sub-Saharan Africa. For the moment I must refrain from applying to the sorcerer-victim relationship an eventual Songhay theory of the self of the sorcerer. As for the rest of the data:

1. The double leaves the body of the sorcerer, and as in the case of the magician, no other double can take its place.
2. This double undertakes a hunt for the doubles of other men. It separates them from their bodies by fright. This offensive is, in

some ways, comparable to the process of the spirit brandishing the bloody skin in front of the dancer at the moment of possession.

3. No double can be substituted for the victim, who quickly regains consciousness. He is thus like the sorcerer in body, but incapable of recovering, as is the sorcerer, his spiritual principle.

4. The appearance for the first time of the death of the double (and consequently his body) as the result of prolonged separation.

5. The existence of a potential world where the doubles of living men associate with the doubles of spirits (or with the spirits themselves). In this world they encounter themselves and fight with or mutually assist one another, thus sharing a secret collective imagination (in contrast to possession dance, where this collective imagination is publicly witnessed).

6. The singular economy of the doubles of victims—consumed, exchanged, or destroyed—is an area whose key remains to be discovered.

7. The forced production of an anal egg, in which is concentrated the sorcerer's power (this again contrary to the magician, who voluntarily spits up his chain).

Before dealing with the other side of the observation process (by the ethnographer-filmmaker), it might be useful to review and summarize the points concerning the notion of *bia*, the double.

Each man has a *bia*, or double, who lives in a parallel world, that is, a world of doubles. This world is the home of the spirits, the masters of the forces of nature; it is also the permanent home of the imaginary (dreams, reveries, reflections), as well as the temporary home of magicians and sorcerers. This reflection world does not seem to extend beyond the limits of the earthly world and, in particular, does not overlap with the world of the hereafter managed by god.

Between the real world and its double, certain connections are possible, whether by the incarnation of spirits during possession dances, by shamanistic incursion of magicians into the reflection world, or by the materialization of a sorcerer at the time of his hunt for other men's doubles.

These two worlds, finally, are so completely interpenetrated that it is nearly impossible for the noninformed observer to distinguish the "real" from the "imaginary." For example, the statement "I met Ali yesterday" can mean equally "I actually met Ali yesterday" or "I dreamed or I thought I met Ali yesterday." And when the observer is first thrown into this exercise, he can disturb or upset both the real and the imaginary.

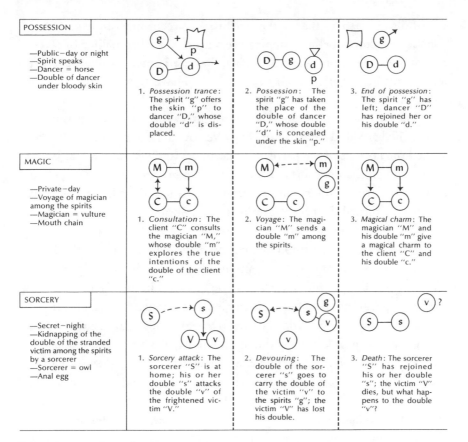

| POSSESSION | | | |
|---|---|---|---|
| —Public—day or night<br>—Spirit speaks<br>—Dancer = horse<br>—Double of dancer<br>under bloody skin | 1. *Possession trance*: The spirit "g" offers the skin "p" to dancer "D," whose double "d" is displaced. | 2. *Possession*: The spirit "g" has taken the place of the double of dancer "D," whose double "d" is concealed under the skin "p." | 3. *End of possession*: The spirit "g" has left; dancer "D" has rejoined her or his double "d." |
| MAGIC | | | |
| —Private—day<br>—Voyage of magician among the spirits<br>—Magician = vulture<br>—Mouth chain | 1. *Consultation*: The client "C" consults the magician "M," whose double "m" explores the true intentions of the double of the client "c." | 2. *Voyage*: The magician "M" sends a double "m" among the spirits. | 3. *Magical charm*: The magician "M" and his double "m" give a magical charm to the client "C" and his double "c." |
| SORCERY | | | |
| —Secret—night<br>—Kidnapping of the double of the stranded victim among the spirits by a sorcerer<br>—Sorcerer = owl<br>—Anal egg | 1. *Sorcery attack*: The sorcerer "S" is at home; his or her double "s" attacks the double "v" of the frightened victim "V." | 2. *Devouring*: The double of the sorcerer "s" goes to carry the double of the victim "v" to the spirits "g"; the victim "V" has lost his double. | 3. *Death*: The sorcerer "S" has rejoined his or her double "s"; the victim "V" dies, but what happens to the double "v"? |

Possession, magic, and sorcery.

▶

### The Self of the Observer and Particularly of the Ethnographer-Filmmaker

In this word of fragile mirrors, standing beside men and women for whom any clumsy action may provoke or inhibit trance, the observer's presence can never be neutral. Whether he wishes it or not, the observer is integral to the general movement of things, and his most minute reactions are interpreted within the context of the particular system of thought that surrounds him.

I have chosen here to begin with the "self" of the filmmaker because recording and then projecting images and sounds introduces a concrete element that books—even illustrated ones—leave out. This is so because the people we study are in large part nonliterate but do know how to look and listen. Over the years, technical advances have resulted in increasingly complex equipment whose operation is increasingly simple. This has led to the use of direct cinema—that is, the synchronous recording of image and sounds—as a tool of ethnographic observation. Since the making of several film studies in Dahomey and Mali, in collaboration with Gilbert Rouget and Germaine Dieterlen, from 1957 to 1965, I have systematically used this technique.

The two pioneers of the technique of direct cinema were the American Robert Flaherty and the Russian Dziga Vertov; during the 1920s, they invented the notions of the participating camera and of kinopravda. Just when the first theoreticians of film tried to define this new "language" in relation to fiction (coming directly from the theatrical tradition), Flaherty and Vertov turned their barely outlined rules upside down by experimenting with cinema in real life.

Dziga Vertov understood that cinematic vision was a particular kind of seeing, using a new organ of perception—the camera. This new perception had little in common with the human eye; he called it the "ciné-eye." Later, with the appearance of sound film, he similarly defined the "radio-ear," a new special organ of recorded hearing. Extending his analysis, we know today that this new kind of audiovisual language can be understood (I should say *ciné-compris,* or "filmically understood") by audiences with no special education. Vertov called the entirety of this discipline "kinopravda" (*cinéma-vérité,* or "film-truth"), an ambiguous or self-contradictory expression, since fundamentally film truncates, accelerates, and slows down actions, thus distorting the truth. For me, however, kinopravda is a precise term, on the same order of kinok (ciné-eye), and it designates not "pure truth" but the particular truth of the recorded images and sounds—a filmic truth *(ciné-vérité).*

At every stage of direct cinema, a filmic attitude *(ciné-attitude)* manifests itself. Contrary to scripted fiction films, the direct cinema filmmaker must be ready at every moment to record the most efficacious images and sounds. To return to the terminology of Vertov, when I make a film, I "film-see" *(ciné-vois)* by knowing the limits of the lens and camera; likewise, I "film-hear" *(ciné-entends)* in knowing the limits of the microphone and tape recorder; I "film-move" *(ciné-bouge)* to find the right angle or exercise the best movement; I "film-edit" *(ciné-monte)* throughout the shooting, thinking of how the images are fitting together. In a word, I "film-think" *(ciné-pense).*

Robert Flaherty, a rough Irish American geologist, used a camera for the first time in the far North among the Hudson Bay Eskimos. He was unaware of these theories, and did not need them, although he had to solve similar problems in the field. From the start, he applied an extraordinarily empirical technique by allowing the Eskimos, Nanook and his family, to participate (beyond acting) in his film *Nanook of the North*. Under incredible field conditions, Flaherty accomplished this kind of participation by building a location development laboratory and projection room. In doing so, he invented the use of the "participating camera," a technique that he saw not as an obstacle to communication but, on the contrary, as an indispensable part of filmmaking in the field.

I have been more or less consciously synthesizing and applying these two methods to my own work in ethnography. Today all the people I film know the camera, and they clearly understand its capability to see and hear. They have helped me during the editing process by screening projections of my films; in Vertov's terms, at the time of shooting they are "film-seen" *(ciné-vus)* when I "film-observe" *(ciné-regarde)* them. In fact, they react to this art of visual and sound reflection in exactly the same manner as they react to the public art of possession or the private art of magic or sorcery.

Long ago, Frazer, in *The Golden Bough,* noted the frightened reaction of "primitives" to being photographed; the reflection might endanger their souls. What does this imply about the moving image, in color, with sound? It is only necessary to have once attended the projection of such a film in the field to understand this kind of emotional shock. One year after its making, I showed my film *Sigui 1969—La caverne de Bongo,* to the villagers of Bongo, in Mali, where I shot it. They relived a past time, animated by a piece of celluloid—reflections of disappeared people, phantom impressions that one sees, that one hears but does not see, or that one does not hear.

I now believe that for the people who are filmed, the "self" of the filmmaker changes in front of their eyes during the shooting. He no longer speaks, except to yell out incomprehensible orders ("Roll!" "Cut!"). He now looks at them only through the intermediary of a strange appendage and hears them only through the intermediary of a shotgun microphone.

But paradoxically it is due to this equipment and this new behavior (which has nothing to do with the observable behavior of the same person when he is not filming) that the filmmaker can throw himself into a ritual, integrate himself with it, and follow it step-by-step. It is a strange kind of choreography, which, if inspired, makes the cameraman and soundman no longer invisible but participants in the ongoing event.

For the Songhay-Zarma, who are now quite accustomed to film, my "self" is altered in front of their eyes in the same way as is the "self" of the possession dancers: it is the "film-trance" *(ciné-transe)* of the one filming the "real trance" of the other. This experience is really true to me, and I know by the control of my camera eyepiece, by the reactions of the audience, whether the filmed sequence is a success or a failure and whether I have been able to free myself of the weight of filmic and ethnographic theories necessary to rediscover the *barbarie de l'invention.*

One can even take this further: Isn't the "image hunt" comparable to the sorcerer's hunt for doubles? And the material that I take such extraordinary care of—the film, keeping it in darkness, dry, at a low temperature— is it not just a "reflection package," a "package of doubles"? If the camera can be compared to the bloody skin of the possessing spirit, then the shipment of the film to the distant processing laboratory can be compared, by contrast, to the devouring of the double by the sorcerer.

The analogy for me stops there, because the next steps are not explicitly a part of African mythology. The "stolen" image comes back several months later and, when projected on the screen, recovers its life for an instant. The reflection is bestowed with such a strange power that its viewing is enough to make a "horse of the spirit" see itself possessed on the screen and immediately enter into trance.

Currently I am at the point of reflecting on my own role as a taker and giver of doubles, as an eater and shower of reflections. I already know that the next step is research to clarify these roles in relation to the self of the ethnographer and ethnography itself. For the moment it is hardly possible to establish a Songhay theory of the self of the filmmaker, but I will be trying to draw up such a profile in my future work with the priests, fishermen, and magicians who have collaborated with me over the last thirty years.

Nonetheless I can show a short film that points out the obvious role played by the camera as a stimulant to possession. [At this point in the presentation, Rouch's film *Tourou et Bitti* was shown. See the appendix to this essay for a description of the film.]

▶───────────────────────────────

## Conclusion

These critical reflections on the self of the filmmaker lead me to expand on the concept of the self of the ethnographer.

In the field, the observer modifies himself; in doing his work, he is no longer simply someone who greets the elders at the edge of the village, but—to go back to Vertovian terminology—he ethno-looks, ethno-observes, ethno-thinks. And those with whom he deals are similarly modified; in giving their confidence to this habitual foreign visitor, they ethno-show, ethno-speak, ethno-think.

It is this permanent ethno-dialogue that appears to be one of the most interesting angles in the current progress of ethnography. Knowledge is no longer a stolen secret, devoured in the Western temples of knowledge; it is the result of an endless quest where ethnographers and those whom they study meet on a path that some of us now call "shared anthropology."

▶ _____

**Appendix: Description of the film *Tourou et Bitti***

On March 15, 1971, the *Sorko* fisherman Daouda asked me to come film at Simiri, in the Zarmaganda of Niger. The occasion was a possession dance to ask the black spirits of the bush to protect the forthcoming crop from the locusts.

Despite the efforts of the *zima* priest Sido, Daouda's father, and despite the use of two special old drums, *tourou* and *bitti,* no one became possessed for three days.

On the fourth day I again went to Simiri with Daouda and my soundman, Moussa Amidou. After several hours passed without possession taking place, I decided to shoot anyway. Night was about to fall, and I thought I would take the opportunity to shoot some footage of this beautiful music, which is in danger of disappearing.

I began to film the exterior of the compound of the *zima* priests, then, without turning off and on, passed through the pen of the sacrificial goats and then out into the dance area where an old man, Sambou Albeybu, was dancing without much conviction. Without stopping I walked up to the musicians and filmed them in detail. Suddenly the drums stopped. I was just about ready to turn off when the *godye* lute started up again, playing solo. The lute player had "seen a spirit." Immediately Sambou entered into the state and became possessed by the spirit *kure* (the Hausa butcher, the hyena). I kept filming. Then old Tusinye Wazi entered the dance area; she was immediately possessed by the spirit *Hadyo*. Still without stopping, I filmed the consultation of spirits by the priests—a sacrifice was requested. At this point I began to walk backward, framing a general establishing view of the compound, now flushed with the coming of sunset. The filming was thus one continuous shot, the length of the camera load.

Looking back at this film now, I think that the shooting itself was what unlatched and sped up the possession process. And I would not be surprised if upon showing the film to the priests of Simiri, I learned that it was my own ciné-trance that played the role of catalyst that night.

(1973)

## The Mad Fox and the Pale Master

Why tell it? Why tell this story of joy and of passion, of humiliation as well as revolt, this story that nobody else will ever tell? Maybe it's because all our youth was a witness to this strange fever that keeps making our heart beat, something that keeps coming back like a recurring memory, a word, a question that still has no answer. Maybe it's also because, for me, to write this homage to Germaine Dieterlen is to go back on the road, to meet Michel Leiris's "Blaise berçant sa laisse" and a manhood that we, neither you nor I, will ever attain because Africa will always remain a phantom.[1] Or maybe it's to listen for the first time to Marcel Griaule speak the words "Bandiagara cliffs," or to find yet again the nostalgic perspective of De Chirico's *The Red Tower*. This is the parallel pursuit whose point of escape could only be the infinite "over there" at the conjunction of research and poetry. It's to smell again the preserving spice of the old Trocadéro Museum before 1937 with its deathly, troubling figures, or to come to the end of the steep paths of the Ashanti forest, and the smell of Lake Bosumtwi, pale as an enigma.

For me all of these things are inseparable, and all anthropological research without its field diary is a castrated work. To talk about the great Dogon adventure without its actors is like reading Griaule's *Masques Dogon* without Leiris's *L'Afrique fantôme*, or Griaule and Dieterlen's *Le renard pâle* without Griaule's *Dieu d'eau*. It's to be a voyeur while refusing at the same time to be seen. So permit me to sketch a field journal whose stopping points, beginning, and end remain unknown to me.

## The Nostrils and the Navel

*Minotaure,* the surrealist journal of the 1930s, had already driven us from Breton's "convulsive beauty" to the funerary rites of the lower Ogol. And the *kanaga,* the Dogon "cross of Lorraine" mask, was already hung in our imaginary museum next to Dalí's *Apparition of Face and Fruit Dish on a Beach* (1938). So as someone who at the time didn't know anything else but the drunkenness of differential equations, I discovered in the Trocadéro Museum some other equations whose three unknowns, the red, black, and white, represented fabulous and secret structures in an imaginary space.

Then came the war. Looking back at it, I think that we had a crazy chance to live through a crazy time. Everything that my generation learned during the previous twenty years was revealed to be an illusion in just one month in May 1940. The army, Verdun,[2] France, honor, dignity, money, church, work, society, family, economic man, libido, historical materialism—everything had been taken away by the winds of one of the brightest springs the world has known. And by a strange paradox I had started my life as an engineer of bridges and roads by blowing up the most prestigious bridges in France. Among them was Chateau-Thierry, so well known to us in the fables of Jean de la Fontaine, and the bridge of the Briare Canal, a stream of steel and water running above the Loire, frozen and still and out of this world like a Magritte painting. Never had a generation of youth been so rich: because we had nothing left, and absolutely nothing left to lose.

In this empty Paris of the German occupation, from 1940 to 1941, the Musée de l'Homme was the only open door to the rest of the world. Once or twice a week, together with my classmates Jean Sauvy and Pierre Ponty, we left the School of Bridges and Roads on the rue des Saints-Père for a bicycle climb through the silent and dead avenues, up to the hill of Chaillot. And if we were lucky, on that afternoon, Marcel Griaule would speak for an hour about the natural totemism of the landscape in the context of the Ethiopian Gondar region and the battlefields of East Africa. And at night, in the museum's first-floor film theatre, Henri Langlois, thin and shy, would present Vladimir Legoshin's film *The Lone White Sail.*[3] And there, too, during this time cutting school, hanging out "in the bush" outside of the plagued city, and outside of the time of shame, Germaine Dieterlen, with a magic lantern, showed us photographs of lost countries.

I don't remember anything of those austere lectures, and I didn't learn anything in this "introductory course in descriptive ethnography." But I can still hear some mysterious phrases: "In Peru the devil creates and sends back the sun," "The swing perhaps originates in the South of India," "There are three types of body decorations: deformations (of the head, trunk, skull), scars (to photograph them well on black skin, you must first rub in millet porridge), amputation (of a finger, for example)," "Extraction of teeth, that's the cult of water," "Earring, a ring charmed under a spell, demon snare trap . . ."

How can I explain the fascination that we could have with such strange notions while all week long we were struggling with the Fourier series, with the problems of structural design, or the use of prestressed concrete? Whatever the irrationalities of these sciences called "human," they were an indispensable counterpoint to the rationality of our engineering discipline. And in this double "college," where the resistance of physical materials seemed like one multileveled surrealist mask behind another, we felt ourselves perfectly at home in the margin. So when chance forced the three of us to become engineers of the public works in France's West African colonies, it seemed to us very natural to go and build bridges in the fantastic country of the Bandiagara cliffs.

One could be fearful of this colonial Africa—it was more Vichyist than Pétain, more Germanophilic than Doriot, more militaristic than in the First World War, more Anglophobic than Darlan, more racist than Montandon.[4] I remember the only advice given to us by the general inspector of the colonial public works department in Dakar: "Above all, don't niggerize yourselves!"[5] But for us, already so much on the fringe of a society that was half crumbled, it was phantom Africa once again. So I didn't feel out of place when fate drove me to travel on the Niger River because it was the shortest path between Bamako and Niamey. Between sand and water, between the hard military buildings and the soft mud palaces, between the absurdity of the uniforms and the timid smiles of the women pounding millet, it was all still the Musée de l'Homme, with its warehouse of African objects.

But when the beautiful boat voyage ended, we had to live in a city that didn't really exist, though it was named Niamey, capital of Niger. At the end of so many weeks and kilometers, we were still faced with a legion of soldiers, with the little schoolchildren singing "Maréchal, here we are."[6] We had to hear from the governor general that I should consider myself a person "mobilized ready to invade Nigeria to give it back to the English." With all that, how could I not sink into despair? How could I not break my head against the mud brick walls? How could I escape from this colonial society that had nothing else except arrogance and mediocrity as its common denominator?

Was it I who chose my first black friends, or was it more they who chose me? Because at that time we were far from the Bandiagara cliffs and the *kanaga* masks. In this apparently Islamized country there were no statues or masks, no altars outside of the mosques. And all through these roads that I drove in my jeep, the scenery, the "poorly treed bush," was always the same. It was "the country of the Père Fouettard"—the black man that's going to whip you—as Albert Londres had once described it.[7]

But there was still this majestic and beautiful Niger River, at the same time terrifying with its crocodiles and welcoming with all its freshness. Slowly, and with a great deal of reticence, I learned how to swim there, to navigate a canoe, and to avoid the mud banks and the cutting oysters, or the terrible steel hook fishing lines of the *mamari* "thieves." Damouré Zika, one of the very young employees of the public works, was my initiator, and we traded knowledge: he was a Sorko fisherman, a master of the river, but I was a better swimmer than he.

So little by little, I became more distant from the European community, sharing my work and play with my first African friends. In fact I didn't understand anything: you couldn't swim over there because of a *karey kyi*, a "man-eating crocodile," yet here, less than fifty meters away, you could dive in complete safety. At night you could go down to the Comacico cinema on a bicycle with a swinging lamp that hooked onto the handlebars. But you had to come back by the main road of the Bureau of Domaines (whose official buildings housed managing offices for public institutions and state properties), to avoid the "soul-eating sorcerers."

And if during the first months I tried to apply the principle of balances to what one clears off and puts back on the road, I quickly understood that the real problem wasn't there. It wasn't "works of art" that we were building but protective coverings for the rainy season. It wasn't "imperial paths" that we were clearing through the bush of the whipper, the Père Fouettard, but paths of sweat and blood, paths where each cut stone and every shovel of dirt was carried on the head, in little baskets, by millions of people. And it was my responsibility to supervise the forced labor of these "good volunteers."

And, I ask again, to what extent were all those precise studies of roads and railroads, of the use of metallic beams and concrete, of any use? When we had to make a bridge, it was more like constructing a masonry arch in the times of the Romans, and our so-called building sites occupied as many people as in the days of the pyramids. There were ten thousand men working on the Fada N'Gourma road connecting Niamey to Ouagadougou in Upper Volta (now Burkina Faso), and ten thousand more working on the Gao road, connecting Niamey to Gao in Mali. Recruited in each village under the threat of surrounding guards, each worker had but a blanket and a certificate of vaccination. They walked hundreds of kilometers to get to the building site. There they stayed three months (or they might return three months later, depending on the capriciousness of the village chief) under the unconditional authority of the site boss.

It was these site bosses that I first discovered. I had never encountered characters like this before except in the worst novels about hard labor camps or the conquest of the American West. The sample went from a decrepit old drunk emptying a bottle in a night, to the young romantic adventurer escaping from the Parisian high school, married to a very young Hausa woman soon to be a mother, to an "exemplary" and gentle Normandy farmer, his wife, and daughter, whose surname was, alas, well deserved: *Karamabu,* "one who beats people until they are dead." Without doubt my curiosity should have overcome my disgust, and I should have studied this strange fauna with which I had to cohabit. But picturesque as they may have been, I skipped the study of the keepers in favor of trying to understand their prisoners.

Then everything went quickly. One morning in July 1942 I received a telegram from a site boss named Pagnouf telling me that lightning had killed ten workers at Kilometer Point 35. Not knowing what to do, I asked one of the most faithful Muslims in the Public Works Department. He said that he wasn't competent to say and that the people struck by lightning had nothing to do with Islam. My friend Damouré gave me the solution. He advised me to go and see his grandmother, a ritual chieftain of the Sorko fishers in the Niamey region. And that is how I met old Kalia Daoudou, a soft-spoken and wise grandmother, who, in her little house of mud and straw in the Gawe section of Niamey, allowed us to discover, Damouré and me, the real Africa.

Under the direction of old Kalia, the ceremony of purification for the ten who were struck by lightning made such an impression on me that I was incapable of writing anything down or taking any photographs. The spirit of thunder who was responsible for this act, through a medium, splashed milk on the burned bodies and gave the reasons for his anger. Then, a few days later, the thunder spirit struck again and on the same river killed a Sorko fisherman in his canoe. This time Damouré and I followed his grandmother Kalia on the banks of the river with a notebook and camera. It was our first ethnographic inquiry: in eight days we developed all of our photos, Damouré transcribed and translated the ritual texts, and the unfolding of this ceremony was minutely described in detail. I sent all of it to Marcel Griaule at the Society of Africanists in Paris.

Germaine Dieterlen answered me immediately. As well as encouraging me to continue inquiries into these things, she sent me a model questionnaire on the cult of water spirits. I will always remember one of the questions: "Do the victims of the water spirits have their nostrils and their navel cut? " Without believing it at all, I asked Kalia, who, to my great surprise said, "Of course! But if you already know so many things, why bother me with all these simple questions?"

So "the nostrils and the navel" was my first passport, the "sesame" that opened the door to my first ethnographic knowledge. This particular day my engineering work seemed completely useless. How could I continue this mediocre routine of being an "empire builder" when there were so many other things to discover? But very curiously, the principles of these two disciplines already seemed complementary to me. So when I naively but passionately began a first inventory of the Songhay gods, I thought about our professor of the resistance of materials, Albert Caquot, who explained to us how he had discovered the strange phenomenon of the principle of resistance to successive stresses. He first described it in a manner that was totally irrational (I would say poetic), and then considerably later, he gave us the precise scientific analysis. For me, both what I learned from Caquot and what I was about to undertake in Africa were about the same principles, those of initiation.

And thirty years later, I still haven't completely resolved the question posed back then by Germaine Dieterlen. In 1969, at Doulsou, on the Niger River, some Sorko fisherman were killing a hippopotamus, and at the same time they wounded a *hasu*, a river serpent. A few days before that, before disappearing, the serpent made ten bull cows who were crossing the river all to fall over in a single instant. At the same time, he also dragged a young boy underwater. When they found the boy's body, the nostrils and the navel were cut.

▶

## The Joking Relationship of the River and the Cliff

It took the coming and going of the war, in particular my expulsion from Niger in 1942 by one of Pétain's governors, to discover that Niger had become my passion.[8] Without any doubt, I had just barely seen a bit of what there was to discover, but the bush was only monotonous if you drove through it by car, and the great river had just begun to reveal its mysteries.

In December, at Bamako, on the way to Dakar where the Vichy government of Niger was sending me for military punishment, I met my friends

Jean Sauvy and Pierre Ponty, both of whom had similar troubles to mine. But we were full of enthusiasm; the Americans had landed in North Africa, and after many hesitations, West Africa had joined the Allied forces.

One afternoon while climbing the imposing Koulouba mountain, we saw the Niger River "glittering in the sun," the way it had blinded its first discoverer, the Scotsman Mungo Park, 150 years earlier. We decided to come back after the "second half" of the war and to descend the entirety of the river in a canoe.[9] Like the military oath others made in Koufra, that was the ethnographic oath we three made in Koulouba, in the total uncertainty of what was going to happen the next day.

But in Dakar we discovered this wonderful man, Théodore Monod, who between my barracks time and free time got me into a small seminar of the Institut Français d'Afrique Noire—IFAN. There I devoured the classics: Barth and Leo Frobenius, the Tarikh histories of the Songhay empire written in the fifteenth and sixteenth centuries, Griaule's *Masques Dogon,* Maurice Delafosse's three-volume *Haut-Sénégal Niger,* and Louis Desplagnes's *Plateau Central Nigerien.* At the same time, I tried to put a little order in my undisciplined notes, as well. There too I met Paul Rivet, while he was stopping between Central America (where he had been in exile) and the provisional Free French government of Algiers. He encouraged me to work on "my thesis" by making a date to meet me at the Musée de l'Homme after the war. But he also let me know that he had scores to settle with Griaule and those who had stayed on in occupied Paris.[10]

I didn't see Rivet, Griaule, and Dieterlen until Christmas 1944, when I was in Paris on a brief leave. Already the decisions had been made, and the Africanists were divided in two. The radicals stayed close to Rivet at the Musée de l'Homme, and the dissidents of the Geographical Society remained around Griaule. In the uniform of an air force colonel, he was burdened, as if stigmatized from a physical deformity, by being named a professor at the Sorbonne by the Vichy government. But he was the only titled chair of ethnography at the Sorbonne, and it was at his house that I signed up to prepare a graduate degree and thesis. To tell you the truth, during those few days of leave in the snow of Alsace, the petty quarrels going on "in the ethnographic chapel" seemed totally idiotic, and just like the image of France at that time. For in its immense majority, the country was just not concerned with these warlike adventures and with us, only its ridiculed heroes.

In the summer of '45 some angry young people found themselves back in Paris, deciding that they would have nothing to do with their own society, for whom they had sacrificed their friends and their youth. Among them, Jean Sauvy, Pierre Ponty, and I decided to abandon the engineering profession. (How can we forget the welcoming of our comrades who stayed on in occupied France in 1940 and who considered us crazies and outlaws—"How are you going to catch up on lost time?" they said). Instead we would prepare graduate philosophy degrees at the Sorbonne, go down the Niger in a canoe, and live and do collective journalism under the name of Jean Pierjean. And in all this pitiful intellectual mess of the winter of '45 to '46, it seemed that only Griaule's damned team had something to bring to us, something we could learn from.

We all found ourselves in the Sahel in the summer 1946, in Bamako. No one of us was richer than the other, hitchhiking by plane to Africa. But we had the unconditional backing of IFAN's Théodore Monod, the only one, along with Griaule, who supported our project to go down the Niger in a canoe. Every week we sent articles and photos that we developed and enlarged in our canoe to the Agence France Presse. Thanks to the small payment "by the line," and our good health and optimism no matter what, we slowly descended what Rimbaud called "les impassibles." Halfway, toward the end of November, leaving our canoe in Mopti, we went up to the Bandiagara, and there, to Griaule's old Sangha campsite.

At the beginning it was a terrible deception: when you come from the river, the climb up the cliffs is a slow incline with no apparent relief. And the architecture of the Dogon villages of the plateau is no more extraordinary than those of the Bozo villages of the river.

We were full of stories to tell, stories of the sources of the Niger River, of the rapids and the capsizing, of the cult of water spirits. But now we very quickly came to understand that our waterway escapades were in no way comparable to this other risky adventure, of the discovery of Dogon metaphysics. Griaule conversed with Ogotemmêli . . . then we left Dieterlen, Ganay, and Griaule to their difficult conversations, and following Geneviève Griaule, we went off to discover the Dogon country.

Of course, it was a great shock as soon as we arrived in Bongo. The fabulous spectacle of the Bandiagara cliffs was a reality that no photograph, no story, no film could really convey. Immediately I lapsed back into an adolescent nostalgia for the mineral landscapes of Dalí, the perspectives and hard light of De Chirico, and the smell of the old Trocadéro. And at our age, afraid to show such childlike enthusiasm, we decided instead to laugh about it.

Without knowing it, we Bozo started up a traditional discourse, a joking relationship, with Griaule's Dogon team. The theme was very simple: all of these totemic alters, all these *tellem* caves of the ancestors, all these caverns of masks, all of this extraordinary decor, all of it was the invention of Griaule and his team. That was the game of the day during the trip to Iréli. What we didn't know then was that this ritual joking between the people of the water and the people of the cliffs would become a cruel premonition. Because when Griaule went back to Paris months later, nobody took seriously what he had just discovered about this mythology, this complicated system of Dogon thought. They thought it was only the creation of the inquirer, a projection of his personal fantasies, bordering on trickery.

After nine months, the river that we had followed, paddling stroke after stroke, came to dissolve into the sea. We came back "tired but at peace"; our oath from Kouluba had been fulfilled. In Paris there was again war in the clan of Africanists. I was finishing my degree and signed up to write a doctoral thesis with Griaule as my research supervisor. I began to work at the library of the Musée de l'Homme.

From Niger we brought, with great difficulty, a collection of objects: paraphernalia and costumes of ritual possession, fishing equipment, and even a very beautiful Mopti canoe freighted with our own money in Wari on a cargo ship owned by Elder Damster. But the canoe was too big, and it stayed in the courtyard of the Musée de l'Homme (one winter day it was covered with snow!) until the day the UN took over the Palais de Chaillot. The cook cut it into pieces to make firewood.

I was feverishly editing our first film, a strange essay in 16 mm black and white on hippopotamus hunting by harpoon. When it was projected at the Musée de l'Homme, I received a great deal of encouragement. The same transpired when I showed it at the Society of Africanists meeting. Germaine Dieterlen said that she saw not only the technique of fishing but a great ritual of the cult of water spirits (that was verified four years later when I was able to film a complete hippopotamus hunt).

Yet I found myself completely neutral in the doubtful combat between the two sectors of Africanists, and soon alone, as well. The journalist combo Jean Pierrejean had exhausted themselves a little in Africa, and Jean Sauvy and Pierre Ponty abandoned me to anthropology. Paradoxically I didn't chose the camp of the resistant rationalists but chose that of my joking relation cousins of the cliffs, the suspect and decried team of Griaule. It wasn't a taste for a crusade but simply because they had more fun. After Griaule's Friday-morning seminar at rue Saint Jacques, we went to drink white wine and cassis at the bar nearby. At those times, I couldn't help thinking of the old Michel Bakunin, asking his Jura comrades to hold off an important revolutionary reunion for a few days because the new white wine of the Vaud country was particularly delicious that very year.

I went back to Africa in 1947 as a research attaché of the Centre National de la Recherche Scientifique (CNRS), with thanks to a scholarship from the "centennial of the abolition of slavery." Together with my friends from Niger, Damouré Zika and Lam Ibrahima Dia, we had the most beautiful horseback ride that one could possibly imagine through the bush. Along the buckle of the Niger River, we relentlessly pursued the spirit traces of Si, of Sonni Ali Ber, the magician king, of Faran Make Bote, the master fisherman, or of Dongo, the spirit of thunder. I met the "wise elders," and I was expecting to discover my own Ogotemmêli someday. But it never happened. Of course, filming the circumcision among the Songhay of Hombori, the "sex soul" was suddenly revealed.[11] And in Wanzerbé, collecting texts of the magic formulae of the *korte,* the hierarchy of "light words" and "heavy words" appeared. But those things were not sufficient for constructing a metaphysical system.

On my return, my colleagues at the Musée de l'Homme saw in my stymied inquiries a supplementary proof of "Griaule's impasse." But Griaule and Dieterlen answered me simply: "It takes twenty or thirty years to penetrate deep knowledge." So I wrote my two theses, leaving "Elements of Songhay metaphysics" as a blank chapter.

I worked in the African Department at the Musée de l'Homme in a strange fever of discovery. The intellectual Paris of the thirties was definitely dead, and surrealism was just a marvelous memory that the new intellectual currents could not replace. The human sciences were committing themselves to the ways of rigor, culturalism, linguistics, structuralism, Marxism. Claude Lévi-Strauss, riding bus 63 from the Sixteenth Arrondisement to the vicinity of the Sorbonne, rehearsed the lecture that he was going to deliver at the Collège de France in front of the sarcastic face of André Breton. André Leroi-Gourhan created, with the Comité Français de Recherche Ethnographique, a regular recruitment of anthropologists, as if until now our discipline was only made of amateurs. And I discovered ethnographic cinema.

Griaule finished *Dieu d'eau (Conversations with Ogotemmêli),* and Dieterlen *La religion Bambara.* When I would arrive each week with the most recent pages of my thesis, I had the impression that I was entering the editing room of a war newspaper: "*They* are going to see this time . . . *They* will finally understand what I'm trying to say." But who were *they?* Without any doubt, they were the same ones that decided, after two years, to hand back my work because I hadn't finished my principal thesis and secondary thesis in time (in fact, I learned very quickly that *they* punished a pupil of Griaule).

It was quite a prestigious stimulant for me. I rapidly ended editing my two theses, and thanks to a grant arranged by Théodore Monod through the l'École Française d'Afrique, I went back to Africa in the company of Roger Rosfelder, a young student of Homburger and Griaule, who was attracted by my first films. In August 1951 we stayed for one month among the Dogon, along with Griaule and Dieterlen. We were to make a film called *Cimetière dans la falaise (Cemetery in the Cliffs)*. All my comrades at the Musée de l'Homme asked me to come back with a report on the "Griaule method." It was, without a doubt, the first time a professor and his assistant would be subjected to scrupulous examination by two of their own students.

Griaule's team was set up in the dispensary; Rosfelder and I and our film equipment occupied the old campsite. We were making the first magnetic tape recordings in Africa with a prototype machine manufactured in Paris by Sgubbi. Each morning Griaule gave us our work for the day. He would ask a musician and traditionalist to come to us, or else he would send us to film their daily routine in the rainy season of the villages of the plain, or in the fallen rocks from the cliff. He was working with his old Dogon informants (alas, Ogotemmêli was dead), and Germaine was working with Dyodo, a Bambara informant. At noon everybody regrouped and exchanged information. We listened. Dieterlen thought aloud, suggesting new and seemingly more audacious and crazy hypotheses from the information than what Griaule was writing down. Griaule commented, rectifying and establishing for himself and for her the new questionnaires for the afternoon.

Day after day the work went along this way, an uncensored "brainstorming" with Germaine Dieterlen acting as a sort of inspired clairvoyant. Griaule was at the same time the commander and the computer.[12] And the Dogon and Bambara informants were passionate participants in an experience whose relevance would be assessed by their reaction. My astonishment gone, I became aware that it was all about an unexpected application of the Socratic method and that of successive approximations. It was in fact the same approach as the one the engineer Caquot had used in elaborating the phenomenon of the resistance of materials—of alternating effort, back and forth, a constant revision and approximation. And so I couldn't help assimilating the whole Griaule-Dieterlen-Dogon ensemble to an "anthropological being," analogous to a "mathematical being" like the development of the Fourier series.

An accident (a drowning, the resultant purification, and the funerary ceremonies) took us for a few days to film at Iréli and at the dam of Gona. We were already thinking of leaving the cliff for the river (I wanted to study a Songhay village during the rainy season). One night when he was in great form, Griaule did an accounting of our present research. He didn't talk about method; he didn't even talk about the approaches that he was weary of. Rather, he spoke of the simple facts that posed some difficult interpretive problems. It was about the first information on the *pontolo,* the "companion star of Sirius," a minuscule satellite likened by the Dogon to the first seed of wild *fonio,* the smallest grain in the world, a wild grass that was the principal food of the distant ancestors. The conjunction of Sirius and his companion would have been useful to the Dogon to determine the exact date of the sixty-year cycle of Sigui ceremonies.

I was already stupefied by this astronomical knowledge of the Dogon, habituated as I was to the river people, whose sky knowledge seemed barely capable of situating the constellation of *albora,* "the man," Orion. Then Griaule, with an enigmatic little smile, said: "And what is strange about this business is that Sirius's companion is invisible to the naked eye." I couldn't help but reply, "If the star's observation is impossible, then the eclipse of the companion and Sirius couldn't determine the Sigui celebration." Griaule didn't respond right away. He looked at me with a dismissive air, and then he simply told me: "I know it is difficult to acknowledge, but if you cannot accept it, you'll never be an ethnographer."

And on this wonderful August night in Sangha, I knew that this man, who was old enough to be my father, wasn't joking. He was answering my worries by another worry, and he was right. This was ethnography, to leave aside one's own system of thought to try to understand the thought system of another. But how could I explain that to my comrades back at the Musée de l'Homme?

That "point of view of Sirius" is no clearer today, even after the most recent celebration of Sigui from 1966 to 1973. During days spent with Amadigné over the last ten years, we scoured the cliffs in search of "observatories." Germaine discovered certain places on the plateau where sites were specially laid out, a difference in the elevation of the stones on the ground representing the solar system. We discovered at the bottom of natural caves these "observation posts" with cradles of stones polished by many repeated visits, all oriented toward the east. From them, sheltered by a great overhang of stone, one can observe the rising of Sirius under the best viewing conditions. And I wondered whether with the benefit of the atmospheric refraction, it might actually be possible to see the *pontolo,* the infinitely small companion of Sirius. But I also knew that even if this optical problem was resolved, the one of adding it all up would still be there, since the revolution of Sirius's companion is a fifty-year cycle, and the Sigui takes place every sixty years.

This uncertainty continues to stimulate my curiosity. And so twenty years after my colleagues at the Musée de l'Homme first posed their question, the only response I can give is that Griaule had started to follow the only ethnographic path possible. And in the difficult study of a strange system of thought, no explanation must be rejected, as irrational as it may be, as sterile as it may seem. And it is surprising to note that even today, particularly gifted young ethnographers do not grasp the point of this principle: "nothing more to say about Dogon society than what the Dogon themselves say." As for those of us who are in fact at the beginning of our approach, getting rid of all our a priori theorizations, the materials that we start to collect now will be able to be exploited (that is, compared or generalized) only in a few years time. And then it will be with the indispensable help of those who are the first concerned, the Dogon themselves.

▶ ───────────────────────────────────────────

### Lake Bosumtwi and the Anvil of Yougo

After my thesis I asked Griaule to accompany me among the Songhay people, to try to determine if they were or weren't part of the "Mande system." We based our idea on one of the first works of Dominique Zahan on the groups of linked populations, the Mandéblon of Kabara, whose collective straw house reroofing every seven years indicates the regrouping place of "the Mandé."

For me, in fact, the frontier between the two systems that I knew was situated in the Akka region, at Lake Débo. On the front side of the mountain, you find patronymically named clans, initiation societies based on age grade, societies of masks, and symbolic representations, but, on the other hand, absence of institutionalized possession dances. On the back side of the mountain, you find an absence of clans and family names, absence of age grades, or of masked societies, few symbolic representations, but, on the other hand, very elaborate systems of possession dances. So here one could be said to come from the west, or one could be said to come from the east. Unfortunately the brutal death of Griaule forbade the realization of this project (and the observations of Viviana Pâques among the northern Songhay have not convinced me that they in fact are Mandé).[13]

In the mid 1950s the Griaule team was spread out. Of course, we knew that Griaule had amassed considerable documents and that with Germaine Dieterlen he had begun the editing of an important book, *Le renard pâle (The Pale Fox)*. And after his tragic end we found ourselves asking if Germaine would be able to complete this interrupted work. Over there in the Bandiagara cliffs, far from the trumpeting of the republican guards at the Saint Clotilde Church, the Dogon of Sangha made a great funerary ceremony for "the Professor." Following the established ritual for dead warriors from abroad, they had invaded the camp, taken Griaule's bush clothing, and dressed a straw mannequin that they installed on the terrace. Then they assaulted the terrace of the dead, mimicking combat with a local musket and bows and spears.

Then, through the crowd and the accompanying cries of women mourners, they took "the cadaver" toward the waterfalls of the Gona river, where Griaule had once had a dam constructed, making possible irrigation to cultivate onions throughout all of Sangha. There, Griaule's effigy was buried in a small funerary cavern just above the gates of the dam opening. And even if the cadaver was a simulacrum, the ceremony was totally authentic, and the sorrow of the mourners was deep. Never, to my knowledge, had an ethnographer anywhere in the world received such a spontaneous homage from those he had studied.

I found Germaine Dieterlen again in 1959 in Abidjan, where she had accompanied one of Griaule's informants, old Ambara. They came with me to Ghana to attend a meeting of West Africanists at the University of Legon. By chance, the Ga fisherman of Accra were celebrating the funeral of a whale that had washed up on a beach at Jamestown. Germaine immediately proposed a strong theory that the Ga were part of the Mandé system. A few days later, visiting the priest in charge of the Ga altars of Accra, she discovered, in the middle of the city, a field of ritual millet in a region where millet had never been cultivated. (The meridian limit for the cultivation of millet is 500 or 600 kilometers to the north.) Then, in Kumasi, seeing a piece of ironwork called the "sword of Osei Tutu" under a ritual fig tree, she said simply, "This is the anvil." And when she asked Prempeh, the Ashanti Hene, if he knew of the existence of the house of Mandéblon at Kangaba in Mali, the king of the Ashanti responded that every seven years he sent a delegation to assist in the ritual reroofing of the Mandé house. And then, back among the Dogon, Germaine Dieterlen and Ambara discovered in a ritual text that the primordial anvil sent by God with the grains of cultivated plants had effectively fallen "in the pond of Kumasi."

If I had been a bit skeptical up until then, I suddenly became very enthusiastic (I had just come out of an austere and deceiving experience of two years of statistical studies of West African migrations, and I needed to get back onto the path of descriptive ethnography). I pointed out to Germaine that near Kumasi there was an unexplained "crater," Lake

Bosumtwi, one of the sacred places of Ashanti country. We went there one day. Following the little path that went down to the bottom of the crater, we saw, moving on the pale water, strange rafts, pegged with wood, as iron was completely forbidden in lake waters. "The anvil!" Germaine said.

Then everything fell into place. Théodore Monod told us that the lake was not a volcanic relic but the point of impact of a meteorite. Someone had just discovered in the surrounding area these glassy and varnished-looking stones whose fall was signaled by meteorites. A team of geologists at the University of Ghana confirmed the hypothesis by the very regular form of the rim of the crater and the great depth of the lake. On the west side of the rim, we learned of the existence of a raised stone, an altar for blacksmiths. This turned out to be where Dogon blacksmiths had to make at least one pilgrimage during their lifetimes, to the very place where the primordial ancestors had gathered the first iron that fell from the sky.

When the research by the geologists estimated that the fall of this meteorite had preceded the appearance of man on the earth by millions of years, I found myself facing the same obvious contradictions that were raised by the case of the companion of Sirius. How could an oral tradition take account of a cataclysm that occurred before the appearance of human beings?

It wasn't until sometime later, in 1965, when preparations for the Sigui began in the Bandiagara cliffs, that we discovered one of the keys to this mystery. The celestial anvil that had fallen into Lake Bosumtwi had re-bounded all the way into Dogon country, at Yougo Dogorou. An enor-mous "dungeon" block of parallelepiped sandstone dominates the village of Yougo like a huge block. In its second fall, this is what crushed the first of God's creatures, the little Andouboulou dwarfs, the predecessors of the first man. And this is why it is from this anvil of Yougo that every sixty years the Sigui starts its tortuous itinerary, which will take it along the cliffs for seven years.

I've snooped around this terrifying rock many times, going around it closely and scrutinizing its every fissure. But in these fractures we could see only reserves of millet and pieces of wooden rungs that each year serve the young people who ritually climb it. During this time Germaine discovered something a few hundred meters below. At the bottom of the fallen rocks there was a perfectly circular artificial pond: Lake Bosumtwi.

But today neither the lake nor the anvil has yet fully revealed its se-crets. Late one afternoon, in February 1966, as Germaine, Gilbert Rouget, and I were going to leave the Yougo range after the first year of Sigui, I re-turned with Amadigné to the anvil of Yougo. The elders of the village, who now considered us as "initiates of Sigui," were accompanying us just for fun. The oldest of them went with us to the great fissure of the eastern face and told us, "This is where the first Andouboulou dwarf still lives, at the bottom of the grotto." And he showed us a crevice ten meters above, an opening with apparently quite easy access. I asked him if we could go in there, and he answered, with a smile, that we could try. So I got close to the cut and put my hand in the interior. Terrified, I backed off. The cavern's interior rock face was completely covered by a veritable rug of black biting bugs. And the Dogon elder, happy at the success of his joke, added, "You mustn't scare them, or else they will fly toward the plain and eat all our crops."

▶

### The *Yasigine*, the Sister of *Sigui*

"The Sigui has gone toward the west, on the wings of the wind." We heard this song for the first time at Yougo with Germaine Dieterlen and Gilbert Rouget, at our first Sigui. We had miraculously obtained authorization to film, and miraculously we found ourselves again on this platform emerging in the plain of Gondo right before the cliff. Miraculously still, we were alone: despite the publicity from the Tourist Office, and the village of tents erected around the Sangha campsite, no one showed up. Germaine and Gilbert were again refashioning the cord bridges where the ravine of Bongo goes straight down the steep serpentine road, twisting turn by turn toward the foot of the Gogoli cascade. I had come from Niamey with my old 403 Peugeot full of film equipment and generators. I was a little late, and when Kimba and I arrived at nightfall at the foot of the Yougo rock, it was already too late to climb it. But the noise of the drums reverberating through the great stone canopies told us that the ceremony was about to start.

Daybreak brought an extraordinary discovery. Nearly deserted the previous year, the village was now packed with young people. They had come from the plain or from far away to the south, from the villages of Ghana or Ivory Coast that had once been abandoned at the time of slavery. They had come to participate in the first Sigui of the 1960s and 1970s. And when Gilbert told me that Germaine, the night before, couldn't help crying as she saw the serpentine procession of the Sigui appearing on the *täi*, the public plaza, it seemed to me that this was the only natural reaction. After all, no outsider had attended the last Sigui, of 1907 to 1914. But some twenty years later, Marcel Griaule and Michel Leiris had devoted months to the study of this extraordinary ceremony, its unfolding, its signification, its customs, its rituals, and its "secret" language, the *sigi so*. Never in the history of the religious sciences had a ceremony been so minutely described without having been directly observed. And here we were, the first spectators of this fabulous opera whose libretto we knew by heart before the curtain even went up. Gilbert and I, although more indirectly involved in this history than Germaine, were also terribly moved. Because, in the end, in the modern Africa of 1966, in a popular democratic republic, there was really no reason why the men of Yougo should listen to the elders call, "The time has come."

I will always remember one of my first experiences of synchronous filming without interruption over several minutes' duration. It was the shot sequence where I discovered the *täi* plaza invaded little by little by the serpentine line of men strictly ordered by age grade. Bare-chested, the men were all dressed in long trousers of bands of indigo cotton. On their necks, ears, and arms they wore the jewelry of their wives or sisters. Their heads were dressed with a white embroidered bonnet, worn much more with the point sticking out than in the "police sketch" that Griaule drew in 1935, worn, as Germaine put it, "like a fish head." In their right hands they brandished a horsetail fly whisk, and in their left hands the *donno*, the single-legged ritual seat. To the rhythm of the drums beaten by the elders, they sang, "The Sigui has flown on the wings of the wind."

All evening, and all night, they danced and drank communal millet beer. And on the perches of the high and narrow terraces, none of us slept. In the morning it was raining. Then the first visitors arrived, friends or tourists who described to us the agony of driving their Jeeps and Land Rovers on the rocky descent to Bongo.

On the third day, we left the Sigui to undertake its first itinerary toward the village of Yougo Na (that we were told was completely packed with tourists). I was filming the statues of the first little men, the Andouboulou, in the small cave of *imisono*, exactly where Griaule had photographed them thirty years earlier. Two uniformed Malian policemen arrived; all the authorizations to film or photograph had been canceled. At this time I could have cried of rage. Gilbert and I went down to Yougo Na to try to get the high authorities to revoke their decision. But there was nothing we could do; the mysterious order had come from Bamako. We had to hand over the films that had been shot.

We then got into this tiny argument: "Our films can't tolerate heat; we've installed two butane refrigerators on Yougo mountain, and if we send the films to Bamako without the refrigerator, they might be destroyed forever." So the policemen went back up with us to see if it was true that we had the refrigerators. And at daybreak, accompanied by a police captain, Germaine Dieterlen and I left in a Land Rover (also equipped with a refrigerator) for Bamako, close to a thousand kilometers away. The next day Germaine obtained a special authorization, and we turned back immediately (without the police captain). The morning of the following day, when we arrived "exhausted but at peace" at the village of Yougo, we were welcomed by shouts of "hooray." The victorious Germaine was really the first Yasigine, the sister of Sigui, the first woman to participate in the first Sigui of the cycle that was starting, and we were able to continue to film.

And since then we haven't stopped following the Sigui. Over the course of seven years, starting from Yougo, we pursued this winding path toward Tyogou, Bongo and Sangha, Amani, Ideyeli, Iamey, and finally toward the canopy of Songo, following the Sigui, "on the wings of the wind."

▶──────────────────────────────────────────

### "The Echo Creator": Cinema in the Cave

At the beginning I thought that it would be enough to shoot one or two films by myself rather than to bring in some other filmmakers. Friends in Paris started to make fun of my escapes to the Sigui, from each February to March, right in the middle of the university academic year. But during all these years I knew instinctively that my real place was much more in this crazy route of the cliff paths than in the university amphitheaters at Nanterre. Marcel Griaule would certainly have said it: "If you really want to observe the Sigui, you have to be there all seven years." And today I think that I was right to prefer the field to the laboratory, experience to theory, ethnography to ethnology, and that what I've taught and will teach to the students who are interested in these problems has been and will be better for it.

Now this cycle is finished, and in sixty years the cry of the fox will again echo at the foot of the anvil. We will not be here to observe it, but there now exists an irreplaceable archive: the seven film documents of the seven years of the Sigui, from 1966 to 1973.

It is still too early to come to any conclusions, but from these films, here are the approaches that we envision:

■──────────────────────────────────────────

### *A Comparative Study of the Different Rituals as Observed over Seven Years*

We thought, just as Marcel Griaule had thirty years earlier, that the ceremony consisted of repetitions, with a certain number of variations (some of which he had discovered in his research). Of these the essential elements were uniforms and ritual objects, initiation of the *olubaru* dignitaries, construction of a new "mother of the masks," and drinking of ceremonial millet beer mixed with sesame oil.

Effectively, from year to year, it is clearly the same scheme, but the infallible memory of the film has brought out significant differences that correspond to information gathered by Germaine Dieterlen on the "itinerary of the ponds" where, after his death, the mythical ancestor was searching for his essence.

The Sigui is, above all, a complete and complex commemoration of the death of the first ancestor after sixty years of life. This ancestor, Yougo Sirou, died (in Yougo, or more exactly, in its Malian double, after the migration of the Dogon of Mandé toward the cliff), transformed into a serpent (the great mask), and searched for its "sex soul" for seven years from pond to pond. Following the path of the serpent, he taught men the high words of the *sigi so* and the male communion of the millet beer. And after having stumbled against the canopy of the Songo, where he drew the first paintings, he came back to die precisely at his own point of departure, at the foot of the stone anvil of Yougo Dogorou.

But without any doubt, this seven-year quest wasn't uniform. By reviewing the fundamental differences of the films of the seven yearly episodes, we think that in fact each year of Sigui has a particular sequence of a grand myth. Relived over seven years by different actors each year, it takes the form of a strange relay of linkages from what happened before to the preparation for what is to follow.

Watching the films one after another with Amadigné Dolo, on the editing table at the Comité du Film Ethnographique at the Musée de l'Homme, we were able to discern the main lines of the sequence. And if I'm reticent to put forward and publish even this first table of double correspondences that we have established, it is because it is still too incomplete, even though it is possible to indicate some differences that already appear pertinent to us.

1st year: Yougo. No tall masks apparent, no leather chest band of cowries.

2d year: Tyogou. Tall mask just carved, not yet painted or stood up; considerable importance of the dance on the *taï* plaza; cowrie chest bands on.

3d year: Bongo. Tall mask carved, painted, and stood up in front of the Sigui cave where the *olubaru* dignitaries have finished their initiation. Very few dances, but moving in file, procession around the altar on the great field that traces Dogon descent; cowrie chest bands.

4th year: Amani. The old tall mask is repainted and stood up; a sacrificed hen at the top. Cowrie chest band mixed with great scarves and new clothes. Very important declamations in *sigi so,* the language of Sigui.

5th year: Idyeli. No tall mask is visible. All the participants, before getting dressed and decorated, spend one night and a day in retreat on a dune, where they bury themselves in the earth. They come back to the village in full daylight, accompanied by the bullroarers twirled by the *olubaru,* in order to bathe in the spring where water always runs. But they dress nearly exclusively with multicolored cloths (instead of with cowrie chest bands).

6th year: Iamey. No tall mask is visible. The men dress in women's skirts, completely covering the trousers of the Sigui. Before going back to the village, they place themselves in a line facing east to listen to the *sigi so.* Then they turn to the west and then again to the east. At the village they drink the beer without sitting on their *donno* seats.

7th year: Songo. All of the villages and surrounding region here have become Islamized. Three men come from Iamey simply to sacrifice a male goat and a goat in front of the cave paintings. They go back by the more direct path to Yougo Dogorou, where they declare to the elders that the Sigui is over. After drinking beer, everyone goes back to their place.

One could thus interpret the different episodes as follows:

1. DEATH of the ancestor near the anvil.
2. FUNERAL for the ancestor, and beginning of the metamorphosis into a serpent; the tall mask is carved and laid down.
3. DAMA, the completion of mourning of the ancestor, end of the metamorphosis into a serpent; the tall mask is painted and stood up.
4. THE WORD, teaching of the *sigi so,* and new death of the serpent; procreation.
5. PLACENTA, the birth of a new form of ancestor, either man or *andouboulou* dwarf.
6. MOTHERING of the ancestor, now a newborn.
7. CIRCUMCISION of the ancestor, who has become a young child and goes back to the hole of the anvil, where he is "still alive" as the immortal reincarnation of Yougo Serou.

Of course these are just working hypotheses (indeed, interpretations with which Germaine Dieterlen doesn't entirely agree). But on the one hand, they permit us to elaborate a new theory of the sixty-year Sigui celebration and its unfolding in time, space, and action. And on the other hand, they make me regret that I couldn't have simultaneously filmed each year's Sigui in each village, to see if the successive unfolding is a development in a series of ritual sequences. Finally, these hypotheses will help us in the second part of the cinematic exploitation of the following documents.

This is about a much more ambitious project, an attempt to edit the totality of all seven years of the Sigui into one film no more than two hours long. Its projection would permit a synthesis in a single viewing, a résumé of the whole ceremony by the intermediary of the technique of cinema. In this way, convergences and divergences would appear, allowing one to verify or disprove this hypothesis about a "series of ritual sequences," which is to say a series of mythic sequences, which is to say the myth of Sigui itself.

Of course this work will only be able to be done with the collaboration of the Dogon by using the technique of feedback, of what I call the "echo creator": the response to a film by those who have been filmed. And here the experience becomes fascinating because in fact no Dogon, other than the members of Germaine Dieterlen's research team, have ever followed the Sigui during these seven years. This is because the Sigui is a series of particular chained links, and the custom is for one to witness a maximum of three Sigui, that of one's immediate village, and the ones of the preceding and following villages. So when we project the ensemble of our films as a first sketch at synthesis, we will be making it possible for the Dogon to see an essential ritual that no Dogon has ever completely seen. We don't know what their reaction will be, although certain informants from the cliffs have let us know that our huge appetite for knowledge should already have brought about our deaths prior to completing this journey. But we are certain that we will open this dialogue to new questions and new answers. Here the ethnographic quest ceases to be a one-way monologue, but following the inspiration of the Yasigine, Germaine Dieterlen, the sister of Sigui, it will become a decisive experience of "shared anthropology."

## The Fox of the Table and the *Dama* for Ambara

We have come for our seventh Sigui, to take it in under the spur of the great canopy of Songo. Already on the ground of the camp at Sangha there has appeared a beautiful drawing in colored chalk, a white, black, and red egg. Separated by a wall like a Dogon granary, oriented from west to east, the points draw a zigzag, like the return of Sigui from Songo toward Yougo. Around Germaine Dieterlen, Goummoyana, the totemic priest of upper Ogol, Amadigné, chief of masks of lower Ogol, and Dyamgouno, the indefatigable walker, are sitting on the ground. With their fingers they are following the contour of the drawings, and they begin the difficult interpretations. This is the trajectory of seven years of the Sigui by groups of three: Yougo, Yendouman, Sangha, then Amani, Idyeli, Iamey, and at last, all alone the seventh year, Songo. Down there the little red character holds the skin of an animal he has sacrificed to Songo and will take back to the point of departure, in Yougo, to warn the elders that the cycle is complete and that this Sigui is finished.

One of the principal informants is not there; Ambara died a few months ago. Earlier his son took us to his house to show us the new mask that he has finished for the *dama,* the lifting of the mourning for his father. And all night the whirring of the bullroarers announce themselves to say, "I eat, I eat," underlining the declamations in *sigi so.* (In the declamation: "last night I recognized Dyamgouno's voice . . .")

Three days ago Lam, Tallou, and I arrived from Niger. We thought that Germaine Dieterlen was no longer waiting for us, but that was to forget the table of divination. At nightfall Amadigné was going toward the great rectangles of earth at the northern exit of the lower Ogol. Imprinted on the sand there is this astonishing journal of the night, by which we questioned the pale fox. The pale fox, the *yurugu,* is the master of necessary disorder, the primal creation, not so loved by God but maybe, in fact, his favorite. He is the one to whom the masked dancers throw a fast *jeté-battu,* a kick of purification, the one that screams every night with the bullroarers because the first bullroarer was his own circumcision scream, as his father held his tail and turned him about.

On these great tables of earth, carefully smoothed out by "the fox's hand" in pieces of acacia wood, "houses" are strictly distributed between the different words like the traditional columns of a newspaper. So this little pile of earth over here is our car; these three little sticks standing up are Lam, Tallou, and I; this hole farther away is Sangha. The questions asked are obvious: "Jean, Lam, and Tallou—are they gone? Are they ill? Have they had an accident? Are they going to die?" A few grains of peanut will attract this little pale fox in the night, this *yurugu* whose traces are the primordial writing. Every night he imprints his answers and his commentary in the earth. He knows everything, he says everything, he has no shame, he is uncensored. If he knocks the stick down, he announces a sickness or the death of the person represented. If he makes the marks of coming and going, it means that the proposed enterprise will begin well but end badly. And if he goes in the right way around the little pile representing our car, it means there will be some delays, but no major accident.

At sunrise, the diviners and those who asked about the future come to read the morning's first edition of the "table of the night." Amadigné bends over the little "houses" where the questions are to be found, and the diviners interpret the set of the four little holes, 1, 2, 1 (that are, the Dogon say, at the origin of geomantic figures). "There's nothing bad; we will arrive the very same day." It is good news. Apourali prepares the most important onion soup; we will arrive just before it gets cold in our plates.

Little *yurugu,* pale fox so minuscule yet so full of science, tireless gnawer of the daily life of cliff villages, nighttime journalist whose information precedes the event, who are you? I have never seen you. I have often followed your traces at the exterior of the tables, but they vanished over the next rocks. I had the very bad intention to watch you one night when the moon was full, but the Dogon quickly warned me that you wouldn't come. So I decided to set up a camera with a flash and trigger attached to a long wire, but the Dogon dissuaded me, saying: "It's the same thing as if you were there; the *yurugu* will know it and won't come, that's all there is to it."

So I gave up on seeing the *yurugu,* but I haven't given up knowing him. To thank me, no doubt, for my discretion, he answers all my questions. Last year, the chief of Bongo, with a little provocative smile, asked him if we would still be alive in one year, and he said "yes." And I went back this year to see the chief of Bongo to confirm *yurugu*'s prediction. Thus I've become one of the disciples of this key character in the system of Dogon thought, this primal protester who began his tumultuous existence by eating his own placenta and since then has made the leaves of the *Acacia faidherbia* fall in the humid season and return for the dry season. As a disciple, I accept the weirdest messages without rationally scrutinizing them as I did once before.

And everything is clarified when the *dama* begins. Here, in the same order Marcel Griaule described some forty years ago, is the long file of new masks. And as I filmed them, I recognized in the viewfinder of my camera the same path you can see in the plates of his book *Masques Dogons.* The drummers have climbed up on the same rocks of the same baobabs, at the northern extremity of the upper Ogol, and play *amma boy,* the "word of God." Here are the *kanaga,* the crosshatched masks that tomorrow, on the *täi* plaza, will hit the rock in the swirl of the creation of the world. Here are the *serige,* "the tiered houses" whose difficult and light dance makes the supple and vertical tall masks ripple like the primordial words at the time of the creation of the world. Here are the *bambara* masks with multiple eyes, military types armed with swords, charged, in fact, with keeping disorder because they represent here the *yurugu,* the pale fox. Here are the "turtledoves" up on their high red-and-white stilts, which advance, successively touching their elbows, according to the Dogon code of atonement. Old Ambara, for whom we celebrate this sumptuous feast, understood the *sigi so* language, and I saw him, one winter afternoon, talk strange dialogue with these doves. The masks scream their cry *"You hou hou"* like the yodel of the Austrian skiers of my youth.

The women move back and take refuge on the terraces, not wanting to recognize their sons, husbands, or brothers behind their masks. Yet three women have stayed in the first row, punctuating the *sigi so* declamations of the elders with their *"You you."* They hold baskets in front of themselves and give the coweries they hold to the dancers with the best masks. They are perfectly at ease among these men, in the middle of this ceremony of men, because they are Yasigine, sisters of Sigui, twins of the fox. One of them, quite old, but with the extraordinary elegance of African grand-mothers, gets up and goes into the crowd. She gets Germaine Dieterlen, who follows her back to sit down next to the other Yasigine because here Germaine herself is also a true Yasigine. Everything is perfectly natural. Germaine is in her place in Dogon society; she entered here forty years ago by chance, by passion, by research, by patience, by following the divinations of the pale fox.

The masks of the fox are busy in full delirium, brandishing their large sabers. And suddenly they are for me these "mad masters," these spirits of European power who twenty-five years ago possessed the young Nigerians of the outskirts of Accra. Tomorrow I will find them dancing on the terrace of the dead one to whom this *dama* is consecrated, dancing on the terrace of Ambara like images in the crazy photos of the *Minotaure* of 1933. And with that I cannot help thinking of the pale master who drove all of us here: Marcel Griaule, whose simulated body lies in a funerary cave above the mouth of the Gona River. That is the same place where these black fibers of the skirts of the *dama* dancers have been dyed. And that too is the same place where, one future day, one will also find the simulated body of the sister of this mad fox, the Yasigine who has not finished posing to me, and posing to all of us, these fabulous enigmas.

(1978)

TRANSLATORS' NOTES

In general, most English phrases that appear enclosed in quotation marks are translations of a French phrase that also appeared in quotation marks in the original. Words originally in italics are often from the Dogon or Songhay languages. For clarity of content, intent, and tone, some sentences have been slightly embellished with the help of Jean-Paul Colleyn and Paul Stoller. For further amplification of the historical details of both Rouch's career and the Griaule school, see Paul Stoller, *The Cinematic Griot: The Ethnography of Jean Rouch* (Chicago: University of Chicago Press, 1992); and James Clifford's essay "Power and Dialogue in Ethnography: Marcel Griaule's Initiation," in *Observers Observed: Essays on Ethnographic Fieldwork*, ed. George Stocking (Madison: University of Wisconsin Press, 1983), 121–56.

1. The "Blaise berçant sa laisse" reference comes from Michel Leiris's book *Biffures*, volume 1 of his four-volume autobiography *La regle du jeu*, published in 1948 (and translated in 1991, by Lydia Davis, as *Scratches*, published by the Johns Hopkins University Press). In the book's first pages, a section called "Songs," Leiris talks about the accidental poetics produced by mishearing words as a child. As an example, he cites a song sung by his brother. It went "Blaise qui partait / En guerre s'en allait," translated (without the rhyme) as, "Blaise was leaving / going off to war." In his creative mishearing, Leiris transposed these words into "Blaise qui partait / En berçant sa laisse," translated as "Blaise was leaving / rocking the beach." What could this "rocking the beach" possibly mean? Leiris expounds on this conundrum for several pages. The other Leiris references in this sentence are to book titles: his 1939 *L'Âge d'homme*, whose title in translation is *Manhood*, and his 1934 *L'Afrique fantôme*, whose title would be *Phantom Africa*.

2. Verdun is where the Germans were halted in 1916 in World War I.

3. Gondar in North Ethiopia was an important site in the African Dakar-Djibouti mission of 1931–1933 by Marcel Griaule and Michel Leiris. It figures in several texts by both. *The Lone White Sail* is the English title of Vladimir Legoshin's 1937 feature film *Beleet parus odinokii;* the French title is *Au loin une voile* or *Au large une voile;* the filmmaker's name is spelled "Legotchine" in French cinema texts.

4. Following an armistice with Germany and suspension of the French constitution, Henri Philippe Pétain became chief of state at Vichy (1940–1944). Pétain's government collaborated with Nazi Germany; after the Allied victory, he was convicted of treason. Jacques Doriot was a particularly prominent collaborator, the leader of the fascist Le Parti Populaire Français during Vichy. Jean François Darlan, another member of Pétain's government, strengthened France's collaborationist ties with Germany. Later, as commander of all French forces, he was in North Africa during the November 1942 Allied landings and brought French North and West Africa over to the Allied side. He was assassinated immediately afterward. Georges Montandon was a racial anthropologist and a member of the administration of the Vichy School of Journalism on rue Notre-Dame des Champs.

5. The French original is "Surtout, ne vous bougnoulisez pas!"

6. The song Pétain made them sing in West Africa, as in France.

7. The reference is to European folklore and the threatening figure of the black servant of St. Nicholas who whips bad boys and girls.

8. The reference to a Dogon-Bozo joking relationship in this section of the paper is both a literary device and an ethnographic reality. The Dogon of the cliffs and Bozo of the river are united by a *mangou* relationship, a formal joking relationship based on an obligation to exchange ritual insults. For some, this relationship is grounded in a myth about how a Dogon mother gave her milk and then her own flesh to nourish an orphan Bozo baby during a famine. For others, the relationship is grounded in the idea that the two groups are united by an oath of eternal solidarity.

9. "La 'deuxième manche' de la guerre," translated as "the 'second half' of the war." Rouch is alluding to the war, sarcastically, as if it were a sports match whose second half would be played after a brief intermission.

10. After the war, Rivet dismissed Griaule from the Musée de l'Homme.

11. Germaine Dieterlen's 1941 book *Les âmes de Dogon* describes the Dogon categories of the soul, e.g., "head soul," "body soul," "sex soul," etc.

12. Rouch's phrase is "ordonnateur et ordinateur," his poesis is partially preserved by "the commander and the computer."

13. Viviana Pâques's book *L'arbre cosmique* investigates the distribution and presence of elements of Dogon cosmology in the neighboring region.

## II  Interviews and
## Conversations with Jean Rouch

# JEAN ROUCH WITH
# LUCIEN TAYLOR

## *A Life on the Edge of Film*
## *and Anthropology*

Anthropologist and filmmaker Lucien Taylor edited and translated his conversations with Jean Rouch, which took place in Paris on December 21–24,
1990.—*Ed.*

LUCIEN TAYLOR: *Why don't we start out with your beginnings.*
JEAN ROUCH: My mother came from Normandy and my father from Spanish!
Catalonia—Ruig is a Catalonian name that means "red." He was an officer
in the navy. Before the war he had trained as a meteorologist, and then he
joined Dr. Charcot's famous expedition to the Antarctic on the boat called
*Pourquoi Pas?* They had no radio connection with the outside world, so
they were totally cut off. There was also a biologist on board, studying
penguins, who would become my mother's brother—after they returned,
my father married his friend's sister. I was born in 1917, during the war.
I consider myself a child of the *Pourquoi Pas?*

I was brought up by parents interested in research, in painting, in taking photographs, and so on. I saw my first film in Brest, where my father
was stationed; he took me to see Flaherty's *Nanook of the North.* The film
had an enormous influence on me. When I was young, I would often dream
that I was in the middle of the snowstorm. A few weeks later my mother
took me to see another film, *Robin Hood,* with Douglas Fairbanks. I remember that I cried when people started dying—my mother tried to explain
that they were actors, and I asked her if the same was true for *Nanook.* So
that was my beginning in cinema—a documentary and a fiction film.

My parents naturally had a large influence on me. Since my father
was a naval officer, we were always moving around. When I was young we
would rarely spend more than two years in the same place, so in a sense I
was forever a new pupil coming from nowhere. I was homeless, in a way,
but at the same time it provided a way to discover the world. I started in

Brest, then I went back to Paris to attend the *lycée,* then I spent two years in Algiers, then I went to Germany, then to Morocco, after which my father was posted as a naval attaché to the Balkans, to Greece, Turkey, and so on. I lived alone here in Paris for my senior year. After my baccalaureate, I joined my father, mother, and sister in Athens and Istanbul. At the time my father was teaching oceanography at the University of Paris. After the war he was appointed director of the Museum of Oceanography in Monaco, where he would be succeeded by Cousteau.

Anyway, I finished my studies in Paris, and I think my father rather hoped I would enter the navy, but in 1937 I was admitted to the École des Ponts et Chaussées, close to St. Germain. It was around this time that I discovered the Cinémathèque—a small room on the third floor somewhere on the Champs-Élysées, and every Friday they screened films. I also discovered the new Musée de l'Homme.

It was a fantastic period because a lot was happening . . . From the start, I was fascinated by the surrealists—I remember when I was about fourteen, I went with a cousin to the Dôme in Montparnasse, and he pointed out this fellow with a blue mustache, wearing an orange jacket and a green shirt, and he said, "Look, that's Salvador Dalí!"—he was an important reference to me. We would often go to the Ursulines to watch films. I remember I went to the first concert Duke Ellington and Louis Armstrong gave in Paris, in 1941 or '42. We discovered jazz, dance, and theater, and cinema. In those days Paris was a kind of paradise.

*What role did religion have on your upbringing? You have described yourself to me as a "Catholic anarchist." Did you connect religion with politics in any way?*
I was brought up a Roman Catholic, but the first time I took communion there were no miracles—God didn't speak to me—well, I had hoped in vain for a revelation . . .

When I was at the *lycée,* we were violently opposed to the Camelots du Roi, who were Royalists, or J.P., Jeunnesse Patriots—they represented an eruption of what would go on to change everything. I was always profoundly alienated from both fascism and Marxism—at the time when André Gide was going to Russia, I was sure that the truth lay elsewhere. To my mind, communists couldn't "afford" the idea of anarchy. I was confident that history would prove them misguided—at the time I dreamed of other places. I knew Rimbaud by heart, and he's taught me a lot—for example, to write a good poem, you have to start from the end, which has become my rule of editing film. I have always edited backwards.

*What was your relationship with the Parisian bourgeoisie?*
Neither my father nor my mother came from a particularly wealthy family.
So I never felt a part of the bourgeoisie. But I learned from my father's
example—when I entered the École des Ponts et Chaussées, I knew that
I would never again have financial problems, that I would always have a
job. That was the advantage of the Grandes Écoles. Most of my mother's
family were artists—so I grew up having to paint and draw. I was very
proud that my first watercolors were shown at a large exhibition in Montparnasse, Le Salon des Indépendants. So I grew up surrounded by artists,
writers, and scientists. My parents and relations were connected to the
avant-garde of the time—this was important to my upbringing. It was natural for me to go to the Cinémathèque, or to visit the Musée de l'Homme,
which utterly enchanted me.

I was never a brilliant pupil, but I was good enough. The École des
Ponts et Chaussées was a wonderful school—I learned that virtually everything had already been invented: prestressed concrete, knowledge of the resistance of materials, and all that. The professors during my time there were
the world leaders of civil engineering. They were consultants to the U.S.

*In your film* Margaret Mead: A Portrait by a Friend, *you ask her about
her "people" throughout the world, and she talks of her "villages" from
Manhattan to Manu'a. You also ask about her "totemic ancestors." Who
are your totemic ancestors, or at any rate your mentors?*
All the surrealists had a big influence on me. I read their books in my teens.
My discovery of Breton's *Manifesto of Surrealism* was very important, as
was *Nadja*. On the other hand, Leiris's autobiography, *L'Âge d'Homme,*
also affected me in many ways—to my mind it was his best work. When I
read it, I just knew he had to be mad. Éluard's *Capitale de la Douleur* also.
You can find quotations from all these "poems" in my films. Magritte,
Dalí, and De Chirico are the painters who most influenced me. De Chirico
took me back to Nietzsche. As I had read Bakunin before Marx, I was
never very interested in Marx—his work seemed obsolete to me. In comparison, Bakunin, who wasn't exactly a theoretician of anarchy but at any
rate urged one not to take power but to destroy it—it was something like
a sentimental intellectual journey. I used to dream of that. Oscar Wilde's
*Picture of Dorian Gray* was also seminal in this regard.

*You haven't mentioned any anthropologists!*
I was too young to hear Marcel Mauss speak; I didn't encounter him until
later. But I discovered Marcel Griaule and Germaine Dieterlen here at the
Musée de l'Homme, during the war. I knew already that they were on to

something significant from the review *Minotaure*. When I first saw the fantastic images of Dogon masks and terraces, that was a tremendous shock. I discovered the Dogon in 1932, at the same time as I discovered De Chirico. For me, De Chirico's paintings were connected with the Dogon landscape.

*In what way?*
It was a dream country. The cliffs of Bandiagara were like the cliffs in Salvador Dalí's paintings, and in Magritte's paintings. All were dreamland. For me the treasure was not in the South Seas; it was in places like the Bandiagara cliffs. Just the name, the "falaises de Bandiagara," was fantastic. It was the country of frogs, of mystery, of people wearing fantastic masks. I later got to know that the Dogon are not afraid of death, and I too learned not to fear it. Unfortunately in our religions, in the so-called *religions reveillées* (Islam, Judaism, Protestantism, Catholicism), there is a moralistic stress on law observance and punishment after death. In the African religions I know, if you do something important in your lifetime, that's enough—you can be immortal.

 No, that is France. :-)

Anyway, at the same time as I dreamed of this, I was enchanted by the idea of building bridges and big dams and so on. After my second year at the École des Ponts et Chaussées, the war started. I was on the Riviera at the time—actually, in Saint Tropez at a lovely hotel of Le Corbusier's. We knew that all that was on the verge of vanishing.

*Did you at the time, or do you now, see any tension between what De Chirico meant for you, of what you say the Dogon meant for you, and your building bridges? Building bridges is communicative infrastructure, modernity, colonialism . . .*
Not at all—for example, De Chirico's lighthouse imagery—this was an architecture of dream. Think of Peter Ibbetson of Du Maurier. I was there at the Surrealist Exhibition with some of my friends—I had the "keys." At this time, at the end of the thirties, I felt that I had been born too late—in Paris the twenties were a fantastic period. I never saw the Ballet Russe Diaghilev, but we were gourmands for everything. We knew that some people possessed the keys to "go back." We were under the influence of the new—in discovering De Chirico I discovered Bakunin, in discovering Bakunin I came back to Nietzsche. Discovering Breton, we discovered Gérard de Nerval. There was this kind of mixing; we discovered people like Novalis and the German romantics.

When I was studying philosophy, I had to read Freud's work on psychoanalysis. I saw that he was not a dreamer himself but was rather exploiting dreams—like Karl Marx. Both Marxism and Freudianism will *well ...*

soon ~~disappear, but that's another point.~~ I've never considered craziness to be pathological, and I always considered it normal to dream. I've always been a very good dreamer; I've even written poems from my dreams . . . In a word, I was a very, very happy young boy—thank God! Traveling with my father to Istanbul, him telling me of the fantastic life he'd lived, all over the world, all his journey—I admired him immensely. He was influential when after the war I decided not to continue as an engineer but to turn to anthropology and film.

*Why did you switch from engineering to anthropology?*
After two years at the École des Ponts et Chaussées, the war began, and I was directed to blow up bridges to stop the German army. I crossed all of France on bicycle, from the Marne River to the Massif Central—a strange way for me to begin my career, blowing up bridges. We went back under the German occupation to Paris to finish our three years at the École. For Easter holidays I would go to Brittany with two friends from the École, Pierre Ponty and Jean Sauvy. We would live on fish, butter, and potatoes and so on. Anyway, one day we were arrested by the local commandant de terre. He thought we were searching for a boat to take us to England. We protested that since we had nothing more than swimming trunks, we hadn't intended to swim to the United Kingdom. Anyway, we weren't able to escape from the occupied areas without the authorization of the commandant, and that was why we decided to leave France officially as engineers in West Africa—as civil servants.

*What was it like to be under German occupation?*
It was horrible. But we knew it was our duty to take them out. At the beginning of the war, we were extreme pacifists. We discovered that what we had learned at school—the invincibility of the French army—was false. The old officers were afraid and were escaping. There was no real battle. In just a month the whole of France was occupied. We were ashamed to have lost the war. The director of our school wrote to each of us saying that the war would be long, and that we should continue at school, or else we would never get our engineering degree, and he was right.

Anyway, we went to Africa and found the colonists there more Vichyssois than the Parisians—which was also the case for North Africa, incidentally. I came to realize that the colonial officers were stupid people. I only had one work of anthropology with me, Michel Leiris's *L'Afrique fantôme,* and I would often dream about his descriptions. Niger was an awful country—the climate was dreadful, quinine tablets had run out, mosquito bites could be very dangerous. I had broken my sunglasses and my colonial helmet, and I thought I might die. Then I was told that sunglasses were unnecessary and were only worn to help those who are manufacturing them.

Niger was a very, very tough country. There was absolutely nothing there—no gas, no cars, no cloth. To have a shirt, you had to make it out of small pieces of cotton. The people there were living in a kind of dream. One day the governor of Niger, a general, said to me: "I know you were a decorated army officer, so you must be prepared to invade British Nigeria." I was responsible for building roads to the north of Niamey up to Lab-bezenga (the border before Gao) and west to Fada N'Gourma in Upper Volta. I was in charge of twenty thousand laborers—working without tools or machinery, they had to carry the earth for the roads in baskets. We made bridges like Romans, just cutting the stones. There was no concrete, no tarmac—no maps, nothing at all. I realized then that the most important problems were not technical but human. The only people around me were Africans. I was a good swimmer, and a doctor friend had told me it was safe to swim in the river Niger. I met Damouré Zika there, with whom I would go on to make so many of my films. He wasn't as fast as I, but he could stay underwater for far longer. He had just got out of school, and I gave him a job as an assistant to the workers.

So while building roads I started to study possession among the Songhay. My closeness to the workers went down very badly with the colonial administration, who thought that my job was just to be an engineer. The governor expelled me from Niger as a Gaullist, because I wasn't a member of the Légion des Combattants—I would listen to the radio from London and so on, actually Brazzaville at this time. Fortunately, I left when the Allies landed in North Africa and in Senegal. I crossed over to Dakar and met my two friends Ponty and Sauvy at Bamako, and we went to the governor's place at Koulouba. We decided that if we survived, we would return and canoe down the river from the source to the sea. In Dakar I was "saved" by Théodore Monod, who was the director of the Institut Français d'Afrique Noire (IFAN). I then went back into the army and spent two years being trained with mines and explosives on the Sénégal River to cross the Rhine. I met Paul Rivet at this time—the founder of the Musée de l'Homme—at a lunch party of Monod's; he was a deputy of the government, a "refugee" in Colombia, on his return to Algiers. I remember reading Griaule's *Masques Dogons* in Monod's library. Senegal was a lovely country. But I had to leave—it was our duty to free France. I went to Morocco and joined the First Armor Division of the new French army. We landed on the Riviera coast close to Marseilles.

During the winter of 1944 I got permission to return to Paris—I visited

Griaule, who agreed to be my doctoral director. I visited Jean Cocteau, who was helping Robert Bresson finish *Les dames du bois de Boulogne;* I went to see Éluard—all these surrealists were veterans of the first war. I went back to Alsace on the bank of the Rhine. I was lucky because in March we built an armored bridge over the Rhine, exactly as we had done over the Sénégal, and then we moved into the German Black Forest, and the Tyrol Mountains, when the war ended. On the day of victory I returned to Paris in my jeep, just to kiss my father and mother and let them know I was alive.

Anyway, I was then sent to Berlin for two months. The town was completely gutted. Monod said the Germans were good musicians and we should ask them to make music and not war. I wanted to make a film about the recently destroyed Berlin—all these ladies, as beautiful as Marlene Dietrich, were prostituting themselves for packets of cigarettes. Quite fantastic! I wrote a page-long script, really just a letter, which Cocteau published in the *Couleur du Temps* section of *Fontaine* in 1945— it was called "Berlin Août 1945." Anyway, five years ago or so, this TV production company wanted to make a film for the inauguration of Channel 7—they had read my script in *Fontaine*. We met at the Café Bulier, and they asked me to return to Berlin to shoot the film. I called it *Couleur du temps*. It's quite a nice film. I showed it later at the Berlin Film Festival and gave them a print.

Anyway, when we returned to Paris after the war, we were very angry with France. I looked for a job, in vain. My two friends and I felt that we owed our country nothing—so we would only do what we wanted to. We felt it was important to be free. We created Jean Pierrejean—our first names—writing three features each week, earning enough to get by. We had a contact at AFP (Agence France Press); they asked us for photographs, and we said we had to fulfill our pact to go down the Niger River. So we gave AFP copyright; they paid for our articles and covered the cost of the trip. Monod gave us transportation, and we spent nine months paddling down the Niger River. We were free to film—we'd bought an old U.S. Army Bell and Howell camera for 1,000 francs in the flea market, and with our income from journalism we bought some black-and-white stock. Four years later, Niger was still being run by the same governor. I decided not to see him. We crossed West Africa to Bamako, and then to Guinea to start at the source of the Niger. We had made ourselves a raft—we didn't even have a canoe—at Kouroussa . . . and as we paddled down, we would shoot film and write articles, developing the photographs ourselves, with a small enlarger from a dry battery—and send them all off periodically, earning enough to buy a canoe.

We crossed all of West Africa, stopping at Bandiagara to visit Griaule, who was with Ogotemmêli in 1946, and at Timbuktu and Gao so that Ponty could return to France, as he had a dental problem. I made my first film in the north of Niger; I would always be shooting film from the canoe, but I had no idea what I was doing. I had lost my tripod early on in some rapids and didn't know how to shoot so as to be able to edit the footage later. We stopped one day just south of the Mali/Niger border, in Ayorou, which I knew pretty well, as I had been there as an engineer. I asked them to build a canoe and to hunt hippopotamuses from it—we returned and filmed them. We crossed into Nigeria, going through the rapids where Mungo Park was killed, and by the time we reached the sea, we were thoroughly exasperated with each other. From there, we returned to Paris in a military plane.

When I got back, I saw that most of the footage was uneditable, so I couldn't make a film about the river journey. Instead I edited my first film about the hippopotamus hunting. I screened it in the Musée de l'Homme to Lévi-Strauss and Griaule, and they felt that film was conceivably a new avenue open to anthropology. Leiris was there—he was enthusiastic and suggested that I show the film at a cellar nightclub in Saint Germain that would often feature bands from New Orleans. I remember taking our own projector for the screening, and that it went down well with these young people who were dancing boogie-woogie. The pianist said that his father, a director of Actualités Françaises, might be interested in funding our work. We signed a contract, giving him control over the editing, the sound, the narration, and even the title itself. The title was absolutely abominable— *Au pays des mages noirs*. The narration was horrible; it was as if it were made by a man following the Tours du France. A shame, but this small film was screened next to Rossellini's *Stromboli*.

*All in all, how do you conceive your relationship to France?*
In 1960 the sociologist Edgar Morin said to me, "Jean, you have made all your films abroad; do you know anything about contemporary France?" He said that I should turn my gaze onto the Parisians and do anthropological research about my own tribe. In fact I really didn't know much about France at this time, as I had spent almost all of my time since the war either in Africa or hard at work in the museum. I saw that Michel Brault and the National Film Board of Canada were working on a similar subject and asked them to come over. Together, we built the first adapted Eclair camera. We made a film at the same time as we made the camera. In *Chronicle of a Summer* I was discovering my own society. I knew that the beginning of what would unravel eight years later was already brewing among the young. So I discovered that there was hope left in France—all these young

people were very intelligent, half crazy, wanting to be happy. Later, in 1968, I felt that perhaps for the first time I was reconciled with my country. Unfortunately André Breton died just a couple of years before May '68. To me '68 was less a political revolution than a poetic revolution, with slogans all over the walls. Anyway, while making *Chronicle of a Summer,* and afterward, in 1968, I discovered I was very close to all these people. We were putting flowers in the beards of Karl Marx and Sigmund Freud.

*How do you situate yourself in relation to the anthropological academy?*
I contest anthropology in my emphasis on the need to share, to produce in a medium that allows dialogue and dissent across societal lines. In *Petit à Petit* I addressed these concerns most directly. I asked Damouré and my African friends to come here to interpret Parisians. When you make films with Africans, you have a strange relationship—a "joking relationship." When I made the Berlin film and gave it to the people in Berlin—that was a joking relationship. My most recent film that I screened in Los Angeles in May this year, *Liberté, Egalité, Fraternité . . . et puis après* is a film about the joking relationship embodied in the concept of "fraternité."

*At the end of* L'Afrique fantôme, *Leiris wrote that he would never again mix anthropology and literature, or science and art. In a sense that's not quite so—*L'Âge d'Homme, *and many of his later autobiographical books, were in some respects an ethnography of himself, his memory, and of Paris. How do you conceive of art and science in your own work?*
I don't think there's any border between the two. All the fiction films I have made were always on the same subject—a discovery of the "Other," an exploration of difference, inspired by Saint-Exupéry's old idea that difference is not a restriction but an addition. The world that you or your great-grandson have to build will be a world based on the principle that "this person is different, therefore we can do something together."

*But at the same time as making films about the Other, are you not also doing an "ethnographie de toi-même"? To me, your personality looms large in many of your films, particularly* Moi, un Noir, Jaguar, *and* La pyramide humaine. *It is infectious, not only for the audience, but— crucially, I think—also for your "actors."*
Certainly—the trouble I have is to . . . I have made many films in the genre of what I call "anthropology/films in the first person." These are based on the idea that when you're filming, there is no reason for people to avoid looking at the camera. Perhaps Bob Gardner's film *Altar of Fire* is unsatisfactory because it is "too well done." The trouble in anthropology, and in film studies, is that we are constructing ever more theory, but theory

increasingly out of sync with practice. Lévi-Strauss never returned to the Nambikwara. Leiris never returned to the Dogon.

*Griaule's later work on the Dogon, after the second war, revolved around his "discovery" and later the mapping out of higher, esoteric levels of Dogon belief. As the director of your doctorate on the Songhay, where there was no comparable* parole claire—*was he a good director?*
Of course . . . but he always thought there would be a *parole claire* there. Initially I was rather ashamed, because I couldn't find one to suit.

*One thing that Michel Leiris was fascinated with was the contradiction, the clash, between different types of cultures. That's why he did a lot of work in the Caribbean; he was interested in what he called "hybrid" social and cultural settings. Many of your films, and particularly* Les maîtres fous, Moi, un Noir, Jaguar, *and* La pyramide humaine, *are about a similar clash between the West and Africa. While most ethnographic films just portray this Other, this primitive, this Africa, in a very facile way, you have always, it seems to me, striven to show that we are involved in a much more complicated interaction . . .*
In fact Leiris went to Martinique, where he became very close to Aimé Césaire, maybe even his best friend. I met Césaire a long time ago at the first meeting of the Artists and Writers from Black Africa, held by Présence Africaine at the Sorbonne, I think in 1952. There was a very interesting clash between Kwame Nkrumah, coming from London, and Diop and Senghor. Nkrumah urged people to fight against tribalism, arguing that *négritude* is a form of tribalism. The American Negroes considered them-selves first and foremost American Negroes. I found the debate overly in-tellectual. One of the most interesting people involved in *négritude* was Léon Damas, from Guyane, and he stood outside this squabble . . . To-gether with Senghor and Césaire at the Sorbonne, going to the *bals Nègres,* they were exiles. Their political notion that only black is beautiful was very popular, but I trace the beginning of the struggle for independence to this time, and I knew that I could have nothing more to do with it. I felt it would be stupid to be a white Negro—perhaps the principal difference between Leiris and myself is that I have returned to the African villagers that I knew and tried to learn more about them. Leiris made his long trip in *L'Afrique fantôme,* but he never returned to Abyssinia. So too with Martinique and Cuba. Leiris was more fascinated by a poet like Césaire than in the Martiniquan people themselves.

*This is interesting, for although surrealism stood firmly against Western civilization, it remained a fundamentally European movement . . .*

Nelson Mandela came to Paris two months ago. Aimé Césaire was there to meet him—for him it was a very important occasion. I see Mandela as the resurrection of the spirit of the young, communist Césaire. What I liked most about Senghor is that in response to political trouble in Senegal, he voluntarily relinquished his position and became a member of the Académie Française . . . The problem with many of these people, and also with the surrealists themselves, was that they permitted politics to intrude into poetry. Buñuel's behavior during the Spanish Revolution was very strange and very sad. Spain was destroyed not only by Franco and Mussolini but also by the "goodwill" of crazy people like Hemingway and Joris Ivens. It was a kind of contest in Paris at the time to prove that you were a man. Morin was a member of the Communist Party, along with Marguerite Duras and others, but he was a militant. While I on the other hand advocated anarchy without militancy. The card-carrying militants were quite blind. In May 1968 I was making a film in Africa, the last film I made about lion hunting. When I heard on the radio that the police had entered the Sorbonne, I said to my friend, "Okay, we must finish the film, as I have to return to Paris." Why? It was insufferable that the police should be inside the Sorbonne. I realized that many intellectuals like Morin, Aron, Sartre, Alain Touraine—while all of them were employed to study society, none of them felt able to have contact with these people. So what is the status of social sciences that weren't able to predict the unrest —like meteorology!

*I'm surprised by the rigid distinction you draw between politics and poetry. Gilles Deleuze wrote five years ago, "No one has done so much to put the West to flight, to flee himself, to break with a cinema of ethnology and say 'Moi, un noir!' at a time when blacks play roles in American series or those of hip Parisians"—he says that "Rouch tends to become a black." Do you not articulate your own intent in this vein, too?*
I realize that for many people, *Moi, un Noir* represented something quite new in cinema, in respect to the relationship between whites and blacks. The film is really about my discovery of Oumarou Ganda, with whom I strangely became very close. He was a veteran of the Stupid War, had run away from home—he was an angry young man like me (he rather younger than I). We knew that there was no easy solution to the problem of racism— all we could do was to try to share our dreams in film. *Moi, un Noir* was the result of an encounter of two people. Oumarou Ganda introduced me to all the people from Abidjan—boxers and prostitutes from Treichville. We thought—I believe rightly—that we got to know Abidjan quite well. The idea was very simple: the camera was the passport to the place. When I showed the first rushes of *Moi, un Noir* to Oumarou, he was really

enthusiastic. He realized this was the way to actively revolt against the world. We put together the narration in two days—for a film that was two hours long at that point. We recorded at the radio station of Abidjan, with the projector shining through the window from outside, so that we could hear Oumarou. He was enchanted and so was able to play so much in his narration. Fortunately it was shot with an old Bell and Howell that you had to rewind every twenty-five seconds—so there were no sentences longer than twenty-five seconds. This structured the narration. This "coincidence" was quite extraordinary—I saw that he would go on to be a filmmaker in his own right. He was one of the best young African filmmakers when he died, a decade ago. Tomorrow, on Christmas Day, I leave for Niamey to observe the tenth anniversary of his death, the first of January, when we will screen *Moi, un Noir*. He was a fantastic guy. "We have nothing in common," he used to say, "I was a private and you were an officer, I never went to school and you are an engineer, you have money and I don't." And I agreed: "Yes, and so what?" Our idea was that even in a slum like Treichville, you can be perfectly happy. It was originally called *Treichville*; Oumarou approved the change of the title from *Treichville* to *Moi, un Noir*. It was the first time that a *noir* was speaking on film—and he was speaking about his own life, or rather about images of his own life. You can't do the same thing in literature, notwithstanding such examples as the book *Baba of Karo*. I'm sure Baba got little feedback from that—and I'm not talking about rights. For me the May '68 revolt was a poetic revolution. The revolt of Oumarou Ganda and myself in *Moi, un Noir* was a poetic revolution.

*Your films on the Dogon—the* Sigui *films,* Ambara Dama, *and so on—are very different. They are less personal, have less to do with contradiction and colonialism, are more conventionally ethnographic verite films. Really you went in on the backs of Marcel Griaule (or at least his legacy) and Germaine Dieterlen.*
I did the same thing myself in my own country, Niger. My doctorate was on possession, and I've made about fifty films you don't know about ritual possession there. Anyway, when much later there was the first coup d'état in Africa, against Nkrumah in Ghana, I knew that it was finished, that there was something wrong in the constitution of power—if you take power, the power takes you. I saw then that the only "way" was to go back to the traditional way of life and way of thinking. This is why I have filmed so much among the Dogon. Also, as Margaret Mead always urged, one should have two fields in anthropology—even if you never do an explicit comparison, it's necessary for objectivity. But I never learned Dogon—I'm not a

very good linguist. I decided to be only a filmmaker, to make the films with Germaine. What I did was to come with my friends—Damouré, Lam, Moussa Amidou—to the Dogon country, and they were as enchanted as I. I discovered another culture. They wanted to be there with me for the filming of the Sigui. When it was finished after eight years, we didn't know what to go on to. So in a sense my films have returned to a more traditional form of anthropology. But I've retained my own sensibility, and approach, which I characterize as intervening to provoke a certain reality.

*What kinds of response have your films elicited when you have screened them to the people in them?*
Because of all the publicity, the Dogon are becoming a kind of emblematic tribe, "the wonderful primitives." The Dogon have now made masks of tourists and cameramen. Last year Germaine screened all the *Sigui* films in four villages. People were enchanted by seeing their rituals on film, ten years later than the performances themselves. The danger is that the films will become a kind of bible, that in fifty years from now when they are preparing for the next Sigui, they will use the film and sound track as reference points. This very thing has in fact happened with Saint Paul and Jesus Christ: the Gospels are better than the original, because they are stories.

*All your films in a sense provoke, rather than "record." I see a difference between France and England here. In his* Méthode de l'ethnographie *Griaule sees the anthropologist as provoking the truths out of his informants: his model is a kind of contest of wills, and the asymmetry of power aside, he respects their resistance to his intrusion. Whereas in the functionalist tradition on the other side of the Channel—and we see this reflected in the Disappearing World series of films—the reality was considered to be objectively out there: you must silently record as if you are as far as possible invisible . . . The presumption is that the observer is very different from the observed; it's rather like looking at a natural history film. There is a substantial difference between the sensibility, and correspondingly the aesthetic, of Disappearing World and most ethnographic films on the one hand and your own films.*
Yes. I prefer not to be a scientist but to participate. I often used to discuss the matter of one's form of participation with Griaule. When I was shooting *Les maîtres fous,* in a remote town in the Gold Coast in 1954, the people participating in this ritual were really crazy. When they killed the dog, Damouré and I were anxious about what might happen next. I asked him jokingly, "There are a lot of babies around; what shall we do if one of these crazy *maîtres* takes a baby to sacrifice?" Another example with

Damouré: when I made my first film about lion hunting, I stopped filming as soon as the lion charged. Immediately I felt very guilty, for I was the only white man there. We were accompanied by Fulani shepherds who would never normally hunt lions—the presence of the foreigner and equipment meant that it was no longer taboo. The lion charged and almost killed this poor shepherd. For the hunters this was quite normal, as this shepherd owned a cow that the same lion had attacked a week earlier. Damouré treated him with penicillin. I stopped filming because I was afraid, but the sound was still rolling. In editing I took the images a frame at a time as a symbol of my fear. So I had the same feeling, that the intrusion of people from outside in something that is very dangerous could create real mistakes, maybe even the death of a man . . . Ethics seem not to exist today in television. I remember this horrible film by Jacopetti, *Africa Addio,* when he asks the mercenary to kill a man in front of the camera during the revolt in the Congo. Also the very famous photo of Frank Capra during the Spanish war; I hope it was staged.

*Did Buñuel ever see any of your films?*
He saw *Les maîtres fous.* He was fascinated and afraid—he liked the dance. He was scared when they killed the dog. He was afraid of blood. Killing and eating a dog is not normal; they were breaking taboos.

*Have you seen* Tierra sin pan? *It's a wonderful parody, even today—or perhaps only in retrospect—of documentary and ethnographic films. What do you think Buñuel was trying to do in this film?*
The cynical narration was written by the surrealist Pierre Unik. It's about misery; it was a very, very poor country. What's strange is that Buñuel was fascinated by this poor country—the village idiot—and he constructed his own fantasy. Buñuel was ready to buy the wonderful, crazy monastery you see at the beginning. For me, the film's about misery and a kind of *"complaisance."* As with the cutting of the eye in *Un chien andalou.* After they shot the film, they ran out of money, and Buñuel edited it himself in his kitchen without a Moviola or anything. He sold the film to my producer, Pierre Braunberger. Braunberger told him he would pay him in three installments, but when the third time came around, Braunberger stalled. Buñuel went to a small hardware store, bought a very big hammer, and went to Braunberger's office. He told Braunberger's secretary that he would count to ten, and that if Braunberger did not appear he would destroy her typewriter. Braunberger wrote out his check in time. It's a true story; Braunberger told it to me himself. After this film Buñuel became a producer in Madrid.

*Did Buñuel influence you?*
*Los olvidados* influenced *Moi, un Noir.*

*In what way?*
His portrayal of desperation and despair. I hate cruelty myself and am upset by the blind man—in some way it is too easy a theme, but Buñuel was like that. *L'age d'or* and *Un chien andalou* had a pronounced influence on me. His ability to cross the barrier between dream and reality is incomparable: the sudden switch to the other side of the mirror. The dream is just as real, maybe more so, than reality. It's what I tried to do in *Moi, un Noir*—or in *La pyramide humaine*—jumping between the two.

*In interviews and often in your own writing, you talk of the effects of technological breakthroughs on your films—the invention of sync sound—and Vertov and Flaherty, an eye and an ear. You seem to have very little to say about the tone, the aesthetic, of your films.*
Well . . . what can I say not to destroy my own . . . ! At the beginning of the social sciences, Auguste Comte argued that we have to consider human beings as things, observe them as if they were things. For years and years this view persisted, in different forms inherited by both Marxism and psychoanalysis, even by most ethnographic films. But my position, which was also Mauss's, is that human beings are human beings—wonderful and mysterious. Mauss disagreed with his uncle Durkheim, who was a Comtist. So this positivist distortion goes back to the beginning. I trace my orientation to Mauss, trying not to theorize about people in such a way as to introduce a gap between observer and observed, but to try to ask good questions, the answers to which will open up new questions. Total knowledge of human beings is impossible.

*Tim Asch and John Marshall once wrote somewhere that the camera could be to anthropologists what telescopes are to astronomers and microscopes to biologists.*
That is Comte, exactly.

*Who also shares your approach?*
Between the wars there were people like Joris Ivens in Amsterdam, Henri Storck, and people meeting in Paris, in Montparnasse, and they were inspired by what Flaherty did in *Nanook of the North* and by what Dziga Vertov was trying to do with *Man with the Movie Camera*. Henri Storck, like Flaherty, made a portrait of Ostende in Belgium, one of the coldest seashores in the world. In Paris, in the twenties, Boris Kaufman and his brother Vertov passed the "sickness" of making documentaries to the

young avant-garde Parisian intellectuals of the time. Every evening they met at the Dôme or at the Closerie des Lilas to discuss their film projects. It was at the Closerie des Lilas that Jean Vigo and Boris Kauffman talked of making *À propos de Nice.* Jean Epstein, coming from Poland, who made *La chute de la maison Usher,* was looking for new projects. This was the beginning of sound recording. Henri Langlois took up the cinema in 1922 with Epstein's *Pasteur,* in 1947 with *La tempestaire.* Turning his back on success, he left for Brittany because we in France had lost our spirit. He discovered *le merveilleux* among the Bretagne fishermen from the beginning of the world . . . Cinema allowed intervention into time, for the first time ever, permitting the construction of a wholly different object. It is this that has always appealed most to me about film.

I first encountered Ricky Leacock while shooting *Chronicle of a Summer.* He's now a great friend, living in my flat. He came to the Musée de l'Homme, and we found out that we were both working in similar ways. But there were still some central differences. In our films we intervened brazenly; Morin was there in front of the camera, speaking to the people, provoking everyone he met. In Leacock's films, he follows his subjects, rather than engaging them. So he remains outside. Actually he's not totally outside. Kenneth Anger was a wonderful dreamer. Unlike Cocteau, he was a provocative homosexual—positively affirming homosexuality as valid. I'm not a homosexual and am not likely to become one. It was clear that he would go on to do something important.

*Luc de Heusch once described you as the "most direct spiritual descendant of Flaherty." And David MacDougall has said that your films (like those of John Marshall and Bob Gardner) reveal a sense of the "wholeness" of other societies. But there's a difference. Flaherty romanticized societies, whereas you try to disrupt any easy conception that other societies are in any simple sense bounded, discrete, and internally homogeneous. If anything, your films show that this presumption derives from our own holistic categories of understanding (Boas's cultural relativism, Malinowski's functionalism, etc.). It's an imposition of distance, surely, that your films disrupt . . .* Flaherty supposed that the world is wonderful, and human beings are wonderful. That was because he was an Irish methodist, or something like that! God's creation could not go wrong. Because I have never had any divine revelation, and because of my experience during the war, I have always felt that the world could be wonderful, but that unfortunately it isn't. Even now I consider that one of the plagues of our times is "goodwill." Goodwill is a sickness. You give something to some people—development agencies and NGOs giving pumps to villages that will break down after a couple of years—and then ask for it back, or ask the villagers to pay for the replacement of the pumps. It's not hypocrisy, exactly, but tactlessness. I'm beginning to realize that the world really is like that, and maybe Buñuel understood it, for he was cruel. The only way to go on is to recognize that the world is at the same time cruel and tender. But there is no solution to this paradox. Chris Marker embodies a form of political goodwill. He's a very nice guy, full of goodwill.

*What do you think of his work?*
It's a kind of provocation, not unlike Alain Resnais in *Nuit et brouillard*. Showing horror, rather as Goya did. The trouble is that Goya and Resnais were real artists, transforming horror to beauty. Marker's a militant and has always felt he can change the world. He is very sad now. What will happen to Castro, one of Marker's heroes? He is an idealist; I'm not. Idealists have a lot of goodwill.

My filmmaking is very different from this other type of filmmaking, whose subjects are something else. The MacDougalls' films on the Turkana are a wonderful positive approach, in which they translate their subjects' words in subtitles. The trouble for me is that the translations are books, the transformation of a written language. But the MacDougalls' films are absolutely honest. They're an example of a husband and wife working together, going to a place, spending a lot of time there, and then making films. That's an example of quality. But these films are something like *Paysans de Paris,* without Aragon, without the talent of a poet, because they are not poets.

I have tried to share my dreams with people, and they theirs with me. The film I'm making now about the Dutch windmills on the banks of the Niger revolves around what I call "poison-gifts"—all the corporations that donate "poison-gifts" under the rubric of "development." My friend Damouré farms rice on the bank of the Niger River, and he had to use a small petrol pump to irrigate the fields. One day when we were there, Philo Bregstein from Holland came to show the film we made together *[Jean Rouch in the Heart of Africa].* He brought with him some Dutch cheese, with a big windmill on the label. I had started to make a film about the drought. I had no solution. I was just filming Damouré, and people migrating to the south to farm millet because there was no rain here. The title of the film is awful, *Madame l'eau.* Philo noticed that Damouré's rice lands were a similar mixture of sand and clay to that the Dutch use to farm tulips. I thought it would be wonderful, as a challenge to development and the drought, to farm tulips on the Niger's banks, and to invent a new type: the black tulip from Niger. This is so crazy because the tulip is totally unnecessary. That's the dream: we will shoot dream sequences of black tulips on the banks of the Niger.

*At the end of your ciné-portrait of Margaret Mead, you asked her: "What of the future and anthropology in the future?" May I ask you the same thing?*

In the future we will realize that we must plan things over many generations. I think we need this not just for physics but also in the human sciences— these very strange people who are human beings, the strangest beings in the world, and we can only ask questions. Perhaps answers will be given in the next Sigui in 2027 by whoever will be there to make another film. The Sigui happens every sixty years—a century with a difference—the old are still around to give their messages to the young. Maybe we should change our calendar, a new century every sixty years. I no longer wear a watch. I once asked the Dogon why they have five-day weeks, and they asked me how many fingers I had.

# JEAN ROUCH WITH ENRICO FULCHIGNONI

## Ciné-Anthropology

This interview was recorded on video in August 1980 to serve as an introduction and commentary to a major retrospective of films by Jean Rouch. Enrico Fulchignoni, who conducted the interview, often moderated film presentations with Rouch at film festivals and university classes. He was active in ethnographic film in Europe, particularly the Festival dei Popoli in Florence, and served on many UNESCO commissions concerning Third World film. He died in 1988 in Paris.—*Ed.*

ENRICO FULCHIGNONI: *In 1895 the Lumière brothers invent a light, mobile camera. An eye that watches, that moves, that jumps, that captures the most mobile aspects of the world. In 1928 someone invents a sound system that is added to this camera. The camera then becomes heavy, the world becomes stiff. There are discussions, there is kammerspiel. It will be thirty more years before a Swiss invents the Nagra, a sound recording machine without a lead casing. A French engineer, A. Coutant, creates a light camera at this same moment, rediscovering the freedom of the original one. This is when Jean Rouch fully becomes Jean Rouch because there is synchronous sound, but above all because he can start to move, to jump, to go off in all directions. We are used to seeing your images with such a dynamic eye that we lose the notion of the immobility of the eye and acquire, on the contrary, the feeling of something closer to wings, or the wind.*
JEAN ROUCH: To be able to leap from one point to another is my essential dream. To be able to go everywhere, to ramble about like you ramble in a dream, to go someplace else. The mobile camera, the walking, flying camera—that's everybody's dream! Simply because making a film, for me, means writing it with your eyes, with your ears, with your body. It means entering into it—being invisible and present at the same time—which never happens in traditional cinema. It's being able to be with friends, with light

equipment, being able to talk to them, have them answer, and not with a clap stick slate, floodlights, staged framing, and so forth. All of that is false! What we're doing right now, for example, is false; you don't stop like this. We should be running across place du Trocadéro, we should go someplace else, we should slip on the winged shoes of Arthur Rimbaud and go off somewhere else and, from that somewhere else, bring back bits of flying carpets that we could share with others—but this is a dream! And in spite of Kudelski, in spite of Coutant, in spite of Brault, in spite of today's Beauviala, in spite of Leacock, we have not yet reached that point. We are still constrained to something terrible, formal; for example, we make films that have a set framing. Why is this framing horizontal? Why isn't it vertical? Why haven't we exploded this stage system that comes from the Italian theater? During the first film I made in 1947, I had the good luck of losing my tripod after two weeks. It was a film on the descent of the Niger River. After I made the film I thought that there wasn't anything that couldn't be filmed without a tripod. The impression continued. Maybe it's simply because I had not formally learned how to make movies.

*Or from a taste for the destruction of all nature of habits. Under the circumstances, it was a destruction of technological rituals, wasn't it?*
No, it amuses me to see if they are useful. Most of the time you find out that they are not. So I tried to make movies in total freedom.

*There is a point that I'd like to raise, because it seems perfect for grasping a certain scientific and, at the same time, poetic value in your films. We get the impression that, in general, beyond what is the evolution of the normal acts we are used to, you are looking for this sort of hidden secret that is the real formula of things, the invisible secret that pushes men to act, to seek. We never have the feeling of being confronted with folklore, with something merely amusing, or funny, but of being placed in a reality that is even more profound than reality.*
I had the good fortune to have as my professor, at rue des Saints Pères, the engineer for construction of bridges and streets, a marvelous fellow who was the greatest specialist on the resistance of materials. It was just before the war, and he told us stories like this one: There's an engineer consultant for a certain number of bridges that the Americans were building from scale models. They called him in to verify the bridges once they were built. One day he goes to see one of these bridges, which has twenty-ton trucks going over it. He makes his calculations and says to himself, "There's nothing that can be done, this bridge ought to fall apart." He goes back to Paris, he thinks, he can't find any solution, then he heads back to the United States, where he learns that that bridge was ten years old, that it had been

opened to five-ton trucks, then seven-ton, then ten-ton, then fifteen-ton, then twenty-ton. Then all of a sudden he has a flash; he says to himself that the material could resist successive stresses by adapting its resistance to the new tensions demanded of it. He does some experiments and discovers the theory of "resistance to successive stresses." I was thus trained by people who were great researchers and who were, at the same time, great poets, because this resistance to successive stresses is nothing less than poetry. I was trained in the school of those who searched to "look beyond accepted ideas, to find out if there is something there." As for my taste for destruction, it is involuntary. I began my career as an engineer by blowing up the bridges on the Marne up to Limoges in 1939, which was not a pretty sight for an engineer. It's a bit of this idea of a certain chaos, a chaos that was perhaps not necessary; it's sort of like sacrilege, if you will. In sacrilege you discover all of a sudden that there were in fact some things that served a purpose, and others that served none at all. So, unconsciously, I apply this double method of sacrilege and of resistance to successive stresses.

*I really like this resistance to successive stresses as a reference to another notion that recurs often in your films: your absolute confidence in the improvisation of your actors, and that extraordinary research you did of a sort of African* commedia dell'arte. *You transported to Africa a technique from the grand Italian tradition of comic actors who embroider on a simple starting canvas, who create a natural comedy, one that has nothing to do with learned comedy, situational comedy, or character comedy.*
It's very simple. There's no formula. Working with people who are champions of the oral tradition, it's impossible to write scenarios, impossible to write dialogues. So I am obliged to surrender myself to this improvisation that is the art of the Logos, the art of the word and the gesture. You have to set off a series of actions to see, all of a sudden, the emergence of the truth, of the disquieting action of a person who has become disquieted. When Albert Caquot discovered resistance to successive stresses, he was faced with an enigma. When I create with Damouré, Tallou, and Lam, we create situations, we create enigmas for ourselves. We pose charades, guessing games for ourselves. At that moment, we enter the unknown, and the camera is forced to follow. It is a very easy recipe, because I myself am behind the camera. In most cases, in most of the sequences I start to film, I never know what's going to be at the end, so I'm never bored. I'm forced to improvise for better or for worse.

*Which gives the impression of tremendous vitality. We always have the feeling of being plunged, with no intermediary, into a sort of Dionysian fertility in which all things are equal. And in the moments of greatest success, we really have the feeling of being everywhere, which provides a richness that cannot be found in the work of other filmmakers who, like many directors of Italian neorealism, demand, consciously or unconsciously, one, two, or three intermediaries in order to see reality. With you, we are immediately plunged into film reality without distinguishing it from the other.*

Yes, that's it exactly. From the moment when necessity obliged me to be alone, I discovered, when they began building cameras with a good view-finder, that I was, behind the lens of my camera, the first viewer of my film. So if I got bored during filming, the viewers to whom I might show the film would be equally bored. I was *the* viewer, so my improvisation was that of a viewer, and the staging was carried out almost without me. With the camera to my eye, I am what Dziga Vertov called the mechanical eye; my microphone-ear is an electronic ear. With a ciné-eye and a ciné-ear, I am a ciné-Rouch in a state of ciné-trance in the process of ciné-filming. So that is the joy of filming, the ciné-pleasure. In order for this to work, the little god Dionysus must be there. We must have luck; we must have what I call "grace." And grace is not something learned; it arrives all of a sudden, it works. What's really curious is that even those people whom I film, even those who watch me filming, know when I make a good film. My African friends, when they see me filming a ritual or something, come up to me at the end to say: "Ah, Jean, today it's a good one," and other times they come and say, "It's a flop!" You cannot provoke grace; sometimes it just comes. It's happened to me often enough that I start making a film, I shoot five minutes, six minutes, a whole magazine, ten minutes, and then I stop for lack of a subject. There wasn't the necessary contact, it's difficult to explain; and it has nothing to do with the cinema of Roberto Rossellini, an intellectual's cinema, carefully prepared in his head, with the intermediary of an excellent director and an excellent cameraman who got splendid pictures, dubbed-in sound that was not the real sound, and the result was something that was perhaps truer than reality. Let's say it's less true than fiction!

*Dionysus has, and in general everything Dionysian has, this double possibility of maximum joy and maximum tragic furor. In some of your films, you have dealt with the two themes: maximum joy, maximum furor, and then maximum tragedy, which is death, like in the film* Les funérailles à Bongo: Le vieil Anaï. *It's the perfect film for understanding one aspect of the problems of death in Africa. To capture death, with all of its mythic components, it's a matter of capturing not just its psychological components, but its symbolic and metaphysical ones, as well.*

There, too, it's not easy. I began to shoot those films about death among the Dogon of the Bandiagara Cliffs in 1951, and it's only thirty years later that I have begun to understand. If you will, this too is a challenge, a poker game, gambling against the stars. It's telling yourself that when you start a task of this sort, it'll take thirty years to finish it. And I am more and more convinced that everything that is shown on television is nothing more than impressions. They are impressions that can be the works of great artists, as are the impressionist works in painting, and Lord knows there are some of those that I like immensely. For example, since you mentioned Rossellini, *Stromboli* is a difficult film. Through *Stromboli* I discovered all the Italian paganism that is barely detected, barely indicated, and that's what I see. But if Roberto had wanted to make a film about paganism and show it, he would have needed not six months of shooting but sixty years. So you need a lot of time. Cinema, the art of the instant and the instantaneous, is, in my opinion, the art of patience, and the art of time.

*As far as the manner in which your films are represented is concerned, the fact of seeing a cycle is extremely important for filmmakers like you who don't simply touch the surface of things.*
Yes, but people are in too much of a hurry. This is perhaps one of the elements that cinema has given to anthropology today. The classic schema of anthropology was: you do two years of fieldwork to get adapted, two more years to learn the language well and to collect material, and then two more years to write a thesis. That makes six years in all. I think that's a mistake. You don't need one lifetime, but generations of researchers.

*Here, we are seeing some completely new possibilities for cinema. I think that if we can escape that sort of fatality of speed and superficiality, which is like a condemnation to eternal wandering that the cinematographer would have been sentenced to by a sort of strange bad luck due to technology, we can enter the domains of a new formation of the human conscience, of a new anthropology that results in a totally changed memory. Before the invention of the gramophone and the camera, that is, of recorded image and recorded sound, there were many infinitely fleeting things in the universe that dissolved after being produced, and in the end, man's memory was unable to capture them. But from the moment when this reality was enclosed in our tape recorders, on our electronic and chemical images, it has been accumulating like the ashes of a volcano.*
I learned the "joy-tragedy" system that you were talking about when I was with the Dogon. At the cliff of Bandiagara, I was able to follow for seven years these ceremonies that take place every sixty years, in the course of which priests are initiated. I noticed that the initiation consisted of upsetting

people and not teaching them anything. They were simply made to retreat into a cave in which there were some raised stones and paintings on the ceiling. It was said that in five years, in ten years, in twenty years, one of them would go back into the cave and say to himself, "I lived under this painting for two months. What does it mean?" At that moment he will ask questions, and only then will he be answered. This is maybe what I have tried to do in my films: to pose riddles, to circulate disquieting objects. If, in a thousand viewers, there is just one who asks the question, then knowledge has been saved. It is possible to succeed in telling the myth and illustrating it, on one condition: that this myth be, as are African myths, so incomprehensible, so poetic, that it will be even more astounding than the explanation to be given of it. It will be a new riddle and thus will be successful. If the myth becomes something very simple, at that moment the cycle is broken, and the myth dies. Take, for example, the *Chanson de Roland* that we all learned in school—it has no connection with the *Orlando Furioso* of Italian marionnette theaters. We started with a myth and now tell the story of Roland as the history of an individual who is, in fact, one of the fantastic heroes of the Sicilian people. André Breton said, just after the war, "What our culture lacks is a myth." In effect, it lacks a myth that could be the foundation of those marvelous rituals we have lost. So this myth, I don't know . . . you mentioned Nietzsche a minute ago . . . When Nietzsche was walking in the streets of Torino and wrote those sublime lines (which I quote from memory) "In autumn, at dusk, when the shadows are low, when the statues come down from their pedestals, (because in Torino there are statues placed almost at ground level), you meet such astonishing phantoms as you will not find anywhere else"—this simple sentence was enough to make a marvelous madman, Giorgio De Chirico, go to Torino to walk around in autumn and, between 1908 and 1917, paint the most extraordinary collection of metaphysical and poetic paintings, opening to dream. And this poetry was made up of factory smokestacks, of the outskirts, of walls of crumbling brick, of smoking locomotives, and of those infinite shadows that announced something more. He too had dreamed of creating a myth, a modern myth that is the world of those avenues. I know there are places in the world where I walk around and I suddenly come upon this peculiar perspective: "grace," a grace which depends on a certain lighting, which depends on a certain mood, which depends on a certain season. So when I make films, it's sort of like that. I would like to paint with movement, with color, moments like those that ask questions of the viewer and give no answer. It is up to them to find it, just as I found it when I was my own first viewer, looking through the viewfinder of my camera. It seems to me that in the filmmaking we are doing—which has been called *cinéma-vérité*, in homage to Dziga Vertov, which has been called "direct cinema," "living cinema," "the contact camera," or whatever—that in this filmmaking, there are all of a sudden these privileged moments that you yourself feel through your viewfinder. And for me, the second moment—which is the moment of truth—is when I am at the editing table, and without my having forewarned her, the editor in front of the little viewing screen stops, rewinds, and looks again. I know that the editor is asking herself the same question that I asked myself in my camera viewfinder; I know it's working, and we can keep on going. On the other hand, if there is no reaction, it's a miss; the grace wasn't there. The ciné-trance was a false ciné-trance, and Dionysus had gone off gallivanting somewhere else.

*After these two surprises—that of the creator and that of the editor—is that of the viewer, the third participant in the miracle, absolutely certain?*
Ah, no! That would be too simple. It happens sometimes, in a way I cannot explain. For example, take the filming of *Chronicle of a Summer* with Edgar Morin, twenty years ago, in 1960. We were looking for a quiet place in Paris because we were experimenting with clip-on lavaliere microphones and with methods for using hand-held cameras in the street. We had decided to film in the marvelous old pavilions of les Halles because it was the fifteenth of August; I think les Halles was closed, so it was silent, tranquil. The camera was placed in the back of a Citroën 2 CV. No one was aiming it. Marceline wore the tape recorder, and she talked alone into her clip-on mike. When Marceline entered les Halles, we pushed the car ahead of her, but a little bit faster than she was moving; we drew away from her, and she remained talking all by herself. At a given moment we let the car stop, and Marceline came closer to the camera. We had not seen or heard anything; we had simply provoked two movements, feelings, emotions, memories. When we saw these images on the screen for the first time, Edgar, still very surprised, suddenly said, "Yes. It's the image of her return." What did that mean? We had chosen, without realizing it, a building that looked like the vaulted roof of a train station. We had fixed the camera on an object in motion, and coming from the other side of horror, Marceline arrived. We did not know that she was telling of her despair when, coming back from the concentration camps, she rejoined her mother and her brother at the Gare de l'Est. This is, for me, the creation of something that goes beyond the tragic: an intolerable mis-en-scène, like some spontaneous sacrilege that pushed us to do what we had never done before. Michel Brault had never

filmed a sequence this way; I myself had never done it, and we will never do it again.

*Yes, but you say "spontaneous." I got the impression that we are really at the boundary between the conscious and the unconscious. You are citing one case here that actually turns up quite often in your films: the setting that you choose determines what hidden forces will manifest themselves. That was the case with Marceline's emotional scene; it's often the case in* Les maîtres fous: *the leafy branches surrounding them stimulate the participants to whip themselves, to hit themselves. I mean, the universe itself collaborates in this spontaneous gush of creative emotion; the setting is never innocent; your characters are never in that sort of neutrality, that emptiness that is so often seen with directors who use large-scale equipment and big sets in which the characters evolve without really being connected to them. I remember in* Anaï, *there's a boy who talks about the future, about what is to come; something in the scene evokes fatigue, the initiation step that must be taken. You chose a mountain, some concrete model to represent that sort of work that one must do to grow up, to become an adult. One gets the impression that your work has a sort of symbolic imagery that connects man to the cosmos.*

I'd say that differently. I learned with the Dogon that the essential character in all these adventures is not God, representing order, but the foe of God, the Pale Fox, representing disorder. So I have a tendency, when I'm filming, to consider the landscape you're talking about as precisely the work of God, and the presence of my camera as an intolerable disorder. It's this intolerable disorder that becomes a creative object. Marceline would never have walked alone, talking all by herself, if there hadn't been a camera there, if she wasn't wearing the microphone, if she didn't have a portable tape recorder. It was provocation; it was disorder. It was disorder because we were breaking an established order, an architecture; and we broke it by asking someone to talk alone in the street (something that is never done); and the pretext, the provocation, was the presence of the camera. The camera is for me, if you will, what lets me go anywhere, what permits me to follow someone. It is something with which one can live or do things that one couldn't do if one didn't have the camera. When my friends and I say today that we use the "contact camera" or "contact lenses," it means that we work with wide-angle lenses, so that we can be very close to the people we film. It ends up reducing our action to an adventure that is the most perfect disorder, since we film with wide angles, that is, seeing everything, but reducing ourselves to proximity, that is, without being seen by others.

We have become invisible by being close and by having an extremely wide view; that's the model of disorder.

*In your respect for ritual, in your respect for the sacred, sometimes you could be seen as someone with a certain reverence. But the presence of the camera as a provocative element, as a demonic element, troubles this lovely image I had of your respect for divinity. Do you think, then, that what counts in creativity is confrontation?*

It's not confrontation; it's a questioning of the established order at all levels. I can give you two examples: First, I've made a lot of films on the phenomena of possession, on precisely those people who practice in the cult of Dionysus today, who know what a trance is. We have lost, you and I, that taste for the thrill, that possibility of escaping ourselves, of living, with our body, the adventure of another, of being the "horse of a god." The paradox is that, maybe because I made films, I have never been possessed. For those who saw them, and I mean the priests and the people I showed them to in Africa, my possession was what I call a ciné-trance, and it was from making all those movements that are absolutely abnormal, from following someone in the middle of a trance arena, from pointing my lens at someone who was about to be possessed, indeed, at that very moment when a possession might take over. The second example I can give comes from the relationship with exact science. I am working right now with Germaine Dieterlen on the thought systems of the Dogon. Little by little we are seeing an absolutely incredible mythology in which one star in particular, Sirius, plays an essential role. All around Sirius, his companion stars slowly emerge. The first one who spoke to me of these companions was Marcel Griaule, my professor at the Sorbonne. He told me, "The Dogon observe Sirius's companion, and what's remarkable is that it is invisible to the naked eye." My reaction was, "Well, then, they can't see it." And Griaule told me, "You are an ass. You'll never be an anthropologist!" That really struck me, but in fact, he was right. He meant, "I claim this, they told me that, I am studying the philosophy of the Dogon, so I am obliged to observe that." He had no answer; he couldn't tell me his choice between this and that. Then the years passed. Since then, he and Germaine Dieterlen discovered that there are three companions to Sirius in Dogon cosmography. Just recently, astronomers have discovered that the aberrant trajectory of Sirius could only be explained if there was another companion, a dead star, a "black star." How did the Dogon know about it? We don't have the answer. This sort of approach is for me the only scientific approach; it's the sole justification for ethnology: to ask oneself questions like this one and to answer, "I don't understand how it works, but maybe one day it will be understood."

*A few years from now, we will have images via satellite of innumerable cultures, not just of the Dogon, not just of African cultures; we'll have innumerable ethnographic films that will come from thousands of different cultures. If all the systems are put in conflict with each other, don't you think that the confusion that will result concerning value judgments might reach a limit that is absolutely unbearable for humanity? Should we have an attitude of incredulity, of skepticism toward all this? Or else answer with aestheticism, like the Renaissance did with the shock of Greco-Roman culture? If we must renounce our Cartesianism, must we accept this trap that is offered to us by the hedonistic component of human nature?*

No. It's not renouncing our Cartesianism; it's considering the possibility that, beside our Cartesianism, beside our so-called scientific explanations, there are others. To ignore them means that we have an imperialist attitude, that we think that ours is the only way to live, that ours is the only way to think. In fact, I think that anthropology, and, perhaps, as you say, thanks to visual anthropology (which allows us to share our culture with other cultures), will help us to discover that we are citizens of a world that is marvelous in its diversity. As long as we are unable to take on this diversity, we will have resolved nothing. But one day we will discover other systems of explication and of science, and our Cartesian science will be enriched by such discovery. Six months ago, in the cliffs of Bandiagara, a crazy American came up to Germaine Dieterlen and said, "Madame, I think the Dogon are right. I have thoroughly studied what you published about the myth: the third companion of Sirius is as 'structurally' necessary to the Dogon myth as it is for astronomers." Perhaps here lies the explanation: it was necessary for the Dogon observing Sirius to introduce an element of disorder, a companion, which determines both the anomalies of the star's trajectory and the anomalies of the creation myth. I don't think we would ever have discovered this without the cinema, because it was indispensable to observe it in the pictures, and above all, it was indispensable to have the Dogon share our ignorance, that is, to show them what we knew, the extent of our knowledge. Of course, they had already had books written about them, but they couldn't read them; but they could look at our pictures and see the state of our knowledge, the stage in our initiation.

*That's a point which I think should be emphasized in your anthropological and ethnographic work—your constant concern with showing images that are not stolen from the people, but, on the contrary, which you share with them as soon as they are realized. What effect do these films have on the public that they depict?*

I always cite the reaction of the filmed participants during the first projection in Africa of *Bataille sur le grand fleuve (Hippopotamus Hunting with Harpoons)*, filmed in 1951 to 1952, and shown to the hunters themselves in 1953, in Ayorou, a fishing village on the border of Niger and Mali. We had brought along all the paraphernalia, a generator, the projector. A sheet on the wall of a hut served as the screen. The villagers, quite naturally, sat in a circle around the projector and the generator. We waited for nightfall. Then, when the generator started running, everybody closed in around the projector lamp. Then an image appeared, not in the middle, but over there, on the sheet. They turned around, and in no more than twenty seconds, they understood the language of cinema. They recognized their village, Ayorou; they recognized themselves. Then all of a sudden, some people who had died since the filming appeared on the screen, and all the people of the village started to cry; we heard such wailing that the sound track served absolutely no purpose. After the first projection, the villagers asked to see it a second time, and they began crying again; then a third time, and then they began to see the film. And then, suddenly, they understood what I was doing. I had by then been working in Ayorou for twelve years; I had written articles about them, a book, my thesis; I had given these things to them. They had taken them politely, but for them these written texts were dead letters, alien things, completely oblique, even when the schoolmaster read them out loud. I remember well the reaction of the head fisherman, to whom I had given my thesis: he had carefully taken out the photographs to hang them on his wall; the rest was just paper, which he used for another purpose. And there, all of a sudden, he saw an image of himself, he understood how I saw him. And the most marvelous dialogue that I had at that moment is when the fisherman began to criticize me. "What? When did you hear music during a hippopotamus hunt?" Following the old tradition of Westerns, at the most dramatic moment of the hunt, I had added a music track, but I had chosen well; the tune was "Gawey, Gawey," the hunters' air. But the fisherman said, "Yes, it's true, but the hippopotamus underwater has very good ears, and if you play music, he'll escape!" At the hunt there must be silence; without it there is no hunt. For me, this was a great lesson. I discovered that I had been the victim of Italian-style theater, with an orchestra in the pit. These people were right. They reasoned in their own thought system, and I, who was making a film about them, had no reason for imposing our system on them. Since then I have almost totally suppressed musical accompaniment, except when it is a part of the action.

I have often repeated this story, for example, to the Japanese. It was during a meeting near Tokyo; also there were Cousteau, Joris Ivens, Ricky Leacock, and, strangely enough, Jacopetti. The Japanese showed an admirable film on the Kula ring of the Trobriands, studied by Malinowski in the past, about the circuit made by these Pacific Islanders who go from island to island in canoes, exchanging shells that have nothing but mythical value. Over these marvelous images they had put what we call in our jargon *"musique à la confiture"* (syrup muzak). I repeated the lesson of the Ayorou fishermen; it influenced all of Japanese documentary cinema, where there is no more *musique à la confiture.* Thus the hunters of the Niger River, armed with harpoons fashioned out of a piece of wood and scraps of iron, managed to completely transform the cinematographic language of a super-developed country like Japan. I made a similar experiment when I showed one of my first black-and-white films to the village of Wanzerbé. There, it was refusal, refusal of our abstraction, the abstract interpretation in black and white. This is one of the reasons I never wanted to use black-and-white video for making films in Africa. Color is life. The world is in color. To suppress color is to be the blank page taking refuge behind writing.

*One thing strikes me in your films. It's the relation to childhood, a relationship of great tenderness that is very different from what we normally see.*
I feel that I have never made the films I should have made on that subject. That is, on these familial relationships, on domestic life; these are the most difficult subjects for me. I'd love to film them, but I don't know how. What struck me when I filmed the Sigui ceremonies, which take place every sixty years, was to see, in one village, the generation of men under sixty down to two-year-old children, all dressed in the same way and all drinking the communal Sigui beer at the same time. I don't think there's a comparable example in our civilization. There is never a reunion of all the men of one generation who receive the knowledge of the survivors of the preceding generation.

*That's one of the most admirable examples of a structure that we are totally lacking. I recall the emphasis you place on initiation rituals, the passage that is made from one generation to another, a fundamental element for the evolution of societies.*
It's the problem of troublesome objects that the Africans multiply and place in the hands of children, without telling them how to use them. Initiation is responding to a question that is asked, and true knowledge is asking a question; that's what we have lost. We pass on a knowledge our pupils do not ask for. Someday we'll have to think about it. The schoolmaster, the profes-

sor, always gives a lecture *ex cathedra,* which, for him, is knowledge. The reason I spoke to you about Albert Caquot is because he was someone who claimed not to know, and who claimed that knowledge, explanation, came to him like that, in a poetic way, like Nietzsche on the streets of Torino, troubled by the long shadows and the statues at sidewalk level.

*What strikes me in films about African civilizations is the effort one must make in order to be able to become an adult.*
I don't agree at all, because initiation is not obligatory; anyone can escape it. This is what most surprised me about the therapeutic side of initiation into possession dance: the one who is sick must ask to be cured. If he is not the one who asks, if it is not he who assumes it, he will never be cured.

*But the transition from one age to another, during which they remain in silence for months, for example, isolated, not having the right to talk to their parents, isn't all that a system that gives them a certain discipline for the future?*
Yes, for those who consent to follow that path, but they are not obliged to. They know that they have to do it if they want to "pass"; it is a necessary rite of passage, but not obligatory.

*But what is the difference that separates them from those who have passed through a traditional initiation?*
That is one of the essential subjects of all of my films: how can cultures survive and continue to be transmitted when they come into contact with another culture as consuming as our own? For example, after *The Lion Hunters,* a couple of English filmmakers reproached me for having left the hunters wearing tennis shoes, or for not having taken away their blue jeans. I, on the other hand, find admirable the introduction of our culture into the middle of other thought systems with which it has nothing in common. Another example: A few years ago in Niger, a good typist knew how to type in rhythm; he used the tabulator pedal like that of a bass, and typed with a beat. As the Nigerians said, in the office of a good typist, everyone is happy. And it's the same thing for filling a tire: these are work and music at the same time. When I made *Jaguar* and *Moi, un Noir,* it was to show this difficult contact between a traditional culture and a so-called industrial culture; and I had no other response but these two fiction films to this essential problem in Africa today.

*There's another serious question, about the things you cannot show if you want to respect the taboos; the essential problem that your great ancestor Flaherty wanted to show in* Taboo.

Of course there are taboos to respect! But can't you agree that to do a film, you must have filled a certain number of conditions?

*Being initiated, for example?*
In fact, it's not exactly being initiated, because from the very moment when you're initiated, you can no longer speak in the same way about the group that you're studying, since you are constrained by a certain rule of secrecy. But there are so many public rituals, why go looking just for the secret ones? I don't at all believe the people who tell you the secret story, *Fantastic Africa, Forbidden Ritual* in Haiti, or films of that type; no, they aren't true.

*In the past thirty years, you've accumulated a remarkable number of films that show different cultures, mainly African. Do you think the future will yield a large place for this type of cinema?*
What I claim is that it is expanding. In every country of the world, it is being produced and diffused. I think we are in a period of transition, that the great adventure of this century will have been the arrival of what we call the "Third World," which, thanks to film, has a right to speak and act, whereas up until now it was submerged by our technical knowledge, by our machines. I always repeat, and this is perhaps the key to my utopia (and I hold to it), that the technical progress that we are now experiencing consists of manufacturing objects that are more and more sophisticated but can be put into an ever-increasing number of hands because they are more and more manageable. Currently in the domain of industry itself, we are in a world of madness, which is completely ridiculous with its technical walls of shame, which make, for example, half the world function at fifty cycles and the other half at sixty, yielding a multiplicity and incompatibility of electrical standards. But in the middle of all this there arrives a mysterious personage whom I would willingly believe to be the Pale Fox of the Dogon. For the Dogon, the Pale Fox invented speech, agriculture, sexual union, joy; he invented funeral rites, and men began to die, so beautiful were these rites. God, in fury, made him open his gullet so that he could tear out his larynx, and trapped him by the tail to drive him crazy. He began to howl, and he became a fox of broken cries: it's the rhombus, the bullroarer that roars on the night of the major rituals. Then he began to speak with his feet, to write: the fox's footprints mark today's divination tables, not with the news of yesterday, as we do it, but with the news for tomorrow. These fox paws, it's 1-2-1, it's the basis of all our computers. I'm quite fond of the idea that it's this same little Pale Fox who introduced the "digital" in our electronic systems. Then there will be marvelous things like video discs that will have the same norms, the same quality as 35 mm film. There will

be books associated with those discs that will cost nothing at all: an hour for less than four francs! We'll have loads of these books. You'll take out a disc that reads *Sigui 1970,* and a little label explains: an old man tells the myth in a secret language, 0265-0270. I'll put it on the machine, and I'll have the sequence immediately. I can read the translation page by page, rewind, or jump to another sequence. It's these video disc books that future generations will read in a hundred years, and I'll receive the best criticisms of my films in maybe two centuries! I like this idea.

▶

## The Beginnings

*Your first film,* Au pays des mages noirs, *is from 1947. Nineteen forty-seven is an important year in France for the recognition of a great director: Bob Flaherty.*
The first film I ever saw in my life was *Nanook,* in 1924. That was my discovery of the cinema. My second ancestor was Dziga Vertov.

*One speaks of Flaherty as a filmmaker of great emotion, and of Vertov as one who denies the emotion of the camera eye.*
My dream, as yet unrealized, is to have the sensitive camera of Flaherty armed with the mechanical eye and ear of Vertov. However, they are not so different from each other, and the antagonism that is attributed to them comes from the political history of cinema. They never met each other, but their emotion was the same. They were on the edge of things; they were poets. Both of them were rejected by their societies. Their approaches were no doubt different, but when we see the result, when we analyze their films today, we discover their singular connivance. *Au pays des mages noirs* is my first film. It was shot in black and white, without sound. The filming lasted nine months (1946–1947), the time it took for the descent of the Niger River in canoes. Actualités Françaises bought the film and reduced its thirty minutes to ten. In the absence of real sound, it was accompanied by idiotic music and a narration spoken by the commentator of the Tour de France bicycle race, in his characteristic voice. They made up the title. Commercially, this film was a great success. My reaction after this film is to say, "No! It's not possible!" The music is worthless; the tone of the commentary is insufferable. It's really an exotic film, a film that should not have been made. I've never shown it in Africa. I'd be ashamed. A subsidy from the CNC permitted me in 1948 and 1949 to realize three films: *Les magiciens de Wanzerbé, La circoncision,* and *Initiation à la danse de possédés.* They were for me my first ethnographic films. In 1951 to 1952, I

took off again to film with the same mechanical camera and with, for the first time, the first portable tape recorder, which allowed my friend Roger to record the actual sound. We returned to the hunt of the hippopotamus with harpoons, with the same fishermen who had been in my first film. This was to be *Bataille sur le grand fleuve*.

*Why did you do a remake of this film?*
Because I had a guilty conscience after the film that Actualités Françaises edited. From an ethnographic point of view, I had three years of experience, and I knew the fishermen of Ayorou very well. The filming lasted four months, following the episodes of that hippopotamus hunt. The use of the same mechanical camera, which had a twenty-second spring-wound motor run, obliged me to shoot very short scenes that are almost edited through the viewfinder. It was then that I understood what Dziga Vertov proclaimed in his manifesto: "I edit my film when I think my film; I edit my film as I am shooting my film." The entire film was shot with a 25 mm lens, which, for 16 mm film, corresponds to the eye's vision, with the perspective of an eye in motion. The images that result are therefore terribly subjective. The viewer finds himself seated in a canoe in the middle of the river, surrounded by hippopotamuses at the distance he would be at if he were really there. This is the film that I showed three years later in Africa and that produced such reactions, particularly against the background music. In this film, I used for the first time the technique of the "participating camera" developed by Flaherty, showing the hippopotamus hunters their own images. This film pushed me in the same direction I followed in 1953 to 1954, when I made *Jaguar* and *Les maîtres fous*.

*What is the relation between* Les maîtres fous *and* Bataille sur le grand fleuve?
The possession dances, which are the means men have to communicate with their gods. From the beginning of my studies in researching the Songhay religion in 1942, I had encountered these peculiar spirits, the Hauka. These new divinities made their appearance around 1927 in the course of traditional possession dances. The Hauka were directly inspired by the French and British army and administration; they represented, in fact, the technical world, the colonial world. From Niamey they emigrated to the Gold Coast, thus following the migratory movements of the young people of Niger who went to the coast to look for work during the dry season. The "mecca" of the Hauka was therefore the region of Accra and Kumasi. I finished my thesis on the Songhay religion, and it seemed essential for me to go to study these phenomena in the field. I left with Damouré Zika, Lam

Ibrahima Dia, and Illo Gaoudel to study these migrations, and, at the same time, to study the Hauka. That's how, in a little village in Accra, with the same Bell and Howell camera and a portable tape recorder, I managed to film *Les maîtres fous* in one day.

*This film,* Les maîtres fous, *is one of your most remarkable films. It bowled over a large part of the French ethnographic film world, on the one hand, and on the other, the world of ordinary spectators.*
In 1955, upon returning to Paris, I presented this film at the Musée de l'Homme, and it was violently rejected by ethnologists there who judged it intolerable, and by some African friends who judged it racist. Then the film was banned in Great Britain and in Gold Coast by British authorities because of cruelty to an animal and insult to the queen.

*The influence of this film was claimed by men of the theater like Jean Genet, who was inspired by it for his plays* Les Bonnes *and* Les Nègres, *and Peter Brook, who used this example to show his actors what the unfurling of the irrational in the body of a man can be like.*
The title of this film, *Les maîtres fous* (The Mad Masters), is a play on words that translates both the word "Hauka" (master of the wind, master of madness) and at the same time the colonial situation where the masters (the Europeans) are crazy. Twenty-five years later, this film has become a classic in Africa. It is shown on the educational circuits in Niger and is considered an anticolonialist film. I broke a lot of taboos with this film. But I could not show it to the Hauka themselves, even though they were the ones who asked me to make it to show during their rituals. *Les maîtres fous* was filmed three years before the independence of Ghana. After that there were no longer any Hauka horses, which were nothing more than a representation of colonial power. Today they have become the servants of Dongo, the god of thunder. They have become characters in history; as have the spirits Koronba, Gourmantché, Haouna, and Touareg.

Jaguar *was filmed at the same time as* Les maîtres fous, *in 1954 to 1965. What does the title,* Jaguar, *mean?*
Jaguar is not the animal but the car, which was at the time the most prestigious car on the Gold Coast, even more so than the Rolls Royce. At the same time, it signified *un jeune homme à la mode,* a stylish, fashionable young man of the world. Filmed at the same time as *Les maîtres fous* (in fact, some scenes from *Jaguar* are included in it), the film was conceived as follows: I wanted both to film the manifestations of the Hauka and to study the migrations of the young people who left Niger to look for work in Gold Coast. At the end of the rainy season in Niger there is no work

available, except for fishermen and hunters. The young people who fought the war in the past now find themselves free and go looking for work. The religion of the Hauka, of the "mad masters," developed among the migrants. It is very difficult to do a documentary on migrations, so we decided to make a fictional film, improvised as we went along. At the beginning we had simply decided who the characters would be—Illo, the fisherman; Lam, the shepherd; Damouré, the gallant—and then we took off for a year, filming a sort of improvised travelogue, shot mostly without sound.

*This film is very important historically, since the three actors will continue to represent, in several of your later films, this group of three African masks, your Harlequins, your Brighellas. There are several themes here: contempt for money, which is, at the same time, desire and derision; the poetics of the discovery of nature, of the discovery of others; and then the innovation of making the authors talk about what's going on, which is extraordinarily refreshing. All of the critics agreed on that point.*
When Rossellini saw this film, he began to dream great things; "This is how to work," he said, "in 16 mm; I've got some money, we're going to set up operations." For a year we dreamed with him.

*Rossellini was fascinated by* Jaguar, *especially the improvisational aspect.* I was equally fascinated by that. The film was shot without sound, and I asked Damouré and Lam to record a sound track at the screening. I thus discovered the possibility of doing an a posteriori commentary, that is, showing the actors their edited picture, which would serve to structure their discussion. The improvisation they did was fantastic.

*It's always that same magic of speech, of the birth of action that exercises its power on the viewer.*
Yes, but that might have been due to the use of the Bell and Howell camera, which, because it only had a twenty-second spring wind, forced us to do a rapid succession of images; and also because of the unified viewpoint resulting from the use of a single 25 mm lens. It was at that moment that I dreamed of shooting with synchronous sound. The idea was to be able to improvise the dialogue directly during filming; to do direct cinema. The film stayed asleep for a long time. When I had completed the sequel to *Jaguar,* entitled *Petit à Petit,* Braunberger decided to link them, given the good press it had received, and run *Jaguar* right after *Petit à Petit.* So, in effect, the film was finished in 1969, almost fifteen years after it was shot. *Jaguar* is my first feature-length film, it's my first fiction film, and it has marked me permanently. All the films I do now are always *Jaguar.* I would like to slightly correct your comment on money. Yes, they did have a casual

attitude about money, but these guys, upon their return, spend their whole fortune; in fact, they act like the bigshot, and later on, they'll get their return. Plus they acquired enormous prestige; they were kings of their village for two days. All the donation scenes are real; everything they gave to Ayorou was money they had really earned. Reality and fiction were continually intertwined.

*In* Moi, un Noir, *in 1957, your second feature-length film, you try to merge not only the action and commentary that people make on the world around them but also a sort of interpretation, seen from within, of the character who tries to reveal himself to himself.*
All of these films follow one another. After the research I did in Ghana, I undertook a similar investigation in Ivory Coast, in 1957, three years before their independence. I had shown *Jaguar* to the Nigerians of Abidjan, and they said, "What's going on in Treichville is even more interesting than what happened in Kumasi." So I got the idea to do a documentary on Treichville showing the contrast between Treichville during the week and Treichville on Saturday and Sunday. Then I met Oumarou Ganda, a docker in the port of Abidjan. We hired him as a statistical researcher on the immigration of Nigerians into Ivory Coast. We began filming the same way we did in *Jaguar*. But in *Jaguar* the actors played roles that were not their own, whereas here I found myself facing someone who was playing his own role, his own life. Thus was constructed this bizarre dialogue with truth, this autobiography on film. Filming entirely without sound, we recorded the commentary the same way we did for *Jaguar*.

Moi, un Noir *appeared in 1958 and received numerous prizes. I think the prestige of this film is due to the unsettling confession of its lead character, but also to its technical innovations.*
It's the first real feedback on the character who recounts his own story. What was important for me was that for the first time, an African spoke on film. I thought of doing the premiere in Treichville itself, but it was impossible. So this film came out in France. It was the era of the Nouvelle Vague. Everything seemed possible for the young French cinema. For example, the sequence in which Oumarou Ganda talks about his war in Indochina was edited without any cutaways or connecting shots. It was an old taboo shattered.

*The liberties that you took resulted in the discovery of new modes of expression, which were later adopted by Godard and Truffaut and are now a part of cinematographic language.*
I had been obliged by constraints to break taboos, to commit sacrileges.

The best result of this film was the discovery made by Oumarou Ganda: having discovered the power of film, he decided several years later to make his own.

La pyramide humaine *is your third feature-length film, shot in Abidjan in 1958 to 1959.*

After *Moi, un Noir,* and having been accused of filming only the lumpen-proletariat, I decided to shoot a new film in the same place, Abidjan, but chose this time the young elite: the senior class of the Cocodi High School. I was using a camera with an electric motor, which permitted me to make longer shots. I started filming scenes that took place outside the school during vacation. And before my very eyes, incredible things appeared: young blacks and whites discovering, all of a sudden, South Africa's apartheid, racism. They began to ask themselves questions about what they were, about their own relationships in class, about their identity; the film was a veritable provocation. The shooting of the second part of the film, the classroom scenes, required synchronous sound, which at that time involved heavy equipment and a large filming team. It was the first time I filmed with synchronous sound, and I discovered the difficulty of dialogues with direct sound.

*It is interesting to see how each time you run into difficulty of a technical nature, you react in a creative manner.*

For the first time I was sharing the filming with another cameraman, and I discovered that the images we made were different. Of course, I was there, but I was not my first spectator in the viewfinder. The young people were so wrapped up in the film that things were terrible. For example, the filming of the scene in which one of the actors disappears by drowning was a mixture of reality and fiction that made me wonder whether I had perhaps gone too far. This film played an important role for me; I felt that I could not continue to film with that technique if I always had to drag around four technicians. It was at this point that Edgar Morin reproached me for filming only in Africa and for not being interested in my own tribe, Parisians. We decided, in the summer of 1960, to make the film that would later be called *Chronicle of a Summer.* Having learned from the experience of *La pyramide humaine,* I absolutely had to have a light, portable camera that would permit synchronous-sound recording. After a month of filming with the same enormous equipment, I asked the producer to call in a Canadian cameraman who was a specialist in handheld camerawork, Michel Brault. We negotiated with an engineer from Eclair, A. Coutant, to build a camera prototype whose functions would be fully discovered only as we were filming. For the first time we used clip-on lavaliere microphones, and the actors carried their own tape recorders. Thus, in a certain sense, we made the first experimental feature-length film. The idea that sums up this experience is the following: you can film anything anywhere.

*This film is the result of technical inventions, but it is equally the result of psychosociological experiments led by Edgar Morin. The discovery of "commensality," that is to say, the idea that people loosen up and talk when they are sitting around a table. How was the choice of actors made?* It was Edgar Morin's little world. At the beginning I didn't have a very good idea of where we were headed. I was discovering my tribe; I was discovering a society that I knew nothing about, like an anthropologist. They would never have said what they did if the camera hadn't been there. From the moment when we could walk in the street, when the camera was free, the actors themselves were free; they could tell stories and carry us along beyond all limits. This film, edited by its images, was a great victory thanks to the arrival of Michel Brault. We all learned from him. From the point of view of editing, we were forced to invent systems so as to maintain the coherence of all the elements we had at our disposal, for an hour and a half. We discovered that we could cut in the middle of a shot, that we could shorten sentences. Before this film, that was unthinkable! With the ciné-eye and the ciné-ear, we recorded in sound and image a *ciné-vérité,* Vertov's kinopravda. This does not mean the cinema of truth, but the truth of cinema. I have never again made films the way I did before. At last we had a technique; we knew how to proceed. It was the "pencil-camera" that you sharpen and write with whenever you want, as much as you can, and wherever you want.

La Goumbé des jeunes noceurs *is the last film that was made in Ivory Coast. What does* "goumbé" *mean?*
*"Goumbé"* is the name of a drum. The "young debauchees' *goumbé"* is an association of young people like the "royal *goumbé,"* previously filmed in *Moi, un Noir.* I had been in touch with those groups of musicians and dancers who organized street dances every Saturday and Sunday evening in Abidjan. The basis of the music is a square drum, the *goumbé,* no doubt of Mandingo origin, and no doubt related to the black slave trade. The *goumbé* became the dance of displaced people. The *goumbé* of the young debauchees of 1965 was a *goumbé* of people who came from Upper Volta, among whom was an extraordinary musician, Sidili Doumbia, who is both a drummer and a singer. For me, this film is the first cinema experiment I was able to do with real synchronically

recorded sound. In it I discovered filming in "shot sequences," filming a sequence without any cuts. I was using a camera with an electric motor, which allowed me to film for three minutes; I could film a dance that lasted three minutes in real time. There is no cutting. It was editing in the movement, by which I tried to have the most effective point of view possible. In *Chronicle of a Summer* we had some long shots, but we didn't have that element because the dialogue was not worth recording for the entire length. In the *goumbé,* what unified the significance was this musical improvisation. This film marked the end of urban sociological cinema and at the same time the end of ponderous and deceiving statistical investigations. I wanted to go back to the bend of the Niger to use these new techniques to record traditional cultures in the process of disappearing or being transformed. One of my old projects was to complete the film *The Lion Hunters*. Begun in 1957, the filming took place over seven years. Every year I filmed, and the next year I returned with the film shot the previous year. It was a collective effort, realized with the hunters themselves, filmed half with synchronous sound.

*Is the prophecy that concludes the film imaginable?*
It's a poetic phrase, because while the hunters told about the hunt, the children fell asleep, maybe because they didn't feel involved. The son of Tahirou, the chief of the hunters, has grown up; he will not be a hunter.

*One of the most striking points in this film is the moment of preparation of the poison. Do they have a precise knowledge of poisons that can kill? Are there magical practices that accompany the preparation of poison?*
Yes, indeed! The poison is made from the fruit of a well-known tree, the strophantus, which is widely used in the majority of arrow poisons in Africa. The chemical technique is complemented by magic: the gestures of the preparation symbolize the death of the lion; the spells pronounced begin with the statement of the "initiation chain" through which his knowledge reaches the hunter. Then he addresses the divinities and the forces of the bush to make the poison effective; the poison takes effect in about twenty minutes. The poetic element is that the lion must die calmly and tranquilly. There is total complicity between the lion and the hunter. The hunter knows the lion; they know his name, they follow his tracks, they spot him. It's he whom the hunters dream about at night; it's a bit like the white whale in *Moby Dick*. And very likely the lion also knows the hunter. These rare relations between man and nature make what is called "animism" understandable. They speak to the lion, and he responds. It is the hero put to death, and the hero is the lion.

## The Dogon

*Nineteen forty-eight was the year of your first encounter with the Dogon, an encounter that would open a whole series of contacts and filming that continue until the present time. From 1951 to 1952 you filmed* Cimetière dans la falaise, *a film that illustrates a funeral ceremony.*
Marcel Griaule and Germaine Dieterlen were working in the Bandiagara cliffs. Griaule, my professor and thesis adviser, asked me to do a film on the life of the Dogon during the rainy season, on culture, and so forth. Roger Rosfelder and I were doing this work when a young Ireli man was drowned in a stream swollen by the rains. It was my first experience, and an overwhelming one, with the Dogon funerary rituals.

*This film has a double interest. The solemn beauty of the ritual on the one hand, and on the other, your enchantment with something that irresistibly recalls scenes of baroque imagery.*
In the courses that Marcel Griaule gave in 1941 at the Musée de l'Homme, there was one magic word: the cliff of Bandiagara. This cliff was associated with the masks of the Dogon, which had unleashed a real artistic frenzy in the 1930s. To discover this place, especially in the rainy season, was something strange and above all very different from all the other terrains I was familiar with up to that point. I began to film the countryside. And then the accident happened. Rosfelder and I had tried to cover the event, but at that time I had a spring-wound camera, limiting shots to twenty seconds. And, for example, it took maybe a minute to bring the cadaver up to the cemetery cave. Every time I rewound the spring in my camera, I changed my viewing angle a bit, just a little bit. Then during the editing, I had no choice but to leave the sequences end to end, even keeping the flash frame at the beginning of each as a sort of cutaway link between shots. It was a bit of a breaking with taboos, from the point of view of cinematographic language, but in the end it worked, because at that moment the essence was more important than the form.

*Does the fact that they are buried there in the cave have some symbolic significance?*
That signifies one thing: the dead from one village are all in one place, they can talk to each other, they exist. At the same time it is a way to protect them from termites, from burrowing animals, from the rain. There was, on my part, an attempt at symbolic interpretation by using elements of the landscape, stone, water, and wind, to express what I felt to be so beautiful

in the appearance of the ceremony, yet so mysterious in spite of all the book-learned knowledge I had about the funerary rites of the Dogon.

*The films that we are going to see now deal with the same ethnic group, the Dogon. How many of them are there, more or less?*
There are about 250,000 Dogon. They settled in the cliffs inside the bend of the Niger River, south of Timbuktu. They speak a Mandingo language; they are originally from Mande. They left the Mandingo mountains in about the fifteenth century, probably after the expansion of Islam, and went back toward the north, to about one thousand kilometers from their place of origin.

*But what, then, is the reason for so much attention given to this group?*
As you could see in the film, the cliff is practically impregnable, and the Dogon found a natural refuge there, which for centuries permitted them to escape influences from the outside. The main idea was to record rituals that were threatened with extinction or radical transformation. When Griaule went to Bandiagara in 1931, he collected oral reports of the Sigui ceremonies that took place in 1910, ceremonies that had never been observed by an outsider. He had brought back a marvelous collection of masks; he had collected texts in *sigi so,* the ritual language of the Sigui; he had filmed a *Dama.* In 1964 and 1965, when I was working with Germaine Dieterlen, we heard for the first time about the approach of the Sigui ceremonies. We knew that it is a commemoration of the invention of death and speech. We also knew that the beginning of the manifestation would take place in Yougo-Dogorou. When in 1966 we went to check on the village, it was empty except for a couple of old people, some women, and some children. The young men were working in Ghana or in Ivory Coast. The supreme religious chief, the Hogon of Arou, confirmed for us the imminence of the ceremonies and, remembering Griaule, authorized us to film them.

*Is the Hogon you mention both a religious and civil leader?*
No, it seems that there is no political leader; it is a society without a state. The Hogon is a religious leader, designated by divination upon the death of the predecessor. He lives in permanent contemplation; he is the witness of all the rituals. In 1967, upon our arrival in Yougo, the village was full. All the men from Ivory Coast and southern Ghana had come back to participate in the Sigui ceremonies. The last Sigui had taken place in 1907, and we were familiar with the schema of the ritual, thanks to the oral traditions collected by Griaule in 1931. The Sigui is observed by all men under the age of sixty, that is to say, all those who have not yet seen the Sigui, but

under the direction of the old men who are over sixty and who participated in the previous Sigui.

*Can you define, in a few words, the aim of this ceremony that takes place every sixty years?*
I'll answer as the Dogon do: you have to see it in its entirety to know what it means. It's an itinerant ritual that takes place every sixty years, and when we began to film it, we knew neither exactly how long it lasted (four to eight years) nor its progression (east to west).

The ceremonies of this first Sigui, *L'enclume de Yougo*, unfolded in three Yougo villages: Yougo-Dogoru, Youg-Na, and Youg-Pilou. Our team was composed of Germaine Dieterlen, Gilbert Rouget, soundman Guindo Ibrahim, and myself behind the camera. At that time I was working on the Songhay; all I wanted to be on the cliff of Bandiagara was a filmmaker. I was not planning to film all of the Siguis, but then, year by year, I was forced to abandon that attitude of the eye that watches without understanding, and our cinematographic collaboration became a real team research effort. The next year we went to Tyogou, a village of the plains. Whereas in Yougo the men were mostly naked from the waist up, here they wore dazzling sashes and cowrie shells. After having followed their procession to visit the sites of ancient villages, we came back to the village for the grand assemblage in the square where the dances took place one after the other. Another new element was the presence of a little girl, the Yasigine "the sister of Sigui," carried on her father's shoulder to represent the community of the women in the midst of the community of men. Something had stunned me in what Griaule had said. He said that in the Sigui, they carved and painted a great mask, the mother of all masks, which is never worn and represents the first dead ancestor who was reborn in the form of a serpent. In Tyogou, it was in front of the cave of the masks, recently carved in the form of a serpent with a tail like a bird's head, but totally unpainted. In the neighboring cave there were three large masks, those from the Sigui in 1908, in 1848, and in 1788.

This second film is called *Les danseurs de Tyogou* because the dance in it plays a primordial role. I had no idea what to say about the great mask. Germaine and I had no explanation. It was while I was editing this second film that I began to see the differences from the first film. I was still determined to do a third one before sending someone else to film in my place. When I arrived in Bongo in 1969 for the third year of the Sigui, the people of Bongo knew that I had drunk the millet beer the previous year in Tyogou and the year before that in Yougo, so I was considered a part of the Sigui. The oldest man in the village, Anaï Dolo, had been Griaule's informant and considered me like his son. He gave me authorization to go into the initiation cave before the end of the retreat. In the first films I had been an outside observer. Here I had a totally different position; I could go wherever I wanted. I made friends with one of the *olubaru*, the dignitaries who were being initiated. They showed me, above the cave of the circumcision, the carved and painted mask of Bongo. At night, accompanied by the roaring of bullroarers spun by the new dignitaries, the new masks of the four villages of Bongo were leaned up against the cave. In the morning everyone could see them: these four masks represented Dyongou Sérou, the first dead ancestor, restored to life in the form of a serpent. This extraordinary ceremony was placed under the patronage of the oldest man in Bongo, Anaï Dolo, who, as I learned later, was then witnessing his third Sigui, which means that he was at least 120 years old.

In 1970, after *La caverne de Bongo* was finished, I took it back to the cliff of Bandiagara, and I showed it to the people of Bongo. It was the first time they saw it. They started to cry because since the preceding year, several people had died. They asked us not to show the women the sequence about the bullroarers, so we put a hand over the lens during that section of the film. I had decided to film the fourth Sigui, in Amani. But I had to ask the Pale Fox for authorization. We therefore had a confrontation, which means we asked the Fox questions on a divination table. The response was favorable.

*This fourth film,* Les clameurs d'Amani, *reveals to us the fundamental myth of the Dogon. Were you aware of the existence of this myth during the three preceding films?*
Yes. Griaule and Germaine Dieterlen had worked on this myth, which is the story of the creation of the world, where singular relations arise between the word and death. We also knew that the men of Amani were the best specialists in *sigi so,* the ritual tongue of the Sigui. It was the first time that I saw a myth recounted in the ritual language by an aged priest. Maybe half of the spectators understood what he was saying, and those who heard without understanding, if they wanted to know more about it, had to go ask the old man to explain, and thus would begin their true initiation. When we arrived in Amani in 1970, the old men who had done the Sigui in 1910 pointed out the route that the procession was supposed to take. They remembered the route so well that they were in the process of knocking down walls that had been built within the last sixty years, because the Sigui procession had to follow exactly the route it had followed sixty years earlier. In Amani there was a mask, but it had been painted the year before. It thus seemed that the mask was connected to a certain year of the Sigui and that

the annual ritual was not simply the repetition of rituals of the previous years. Here there were no cowrie shells as there had been in Bongo, but double sashes worn across the chest. It was while I was making this film, and especially while editing it, that I realized that there was no relation between the four Siguis that we had just seen, and that each one represented something different. But we didn't know exactly what. The next year, 1971, we were in Idyeli, a village at the base of the cliff, near a permanent spring whose gardens came to die in the sand of a high dune. At Idyeli there was no mask, it had not been brought out; the dignitaries were not in a cave but in a straw shelter at the entrance to the village, facing the dune, which was to play an essential role. One night we heard the sound of the bull-roarers, and the next morning the village was completely empty. The men over sixty who had remained in the village gave us authorization to rejoin the men on the dune, because it was there that the Sigui was beginning.

For this fifth Sigui, *La dune d'Idyeli,* we spent the whole day on the empty dune without drinking or eating. In fact, the dune was dug full of burrows in which the men hid. They stuck their heads out like rabbits. In the shade of a tree, curled up in a fetal position next to their bullroarers, slept the dignitaries, the *olubaru*. They were waiting for the wakening, for birth. Around three in the afternoon, an old man came from the village, and the *olubaru* turned to the bullroarers. The old man cried out in *sigi so,* and all of a sudden the entire dune was covered with people. New men came out of their placentas of sand, and accompanied by the bullroarers, they went back to the village in procession. They washed and dressed themselves; it was the birth of a new generation. We had never seen this. This had nothing to do with what had happened in the other villages. I was sure now that we were following year by year the essential sequences of the myth. We had to go on. To film the sixth Sigui, *Les pagnes de Yamé,* in 1972, I was prepared to go anywhere. It took place on the plateau, in Yamé, a village that was already strongly Islamized. There the men who came from the neighboring villages dressed up as women. Some even wore their sashes. It was the year of the mothering of the new generation. The most dramatic moment of the ceremony was when the men lined up facing one of the old men who said, in *sigi so,* "The Sigui has come from the east, he has come on the wings of the wind." The men turned toward the east, then toward the west, and they waited a moment, then they turned back toward the east. I spent a long time trying to understand what that meant; that the Sigui had arrived at his western boundary. They had turned in the direction where traditionally the Sigui was supposed to go the next year, but where he would not go because of Islam.

So the men of Yamé went to take millet beer to the villages, to let the faithful ones who could no longer make the great ritual drink from it. The seventh ceremony in 1973 was supposed to take place in Songo, between Bandiagara and Mopti, in thoroughly Islamized country. Amadigné Dolo, the chief of the masks in the village of Sangha, came that same year to work with us in Paris, on the first six films. We then learned that the most important moment in our fortunes had been the divination in the fourth year, before the voyage to Amani, because that would be our fourth Sigui, and no one had ever seen more than three Siguis. We began to build hypotheses: the six Siguis represented six very different successive sequences of the myth. The first Sigui is the fall of the anvil, it's the death of the first ancestor, it's the ritual that immediately follows death. It's like in the *Cimetière dans la falaise.* The second Sigui, the dance in the square with the mask that has not yet been painted, is the funeral dance with the dancers of Tyogou. The third Sigui, where the masks are painted, decorated, is the *Dama.* It's the fabrication of the masks, identical to the one that is done every five years. In the *Dama* the ancestors are represented by the masks, as they were on that day by the great serpent mask representing the first dead ancestor. So the first year is death; the second year, the funeral, that is to say, the soul of the dead man is entrusted to the spirit of the water; a mask is made in every village, but it is not painted. The third year, in the *Dama,* the masks enchant the soul of the dead man so that it begins its journey to the hereafter. The fourth year, the word and the dance of the serpent, is procreation; it's the preparation of a new generation. The fifth year is birth, the men come out of their dune-placenta, go wash themselves and dance, a new generation is born. The sixth year, everyone is dressed like a woman, it's the mothering, the child is in his mother's arms. Thus one last element was lacking, the circumcision, which was to take place in the seventh year in Songo. 1973 was a big drought year in Mali. The government forbade us to film and photograph all the ceremonies. So we came back the next year, in 1974, to film a reconstruction of what had happened the year before. The *olubaru* of Yamé, dressed in normal Dogon attire, went to Songo and sacrificed a goat at the foot of the cliff where the paintings are located. Then they went to touch up these paintings. Next they went to Yougo to have their gourds filled with the millet beer prepared there. The cycle was completed, the serpent was biting its tail, it could all begin again sixty years later. Symbolically they made the Sigui: the sacrifice was to purify them so that they could go on to finish this seven-year chain. Thus, in seven hours, I filmed the event they had made the previous year. With three Dogon, we went to the cave of Songo. They began to tell of the paintings, what they represented. I had confirmation of the fact that there were indeed seven different years that represented seven different episodes of the adventure of the death of the first ancestor, and then they took off across the Dogon country singing these marvelous songs: "The Sigui has come on the wings of the wind, the Sigui has left on the wings of the wind."

*Are there initiations? Lessons? Somebody who explains to them what they're supposed to do?*
The ancient ones are there. There are always people who are older than sixty, who have seen the previous Sigui. Every sixty years every village reproduces what happened sixty years earlier.

*Is there a reason why all of this is repeated every sixty years?*
The reason given in the myth is that they had done a Sigui for the first dead ancestor, and then the second one died sixty years later. They decided to do the same thing for the second that they had done for the first. It is the length of a human lifetime. What we have just seen is the transition from one "century" to another, the transmission of knowledge from one generation to another, every sixty years. And being sure that there will be survivors, we are sure that the knowledge of this new generation will be passed on to the next, and so on until the end of the world. The adventure of a village community; all the males from age two to age fifty-nine all dressed alike, all drinking beer, and so on.

*Where does the presence of the Fox come in?*
It comes in the dances. The kick that they give is kicking the Fox. Because for order to exist, disorder is necessary; that's the Fox, master of disorder. The Sigui follows a route from year to year, a serpentine line from the top of the cliff to the bottom, if you will. The Sigui follows for seven years a route that looks like the pattern the dancers follow for three days when they come into the village square. These films pose many questions. One of the most important is that the Dogon themselves never see more than three Sigui. So we are preparing a film synthesis that will break this taboo for Dogon spectators. It's a question of transmitting knowledge that goes beyond the rules of classical ethnology. Maybe if, in the history of the Dogon, one of them had followed all the Siguis, it would have resulted in tremendous disorder. Maybe it's that once the global knowledge of these separate knowledges would be transformed into a power that might truly regroup the Dogon under one single commandment, Dogon society would become the Dogon state. With the knowledge diffused, power too is diffused. But these are still hypotheses. The next stage is the two films on death rituals that have presented us with the final questions. In 1972, when we were filming the sixth Sigui, *Les pagnes de Yamé,* we learned that the funeral of Anaï Dolo, the oldest man in Bongo, who had died six months earlier, was

going to take place. There are three essential ceremonies after the death of a man: the burial in the cemetery, the funeral that takes place six months after death, and the fabrication of new masks and their dance, the *Dama*.

*What is the significance of the statue that is on the terrace in* Funérailles à Bongo: Le vieil Anaï?
That signifies that the dead man himself is presiding over his own funeral. The dead man was placed in the funeral cave. They washed away the stains of physical death. The soul does not leave the village during the six months between death and the funeral. It remains on the terrace of his house. At the funeral, the dead man is asked to leave, so he presides for one last time over the great ritual. Before him, before the statue, the men mimic one of the great events of his life: the 1895 battle against the French army, in the course of which Anaï had been wounded. The little group in the center of the dance circle represents the Dogon; all the men going around them carrying guns represent the French army. In the end, Anaï is wounded. It is his great-grandson who plays his role; he falls and takes one last shot with his gun. When the combat ends, everyone sings the praises of all the combatants. The next day the statue is taken down from the terrace. This means that the soul of Anaï may begin to leave. One evening, one of the members of his family, the oldest man in the village, recites the *tégues* of Anaï—his ritual slogans, which are all at the same time the sayings of God, the adventure of the creation of the world, the history of the Dogon, and the portrait of Anaï himself. I filmed this sequence with a spotlight attached to my camera and with a pressurized gas lantern. Unsure whether or not we'd get a picture, we translated the text. I illustrated it, sentence by sentence, by going to film all the places that were mentioned. The dead man would be ready to leave the village after one last ceremony on the public square. Another mannequin, made of wicker wrapped in a blanket, is placed on a litter. It represents the first dead man on his litter made of antelope horns. "The first ancestor must be buried." Now Anaï is going to rejoin the spirit of the waters in the pond, where he will await the next ritual, the *Dama*. At this point, mourning is provisionally lifted; normal activities may be resumed in the village.

*This transition from a human time to mythical time is fascinating!*
Yes. He has to get back to the first ancestor. They don't do this for everyone who dies, just as they only enact the battle with the French for the last survivors. There will be one more in Bongo, for Anaï's little brother who

was six or seven years old when the French arrived. He's the old man who is telling Anaï's story.

*And every time they will evoke the mythical time?*
If it's a *Moulouno* or if it's a mask chief, it will be evoked as far back as Diongou Serou, the first ancestor, whom we saw represented in the form of a serpent, who was the first dead man and thus was the one for whom the first rituals were performed. I made the end of the film by filming the great-great-grandson of Anaï, who had been designated to be his *nani,* his "correspondent." Anaï is dead, his soul is in the pond, but someone in the village must assure him of a good journey toward the land of the dead in the coming years; that is the *nani*'s role. The next film, *Ambara Dama,* was shot in 1974, after filming the last Sigui. It dealt with one of the great ceremonies described by Marcel Griaule, a *Dama,* a giant mask celebration. This *Dama* was given for one of Griaule's first collaborators, Ambara Dolo, who died in 1971. The *Dama* is a very complicated ceremony that closes the Dogon mourning period. After the funeral, the soul of the dead man leaves the village and stays nearby, in the pond. There it discovers the other dead men. But they come back to walk around the village. After a certain period, the village is crowded every night with these wandering souls. Thus it is necessary to make them leave the village. Every five years the village is cleared of these marauding souls, and a *Dama* is organized, a mask celebration. *Dama* means "dangerous thing," "forbidden thing." Marcel Griaule, in his thesis, had minutely described some ceremonies at Sangha, and when I began filming in the same village forty years later, I saw exactly what he had described. The only way to do a commentary was to take Griaule's very texts. The *Dama* represents the way in which the men "enchant" the souls of the dead with the mask dances so as to lure them far away, but at the same time it represents the contagion of death, because the rituals are so beautiful that men want to die so that these seductive ceremonies will continue to be practiced. Ambara was the first informant who worked with Griaule and Germaine Dieterlen. He was the one we had followed for days and days in the caverns. He was one of those who could read the signs of the paintings, who told the great picture book of the paintings in the caves. He had participated in the Sigui at Yougo-Dogourou in 1908, so he was born between 1900 and 1904. He died at the age of seventy.

The Dogons are probably the last ones, as a result of their isolation, to have preserved these ancient systems of masked representations. We must go back to the myth: the inventor of the masks was the Pale Fox, the

master of disorder. He had stolen seeds from the testicles of God, his father, in order to plant them. God, furious, decided to get rid of him. But
the spirit of the water, master of order and fertility, made a tree grow, the
*sa* tree. The Fox discovered that the bark of the *sa* becomes red when it is
removed. The first masks were made by the Fox when he discovered the
red fibers. He said to himself, "I am stronger than my father. God is dead."
He went back up onto the terrace and danced to his father's death with a
mask made from the red *sa* fiber. But God was not dead, and he chastised
the fox: he tore out his larynx, spun him around like a rhombus, and he
became the Fox. But he's the one who invented the first mask. These masks
represent the passage from fire, from the sun, from something astonishing
to something fresh, to the total purification of the souls that leave by following these scarlet masks, which are, as Ogotemmêli said, dancing pieces
of the sun. The red masks are made every five years. They are prepared
three or four months before the date chosen for the *Dama*. All of the old
masks are abandoned except for the mother of masks, the great Sigui
mask, which is remade every sixty years. The mask represents the myth.
The dances have no connection with the Sigui dances; all the people are
different. The mask wearers are anonymous. The Ambara *Dama* in 1974
was an exact replica of the *Dama* of the hunter Manzon observed by
Griaule in 1935. This showed us the mask society's total conservation
of such an important ritual.

*Behind the mask there is someone who must remain in secret.*
Yes, and the mask is a dangerous thing. The mask is something that can enchant death, and enchanting the souls of the dead is the same as enchanting
the souls of the living, making them disappear. According to the myth, this
*Dama,* invented by the master of disorder, became so fascinating that the
people of the village of Sangha, who were immortal, bought a cadaver so
that they could have a marauding soul and so that they could enchant it
with these marvelous dances. But from that point on, they began to die.
Art is a fatal seduction. That's why the *Dama* is dangerous.

*The beauty of a ritual can render it universally intelligible.*
Yes, but you cannot explain this beauty if you do not know the myth. The
myth is there, it is underlying, but you do not understand it. The last part
of the funeral rituals begins on the next day when the soul leaves the village and goes toward the abode of the dead in Manga. The *nani* or "corre-
spondents" of the dead accompany them along the way and go off from
time to time to bring them food. The Dogon say that it takes sixty years
to properly make the journey of the dead.

*This idea of death slowly dissolving is one of the most beautiful poetic transpositions that man's creativity has ever conceived. We talk of memory, oblivion! They say it is there, it is moving away, so you have to push it gently.*

The soul has left, but the vital force remains in the paintings, which take on new masks, and which will give a bit of Ambara's vital force to all the masks to come. So this is the great course of the Dogon funeral rituals. When I saw these films again with Germaine Dieterlen, we realized that we had approached the problem backward. Until that point, what we had done for almost thirty years was to amass cinematographic documentation in considerable quantity—a bunch of analyses of rituals that we had attempted to explicate and comment on according to the corresponding Dogon myths. What we now have to do is try to tell the myth while illustrating it, in particular with the corresponding rituals. And it was no doubt indispensable, when faced with such a complicated myth, to start with these slightly naive analyses of the rituals, because this permitted us to better understand a particularly complex myth. We have already begun to shoot the first pictures of this film, which will probably be called *Le renard pâle (The Pale Fox),* and which begins at the very beginning of the world, when there was nothing, neither earth, nor air, nor water, nor fire, nothing but a grain seed, denser than you can imagine. And then comes the explosion.

▶ ——————————————————————————————

**The Fictions**

*The fundamental element of the three films,* Petit à Petit, *made in 1969,* Cocorico, Monsieur Poulet, *made in 1974, and* Babatou, les trois conseils, *made in 1977, is the presence of the characters you've been following since the beginning, and who have played a fundamental role in your work. Who are they?*

Damouré Zika, a Sorko fisherman whom I met in 1941 on the Niger River, introduced me into the circle of fishermen through his grandmother. Lam Ibrahima Dia went down the river with us in a canoe, in 1946 and 1947. Tallou Mouzourane joined our team during *Bataille sur le grand fleuve.*

*So here are three characters who correspond to three completely different personalities: three faces, three different ways of behaving, and probably three different ethnic groups.*

Damouré is Sorko, Lam is Peul, Tallou is Bella.

*Do you think there is any analogy between these three characters and those of the commedia dell'arte? Those typical characters, those masks, they facilitate the elaboration of plots, of canvases that can be infinitely multiplied.*

In fact, Damouré and Lam have been in other films, those of Moustapha Alassane and those of Oumarou Ganda, and they always play the same role: themselves.

*The three have another element in common: improvisation. In the commedia dell'arte, the characters, by knowing each other so well, learn to polish up their linguistic craft. Does this happen in the same way?*

No, because there's more than just language. There are gestures, action, and above all, what does not exist in the commedia dell'arte is the director who improvises his staging. We never know the story before we start filming. When we filmed *Cocorico, Monsieur Poulet,* those were real episodes of the trip, for example, real car breakdowns that served as the basis for our improvisation. This was how we had made *Jaguar,* and we proceeded in the same fashion for *Petit à Petit.*

*In* Petit à Petit, *there was something beyond the invention of the accidents; there was a deliberate theme. The theme of an African confronting a Western situation.*

In fact, there was no theme: in reality Damouré came to Paris to do an internship for UNESCO. That was how we got to film Damouré in Paris. Here again we could not do a documentary. So we had decided to do a sequel to *Jaguar:* the society of *"Petit à petit l'oiseau fait son bonnet,"* created in *Jaguar* by Damouré, Lam, and Illo, becomes important and sends its president, Damouré, to see how people live in multistory houses, because they want to build a skyscraper in Ayorou. That was our only starting point.

*That's really all you knew?*

No, we had decided at the outset that Damouré and Lam would not agree to play businessmen unless they could abandon everything at the end of the film; just as in *Jaguar* they only went to Gold Coast on the condition that they be able to give away all their gains when they got back. So we left for Ayorou, where we had created a fictitious import-export business, and then Damouré, the director, takes the plane to Paris. All this was really filmed at that moment. Then filming stopped. Damouré began his internship at UNESCO and, at the same time, discovered Paris all by himself. During *Jaguar,* he had written a travel journal (*Mystérieux et dommages d'affaires,* published at the NRF); in the same way, he kept a journal of his life in Paris. It was an explorer's log, a precise rendering of a cruel voyage to wonderland. Starting with this text, we built our story. There are two versions of this film. One that lasts four and one-half hours, and the other that came out in the theaters, lasting an hour and one-half.

*What was the Africans' reaction to this film?*
Their reaction was pretty hostile. The end of the film was a total misunderstanding. It was a question not of backing up but only of taking time to stop and think. The film was a really popular success in African theaters.

Cocorico, Monsieur Poulet, *the film that enjoyed the greatest success . . .*
That was perhaps the most fun film to make. We wanted to show how a chicken dealer (Lam's actual profession at the time) lives. The whole film unfolded in a bizarre way because we were overwhelmed by incidents in the improvisation. Lam's car had no brakes, no headlights, and no registration. It was really a patience-mobile that forced us to stop when we least expected. The introduction of the character of the devil of the bush came up in Lam's reflections when we broke down. "Let's not stop here," he said every time the car refused to go on, "there are devils here!" The entire story was improvised step by step as we filmed.

*In the film there is an extraordinary element—the constant dismantling and rebuilding of the car. There hasn't been a thing like this on film since Charlie Chaplin.*
That car should never have been on the road! There were no special effects; the dismantling of the car was effectively carried out in one day. The first river crossing, underwater, was Lam's idea; the second, in the tarp, was mine; and the third, where we used the air tanks as floaters, was Damouré's idea.

Babatou, les trois conseils *is your latest feature-length film. It too was realized with the help of some of your old collaborators.*
The idea was to make a film that was both historical and at the same time a son of *Jaguar.* When we studied the migrations from 1951 to 1961, we learned that these southward migrations had been started in the middle of the last century by a great expedition of conquerors, the Zarma and the Songhay, who had come from central Niger. Gazari, Alphahano, and Babatou were the legendary leaders of these wars in the Gurunsi lands (in the northwest part of modern-day Ghana). At the time of the European conquest, Babatou fought the French, the British, and the Germans in turn. Within the framework of the wars of the Babatou, we have placed the story of the three counsels, which is one of the Oriental tales that has

spread widely throughout black Africa. An old man exchanges a captive for three essential pieces of advice: "If you arrive in a village at sunset, go no farther, stop there; if you arrive at the edge of a river in spate, wait until the water goes down before crossing; if you get angry at night, wait until morning before doing anything."

In making this film, we considered the question of language: should the actors speak French or an African tongue? The warriors of Babatou, when they were in the Gurunsi lands, had to use a lingua franca, Dioula, which was in fact something like the broken French spoken in this film, but which many West Africans can understand without subtitles. Relations with women were probably like this. These people had a great number of wives, and the children who were born belonged neither to one nor to the other, neither to the father's family nor to the mother's. There is even an ethnographic section in this film, a traditional warrior's burial. I asked a *Zima,* an animistic priest, to reconstruct the ceremony through which the soul of the dead is allowed to remain on earth to protect the living. He made the ritual sacrifice, but of course, the cadaver was fake. The film has not yet been distributed. It was selected for the Cannes Festival in 1978. I showed it in Niamey. At the end of the screening, as always happens in Africa, the viewers discussed the film and figured out the moral. It was a child who discovered the moral. He said, "I'd say that the moral is that you should follow the advice of your elders, but not too much!"

▶

## The Creative Trance

When Rouch reviewed the text of his oral interview with Enrico Ful-chignoni, he decided to add a written conclusion. A portion of this added text comes from his essay "On the Vicissitudes of the Self," which appears in its entirety in part 1 of this collection.—*Ed.*

One of the essential parts of the work I have been able to do is the research on the phenomena of possession. *Yenendi: The Rainmakers* is the third film that I directed. It's a rain ritual, filmed in Simiri in 1951 and 1952. You see how men, possessed by the rain genies, speak in the name of these divinities of nature and make a contract about the upcoming rainy season. This was the first attempt to show the phenomena of possession, to show the trances as we saw them in *Les maîtres fous. Tourou et Bitti, les tambours d'avant,* on the same subject, possession, was made thirty years later in the same village of Simiri. It's a ritual that takes place before the rainy season to ask the spirits of the bush to protect the coming harvest against locusts and against curses. These two films show what cinematographic technique has become today. In the first there are very short shots with an impersonal ethnographic narration that tries to explain the ritual and to illustrate it with the arrival of the rain. In the second one, I used a ten-minute shot sequence that I started five minutes before the essential event, the possession trance. It is done in real time. In these two films, the same characters appear. The woman who is possessed by the rainbow in the first film is the priestess of the harvest in the second. Douada Sorko, the priest of the second ritual who speaks with the spirit of the bush, is the same person we see in the first film wearing a colonial helmet and shaking a hatchet with bells on it. When I filmed the second ritual, I myself was in a sort of trance that I call a ciné-trance, the creative state, which allowed me to follow very closely the person who was about to be initiated. The camera played the role of a ritual object. The camera becomes a magic object that can unleash or accelerate the phenomena of possession because it leads the filmer onto paths he would never have dared to take if he did not have it in front of him, guiding him to something that we scarcely understand: cinematographic creativity. I wrote an essay in 1971 about the film *Tourou et Bitti,* dealing with the vicissitudes of the person of the possessed, of the magician, of the sorcerer, of the filmmaker, and of the ethnographer. It seemed to me in particular that the individual observer who confronted the phenomena of possession, of magic and sorcery, merited critical examination himself. It is necessary to state my position, within the limits of my current knowledge, on the Songhay-Zarma theory of the person in the crisis of possession, founded on the notion of a "double," or *bia,* who represents shadow, reflection, and the soul, all at the same time.

The elements of this are the temporary substitution of the person by the spirit's double (or by the spirit itself); the conservation of the substituted double in a fresh skin of protection; the role of music and dance as the call of the spirit or of the double of a spirit who is not yet incarnate. One could say that every man has a double, a *bia* who lives in a copy of the world, in the domain of spirits, the masters of the forces of nature, the permanent domain of the imaginary, temporary domain of magicians or of sorcerers. This reflection of the world does not seem to go beyond the limits of the earthly world; it does not flow into the world beyond which is ruled by God. Between the real world and its double, connections are possible either through the incarnation of spirits in the course of possession dances, or by a magician's trance, or by the materialization of the sorcerer during his hunt for other doubles. These two worlds, in the end, are so interpenetrative that it is almost impossible for the uninformed observer to distinguish the real from the imaginary in them. "I met Ali yesterday" can just as easily mean "I really met Ali yesterday" as "I dreamed about, I thought about, Ali yesterday." And when the observer gets used to this gymnastic, he disturbs the real as well as the imaginary.

In this universe of fragile mirrors, next to men or women who can with one clumsy motion unleash or stop the trance, the presence of the observer cannot be neutral. Whether he wants it or not, he himself is integrated into the general movement, and his slightest actions are interpreted with reference to this particular system of thought. All the people I film today are familiar with the camera and know what it is capable of seeing and hearing. They have also seen successive screenings of the films in the course of their editing. In fact, they react to this art of visual and sound reflection in the same way they react during the public art of possession or the private art of magic and sorcery. The person of the filmmaker is transformed before their eyes as he focuses on them. He no longer speaks except to shout such incomprehensible words as "roll" or "cut!" He no longer watches except through the intermediary of a strange appendage, a camera and its viewfinder, and he no longer listens except through the intermediary of a shotgun microphone.

Paradoxically it is thanks to all this equipment, thanks to this new type of behavior, that the filmmaker can be integrated into the ritual. This strange choreography, if it is inspired, renders the cameraman and his assistant, the soundman, not invisible but actually participants in the ceremony in process.

Thus, for the Songhay-Zarma, who are quite used to cinema, my person is altered before their eyes just as the person of the possession dancers is altered, to the point where it is the ciné-trance of one filming the real trance of the other.

We can go even further: isn't this image hunt comparable to the sorcerer's hunt for "doubles"? And the film that I keep with extraordinary care (darkness, low temperature, dryness) is a "packet of reflections," a "packet of doubles." If the camera can be considered a part of the bloody skin of protection, then sending the films off to distant laboratories can be considered, on the other hand, like the sorcerer's devouring of the double.

For me the analogy stops there, because the succession of operations is not explicitly handled in African mythologies. This "stolen" image comes back a couple of months later and, on the screen, comes back to life in an instant.

That's where I am at the moment in my thoughts about my role as taker and giver of doubles, of eater and then exhibitor of reflections, but I know this is a matter of research that could be relevant to shedding some light on the singular relations between ethnography and the ethnographer.

The port of Ayorou on market day (*Au pays des mages noirs*, 1946–1947).

Hippopotamus hunters spearing fish (*Chasse à l'hippopotame*, 1947).

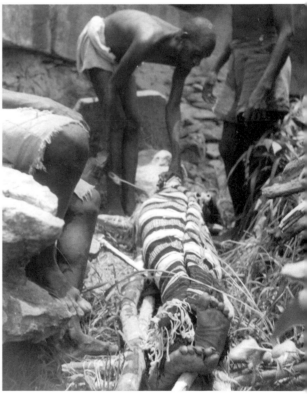

Dogon men preparing for the burial ritual (*Cimetière dans la falaise*, 1950).

Offering to the spirits during a rainmaking ceremony (*Les hommes qui font la pluie*, 1951).

Hippopotamus hunting on the Niger River (*Bataille sur le grand fleuve*, 1952).

Hunters' boats on the Niger River (*Bataille sur le grand fleuve*, 1952).

Possessed Hauka spirit in the body of his medium (*Les maîtres fous*, 1955).

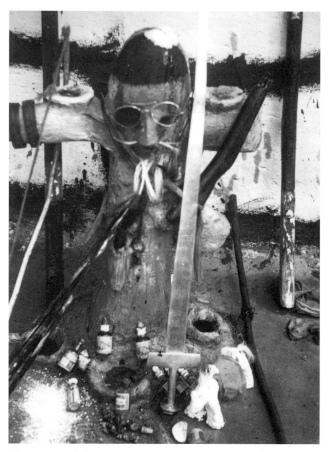

The statue of the governor-general (*Les maîtres fous*, 1955).

Oumarou Ganda as Edward G. Robinson (*Moi, un Noir,* 1958).

White and black students in the classroom (*La pyramide humaine*, 1959).

Students parting at the airport (*La pyramide humaine*, 1959).

One of the lion hunters (*The Lion Hunters*, 1957–1964).

Rouch and hunters on the trail (*The Lion Hunters*, 1957–1964).

Damouré, Lam, and Douma—the company of Petit à Petit (*Jaguar*, 1957–1967).

Angélo and Edgar Morin in conversation (*Chronicle of a Summer*, 1960).

Morin and Régis at the table (*Chronicle of a Summer*, 1960).

Michel Brault walking the camera (*Chronicle of a Summer*, 1960).

Rouch and Morin in the Musée de l'Homme (*Chronicle of a Summer*, 1960).

Dogon men's ritual dance (*Sigui 1: L'enclume de Yougo*, 1967).

Rouch filming with the Coutant Eclair NPR camera (*Petit à Petit*, 1968–1969).

Safi Faye driving in Paris (*Petit à Petit*, 1968–1969).

Rouch cues the microphone closer while filming Damouré and Lam (*Petit à Petit*, 1968–1969).

Damouré and Lam discuss the meaning of Paris (*Petit à Petit*, 1968–1969).

A Bugatti in Paris (*Petit à Petit*, 1968–1969).

Dogon *olubaru* dignitaries in the Sigui (*Sigui 4: Les clameurs d'Amani*, 1970).

A Dogon elder speaks *sigi so*, the ritual language (*Sigui 4: Les clameurs d'Amani*, 1970).

The drums *tourou* and *bitti* and the *godje* bowed lute (*Tourou et Bitti*, 1971).

Musicians and possessed medium (*Tourou et Bitti,*
1971).

Ritual rifle shots (*Funérailles à Bongo:*
*Le vieil Anaï, 1848–1971,* 1972).

Funerary cradle (*Funérailles à Bongo: Le vieil Anaï, 1848–1971,* 1972).

Village procession (*Sigui 6: Les pagnes de Yamé*, 1972).

Rouch in Mali filming ritual objects in the Dogon Sigui ceremonies, circa 1972.

Floating Lam's Citroën 2 CV across the river (*Cocorico, Monsieur Poulet*, 1974).

Cave paintings at Songo (*Sigui 7: L'auvent de la circoncision*, 1974).

Ritual dance of the Dogon *serige* masks (*Le Dama d'Ambara*, 1974).

Dogon dance procession with *serige* masks (*Le Dama d'Ambara*, 1974).

Rouch filming Damouré and Lam (*Babatou, les trois conseils,* 1975).

It is hardly possible for me to establish now the Songhay theory of the person of the filmmaker, but I will try to sketch a profile in the course of later films with the Zima, the Sorko, and the Sohantye who have collaborated for more than thirty years in my research. All I can say today is that in the field, the simple observer modifies himself. When he is working, he is no longer the one who greeted the old men at the edge of the village. To take up the Vertovian terminology, he is "ciné-ethno-watching," he "ciné-ethno-observes," he "ciné-ethno-thinks." Those who confront him modify themselves similarly, once they have placed their confidence in this strange habitual visitor. They "ethno-show" and "ethno-talk," and at best, they "ethno-think," or better yet, they have "ethno-rituals." It is this permanent "ciné-dialogue" that seems to me one of the interesting angles of current ethnographic progress: knowledge is no longer a stolen secret, later to be consumed in the Western temples of knowledge. It is the result of an endless quest where ethnographers and ethnographees meet on a path that some of us are already calling "shared anthropology."

▶

## The Staging of Reality and the Documentary Point of View of the Imaginary

In March 1981 Rouch decided to update his conclusion a second time. He wrote this text in Paris as his final thoughts on the interview.—*Ed.*

For me, as an ethnographer and filmmaker, there is almost no boundary between documentary film and films of fiction. The cinema, the art of the double, is already the transition from the real world to the imaginary world, and ethnography, the science of the thought systems of others, is a permanent crossing point from one conceptual universe to another; acrobatic gymnastics, where losing one's footing is the least of the risks.

In filming a ritual (for example, a possession dance among the Songhay, or a Dogon funeral), the filmmaker discovers a complex and spontaneous stage setting whose creator he most often knows nothing about. Is it the priest seated in his armchair, is it the nonchalant musician, is it the first dancer? He doesn't have time to look for this indispensable guide if he wants to record the spectacle that is beginning to unfold and cannot be stopped, as if animated by its own perpetual motion. So the filmmaker stages this reality like a director, improvising his shots, his movements or his shooting time, a subjective choice whose only key is his personal inspiration. And, no doubt, a masterpiece is achieved when this inspiration of the observer is in unison with the collective inspiration of what he is observing. But this is so rare, it demands such a connivance, that

I can only compare it to those exceptional moments of a jam session between Duke Ellington's piano and Louis Armstrong's trumpet, or fiery encounters between strangers that André Breton sometimes gives us accounts of. And though I may have succeeded in this sort of dialogue once in a while, for example in *Tourou et Bitti,* a shot sequence of a possession dance, I still have the taste of this effort in my mouth, and of the risk taken so as not to stumble, not to screw up my focus and lens setting, to be drifting as slowly as possible and then to suddenly fly with my camera as alive as a bird. Without that, everything had to start over, which is to say that everything was lost forever. And when, exhausted by this tension and this effort, Moussa Amidou put down his microphone and I my camera, we felt as though the attentive crowd, the musicians, and even those fragile gods who had haunted their trembling dancers in the interval, all understood the meaning of our research and applauded its success. And this is probably why I can only explain this type of mise-en-scène with the mysterious term "ciné-trance."

In the course of directing a fiction film, where everyone "acts," the same phenomenon occurs regularly if one applies the techniques of cinematographic reporting to the recording of the imaginary. In traditional cinema, this work is done a priori when the director makes his shooting script, trying to put on paper the series of images that would lead the viewer to follow a precise itinerary. And it suffices to refer to Einstein's scratch paper to discover the complexity of such a task (which the *cinéphiles* at the cinematheque follow in reverse, starting with the known and recognized work, and working back to the yet uncertain sources of the work). Then the same patient research must begin all over in the preparation of the sets and in the play of the actors, repeated a hundred times. I must say that I have always been astounded by this mole's task, which is supposed to end up in a film whose quality is meant to be, like true elegance, invisible. I am also thinking here of the American musical comedies that demand days and weeks of careful preparation to end up with five unforgettable minutes of a shot sequence of Gene Kelly dancing in the rain. It astounds me even more that I am totally incapable of doing the same.

The only possible way for me to approach fiction is to treat it the way I think I know how to treat reality. My golden rule is "one take," only one angle per shot, and everything filmed in chronological order. Inspiration now changes sides, it is no longer solely up to the filmmaker to improvise his shots and his movements, it is also up to the actors to invent the action that they are as yet unaware of, dialogues that are born of the preceding retort. This means that the atmosphere, the humor, and the caprices of this capricious little devil I call "grace" play an essential role in the reaction and interreaction, which can only be irreversible. Here again it is impossible to back up, impossible to not take into account all the hazards one meets on the way. Thus in *Cocorico, Monsieur Poulet* we gave up trying to foresee the thread of our story because the continual breakdowns of our star-vehicle modified the preplanned scenario at each instant.

But at the same time, what a joy it is, what a "ciné-pleasure" for those who are being filmed, or for the one who is filming. It's as though all of a sudden, anything is possible; to walk on water or take four or five steps in the clouds. So invention is continuous, and we had no other reason to stop than a lack of film or the mad laughter that made the microphones and cameras tremble dangerously.

And when the film was finished and Damouré, Lam, Tallou, and I discovered that our laughter was contagious and that the viewers shared our joy, we were happy as only madmen and children know how to be: we had succeeded in snatching a couple of feathers from the marvelous unknown bird, we had succeeded in *sharing our dreams*.

For me, there is no other way to make a film.

# JEAN ROUCH WITH JOHN MARSHALL AND JOHN W. ADAMS

## Les maîtres fous, The Lion Hunters, *and* Jaguar

Filmmaker John Marshall and anthropologist John W. Adams interviewed Jean Rouch in English in September 1977 at the Margaret Mead Film Festival at the Museum of Natural History in New York. They asked Rouch to present his story of the making of *Les maîtres fous, The Lion Hunters,* and *Jaguar.* At the time, these three films about Africa were Rouch's best-known works among North American students and teachers of anthropology. John W. Adams begins each section with a brief anthropological introduction to the films; Rouch's comments follow.—*Ed.*

▶

### Les maîtres fous

*Les maîtres fous* (1953) is perhaps the best-known film by Rouch. Within twenty minutes it shows some of the urban background of a possession cult known as the Hauka, then presents their biggest ceremony of the year, held on a Sunday in the suburbs of Accra, Ghana. There the "horses" are possessed by spirits of colonial administrators and enact a drama that becomes a reflection of that regime through the eyes of cult members. The film concludes with scenes of the "horses" the next day and contrasts their happiness and tranquillity on the job with the violence of the ceremony. It suggests that the ceremony is a form of catharsis. An early report, "Culte des génies chez les Sonray" (from *Journal de la Société des Africanistes* 15 [1945]: 15–32), became the basis for research that culminated in Rouch's doctoral dissertation, published in 1960 in Paris under the title *La religion et la magie Songhay.* These publications place the cult in the context of the traditional religion and show that it is a contemporary reworking within the colonial situation of themes and practices of the traditional religion. The film *Jaguar* shows more of the urban milieu within which the ceremony took place. (The reference under *Jaguar* also discusses the cult.) A review of *Les maîtres fous* was published in *American Anthropologist* 73 (1971): 1471–73.

I first came across the cult when I was doing a film on hippopotamus hunting among the Sorko *(Bataille sur le grand fleuve)*. At the beginning of that film there is a woman in trance, and at the end there are three fishermen. I showed it later in Accra, and I think there were some Hauka in the audience; at any rate, the Hauka priests heard about it, and they cabled me in Togo, where I was at the time, to come and film their ceremony, which they planned to use as part of their ceremony. I had seen maybe one hundred ceremonies, and I knew the people very well, but I had never seen them eat a dog. They had only eaten a dog two or three times before. They did that, of course, because the British would not eat dogs, just as before they had eaten wild pig, which Muslims refuse to eat.

Once I saw in Kumasi, in the center of Ghana, the military parade of the Hauka, which was fantastic. There were altogether one hundred of them possessed, with their guns, all making a parade and shouting, but unfortunately it was at night, and I could not film it. Normally they go every Sunday in the suburbs, where sometimes a few are possessed. But the ceremony we filmed, the biggest one of the year, was held on a special farm. At the end of *Les maîtres fous* the truck driver says quite spontaneously, "Let's have one of these—major ceremonies—every six months instead of only once a year," which indicates how these possession religions come from the people; in other words, it isn't a priest who decrees. It takes them about an hour to induce trance, occasionally three hours, or even, I remember once, two days! And when they are in trance they speak a strange language, which is part French. They make the foam in their mouths while they are in trance by moving their tongues and swallowing very fast at the same time, but you can't do it unless you are in trance.

The cult is an African expression of our culture. The title of the film is a pun. It means the "masters of madness," but the British colonial masters are the ones who are mad! There's an attitude of both mockery and respect in *Les maîtres fous;* they're *playing* gods of strength.

When the young African students, and those who work on salary, were schoolboys in their own villages, learning our culture, the Hauka was a fascinating kind of model to follow. Europeans are not supposed to be afraid of anything. They don't care, they break taboos, they do what they want, and I think that the Hauka represent the same behavior, which is very important: people who are afraid of nothing, people who don't care. A lot of them were possessed by Hauka when they were in school. At the peak of the movement there were maybe one hundred Hauka gods, with newcomers all the time; and there were roughly 50,000 to 100,000 boys going every year to work in Ghana, and among them maybe 30 percent were possessed, but all the others were followers, "the faithful," who were there every Saturday and Sunday seeing an entertainment which was better than cinema, full of fantastic things, like when they take the dog meat from the pot of boiling water and are not burned.

In the film there is only one woman who is possessed, and the reason is that it was made in Accra about a particular group of migrants who were men; the only girls were prostitutes who followed them. But in the traditional religion there are more women than men, and even now the majority of the gods' "horses" are women. When we were filming, there was no policy of deliberate discrimination against women; in fact, it was open to everybody. Even if I had been possessed, I would have been a member of the sect, though I'm white.

Women are possessed by the same gods as men; there is no difference. In the film, the girl is possessed by a man, Captain Salma, the first French officer to be district commissioner in Niamey (from 1901 to 1905); he was married to an African girl. And there is a man who is possessed by Madame Salma, a very well known Hauka. Women are not possessed by a discrete group, as opposed to the men. And you're not possessed by only one; you can have five gods in your panoply, but most people have only two or three, and they are always the same ones. It's a question of personal character, which suddenly decides what type of god will possess you.

When the cult first appeared in Niger in 1925, the priests of the traditional religion were violently against it because, for example, when the priests were asking Dongo, the thunder god, to speak of rain, all the Hauka were coming and shouting and speaking of something other than the requests of the chiefs of the village. So the chiefs complained to the French administrators. The story is that around 1928 the district commissioner of Niamey, now the capital of the Republic of Niger, sent his guards around to the villages to collect all the Hauka and to bring them to Niamey, and when they were assembled he said, "Dance, I want to speak with Hauka." So they performed a ceremony in front of him. They became possessed, and he asked the gods to weep and to take their tears and put them on the Hauka. The possession crisis stopped immediately, of course, and the commissioner said, "You see, there are no more Hauka, I am stronger than the Hauka." Then he put them all in jail.

When they were in jail, one man became possessed and said, "I am a new Hauka, I'm Corsasi" (the Wicked Major). The name of the district commissioner was Crocchicia, which is a Corsican name, and the man said, "I'm Corsasi, I'm stronger than all the other Hauka, we have to break out of jail." The jail walls were mud; they broke jail, went outside, shouting, and Crocchicia had to use all his guards to keep them quiet. They were kept in jail for two months and then sent back to their own village. But when they went back, the cult increased very quickly. They were martyrs, you see, and when you fight against a cult like that, you just give it publicity.

The French thought the Hauka might constitute a serious threat, because often in the colonial period some priests of Islam would start to preach the holy war, the jihad. I spoke to Governor Crocchicia myself at the end of his life about what had happened in Niamey. He was very old, and all he said was, "Oh yes, I remember this boy shouting. . . . They said they were devils. . . . But we did it."

Later they had the same trouble with the British administration, and in '35 or '36 the British district commissioners made exactly the same mistakes: they put all these people in jail, and so on. And that very night there were fires all around the town; the Public Works Department in Accra was destroyed, and the Hauka—when they were possessed—said, "We are responsible. . . ." They did it to show that they were strong. So to avoid further trouble there was a kind of *accord* among the Hauka priests to perform their ceremonies only on Saturday and Sunday, and only in certain places.

I shot the film in two days in 1954, using the old Bell and Howell, which had to be rewound every twenty seconds. Jane, my wife, was with me, so was Damouré, who did the sound recording, and we were all very disturbed. We drove back at night in a small car, and it took maybe an hour. But first we had to walk half an hour to get to the car, and everyone was tired. We drove Gerba, the "loco driver," back home, just like after a party, and there was an incredible smell of dogs and perfume in the car because they drink perfume during the ceremony. I said to Damouré, "We really made a very bad film, it's very cruel," and it was only then that we decided to go out the next day to see what the boys were doing.

But with us among my staff was a young lad named Tallou, who later acted in *Cocorico, Monsieur Poulet* (1975). He was shocked: "Everything is fake. All this is fake." And Gerba said to him, "Tallou, be careful. You shouldn't say that because the Hauka will take revenge." And two weeks later Tallou was possessed! It was a savage trance; it caused a lot of trouble because he was possessed in the middle of Accra, and he started to fight his friends. We found him spending the night in the cemetery outside the town, and I brought him to Mountyeba the priest, who said, "Yes, he's possessed, but you have to wait maybe a year before his initiation," and he also told me, "You are responsible because you brought him here. The best thing to do is to take him back to his own village." He gave me some perfume and other things and explained how to quiet Tallou if there was a crisis. So I sent Tallou with my driver Lam (who *also* played in my films!). They went back to Niger by train and lorry, and during the journey, he was possessed two or three times, and Lam had to quiet him by pouring perfume on his head and saying, "Be quiet, be quiet." It was two years before Tallou was initiated. One of the last Hauka was a French general who was commandant during the Indo-China war. And the very last was called General Marseilles, because some African troops who were going to Indo-China stayed in Marseilles, France. Tallou was possessed by General Marseilles, the last of the Hauka.

I couldn't show the film, first because of British censorship, which equated the picture of the governor with an insult to the queen and to her authority; and I couldn't show it also because when I projected the film—I'd done experiments about this—the people who went into trance did so in an uncontrollable and almost dangerous way. It is a kind of electroshock to show a man a film of himself in trance.

But I think that the priests knew all this quite well and that they wanted to use it for its therapeutic value. Perhaps they might have been able to control it. I'm sure they knew they were playing with fire, but it was probably their intention to go beyond what had been done before. You see, when they first decided to eat a dog, it was really breaking a very strong taboo. They were doing something very bad, and maybe if they had used the film there would have been a fantastic emergence of all the Hauka power at the same time. Well, they were ready to try a kind of experiment because they felt they could command any aspect of European-based technology, including cameras and films, and so it would have been a challenge. My hypothesis is that they would have used a camera in the cult just as they used a gun: a crude wooden camera, and it would have been a normal part of the cult, if this movement had not been stopped by independence. But it was.

Well, when *Les maîtres fous* was first shown in Paris, at the Musée de l'Homme, by Professor Marcel Griaule, there were some African students around, keeping an eye on the museum, and they said it was an affront to their dignity. But it's now shown at the Cultural Center in Niger, and frankly I think it's better to eat a dog on Sundays and to be quiet during the rest of the week than it is to be sending people to concentration camps. In fact, the uprisings in May '68 were a kind of possession by things that were otherwise inexpressible.

I remember the reaction of Claude Chabrol, the French filmmaker, who called Braunberger, my distributor, and said to him, "I want to meet Jean Rouch, because he's a fantastic filmmaker. What a setup! How can he direct actors like that?" Because he thought it was a fake. You see, it's impossible to predict the reaction of an audience. Jean Genet's was to write *Les Nègres*. Peter Brook used it to train his actors for *Marat/Sade*—though Lacan has said it has absolutely nothing to do with our mental disease—and I asked Peter Brook if his actors became possessed, and he told me that they would never admit it because they want to be only actors.

The film in fact shows the very end of the Hauka development because it was only two or three years before the independence of Ghana. When the country became independent, the Hauka still continued, but there was no more colonial power, and there was never a Hauka called Kwame Nkrumah. It was really a cult of the colonial period. It's very interesting because we seldom assist at the birth of a new cult and never at its death. Five or ten years later I showed the film, not in Accra, but back in the villages, and they were very moved by it.

After independence, the new Ghana government thought that there were too many foreign workers in Ghana, so they started to control migration. Fewer and fewer boys went to Accra to find jobs, and the Hauka boys who were settled in Accra went back one after the other to their own country, and they brought back their Hauka with them to their own villages. But three years later, in 1960, their own country was independent, and the Hauka no longer had the same success as before. When they came back, the traditional priests assimilated the Hauka. So Dongo, the god of thunder, is now considered to be their father. And the story is that Bilali, another aspect of Dongo, when he was in Mecca, had a lot of sons who came to Africa. They say that Bilali actually sang Hauka songs and did Hauka rituals when he was in Mecca. The Hauka were the enfants terribles of Bilali, but now they are with us; we are all together in the same family. And even today in the very remote traditional villages, the Hauka still play an important role.

I've been working in Simiri, one hundred miles north of Niamey, where I have made a lot of films. One was about the drought in this area, because they are rainmakers (*Sécheresse à Simiri,* 1973–1974), and when I showed the film to the people there, last year, I learned that the rain was being kept in the hat of the chief and that he was responsible for the drought. And I learned that the chief keeps a white horse in his compound that is never mounted. It's the real horse of the spirit of the village, and near his stable is a black bull. Every seven years they have to slaughter the black bull and pour its blood on the horse. Of course the horse sometimes dies, and then they have to get another one. I heard that the next ceremony will happen in a year and a half, and that one year before the ceremony, the black bull is freed. He goes into the bush, where he spends the whole year. When the time for the ceremony arrives, the Hauka of the village possess the boys and girls, and it is the Hauka who have to go into the bush and find the bull and bring him back to be slaughtered. I tell this because it shows the role that the Hauka play now in a very important and certainly very old ceremony. The Hauka are in fact not responsible for creating the ceremony, but they're incorporated into it. They still do audacious things. So the village will send Europe's best soldiers out to catch the bull!

Five years ago there were newcomers exactly as the Hauka once were newcomers. In small villages new gods appeared who called themselves Sasale. The Sasale were originally a group of former slaves who are very famous in Niger because they danced for the chiefs. And when they danced they took off all their clothing and they sang sexual songs and danced sexual dances. And the spectators paid them to stop. You see the idea: it's a kind of striptease, only you pay them *not to go on!* Well, when the Sasale possess the boys and girls, they do the same thing; they start to take off their clothes, and they start to make love when they are possessed. It was considered shameful, it was forbidden by the Niger police, and they were put in jail, and the same story started all over again, and of course it only became more and more important.

The Sasale were in fact the ghosts of famous singers, prostitutes, playboys, who had died some years before and come back. The first one was named Alibiyo, which means "The Black Ali." He was a young and very handsome man who had been propagandist of the RDA, the Rassemblement Démocratique Africain, a political party in the fight for independence in West Africa. He died just after independence in '61, and the minstrels, guitar players, fiddle players—the griot—composed a very famous song about him called "Alibiyo." The Niger army was looking for traditional tunes to play and chose "Alibiyo." When Alibiyo appeared three years later, he said, "You are calling me all the time, even the army is calling me. Well, here I am, I'm Alibiyo the playboy," and that was the beginning.

This new religion is starting the same way: it's absolutely underground because the government is against sex. I began a film about it, but they asked me not to show it because of course the people were all, well, they were not making love in front of the camera, but all the dances, all the songs, were about sex: "Look at my clitoris," "Oh, your testicles are wonderful," and so on. It was really something. You see, it happens all the time. These religions are a kind of *inconscient collectif.* The people can't explain what they're doing; they can only show what they're thinking of, and it means that during these years from the twenties to independence, they were thinking of power—military, administrative, bureaucratic power—and now they are thinking of sex and death.

The Hauka introduced the idea of people who are outlaws, in the exact sense of the word. (It's important in one's myth to have people who are outlaws.) But now that the Hauka are inside the law, because they are the sons of Dongo, there are new outlaws of sex and death, the Sasale. Even in the present political situation, it's still working, it's still there.

▶ ─────────────────────────────────────────────────

### The Lion Hunters

*The Lion Hunters* (1956–1965) opens with shots of a Land Rover entering the "land of nowhere," heading toward a village where preparations are under way for a Gow hunting party (making arrows and poison, target practice, and so forth). In the second part, the hunters go out and kill a number of animals, including three lions, but the lion named "the American," which they had hoped to kill, eludes them. The identity of the Gow hunters and their relationship to the other peoples in the area are not fully explained. Rouch's field notes, deposited in the Musée de l'Homme, have not been written up, and the only printed material is a collection of folklore (*Les Gow, ou chasseurs du Niger . . .*, by Auguste Victor Dupuis-Yakouba, Paris, 1911), which suggests in the origin myth only that the Gow hunters may be illegitimate sons. Rouch elaborates on the comment in the film that the men who kill lions lose their sons, and sketches briefly something of the political relationship of the Gow to the Songhay millet farmers of the area. During the interview, Rouch drew our attention to a publication about a similar group of (Manding) hunters by Youssouf Cisse, "Notes sur les sociétés de chasseurs Malinké" (*Journal de la Société des Africanistes* 34 [1964]: 175–226), which explains why they fear that they will lose their sons. *The Lion Hunters* was reviewed in *American Anthropologist* 74 (1972): 1567–68.

The film was made in a very specific place, which is at the exact boundary of three states: Niger, Upper Volta, and Mali. There are many lions there because it's so remote. To give you an example, we left Niger in the morning, the lion killed an animal in Upper Volta, and the lion was killed in Mali, just crossing the border. There are no boundaries, no border control, only a tree.

The narration on the American version is a translation of the narration, which I did for the French version. *The Bush Which Is Farther than Far* is a translation of *Gandji Kanga Mooru Nda Mooru*, which is the actual name. We were just at the boundary of the millet-farming area and the bush. The nomads go into the bush, which is farther than far. But *le pays de nulle part* was a nickname that we gave the place: the Land of Nowhere. I said in the commentary that there were mountains without any name, and that we called them "Mountains of the Moon," or "Mountains of Crystal." You see, I wanted to express in the commentary the fact that we were included in this adventure, and that we put all our own fantasies into it, because we kidded around about these things, just joking. Maybe I was very ambitious, but my idea was to start from the beginning, to tell the story as they would tell it to their own boys, and it was to be the story of this particular hunting party in which Rouch was filming.

Nowadays, there are Songhay, Gow, Tuaregs, Bella, and Fulani nearby. The Songhay are millet farmers. The Gow aren't a tribe; they are just a group of Songhay who hunt lions. Then there are two nomadic tribes: the Tuaregs and the Bella (who are slaves of the Tuaregs), in addition to the Fulani-Djelgodji, who are the last Fulani nomads to penetrate inside the belt of the Niger River.

The Songhay own the land on which the Fulani pasture their cattle, so the Fulani have no right to the lions. The same with the Tuaregs. They pay the Gow to hunt, and when they kill a lion, the Gow receive maybe two or three bulls, which they pasture with the Fulani herds. The Gow also get the heart of the lion, which they can sell for as much as a thousand dollars, but the Fulani don't know that. The head of the hunters goes every year to Ghana to sell the lion hearts, the skins, and so on, and he brings back clothes and gifts to the Fulani. He is a very wealthy man.

But the Fulani don't care; to them it's a magic business. They want only one thing: to go into this area with their cattle and to be at peace with the farmers, and to be at peace with the lions. Yet the Fulani say that if there were no more lions, they would have to leave the country. After the drought, the lions crossed to the other bank of the Niger River, and the Fulani followed. They said, "The lions know where there is good grass, small water holes. Where there are lions we have good meadows, good pasturage, good grass for our cattle, because the lions know where they can find antelopes, which need the same grass."

I wanted to make a film about the Fulani, but it was impossible. You cannot go with them at night when the cattle are there because they are speaking with the lions, fighting them. They tell you the story of these encounters, but you cannot film them. Even very small boys, perhaps seven years old, come back and say, "Tonight I fought a lion with my club."

The Fulani have no right to *kill* lions because they are shepherds, so the only thing they can do is to fight them with their clubs and stones and hope the lion will go away. But if they use spears, it's finished; the lions will attack. You see, there's a kind of agreement between the lions and the shepherds, a kind of contract: the lions can kill the cows or the bulls who are not in good condition, but if a lion kills not to eat but for its own sake, then they can call the Gow to kill it. Technically, of course, they could do it themselves, though it's not so easy.

Normally the Gow stay home and wait for one of the shepherds to come. When there is a lion, the Gow know what happened; they know exactly how many lions were there. If they know the lions, they know the track, they know the way the lion kills the animals, they know exactly what is the mood of the lion, and so on. That is the magic knowledge of the bush, to know this kind of thing and decide to, well, to go in this direction to find him. But for example, I was in Yatakala when a man came from Mali, maybe sixty kilometers away. "Well, there is some trouble with a lion." So Tahirou sent one of the Gow on horseback to see what was going on. And two days later the man came back and said, "There's a group of lions there, but they are absolutely normal; we must not interfere with them."

The hunters are recruited because they are interested. Anybody can be a Gow if he has enough courage and enough technique to kill a lion. That's the difference between a Gow and other groups: they are not a descent group; they are just hunters, a professional caste, but not like the blacksmiths, because a blacksmith has to be the son of a blacksmith. It's just an open caste for people of knowledge. In the beginning of the area, the hunters played a very important role as leaders, and what was important was that their power was not hereditary. The narration of the film says: "If you kill lions, you will lose all your children, all your boys will die." So you cannot have descendants. The chief was the best hunter, but there were no "sons of the best hunter" to succeed him because he had no sons. (In fact it happened that Isiyaka lost one of his sons during the next year after killing the lion in the film, but he knew that was the risk he ran.) They say that in the beginning, the founders of state power in West Africa were hunters. And one day they preferred power to hunting. Then their sons could live, and when they died, they asked the people to take their sons to be chiefs instead of themselves. That was the end of this wonderful time when there was no hereditary power. There was power only in the sense that the best hunter was the chief.

The Gow don't own the lions on their land. They are hunting lions; the lions are hunting something else, and sometimes the lions are hunting Gow, to kill them! It happens. There are not many lions now, but twenty or thirty years ago there were. All the people farmed, but during the dry season, when they had nothing to do, the men made war or went hunting. To hunt a lion is to be a really big hunter. And the lions are considered almost like domestic animals.

They say that the lion was the model of human society. The lion is polygynous: he lives with his son, and the lioness very often does all the work for them. But the lion is the chief of his territory, and he has to fight against the other lions, just to keep the place for a lioness. And they say that when the cubs roar there is rivalry between the lion father and his son, and at the same time the lion has to fight against his son. Normally, though, the son goes out with his twin sister to found a new family. And they say that in ancient times, men's communities started in the same way; all the children were twins. And the first marriage was between twins; it was the beginning of the family. In the human social organization, the males were hunters, doing exactly the same thing as the lions, and it was a model they followed. And sometimes the young lion, if the father lion is old, fights against his father, and if he can kill his father, he has to eat him. Then he is a chief. And they say that when you find the body of an old lion, in the bush as if it had been eaten, that it is not the hyena or the jackals who did it, for they cannot eat lion meat, but it was the lion's son. Well, that's the myth.

The story is that the poison, the *boto,* was given to the first man by a female elephant that gave him the secret because she was jealous of another female elephant that was in love with her husband. And the female elephant asked the man to prepare poison. The man became a close friend to this elephant, and when everything was ready, he said to his father, "Tomorrow I'll go and kill the big elephant." And his father said, "Tell me the whole story." And he said, "I saw the female, she gave me the *nagyi* and everything to make poison, and I have to put it on my spear." And the father asked his son, "How many spears did you bring with you?" "Only one, that's enough." And the father said, "My son, take two and be careful." Then the boy went into the top of a tree. The female asked her husband to come this way, and when he was under the tree, the man threw his spear, and the male elephant died. And then the female elephant tried to attack the tree with the hunter in it, but fortunately he had a second spear, and with the second spear he killed the female who had given him the secret of the bush. That's the story.

They prepare the poison inside a magic circle to avoid all influence of the bush. There are certain small bush spirits, *atakurma,* who are the shepherds of the wild animals, and who spy on the Gow for the lions! When the Gow prepare the poison, they are not really invisible, but they are secret. The poison itself is strong enough to kill a lion, from a chemical point of view, but they put in something else, and that's their own magic. And maybe the small *atakurma* see that and go tell the lion, "Well, there is no way out." But when I asked the Gow to explain it, they just laughed, which means, "We don't want to give you the answer."

When it's finished they break the jars that had contained the poison, and walk around on them. I said to one of them, "If you are hurt, you'll die," and he said, "Yes, of course, I'll die." But that's the game: to play with the poison to show that you are stronger than the poison. Actually, though, they have an antidote, because when they shoot a lion there are spent arrows on the ground, and if they are barefoot, they can be hurt by an arrow and die. So they carry this counterpoison with them. I asked them what it is, but they wouldn't tell me. Only that they take the charcoal that is used to make the fire to boil the poison. That's all: this charcoal is the counterpoison. Which in fact is not true. There is something else. But they don't want me to know the secret, because when these people were warriors, they prepared the antidote to cure people hurt by the poison. That's the big secret.

The Gow poison is really very effective, an alkaloid to stop the heart. After ten minutes the lion is absolutely stunned. What's strange is that this alkaloid (from the fruit of a *Strophantus* tree) contains some of the same chemical components as cortisone. It's been analyzed. And they use the fat of the lion to cure rheumatism. Which means that when you kill a lion, his body becomes a kind of laboratory when he's dying, producing this fat to cure rheumatism. Maybe we can use it in the pharmacy! It'll be a blessing to the lion population, a boom on lions!

Among the Gow there is only one person who knows the secret of the poison, Tahirou, who is very old and is now ready to give the secret to another man. At the beginning of the film, when he is speaking the "initiation chain," he says, "Bulason gave the secret to Koro, and Koro gave it to me." Koro was his father, but Bulason was not his grandfather. Of course, Tahirou will try to give his secret to one of his kinsmen, a nephew, for example, but it's the hunters themselves who decide.

I don't know how they decide, but it's certainly the one who "knows" and who has luck. It's very important to have luck. It won't be Isiyaka because he has no luck, though he's a good hunter and a good fiddle player. Wangari, the younger brother of Isiyaka, has good luck because he's laughing all the time. When you have a jolly fellow like that around, it's good. And he knows more than Isiyaka about the bush. Tahirou in fact is not a very good hunter; he knows things, he has contact with lions, can read their tracks, and so on, but actually he is a very bad archer, though the commentary does not say so. But at the end of the film, when they all come back to the village, the lion is *said* to have been killed by his arrow because

he's the chief. Every hunter knows quite well, though, that he had absolutely no arrow in the lion when they killed it, but he gets the heart, which will
be sold for a very large amount of money. The villagers say, "O Tahirou is
the best, he's the chief, his arrow was in the heart. . . ." But we knew that it
was Isiyaka. The narration says only that Isiyaka, the fiddle player, is really
the best shot. But he isn't a "good hunter" because he has no luck.

Tahirou decides when to start the hunt, and he stops it when there is
something wrong. For example, when they killed the hyena, he said, "It's
very bad, we have to be careful. . . ." They say the hyena is the most intelligent animal in the bush and that it's very dangerous. The men were absolutely terrified of it and stopped for two hours, but it was not necessary.
Of course the hyena was very angry, but it was not dangerous at all. They
said, "The hyena should die very quickly." They never did that with the
lion later on. They shot in a second arrow very quickly just to finish him
off. We came back to the Fulani camp, and that was the beginning of our
bad luck. Tahirou was not speaking. And for two weeks, nothing happened, everything went wrong. We "lost the tracks," and for the Gow, "to
follow the track" means to go out alone to kill a lion one-on-one. That is
the correct—the Gow—way to do it, but they told me I couldn't go on a
real hunt till I'd been on a hunt like this. So they kept saying, "We cannot
follow the track and see where the lion is."

You see, my filming of the hunt was my own initiation as a lion
hunter, and my intention in editing the film and in the commentary was to
try to give the audience a feeling of what I myself felt as I was learning the
way of the lion hunt. I said all this in the original French version, but the
American distributor cut out the parts where I explained it! Twenty minutes are missing, and there are also two reels absolutely out of sync: when
the boys are training with bows and arrows, and the last reel.

The missing reels come just after the making of the poison. The Gow
gather together to decide what kind of hunt they will make, and then they
show some of the different ways. For example, they build a kind of mud
bunker just in front of the water hole where the lions come to drink; it's
not a reconstruction, but they are playing. However, when the hunters are
inside the bunker at night, they have no lights, so it was impossible to make
the film that way. The other way is to sit on top of a tree near where a donkey or some other animal has been killed by a lion and just wait there at
night. But again you cannot film it because it's dark. They said, "We cannot go out alone because you're not lion hunters." So we decided to make
a film showing them using traps. I follow them to Ghana where they buy
their traps, and I show the men making the traps in Swedru. (They are
European traps by origin: the Portuguese brought the technique.) Then

we start the hunt. But every time it's failed. So they went to see a man who tells the future by throwing cowrie shells, who said that there was a member of the staff who was against the hunt because he was acquainted with the lioness and did not want to hunt. And when he described this man, everybody knew who he was, but we had to stop. Then you see the cable (which was actually sent), and the film continues as I made it.

I had authorizations to make the film from Upper Volta, Mali, and Niger. And they sent an officer there from Mali with two frontier guards with guns. But the Gow asked us never to have a gun with us because it's so dangerous. They said, "If the lions smell the odor, they will attack the man directly." Well, I don't know if that's true, but there was some anxiety on the part of the Gow. So we had absolutely no guns, nothing. I was very annoyed because when the lion charged, the two guards with their guns ran away very quickly, and Damouré had to cure them afterward because their legs were full of thorns from the grass in the bush. It was a shame. (If you look carefully at the film, you can see one of these men with a gun. I kept it in because it was true. But it was shameful for them to have behaved like that, and we had some trouble about it later with the authorities.) At the beginning of my filming, the Gow smelled the camera, and they said, "That's exactly the same odor as a gun, you have to be careful." So for the entire time I put herbs on my camera just to avoid the smell.

In fact my presence among the Gow was the cause of an accident with the Fulani herdsman. He saw me with the Beaulieu camera, which had a small zoom, and thought I had a magical weapon with which to kill the lion. He said, "Well, this man is not a Gow, yet he's following the Gow, so we can go along, too." They wanted to know what would happen. That was the real cause of the trouble, because they are not supposed to follow the Gow.

The reason why the film took so long to shoot is that year after year we went there, but it was impossible to start the hunt because there was no *scandale,* as they say, for example, that a lion had killed a camel and then did not eat the camel. The lions would eat more cattle if the Gow just killed lions without any reason. That's the tradition.

For dramatic or aesthetic reasons, we changed the actual order of events. The first shot of Isiyaka playing his fiddle in sync sound was maybe the last shot I filmed. I used it at the beginning and at the end, when the boy fell asleep, but I shot them just at the end of the shooting. The last hunt in the film, for the lioness of Fitili, happened one year *before* the hunt for the other lioness. Every year that I was shooting the film, I would go with a copy and a projector to Yatakala and show the film to the Gow. After seeing the first cut, they said, "Well, it's a pity you can't see more lions. We'll have to go out and get some more lions." So then we made the part in which the lion "vomits his death." But we decided to stop the film there because the Gow kept asking us to come every year and make a kind of annual report of the lion hunt!

The narration of *The Hunters* was truly wonderful, John, the way you made a film tell a story, and in the French version I tried to do it the same way. My commentary was improvised as usual, and I spoke it myself. The idea was to remove myself because I am not an actor. I wrote out the main things to say, and I roughly knew the text; then I improvised in front of the screen, in five-minute sequences. And I was very impressed by the fact that when you do it that way, just trying not to make mistakes, just trying to speak good French, that if you are in good voice, you are very moved. I think that's why I hate the English-language version, because it was by a Canadian who tried to play a role. It's not too bad, but I don't like the way all that false drama intrudes. But anyway, that's why I recorded the commentary for *Les maîtres fous* myself, even in my bad English, but the trouble was that it was not improvised, I had to read it.

When I started the film in '57, I shot the first poison preparation using only the small Bell and Howell camera, which meant that nothing was sync sound; and all the shots were very short because I had to rewind the camera constantly. From my point of view, the film was edited in the camera during the shooting. I would change my angle all the time, so that there would not be too much to do in the editing. But when I finished the film, sync sound, in '65 using the Beaulieu, I had a problem editing it because all the sequences of technical processes in the first part of the film were shot with this new camera, and the shots were much longer.

For example, the preparation of the bow and arrow was made after the rest of the film itself, and the shots with the blacksmith were very long. But we edited it in the same way as the first footage because it was in the same part of the film. I was upset because there was a very good sequence that lasted maybe three minutes in which you can see the making of an arrow from beginning to end in one shot. But I had to cut it up because I had to respect the first shooting. So the editing style is very *elegante*. I like the girl (Josée Matarassa) who did it very much because it's difficult to edit a film like that, and there was important work, which she had to do on it. But when I made this film, I realized that there was a big difference in the two approaches: silent film and sound film. In the last film I showed yesterday night (*L'enterrement du Hogon*, 1972), the shots are very long because it's the only way to film now, I think.

I regretted having to reedit the footage in *The Lion Hunters* so much that I made the second film about hunting "the American" [called in

Songhay simply the White Man—*Ed.*] entitled *Un lion nommé "l'Améri-cain"* (1968) just to use the long sequence about the death of the lion and to show exactly what happened during the whole time in sync sound. In it you see us going out in the Land Rover, and Damouré asks the hunters to tell us when they are on the track, and Isiyaka says, "You see, that's the track of the American, because when we were with Rouch, he had a leg caught in the trap, and you can see where he was hurt. That's the American." It's all very clear, and at the end of the film, Damouré interviews Isiyaka, and there is the lioness, dead, and he says to Isiyaka, "Well, it's not the American." And Isiyaka says, "No, the American went into another bush. But maybe next year we will kill the American." And it was the beginning of the myth of the American. But I think all that is very difficult to put in a film. It was the last attempt to kill the American. We killed another lion, yes, but the American was killed by a Mali hunter, using a gun, one year later.

It's very strange because Tallou was working with me when I made *Un lion nommé "l'Américain."* (You remember he became possessed by the Hauka.) And when we were right in front of the lion, ready for action (he was carrying the Nagra), he became possessed again, and his new god was called the American! And Tallou started to roar like a lion: "The American!" And the lion was very astonished. Tallou was possessed because he was afraid; you see that assimilation. He was mimicking the American. Now the American is a kind of myth: every big lion is the American, and the spirit of the American is, I don't know, perhaps a Hauka.

There's nothing profound about the second film. Wangari and Tahirou sing for the lion and for the hunters and so on. It is based essentially on a very long five-minute shot of the death of the lion. But the film is not dramatic, and that's the trouble: truth is less dramatic than editing. I know that. But I go for the truth and then try to find drama inside the truth. It will happen, but it's unpredictable. For instance, I made a small film, only ten minutes long, of a possession dance in one shot (*Tourou et Bitti*, 1967). I started to shoot just five minutes before the trance began. It's dramatic because something happened in the middle of the shooting. That's the way to make films: you have to start just before the event, and the fact that you are shooting evokes the event. But when you shoot like that, very often it's a mess. One time I started, and just when there was no more film in the camera, the trance happened. But anyway, I think that's the way you can film the drama.

As I said, the correct way to hunt a lion is one-on-one, one hunter, one lion. Well, you can do it if you have the courage. I didn't know the way to do it, not really, and there was the question of sound equipment. If you could use a Nagra in your pocket and could be alone with a hunter like that, you might be able to film it, but I cannot say that I would stay in front of a lion that is charging. When I was shooting the lioness hunt, I was using the Beaulieu and a Nagra, but it was not sync sound. It was too difficult at that time. But if I could use a crystal system, with an Eclair and a Nagra, and could be absolutely independent, certainly, I would try to shoot the whole film, everything, even if I were frightened. Even if I were running, I would continue my shooting. Maybe it would be a very strange film, but the drama would be inside!

When I was shooting the Fitili lioness, I really was frightened. She was jumping around like a grasshopper. Even a small lion is dangerous, and if you are hurt, it's very infectious. When she started to jump, I stopped the camera, but the soundman didn't stop, so there was something in the action that I missed. Of course I hoped audiences would believe me, but many people don't believe that it actually happened that way. Well, I think there's less than one minute lost between the moment I stopped and the death of the animal. Isiyaka got his arrow in very quickly, but at the time I didn't know exactly what to do. I was a student in lion hunting, too! I didn't know the way.

They say that if you stand absolutely still, you're all right. If you are afraid, you can take a small tree, or just a branch, and hold it in front of you, and the lion will just roar, and lie there like a dog. In the bullfight there are clowns who stand quietly in the middle of the arena, and if the bull is just standing around, they have only not to move, and they're safe. I think it's the same thing, but, well, if you are making a film. . . . I even thought of using a helicopter, but what would that mean? A helicopter would make it all very stupid. Besides, I'm very happy to know that there is something like that which nobody can film. I've never seen a kill one-on-one, but they tell the story all the time. Tahirou killed one hundred lions that way; he killed ten lions a year, alone, and came back alone.

▶ —————————————————————————————————

## Jaguar

*Jaguar,* filmed at the same time as *Les maîtres fous,* marked a departure by Rouch from straightforward recording of factual information. Three of his friends play the roles of young Africans who go down to the Gold Coast each year during the dry season; the film shows them responding to other ethnic groups along the way and to the city where they find work. It was filmed as part of Rouch's study of these migrations that has been published principally in "Migrations au Ghana (Gold Coast) (Enquête 1953–1955)"

(*Journal de la Société des Africanistes* 26 [1956]: 33–196). *Jaguar* was reviewed in *American Anthropologist* 76 (1974): 697–98.

I think there are two kinds of truths: dramatic truth and documentary reporting, but pure documentary is very rare, and maybe it's inevitable that a film has some drama in it. A film like *Jaguar* was fun. It was shot as a silent film, and we made it up as we went along. It's a kind of *journal de route*—my working journal along the way with my camera. We were playing a game together; we were all in the same car going down to the coast. I remember I had a big discussion with my wife Jane, who was with me at the time (it was her first trip to Africa), because she said, "The Truth is more important: why aren't you making a documentary instead of asking these people to play roles that are not their own?" And I explained to her how very difficult it is to show all the things I wanted to show about these migrations in a documentary.

I asked them to act, and it was very easy for them to do it, but we were always in a false situation. For example, when the boys were crossing the border at the customs office by the police station, I just went up and said, "I am shooting a film of some people, do you mind?" And they said, fine. They didn't know what was going on: when the boy crossed the border, I was actually filming the man in front, and he didn't see what happened behind him. So they did cross the border illegally, but I was with the camera, and if something happened, everything would have been all right— they had identity cards and so on. But we were so happy about it that we never went back to cross legally. We were absolutely happy because we knew that it was possible.

A second example in the film: Suddenly you see Damouré Zika with a Rolleflex taking photographs of Kwame Nkrumah. Well, it's absolutely unbelievable that a migrant would be able to do that. Where could he find a Rolleflex if he was working in timber? But we decided to do it, and he came there with his Rolleflex and was filming among the staff of the so-called international photographers. He was making photography, so he was invisible, and we were so happy to be there with absolutely no newspaper card, or anything like that. But the people knew me, and they knew that I was making a film of the election (*Baby Ghana*, 1957). So we were using the camera as a kind of passport to fantasy or to truth; I don't know which, exactly.

We shot the film like that in one year. The narration was done later on, and the film was not edited on a bench but was actually filmed in the camera in the final order you see on the screen. I brought the film back two years later and projected it to the boys in Accra. We improvised the commentary in one day, and it was first-class. The man in charge of the film unit in Accra was an English filmmaker, Sean Graham, who worked with Grierson, and he was very nice, and very kind. He said we could use the auditorium to make the recording. And I projected the print and at the same time recorded the commentary on a Nagra (the first model, which was powered by a spring that you had to wind). Sean said, "Well, I never saw such genius in improvisation." Because the boys were like that; they were just improvising this. That was the film. The sequences were not very long, so rationale for the narration was just the frame, and that was very good. But I'm sure, for example, that if this film had dialogue, there would have been long explanations about everything.

There is a wonderful scene that I love, when they are on the beach just before crossing the border. They discover the sea; they are swimming in the surf. There's a sunset, and walking back along the beach, they see a sea star. They really had not seen one before. And Damouré actually looked at it and put it on his head. That was what he did when the film was shot. But when he recorded the narration, he said, "You see that's the star of the sea, the snow star, *l'étoile des neiges.*" At this time there was a very popular tune in France called "L'étoile des neiges," and he said, "It's l'étoile des neiges," the snow star in the middle of the sea. That's what I call natural poetry. I don't remember what he said at the time he was putting the star on his head, but he certainly didn't say that, only when he saw the film later on.

It was just at the beginning of independence in Africa, and all the scenes with Kwame Nkrumah are absolutely unique nowadays. About five years ago I saw the son of a minister of Kwame Nkrumah, who is now working for the Ghana TV system. He said to me, "Jean, you have to keep your film very firmly because when there was *le coup d'état* with General Ankra they destroyed all the films about Nkrumah. All the records, all the old photographs were destroyed, even in the laboratory in London." Sean Graham said to me last year that he had saved a part of his own films (1977). We were very close to Nkrumah at this time, and I knew him quite well, and there was no trouble. It was the beginning of a fantastic *fête revolutionaire,* an explosion of joy, with people dancing in the streets, and so on. And there was no problem for us, and maybe that's the difference between *Jaguar* and, say, *Come Back, Africa* (1959). Because I think that when Lionel Rogosin made his film about apartheid in South Africa, he was in a very difficult position himself. I'm not sure, but I suspect that he was trying to put his own feelings about discrimination and racism in the film, more than the people themselves did.

I think also that in *Come Back, Africa* the ending is highly dramatized:

it says "there is no way out." In *Jaguar* there is not that feeling: something could happen. It was maybe also the difference of my own feelings. I think that when Lionel was making his film, he felt guilty. And when I look at *Come Back, Africa,* I'm sad, I feel guilty myself. In *Jaguar* we are not guilty.

When I was in Johannesburg two weeks ago, my first visit to South Africa, I was there like a migrant because I had no passport. I had no right to go to Johannesburg and walk the streets to see what was going on. And really I had exactly the same feeling as I had when I met some German people just before the war: to be in front of a group of men who had decided to stay there, not to move, and who had the law with them.

At the same time I discovered something I did not know: the majority of these people in Johannesburg were Jews. And for a man like Lionel Rogosin, who suffered racism in this country, it was very difficult, he said, to discover that Jews, among all the others, were responsible for apartheid. He felt guilty, and that may be the point. You see, when I made *Jaguar,* I didn't feel guilty. It's not my fault that my father or my grandfather came to conquer West Africa. I'm not guilty; that's the difference. Maybe it's because—well, not education—but maybe because I "did a war" that I have nothing to do with all that. Lionel has not, you see. If I were making a film in South Africa, I'd try to make it in the *Jaguar* way to show that there is a way out, just on the margin. If you are marginal, you can go on.

Recently I shot in Maputo in Mozambique two reels *(Makwayela)* about a group of people who work in the mines of South Africa. They were working in a bottle factory at the time, and they were singing and dancing the story of their migration to South Africa. I shot the film in 16 mm as a study film for the people of the new Institute of Cinema of Mozambique. I was there with some people who had escaped from Brazil, from Portugal, and so on, and they were trying to find their own revolution in Mozambique. We were confronted by workers who went to South Africa under difficult conditions but were singing. And I realized that they were the same as the boys in *Jaguar,* and that I knew all the tricks they knew. And it was fun because they do exactly the same tricks. For example, when I was in Ghana, I discovered that the people who work in the gold mines thought that it was too exhausting to work in them all the time, so they used only one labor card for three friends. Which means that every day it was another worker of the same name. Because you can afford to work in the mines only one day instead of three. But if you want to do that, you have to have the same bed, which means that you have to share everything. That's the *Jaguar* way. These guys did exactly the same thing.

And curiously all these young people from Mozambique were absolutely afraid because we were joking about such conditions. They said,

"But Jean, they were living in slums," and so on. So I asked them—I don't speak Portuguese, but someone was translating—and they said, "Well, but that was the only way to save money, and that was the only way to save our health, we just found tricks." It's the same thing in Paris in the Renault factory. Everywhere they find a way. The best testimony we had about concentration camps after the war was from people who discovered that having fun was the only way to get out alive; that was the most important testimony: fun among death. But it's very difficult to put that in a film, really difficult, but maybe that's also the challenge. Well, my dream would be to make a film about South Africa, but I don't know how to do it because the situation is tragic. It's a terrible situation, but I'm sure that human beings can find in any situation a small path to go out, and you only need one. (I had exactly the same idea—this kind of psychodrama—in my film *La pyramide humaine,* which is about racism.) You see, I think that if you want to show a very dramatic situation, you have to show at the same time fun happening, even if it's very tragic.

I remember during the war when we entered Germany. I was in a small force, and some people said that there was an SS group in a monastery, and we went there, and we were maybe twenty or twenty-five, some American soldiers and some young French soldiers who had escaped from Paris, with two half-tracks and a small tank. But they were not German; they were *French* SS. And the man who was in command of the SS was a colonel in the French army, and his name was de Turenne, which is of course a very important name in France. He had only one leg and was really a kind of "last soldier." It was a very dramatic moment because they were one hundred and we were very few. But they had no way out, and this man knew very well that he was a prisoner and that he would be shot in the coming days. It was very dramatic.

I said to him, "Well, you must ask your boys to come here." It was really a meeting of all the French people who were with the German occupation army against the French patriots. They were ugly people, and they started to bring their guns, their *matraques,* every horrible weapon they used, and the man turned over to me a French flag, which had a black Greek letter gamma in the middle. It was really horrible, but suddenly it was very quiet.

There were two incidents that I remember quite well. The first was an old gentleman in civilian clothes who said to me, "*Mon lieutenant,* I'm not a fighter, I'm only a *collaborateur!*" That's so strange, a man who's in that kind of business saying, "I'm only a *collaborateur!*" Well, it was impossible not to smile. . . . And the second thing that happened was that a sergeant from Paris, with a fantastic Parisian accent, opened a window and shouted,

"Mon lieutenant, j'ai trouvé des Gauloises." I've found some Gauloises! Even the Colonel de Turenne was obliged to laugh, and he was laughing perhaps for the last time of his life, because he was dying.

Well, of course I was very courageous for this time because we laughed, and something happened in the middle of all that horror. Maybe that's the reason why I always try to find situations like that, but I don't know if it's right, I don't know if I'm following the right track. You see, it was the same thing with the Hauka in prison, exactly the same thing. And you see, we share this, Damouré, Lam, and I, because we did that all our lives. We are *en marge*, we are marginal, and that may be the reason I have this feeling.

But anyway, it was very amusing.

## JEAN ROUCH WITH DAN GEORGAKAS, UDAYAN GUPTA, AND JUDY JANDA

## *The Politics of Visual Anthropology*

Dan Georgakas, Udayan Gupta, and Judy Janda interviewed Jean Rouch in English in September 1977 at the Margaret Mead Film Festival at the Museum of Natural History in New York. The questions and responses relate to the seven films by Rouch featured over three evenings at the festival that year: *Les maîtres fous, Moi, un Noir, Chronicle of a Summer, The Lion Hunters, Jaguar, Petit à Petit,* and *Cocorico, Monsieur Poulet.—Ed.*

*You are best known in the United States for* Chronicle of a Summer. *The more we learn about the film that launched* cinéma-vérité, *the more controversial and intriguing it becomes. For instance, some of your own comments after the screening at the Museum of Natural History raised questions about the fundamental verite of the film. You stated that the secretarial scenes in the film were shot at the offices of* Cahiers du Cinéma. *You also talked at length about the individuals in the film, many of whom went on to become filmmakers, and others like Régis Debray to become prominent Marxist personalities. Rather than the mood of the Parisian "tribe" at the end of the 1950s,* Chronicle of a Summer *actually renders portraits of people in the political and artistic avant-garde. At the same time, there is little footage within the film that demonstrates that these are exceptional people. One minor point is that they never use words like "socialism" or "communism." Could you expand on how the film evolved from an idea to this reality?*

At the beginning, when we first started thinking about such a film, I said to Edgar Morin, my collaborator, that I didn't really know many industrial workers. Edgar said he would arrange for that. I only learned later on that the people he chose all belonged to the same group as Morin, Socialism or Barbarity (Socialisme ou Barbarie). This turned out to be critical for the film's development, but it wasn't clear to me at the beginning. I think you are wrong when you say they didn't mention communism. At one point, a worker is unhappy because he is doing nothing, dealing only in papers. Morin says, "Remember when we were militants in the same party? We did something. Now, where are we?" This is a reference to the fact that they had both been in the Communist Party. Morin and the others left the party in disgust after it supported the suppression of the Hungarians.

*That doesn't come across so clearly, but you are admitting that it's not about the Parisian tribe after all.*
It's a tribe all right, but a specialized tribe [laughter].

*Perhaps a subtribe?*
Yes, I like that. Fortunately, it was a tribe of substance. In their attitudes, you can see what will explode all over France in May 1968.

*There are some troubling implications here for documentary filmmakers, particularly anthropologists. When anyone goes to a foreign place and a guide tells them, "Let me take you to a group of typical workers," or "Let me show you an important ritual," how do we know what we are seeing? Here you were in your own country and working with a dear friend, and in some degree he took you in. He said, "Here are some workers," and they turned out to be of a political tendency whose virtue was that it was not typical at all.*
You are absolutely right. Perhaps we should add some subtitles to identify 'the party' as the Communist Party.

*There's more to it than that.*
I would say that it was clear who they are to a French audience. This group was not quite illegal, but it had to be cautious. At that time, the Algerian War was the major political issue, and these people were aiding the revolutionaries. We could not speak to that question because of their own security and the security of the Algerians. The French audience of that time would have no trouble understanding what the speakers represented. Showing it now or in another country, problems emerge which weren't an issue then.

*Let's turn to some of the techniques you used. One of the most striking sequences was clearly staged by you as a "director," even though the "actors" didn't know what was coming. We're thinking of the scene where you ask the African students to interpret the meaning of the tattoo on Marceline's wrist.*
That was a provocation. When I first saw the film, I noticed that I was smiling a very cruel smile when I intervened. That smile sometimes embarrasses

me even now. You see, we were having lunch outside the Musée de l'Homme, and the subject came to anti-Semitism. As soon as it began, I knew I would ask the question about the tattoo the Nazis had put on Marceline's wrist because I knew the Africans did not comprehend our concern about anti-Semitism. When I posed the question, the isolation and assumptions of cultures emerged dramatically. It's not quite apparent in the film, but before that moment, people were jovial and laughing. Suddenly the Europeans began to cry, and the Africans were totally perplexed. They had thought the tattoo was an adornment of some kind. All of us were deeply affected. The cameraman, one of the best documentary people around, was so disturbed that the end of the sequence is out of focus. I stopped filming to give everyone a chance to recover. Now, is this a "truthful" moment or a "staged" moment? Does it matter?

*The long sequence in which Marceline walks by herself, talking into a tape recorder strapped to her body, is like a cinematic stream of consciousness. There are many such experiments in the film. Where did you get your ideas?*

Morin must be given a lot of credit. He proposed to make the first sociological fresco film, a film without the convention of stars or leading performers. He wished to deal with anonymous people as much as possible. I told him this was not possible. When you begin to speak with any person, even a cop, the man is not cops, he is a cop. You can't get around that. So while we can oppose the star system and what it implies, we cannot deny individuals their humanity and personality. We had many discussions on this point. Each day we would project the rushes before doing any new work. We had a lot of give and take between us and the producer Dauman and the people in the film. We had all these ideas we wanted to deal with, more than we ever got in.

For instance, there was a wonderful sequence in which we spent a day with the factory worker Angélo. We couldn't shoot inside the factory because Angélo's politics were well known and both the company and the union were against him. The men who participated had to be secretive. We shot only at the entrance. Then we followed Angélo to his home in a working-class district. There were twenty minutes spent showing him taking a bath. That would be a very good short film in itself, a twenty-five-minute study of a man coming back from his work to his home and a warm bath. But we had to cut it out. Another thing, since making that film, I am not allowed into a factory with my camera. I, too, find myself opposed by both management and the union.

*At the museum you indicated that the making of the film involved the simultaneous making of a camera.*

Oh yes, that was one of the best parts of making that film. We are now talking about the late fifties, when cameras were heavy and static. I had gone to a film meeting in California where I met Michel Brault, who showed the film *Les raquetteurs,* and he asked me to stop back in Montreal on my way home. I took up the invitation and saw the first films made by the young filmmakers of Quebec. They were using a new type of wide-angle lens. Before then, there had always been the problem of distortion. They had also begun to take the camera from the tripod and go "walking with the camera." I loved that. The cameras were still noisy, but if you wrapped a trenchcoat around them, something could be worked out.

Back in France, Morin approached me about his idea for a film. I began with a very excellent cameraman, but when I wanted him to "walk in the streets," the poor man refused. It was too much of a challenge for him. I then told Dauman, our producer, that the only one who could do what we wanted was Michel Brault. What a comment on the vaunted French cinema! We had to go to Montreal to get a competent person. During the same time I spoke with André Coutant, who was father of the Eclair Cameflex 35 mm camera. He said there was a new camera that might interest me. It was a military prototype built for use in a space satellite. That meant it was very light, dependable, and steady. Unfortunately it had a magazine of only three minutes. I asked him if he could build a model with a larger capacity. He said he would try. So we began to make our film with a camera that didn't totally exist. We had a contract with the manufacturer that they would not be responsible for any scratches made on the film, but Coutant agreed that he would personally repair the camera every night. After shooting, Edgar and I would bring it back to him and tell him what problems we had encountered, what new ideas we proposed. The creation of the camera proceeded with the creation of the film. I was overjoyed with the result. It was doubly wonderful because I was in front of these people who were always so serious, and I was joyous at seeing the camera being born. That was one problem I felt about them, especially Morin. They didn't see the pleasure you could have in life.

*One thing that was clear seeing several of your films on three consecutive evenings was that* Chronicle *has a very different look than the others. Generally in your African films, we are given long-distance shots of people active in a religious ritual or some other rite involved with nonrationalist values. In* Chronicle *the subjects mainly talk, and they talk about complex philosophical and psychological ideas. The action is generally indoors, and there are many close-up shots.*

Part of the explanation has to do with the camera. When we began the film, the camera was still on its tripod. I thought the effect was much too static, so I began to move it as people spoke. How they looked and what they did with their hands seemed important, so I did close-ups. After a while, we went outdoors and walked in the street. At the end of the film there are no close-ups. Even when we shot the participants viewing what we had completed of the film to that point, there are no close-ups of Marilou, Marceline, or any of them. I don't disagree with the thrust of your question, though. Remember, I didn't know these people personally, and they began to speak of very intimate problems. I was somewhat embarrassed by that. The first Marilou sequence was shot right after I met her for the first time. In the second, we were alone at Marceline's flat after dinner. She was talking so nervously that I had to react. So I took those big close-ups, to try to get inside. I was very upset by that experience. You are right. I never do close-ups like that in other films, but that is true even for other films about France.

*It struck us that the film about France emphasizes how the European thinks, while your films on Africa emphasize how the African behaves.*
This is an interesting point, and I must say it is the first time the question has been put to me. Normally, I would not see so many films one after the other. As I have said, other films I have done in France do not have so many close-ups. Another thing, at the beginning we shot people at 100 meters, and they did not know we were shooting them. They thought we were a group of people who had a camera. I disliked that very much. We wanted to do something that was spontaneous, but that was more like candid camera, something sneaky. Our caution goes back to the fact that Angelo and his friends had so many enemies that we had to be protective of our subjects. Perhaps the close-ups were a kind of backlash.

*That still doesn't explain the African films where nobody ever talks directly to you. How accurate is that, given the strong oral traditions of African culture? What we see in the films is a kind of homage to the primitive, to the past, to the exotic. Aren't Africans as articulate as Europeans? Isn't there a modern African society with elements as creative as the group that called itself Socialism or Barbarity?*
You are asking good questions. The explanations come on several levels. One immediate response I have is that I have decided not to make political films about postindependence Africa. After all, these are not my countries.

I think it is imperialistic to project your political values onto Africa. That kind of film must be done by Africans. I have been tempted to break my own rule. I had quite good relations with Kwame Nkrumah and started to make a film about him. In *Jaguar* you can see part of the coup d'état. After that coup, everything about Nkrumah was destroyed. I had the idea of doing a film about him while he was in exile. After three months, I saw that it was wrong for him. It would have been impossible to show that film in the one country where it most mattered. And who was I to make such a film? It would be a shame for him and for them.

*What about the dialogue in earlier films, during the preindependence era?* At the time we could not do it technically. When we made *Chronicle of a Summer,* the first independence had already taken place in Ghana, three years earlier. I understand what you are trying to get at, but there are terrible problems involved. If I were to do a film now about the political regimes of Africa, it would be a spectacle of disasters, one after the other. It's embarrassing for a European to make a film like that. I don't think it's my own cowardice either, although some people have said I am not courageous. I don't know. I'm censoring myself all the time. In *Cocorico, Monsieur Poulet* we had a sequence where the police bargained up their bribe from two chickens to three. When we saw the rushes, we decided to take it out, even though it was an honest and accurate representation. How to deal with such corruption is a real dilemma for people who make films in Africa, even for the African filmmakers.

*Let's take the same issue from a different perspective. What is your conception of the narrative, even in the strictly anthropological film? Your comments on* The Burial of the Hogon *and* The Mad Masters *did a great deal to enlighten us about your aims and what the films were all about. When we watched the films beforehand, we were puzzled by many of the images. We were like those Africans who had no way of understanding the tortured history symbolized by that tattoo on Marceline's wrist.*
But the alternative is so boring—to say, "In the village of so-and-so, blah-blah happened." My ideal would be a film that everybody could comprehend without any narration. Language is such a problem. We can't even accurately translate exactly what people are saying in another language. Then, too, I am using more and more feedback. When films are shown to the subjects, narration angers them. Nonetheless I sympathize with your question. It is almost as if the films were still not complete. Something has to be done with them. I have a new film about drumming where I use a different kind of narration. I give a very subjective response to what I am filming.

*It's still not clear whether you think narration is good or bad.*
My dream is to show in a film what can be understood directly without the aid of narration, to explain everything that needs explanation by filmic devices. But I am perplexed. If people speak, you need to translate. I have one film in which I have created a very precise translation that is on a sound track that is cut in right after they speak. I try to speak the translation in the same way the people speak. That is as close to simultaneous translation on film as you can expect. Stereo would be a better solution. One track could have the original language and the other a translation.

*One of your other partial solutions gave us problems. In* The Mad Masters, *near the end, you comment that the ritual helps the people to be good workers and to endure colonialism with dignity, that it provides some psychological accommodation. Clearly, one of your aims was to deal with the viewer who would be appalled at seeing people drinking dog's blood. You wanted to show the positive psychic benefits to the individuals involved. Our reaction, though, was that people should not be accommodated to endure colonialism. Is it not far better for anger to explode on the job than to be let off in some harmless religious rite? Is it not better if they were "bad" workers who "accidentally" broke their tools and were "lazy"?*
Quite right. I no longer care for that ending. Originally that commentary was impromptu. I wanted to explain that the ritual was a method that allowed them to function in normal society with less pain. I wanted to make it clear that they were not insane. An important point that got lost was that therapy for the Africans is not a one-to-one private consultation like you have in psychoanalysis and most Western therapies. The therapy we filmed was a public ritual done in the sun. That aspect is one of the most important things we Westerners need to learn. But I can't very well fiddle with the commentary now. The film has existed as is for more than twenty years.

*We've come to the conclusion that your body of work is much more exciting as cinema than as anthropology. In every film there is some new experiment. Most of the time, as in* The Lion Hunters, *there is an imposed dramatic structure. The action builds to a traditional climax. That's effective cinema, but does it describe the tribe accurately? Doesn't a lot get lost for dramatic values?*
This is one point where I disagree with you completely. Good anthropology is not a wide description of everything but a close identification of one technique or ritual. The rituals are supposed to be dramatic. They are creations of the people who want them to be interesting and exciting. In *The Lion Hunters,* twenty minutes have been left out. Those sequences showed

the position of the trap, why they use traps, why they hunt in the first place. But you can explain that sort of thing in writing very well. What you can't get in writing is the drama of the ritual. Writing can't have that effect. That's the whole point of visual anthropology.

*What about the distortions? For instance, your films exclude the role of women.*
If you want to make films about African women, you have to be a woman. A man cannot enter the woman's society. It's just impossible. It is forbidden. Men are not even allowed to have intercourse with their wives when a hunt is about to begin. It is the male society I can be a part of, so that is what I film. There are many things that have to do with women that I could never show.

*If you could intervene in* The Mad Masters *and show the footage of real colonial officials, why isn't it possible to use similar devices to speak about women?*
That's easier said than done. When I show the water was poured from the well by the wicked women, what visual intervention could be made? Or when we say the poison of the female is stronger than the male poison, more exposition might just confuse matters, because that is not the direct subject of the film. You must understand that there are wonderful women's ceremonies that men are not allowed to view. Obviously they would not allow even a woman to film them if men were to be allowed to see the film afterward. I have one old woman who tells me some things, but she is allowed privileges because of her great age. I have many problems with my students about such matters. I have to explain to women that during their menstruations they are not allowed in some locations. They have to be out of certain villages altogether. What a dilemma for a European woman who wants to work in Africa.

*Since we've talked about the different ways people interpret the same images, this might be a good place to talk about the influence your work has had on others. Most people in the United States do not realize that Jean Genet was very affected by seeing* The Mad Masters.
Now I am embarrassed in a different way, but Genet's *The Blacks* was directly influenced by *The Mad Masters*. The idea in his play was that the blacks play the masters, as in the ritual. Possession, after all, was the original theater, the idea of catharsis. Genet seized upon the idea of mockery and exchanged identity. That wasn't exactly what the original was all about, but Genet worked the material to his own end.

*What do the Africans have in mind when they take part in the ritual?*
They insist they are not engaged in mockery or that they have any notion
of revenge. I believe that is true, at least on the conscious level. The history
of the cult is very complex. It goes back to Africans who went to Mecca.
The entire rite, the foaming at the mouth, the sacrifice of the dog, and all
the shouting is considered to be the action of spirits which have possessed
them. These are powerful new gods who most certainly are not to be
mocked. When the cult began, the Islamic priest saw them as heretics and
persecuted them. The French administration joined in because they did not
like the revival of strong animistic faiths that might turn political. So it was
a forbidden cult almost from the start. Many of the original cultists, members of the Hauka, became migratory workers and had to go far from their
homelands. Everywhere they were banned, and as usual, the more they
were banned, the better it was for the cult. The first compromise was to
agree to do it only once a week, on Sunday, at a specific location. Later the
cult declined, and the rite took place only once or twice a year. The Hauka
movement broke taboos, whether it was eating a dog or modeling behavior
on the colonial example. It was like Buñuel's attitude to the church. You
cannot feel sacrilegious if you do not respect your opponent. What the
Hauka did was very creative and implicitly revolutionary, just as the authorities feared.

I only met Genet twice, but I knew the actors in his play, and we discussed the film quite a bit. Genet was an ex-convict, so he knew about systems within systems and how one resists. I think the film showed him a
way to resolve some of his contradictory feelings. What we got on film was
one of the last moments of the cult. After independence, there was no more
colonial power and thus no model. But there is something extraordinary
about that ritual they invented. Every sort of force has attacked them and
me for filming them—the colonialists who don't like the portrait, African
revolutionaries who don't like the primitivism, antivivisectionists who
don't like the sacrificial murder, et cetera, et cetera.

*Peter Brook was another person who had a profound reaction to the film.*
His response was quite different from Genet's. He saw the film when he
was staging *Marat/Sade* and asked all his actors to see the film and model
their playing on it. Later we talked together often, and he went with me to
Africa. He tried to create a new theater without using any recognizable
words. He was fascinated by the Hauka, who had invented an artificial
language, part pidgin English, part broken French, part who knows what.
Yet people understood the language. I've hypothesized that before this century is over, there will be a movement among blacks in the United States

that will use such a language. But Peter Brook was not doing politics. He was interested in theater. His play dealt with a revolutionary period in which power belonged to his subject. He wanted the actors to act as if they were possessed even though they were not. A friend of mine said that if you are moved when you act, you are finished. You have to act to be moved, but not to be moved when you're acting. You have to believe in the roles you are playing. With the Hauka, there is no acting. They believe they are the spirits during the possession. I told Brook that if his actors were too successful in giving up their identity, they might become possessed. Then what would he do? He was not a doctor or a priest. I thought he was playing with fire.

One last thing we should say about the Hauka is that they are no longer in Ghana. They were expelled when they weren't needed as workers. They returned to Niger and took a specific role in each village. Since there is no more colonial power, they have no models and are returning to traditional cultures with an Islamic bent. They and the film I made about them have had a tremendous impact, however. Reaction to that film was one of the sources of my idea to have African anthropologists come to France to film our tribes and rituals.

*You've helped a number of Africans begin careers in film. Would you tell us something about them?*
Well, there is Oumarou Ganda, the main figure of the film *Moi, un Noir*. He created a narration for the film that works at three levels. The first is a description of what you see, the second is a kind of dialogue, and the third is a statement about his own condition. He's gone on to make films on his own. Another person I've worked with is Moustapha Alassane, who is a kind of renaissance type. I believe some of his films are available in the United States.

*We indicated earlier that we thought your films posed very interesting cinematic questions but we were not so certain about their virtue as anthropology. We were thinking in terms of what an anthropological film can and cannot be. Does it just record raw data, or does it interpret? To make a film always involves a selective process and conscious intervention at specific points. That must conflict with an attempt to present anthropological fact.*
Most people refuse to recognize that any anthropology must destroy what it investigates. Even if you are making a long-distance observation of breast feeding, you disturb the mother and her infant, even if you don't think so. The fundamental problem in all social science is that the facts are always

distorted by the presence of the person who asks questions. You distort the answer simply by posing a question.

*If the very presence of the observer causes so much distortion, the presence of a camera must magnify the distortion.*
Absolutely! But I think this new distortion can be positive. Let's make a comparison between classical anthropology and visual anthropology. In the first, you take a professional from a prestigious university, and they go to some remote place, where people are usually without a written language. Just by making an investigation, the people of the places are embarrassed and have their routine disturbed. When the survey is completed, the anthropologist goes back to the university, writes the dissertation, and possibly wins distinction in the field. What is the result for those who were surveyed? Nothing. There is no feedback from the disruption the anthropologist has created. The subjects will not read the survey. With a camera, there can be a far more fruitful result. The film can be shown to the subjects. Then they are able to discuss and have access to what has happened to them. They can have reflection even if the film is bad, for however incompetent the film may be, there will be the stimulation of the image you give of them and the chance for them to view themselves from a distance, up there on the screen. Such a distortion changes everything. In the first example given, there can be some reward for the researcher and for science in the abstract. In the second, you can have all that and benefits for the people, too.

There is another problem related to all this, which your readers in particular should appreciate. Six or seven years ago, I attended a conference in Montreal sponsored by the African Section of the American Anthropological Association. That meeting was disrupted by people acquainted with the Black Panther Party. They argued that we were new slave traders. They said that by making a survey of any given tribe and becoming an expert, the anthropologists could gain prominence and teaching posts and writing contracts that would be lucrative for a lifetime. Often, the fieldwork never amounted to more than a few years' work. One American black replied that he was in a different category because he was making a study of workers. The reply was that his work might be even more damaging. It was argued that his reports would be of most value to businessmen and governments who needed data to further exploit and control the workers. I think those arguments were right in one sense, but the solution is not quite as simple as they wanted to make out. Do we stop all research because we cannot control the use of our findings?

Then there is still another kind of exploitation. Some ten years ago, a musicologist recorded a wonderful song of the Watusi. It was published in a very small edition of scientific records. Eventually, the Rolling Stones heard the tune. They liked it so much, they recorded it and made a lot of money. Naturally, the Watusi never earned a cent. They were certainly exploited. The musicologist had made the original recording with good intentions, and the Stones obviously respected the music, but the rip-off occurred. When you record an oral tradition, there are no copyrights and often no original or single creator. This is true for stories, as well. When you are making an anthropological film, the problem is just as severe. The people allow us to film them, but once it is done, the film goes to the West, and the people have no control over what is done with the images of their lives. Often the people who made the film have been given grants or get professional stature. Should the people be paid, too? Or is that another kind of insult?

*Once more you address the problem as an artist might, the question of who "owns" a creation.*
Well, I've been concerned about this problem a long time. On *Moi, un Noir,* I insisted that 60 percent of the profits go to the actors because they wrote the scenario. They did everything in the film. But even if the contract is observed, we have now created the idea that culture is something to sell or to buy, an idea the Africans never had. This is a long-range distortion that will become increasingly important. Nobody seems to care about this. Consider this possibility: today we make a film in a "backward" region. Ten years from now, the inhabitants of that region may see it on television, perhaps via some orbital satellite. Most likely they will still be poor. What has been the benefit for their culture? And now the African national governments create another distortion. They say if something is done within their borders, it is part of the "national" culture. This is really absurd because a tribe may be cut into three parts, with its people becoming citizens of three separate political states. The people shown in the lion-hunting film have been divided among the states of Upper Volta, Mali, and Niger. The students at each respective national university consider the culture of the tribes in their particular country to be part of their "national" culture. I believe African anthropologists trained in such universities may ultimately prove more destructive than the Europeans.

One solution I propose to this is to train the people with whom you work to be filmmakers. I don't think it's a complete answer, but it has merits in that it leaves the people with something rather than just taking from them. That would mean that anthropologists would have to have training not only as filmmakers but as teachers of filmmaking. Of course, we can't expect miracles. I once had an African student ask me if much money could be made from film. I told him that if I taught someone how to use a pencil, it did not mean they would become Victor Hugo, only that they could write.

*This matter of rights has cropped up often in discussions of cinema verite made in the United States. For example, Fred Wiseman makes a film about welfare recipients and becomes a "hot" television property. What about the desperate people he has filmed? They remain as before. Having helped yet another professional to a successful career.*

That's the problem. Let me go back to *Chronicle of a Summer.* I brought that very problem to Dauman. He solved it as a businessman might, and it was not bad. Marceline, for instance, was paid for six months, and that was how she got her first job in films. Her story had a very happy ending. She stayed in film, married Joris Ivens, and has made films in Cuba and Vietnam. Angélo could not get work because of the film, and Dauman helped him buy a shop because he felt responsible. We did things like that. Next year will be the eighteenth anniversary of that film, and most of the people in it have prospered because of their involvement.

*Would you tell us something about the film that had its American premiere at the museum—*Cocorico, Monsieur Poulet?
The subject of this film is the "marginals" of Africa. I have come to the conclusion that changes in society are due primarily to those few people who are on the fringe of society, those who see the economic absurdity of the system. I regard them as a kind of populist avant-garde. They have to find some way to make a living without being trapped by the system. They are marginal. The plot deals with how three men go with their car into the countryside to buy chickens for resale in a large city. The three men in the film helped me write and film the story. The car you see belonged to Lam, the main character. He would go in a fifty-mile radius looking for chickens, fish, and millet. That car had no license, no brakes, no lights. I thought it would be most interesting to show the routine of this marginal economy.

*In the film the chickens he buys are from a contaminated area. Do you endorse that kind of marginalism?*
There was no contamination. That problem happened two years earlier when there was an epidemic. There was a forbidden zone for perhaps a month. The sign in the film was one we made ourselves. We just put it in at the end as a joke.

*That created a real problem for those of us unfamiliar with the situation. What we see seems to reinforce basic prejudices against Africa. The women cast evil spells. The police are inept. The merchants have a dangerous car held together with spit and glue. People trade in contaminated chickens. Your idea of showing the "hippies" of Africa doesn't register.*

Perhaps this is your own Western prejudice.

*That may be true, but* Cocorico *is presented as a fiction film, not as anthropology. We are all aware that Africa is in transition, and in this fictional work there doesn't seem to be anything positive going on, concretely or in consciousness.*

From my point of view, it is absolutely positive. Africans have had a history of seeing national and international experts come and tell them that their family life is not good and that they do their work incompetently. Lam and the others had seen many such people come and go. They knew that most of these experts never ask the farmers why they are using a particular technique. I can't see how you can make changes until you learn the habits of the people. I believe there is a prejudice against native African culture. You would think a field had never been planted or that advanced cultures had never thrived. If you want to change African farming methods, you must make a twenty-year commitment at the least. How many engineers, specialists, and experts are prepared to spend so much time in a single African nation? Not many. Most prefer to make a fast survey, write a report, and go home. Cocorico shows some of the schemes and strategies used by the common African.

I think the relationship Africans have to their machines is much more positive than the ones in Europe. Lam is a very good mechanic. He can ask anything of his car. It was no problem for him to take the car apart in order to cross the Niger. He did it all by himself. He went to some care about keeping the water from the oil and the cylinder, but he knew what to do. He felt free to rip the car apart because he knew he could put it together with just the simple tools we showed. I could make a film about an African who repairs transistors. He has no formal training, but he has a system with a small loudspeaker like the one in a tape recorder. It is run on a battery and hums when there is a defect in the circuit. This is a spontaneous approach to electronics. You do not have to know the principles of physics to deal with an auto engine or to repair a transistor.

*In the film it seemed that the Africans treated their car like the stereotyped "dumb hillbillies" of Appalachia who are used as comic relief in Hollywood films and on American television.*

I don't know what the relationship between auto and human is in the United States, but in France, if a car is stuck or if there is a flat tire, there is a catastrophe. In Africa, however, it's a joy because you stay there. A person will say, "Good, we are stuck. Now we can stay a few days and meet people whom we never met before and will never meet again." Back in the early forties, we ran cars on a kind of charcoal gas because there was no petrol. We were stuck all the time. At first I would be furious, but I learned the African way, and now I don't mind such things. I don't even wear a watch. That's the kind of perspective I tried to capture in the film.

*What has been the reception of the film in France?*
When the film opened in Paris, I happened to be in Africa. So there was no press conference for the film, no publicity of any kind. Still, it opened in three theaters, and in two months there were fifty thousand paid admissions. The only prints of the film were bad 16 mm prints without subtitles. One of them was used here. The distributor became ambitious and thought to have the film blown up to 35 mm. Five prints were made. Unfortunately the distributor went bankrupt and did not pay the lab. The prints are now blocked, and I am trying to make an arrangement with the laboratory. We are also working to get commercial distribution in Africa.

*Earlier you spoke about making a camera while doing* Chronicle. *You sounded like Lam dealing with his car. Through the years, your equipment has changed quite a bit, hasn't it?*
I began making films with 16 mm because at that time I had no money for 35 mm. That was in 1946, when 16 mm was strictly amateur. Later I got hold of an old American army newsreel camera with an excellent lens. I shot all my earliest films with that camera. What a time we had. There was no editing table or splicer at that time. You had to cut the film by sticking it with your finger. There was no viewer, so I projected the film with a regular projector and cut and cut. There was no sound except with 35 mm. When I completed my second film, I asked some African workers in Paris to play music as they watched a projection. That was a stupid idea, but it gave me genuine African music as an accompaniment, and that was an improvement over nothing.

With the third film, I used the earliest Nagra, the one with a winch. It was supposed to be portable, but there was a handle to turn, and it weighed more than fifty pounds. The film had no sync sound, but there was an attached reel to take up music. Then you had to transfer the sound from the tape to the kind of recording disc used at that time in broadcasting stations. Sometimes I improvised commentary and mixed the sound track. Luckily, television used 16 mm equipment, and with the television boom we got major improvements—the first good splicer, the first viewer, the first sound mixer. Still we wanted real sync sound that was portable. We still had equipment that weighed a ton and required a crew of five if we wanted sync sound. We tried all kinds of tricks to get around the problem. One film called *La pyramide humaine* used a technique that really sounds funny now. The camera was put on a tripod in a blimp, and all the people stood around at the same distance so that you could go from one to the other without any problem of focus. You could have people talk with the camera that way. We used that technique more than once, but it was limited. I'm talking of the fifties now. It was when I was editing that film that we decided to shoot *Chronicle of a Summer.*

*And that was when you built the Eclair.*
Yes, I am so pleased to think about that. By the end of the film, Michel went back to Montreal with a new technique, and we all had a new camera. Everyone learned so much from that experience. I learned to "walk" the camera. I learned to use the wide angle. After that film, French cinema was never quite the same. Everyone wanted to walk with the camera, even if they had the camera on a tripod and rolled it in a wagon. We got them to think about what "truth" in film was. Afterward Coutant made further improvements, and we got the small Eclair. Unfortunately, because of deaths, the main engineers left Paris and went back to Grenoble. They started their own company and have built new cameras. Coutant is still a young man, and he's full of new ideas all the time—crazy, wonderful ideas. He works with Godard.

We all feel there are no secrets. Everyone is capable of learning what there is to learn. If you are going to use a camera, you should know how to repair it. The idea with the new cameras is to have you spend at least a day at the factory. You mount it by yourself and dismount it, three or four times until you know it perfectly. You know what you will film. You know how to readjust the camera, how to fix it. You know that there is a machine and it has no magical insides. If something goes wrong, you can change it like you change a flat tire. There are many films still to be made and many improvements in cameras. Coutant has a three-year plan in mind with a technological breakthrough set for each year. He would like to see a camera with the sound quality of Nagra 4, a camera without cables, a focus mike that could connect with the focus on the lens, and a three-zoom lens with a corresponding sound focus. What is important in the kind of work I have done is to record rituals and ways of living that are rapidly disappearing. With the new equipment, we will be able to make much better films, and the people in those films will be able to make them, too. I look forward to more and more of that.

*III   Chronicle of a Summer:*
*A Film Book by Jean Rouch and*
*Edgar Morin*

# EDGAR MORIN

## Chronicle of a Film

In December 1959, Jean Rouch and I were jurors together at the first international festival of ethnographic film in Florence. Upon my return, I wrote an article that appeared in January 1960 in *France Observateur,* entitled "For a New Cinéma-Vérité." I quote it here because it so clearly conveys the intentions that pushed me to propose to Rouch that he make a film not in Africa this time but in France.

▶ ─────────────────────────────────

### For a New *Cinéma-Vérité*

At this first ethnographic and sociological festival of Florence, the Festival dei Popoli, I got the impression that a new *cinéma-vérité* was possible. I am referring to the so-called documentary film and not to fictional film. Of course, it is through fictional films that the cinema has attained and continues to attain its most profound truths: truths about the relations between lovers, parents, friends; truths about feelings and passions; truths about the emotional needs of the viewer. But there is one truth that cannot be captured by fictional films, and that is the authenticity of life as it is lived.

Soviet cinema of the grande epoque and then films such as *Le voleur de bicyclette* and *La terre tremble* tried their utmost to make certain individuals act out their own lives. But they were still missing that particular irreducible quality that appears in "real life."[1] Taking into account all the ambivalences of the real and of the imaginary, there is in every scene taken from life the introduction of a radically new element in the relationship between viewer and image.

Newscasts present us with life in its Sunday best, official, ritualized, men of state shaking hands, discussions. Once in a while fate, chance, will place in our field of vision a shriveled or a beaming face, an accident, a fragment of truth. This scene taken from life is most often a scene taken from death. As a general rule, the camera is too heavy, it is not mobile enough, the sound equipment can't follow the action, and what is live escapes or closes up. Cinema needs a set, a staged ceremony, a halt to life. And then everyone masquerades—equipped with a supplementary mask on the camera.

Cinema cannot penetrate the depth of daily life as it is really lived. There remains the resource of the "camera-thief," like that of Dziga Vertov, camouflaged in a car and stealing snatches of life from the streets;[2] or like the film *Nice Time*, stealing kisses, smiles, people waiting outside Picadilly Circus. But they can't be seized or caught like scattered snapshots. There remains the resource of camouflaging the camera behind plate glass, as in the Czechoslovakian documentary *Les enfants nous parlent*, but indiscretion seems to halt the filmmaker just as he becomes a spy.

*Cinéma-vérité* was thus at an impasse if it wanted to capture the truth of human relations in real life. What it could seize were the work and actions in the field or the factory; there was the world of machines and technology, there were the great masses of humanity in motion. It is, in fact, this direction that was chosen by Joris Ivens, for example, or the English documentary school of Grierson.

There were some successful breakthroughs into the peasant world, as in Henri Storck's *La symphonie paysanne* and Georges Rouquier's *Le farrebique*. The filmmaker entered a community and succeeded in revealing something of its life to us. There were some equally extraordinary breakthroughs into the world of the sacred and of ceremonies, for example, Rouquier's *Lourdes* and Jean Rouch's *Les maîtres fous*. But documentary cinema as a whole remained outside human beings, giving up the battle with fictional film over this terrain.

Is there anything new today? We got the impression at Florence that there was a new movement to reinterrogate man by means of cinema, as in *The Lambeth Boys*, a documentary on a youth club in London (awarded a prize at Tours); or *On the Bowery*, a documentary on the drunkards in a section of New York; or *The Hunters*, a documentary on the Bushmen; and, of course, the already well known films of Jean Rouch.

The great merit of Jean Rouch is that he has defined a new type of filmmaker, the "filmmaker-diver," who "plunges" into real-life situations.[3] Ridding himself of the customary technical encumbrances and equipped only with a 16 mm camera and a tape recorder slung across his shoulders, Rouch can then infiltrate a community as a *person* and not as the director of a film crew. He accepts the clumsiness, the absence of dimensional sound, the imperfection of the visual image. In accepting the loss of formal aesthetic, he discovers virgin territory, a life that possesses aesthetic secrets within itself. His ethnographer's conscience prevents him from betraying the truth, from embellishing upon it.

What Rouch did in Africa has now begun in our own Western civilization. *On the Bowery* penetrates the real society of drunkards, who are really drunk, and the live location sound recording puts us right in the middle of a live take on what is really happening. Of course, it is relatively easy to film drunken men who are not bothered by the presence of a camera among them. Of course we stay on the margin of real everyday life. But *The Lambeth Boys* tries to show us what young people really are like at play. This could have been achieved only through participant observation, the integration of the filmmaker into the youth clubs, and at the price of a thousand imperfections, or rather of the abandonment of ordinary framing rules. But this type of reporting opens up a prodigiously difficult new route to us. We have the feeling that the documentary wants to leave the world of production in order to show us the world of consumption, to leave the world of the bizarre or the picturesque in order to research the world of intimacy in human relations, or the essence of our lives.

The new *cinéma-vérité* in search of itself possesses from now on its "camera-pen," which allows an author to draft his film alone (16 mm camera and portable tape recorder in hand). It had its pioneers, those who wanted to penetrate beyond appearances, beyond defenses, to enter the unknown world of daily life.

Its true father is doubtless much more Robert Flaherty than Dziga Vertov. *Nanook* revealed, in a certain way, the very bedrock of all civilization: the tenacious battle of man against nature, draining, tragic, but finally victorious. We rediscovered this Flahertian spirit in *The Hunters,* where pre–Iron Age Bushmen chase game that escapes them.[4]

We chose this film for an award not only for its fundamental human truth but also because this truth suddenly revealed to us our inconceivable yet certain kinship with that tough and tenacious humanity, while all other films have shown us its exotic foreignness. The honesty of this ethnographic film makes it a hymn to the human race. Can we now hope for equally human films about workers, the petite bourgeoisie, the petty bureaucrats, about the men and women of our enormous cities? Must these people remain more foreign to us than Nanook the Eskimo, the fisherman of Aran, or the Bushman hunter? Can't cinema be one of the means of breaking the membrane that isolates each of us from others in the metro, on the street, or on the stairway of the apartment building? The quest for a new *cinéma-vérité* is at the same time a quest for a "cinema of brotherhood."[5]

P.S. Make no mistake. It is not merely a question of giving the camera the lightness of the pen that would allow the filmmaker to mingle in the lives of people. It is at the same time a question of making an effort to see that the subjects of the film will recognize themselves in their own roles. We know that there is a profound kinship between social life and the theater, because our social personalities are made up of roles that we have incorporated within ourselves. It is thus possible, as in a sociodrama, to permit each person to play out his life before the camera.[6] And as in a sociodrama, this game has the value of psychoanalytic truth, that is to say, precisely that which is hidden or repressed comes to the surface in these roles, the very sap of life that we seek everywhere and is, nonetheless, within us. More than in social drama, this psychoanalytic truth is played for the audience, which emerges from its cinematographic catalepsy and awakens to a human message. It is then that we can feel for a moment that truth is that which is hidden within us, beneath our petrified relationships. It is then that modern cinema can realize, and it can only realize it through *cinéma-vérité,* that lucid consciousness of brotherhood where the viewer finds himself to be less alien to his fellow man, less icy and inhuman, less encrusted in a false life.

In Florence I proposed to Rouch that he do a film on love, which would be an antidote to *La Française et l'amour,* in preparation at that time. When we met again in February in Paris, I abandoned this project, as it seemed too difficult, and I suggested this simple theme: "How do you live?" a question that should encompass not only the way of life (housing, work) but also "How do you manage in life?" and "What do you do with your life?"

Rouch accepted. But we had to find a producer. I laid out the idea in two minutes to Anatole Dauman (Argos Films), whom I had recently met. Seduced by the combination of Rouch and "How do you live?" Dauman replied laconically, "I'll buy it." I then wrote the following synopsis for the filming authorization, which we had to request of the CNC (Centre National de la Cinématographie).

This film is research. The context of this research is Paris. It is not a fictional film. This research concerns real life. This is not a documentary film. This research does not aim to describe; it is an experiment lived by its authors and its actors. This is not, strictly speaking, a sociological film. Sociological film researches society. It is an ethnological film in the strong sense of the term: it studies mankind.

It is an experiment in cinematographic interrogation. "How do you live?" That is to say, not only the way of life (housing, work, leisure) but the style of life, the attitude people have toward themselves and toward others, their means of conceiving their most profound problems and the solutions to those problems. This question ranges from the most basic, everyday, practical problems to an investigation of man himself, without wanting, a priori, to favor one or the other of these problems. Several lines of questioning stand out: the search for happiness; is one happy or unhappy; the question of well-being and the question of love; equilibrium or lack thereof; stability or instability; revolt or acceptance.

This investigation is carried out with men and women of various ages, of various backgrounds (office workers, laborers, merchants, intellectuals, worldly people, etc.) and will concentrate on a certain number of individuals (six to ten) who are quite different from each other, although none of these individuals could rightly be considered a general "social type."

Considering this approach, we could call this film "two authors in search of six characters." This Pirandellian movement of research will be sensitive and will serve as the dynamic springboard for the film. The authors themselves mingle with the characters; there is not a moat on either side of the camera but free circulation and exchanges. The characters assist in the search, then dissociate themselves, then return to it, and so on. Certain centers of interest are localized (a certain café or group of friends) or are polarized (the problems of couples or of breadwinning).

Our images will no doubt unveil gestures and attitudes in work, in the street, in daily life, but we will try to create a climate of conversation, of spontaneous discussions, which will be familiar and free and in which the profound nature of our characters and their problems will emerge. Our film will not be a matter of scenes acted out or of interviews but of a sort of psychodrama carried out collectively among authors and characters. This is one of the richest and least-exploited universes of cinematographic expression.

At the end of our research, we will gather our characters together; most of them will not yet have met each other; some will have become acquainted partially or by chance. We will show them what has been filmed so far (at a stage in the editing that has not yet been determined) and in doing so attempt the ultimate psychodrama, the ultimate explication. Did each of them learn something about himself or herself? Something about the others? Will we be closer to each other, or will there just be embarrassment, irony, skepticism? Were we able to talk about ourselves? Can we talk to others? Did our faces remain masks? However, whether we reach success or failure in communications during this final confrontation, the success is enough, and the failure is itself a provisional response, as it shows how difficult it is to communicate and in a way enlightens us about the truth we are seeking. In either case, the ambition of this film is that the question that came from the two author-researchers and was incarnated by means of the real individuals throughout the film will project itself on the theater screen, and that each viewer will ask himself the questions "How do you live?" and "What do you do in your life?" There will be no "THE END" but an open "to be continued" for each one.

In the course of subsequent discussions, Dauman, Rouch, and I reach an agreement to proceed with some "trial runs." I propose some dinners in a private home (this will be in Marceline's apartment). The starting principle will be *commensality,* that is, that in the course of excellent meals washed down with good wines, we will entertain a certain number of people from different backgrounds, solicited for the film.[7] The meal brings them together with the film technicians (cameraman, sound recordist, grips) and should create an atmosphere of camaraderie. At a certain given moment, we will start filming. The problem is to lift people's inhibitions, the timidity provoked by the film studio and cold interviews, and to avoid as much as possible the sort of "game" where each person, even if he doesn't play a role determined by someone else, still composes a character for himself. This method aims to make each person's reality emerge. In fact, the *commensality,* bringing together individuals who like and feel camaraderie with each other, in a setting that is not the film studio but a room in an apartment, creates a favorable climate for communication.

Once filming begins, the actors at the table, isolated by the lighting but surrounded by friendly witnesses, feel as though they are in a sort of intimacy. When they allow themselves to be caught up in the questions, they descend progressively and naturally into themselves. It is pretty difficult to analyze what goes on. It is, in a way, the possibility of a confessional but without a confessor, the possibility of a confession to all and to no one, the possibility of *being* a bit of one's self.

This experience also takes on meaning for the person being questioned because it is destined for the cinema, that is to say, for isolated individuals in a dark theater, invisible and anonymous, but present. The prospect of being televised, on the other hand, would not provoke such internal liberation, because then it is no longer a matter of addressing everyone and no one, but a matter of addressing people who are eating, talking.

Of course, no question is prepared in advance. And everything must be improvised. I propose to approach, through a certain number of characters, the problem of work (the laborers), of housing and vacations (the Gabillons), of the difficulty of living (Marceline, Marilou). Rouch chooses the technicians: the cameraman Morillère, who works with him at the

Musée de l'Homme, the sound recordist Rophé, the electrician Moineau. We start at the end of May, as soon as Rouch finishes *La pyramide humaine*.

The first meal concerns Marceline, who also plays the role of all-purpose assistant during this preliminary phase. In spite of the dinner, all three of us are very tense and intimidated. It is the beginning of this meal that appears in the first sequence of the film (the essential part of the rest of that conversation is also reproduced in this volume). At the screening of the rushes, we are disappointed. Marceline has narrated episodes of her life, but she has not revealed herself. My first questions were brutal and clumsy; Marceline closed up, and I went back into my shell. It's Rouch who revived the dialogue.

At the second meal, we have Jacques Mothet. Jacques is a P2 at Renault and belongs to a group called "Socialism or Barbarity." I think he is the only one since Navel to describe in an illuminating way what goes on in a factory. I do not share the views of Socialism or Barbarity, and Mothet considers me with a certain distrust. It was on my insistence that he agreed to participate in this trial. In the course of the meal, a lively discussion pits him against Moineau, our electrician, who scorns factory workers, having emancipated himself to find an independent profession. We get so caught up in the discussion that it does not occur to us to film; we realize too late that we have let something essential escape. We ask Jacques and Moineau to take up the debate again. We film, but there is no longer the same spontaneity.[8] [A short fragment of this scene was integrated in the film. Moineau is cut out; Jacques talks about workers who unsuccessfully try to leave the factory. This fragment is edited together with a later discussion that brings together Jacques, Angélo, and Jean.]

The third trial run is with Marilou. Marilou has been adrift for several months, and during this time I have not had a conversation with her. To my mind, Marilou confirms the idea that the best are those who live with the most difficulty. It suffices here to say that for me the question "How do you live?" necessarily and fundamentally implicated Marilou. The naive viewer will be surprised if I say that ordinarily and especially in public, Marilou is shy. What happened that evening was an unforeseen and distressing plunge, of which the camera evidently only recorded that which emerged in the language and on the face of Marilou.[9] (In the film script that follows, we have almost fully restored my dialogue with Marilou that was cut from the film.)

For the fourth trial we invite Jacques Gabillon and his wife, Simone. I knew Gabillon during the time when I was the editor of the *Patriot Resistant*, the journal of the FNDIRP (Federation of Resistant and Patriotic

Deportees and Internees). From Bordeaux he came to Paris, where he had great difficulty finding work and housing. Since then he has been an employee of the SNCF (the national railroad) for several years. I have the impression that Simone and Jacques invest a large portion of their aspirations on vacations, which are made easier for them by the availability of free railroad tickets. In fact, they are leaving this very evening to spend the Pentecost holidays in Brittany, and we are hoping to hold them here right up to the last minute, so that the camera could record live their fear of missing the train. Through them we plan to raise the issue of modern-day vacations. But I start by talking to them about the question of housing, and the conversation takes an unexpected turn (bedbugs). At this point there is a camera failure, and they leave without attacking the question of vacations. [A section of this scene was put in the film at the beginning of a second Gabillon interview, which we filmed later, at the end of June or early July.]

We want a student. Marceline insists that we take Jean-Pierre. I hesitate because he is too close to Marceline. Rouch says Jean-Pierre is okay. I give in to their opinion (I won't regret it). At the same time it will eventually be a matter of a new trial run with Marceline, who had overcomposed her character in her first trial. We do not forewarn Marceline that she will be included in the course of this dinner. We only tell her to remain seated next to Jean-Pierre. We find that it is difficult to begin a conversation with him. I try to ask him what his reactions are to people of my age. After a few abstract exchanges, Jean-Pierre talks about his feeling of impotence and evokes the woman that he had been unable to make happy. Then I address myself to Marceline, who is very moved. [The last part of this interaction is almost totally preserved in the film.]

Finally we film an encounter between Marceline and Marilou in the presence of Jean-Pierre. Marceline and Marilou had met a month or two earlier and liked each other. Then there was a cooling of this friendship, which I attributed to the first trial runs. (We had been moved by Marilou's trial run, disappointed with Marceline's.) I thought it healthy to open up an explication in front of the camera, during a dinner, of course, in hopes of provoking a revival of the lost friendship by means of a frank explication. In fact, I provoked an even more marked confrontation, in which each one in turn retreated into her solitude. Nothing from this discussion, perhaps the first real argument that has been recorded on film, was included in the final film.[10]

The "trial runs" are finished. We don't know yet that what will end up being the essence of our film has already been shot. The producers have decided to continue but on the condition that Rouch agree to take on a cameraman of great talent (Sacha Vierny) and a master editor (Colpi). I myself would agree, as I accord small importance to such matters, but Rouch, who can only work with technicians that he gets along with well, wants to choose his own. After exhausting discussions, Rouch accepts Viguier (cameraman for *Lourdes* by Rouquier) and Tarbès.

At the same time, Rouch is negotiating with Pierre Braunberger, producer of his preceding films, who does not want Rouch to undertake anything before reworking the editing of *La pyramide humaine*.

Besides this, Rouch and I are beginning to have our differences. For him, the words spoken in the course of the trial runs should illustrate the images. He has had enough of filming in place, in a room with a camera on a tripod. He has had even more than enough of seeing that everything filmed so far is sad; it needs joyful things, gaiety, the other aspect of life. He thinks the film should be centered on two or three heroes; otherwise the spectator runs the risk of being lost in a succession of images, unable to relate to characters he knows nothing about. If necessary, we would establish a plausible plot, as in *La pyramide humaine*. On top of this, Rouch wants to finish up some research that is close to completion: to film in the street with synchronous sound, that is, for example, to capture the conversation of two friends who are walking down the Champs-Elysées. Finally, in the end of June, beginning of July, Rouch thinks that some considerable event may evolve in the course of the summer (generalized conflict starting with the events in the Congo? Peace in Algeria with the conversations of Melun?), and that we must film *Summer 1960* as a chronicle of a capital moment in history.[11]

As for me, I think that the trials are interesting only if the words emerge from the faces, in close-ups, of Gabillon, Marceline, Jean-Pierre, Marilou, Jacques. I think that we must now go to Jacques's actual workplace, that is, to the Renault factory, and maybe film other places of work, such as the offices of the SNCF, where Gabillon is employed. We should also go to leisure places, in the streets of the city. We should attack the political problems that weigh down this summer of 1960—the Congo, the war of Algeria—but I would not like the theme of "How do you live?" to dissolve into the "chronicle of a summer." Neither would I like it to dissolve into two or three people, nor would I like it to be characters, but multiple presences. This means pursuing a survey on three levels: the level of private life, internal and subjective; the level of work and social relations; and finally the level of present history, dominated by the war in Algeria. The film should be a montage of images in which the question "How do you live?" is transformed into "How can one live?" and "What can one do?" which would bounce off the viewer.

Pressed from all sides, in different directions, by two producers, and by me, Rouch establishes a perilous modus vivendi with Braunberger and accepts Viguier-Tarbès from Dauman. While I am forced to be away from Paris, he films on the Champs-Elysées, in synchronous sound, Jean-Pierre and his friend Régis taking a walk; introduces them to some other young people, among whom is Marilou; and finally films a fourteenth of July dance with Jean-Pierre, Régis, Marilou, Landry, and Marceline.

After the Champs-Elysées filming, a triangular discussion opposes Dauman, Viguier, and Rouch. Dauman complains about the poor quality of the picture. From that point on, he wants to block any more technical improvisation and threatens to abandon the film if "drastic" measures are not taken.

I take advantage of the crisis to revive the meals, this time collective meals. At the discussion on Algeria (in addition to Jean-Pierre, Régis, and Marceline) Rouch introduces Jean-Marc, a young filmmaker, and I introduce Céline, a Communist student. This discussion was in fact quite lively, violent, and at certain moments pathetic, at others comical (I was drunk by halfway through the meal); Viguier and the sound recordist, Guy Rophé, participated quite spontaneously. [Only a few pale tatters of this discussion remain in the film, since we have omitted the sections where certain of the young people got very heavily involved.]

The discussion on the Congo is filmed in the open air, on the terrace of the Totem, the restaurant at the Musée de l'Homme. Rouch has introduced Nadine, Landry, and Raymond, who appeared in *La pyramide humaine* while they were high school students in Abidjan. Two discussions result, one an unforeseen discussion on sexual relations between blacks and whites, and the other on the Congo, the first ending the moment Marceline explains the meaning of the number tattooed on her arm.

At this moment, Viguier and Tarbès level the camera at Landry's suddenly solemn face; they then frame the face of Nadine, who has begun to cry near Landry. At that second, the film in the camera runs out, and we could only capture the beginning of Nadine's emotion, as she hides her face in her hands.

Two remarks: (1) In this type of filming, the framing must follow the event. In ordinary films the event is circumscribed by a preestablished frame composition. Here, however, everything depends on instinct, on a sort of telepathic communication that is established between the cameraman and the scene. It is the cameraman's responsibility to capture the significant face, which is not necessarily the speaker's face; in the course of filming, Morillère, Rouch, Viguier, Tarbès, and (later) Brault all had some of these inspired moments that involved more than talent: sympathy and communication.

(2) The expression on a face in tears is radically different in acted cinema and in lived cinema. In acted cinema, the actor forces the expression on his face to signify his tears; even when he is really moved, he exaggerates his emotion so as to convey it. In real life, we make tremendous efforts to dissemble tears: we hold back sobs, tighten our facial muscles; we inhibit instead of exhibit. This was revealed at the playback projection of the scenes where Marceline (the dinner with Jean-Pierre), Marilou, and Nadine (fleetingly, because there was no more film) are in tears.

Around the twentieth of July, we lose our cameraman. However, I have already made arrangements with the Renault Corporation so that we can film in their factory workshops. We have to film before July 28, the date when the factory closes for vacation. I had already asked Jacques to pick out some young workers to do a discussion-dinner on their work, and there was only one evening—or night, rather—when we could get them together after work let out.

Argos Films assigned us a director of production, who has the disagreeable job of overseeing the technical conditions of the filming. He is ordered to authorize filming only if a clap stick slate is used: this order was not always respected. It is a director of shorts, Heinrich, who accepted this job so as to watch Rouch film and to get to know his methods. As I insist on the need for the workers' meal, Heinrich calls on two television cameramen. We go to the factory exit to look for Jacques, who introduces us to Angélo and Jean. The technical preparations are difficult. It is late. We are tired. At around three in the morning, we film a discussion that reveals Angélo and Jean to us. [Only a thin fragment of this discussion is integrated in the film.]

We have forty-eight hours before vacation closing to film in the Renault factories at Billancourt. We hire Coutard, who worked with a handheld camera in Godard's *À bout de souffle* and is free for a few days before he has to begin *Le petit soldat*. What we have to film, unlike industrial documentaries, is not machines but the faces and hands of the workers. The vacant faces of those who do mechanical work, the specialized workers, appendages of their machines, eternally repeating the same gestures. We should also film the relationships between boss-foremen and workers, but this is impossible; we would have to camouflage microphones and cameras in every corner of the shops.

Following Jacques's indications, I keep an eye out for the most significant scenes. While Coutard's assistant cameraman, Beausoleil, sets up a camera on a tripod with a microphone fixed next to it, Coutard and Rouch wander among the machines. Coutard, with 35 mm camera in hand, ultrasensitive film (which needs no lighting), and telephoto lens, shoots scenes

of the factory without being noticed. We also film the great vacation exodus from the factory, with three cameras set up at different points. We accumulate almost an hour and a half of film. We have not filmed Angélo,
Jean, and Jacques at their machines, for fear of unfavorable reactions from
the management, either for them later or for us at the moment.

Shortly thereafter—or shortly before?—we have a dinner with the
Gabillons, again at Marceline's apartment, where we bring up several different subjects about happiness and about work. Jacques Gabillon talks about
"two men" who are in him and of the modern-day man, "a bunch of identity papers." [Part of this meal makes up the second half of the Gabillon
sequence.]

In the meantime Rouch and Dauman reach an agreement to hire the
Canadian cameraman Michel Brault. Brault had shot some short films with
a handheld camera and in synchronous sound for the Canadian National
Film Board. Rouch knew him and admired his work. After several intercontinental telegrams and phone calls, Brault agrees to come and arrives in
Paris at the end of July, beginning of August. This is the chance for Rouch
to victoriously resume his filming experiments in the street, in nature, with
synchronous sound. This time Rouchian "pédovision" will replace my
"commensality." (This is what we call the two methods used in this film.)

The fifteenth of August approaches. Rouch wants to film Marceline
alone in the streets of deserted Paris on August 15. Marceline proposes
going to the Place de la Concorde, where Dmytryck is making a film about
the German occupation. It is studded with Wehrmacht direction signs; there
are extras dressed up as German soldiers. We arrive at the Place de la
Concorde on August 15, but Dmytryck's filming ended the day before;
the German signs have disappeared, no more Wehrmacht.

Rouch inaugurates the new methods: Marceline will have a tape recorder slung across her shoulders, connected to a clip-on lavaliere microphone brought by Brault; she will walk along, talking to herself in a low
voice. Brault films her from Rouch's Citroën 2 CV with Rouch at his side.
Heinrich, Rophé, his assistant, and I push the 2 CV for the dolly shot. We
continue at the Place de l'Opéra, hardly deserted: August 15 was quite
populated this year—not only tourists, but Parisians as well. I propose a
quiet street in the Sentier, rue Beauregard (where a few unknowns begin to
gather), and then Les Halles, where the strangely dead setting, a sort of station from a nightmare, makes Marceline recall the transport to Auschwitz
and the return. To establish contact with normal life, Rouch makes
Marceline walk under the Arcades on the rue de Rivoli, where she continues to talk to herself whenever inspired by the store windows. [In the

film we have kept the Place de la Concorde and Les Halles sequences from this filming.]

Once again Rouch is struck with the desire to leave the "sad" problems and look for something else. He takes advantage of a meeting in Saint Jean de Luz with Braunberger to take off with Nadine, Landry, and Brault. He films several scenes between Nadine and Landry on the road, at the seashore, where Nadine and Landry are supposed to be two student hitchhikers who take off to the south of France on vacation. [From this shooting there remains a fragment of the bullfight in the final film.]

Rouch wants to film Saint Tropez, continuing the hitchhiking adventure of Landry and Nadine, and reintroducing Marilou, Jean-Pierre, and Marceline. As this idea holds absolutely no appeal for me, he tries to win me over by saying that we'll film my little daughters in Saint Tropez, discovering some new starlets. What finally makes up my mind is the idea of Landry as "black explorer of France on vacation."

Meanwhile Rouch has the idea of a pseudo–Brigitte Bardot, whom we will put in the setting Saint Tropez. This idea appeals to Dauman, who sets out to look for pseudo–Brigitte Bardots; his associate Lifchitz goes off on his own hunt. We run the risk of being inundated with false BBs, but Argos Films, to economize, hires only one—the real Sophie Destrade.

While the Saint Tropez expedition is being prepared to Rouch's great joy, I learn that Marilou is leading a new life. She no longer feels as lonely as before and has met a young man with whom she is in love. I propose a new dialogue with Marilou, which takes place in my home. Marilou has forewarned me that she will not talk about her friend; her apprehension makes her very nervous. (We had to wait two hours before the equipment was ready to function, and she had to get back to her office.) As she spoke her facial expression changed from joy to fear to the sadness of memory to hope. ["Marilou Is Happy" sequence.]

Marceline has stayed in Paris while Jean-Pierre is on vacation with Régis in the south. She thinks Jean-Pierre is drifting away from her. She has family problems. We film a conversation with her, but she has been, unconsciously, influenced by the rushes she has seen of Marilou. [This dialogue with Marceline was not integrated into the film.] From this point on, we no longer show the rushes to the participants, except to Angélo, who has a skeptical, even ironic, interest in our enterprise.

Rouch, Brault, Marilou, Landry, Nadine, and Catherine take the "Caravelle" airliner. Rouch introduces Catherine, who is a happy woman: she has no problems, he says (unfortunately she will have some problems in Saint Tropez). In the plane, Rouch films a conversation between Catherine and Landry, who pretend they are just meeting. He films Marilou and Landry. In the train from Nice to Saint Raphaël, he films again. [Nothing of all of this is preserved in the film.]

At this point Rouch and I have a clear difference of opinion. Rouch wants to film a surrealist dream with Marilou, where she wanders alone in the night, dances, goes for a walk in the cemetery, meets a man who is wearing the mask of Eddie Constantine; the man pursues her, unmasks himself, and it's Landry. I tell him that I am against this scene, as any fiction falsifies the very meaning of what has already been filmed. Rouch films Catherine water-skiing. I grumble. Finally we reach an agreement: I'll stick to everything having to do with "Landry, black explorer"; I'll stick to the false Brigitte Bardot and to the staged publicity photographers attracting the crowd of tourists; I propose a collective discussion on the theme of Saint Tropez, and I maintain that we must film a dialogue between Jean-Pierre and Marceline.[12]

The Saint Tropez discussion takes place on the terrace of a hotel, but the film used to record this discussion was, by mistake, mostly ultrasensitive film. [The film retains a brief moment of the usable segment, and Sophie's comments in the discussion are used as voice-over while she walks at l'Épi beach.]

I revive the theme of happiness in a conversation filmed with my two daughters, with Landry intervening. [A fragment of the conversation was preserved in the film.]

During these two days of filming, Marceline and Jean-Pierre are having difficulties in their relationship. I ask them again if they would agree to try to work out their relationship in front of the camera. I tell Jean-Pierre separately that this scene, where for the first time the camera would film a couple's discussion, would be meaningful only if it were not thought out in advance. Since for some time Marceline has had the tendency to compose her own character, Jean-Pierre would have to avoid allowing the climate of their dialogue to become too literary. What would Marceline and Jean-Pierre decide? I don't know. We waited until the last minute to tell Jean-Pierre and Marceline that it was their turn, and Rouch chose a little nearby jetty. There is a strong mistral on the embankment. Jean-Pierre and Marceline sit side by side. Rouch is listening in through headphones; he's the only one who can hear the dialogue. Brault is lying three meters away with the camera, and I myself at three meters' distance can hear nothing. Jean-Pierre has the clip-on lavaliere microphone. From time to time Brault says "cut," and he changes angle; Jean-Pierre responds by clapping his hands to slate the next scene. [This scene was condensed in the editing, not by choosing one continuous segment but by selecting and juxtaposing different moments. The viewer also sees frequent shot changes, and under these conditions it is difficult to escape the idea of staging, especially since it is difficult to believe that a couple could agree to give themselves up in such a way to the camera. This sequence, which was cut out by Argos in the copy passed on exclusively to the Agriculteurs, is kept in the other copies.[13] It shows much more pointedly than the other sequences the problems of conventional cinematic editing in relation to our filmed material. In spite of the misunderstandings it might engender, I think this scene necessary because it witnesses an extreme point of our enterprise.][14]

We return to Paris. Argos (in a new repressive phase) wants to limit our filming days. Rouch cannot film if he feels pressured. I suggest to Rouch that he accept the limits; if we have not completed our program, Argos will be obliged to make us finish the film. But interminable discussions continue.

Nonetheless, I establish a filming schedule in a spirit of compromise with Rouch: since Rouch wants some "heroes," I make an effort to put some emphasis on the worker-heroes Angélo, Jacques, and Jean. At the same time, to revive the theme of "How do you live?", which has already been considerably compromised, I propose interviews in the street where Marceline and Nadine stop passersby and ask them, "Are you happy?" Again I take up the theme we had already planned, of encounters among our characters: worker-student encounters, encounters of women among themselves, encounters of men, to lead up to the grand final encounter. To start, we are going to approach the question of the return from vacation. Rouch accepts this program: he also wants to film conversations on the terrace of a café (Les Deux Magots), in a department store like Galeries Lafayette, and an encounter in the women's shop that Catherine has on the Left Bank. The film crew for this last shooting period is made up of Brault (cameraman); Rophé (sound; in his absence either Rouch or Boucher take care of it); and Morillère and Boucher (general assistants), who are attached to the committee on ethnographic film. Rouch has arranged with the engineer Coutant the possibility of working with his new prototype electronic 16 mm camera, which is lighter and, more important, *soundproof,* that is to say, we can film anywhere, without a "blimp" to absorb camera noise.

The end of vacation means first of all back to school: we film Irène, Véronique, and their little friend Dominique leaving the Fénelon high school during the first days of school and walking home on rue Soufflot. The Rouch technique is in full force here. Véronique has the clip-on microphone and a tape recorder slung over her shoulders; they walk freely. Brault, guided by hand signals from Rouch, follows or precedes them, filming up close with a wide-angle lens. Thus in this procession where filmers and filmees almost form one body, the normal movement of passers-by is almost undisturbed, the characters in movement feel at ease with the camera, their comments are directly related to the spectacle in the street (a *France-Soir* headline, a cinema poster, a shop window, etc.). The sound leaves something to be desired: every step Véronique takes jostles the tape recorder; we can hear a sound like a heartbeat, certain words are barely audible. We also film Véronique and Irène doing their first homework, questioned by Nadine on their first days back to school and on the characters in the film. These scenes were not included in the film. I would have liked to see them ask more about the opinion of the two little girls on the world of adults, on their own "How do you live?"

The end of vacation is also Jean-Pierre preparing for his philosophy exams, which he failed in June. An important theme: if Jean-Pierre fails them again in October, he will lose his deferment and be called up for military service, that is to say, Algeria. We film a discussion scene at Jean-Pierre's desk with Régis. They talk in ironic terms of philosophy; they consult the list of signatures for the call of the 121; they blame Rouch and me for not signing, trying to get a rise out of us. Then we film Jean-Pierre coming out of his exam. He leaves the Sorbonne; Régis is waiting for him in the square with the tape recorder over his shoulder and clip-on microphone on his lapel. Brault films their encounter and follows them. While they head toward the Seine on small side streets, they talk about the written dissertation, then about one thing or another in a half-serious, half-joking tone. On the quays of the Seine, Régis asks Jean-Pierre what his plans are for the future and whether he imagines himself joining in. Jean-Pierre does not want to join in. They walk away along the quays "toward the east, toward the future," says Régis, who will, in the next year, belong to the Communist Party. When Jean-Pierre finds out he has passed, we film Rouch, Morin, and Jean-Pierre walking in the gardens of l'Observatoire. Jean-Pierre is questioned about his plans for the future. [None of these scenes are in the final film.]

The end of vacation is Marilou returning home; her fragile happiness seems to have consolidated a bit. We shoot a scene in a hotel room on rue Gît-le-Coeur, where she goes to see her friend Jeanne, whom she hasn't seen since she got back. Jeanne asks her questions about her vacation, her plans. Marilou is relaxed, cheerful. [This scene, kept almost up to the last minute, was finally not included in the film (to my great regret, since it showed Marilou smiling and joking), as with almost all scenes dealing with the return from vacation and events that follow the vacations.]

The end of vacation is also the Gabillons returning with souvenirs and photos of their vacation in Spain. We go to the Gabillons' apartment, in their low-cost housing development in Clichy, and we film their breakfast and ask them to bring out their photos and talk about their vacation. [This scene was not included in the film.]

In filming the return from vacation, we took advantage of the chance to film daily life. Marilou and her boyfriend getting washed and dressed in her little room; the camera follows them down the service stairs (the longest stairway traveling shot that has ever been done, Brault's camera following Marilou's hands on the banister rail), in the street, then Marilou walking up the Champs-Elysées, going into her office (at Cahiers du Cinéma), working on some letters, and typing. [Some of these shots were included; one at the beginning of the first Marilou sequence, the others at the end of the second Marilou sequence.]

Daily life: that means filming the life outside work of Angélo, Jean, and Jacques. We start with Angélo, whom we meet at the exit of the factory and who is then followed by Brault in the street, on the bus, at home, without interruption until nightfall. We don't know where Angélo lives, and we discover the interminable stairway that goes up to the Clamart plateau (we could not have found such a setting if we had searched for one like it), the suburban streets that change from urban to rustic, and finally the little cottage where Angélo lives with his mother. We also discover how Angélo spends his time: doing judo exercises (he is a judoka amateur), playing guitar, reading (a life of Danton), then dinner and bed. Since Angélo gets up at 4:45 the next morning, he goes to bed early. We tell him to leave his key in the door so we can film him waking up. At three in the morning, Morillère comes to wake me up while Boucher waits in the street. Completely naked, haggard, I open the door for him; he flees. I catch up to him and then call Rouch. I tear him from his sleep. Rouch phones Brault. We pick up Rouch and Brault in Dauphine and cursing the film, empty stomached, we hurry to Clamart. In the darkness we penetrate like burglars into Angélo's little garden. Boucher steps in manure, stifling his curses. We finally enter the bedroom on tiptoe, holding back our laughter. Brault hoists his camera up to his shoulder, and that's the signal: we turn on the lights. While Brault shoots, we see Angélo coming out of sleep under the effects of the light. When he discovers us, flabbergasted, he curses at us, and we burst into laughter. [This shot of his waking is retained in the film. It does not strike the spectator, who cannot tell the difference with a fake movie alarm clock ring.] Angélo has his coffee with milk, brought to him by his mother, then gets up, washes, gets dressed, leaves the house, takes the bus, et cetera . . . the camera follows him up till the moment when he disappears into the factory by the great door on the Place National, while we see, as though a director had prepared everything, two guards in uniform watching the entrances and, in front of the door, a worker distributing leaflets. [A certain number of shots from this Angélo filming were preserved and edited into the final film.]

This same morning, Angélo is called in by the management of his shop, where he is informed that he has been transferred to another, very tough shop. Did this bullying have anything to do with our cinematographic intervention the day before, at the factory exit? (The shop foreman said to him, "So, we're making movies now?") The next morning Angélo comes to find me and explains the affair. As Rouch is supposed to come with Brault a bit later, I tell him that we absolutely must film. They arrive, and Angélo explains what happened to Rouch in a three-sided discussion. They ask him about his future. Angélo, discouraged, wants to leave the tool machines. Could we find him work? We'll have to look around. [An important part of this scene was included in the film. Even though chronologically it takes place after vacation, we put it in before the vacation sequences, given that we wanted to include it and that we wanted to end the film at the end of the vacation.]

Following this incident, Jean, the young worker-turned-draftsman, no longer wants to be filmed. He will only agree to participate in a discussion between students and workers. We film Jacques waking, getting up, leaving for the factory; he lives in Montmartre and goes by motorbike to Billancourt. We follow him in two cars, one behind, lighting him with its headlights, the other either beside him or slightly ahead, with Brault filming. [None of this is included in the film.]

Taking advantage of the last weeks of good weather, Jacques, his wife, their children, Angélo, and sometimes other friends often go to Fontainebleau forest, near Milly, for the weekend. Even though Rouch is again deeply involved in worker life, I insist that we go to Milly-la-Forêt. Rouch organizes a parallel expedition with Nadine, Catherine, and Landry. We leave in several cars and with two cameras (Brault and Morillère). We have a picnic and film what is going on (rock climbing, climbing down with ropes, children's games, songs). [One part of what was filmed here constitutes the Milly-la-Forêt sequence in the film.]

Are you happy? Since the beginning of the film, Rouch has thought that Nadine could be a sort of woman-sphinx who would ask a riddle of passersby in the street. To my mind, this question should be "Are you happy?" asked by Marceline and Nadine together (one alone would be intimidated) in different areas of Paris. The camera would be hidden in a car; the microphone would be visible. We film at Place du Panthéon, rue Soufflot, Place de la Bastille, at Ménilmontant, at the Passy metro, at Place

Victor Hugo. [A certain number of these interviews constitute the "Are You Happy?" sequence.]

At the same time, we envisage several surveys in greater depth on the theme of "How do you live?" Marceline obtains the consent of a postal service employee to interview him and his wife in their home [not included in the film] and of a garage mechanic, whom she interviews in his shop [a good part is included in the film]. Rouch knows a happy young couple, the Cuénets, who are also interviewed [this interview is, for the most part, included in the film]. At around the same time, we record a walking dialogue between me and Rouch at the Musée de l'Homme where we try to tie things up. [This dialogue was not included in the film.]

I am keen on the encounters, and I envisage an encounter between workers and students, an encounter among the women who participated in the film, and an encounter among the men, before the general encounter. Material obstacles and the time factor (Argos makes it clear that everything must be finished by the end of October) prevent us from organizing all but the student-worker encounter. One Sunday noon we organize a lunch at the restaurant of the Musée de l'Homme with Angélo, Jean, Régis, and Jean-Pierre. After some embarrassing slow starts, the conversation livens up.

Angélo and Jean attack the students for their arrogance with regard to workers. Jean-Pierre and Régis explain themselves. [This discussion was not included in the film.] At a neighboring table sat Landry. Rouch wants Angélo and Landry to meet each other. We all go to my house, and Rouch sets them face-to-face on a step of the stairway. Angélo had very much liked the rushes where Landry appeared, commenting on the bullfight, moralizing to the little girls, talking about his black skin. Angélo seemed like a good guy to Landry, who had likewise seen him on the screen. In fact, a friendship was born before our eyes, under the eye of the camera. At the same time Angélo fully expresses his protest against both the conditions of the workers and what he sees as the false compensation for these conditions, this embourgeoisement symbolized by the possession of a car.

Rouch prepares the filming in Catherine's shop, where Nadine, Sophie, and Marceline are supposed to participate. There is a tension between Marceline and Catherine ever since Saint Tropez. On top of that, Marceline is critical of Catherine's "bourgeois lifestyle." I tell Marceline that she may "attack," but I also tell her that it would be better not to touch on any private problems. The camera is hidden in the back of the shop; the microphone is also hidden. Marceline, Nadine, and Sophie are among the clients (who are unaware of the filming); they try things on. Suddenly Marceline attacks. Her accusations become more and more precise and intimate, whereas Catherine is very relaxed. Nadine, feeling uneasy, says to Marceline,

"We're leaving," and they depart. [We baptized this sequence "Thunder over the Petticoats." It was not included in the film. A part of the sound track is pretty inaudible; the shop door was left open for several minutes, and the street noises drowned out the words.]

A few days later Rouch films a conversation on the terrace of the Deux Magots, without disturbing the regular customers (camera camouflaged in a car parked on the sidewalk, microphone camouflaged under a handkerchief). Marceline and Nadine comment on the outburst that occurred at Catherine's. One afternoon, a couple of days later, we film at the Old Navy, a café where Marceline is a regular. We record a conversation between Marceline and Marilou on the terrace using the same method. Marceline talks about Jean-Pierre; she says that they have reached a new agreement, founded on freedom and mutual trust. We also film a breakfast in bed with Marceline and Jean-Pierre, then their rising and morning ritual. [None of these scenes, each of which uncovers a new aspect of Marceline, was included in the film.]

At last we shoot the final encounter. I had dreamed of a sort of confrontation in a large room after projecting the film, with multiple cameras and microphones recording not only the reactions to the film but also the conversations that would start up spontaneously and according to the affinities among the different characters. A big final scene where the scales would fall and consciousness would be awakened, where we would take a new "oath of the tennis court" to construct a new life.[15]

Of course this is no longer feasible. It is no longer possible to show the entire film. Of course nothing has been edited, and we must hurry to finish before the deadline. We choose the shortcut of using the rushes that were specific to each of the characters. Marilou happy, Marceline–August 15, Jean-Pierre and Régis coming out of exam, return from vacation–Gabillon, Milly-la-Forêt, and a few other fragments. The reunion takes place in the projection room of the Studio Publicis, in the basement. After showing the film, we open the discussion. [This was abridged in the film, but all of the critical aspects were retained.]

In this sequence, voluntarily or involuntarily, Angélo, Marceline, and Marilou all say something essential about themselves, each one revealing in a word just what they had done in the moment when the camera's eye was trained on them. I feel that Rouch is distressed by the criticisms. We separate at the Champs-Elysées; it is raining; it's the last reel, Brault films the wet, glistening sidewalk, which reflects the passersby. The unfinished film is completed. Nearly six months of effort, of passion, of arguments, of camaraderie, of experience, of research abruptly become memories. I will no longer wake Rouch at 8 A.M.; Brault will take off for Canada. Each person goes off on his own. It is autumn.

The film is finished.

Renault lays off two thousand workers. Angélo is one of them. I tried to find him work, first doing odd jobs for some friends, while waiting. He almost learned how to make tapestries in the studio of a friend, Yvette Prince, but the studio was going through a difficult period; he did a stint as a warehouse man for a publishing firm, where he began to show his demanding spirit; he was fired ("What do you want?" he asks me philosophically, "I'm a revolutionary"). Nina Baratier, a film editor, found him a place as stagehand at the Billancourt studios in the early spring. He wants to get away from the machines, and we are trying to help him. One day Angélo disappears from the studios. He had found a skilled worker job in a little metalwork factory, much smaller than Renault. He was supposed to get married. He has since gotten married.

The intervention of the film has thus had a pretty powerful effect on Angélo's life. In the first phase, it crystallized his revolt against the alienation of manual labor, in the hopes of escaping machines. For several months he experienced other types of work (warehouse man, stagehand). He was able to see the possible significance of a choice between an independent but chancy job and a subordinate but regular job; between his qualification as a machinist and those of other jobs for which he had no technical training. Of course I did not push him in any particular direction; I always looked in the direction he indicated. If he does finally return to the machines, it will be less by force than by his own choice.

Marilou is trying hard to hold the ground she has gained. The couple has some difficult money problems. Recently, Marilou has had the opportunity to learn a skill that is much more interesting and freer than secretarial work: studio photography.

Marceline, the film finished, could not return to her applied psychosociological surveys. Argos helped her out. She is looking for work she would like; in fact, she could be an actress. Jean-Pierre lives with her.

Jean-Pierre passed his exams and is pursuing his degree. He is looking for a job that would not keep him from preparing for his next exams.

Landry, after having spent the last year in a provincial high school, is taking a private course in Paris. Nadine is going to take her baccalaureate exams in philosophy. Gabillon took a trip to Greece. He would like a more interesting job and hopes to get into the European railroad agency. Régis went on vacation to Cuba and upon his return joined the Communist Party. The Cuénets are going to have a baby. All of them regret that the film only showed a one-sided view of themselves. They all feel they are richer, more complex, than their images on film. This is obviously true.

▶

## Editing

We have more than twenty-five hours of film, almost all of it 16 mm. Now we have to extract a film of normal length (one and one-half hours). It's not only a technical problem (the transformation of real time into cinematographic time, the new significance presented by images when edited, the type of editing to choose, etc.); it's also the problem of the meaning of the film. Anything is possible with our enormous corpus of multiple, uniform material.

Everything becomes complicated, and once again a three-sided crisis breaks out. Argos Films wants to have one "editor in chief" who will give the film an "incontestable technical and artistic quality." Rouch refuses the editors they propose and wants to choose the woman who edited his earlier films. Rouch can only work with people he chooses according to his affinity and compatibility. At the same time, Rouch announces that he has to go to Africa for two months; Argos opposes his departure, which would immobilize the editing. For my part, I want to work on the editing from a position of equality with Rouch, because I fear that the "How do you live?" sense of the film might disappear.

For Rouch, the guiding thread should be one or two "hero" characters in the film. He even suggests me as the hero of the film, off in search of the unfindable truth. General ideas bore him; what he is always interested in is the living detail, spontaneity. He wants to proceed by approximations, that is, by successive elimination of images until the normal duration is reached, just as he did in *La pyramide humaine*. He does not want to feel bound in advance by any norm, any idea. On the contrary. On the other hand, I feel that a large part of the richness of *La pyramide humaine* was lost in the editing, to the benefit of the heroine, to the benefit of the plot. I value those themes I would like to see expressed.[16]

I don't have a real plan, but a sort of structure that I rediscover at every stage of the elaboration of the film. Thus, for example, at the end of July, Argos Films asked for a schema of the editing, as assurance that we were not simply filming at random. I improvised a text where the following themes were presented in succession: (1) monotony: shades of gray; (2) factory and office work; (3) the difficulties of living (loneliness and happiness); (4) love; (5) the sounds of the world in summer, 1960; (6) on the road again.

Later on, once the editing had begun, Rouch and I would be interviewed by *France Observateur*. This interview conveys our differences as well as our agreement, as evidenced in the following extract:

*What is the importance of the editing of this film, given that you have twenty-five hours of rushes?*

ROUCH: There's the crucial point! We are in conflict, Edgar and I—a temporary and fruitful conflict, I hope. My position is the following: The interest of this story is the film; it's the chronology and evolution of the people as a function of the film. The subject itself is not very interesting. It is difficult to bring together the testimonies, because they are often heterogeneous. There are people who cheat a little, others not at all. To bring together their testimonies would be to falsify the truth. I'll take a simple example: we asked people one question, among others, "What do you think of your work?" Most of these people said they were bored in their jobs. The reasons they give are very different: intellectual reasons, sentimental, physical reasons, et cetera. Bringing these reasons together, in my opinion, is less interesting than the individuals themselves and finding out the motives behind their responses. There are some marvelous contradictions in certain scenes of the film; sometimes people contradict themselves in a fantastic way. For example, Angélo, the worker who has been let go by Renault, is talking with Landry, the young African. Landry says to him: "You're at Renault? . . . Ah, it's well known in Africa, the Renault Company! You don't see anything else . . . 1,000 kilos, Dauphines . . ." And all of a sudden Angélo, before even replying, breaks into a smile and says: "Oh yeah? You've heard of the Renault Company?" It's inimitable!

So from the point of view of editing, my idea is the following: with some rare exceptions, it is almost impossible to upset the filming order. The people evolved in such a way that, if we want to become attached to them, it is necessary to show them as a function of their evolution. In fact, the whole film was conceived that way. That's how I see the film. And that's why I center it on the summer: it begins in spring and ends in autumn. It's the evolution of a certain number of people throughout events that could have been essential but were not. We thought in the spring that the summer of 1960 would be essential for France. It wasn't, but even with this sort of disappointment, this evolution is nonetheless, to my mind, the subject of the film.

So the editing that I am doing at present, which can, of course, be changed, is much more a chronological editing as a function of the filming than editing as a function of the subject or of the different subjects dealt with in the filming.

MORIN: I think that we must try to maintain in the editing a plurality. The great difficulty is that there are in fact many themes. What I would like is to concentrate this collective halo around the characters. In other words, I would not, in the end, like to see everything reduced to purely individual stories, but rather there should be a dimension, not so much of the crowd, but of the global problem of life in Paris, of civilization, and so forth.

What I would like is that at every moment we feel that the characters are neither "film heroes" as in ordinary cinema nor symbols as in a didactic film, but human beings who emerge from their collective life. What I would like is not to situate individualities as we see them in normal films—in classical, fictional narrative films—where there are characters and some story happens to those characters. I would like to talk about the individual characters in order to go on to a more general problem and then come back from the general problem to the individual.

This means doing a sort of *cinéma-vérité* that would overcome the fundamental opposition between fictional and documentary cinema. In fictional cinema, the private problems of individuals are dealt with: love, passion, anger, hatred; in documentary film until now only subjects external to the individual are dealt with: objects, machines, countrysides, social themes.

Jean and I agree at least on one point: that we must make a film that is totally authentic, as true as a documentary, but with the same concepts as fictional film, that is, the contents of subjective life, of people's existence. In the end, this is what fascinates me.

Another thing that fascinates me on the theme of *cinéma-vérité* is not just reviving the ideas of Dziga Vertov or things of that genre, but—and this is what is really new, from the technical point of view, in what Jean has said—it is that *cinéma-vérité* can be an authentic talking cinema. It is perhaps the first time that we will really end up with a sketch of talking cinema. The words burst forth at the very moment when things are seen—which does not occur with postsynchronization.

ROUCH: In the empty Halles, when Marceline is talking about her deportation, she speaks in rhythm with her step; she is influenced by the setting, and the way she is speaking is absolutely inimitable. With postsynchronization and the best artist in the world, you would never be able to achieve that unrelenting rhythm of someone walking in a place like that.

MORIN: In addition, it is a film where there are no fistfights, no revolver shots, not even any kisses, or hardly any. The action, in the end, is the word. Action is conveyed by dialogues, disputes, conversations. What interests me is not a documentary that shows appearances but an active intervention to cut across appearances and extract from them their hidden or dormant truths.

ROUCH: Another extraordinary thing that you've forgotten, and that's understandable, is the poetic discovery of things through the film. For example: a worker, Angélo, leaves the Renault factory, takes the bus to go home, and gets off at Petit-Clamart. To get to his house, he has to climb up a stairway, an unbelievable stairway, and this ascent—after all, it's only a worker on his way home—becomes a sort of poetic drama.

MORIN: Our common base is that neither one of us conceives of this film as merely sociological or merely ethnographic or merely aesthetic, but really like a total and diffuse thing that is at the same time a document, an experience lived by each person, and a research of their contact.

Rouch proposes to me an alternate method of working: he'll start on his own to make a preliminary selection of six to eight hours, head to tail, before he leaves for Africa in three weeks. Then he leaves me to edit during his three-week absence. And so on, from confrontation to confrontation, we will reach an agreement.

The Rouch-Dauman agreement on the editor in chief having not been achieved, we will work with Nina Baratier, who has been taking care of the film since August, assisted by Françoise Colin. Thus begins the first phase of editing.

Rouch comes up with a stringout of about seven hours. At the screening I see that many sequences that I consider essential have been eliminated and that others that seem uninteresting have been chosen. I feel as though everything is caving in. I, in turn, then take the editing, reestablish some of the eliminated sequences, and eliminate some of those that Rouch had retained, to end up with about four hours of screen time. Now Rouch is dissatisfied.

He takes over the editing, makes a four-hour version starting with the introduction of the characters, and follows the chronology of the film in their wake. The introductions are disappointing. I resume editing and in a couple of days have a schema that starts with the "Are you happy," follows the theme of work, political problems (Algeria, the Congo), personal life, to end up with a conclusion in which, in a few flash images, each of the characters expresses his revolt. The last image: Angélo fighting alone with a tree. The screening is disappointing. On the way we have made concessions to each other: Rouch reestablished some moments that were important for me; I did not cut some moments that he is fond of.

Finally we reach an agreement on a compromise of principles.

Compromise: the film will not be a mosaic-type montage as I wanted it, made up of opposing sequences, sustained by the guiding theme "How do you live?" nor will it be a biographico-chronological montage as Rouch wanted. It will be something mixed, between the two. We agree on the fundamental sequences that I, for my part, would like to include almost in their entirety, without condensing them. I propose a compromise schema, abandoning the final montage on "resistance" and the ultimate symbol of Angélo fighting with the tree, and adopting the three-part chronological order: before vacation, the vacation, after vacation.

But by now the debate between Rouch and me is no longer taking place in private. Argos Films intervenes, sometimes mistrusting Rouch and wanting to oversee his work (which he refuses), at other times being enthusiastic over Rouch. According to these alternating attitudes, Rouch is either a clumsy *bricoleur* or an inspired improviser. Dauman gives me no credit for my capacities as neophyte editor but thinks at times that my contribution is efficient and at other times that I am an abstract theoretician who is massacring the film. Dauman is sometimes Rouchist, sometimes Morinist, quite often groans to see our combined incapacities, and is constantly railing against Nina Baratier. In the beginning Nina Baratier sides sometimes with Rouch and sometimes with me when it comes to eliminating scenes she doesn't like or keeping ones she likes; in a second phase, she thinks that Rouch and she deserve total confidence.

The successive versions were shown to different people, among whom Azar and Roger Leenhardt would play a significant role. Argos wants Azar to be the editor of the film, but Rouch, already at odds with me, wants to have a free hand. Azar formulates essentially the following remarks:

1. What is extraordinary and unique for him are the moments when the faces in close-up express some emotion. The moment when happiness erupts on Marilou's face is one of the four moments in cinema that have most impressed him in his life. He also thinks that the high points of the film consist of Jean-Pierre's monologue and Marceline on August 15. Gabillon is moving. He doesn't like Angélo much; he finds him to be a ham.

2. Next to these sections, everything that is "cinema" is not only secondary but risks killing the best parts. In any case, the section following the vacation segment is of no interest. The film should end on a strong beat, at the end of vacation. At the end of a dramatic progression, we should finish with Marceline on August 15 and Marilou happy.

Leenhardt's remarks are different. The film must be intelligible: from the start the subject should be clear, the problem plainly stated. In this sense he favors the introduction that Rouch is proposing, the beginning of our first dialogue with Marceline, where we reveal our purpose. There must also (and here Azar is going in the same direction) be a dialogue at the end of the film that conveys the authors' conclusions.

The experimental screenings also bring out the fact that our few critical spectators believe much more strongly in the truth of those scenes in which Rouch and I appear in front of the camera, participating in the dialogue with our characters. They feel that the scenes in which we do not appear, like the jetty at Saint Tropez, are "acted."

These remarks have some influence on us. We will maintain our presence in the picture, which we had earlier had a tendency to eliminate (except when Rouch was considering making me the "hero" of the film, off in search of the elusive grail). Rouch will retain his introduction (the first dialogue with Marceline), but immediately afterward will come the "Are you happy?" sequence. The conclusion will be our dialogue at the Musée de l'Homme (it is not until later that this will be replaced by a new dialogue filmed subsequently). Rouch will come around slowly to the idea of cutting the after-vacation, which satisfies me inasmuch as this gives more room for the trial runs, which will take a central position. As for me, I will slowly accept the reduction of the social-worker part and the suppression of any normative theme in the conclusion. We reach an agreement on an editing plan.

Because Rouch has to leave for Africa for a while, and because Dauman demands an editor, Rouch chooses Ravel. For fifteen or twenty days, Ravel works alone with Nina Baratier, following the plan that we have established together, but having a fair amount of freedom of composition. I will not intervene during this period except to insist on the need to make a minor change in the "Are You Happy?" sequence. Ravel therefore edits the first half hour of the film in the present order of succession (with the exception of the Landry-Angélo dialogue, Angélo's dismissal, and a few other modifications). Rouch and I will be satisfied.

Rouch comes back from Africa. He intervenes directly at the editing table and immediately orients Ravel on the montage of the vacation sequences. The editing speeds up; a copy must be ready for the Cannes festival; I defend my stand on the parts that I judge essential, such as the Algeria discussion, the discussion on the Congo and racism. Algeria poses some particular difficulties: how to render the tumultuousness of this discussion and above all its dramatic character when we must cut the passages that might be dangerous for our young participants? How to avoid having the censors cut the scene completely? We also have many discussions about the vacation sequence, but I leave the bullfight to Rouch (I would have kept one minute or cut it entirely) and the little dialogue between Catherine and Landry about Saint Tropez. The scene of Marceline and Jean-Pierre on the jetty is edited in the conventional cinema style; it would no doubt have been better to show one long uninterrupted segment. Little by little the post-vacation sequences are eliminated or are aired before the vacation. We go on to the mixing, and a copy is printed, which is screened at Cannes.

This copy will not yet be the definitive version. The group discussion in the Studio Publicis is not yet included, and there are still a few postvacation episodes, like Angélo's dismissal, Marilou's visit with her friend Jeanne, at home with her boyfriend, Marceline and Jean-Pierre waking up.

The Publicis discussion had been abandoned along the way. I was not particularly attached to it, Rouch having said that it was uneditable. But after Cannes, after a screening at the Musée de l'Homme and at UNESCO, we feel that the end of the film is weak.

For me the weakness begins at the moment when we get to Algeria; for Rouch, it is only the end that needs work. He proposes to look at the screening of the Publicis discussion again, and we are finally in total agreement on this point. It is absolutely necessary. At the same time we eliminate the last postvacation element. A new discussion divides us on Marilou Happy, which I think has been sabotaged in the editing, and we reestablish in part what I ask for. However, we cannot retain the Marilou-Jeanne scene, which probably brings nothing to the film but does show Marilou relaxed and cheerful. All we have left is to film a new conclusion, an improvised dialogue at the Musée de l'Homme after the screening of the Publicis discussion and taking into account (implicitly) the reactions of the first viewers. We are in the beginning of June 1961, one year after beginning "How do you live?" The film will definitely be called *Chronicle of a Summer,* even though the title does not reflect the subject. But Argos has decided it. "How do you live?" is too TV, it seems. I leave for Chile on June 20. Finally we film a supplementary scene, a last dialogue between Rouch and me at the Musée de l'Homme. On this occasion we used a wireless microphone and therefore did not need to carry the shoulderbag tape recorder as we walked. We were told that this conclusion scene was necessary. The day before filming it, we reviewed the final sequence of the group discussion at the Studio Publicis. Rouch and Ravel finish editing the Studio Publicis part, the final discussion, and with a few more modifications, they put the definitive version of the film in order.[17]

▶ ───────────────────────────────────

## Post-*Chronicle*

*Chronicle of a Summer* is finished. It is already slipping away from us. Lately we are free to add a postscript, for example, to take the unused film to make one or two supplementary films that could be shown in ciné-clubs. Or maybe we could establish a long version (four hours), again for the ciné-clubs or for private showings. Maybe we will do it, but the film is slipping away from us, that is to say, we must accept it as is.

As for me, I am divided between two contradictory feelings. On the one hand, I feel dissatisfaction in view of what I had ideally hoped for; on the other hand, I feel deep contentment at having lived this experience, adhering to the compromise that such an accomplishment presupposes. Without Rouch, the film would have been impossible for me, not only because it was Rouch's name that convinced the producer to try the adventure, but also and above all because his presence was indispensable for me, and there again not only from the technical point of view but also from the personal point of view. Although intellectually I can distinguish what differentiates us, I cannot practically dissociate this curious pair we formed, like Jerry Lewis–Dean Martin, Erckman-Chatrian, or Roux-Combaluzier.

We must also express our gratitude to Anatole Dauman. Thanks to Argos Film, Rouch and I were able to carry out decisive experiments in our respective researches. It is thus impossible to dissociate the "Argonauts" from *cinéma-vérité*.

This film, which is slipping away from us, now appears before critics and viewers. It presents us once again with problems, indeed with new problems. These are not aesthetic problems but questions more directly related to life. Because unlike other films, the spectator is not so much judging a work as judging other human beings, namely, Angélo, Marceline, Marilou, Jean-Pierre, me, Rouch. They judge us as human beings, but in addition they attach this moral or affective judgment to their aesthetic judgment. For example, if a spectator doesn't like one of us, he will find that person stupid, insincere, a ham; he'll reproach the character for being at the same time a bad actor and an unlikable individual. This confusion of levels at first upsets us but reassures us at the same time, because it expresses the weakness and the virtue of this film. It shows us that, no matter what, though we have been doing cinema, we have also done something else: we have overflowed the bounds of cinéma-spectacle, of cinéma-theater, while at the same time sounding the depths of its possibilities; we are also a part of this confused and jumbled thing called life.

This film is a hybrid, and this hydridness is as much the cause of its infirmity as of its interrogative virtue.

The first contradiction holds in the changeover from real time to cinematographic time. Of course the real time is not the total time, since we were not filming all the time. In other words, there was already a sort of selection in the filming; but the editing obliges us to make a selection, a more difficult composition, more treacherous. We choose the times that we find the most significant or the most powerful; of course, this theatricalizes life. On top of that, the close-up accentuates dramatization. In fact there is more tension in seeing close-ups of Marilou, Marceline, or Jean-Pierre than in being present in the scene itself, because the close-up of the face concentrates, captures, fascinates. But above all we realize that though the editing can improve everything that does not develop through the length of the film, it also weakens and perverts the very substance of what happened in real time (the jetty at Saint Tropez, Marilou unhappy, or Marceline on August 15, for example). Additionally, the compromise that Rouch and I made on the characters works to their detriment. The viewer will not know them well enough, and yet will arrive at a global judgment on their personalities; they are sufficiently (i.e., too) individualized to avoid such judgment. Thus Jean-Pierre, Marilou, Marceline, Angélo, Gabillon will be perceived globally by means of mere fragments of themselves.

These judgments, as in life, will be hasty, superficial, rash. I am amazed that what should inspire esteem for Jean-Pierre or Marilou, namely, their admission of egoism or egocentrism ("egoism" for Jean-Pierre; "I reduce everything to my own terms" for Marilou), will paradoxically produce a pejorative judgment of them. It seems we have underestimated the hypocritical reaction, and as a result I tell myself that the real comedy, the real hamming, the spectacle, takes place among the petit bourgeois who play at virtue, decency, health, and who pretend to give lessons in truth.

But I must not let myself follow that miserable downslide of the human mind that always transfers blame to others. Errors in judgment of which the characters in the film are victims are provoked because we both over- and underindividualized our characters, because certain tensions whose origins are unclear emerge in the course of the film, because there is a whole submerged dimension that will remain unknown to the public. Without intending to, we have created a projective test. We have only provided a few pieces of a puzzle that is missing most of its parts. Thus each viewer reconstructs a whole as a function of his own projections and identifications.

As a result, while this film was intended to involve the viewer, it involves him in an unforeseen manner. I believed that the viewers would be involved if they asked themselves the question "How do you live?" In fact, the reactions are more diverse, and this diversity is not just the diversity of aesthetic judgments; it is a diversity in *attitudes* toward others, toward truth, toward what one has the right to say, and what one should not say.

This diversity marks our failure as well as our success. Failure, because we did not come away with the sympathy of the majority, because, thinking we were clarifying human problems, we provoked misunderstandings, even obscuring reactions. Success, because to a certain degree Rouch and I gave these characters the chance to speak and because, to a certain degree, we gave the public a liberty of appreciation that is unusual in cinema. We did not merely play the divine role of authors who speak through the mouths of their characters and show the public the sentiments they should feel, their norms of good and bad. It is also because there is this relative freedom, and not only because we filmed under the least cinema-like conditions possible, that we have approached the cinema of life. But in approaching thus we have also approached all the confusion of life.

We have also modified the relationship between actor and spectator, which is like the relationship between an unseen God and a passive communicant. We have emerged from mystery, we have shown ourselves, present, fallible, men among others, and we have provoked the viewer to judge as a human being.

Whether or not we wanted it so, this film is a hybrid, a jumble, and all the errors of judgment have in common the desire to attach a label to this enterprise and to confront it with this label. The label "sociology": is this a film that (a) wants to be sociological, (b) is sociological? Those for whom sociology signifies a survey of public opinion on a cross-section sample of the population, that is to say, those who know nothing about sociology, say: We are being tricked, this isn't a sociological film, the authors are dishonest. But we have in no way presented this film under the label "ethnographic" or "sociological." I also do not see why film critic Louis Marcorelles denounces my "false sociological prestiges." I never introduce myself as a sociologist, neither in the film nor in real life, and I have no prestige among sociologists. We have not once, to my knowledge, pronounced the word "sociology" in this film. Our banner has been *cinéma-vérité,* and I'll get to that. Our enterprise is more diffuse, more broadly human.

Let's say to simplify things that we're talking about an enterprise that is both ethnographic and existential: ethnographic in the sense that we try to investigate that which seems to go without saying, that is, daily life; existential in that we knew that each person could be emotionally involved in this research. Any filmmaker could have posed the question "How do you live?", but we wanted this interrogation to be minimally sociological. This minimum is not just an opinion poll, which not only achieves only superficial results when dealing with profound problems but also is totally inadequate for our enterprise. This minimum is first of all a preliminary reflection on the sociology of work and daily life. Next it is an attitude that is engraved in one of the fundamental lines of human sciences since Marx,

Max Weber, and Freud. To simplify: for Marx, it is crisis that is revealing, not normal states. For Max Weber, a situation is understood by starting not at a middle ground but with extreme types (which Weber constructed theoretically by the method of utopian realization and named "ideal types"). For Freud, the abnormal reveals the normal as one exacerbates that which exists in the latent or camouflaged state of the other.

If a good part of the film's viewers refuse, reject, or expel from themselves what they consider a "pathological" case that is in no way representative or significant, this indicates not an error in our method but rather the difficulties involved in consciousness of certain fundamental givens of being human. The real question is not whether Marilou, Angélo, Marceline, and Jean-Pierre are rare or exceptional cases but whether they raise profound and general problems, such as job alienation, the difficulty of living, loneliness, the search for faith. The question is to know whether the film poses fundamental questions, subjective and objective, that concern life in our society.

■———————————————————————————————————

### Psychoanalysis, Therapy, Modesty, Risk

I have written that in certain conditions the eye of the camera is psychoanalytical; it looks into the soul. Critics have reproached us for doing false psychoanalysis, that is, of knowing nothing about psychoanalysis. Here we are dealing with a myth of psychoanalysis, just as there is a myth of sociology. Psychoanalysis is a profession and a doctrine with multiple tendencies, all strongly structured. Our venture is foreign to psychoanalysis understood in its professional and structured sense but does go in the direction of the ideas that psychoanalysis has helped to bring into focus. Otherwise we have gambled on the possibility of using cinema as a means of communication, and the therapeutic idea of our plan is that all communication can be liberation. Of course I was aware, and am even more aware since the film has been screened, of all the difficulties of communication, the boomerang risks of malevolent interpretations or of scornful indifference; I know that those I wanted recognized were sometimes disregarded. I know that if I were to do it again, I would do it differently, but I also know that I would do it. And I reaffirm this principle: things that are hidden, held back, silenced, must be spoken; J. J. Rousseau is worth more than Father Dupanloup; *Lady Chatterley's Lover* is worth more than the censorship that prohibited it. We suffer more from silencing the essential than from speaking.

The need to communicate is one of the greatest needs that ferment in our society; the individual is atomized in what Riesman has called "the lonely crowd." In this film there is an examination of stray, clumsy communication, which our censors have called exhibitionism or shamelessness. But where is the shame? Certainly not in those who make themselves the crude and ostentatious spokesmen of shame: shame does not have such impudence.

But finally one question is asked: do we have the right to drag people into such an enterprise? I will answer that it is first a matter of characterizing this enterprise, that is to say, the risks it involves. Is it an enterprise of vivisection or poisoned psychoanalysis? Or is it, on the contrary, a game of no importance? Does it involve the same sort of risks as taking passengers in a car on vacation roads or leading an expedition into a virgin forest? How can they judge the harmful consequences, those who know neither Marilou, nor Angélo, nor the others? Having thought it all out, I'd say that the greatest risk depends on those who criticize Angélo, Marilou, et cetera; that is to say, their inability to love them. Of course we exposed Angélo, Marilou, Marceline, and Jean-Pierre to this risk because we overestimated the possibilities of friendship. But even in the case of Marilou and of Jean-Pierre, unknown friends are born to them.

In the end, anyone who lives with a woman, has children, recruits adherents to his party, whoever lives and undertakes anything makes others take risks. Each of us risks the destiny of others in the name of their interests and their morals. The ultimate problem is that of each of our own morals.

■───────────────────────────────────────────

### Bourgeois or Revolutionary Film?

This film is infrapolitical and infrareligious. There is a whole zone left unexplored by the film. If we had been believers, we would not have neglected belief. On the political level, the question is different. We did not want, for example, to present the worker problem at the level of political or union affiliations or of salary claims, because conditions of industrial work should be questioned at a deeper, more radical level. Taking into account this infrapoliticism, we were the only ones in filmmaking to question the war in Algeria and to thus attack the central political problem of the hour.

It was possible to judge this film variously: reactionary or revolutionary, bourgeois or leftist. I don't want to get dragged into defining right now what I understand by reactionary, bourgeois, Left; nor to polemicize with those who find the film reactionary. I would say only that the meaning of the film is clear if one conceives of it as contesting both the reigning values of bourgeois society and Stalinist or pseudoprogressive stereotypes.

### Optimism? Pessimism?

It is true that Rouch was naturally carried toward what is cheerful and light and that he was the spokesman of "life is beautiful," while I was naturally carried toward what is sad or sorrowful. The reason for my quest to approach the difficulties of living is not just that happy people have no story to tell but also because there are fundamental problems that are tragic, ponderous, and must be considered. But to confront these problems is not to despair. What disheartens me, on the contrary, is that everyone who is not subjected to the piecework without responsibility or initiative, that is, typical of the laborer or the civil servant, readily takes it for granted. What disheartens me are those people resigned to the artificial, shabby, frivolous life that is given to them well defined. What disheartens me are those who make themselves comfortable in a world where Marceline, Marilou, Jean-Pierre, and Angélo are not happy.

That these may be "my" problems, that my problems should have taken form in this film (at least in an elementary fashion), does not mean that they cease to exist independently of me. That I may have difficulties in life, that I may not really be able to adapt—this does not necessarily mean that I cannot step outside of myself; it may also sensitize me to the problems of others. In any case I drew two "optimistic" lessons from this experience. First, an increased faith in adolescent virtues: denial, struggle, and seeking. In other words, Angélo, Jean-Pierre, Marilou, and Marceline have inspired me to resist the bourgeois life. The second is the conviction that every time it is possible to speak to someone about essential things, consciousness is awakened, man awakens. Everyone, the man in the street, the unknown, hides within himself a poet, a philosopher, a child. In other words, I believe more than ever that we must relentlessly deal with the person, denying something in the person, revealing something in the person.

### Cinéma-Vérité?

Finally we come to the problem of *cinéma-vérité*. How do we dare speak of a truth that has been chosen, edited, provoked, oriented, deformed? Where is the truth? Here again the confusion comes from those who take the term *"cinéma-vérité"* as an affirmation, a guarantee sticker, and not as a research.

*Cinéma-vérité:* this means that we wanted to eliminate fiction and get closer to life. This means that we wanted to situate ourselves in a lineage dominated by Flaherty and Dziga Vertov. Of course this term *"cinéma-vérité"* is daring, pretentious; of course there is a profound truth in works of fiction as well as in myths. At the end of the film, the difficulties of truth, which had not been a problem in the beginning, became apparent to me. In other words, I thought that we would start from a basis of truth and that an even greater truth would develop. Now I realize that if we achieved anything, it was to present the problem of the truth. We wanted to get away from comedy, from spectacles, to enter into direct contact with life. But life itself is also a comedy, a spectacle. Better (or worse) yet: each person can only express himself through a mask, and the mask, as in Greek tragedy, both disguises and reveals, becomes the speaker. In the course of the dialogues, each one was able to be more real than in daily life, but at the same time more false.

This means that there is no given truth that can simply be deftly plucked, without withering it (this is, at the most, spontaneity). Truth cannot escape contradictions, since there are truths of the unconscious and truths of the conscious mind; these two truths contradict each other. But just as every victory carries its own defeat, so every failure can bring its own defeat. If the viewer who rejects the film asks himself, "Where is the truth?", then the failure of "How do you live?" is clear; but maybe we have brought out a concern for the truth. No doubt this film is an examination whose emphasis has been misplaced. The fundamental question that we wanted to pose was about the human condition in a given social setting and at a given moment in history. It was a "How do you live?" that we addressed to the viewer. Today the question comes from the viewer who asks, "Where is the truth?" If for a minority of viewers the second question does not follow the first, then we have both supplied something and received something. Something that should be pursued and thoroughly investigated. To live without renouncing something is difficult. Truth is long-suffering.

◆————————————————————————————————

## NOTES

Unless otherwise indicated, notes to this chapter were written by Jean Rouch.

1. The French is *pris sur le vif.—Ed.*
2. In fact it seems to me that the camera-eye experiments by Dziga Vertov and his friends ran up against equipment that was too heavy and difficult to handle. The camera in the street was visible to those it filmed, and this seemed to the authors to invalidate its results. Since then both technical manageability and people's reactivity to the camera

have evolved considerably. We must also mention Jean Vigo, whose *À propos de Nice* is quite a fascinating endeavor.

3. This image of the filmmaker-diver has always pleased (and flattered) me. The filmmaker with his equipment does indeed look like a deep-sea diver or like an interstellar voyager, but one who navigates in a "non-silent" world.

4. *The Hunters,* produced by the team of the Film Center of the Peabody Museum (Harvard University), comprising John Marshall, Professor Brew, and Robert Gardner.

5. The French is *cinéma de fraternité.—Ed.*

6. This notion of the play of truth and life before the camera, pointed out by Edgar in 1959–1960, is a capital one. Starting, no doubt, at the moment when Edgar sensed it in the drafts presented in Florence, it has been possible to pursue this play, no longer with only men who are alien to our culture (thus brothers to the spectator). From this contact in Florence came the experience of *Chronicle of a Summer.*

7. At the beginning, this fine meal idea was destined more than anything to satisfy the demonic gourmandise of Morin, thus to get him in the mood for conversation. In fact it allowed a feeling of trust to develop among the actors and the crew, which was indispensable for suppressing inhibitions before the camera (always present and ready to record at any moment).

8. This is one of the major obstacles in this cinema based on complete improvisation. When we do not film a scene as a result of carelessness, or when the filming fails for technical reasons, the new takes are never as good as the original. We eliminated all of them in the final editing. (In *La pyramide humaine* I also suffered terribly from this difficulty; certain remade scenes had to be kept, and these are the worst in the film.)

9. I was behind the camera during this scene. We were then using an Arriflex camera with an enormous soundproof case. Morillère was at my side, holding focus. When Marilou spoke of suicide, the silence that followed was so necessary that no one spoke. Morillère and I exchanged a glance that meant "we won't stop," and when Morin finally broke the silence, everyone breathed again.

10. This beautiful scene had to be eliminated because the pretext of the discussion was the screening of the film *L'etoile,* which Marilou and Marceline had just seen. The references to this film were too frequent to avoid making this section an overly specific discussion.

11. It was a gamble; we lost. Indeed, the summer of 1960 was to represent for us an essential moment in the history of France, and to show us the repercussions of this adventure on the heroes already associated with our enterprise seemed to me to become the principal subject of the film. Nothing remains of this except the Algeria-Congo discussion and the title, *Chronicle of a Summer.*

12. Although all this Saint Tropez period was terribly depressing for Edgar, who felt threatened by the fiction of psychodrama, it was terribly exciting for Michel Brault and me as we invented our new tools. We came back from Lausanne, where Stefan Kudelski, inventor of the Nagra tape recorder, excited by the enthusiasm of Michel Fano (sound engineer), Michel Brault, and me, let us glimpse the cinema that was to be born a year later. Marilou's dreams, fake encounters in the plane and the train, the false BB—these were as much experiments in synchronous-sound filming in a plane, on a train, in a crowd, et cetera; the first in the world and since much imitated.

13. Les Agriculteurs was a movie theater known for screening experimental and innovative films. The scene mentioned here is included in the film script that follows; it does not appear in English subtitled prints of the film circulated in the United States.—*Ed.*

14. To my mind, this scene is one of the most beautiful in the film, along with the one of Marceline on August 15 (of which this is the opposite). We made the error, in editing, of trying to condense it (it lasted almost half an hour in the rushes), respecting a certain cinematographic language (changes of angles between different shots).

15. The *serment du Jeu de Paume* was sworn on June 20, 1789, by the deputies of the Third Estate not to separate after giving a constitution to France. Because the king prohibited access to the Salle des Menus Plaisirs, where they usually met, they went to the nearby Jeu de Paume.—*Ed.*

16. In fact I had the same anguish over the making of *Chronicle* that I had earlier felt with *Moi, un Noir* and *La pyramide humaine,* that of amputation. This is, no doubt, the greatest stumbling block of all these improvised films, with no scenario or preplanned continuity: to reduce to one hour and thirty minutes an enormous body of material whose value is its authenticity, that is, the length, the hesitations, the awkwardnesses. In a film shot in silence, like *Moi, un Noir,* the problem is already difficult; in a film shot with direct sound like *Pyramide* or *Chronicle,* it's an incredible headache. I knew only one effective method of approach, successive approximations that alone allow us to "see" the film reduced to a human screening time. This was my greatest fear about having one editor in chief who would rethink the film.

17. I see that Edgar has slightly exaggerated the

oppositions we faced in his chronicle of *Chronicle*. "Coauthoring" is not simple team-work where the two partners agree. It is a more violent game where disagreement is the only rule, and the solution lies in the resolution of this disagreement. It is also necessary for the arbiter (or the producer) to have an open enough mind to follow the game while sanctioning its only faults. Alas, a film producer, caught between patronizing intolerable artists and financial imperatives, cannot be impartial.

# JEAN ROUCH

## The Cinema of the Future?

Making a film is such a personal thing for me that the only implicit techniques are the very techniques of cinematography: sight and sound recording, editing the images and recordings. It is also very difficult for me to talk
about it and, above all, to write about it. I have never written anything before starting a film, and when for administrative or financial reasons I've
been obligated to compose a scenario, some continuity plans, or a synopsis, I have never ended up making the corresponding film.

A film is an idea, flashing out or slowly elaborated, but one that cannot be escaped, whose expression can only be cinematographic. On the
road from Accra to Abidjan, the sun plays in the leaves of the trees, kilometers follow upon miles, corrugated iron replaces the meandering asphalt.
I've passed by here twenty times. I am driving; next to me someone has
fallen asleep. And so, in the ever-changing, ever-renewed scenery, other
scenes appear, other characters. Thus in a few hours of fatigue and dust,
I have seen and heard a draft of *La pyramide humaine* that is much more
like the film finally realized than any "plans" I might have written.

Or else it's in a bar, in Treichville, a Sunday night; a friend and I have
wandered in, in pursuit of the splendid festivities only the people of these
parts know how to put on, in the middle of the sordid streets, in the middle
of the slums. The contrast between the ephemeral Sunday gaiety and the
daily misfortune is so strong that I know it will haunt me until the very
moment when I am able to express it. How? Go out of this bar and shout
in the streets? Write a general book for the public on this investigation we
are now doing on the migrations in Ivory Coast, which, otherwise, if it ever
sees the light of day, will interest only a few specialists? The only solution
was to make a film about it, where it would not be me crying out my joy or
my revolt, but one of these people for whom Treichville was both heaven

and hell. So in this bar ambience on a lugubrious evening in January 1957, *Moi, un Noir* appeared to me as a necessity.

And all the other films, coming upon me suddenly, on the roads of Africa or on the rivers, baptized in that strange contact with the countryside or climates, where the lone voyager discovers what he was looking for with such insistence, that dialogue with himself, with his own dreams, that faculty of "intimate distance" with the world and with mankind, that faculty that anthropologists and poets know so well and that allowed me to be both "entomologist" observer and friend of the *maîtres fous,* the game leader and primary spectator of *Jaguar,* but always on the condition that I not determine the limits of the game whose only rule is to film when you and the others really feel like it.

The camera (and for a few years now the tape recorder) have thus become indispensable tools for me, as indispensable as a notepad and pencil, each having its specialty, its time for use, its limit (I spent several months without filming anything in Africa, because nothing was happening; then one day either something "happened," or else I was unable to escape certain ideas that I had to express).

This almost insurmountable difficulty that I have verbally expressing what a film will be before it is made is without doubt the cruelest of trials for those around me and those who collaborate with me. Each time I have found myself in these situations, conflicts have exploded, and I have not known how to stop them, caught between the desire to remain faithful (perhaps too superstitiously) to a method that has proved itself and the desire not to play the tyrant with collaborators who were and could be nothing other than friends. And each time I recommenced the same impossible dialogue between the incommunicable and those to whom I had to communicate it. So as an introduction to *Chronicle* I don't know how to do anything here but to set up a sort of ledger of a certain cinema that one could call ethnographic.

It may seem presumptuous to write about an experience that is not yet finished, an experience that is still in progress, but I think it is necessary to make the point. In fact ethnographic cinema was born at the same time as the cinema with Marey's chronophotographic rifle, among whose first users was an anthropologist, Dr. Regnault, who used it to study the comparative behavior of Europeans and Africans.

After this, the cinema was directed along other routes, and it is certain that documentary film remained, in spite of everything, a separate category. I must here salute the father of ethnographic cinema, Robert Flaherty, who made the first ethnographic film in the world, *Nanook of the North,* in extremely difficult conditions. Thus at the very beginning, Flaherty undertook an endeavor that was not, unfortunately, much followed thereafter. He thought that to film men who belong to a foreign culture, it was first necessary to get to know them. He therefore spent a year at Hudson's Bay among the Eskimos before filming them. He also experimented with something that we are only beginning to apply methodically: showing the finished film to those who appear in it. At that time laboratory work was an extremely delicate process. Flaherty did not hesitate to build a laboratory right in his little cabin by Hudson's Bay, where he developed his own films. According to his own account, he dried them by running in the wind. Because he did not have a sufficient source of light (at that time copies required a considerable light source), he pierced a hole in the wall of his cabin and used sunlight to print copies of the film. Thus he was able to project the first version of *Nanook of the North* for Nanook and his family. But this first version was seen by no one else because, as you may know, a fire ravaged the cabin, and the film was completely destroyed. At that time, Flaherty was an engineer-geologist. He did not hesitate to start over (he was of Irish origin and therefore particularly tenacious), and with backing from Révillon furs, he was able to set up another experiment and realize for the second time the *Nanook of the North* with which we are familiar today. Five years later, Flaherty made *Moana of the South Seas. Nanook* had been a considerable commercial success, and Flaherty found himself encouraged by American production companies to go make a film in the South Pacific. He went to the Samoan Islands, spent a year there without filming, and at the end of a year, having learned the language, he began to film the daily life of the inhabitants of the Samoan Islands. He applied the same method: he developed the films on the spot, edited them, and then showed them to the people he had filmed, as they were developed. *Moana,* unlike *Nanook,* was an absolutely complete commercial failure, and most of Flaherty's later films had only modest commercial success. Flaherty died a couple of years ago on an extremely modest small farm in Vermont where his wife, Frances, still lives. At the time of his death he was preparing for a film expedition to sub-Saharan Africa.

During the same period, the 1920s, another team of enthusiastic filmmakers was trying to use the camera to the limits of its possibilities in the Soviet Union. This was Dziga Vertov's group, and sometime around 1929 they wrote a manifesto: "the camera-eye." The camera was an eye, a new eye open on the world, which allowed anything to be seen. Dziga Vertov's endeavors were severely condemned by the Soviet Union at that time, but his films nonetheless spread throughout the entire world. They carried a new banner: *kinopravda,* or *"cinéma-vérité."* It was an absolutely crazy endeavor, but a fascinating experiment, and Vertov's film *The Man with a Movie Camera* will remain the first attempt to put the camera in the street, to make the camera the principal actor, the object of this new cult of total cinema where the knicker-clad priest is the cameraman.

Some people thought this experiment was a failure because the people in the street looked at the camera, because the camera was a far too heavy object, and because simultaneous film sound was not yet invented. Georges Sadoul recently told me that Vertov had foreseen, in his unpublished manuscripts, the possibility of recording synchronous sound with the arrival of talking movies. This would open a new chapter of the "ciné-eye": the "ciné-eye-and-ear." This is in fact what we are trying today.

I must add a third master to this preamble. During the same period, in France, Jean Vigo was also trying to use the free camera to simply show the behavior of his contemporaries through their culture in his film *À propos de Nice*.

Out of these three efforts, ethnographic cinema was born. But this birth was difficult. Once the technique had progressed, cinema was divided in two branches. On the one side, under the influence of Flaherty, and in spite of him, "exotic" cinema was born, a cinema based on the sensational and on the foreignness of foreign people, a racist cinema that was ignorant of itself. On the other side, that of ethnography, under the impetus of Marcel Mauss, cinema was engaged in an equally strange course, that of the total research investigation. Mauss recommended to his students that they use the camera to record everything that went on around them. They should not move it, it was a sure witness and it was only by shooting these films that one could study certain gestures, behaviors, and techniques. During this period Marcel Griaule nonetheless brought back from Dogon the first French ethnographic films, followed by those of P. O'Reilly, oceanographer and cinematographer. Unfortunately, the war interrupted these projects, and it was not until after the war that there was a new evolution.

It was a revolution, the revolution of 16 mm. During the war, news cameramen used 16 mm cameras with great success, and their films could then be enlarged to standard format 35 mm. From that point on, the camera was no longer that cumbersome object that Vertov's friends could not parade in the streets without its being noticed. It became a small tool, as easy to manage as a Leica, or as a pen, to recall the model of the "prophet" Alexandre Astruc. The use of color also permitted the filmmaker to stop worrying about questions of lighting: no matter what angle on the shot, with color, all shot perspectives came out right.

At this time a certain number of young ethnologists decided to use the camera, and strangely enough, at the same moment in France, in Belgium, in the United States, in Great Britain, and in Switzerland, these ethnologists all had the same idea in mind: to capture the most authentic images possible while respecting the rules of cinematographic language. It was thus noticed that there was little difference between ethnography and cinema. I have stressed this countless times: when the filmmaker records on film the actions or deeds that surround him, he behaves just like an ethnologist who records his observations in a notebook; when the filmmaker then edits the film, he is like an ethnologist editing his report; when the filmmaker distributes his film, he does the same as the ethnologist who gives his book to be published and distributed. Here there are very similar techniques, and ethnographic film has truly found its course in them. The possibility of easily recording sound also brought a new element. Around 1949, manufacturers were perfecting autonomous tape recorders, allowing, in principle, for an ethnographer to portably record image and sound.

In France, at the Musée de l'Homme, my colleague Roger Morillère has been giving a course in cinematographic initiation to students in ethnology for the past ten years. Sound-cinema has become one of the techniques taught to future researchers just as they are taught to study kinship or prehistory, or to collect objects. Already we have successes which must be hailed: the French films of Morillère, of Monique Gessain, of Father Pairaut, of Igor de Garine, of Daribenaude, of Guy le Moal; the Belgian films of Luc de Heusch, the Swiss films of Henri Brandt, the Canadian films of the marvelous team of the National Film Board, the American films of Marshall and Gardner, the films of the Italian sociological school, and so on. It must be said with a certain pride that these films made on a minuscule budget (an ethnographic film in 16 mm costs 1.5 million old francs and 200,000 francs in the filming) nonetheless succeeded in having an influence on two levels. On the level of ethnography itself, I remember that in the beginning, when my friends and I had just started to handle the cameras, whether here or in Belgium or in Switzerland or in Great Britain or in the United States, a certain number of classical ethnologists felt as though we had introduced a "magic lantern" into our discipline, a sort of toy, and that film could at best serve to illustrate lectures or seminar talks. But by making films, we showed the skeptics that the cinema was an irreplaceable tool of inquiry, not only for its ability to reproduce indefinitely what had been observed, but also in rediscovering the old Flaherty technique, for the possibility of screening the reported document for the people who had been observed, and to study their behavior in the images with them.

At the level of commercial cinema, our influence was also important. First of all, we were responsible for the decline of a certain number of cinematographic enterprises that were monumental swindles, such as those of the "Lost Continent" series, "Green Magic" Walt Disney films, and so on. I think that this purge was very efficient because no one has the right to exploit lies in order to make money. One might say that cinema is an art of lying, but then it should be made clear: it's fine to make a "Tarzan" series (I like Tarzan films quite a bit) without claiming to make a documentary film.

But there is another effect: we have indirectly contributed to the birth of what has been called in France the "Nouvelle Vague." What was going on in the Nouvelle Vague? It was almost entirely a question of the economic liberation of commercial cinema and of the traditional norms of the cinematographic industry. We had predecessors in this domain. Melville, for example, was able to shoot *The Silence of the Sea* by using expired film stock. In fact, around 1949 to 1950, it was impossible to shoot a film in 35 mm without having a filming authorization, without having a minimum crew, without having a permit to purchase the film. To make a film at that time required a budget of around 60 to 100 million old francs. We showed that with ridiculously small means we could make films that were perhaps not of an extraordinary class, or of remarkable quality, but cost infinitely less.

To give you an example, a film like *Moi, un Noir* came to about four hundred thousand francs in the filming. The interest in this technique of 16 mm enlarged in color was that it permitted a two-stage financing. You make a 16 mm film. If it is no good, you have only lost half a million. If it is good, there is still time to invest money in enlarging it, and you then know what you are investing money in and what you are taking a risk on.

But in all of this, something was lacking: direct synchronous-sound recording. We were working on this problem, in France and abroad, for a great many years, and it seemed insoluble for two reasons. The first was the need to film synchronous sound in the studio because the microphones are sensitive to wind, to atmospheric conditions, and to outside noises. The second was the weight of the equipment. With 16 mm we were freed of the weight problem, but the camera made a noise like a coffee grinder, and it was impossible to film and record sound at the same time. For example, in *La pyramide humaine* we used a "blimped" 16 mm camera, enclosed in an enormous case weighing about forty kilos, and we did as many sound and picture takes as possible indoors so as to avoid the outside noises. When we were in Abidjan, I remember well that all we had to do was start shooting a scene for a truck to pass 100 meters away and for the sound engineer to shout, "Stop! This is impossible!" We did, however, find a system: the camera was set on a tripod at an equal distance from the principal protagonists, and when a dialogue started, we did not interrupt the filming but

simply asked the actors to wait until the camera was on them before responding to the question or statement pronounced by another, but this
staticness itself was paralyzing.

During this same period in Canada and in the United States, people
sought the solution to the same problem. Last year in August this solution
appeared in three countries at the same time: in Canada, in the United
States, and in France.

In France the inventor André Coutant specialized in building lightweight cameras for rocket flights. He had the idea of using one of these
light electric cameras to make a soundproof camera. He presented us with
a prototype of a camera that was not yet perfectly soundproof but weighed
1.5 kilos. It had a 120 m magazine and ten minutes of running time, and
thanks to a housing constructed by my friends Morillère and Boucher, it
made little enough noise to be used outside, even very close to a microphone. Our friend Michel Brault, a Canadian cameraman, came to Paris
at that time and brought the small, clip-on lavaliere microphones used by
Canadian and American television. These microphones are not visible. We
had resolved Dziga Vertov's problem: we were able, with the camera housing, to walk around anywhere, to film with synchronous sound in the subway, in a bus, in the street. Michel Brault also brought us a technique that
he had perfected some time earlier in Canada: the walking camera. He had
been practicing for a year to walk forward, backward, and sideways so well
that the camera in his hands became absolutely mobile. Another advantage: the camera in its housing was minuscule. We could film in the middle
of the street, and no one knew we were shooting except the technicians and
the actors: this is how *Chronicle of a Summer* was technically possible.

From this point on, ethnologists and sociologists will be able to go
to any part of the world and bring back images such as have never before
been seen, images in which there will be this complete union of sound and
image, of action, of setting, and of language. We have at our disposal a fantastic tool in perpetual progress (wireless microphones, cameras with automatic focus and aperture setting, etc.).

For the moment (I am, of course, addressing ethnographers now),
we must be able to use it as rapidly as possible before certain practices in
threatened cultures have completely disappeared. I think it is necessary to
accelerate our effort at this school directed by Morillère at the Musée de
l'Homme, where we can train ethnographers and perhaps even filmmakers
in these new cinema techniques.

Where are we going? I must admit that I have no idea. But I think that
from now on, right next to industrial and commercial cinema and intimate-

ly linked to the latter, there exists a "certain cinema" that is above all art and research.[1]

I have said very little about *Chronicle of a Summer* in this essay, leaving this task to Edgar Morin, whose meticulous testimony could only be done by him, because, returning to what I said at the beginning, the film is a means of total expression for me, and I do not see the necessity for me to write before, during, or after filming.

◆────────────────────────────────────────────────

**TRANSLATORS' NOTE**

1. The "certain cinema" that Rouch speaks of is elaborated in his articles "The Camera and Man" and "On the Vicissitudes of the Self," presented earlier in this book.

# Chronicle of a Summer: *The Film*

We have the good fortune to publish in this volume the text of the dialogue from several important scenes of *Chronicle of a Summer* that do not figure in the version of the film shown in theaters. These scenes have been incorporated here where they fit in quite naturally. To distinguish them from the dialogue of the film, they are set in bold italic type.

E. M. and J. R.

The transcript has been additionally modified to conform to the English subtitled print of the film in U.S. distribution.—*Ed.*

▶────────────────────────────────────

## Introduction

*The film opens with views of Paris and its industrial suburbs, at the end of a summer night. Factory smokestacks. The sound of sirens. Day breaks. The crowd of workers and employees headed for work surges from every subway exit. Titles. Off-screen is heard the voice of*

ROUCH: This film was not played by actors, but lived by men and women who have given a few moments of their lives to a new experiment in *cinéma-vérité*.[1]

▶────────────────────────────────────

## Marceline

*A dining room. The end of a meal. Behind the partially cleared table, Edgar Morin and Jean Rouch are seated on either side of Marceline.*

ROUCH: You see, Morin, the idea of gathering people around a table is an excellent idea. Only I don't know if we'll manage to record a conversation that's as normal as it would be if the camera wasn't present. For example, I don't know if Marceline will be able to relax, will be able to talk absolutely normally.

*Marceline turns to Morin.*

MORIN: We've got to try.

MARCELINE: I think I'm going to have some difficulty.

ROUCH: Why?

MARCELINE: Because I'm a bit intimidated.

ROUCH: You're intimidated by what?

MARCELINE: I'm intimidated because . . . at a given moment I have to be ready, and, well, I'm not, really, I guess . . .

ROUCH: At this moment you're not intimidated.

MARCELINE: No, right now I'm not.

ROUCH: Okay, so you're not intimidated now. What we're asking of you, with great trickery, Morin and I, is simply to talk, to answer our questions. And if you say anything you don't like, there's always time to cut . . .

MARCELINE: Yeah.

ROUCH: You don't need to feel intimidated.

MARCELINE: Yeah, but I'm less now than I was a couple of minutes ago because I wasn't attacked head-on, I guess . . .

*She laughs. Jean Rouch laughs, pointing to Morin.*

ROUCH: It's this ruffian. Okay then, go ahead, Morin, attack!

MORIN: Okay, I'll attack anyway. You don't know what questions we're going to ask you. We ourselves don't even know too precisely. What Rouch and I want to do is a film on the following idea: How do you live? How do you live? We start with you, and then we're going to ask other people. How do you live? That means, how do you get by in life? We're starting with you because you are going to play an integral role in our enterprise, in our film, and because we have to start somewhere . . .

▶ ─────────────────────────────────────────────

MORIN: *Listen, Marceline, it's impossible to see you without noticing a number tattooed on your arm. It means that you have lived through what may be the worst trial a human being has endured. And I remember that not long ago you and I saw a film called l'Étoile. It was a story about deported people, and I know that you were terribly upset by the film.*

MARCELINE: *Yes, for sure . . . I was particularly upset by that film because it happens that I saw it at a given moment, but now I realize that I relive with incredible clarity old images of Auschwitz . . . and I have no idea why . . . I don't know what the period I'm living at this moment corresponds to. I don't know, for example, I can forget it for a while, or live with it, but without thinking much about it, because I think . . . well, I couldn't go on living if I was always thinking about it. There was a whole period in my life when I was really obsessed . . . in my daily life as well as in my sleep because it was almost unbearable. And at this moment . . . I don't know . . . I don't have the words to explain.*

MORIN: *Listen, Marceline. We don't want to question you about this deportation. It's about the fact that you were deported when you were quite young.*

MARCELINE: *Yes.*

MORIN: *You were fourteen and you never turned fifteen . . . you never lived as a fifteen year old like everyone else. Deep down, this fact has had an effect on you, when you first came back among us and maybe even still today. You say that today you're in a crisis period where these images are more vivid than at other moments.*

MARCELINE: *Yeah.*

MORIN: *But we'd like to know how, not only in this particular crisis, but how you've managed to live in this normal world after coming out of that world of madness.*

MARCELINE: *Well . . .*

ROUCH: *Marceline, go ahead and tell us about your present life, what you do, et cetera.*

MARCELINE: *Well, I live . . . I don't know . . . I live sort of in disorder, I guess . . .*

▶ ─────────────────────────────────────────────

*Close-up of Marceline, then of Rouch.*

ROUCH: What do you do all day? For example, when you get up in the morning, what do you do?

*Close-up of Marceline.*

MARCELINE: Usually I work.

ROUCH *(off-screen):* What sort of work?

MARCELINE: I do psychosociological surveys for an applied social psychology firm. I do interviews, analyze the interviews, and eventually write up summaries of them. Which takes up quite a bit of time, I think.

ROUCH: Is it interesting?

MARCELINE: No, not a bit.

ROUCH: *So why do you do it?*

MARCELINE: *I do it because . . . I've got to live, I've got to feed myself, house myself, it's so . . . those are the only reasons I do it. And then it happens that, the fact that . . . at least I think partly because of my past . . . the fact that when I came back from being deported I found myself quite alone in life . . . I didn't have the chance to do what I wanted to do . . . at least to have some direction.*

ROUCH: *What would you have liked to do?*

MARCELINE: *I don't know, I have no idea. Deep down I think I could have had some desire of . . . no, I think not . . . I think I'd be lying . . . I mean, I think . . . I think that . . . I mean, I think maybe there is a certain instability in me and anyway the past has made any readaptation pretty difficult.*

MORIN: *Marceline, you do surveys, you have a little tape recorder over your shoulder and you go interview people, for this company or that company, and then, when you're not doing surveys you can often be found in a café called the Old Navy.*

MARCELINE: *That's right.*

MORIN: *When you have time to kill, when you're alone, you go to the Old Navy?*

MARCELINE: *Yes.*

MORIN: *That café on the Boulevard St. Germain?*

MARCELINE: *Yes.*

MORIN: *What do you find there?*

MARCELINE: *What I find there, well, it's pretty difficult to explain because basically, I think it's a place where people go partly for . . . I don't know how to tell you, it's a place where I go when I'm alone, or when I don't want to be alone . . . I know I'll find people I know there, it's a kind of haven, a refuge, a discussion ground . . . I mean, when I go to the Old Navy, like some evening when I have nothing to do, I'm pretty much assured that I will not eat alone, maybe I won't go home alone. I don't know, but maybe I'll go to the movies too, maybe I'll do something.*

MORIN: *It seems to me that you are very scared of being alone, and there's one thing that strikes me, that you know loads of people, a lot more people than, than people who know a lot of people know . . . and I think that's . . . this has some meaning, doesn't it?*

MARCELINE: *Yes, I think it must have some meaning. I think I must need to be surrounded like that, and more than that I like people a lot, I like to see them, I like to be with them. You say I know a lot of people . . . yes, I know a lot, because . . . I've been hanging around St. Germain for fifteen years,* more or less . . . well, let's not say fifteen because I came back from deportation in '45 . . . I must have started in '46 or '47, so, of course, I mean, naturally I've known tons of people.

ROUCH: *You say you know tons of people. Do you have many real friends?*

MARCELINE: *No. I have really very few friends. I mean, I must have one or two, and that's it.*

ROUCH: *But Marceline, aren't the people at the Old Navy all just like you?*

MARCELINE: *Yeah, I think so . . . well . . . more or less.*

ROUCH: *Basically it's a society of loners?*

MARCELINE: *That's right. It's a society of loners and of people who don't fit in. And in general I must say that some of the people there are much younger than I am, of course . . . because some are students, some are actors, et cetera. So I must say that I am one of the—at least at the Old Navy anyway, maybe not in other bistros in St. Germain des Prés—I'm one . . . I mean probably . . . I mean it sounds stupid to say this but, well . . . I'm one of the oldest . . . (she laughs).*

MORIN: *No, but I'm going to ask you a very indiscreet question . . . it's your attitude toward men . . .*

MARCELINE: *My attitude toward men?*

MORIN: *Yes.*

MARCELINE: *What is my attitude toward men in general?*

MORIN: *Yes.*

MARCELINE: *I've known a lot of them, I've never found one (laughter), so I think I've given up searching (laughter).*

MORIN: *You were searching?*

MARCELINE: *When I was younger, yes.*

MORIN: *You aren't searching anymore?*

MARCELINE: *Oh, there's always the desire deep within me to find someone, maybe, but I think my many experiences have scarred me a bit, and even if I have trouble . . . I mean I think that in getting older I've become less absolute, less exclusive, less possessive, less demanding, less intransigent, so maybe I could be content sometime to accept living with someone who doesn't bother me too much, who desires me, who gives me breathing room . . . but at the same time the men I could . . . I don't know . . . I could live with are already all married . . . so . . . I'm old, so it's difficult.*

MORIN: *That is to say, you're thirty-two.*

MARCELINE: *Yes, I'm thirty-two. But at thirty-two, well, I don't know . . . men between thirty-five and forty are all married off, so . . . so my attitude with men . . . well, I think it's the attitude of a woman . . . I mean . . . I meet a man I like, well I certainly sleep with him, but I've become much more picky with age too, so I sleep with them less often. (laughter)*

MORIN: *What are you looking for?*

MARCELINE: *Well, you certainly ask it brutally . . . what I am looking for . . . I have no idea what I'm looking for, I just want to live life, that's all.*

MORIN: *You live from day to day?*

MARCELINE: *Ah, yes, that's it . . . I even live for the instant. (laugh)*

MORIN: *Would you like to live any other way?*

MARCELINE: *But when I was younger I think that . . . I mean for a long time I thought that . . . yes, that's it, I think . . . for a long time I thought that a man could help me live, could help me somehow to overcome my past, and then now I begin to not believe that so much. Inasmuch as, of course, given the places I frequent . . . given that the people I meet are all more or less neurotic, so . . . the only man I had in my life who wasn't my husband . . . I stayed with him for eight months . . . then I left. I absolutely could not live . . . he made me sweat.*

MORIN: *Why?*

MARCELINE: *He annoyed me because . . . first of all our lives . . . really we had no affinity . . . we had no common desires . . . everything he wanted I found laughable . . . success, a career in Madagascar . . . things like that . . . I couldn't give a damn . . . I mean I wasn't interested. And then when I first met my husband I had just come out of a serious nervous depression . . . I mean, it was my first nervous depression . . . in fact the only one I had, it was several years after I returned from deportation, I was just back from the sanatorium . . . so I had had this nervous depression. Then I met this big young engineer who built dams and who looked at the soft blue line of the mountains like that, who thirsted for the vast horizon. He was nevertheless extremely kind, extremely nice, and then, since I was small, he confined me to a role as a little girl that I absolutely could not accept. Uh . . . the word 'Jew" had no meaning for him . . . he had absolutely no understanding . . . the war he spent in high school or with some boy scout troop, so really we were not similar. So I left, I left him after eight months because I was bored, it's not so much that I was bored with him as . . . basically we didn't understand each other. With that I think he'll meet a girl who will suit him fine, but not me. And I was inevitably drawn back to the Old Navy. I rediscovered the Old Navy. I rediscovered St. Germain . . . well, of course I had an extremely hard time because he had cut off my supplies, so starting then I really began to work . . . I've . . . in fact that's sort of how I learned my current profession, I don't know, I ended up in a joint where they paid me 100 francs an hour to transcribe diagrams, studies, and so, fine, so I was paid 100 francs an hour, and then there was no more work, so I started to mimeograph reports, and then I read some kind of investigation reports, things like that, and then when there was . . . the day when there were no* more reports to duplicate, they kicked me out . . . there was no more work, so I was . . . out of sheer nerve I went to see the head of the psychology service, then I said that . . . that it didn't seem so difficult to me, that stuff, that I could surely do it, so he said, "Diplomas, no diplomas," then he said I seemed too timid. I must admit that physically I was very different . . . now I'm a bit aggressive what with the red hair, whereas back then I had my hair pulled back, no makeup . . . I was a poor little ragamuffin wandering around the streets . . . I begged him to take me on anyway . . . I told him I didn't care whether I was paid 100 francs an hour but that he had to try me, he had no right to refuse me. So he tried me, and it worked out very well, and there it is, that's how I learned this job after being a waitress in a milk bar, after typing manuscripts, after doing loads of things, anything to make a living.

MORIN: *Do you want to get out of that, or do you want it to keep on?*

MARCELINE: *I think that no matter what I do in life, even if . . . I don't know, I manage to do something I can . . . I mean something I might like, which might interest me, then there will always be a part of me that will be . . . what it is . . . I mean that unlike most of the people I see around me, I have known a lot of people who at some point have become famous, whether they do something, I don't know, make films, write books, paint, et cetera . . . they have a name. At that point all these people stop coming to the Old Navy to . . . I think that to a certain degree they are tied up elsewhere, but at the same time, perhaps they need it less . . . I don't know. At the same time the Old Navy for them represents a time in their lives that they want above all to forget . . . little by little they become bourgeois, they buy cars, they even buy country homes, apartments, they have children . . . and I think that all these elements make them want to forget that moment in their lives, and they don't go to the Old Navy anymore . . . and for them, to go to the Old Navy is no longer any big deal. So I don't know what might happen to me . . . I suppose that . . . I'm nevertheless just as optimistic . . .*

MORIN: *But notice, your number, you keep it, because there are women now who were deported and who have their numbers removed from their arms.*

MARCELINE: *Yeah, yeah, I know . . . I know they can do some kind of a graft or else take it off with electrolysis . . . I saw a girl, in fact, who had had a number and who had an enormous scar that was really ugly. Me, I always considered, at least . . . did I really consider it? . . . there were moments when I wanted to get rid of it, and then, I don't know, I mean, it . . . well, I don't know.*

*Medium shot Rouch, addressing Marceline.*

ROUCH: When you go out in the street in the morning . . .
MARCELINE: Yes . . .
ROUCH: Do you have an idea of what you're going to do during the day?

*Shots of Marceline walking in the street. She walks with her back to the camera, which follows her. The day is gray. We see that it has been raining. Marceline is wearing a raincoat and wears a satchel slung across her shoulders. Over these images, we hear, off-screen, Marceline's laugh as she responds to Jean Rouch, then her voice.*

MARCELINE: Listen, there are times when I go out in the street in the morning when I have things to do, but there is no guarantee I'm going to do them. I mean, I never know what I'll be doing from one day to the next. It's like I live thinking that I don't know what tomorrow will bring, and then, for me adventure is always just around the corner.
ROUCH: And if we asked you to go into the street and ask people the question "Are you happy?" would you go?

*Marceline continues to walk down the street, her back to the camera, following Rouch's off-screen question.*

▶

**Are You Happy?**
*Metro Passy*

*The picture answers Jean Rouch's question. Marceline, wearing the raincoat in which we saw her in the preceding sequence, calls out to passersby near the Passy metro station. The satchel she is carrying is a tape recorder case, and she holds a microphone in her hand. She is accompanied by Nadine, who is taking part in the film as interviewer. Marceline speaks to a passerby:*

MARCELINE: Are you happy? Sir, excuse me?
MAN: What the fuck do you care . . .
MARCELINE *(to Nadine):* He said what the fuck do you care . . .

*Nadine laughs. Marceline and Nadine approach a young boy.*

MARCELINE: Are you happy?

*The young boy draws back in fear.*

MARCELINE AND NADINE: Hey, don't be afraid! We don't want to hurt you!

---

### Place Victor Hugo

*Marceline calls to a middle-aged woman, passing by.*

MARCELINE: Ma'am . . . excuse me . . .
WOMAN: Eh, I don't have time, I'm already tired enough.

---

### Place De La Bastille

MARCELINE: Are you happy, sir?
PASSERBY: Oh, don't give me all that stuff!

*Marceline stops an unassuming-looking man, about fifty years old.*

MARCELINE: Are you happy?
MAN: Always, yes.
MARCELINE: Really?
MAN: Yes, of course!

---

### Place Du Pantheon

*Marceline speaks to an old woman, who is afraid of the microphone.*

MARCELINE: Are you happy?
WOMAN: Oh yes. Well, things are okay . . . those contraptions!

---

### Menilmontant

*A young woman pushing a baby carriage.*

YOUNG WOMAN: It depends what you mean by happy . . . Happy? I'm happy in my home life. Yeah, and so?

## Bastille

*A woman around sixty years old. She tries to avoid them.*

NADINE: Please, ma'am, do us this favor.

WOMAN: Of course . . . can't you tell? Can't you see it on my face?

MARCELINE: Yes, you have a very bright face.

WOMAN: So I'm happy, happy to be alive, even though I'm sixty years old.

NADINE: You're sixty?

WOMAN: Yes, and even though I travel twenty kilometers every day to come work in Paris.

NADINE: No kidding?

WOMAN: I'm glad to have my health . . . that's the main thing . . . and a kind husband.

## Metro Passy

*A woman, on the metro platform.*

WOMAN: It depends.

MARCELINE: It depends on what?

WOMAN: It depends on what . . . you know, question of money, no; you're never happy when you're a worker.

## Saint Germain de Prés

*A man around fifty years old.*

MAN: Sometimes I've got plenty of troubles.

NADINE: And still you're not unhappy?

MAN: I've lost my sister, forty-four years old, yes, my dear! And I am really upset . . . believe me. Now I don't even try to understand.

## Place Victor Hugo

*A young man wearing glasses—no doubt a student.*

MARCELINE: Are you unhappy?

YOUNG MAN: What do you mean, unhappy? What for?

NADINE: Are you happy or unhappy?

YOUNG MAN: It depends what philosophy you adopt.

MARCELINE: Oh, we're doing a study on the theme of happiness.

NADINE: Yeah.

YOUNG MAN: On the theme of happiness? And you aren't going to cite any names? Well . . . I don't know . . . if you take Descartes . . .

NADINE: Oh no, no, no . . . oh my, no!

YOUNG MAN: You see, I'm in the middle of reading this!

*He shows a book that he pulls out of his pocket.*

■ ————————————————————————————————————————————

## Bastille

*A fun fair. In front of a merry-go-round, Marceline and Nadine interrogate a friendly young cop.*

MARCELINE: Are you happy?

COP: No.

MARCELINE: No, you're not happy, why? We're doing a sociological investigation.

COP: A lodging investigation?

NADINE: No, sociological.

COP: Off-duty it would be okay to answer, but in uniform . . .

MARCELINE: You aren't allowed to answer?

COP: No, not in uniform . . . off-duty I would have answered.

■ ————————————————————————————————————————————

## Saint Germain de Prés

*A middle-aged lady, unpretentious, but elegant.*

LADY: On the theme of happiness? I've had happiness. I've had unhappiness. I've had a bit of everything in my life. It can't be any other way, eh? You've got to take the good with the bad, eh?

■ ————————————————————————————————————————————

## Rue Beauregard

*An old man, almost miserable looking.*

MARCELINE: Why are you unhappy, sir?

OLD MAN: Because I'm too old.

MARCELINE: Really?

OLD MAN: Yup, seventy-nine years!

MARCELINE: No?

OLD MAN: I swear it, yes, I'm from '82.

*He seems completely terrified by the mike, which Marceline holds near him. The young women laugh.*

NADINE: Don't be afraid, no, don't be afraid, it's the microphone! It's the microphone!

MARCELINE: And do you think that when you're eighty . . . when you're seventy-nine years old, you're unhappy?

OLD MAN: Oh, well, I lost my wife, too . . .

NADINE: So you're alone?

OLD MAN: Ah yes, I'm alone. And then there's the rent, 6,318 [francs] every month. I'm in a hotel . . .

■──────────────────────────────────

### Saint Germain de Prés

*Two young women, elegant and cheerful.*

MARCELINE: Are you happy?

ONE YOUNG WOMAN: Yes.

NADINE: And you, miss?

OTHER YOUNG WOMAN: Me too, of course. We're young, and it's a beautiful day.

▶──────────────────────────────────

### The Garage Mechanic

*A car repair shop. Medium shot of the front of a car with its hood up. Back to the camera, the garage mechanic, in blue coveralls, is leaning over the engine. His wife is standing near him, screen left. They both must be about thirty-five. Marceline arrives and comes toward them, facing the camera.*

MARCELINE: Good morning. I was sent here by Daniel; he said you had agreed to be interviewed.

MECHANIC: Yes.

*Medium close-up of the mechanic.*

MARCELINE: I'm going to ask you to answer just one question for me: are you satisfied with your living conditions?

*The mechanic casts one last glance at the motor.*

MECHANIC: There's not much to be done about it.

*Medium shot, over Marceline's shoulder to the mechanic and his wife.*

WIFE: We aren't lacking anything. We've got everything we need . . . what we want, well, it's to move up . . . I mean it's . . .
MECHANIC: No, in a certain sense we're not complaining . . . to say we're complaining . . . we're not complaining. Us, we don't complain. I mean to say that . . .
WIFE: I think that to get somewhere in life, to do something yourself, you've got to work.
MARCELINE: Yes.
MECHANIC: No, but that's out of the realm of living conditions. About living conditions, we get by because we cheat a little, eh? Because we do a bunch of things that we really shouldn't do.

*The wife is shocked.*

WIFE: Oh, you're being funny, saying that . . .
MECHANIC: It's the truth . . . You ask me a question, I answer it for you.
WIFE: Obviously.
MECHANIC: Now, living conditions . . . well, it's practically impossible if you stick to the rules . . . that's what I think.
MARCELINE: Yeah . . .
MECHANIC: I mean that if I bill all my clients . . . if I bill everything normally, then making a living is impossible . . .

*The young woman seems scandalized and most of all very worried. She taps her husband lightly and looks toward the camera with apprehension. A friend of the mechanic—a worker or somebody connected with the garage—is near him. Marceline questions him. (Opposite angle to medium shot of the men.)*

MARCELINE: And you, sir, are you happy?
MAN: Oh, from time to time. It depends on the moment . . . on circumstances . . . I manage.

*Close-up of Marceline, to three-shot, with the wife in profile.*

WIFE: When you get right down to it, Paris is not all that much fun. The atmosphere, the lack of sun . . . we still have a life that's, well, too . . .

*Close-up of Marceline, to medium shot of the two men behind the gaping hood of the car, wife in profile.*

MECHANIC: People are crazy, they're nuts. They work all week, then they don't do anything on Sunday. They don't want to wreck the car. They park along the side of the road, they take out their little table, their little chair, they set themselves up so they won't wreck the car, because on a little back lane, they'd wreck it. So they sit there, they use five liters of gas and they take three hours to get home. You think that's normal?

*Close-up of the two men, over.*

MARCELINE: And you live differently, you two?
MECHANIC: I try . . . we try.
MARCELINE: Yeah? . . .
MECHANIC: We're interested in useless things that don't get you anything, just for the fun of it.
MARCELINE: What do you mean by useless things?
MECHANIC: Well, we've got some friends . . .
FRIEND: Putter around . . .
MECHANIC: We mess around doing things for no reason. We spend time doing nothing.

▶────────────────────────────────────────────

**Maddie and Henri**

*A door opens to reveal a young woman, and behind her a room visibly close to the roof. In the back of the room a young bearded man is seated. Marceline and Nadine enter:*

MARCELINE: Hello.
YOUNG WOMAN: Hello.
NADINE: Hello, we're here for the survey you were told about . . . hello . . . here we are.
YOUNG WOMAN: What are your names?
NADINE: I'm Nadine, and this is Marceline.
MARCELINE: And I'm Marceline. And you?
YOUNG WOMAN: Maddie . . . and he's Henri.

*Marceline asks her question—are you happy? Close-up of Henri, who answers:*

HENRI: Me, I don't know . . . happiness isn't a goal . . . I don't set up happiness as a goal for myself . . . I try to live as normally as possible . . . I mean as true to myself as possible . . . at the moment there are two of us . . . that hasn't changed a thing in my concept of happiness . . . I try to find it for two, whereas before I was looking for it alone . . . and that's it.

MARCELINE: And how was your life before?

*Close-up of Maddie, later cutting away to close-ups of Henri and Marceline.*

MADDIE: Until I was seventeen, I lived with my parents and then some friends, and I decided to start a business that was going to make us get rich quick . . . of course! Because working a lot . . . that is not very interesting . . . because it's really a waste of time . . . for earning money in particular. So we had a big cabinetry shop and with big old Louis Philippe bureaus that we cut up, that we dismantled completely . . . we managed to make Louis XVI bureaus, because the wood was 100 years old and people were fooled by it . . . 100 years or 150 or 200 years, it doesn't matter . . . So we transformed them, for example, by adding some columns on either side . . . we left only three drawers . . . You know on Louis Philippe's there are five drawers. Then in the end, using only the old wood, we managed to even reconstruct some Louis XIV pieces, by bending the old wood, adding curves and new veneer . . .

NADINE: And you made money in this venture?

MADDIE: Oh, the people who were with me made a lot, but in the end I got out . . . people are even suing since then . . . I mean to tell you that all this . . . to say that the business world is hideous . . . in fact I'm very happy not to have gotten anything out of it . . . except for the experience so that I never again get started in ventures like that . . . it's not worth it.

*Maddie gets up, and we see her in the foreground, getting a bowl of fruit from a table. Henri is talking in the background.*

HENRI: Me, I'm a painter. I'm not a theoretician. To understand something, I need to make it, to participate in it . . . so . . . I like painting, and so I do it to try to understand others a bit . . .

*Maddie returns toward Henri, Nadine, and Marceline on the terrace and offers some fruit.*

MARCELINE: I'll take one grape, I'm not hungry at all . . .

MARCELINE *(off-screen):* What do you do every day?

*Maddie is seated, Nadine at her right, Henri at her left; Marceline faces her, holding the microphone.*

MADDIE: So there you have it, it's been exactly a year and a half that we're together . . . so it's sort of been our honeymoon. We've usually stayed in bed until one in the afternoon . . . read old books, and every afternoon we've painted . . . but painting, that's only for the last six months.

HENRI: You're forgetting about our jaunts.

MADDIE: Because besides that we wanted to travel a bit, all over. Last year we left in May. It was our honeymoon trip from May up until . . . until the end of September . . . we went to the Camargue . . . we rented a studio . . . well, in an old house, with an old lady.

MARCELINE: Aie! You went to Saint Tropez?

*Close-up of Henri.*

HENRI: Completely broke! And there we had to get by, we had to live . . . and the great discovery was to realize that we could live down there just like we live here now . . . I mean we did odd jobs . . . I painted names on boats . . . things like that. I worked two hours a day . . . we led a life of luxury.

*Close-up of Maddie.*

MADDIE: And then we lived on that for the whole day . . . we sunbathed, we painted . . .

*Close-up of Henri.*

HENRI: We don't think about the problem of happiness . . . maybe that's why we consider ourselves happy, because we don't think about the problem of happiness, which is a pretty empty word. Because to consider the problem of unhappiness . . . the problem of happiness, is to consider the problem of unhappiness . . . and the problem of unhappiness is ridiculous. It's a word that should be struck from the vocabulary, unhappiness. There is sorrow . . . there's everything you want . . . but not unhappiness . . . or happiness either.

*Henri gets up and walks to the foreground; the camera follows him, panning left toward an odd cabinet with a glass door, which he opens, and he flicks a switch. It's an antique music case in which an enormous toothed wheel begins to rotate. In the background, Maddie is still talking.*

MADDIE: You see, for example, we have no money, and yet I know very few people in our group of friends, who earn, by the way, some hefty sums every month, who have a library or a record collection like ours, because as soon as we sell a little painting, it's really to enrich our universe with belongings, with objects.

*The camera stops on the music machine, filming it in successive extreme close-ups, while we hear the music continue its little mechanical round. Downward wipe to black.*

▶————————————————————————————————————

**The Workers**

*Part of a close shot of a photo of Marlon Brando stuck to a wall. The camera tilts down to a group of young workers at a table with Jean Rouch and Edgar Morin (close-up of Jean, with inserts of Morin, and then Jacques).*

JEAN: When I think that you have to get up in the morning at the same time every day . . . let's say at six o'clock . . . then you have your coffee . . . you take the same route every day to get to the station . . . you walk up the stairs, you get on the train, then you arrive, . . . you go in the same door every day. Then the time clock, you punch in every day. Then after that you sit down at your drafting table, and you start to draw. And then at noon you start over every day, you talk, and then that's it, you go eat and then you come back, and then in the evening you take your train, you go home and then you eat . . . then you go to bed, and it's always the same, I mean, I find it ridiculous. I find it . . . When I get here in the morning, when I get to the door of the factory . . . I don't know . . . I feel like there's something . . . I feel like rebelling, and then I tell myself . . . after all, I don't give a damn.

*Close-up of Jacques.*

JACQUES: Me, I've never heard a guy tell me his work was interesting.
MORIN: But Angélo, do you feel the same way he does?

*Close-up of Angélo, panning from Jean.*

ANGÉLO: Yeah, just about . . . yeah . . . but I think that.

*Medium close-up of Jacques with cutaways to Angélo.*

JACQUES: Well, there are lots of guys who want to become . . . to climb the ranks . . . to get from workers to technicians, from technicians they think they'll get to be . . . I don't know . . . engineers, maybe. So they take courses . . . that's what they're hoping for . . . but to leave to go where? To shop around? There are many who leave to go shop around and then they come back . . . there are some who leave to go start a business . . . some succeed . . . some don't succeed, and they come back. The problem is the same for people who work in the office. For all the people who work in whatever part of the factory, it's the same. It's that the work is so fragment-ed, it's gotten so small, if you like, that we end up doing a job that's mo-notonous . . . that's boring . . . and it's always the same.

*Close-up of Angélo.*

ANGÉLO: Well, I think that . . . me, I do twenty-four hours a day. Because you do nine hours a day, that's true, but the rest of the hours you use to sleep, and you sleep so you can go work, so it's all the same . . . and all of it is work . . . I think he's right.

▶ ————————————————————————————————

**Angélo**

*Angélo's bedroom, at home in Clamart, in the morning. An alarm clock rings. Angélo emerges from the sheets, stretches. His mother comes in car-rying his breakfast tray. They kiss each other.*

ANGÉLO: How are you?
MOTHER: Fine, how are you?

*The mother leaves the room. Angélo eats his breakfast, then lights a ciga-rette and takes a couple of drags before he gets up.*

*Rapid succession of shots: Angélo finishes washing, gets dressed, and leaves the house.*

*We follow him, as does the camera, down the street. Day has not yet bro-ken. The factory entrance, which groups of workers penetrate silently. We see Angélo enter. A worker at the door distributes leaflets.*

*The factory. Flashes of the workers at work in front of their machines in full action. Lathes, milling machines, plating presses . . . melting iron. Trolleys. Wagons.*

*The break. Workers, sitting in different corners of the shop, eat sandwiches. One leafs through a newspaper as he eats.*

*End of the day. The workers leave the factory. We follow Angélo in the street. He is waiting for the bus. Quick shots of the ride. When he gets off, Angélo climbs a long stairway squeezed between gardens. Some children are playing on the steps. Angélo says hello to some of them in passing.*

*When Angélo reaches the top of the stairs, we discover, from that point, an immense panoramic view down onto the roofs of Paris.*

*At the end of a little street also lined with gardens, Angélo reaches the house where he lives. We then see him in the courtyard, in a white judo suit. He is practicing judoka movements: shoulder butts, wrist manchettes, falls. Some sort of heavy bearskin hangs from a tree, and the tree itself serves as his partner. Angélo seems to be fighting with the tree.*

*Angélo's room. He stretches out on the bed, picks up a book with an ancient binding, opens it. We can make out a title:* Danton.

*Dusk. Lights go out in Angélo's room.*

▶ ─────────────────────────────────────────

### Angélo and Landry

*The staircase of an apartment building. On the first steps are seated Landry, a black African, and Angélo. Standing and facing them at the foot of the steps, Edgar Morin.*

MORIN: Angélo, you saw Landry at the screening of the rushes;[2] you wanted to meet him . . . well, here he is now, go ahead!

*Close-up of Angélo, then Landry.*

ANGÉLO: What are you doing in France now?
LANDRY: In France I'm at Villeneuve-sur-Lot college, in Lot-en-Garonne. It's a place where I'm quite happy.
ANGÉLO: I work at Renault.
LANDRY: Ah, you work at Renault! Well, well, my friend! They sure talk about Renault in Africa. The Renault company, what do you know, what do you know!
ANGÉLO: It's got a big reputation.

*Series of close-ups alternating between Angélo and Landry during the following response.*

LANDRY: Oh, a very big reputation; for Africans it's the only automobile manufacturer that exists. Besides Renault there's nobody . . . Yes, but, I don't know . . . for myself, I would never consider working in a factory. Because I imagine that . . . in a factory you're there, you're closed in, you're there all day long, the noise of machines and all there . . .

*Close-up of Angélo.*

ANGÉLO: You're absolutely right. It's disgusting. I wonder how we manage to stay in a factory, like you say, closed in. We're closed in, we're controlled. There's a kind of discord that already divides workers. And on top of that, there's the management harassing us, always in back of us, the foremen, that's right, it's really disgusting. And you're right when you say that you wonder how we manage to stay in a factory; it's really tough, only you've got no choice, sometimes there just isn't anything else. Uh . . . when you first came to France, and you were doing absolutely nothing, you didn't know the place, you didn't know anyone, eh? That's just what I'd like you to tell me a little about.

*Close-up Landry.*

LANDRY: Ah! When I first came to France, I didn't know anyone, I mean . . . I didn't know anyone. I wasn't really familiar with life in France, and I was obliged to get by . . . I mean to pull myself through. In my condition it's pretty difficult. An African in France is not . . . there's . . . for him the big problem is a question of adaptation.

*Alternating close-ups of Angélo and Landry throughout the following exchange.*

ANGÉLO: I also have the impression that in life you have . . . there are people who have inferiority complexes.
LANDRY: When I talk about inferiority complexes, that's me exactly, I mean . . .
ANGÉLO: Yeah, I understand, but there's a thing I want to ask you. Could I maybe use *tu* with you? Do you mind?
LANDRY: Yes, of course, at this point! . . .
ANGÉLO: There's a thing I want to ask you, and that's, do you still have this complex?
LANDRY: Uh . . . me, no, I no longer have a complex because when I arrived in France I realized that the French in Paris were not the same as the French in Africa and—
ANGÉLO: It doesn't bother you a bit . . . you're black, and you don't give a damn.
LANDRY: Oh, I don't give a damn! Like I said, I've got a system. I knock on a door, and when it opens, I walk in. When it insists on staying shut, I turn around. It's simple.
ANGÉLO: Oh, you're right. You're really okay. I like you a lot. Listen, I'm going to say, what do you think about workers?
LANDRY: Uh, workers, well, I, workers in France, I'm not exactly familiar with them . . .
ANGÉLO: You're not familiar with them . . .
LANDRY: Ah, but . . . I don't know how it works in France . . . because here

in France I've seen workers, even the lower-income worker, he's got a car. And so every evening you see him, he's very happy . . . so I don't know how it really works and . . . I don't know if it's the same as in Africa . . .

ANGÉLO: You're right . . . you see, I work at Renault, and you've got to figure, you know, 80 percent of the guys who have their car . . . because I must tell you, it's that in France . . . the guy is an individual. He works for himself . . . y'know . . . he thinks only of himself . . . the guy's got his salary, you see, he works . . . he works . . . for himself, the guy . . . and he works hard, eh? So he saves up some dough, you see, he deprives himself of certain things, you see . . . he wants to play, like, that kind of guy, you know, who has dough . . . who's got some bread . . . you see. He's a pitiful guy . . . he's really a pitiful guy. The rest of us, we go to the cafeteria, you know, but me, I don't give a damn . . . I've got absolutely nothing . . . I've got absolutely nothing . . . I'm a poor guy, but I eat. At the cafeteria at Renault, you see, the guys at the table . . . you know they eat . . . just . . . an appetizer . . . you know, that's all . . . and a bit of bread. That's all, but they've got one thing . . . they've got their wheels . . . so you imagine . . . you say to yourself, you say . . . yeah, but shit, these guys in France . . . the proletariat in France . . . he's got some dough . . . he's got some dough . . . he makes a lot . . . he makes a lot of bread . . . he can buy himself a car . . . he can buy himself a car . . . he can pay for his apartment. Don't believe it! He is one unhappy guy . . . he's a pitiful type. Believe me! I live with these people . . . I live with them . . . they're a pitiful bunch. Look, you've got other things like . . . you go into a café or a restaurant . . . more like a restaurant. You see the guy really well dressed . . . with all that, you say . . . at least this guy must have some money. He's a pitiful guy . . . don't have any illusions . . . he's a pitiful guy . . . most of the time he's a pitiful guy, well, that's my opinion . . . he's an unhappy guy . . . he's a guy who's deprived himself so he could buy a suit, you see . . . well dressed. The gossips and you see the whole deal. It's a sham, all of that . . . it's a joke . . . the guy . . . because . . . why is it a joke? It's a joke because on Monday he's going to start over like a pitiful guy in a shitty factory . . . filthy . . . Like when you see him inside a factory, and you see the outside, it's no longer the same guy . . . you see?

*Final close-up of Landry, agreeing, vaguely disturbed.*

▶

## Gabillon

*A dining room. At the table facing Edgar Morin is Jacques Gabillon, his wife, Simone, and their little boy.*

MORIN: Go on and serve your kid! He's got nothing left to eat!

MME GABILLON: What do you want, my love?

CHILD: Some cucumber . . .

GABILLON: Cucumber!

MME GABILLON: Okay, then.

GABILLON: You're a cucumber lover.

*Profile close-up of Morin, with cutaways to Gabillon.*

MORIN: I remember . . . eh? . . . For years, the housing problem . . . how much it bothered you . . . how much it weighed down your life. And then now you're in Clichy. Low-cost housing is better anyway. It's bright, it's peaceful, et cetera . . . but could you talk to us about that problem?

*Close-up of Mme Gabillon during her husband's response.*

GABILLON: It was sheer anguish, the housing question, it was distressing . . . Not to have a home . . . to be in some ways at the mercy of others. It's something absolutely terrible. Well, first of all when you're in a . . . in a boardinghouse . . .

MME GABILLON: Oh, listen, you don't remember! . . . There were some walls that were so thin you could hear everything the neighbors were saying next door . . .

GABILLON: Of course . . . of course . . . it's true.

MME GABILLON: We didn't even have heat in the room.

GABILLON: It's true.

MME GABILLON: And then we had bedbugs . . . I was so terrified that I wanted to sleep outside.

GABILLON: But I didn't want you to sleep outside . . . you wanted to go up to the park on the hill . . .

MME GABILLON: Well, I would have preferred.

GABILLON: The park . . . though . . . in the eighteenth . . . down there . . .

*Close-up of Mme Gabillon.*

MME GABILLON: Oh, it was awful! I had never seen bedbugs in my life. The first time I saw . . . it was one day . . . I woke up at about five in the morning. I mean before I had a couple of little . . . a couple of little bumps on my arms . . . I didn't know what they were . . . I thought they were some weird pimples, and then one fine day I woke up at five in the morning, and I turned my head and saw some kind of bug climbing behind my bed . . . I'd never seen any bedbugs . . . never . . . I let out an ear-piercing scream. You remember . . .

GABILLON: I didn't care. I'd seen bedbugs, of course.

MME GABILLON: But I hadn't.

GABILLON: I had seen them before, but Simone hadn't, eh?

MME GABILLON: Oh no, it was awful! . . . to see such things!

*Close-up of Gabillon.*

GABILLON: Then it's terrible because she wanted to go out like that and sleep on the grass . . . on the lawn . . . in the park, down there . . .

MME GABILLON: No it wasn't . . . yeah, but the Buttes Chaumont,³ it wasn't . . .

GABILLON: And me, I didn't want to. I didn't want to because for me the Buttes Chaumont, you know, it's something . . . it left me . . . how can I explain, it was a risk, you know? . . . to be left somehow at the mercy of the night . . . and anyway, I didn't want to leave her in the park, on the lawn, eh?

*Close-up of Mme Gabillon.*

MME GABILLON: As for me, I preferred that to the bedbugs. Oh, I would have preferred that. And then I talked about them at the office, and I had a friend who said, "Oh my god, a bedbug makes . . . it's weird . . . it's like a drop of blood running down your body." And all night I thought about that. I got to sleep around four in the morning thinking I'd feel a drop of blood fall on me . . . it was awful!

■————————————————————————————

### Are You Happy?

*Close-up of Edgar Morin, then close-ups alternating between Gabillon and his wife during the following replies.*

MORIN: I was wondering something. Are you happy?

MME GABILLON: More or less . . .

MORIN: And you?

GABILLON: More or less . . .

MORIN: So what's missing?

MME GABILLON: Oh, I'm ashamed to say it . . . money.

MORIN: And you?

GABILLON: To do what I'd like to do . . .

MORIN: Which is?

GABILLON: To devote time to what interests me . . .

MME GABILLON: Yeah, but it's the same thing! Because if we had money, he could dedicate himself to whatever he wants . . . I mean . . .

MORIN: Right now what are you happy with?

MME GABILLON: Well, I suppose that in spite of everything, I'm pretty spoiled by life . . . because . . . I love my husband . . . I love my son . . . I have a job . . . a small job, but I like it . . .

GABILLON: For me, work is time wasted.

*Close-up of Gabillon during Morin's question, then alternation of close-ups again, according to which person is speaking.*

MORIN: Okay, but if you remember . . . you struggled . . . we struggled in the same party. We hoped for another kind of life . . . we hoped for something different . . . and then?

GABILLON: Yes, of course.

MORIN: So we bury it?

GABILLON: Ideals are not always . . . they're not always . . . not even often attainable. So of course we accept . . . we accept or no, we don't accept the life that is made for us.

MORIN: You have to adapt?

GABILLON: You have to adapt. I admire and envy people who precisely can adapt totally. Me, I'm reduced to a sort of . . . a split, you know, internally, an intimate split, and I abandon one part of me, you know? . . . that I adapt.

MORIN: And the other part—what does it do?

GABILLON: Well, I keep it . . . up till now . . . I protect it, more exactly . . . I protect it!

MORIN: And what is this part?

GABILLON: Well, it's the authentic part of me . . .

*Off-screen voice of Gabillon over close-up of Morin, then slight pan toward Mme Gabillon, finishing on close-up of Gabillon with Mme Gabillon.*

I think that the tragedy of our age is that we choose our work less and less. You don't enter into something . . . you fall into something because you've simply got to have . . . if not a title . . . but a position, an official job . . . because you need an ID card . . . you need a work card. A man today, what is a man? A packet . . . a packet of . . . he's an ID card . . . a bunch of forms . . . that's today's man, isn't it? Not everybody can be an artist, nor can everybody be a craftsman. It's a maneuver so you have to beat boredom . . . the whole day long . . . a job that's uninteresting, a job to . . . how shall I put it? . . . in which you find no interest, that has no meaning. . . . And yet obviously you have to do it, this job. . . . You have to put up with it, right, until six P.M.

MORIN: Yeah, but after six o'clock?

GABILLON: Well, after six o'clock you try to become yourself again . . . you become yourself again. You have a job until six o'clock, and then afterward you're a whole other man . . . a whole other person.

*Close-up of Morin, smiling.*

MORIN: And what does this man do?

*Profile close-up of Gabillon with close-up inserts of Mme Gabillon.*

GABILLON: Well, this man, he vibrates, he exists. He's maybe a prisoner elsewhere. He's a prisoner of the first man, right? It's the first one who passed him the handcuffs. But I think that more and more you have to, you have to . . . how shall I put it? Cut down your participation, you know, in work, in work, in official work, and give even more on the side . . . to what I call the marginal life . . .

*Close-up Morin.*

MORIN: Because for the rest you think . . . is there anything you believe in?

*Close-up Gabillon.*

GABILLON: I believe in life . . . I mean, I believe . . . in the possibility of being fulfilled in spite of everything, in . . . and because of it!

▶───────────────────────────────────

## Marilou

*[This exchange between Marilou and Morin, which has been shortened considerably in the film, is reproduced here almost in its entirety. Marilou knew nothing of the questions she would be asked. Morin didn't know where he was heading. The first question was anecdotal and superficial, but Marilou, who could have avoided answering it, responds with extraordinary candor, which takes this exchange beyond the bounds of the conversation or the interview.]*

E. M. and J. R.

▶───────────────────────────────────

MORIN: *Listen, Marilou . . .*
MARILOU: *Yes, my father . . .*
MORIN: *I'm going to ask you a question.*
MARILOU: *Go ahead.*

MORIN: *On Friday, last Friday at three in the morning, I saw you at St. Germain des Prés with two men . . . And as I happen to know that the next day you had to be at work at nine in the morning, that you are a secretary for a magazine, I ask you the question: how do you live?*

MARILOU: *That's a question I don't ask myself. I live like I live; it sometimes happens that I'm out late every night, that I still manage to get to work, it sometimes happens that I go to bed very early, it doesn't change me in the least; makes absolutely no difference in my life.*

MORIN: *It was in July 1957 that you arrived in Paris with your suitcases. You didn't know French; well, you had learned some in school.*

MARILOU: *Yes, it was the fourteenth of July in 1957. I arrived on the fourteenth of July, I didn't know a word of French, I had some addresses, but I didn't know anyone; I arrived and I went to the first address and no one was there, I went to the second address, there was a girl who spoke English. She said, "You must be tired, come in and rest." . . . I rested. I phoned the first address because it was some friends, some comrades, political friends, I went back there and I lived at the beginning with a Spanish refugee, I learned French in political surroundings . . . it was . . . it was really great, and I didn't notice that I was making an effort to adapt because there were new relationships to be made, new people, even the language, it was a really euphoric period up to the point when I began to express myself in French, and the mechanism of repetition started up. I realized that at Concorde or at Montparnasse or Etoile or St. Germain des Prés . . . the problem was the same as in the smallest café, on the smallest street of the most remote little hamlet in Italy, and that it had done me no good to have come to France.*

MORIN: *I first met you in October '57, in sum those were your early days in Paris?*

MARILOU: *Yeah.*

MORIN: *It was at the town hall in Clichy.*

MARILOU: *Yeah.*

MORIN: *It was by chance, there was a debate about Poland.*

MARILOU: *On Stalinism.*

MORIN: *With our friend Claude.*

MARILOU: *Yeah.*

MORIN: *And you worked as a secretary.*

MARILOU: *Yeah, a crummy joint.*

MORIN: *I saw you then, and it's been over three years since.*

MARILOU: *Yeah.*

MORIN: *You're a Parisian now, at least you're no longer . . . you're more Parisian than Cremonese, I mean . . . has something new happened for you?*

MARILOU: *Yes. Nothing scandalizes me anymore. In Italy I was into politics and was really scandalized (now, I don't like that word) by a certain social situation. I really thought I could do something; I pursued it in France. I belonged to leftist groups in France; for the past two months, I've been out of politics altogether! . . . I find it laughable . . . I find that . . . I discover that I don't know how to say . . . a logic in things, and I tell myself all the time, fine, it's like this, if you like it, fine, if you don't like it, all you have to do is avoid it. Yeah, but otherwise you just keep on walking, that's all.*

▶ ─────────────────────────────────

*We see Marilou going out of her maid's room and leaving the building she lives in. We follow her on the street. We find her at her office of Cahiers du Cinéma, where she is a secretary.*

*Over a medium close-up of Marilou sitting in front of her typewriter, we hear Edgar Morin, whose voice continues over close-ups of Marilou in inserts, then alternating with close-ups of himself.*

MORIN: Marilou, you are twenty-seven years old, you came from Italy to France three years ago, and for the past three years you have been living a totally new experience. When you were in Cremona, you lived with your father, a petit bourgeois, to boot. Here in Paris you live in a maid's room, without running water, you have had the experience of being a foreigner, and you have met some men; you have learned some things; you've gotten to know Paris, you've had some new friends, and so, what I want to say is, what is there that's new for you?

*Close-up of Marilou, the face, attentive, leaning on one of her hands.*

MARILOU: You've mentioned the difference between my bourgeois life in Italy and my maid's room in Paris. In fact, my maid's room has done something for me. I spent one winter . . . several winters, in fact, with no heat . . . it was cold. It was the first time I lived without comfort. It was a relief the first year . . . I was overwhelmed by bad conscience when I first came to Paris . . . and . . . I don't know . . . it was silly, but it did me good to be, to be uncomfortable . . . and then, and then . . . I think . . . it was also the first time I worked. The first times when I woke up at seven o'clock, even if I was exhausted, I was almost happy to take the subway . . . to find myself in the bustle. I think that really I felt myself a part of something. But that didn't last too long. Now I'm sick of my maid's room, I'm sick of being cold in the winter . . . I'm sick of being in the subway at rush hour. I don't find anymore . . . communication, I find . . . it all disagreeable, it's all for nothing . . . and . . .

*Close-up of Morin.*

MORIN: Yeah, but listen . . . I mean . . . Are you pursuing something? Do you have some goal? . . .

*Close-up of Marilou.*

MARILOU: Really, to be honest, I don't know . . . There are moments when I happily tell myself that I came to Paris . . . and it's true, I have the impression that I've recovered lost time. I felt sort of out of phase with everything when I first came here, and I was closed up at home . . . isolated . . . when I was in Italy. And I used up my inner resources, so I wanted to go crashing into reality . . . I did it . . . and I thought it was good. And now I wonder if I had to do it that way. I drink, for example, . . . that too I find . . . I don't know . . . I wanted to free myself of alibis when I came to France, I wanted to live, not by compensation . . . I wanted to live because I wanted to live . . . you know, then . . . Now I've destroyed bit by bit the false mechanisms, the alibis, and I recover them by drinking or by sleeping around, by some irrational attitude, by doing fucked-up things basically . . . using foul language doesn't help, so, that's it—.

▶ ───────────────────────────────

MORIN: *Yes, but still you see I don't agree with what you're saying. There's something in you, because here you've got friends, there are people who really like you, you're not alone, so in the end what are you seeking to overcome? You know you have help . . . I don't understand now if you're wishing this state on yourself . . .*
MARILOU: *I know there are people who love me, that's not what's important, it's feeling it. There are moments when I don't feel it, where I feel cut off from everything, where I feel that something isn't working, something fundamental is not working . . . and it comes before something happens, and so I don't give a damn whether people love me or not . . . it's not important, you see?*
MORIN: *Yeah, but then I say, what does there need to be for things to work right? What does there need to be for things to work right?*
MARILOU: *I need to feel, in a given situation, like I am in the real world, whereas I constantly feel like I am in the imaginary.*

▶ ───────────────────────────────

*Close-up of Marilou from Morin's profile point of view.*

MORIN: You say you are in the imaginary. But what does reality mean for you? Is it to have a job that really interests you? To do what you really want? Is it to . . . to . . . live with a man that you love rather than living day to day like this, sleeping with guys? I don't know, what is it?

MARILOU: But one flows from the other, clearly. It's to have a job that . . . that doesn't scare me. It's to live with someone who . . . no matter how long . . . whether it be for an hour, two hours . . . a month . . . fifteen days . . . and knowing that I'm with him . . . that I have the possibility of communicating with him . . . that there are no phantoms to prevent my enjoying him. It's . . . it's above all . . . to come out of myself . . . to live or die, even . . . provided that it puts me in touch with something that . . . makes me get outside of myself, that's all . . . I reduce everything to myself for the moment. I don't even have the right to . . . not even the right to kill myself, you know, it would be false . . . absolutely false . . . and . . .

*Long close-up of Marilou, who is silent, biting at her lips, on the verge of tears, under the gaze of Edgar Morin, who is immobile, and also silent. Then . . .*

MORIN: But why do you reduce everything to you?
MARILOU: What?
MORIN: Reduce everything to you?
MARILOU: If only I knew!

*Prolonged close-up of Marilou, silent again, edgy, anguished.*

▶————————————————————————————

*Intervention of Rouch, who, after baiting this Morin-Marilou dialogue, remained silent and out of the conversation. Marilou is in tears, but her face is very calm.*

ROUCH: *Ask a question now, anything, about the pope. Ask the question now, and don't get close to her, ask the question.*
MORIN: *Okay, now listen, Marilou . . .*
ROUCH: *No, you're moving closer, Morin, stay back. Morin, move back. Start the question over.*
MORIN: *Listen, for tonight we're going to ask you something a little lighter, okay?* (Laughter) *What do you think of the pope, of anything you want?*

*Questioning face of Marilou.*

MORIN: *Because the pope is Italian.*
MARILOU: *I don't care about being Italian. I'm Italian by chance, and I don't give a damn about the pope either.*
MORIN: *You're not Italian by chance.*

MARILOU: *No, it's by chance.*

MORIN: *But I see that when you prepare a dish of pasta-scouta, you prepare the sauce as though you were.*

MARILOU: *It's all a show for friends. Italians are supposed to know how to make spaghetti, so I make it, so everyone thinks my spaghetti sauces reveal the purest Italian tradition . . . well, the last time, I put vodka in it. So there, I'm quite pleased with myself (laughter).*

MORIN: *Do you feel as though you've said things . . . lots of things or not many things.*

MARILOU: *I can't say anything at the moment . . . I don't know where I am . . . I can't say anything.*

MORIN: *Do you think this film could help you say something?*

MARILOU: *I don't know. You are all very nice, that's all I can say.*

▶ —————————————————————————————————

## Jean-Pierre

*The balcony of an apartment building in the seventeenth arrondissement. Back to the camera, Jean-Pierre is looking down at the street. He has a glass in his hand. He takes a drink, then goes back into his room and toward his worktable, which is scattered with books and papers. He sits down and takes a cigarette, which he lights. Off-screen, we hear the voice of Edgar Morin, while Jean-Pierre stands up again.*

MORIN: Jean-Pierre, you are a student, you are twenty years old, and I wonder how you get by in life.

*Close-up of Jean-Pierre. It is now another scene—a dining room, the end of dinner. After a moment we discover the presence of Marceline and Morin, by insert close-ups.*

JEAN-PIERRE: Well, it is true that I live . . . Yes, in fact I do live . . . I live . . . I live no doubt much better than most students my age live. But I live, I mean I live so long as I accept some terrible compromises . . . I live only so long as I accept . . . I accept that things are not what I had wanted them to be . . . As long as I accept . . . well, being fucked over, you know! . . . There aren't, there aren't any problems . . . In fact I think that all the guys . . . all the guys who are my age now . . . even some older ones . . . manage to live serenely, if you will, only as long as they accept the necessity of being fucked over . . . But otherwise when I talk to you about impotences . . . I mean . . . they're real impotences, you understand . . . Like the fact that I go and blow my exams . . . I don't know, I mean . . . Like I tried to live with a woman . . . I tried to make her happy . . . that she wanted to make me happy . . . that we tried to be happy . . . then that it dissipates, it becomes absurd. They're impotences, you know . . . like on the political level, too . . . and again, I don't give a damn now . . . I mean, it's somehow much less important . . . that all my political needs, you know . . . are attenuated, are scattered . . . Sure I have needs, but to say that I am really unhappy that . . . that I am close to doing some very concrete things, some effective things, in the end, it's truer, you know . . . I have . . . well, I mean I have loads of very intellectual justifications for all that . . . I mean like I've seen those of your generation . . .

*Close-up insert of Morin.*

I've seen what their political involvement produced . . . I mean . . . their powerlessness in the face of barriers . . . I don't want it anymore . . . I mean . . . I've seen too many people like that, y'know, who . . . who were reduced to the point of crying by all that . . . to the point of being traumatized . . . of not knowing what to do any more . . . You are almost all like that, in fact, on that level . . . so me, I don't want it . . . and that is an intel—intellectual justification . . . though I know very well that in a much more interior way . . . it's not that at all . . .

*Close-up insert of Marceline.*

. . . a sort of absence . . . a sort of absence of courage . . . Even on the emotional level . . . there is selfishness. Even though you've dreamed of moments of passion . . . of beautiful things . . . You realize . . . at least I'm obliged to realize . . . I mean . . . that everything is made in half-tones . . . I mean half-tones . . . and really neutral shades . . . There's no black and white . . . it's just shades of gray . . . I mean a little darker gray . . . a little lighter gray . . . It's sickening . . . d'you understand?

*Close-up of Marceline, silent, who nods her head in agreement. Then to Marceline:*

MORIN: D'you have something to say, Marceline?

*Close-up of Marceline, who we feel is close to tears.*

MARCELINE: I have to say that I feel very responsible for that . . . because it's partly through me that you . . .

*Close-up of Jean-Pierre.*

knew all those people who were ready to cry after their political experiences . . . Me too, in fact . . . And then when you talk about having wanted to make a woman happy . . . I know it's me . . .

*Close-up of Jean-Pierre as Marceline speaks.*

. . . so I feel a bit responsible . . . for all your helplessness inasmuch as . . . well . . . I made you leave the path that maybe you should have stayed on . . .

*Close-up of Morin.*

MORIN: No, but it's true . . . I think that Jean-Pierre says the word "impotence" and that Marceline must think . . . of the word . . . "failure?"

*Close-up of Marceline, who has a bitter smile.*

MARCELINE: I do have a feeling of failure after so many years . . . though when I met Jean-Pierre I really didn't want it to be like that . . . I so much wanted him not to have the twenty years that I had had . . . I . . . thought I could make him happy . . . that in spite of everything, it was possible.

*Tilt down to close-up of Marceline's arm, on which we can distinguish a tattooed serial number, then back to face close-ups of Jean-Pierre and Marceline.*

I loved him deeply . . . I love him still, in fact . . . but then . . . it's still a failure. And it's not just a failure for me . . . it's a painful experience for him . . . because I still think he loves me a little, maybe . . .

*Close-up of Jean-Pierre, eyes lowered.*

▶ ────────────────────────────────

**The Algerian War Question**

*A long table surrounded by numerous guests, among whom the camera allows us to recognize Edgar Morin, Jean Rouch, Marceline, Jean-Pierre . . .*

ROUCH: We've reached the point where the film, which up to here has been enclosed in a relatively personal and individual universe, opens up onto the situation of this summer of 1960.
VOICES: Yeah, yeah . . .
ROUCH: So, shall we go ahead?
MORIN: Yes, but I'd really like to know what they think.
ROUCH: Let's go!
MORIN: Okay. Let's go . . . here we go, here we go . . . here we go . . . I don't know, but if I were a student . . . y'know . . . right now, the men in particular. I mean old enough to do military service, I'd be thinking about

the events in Algeria . . . I mean about the war in Algeria . . . You don't give a damn about this issue, about the war in Algeria, do you?

*Close-up of one of the young people, Jean-Marc.*

JEAN-MARC: No, we do give a damn . . . if only for this reason, that one day, I mean, I don't know, next year, in two years, in ten years, well, there will be great subjects for films on the war of Algeria! *(Over close-up of Régis.)*
MORIN: So you're an aesthete? That means you're talking about the future films that you'd like to make about the war in Algeria, well that's fine . . .

*Medium close-up of Céline and Morin, vehement.*

CÉLINE: If only the majority of the French would show their opposition . . . would show it publicly.
ROPHÉ *(sound recordist)*: But to what end?
CÉLINE: To put an end to this absurd war.

*Close-up of Rophé, in profile.*

ROPHÉ: I don't see why France should abandon tomorrow what I call her rights . . . because it is still her rights.

*Close-up of Jean-Pierre, with Céline, attentive in the background.*

JEAN-PIERRE: That this war has to end by means of negotiations is clear . . . every war ends by negotiations . . .
ROPHÉ: The GPRA[4] is probably not capable of stopping it.
JEAN-PIERRE: But that's not the point!
ROPHÉ: It absolutely is!
CÉLINE : But this war has to stop!

*Close-up of Régis, with insert of Céline.*

RÉGIS: This war has been going on for six years, that's the first thing to be said, and people are always forgetting it . . . Saying that we're installed in a sort of mutual habit . . . a sort of resignation to a state of fact. In fact there are crimes going on out there that are not by mistake . . . they're facts, and most people refuse to see them.

*Medium close-up of Viguier, a cameraman, with Morin.*

VIGUIER: There is an Algerian problem, and there is a student problem . . . the two problems have become mixed up, and that is an enormous problem, because it is a problem which touches you, particularly you young people, and what I reproach you for in this problem is for not playing your part . . . In my opinion you are not playing it because your hearts are not in it.

*Close-up of Jean-Pierre, who is visibly wounded by Viguier's intervention.*

JEAN-PIERRE: Yeah, but you're talking in the name of a myth of youth . . . you're talking more about a myth of youth!
VIGUIER: There is no myth of youth?
JEAN-PIERRE: Yes there is! From your own lips we feel . . . I mean we hear the myth of youth . . . rising youth . . . glorious youth . . . active youth . . . aggressive youth . . . But why?
VIGUIER: Active youth . . . I'm all for it!
JEAN-PIERRE: But why? Just because we're twenty years old, we can do anything? Because we're twenty we're available? But it's not true!
VIGUIER: We all have rights.
MORIN: As far as this question of the war in Algeria is concerned, everyone is dirtied right now, even those who think they have clear-cut opinions . . . firm opinions . . . solutions . . . France is pretty dirty . . .

*Close-up of Régis, turned toward Morin, with inserts of Céline, Rophé, and Morin.*

RÉGIS: To get out of that mess you're so complacent in—
MORIN: I'm sorry, my friend . . .
RÉGIS: You have to carry your stone against the absurd, and that's a task each of us can do without worrying about the problems of the group. You don't start out from the group or from abstract words, you start out from what each person is. You've got to wager and you've got to make the French wager on the idea that men can finally put an end to this war.

*Sound effects of machine-gun fire. Succession of rapid close-ups of newspaper headlines: "The Tough FLN Men Counterattack," "Tight Negotiations with FLN," "Negotiations Broken at Melun," "Desperate Messages from Whites in Congo," "100 Dead in Congo."*

▶ ─────────────────────────────────────────

**Racism in Question**

*The same restaurant terrace. Another day. Another table. Rouch, Morin, Marceline, Nadine, Jean-Pierre, Régis. And also Landry, and several other young Africans.*

MARCELINE: Personally I would never marry a black.
ROUCH: Why?

NADINE: For the children?

MARCELINE: No, not at all, absolutely not . . . not at all . . .

ROUCH: Why?

*Medium close-up from Marceline's profile and point of view. In the middle ground, turned toward her, are Jean Rouch and Landry.*

MARCELINE: Well . . . why . . . Because for me it has nothing to do with . . . I'm not racist. I understand perfectly that one can love a black.

VOICES OFF-SCREEN: But . . . but . . .

JEAN-PIERRE: But! . . . But! . . . You don't like Negroes . . .

MARCELINE: No, no that's not true . . .

ROUCH: You're racist at a sexual level . . .

MARCELINE: No, I'm not racist in matters of . . . It's not racism. I cannot have . . . I can't have sexual relations with someone I don't find . . . I can't do it with someone I don't find attractive.

ROUCH: So you don't find blacks attractive . . .

*Insert close-up of Landry.*

MARCELINE: For a long time I thought it wasn't possible, and I still think so . . . only because I don't want to . . . that's all . . . it's a question of desire . . . only, I remember, two years ago, on the fourteenth of July . . .

*Laughter.*

ROUCH: Ah, ah . . .

VOICE OFF-SCREEN: A weakness?

MARCELINE: No, I didn't have . . . No, not at all . . . But I remember that for the first time . . .

JEAN-PIERRE: Be brave.

MARCELINE: No . . . for the first time at a fourteenth of July ball, I danced with a black.

JEAN-PIERRE: And were you moved?

MARCELINE: And . . . the way he danced was so extraordinary . . .

ROUCH: Come on, go ahead, . . . go on . . . go on . . . *(laughter)*

*The framing favors Landry.*

LANDRY: Fine . . . well, here's why I don't agree . . . you see, the . . . for example, the blacks who are in France, in general when they go to a dance, people like the way they dance . . . But I wish they'd like blacks . . . for other reasons than the way they dance . . .

MARCELINE: But I agree completely.

*Close-up of Morin in profile, looking toward the others from the far end of the table.*

MORIN: Fine . . . but we're basically getting to the question that we're here for . . . I mean we're here to discuss the Congo . . . among our African friends . . . But before we discuss that . . . I wonder . . . in spite of the fact that for days now the press has been talking about these events in large headlines whether we in Paris . . . uh . . . whether we really feel concerned about this . . . I'd like to know whether Jean-Pierre, for example . . . whether Marceline . . . or Régis . . . feel concerned, and how they're concerned, about this . . .

*Medium shot of Rouch and Régis from Jean-Pierre's point of view.*

JEAN-PIERRE: I know that I felt concerned one time, quite physically because I was watching the TV news. And after the speaker showed a couple of pictures, announced a couple of events, he concluded by saying in a dry tone, "We can see what these people are doing with their independence."

*Medium shot of Landry, with Jean Rouch and Nadine.*

LANDRY: The Belgian arrived in the Congo . . . he said to himself, "Okay fine . . . money to be made." No, he didn't even say that. First of all, he said, "No elite, no worries" *(laughter)*.

*Close-up of Nadine, to two-shot of Nadine and Landry.*

ROUCH: And you, Nadine. What do you think?
NADINE: I agree with Landry.
ROUCH: You've been to Léopoldville . . .
NADINE: Yes, I've been to Léopoldville.
ROUCH: For how long?
NADINE: For one year. I was a boarder with those nuns who were raped. (She smiles, then is serious.) No, it was horrible, I mean, because it's, the fact is that there the Africans were completely caged in. They were not allowed to come into certain areas. It was really horrible.

*Profile close-up of Régis.*

RÉGIS: Does a native of the Ivory Coast feel involved in this, as a black, because a black from the Belgian Congo is doing . . . I mean . . . Is there really a racial solidarity? Do you feel responsible, or not?

*Close-up of Landry.*

LANDRY: Oh, yes . . . I feel responsible.

RÉGIS: Really?

*Raymond, one of the young Africans, intervenes.*

RAYMOND: It's true that you can reproach them for violence . . . but it's a question of anger . . .

*Close-up of Landry.*

LANDRY: It would be another story between Congolese and Ivorians . . . A Guinean, for example, would not feel engaged. But as soon as it's a white mistreating a black . . . you understand . . . I mean, all the countries, you see, the states of Africa were colonized . . . so as soon as they see a country mistreated by the whites . . . Well . . . immediately it's as if it was, you see, as if it was them who were suffering the pain of the others . . . so right away, it's like that!

*Close shot of Marceline in profile.*

MARCELINE: I understand that very well, because while the example is not completely, completely a good one . . . but if there is a manifestation of anti-Semitism in any country in the world . . . well, then I'm involved . . . I can't allow it . . . whether it be a German Jew, a Polish Jew . . . a Russian Jew . . . an American Jew . . . it's all the same, for me.

*Medium close-up of Jean Rouch, panning to a two shot with Landry.*

ROUCH: We're going to ask Landry a question . . . Landry, have you noticed that Marceline has a number on her arm?
LANDRY: Yes.
ROUCH: What is it, do you think?
LANDRY: No, I . . . I have no idea . . .
ROUCH: No idea . . . Okay, and you, Raymond . . . what do you think?
RAYMOND: Well, I don't know exactly . . . I know that there are sailors who usually have numbers on their arms . . . and since she's not in the navy . . .
ROUCH: Why? So, what is it that . . . Why? Do you know more or less what it means?
RÉGIS: Affectation . . .
ROUCH: Affectation?
RAYMOND: Maybe, yeah . . .
RÉGIS: But why a number, anyway?
ROUCH: Why a number?
MARCELINE: I could have put a heart?

JEAN-PIERRE: It could be her telephone number . . .

MARCELINE: I could have put a heart.

RAYMOND: That couldn't be a telephone number because it's too long . . . 78-750.

*Close-up of Marceline's arm, then medium close-up of Marceline with Régis in the background.*

MARCELINE: Well, first of all the . . . This isn't a V . . . it's a triangle that is half of the Jewish star . . . I don't know if you know the Jewish symbol that's a six-pointed star . . . And then the number . . . well, it's not my telephone number . . . uh . . . I was deported to a concentration camp during the war, because I'm Jewish, and this is a serial number that they gave me in that camp . . .

*Quick pan to close-up of Landry, who lowers his eyes.*

ROUCH: So?

RAYMOND: It's shocking . . .

MARCELINE: Raymond, do you know what a concentration camp is?

RAYMOND: Yes . . . yes . . . I saw a film . . . a film on them . . . on the concentration camps.

*Close-up of Marceline's hand, stroking a flower.*

RÉGIS: *Nuit et brouillard, Night and Fog* . . .

RAYMOND: I think, *Night and Fog* . . . yeah . . .

*Freeze-frame of Marceline's hand.*

▶ _____

## La Concorde

*The Place de la Concorde, almost deserted. It's the fifteenth of August, in the morning. From the center of the square, Marceline comes toward us, slowly. She is walking with eyes lowered, looking at the ground. We hear her voice, tired and sad.*

MARCELINE: This Place de la Concorde is as deserted . . . as it was twenty years ago, fifteen years . . . I don't remember any more . . . Pitchipoi . . . You'll see, we'll go down there, we'll work in the factories, we'll see each other on Sundays, Papa said. And you, you would answer me, you're young, you will come back . . . me, I surely won't.

*She is humming and walking faster. The camera continues to follow her in a backward traveling shot.*

And then here I am now, Place de la Concorde . . . I came back, you stayed. *(She sighs.)* We'd been there six months before I saw you.

*Close-up of Marceline, still walking.*

We threw ourselves in each other's arms . . . and then . . . that filthy SS man who flung himself on me, who hit me in front of you . . . you said, "But that's my daughter—that's my daughter." Achtung! He threatened you with the same treatment . . . you had an onion in your hand, you put it in mine and I fainted . . .

*Another scene. An intersection. Marceline walks at a distance from us. We hear her voice humming "Les grands prés marécageux." . . . She sighs.*

Papa . . . When I saw you, you said, "And Mama? And Michel?" You called me "your little girl" . . . I was almost happy . . . to be deported with you . . . I loved you so much . . .

*We recognize the vaults of Les Halles. The camera, preceding her again, moves away from her quickly. Marceline is soon nothing more than a small, solitary silhouette in the empty market stalls, immense and dreary, yet we still hear her voice.*

Oh, Papa, Papa . . . How I wish you were here now . . . I lived through that thinking that you'd come back . . . When I came back it was tough . . . It was tough . . . *(She sighs.)* I saw . . . saw everyone on the station platform—Mama, everybody. They all kissed me. My heart felt like a stone. It was Michel who moved me. I said, "Don't you recognize me?" He said, "Yes, I think . . . I think you're . . . Marceline . . ." Oh, Papa . . .

*Black.*

▶

## The Fourteenth of July

*A festival setting. Nighttime ball at a street intersection. Brouhaha. Lights. Accordion music; waltz dancing. We recognize, among the dancing couples, Marceline and Jean-Pierre, and Marilou.*

► ──────────────────────────────────────────────

**Marilou Is Happy**

*A French window opening onto the street. It is daylight. Over this image we continue to hear the sounds of the fourteenth of July festival. We are inside a room. Edgar Morin approaches the window and closes it, at the same time cutting off the festive sounds. He comes back inside, and we discover Marilou sitting nearby. Morin sits down facing her.*

MORIN: Well, Marilou. It's been a month since we had this discussion together. And now it's August, and, well, something has struck me . . . Two evenings ago we were walking down the street, and I was talking to you about a question in this film that I told you I had asked my friends Jacques and his wife. The question was "Are you happy?" and I told you that they had replied, "More or less," and you said, "Me too, I could answer, 'More or less.'" And yet when I saw you, it must be . . . fifteen days ago, you were in fact quite depressed, you didn't seem at all well . . .

*Silence. Marilou smiles.*

Could you answer, "More or less"?

*Medium close-up, from Morin's point of view, of Marilou, whose voice trembles a bit.*

MARILOU: Yes . . . once again I don't know what's happening to me . . . Like I didn't know the evening of the fourteenth of July. I had all the faces of all the people I ever knew coming toward me . . . I didn't know where to put them . . . and I believed everything was fucked up . . . I think I overcame a hurdle that night. Then there were one or two empty days . . . and then all of a sudden everything fell into place, I started seeing people again . . . I came out of the fantasy world, and now everything has become so simple and easy!

*Close-up of Marilou as Morin asks the questions:*

MORIN: All of this came abruptly? All by itself? . . . It happened all by itself?

*Marilou hides her face in her hands. Her smile fades, then returns; tilt to her hands, playing with a charm, then back to her face.*

MARILOU: Ever since I started to have people around me . . . to feel a part of things, I have become ready . . . ready for everything, for . . . I don't know, for friendship . . . for love, too . . .

MORIN: Is that what changed things?

*Marilou's face becomes radiant. Her eyes sparkle. We can see that she is full of a joy that wants to explode, that she'd like to shout out, but that she is controlled.*

MARILOU: Yes, that's it . . . that's it . . . But what's stronger than anything else . . .

*Marilou buries her face in her hands again. A cloud of anguish passes over it.*

is the fear, in spite of everything, it's the fear . . . like it's happened to me a thousand times, of again finding myself completely alone, completely alone, completely isolated.

MORIN: I don't think so.

*Silent close-up of Marilou's face, which has become radiant again.*

MARILOU: What do you want me to say . . . You can't talk about these things . . .

MORIN: No . . .

*There follows a series of images of Marilou in the street, leafing through a newspaper as she walks, then throwing it away. The garret window of a little room, on a roof. Marilou pokes her head out and closes the window. In the room, Marilou and her friend are getting ready to go out. We follow them down the stairs, which they descend while playing with their hands on the banister. We end with shots of their hands clasped between them as they walk down the street.*

▶ ━━━━━━━━━━━━━━━━━━━━━━━━━━━━━━━━━━━━━━

**Angélo Gets Pushed Around**

*Some shots of Angélo walking down the street. Off-screen voice of Jean Rouch, over inside close-up of Angélo.*

ROUCH: Angélo, Edgar tells me things aren't going well . . . What exactly is going on?

*Close-up of Angélo, then of the group of Angélo-Morin-Rouch.*

ANGÉLO: Well, now, at the shop . . . I'm . . . I mean . . . I went back to work after you left. They came up and they said, "They want you in the office." So I thought, first off . . . I thought it must be about some work problem. I said to myself, "Okay . . . I must have screwed up a series of pieces, so they're going to chew me out." But it wasn't that at all. They start to say this, I mean the boss says, "So we're making movies now." So I say, "I don't see what that's got to do with my work." He says, "Okay, let's forget it. That's not the problem. The problem is that we're going to change your shop assignment, we're going to put you someplace else because there's no work." And then they don't let up hassling me . . . I mean, yesterday the foreman came looking for me, and he says, like this, "Okay, you've got ten pieces to make . . . If you make me those ten pieces this morning, then fine, I'll leave you alone." So I made him the ten pieces, on the milling wheel, which was all fucked up . . . and when I finished these ten pieces, about one in the afternoon, he brings me twenty more and says, "You're here to work." So that was too much for me to take . . . I was going to punch him out, because I could see that he was just there to give me shit, so I took time off and left . . . I left because Jacques, you know, and Gontrand, he told me like, he told me . . . "You've got to get out of here, take some time off, go rest a bit, because if you don't, you're really going to give them a hard time, and at the moment you'd better not." And that's it . . .

ROUCH: If you stay at Renault, what kind of future will you have?

ANGÉLO: Absolutely nothing.

*Close-up of Angélo over the following:*

ROUCH: Someday you could be what, you could be a shop foreman?

ANGÉLO: Absolutely not, I haven't got a chance.

▶

**France on Vacation**
*Paris*

*First some shots of factory workrooms. On the walls are hung signs on which we read "Vive les vacances," "2 au jus." . . . Subway exits. Taxis. People loading cars. General atmosphere of a happy stampede.*

*Followed by a silent shot of Edgar Morin, standing beside a sidewalk. He is reading a newspaper headline: "Desperate Messages from Whites in Congo." . . . Near him is Marceline.*

■

**The Seashore**

*A woman on water skis speeds toward us and collapses at the feet of the camera, which follows her, to reveal Landry and Nadine paddling around.*

*Off-screen voice of Jean Rouch over image of Landry coming out of the water.*

ROUCH: And that's how Landry has become the black explorer of France on vacation.

---

### The Bullfight

*Arenas. Bullfight atmosphere. A crowd in the grandstand yells, gesticulates, applauds. We recognize Landry and Nadine. Close shot of Landry and Nadine commenting on the bullfight, amid loud background ambience on the sound track.*

LANDRY: This is horrible, horrible.
NADINE: So you see . . .
LANDRY: But look . . .
NADINE: Okay, then he stabs him in the neck . . . that's to finish him off.
LANDRY: Why? . . . Oh . . . ah!
NADINE: Oh!
[LANDRY: But what are the passes for? Does that tire the animal out, or is it . . .
NADINE: No, it's the matador who . . .
LANDRY: Ah . . . yes . . .
NADINE: Go on!
LANDRY: Now I like this, I like the passes. You see, if everything could consist of just the passes, I would have liked it, but killing the animal, I'm not for that.
NADINE: But you've got to kill it . . .
LANDRY: What do you mean you've got to? But those people down on the side, they're bloodthirsty. They're just waiting for him to kill the beast . . . the blood . . .
NADINE: No, no . . .
LANDRY: Oh yes they are . . .
NADINE: There are people who come just for that but . . . doesn't that look good?][5]

*Close-up of Landry and Nadine intercut with other spectators.*

LANDRY: Oh, shit!
NADINE: Look, look! Oh, that was marvelous . . . Bravo!
LANDRY: Here it is, here it is . . . watch it, watch it, this is it . . . oh, watch

it, look out there! . . . Oh good, he didn't get it then . . . look, oh . . . I like these passes . . . I like these passes . . .

NADINE: It's beautiful, isn't it? Oh, he's cute, I like him a lot . . . Oh, this is great!

LANDRY: That's fantastic . . . That's a sight to see, you see, that's a sight to see . . . They came here to see the beasts die, . . . and it's done! . . . Ah, yes . . . These are the pleasures . . . the pleasures of life in the provinces.

*The crowd in the grandstands.*

■————————————————————————————————————

## Saint Tropez

*Landry and Catherine (the water-skier) walk slowly along the port.*

LANDRY: You see, Saint Tropez is a city, it's kind of a village, too, it reminds me quite a bit of black Africa, you see the old houses, the red tiles, and all that . . . Ah! Saint Tropez—they talk about it all the time in my deep forest, in my African bush, I've heard talk of Saint Tropez. I find it kind of curious that you see all the women in Saint Tropez wearing bikinis, I mean they do everything to attract attention.

CATHERINE: Yeah, and then they put on these outrageous outfits, with the excuse that they're in Saint Tropez.

LANDRY: Exactly. And when I think that back home, you know, in Africa when . . . because in certain regions of Africa there are women who wear leaves, you know, as panties.

CATHERINE: Yeah.

LANDRY: You see, and there are some colonials who make fun of us, who make fun of these women, but it's funny. You see, a woman in a bikini, she's not hiding anything, a woman in a bikini.

*We see, as they do as they walk along, a crowd of vacationers in shorts and bikinis, crowding around a group of photographers for whom a pretty girl poses while standing in a boat tied up at the pier. Sophie, the cover girl, Catherine, Landry. Sophie is explaining herself to Landry.*

SOPHIE: It's not much fun being a model, but I'm getting used to it . . . I've got to make a living, and publicity photos, they bring in a bit of money . . . that's why I do it.

*All three are walking away from the port, still talking, followed by the hordes armed with cameras, bombarding Sophie.[6] A terrace. We find Morin, Rouch, Catherine, Landry, Sophie.*

MORIN: Catherine, you're not saying anything . . .

CATHERINE: There are a lot of things I don't want to think about . . . I want to go swimming . . . go water-skiing . . . and then, especially here . . .

MORIN: Okay, but I'd still like to hear our dear Sophie's opinion . . .

ROUCH: You see, all these people talk about things . . . Do you really know Saint Tropez well?

*Close-up of Sophie on her first words, then we hear her voice off-screen while in the picture we see her walking in Saint Tropez, crossing the deserted terrace of the Epi Club, then inside, then another terrace overlooking the beach, where Sophie arrives, sits in the sand, and begins to dip her feet in the edge of the water.*

SOPHIE: I can't really say I know it very well, because you really need to have lived several months in a place to know it well . . . But, I mean . . . I came here last year . . . because I was doing some gigs in the casinos around here . . . and I had a little villa . . . Now, you know, in the street . . . we ask everybody, "So you're having a good time in Saint Tropez?" So it sounds really good to answer, "We're really bored stiff here." It's a kind of snobism to answer, "We're bored," because at the moment it's the rage to say, "We're bored in Saint Tropez." . . . that's it . . . I mean, people are bored everywhere . . . but now if you're bored, it comes from yourself . . . Because you're . . . you have an internal, personal life . . . you're not bored any place . . . And here . . . there are lots of movie stars, and therefore lots of directors . . . so . . . all the little girls from Paris come down here with their little bikinis . . . their tight little pants . . . yeah . . . yeah, sure, always very simple . . . and their little low-cut strapless bras . . . their long hair . . . their eyeliner, y'know, their eyelashes like this . . . right in style . . . So they always hope they're going to meet some director . . . Naturally . . . They've got everything . . . except a head with a bit of brains . . . Of course, that's not given to everybody . . . *(laughter)* . . . right, Marceline? So then fine . . . What more can I tell you now? . . . That Saint Tropez is really a charming place . . . with incredible countryside . . . Of course, it's a shame there are all these people here . . . But these people are other places, too . . . So why be against Saint Tropez? . . . Me personally, I'm not bored in Saint Tropez . . . So there . . .

▶ ─────────────────────────────────────────

**Irène and Véronique**

*Saint Tropez. Sitting at a table in a garden are Edgar Morin and his two daughters, Véronique (age twelve) and Irène (age thirteen).*

*Alternating close-ups during the dialogue.*

MORIN: You know that Rouch and I, we're making a film. It's called "How You Live."

IRÈNE: Yeah, I've heard some vague mention of it.

MORIN: Okay, so here's the problem: we don't agree because Rouch thinks that life is funny, and I think that life is not so funny.

IRÈNE: You're kidding . . . That's a bit much . . . I think that, on the contrary, I think that Rouch is right.

MORIN: Life is funny?

IRÈNE: Yeah.

MORIN: Why is it funny?

IRÈNE: Well . . . Maybe I said that because we're on vacation, now that I think about it.

MORIN: And besides vacation?

IRÈNE: Well, besides vacation . . .

VÉRONIQUE: Besides vacation . . . oh . . . we don't know much about it. We're not in your position . . .

IRÈNE: Well, I don't know . . . You go out in the evening with Mama, isn't that fun?

VÉRONIQUE: But why do you find life sad all of a sudden?

*Landry arrives and comes to sit with them.*

MORIN: Ah, here's a friend, Landry.

LANDRY: Hello, Morin.

MORIN: But I think you, that . . . you . . . you don't know much about the life of . . . French children?

LANDRY: No, not a thing.

MORIN: These two girls here, twelve, thirteen years old . . . it must surprise you to see them? It must not be like this back home in Ivory Coast?

*Medium three-shot of Landry facing Morin, with Véronique between them.*

LANDRY: Oh no, back home it's not like this . . . You know . . . Where I live, a girl starts living when she's, already when she's six years old.

*Close-up of Landry.*

And even when I was seven years old I already knew how to cook.

*Irène faces Landry; camera pans to Landry in close-up for his response.*

IRÈNE: Well, we only do work for school.

VÉRONIQUE: We don't work for our parents.

IRÈNE: Of course, we clear the table once in a while, we do things like that, but not very often.

LANDRY: And that's a mistake. You have to learn. You can't be content with an easy life . . . you know . . . Because you have to realize that later, you see, you'll have to do more in life than just clear tables.

▶

## On the Bottom of the Sea

*The jetty at Saint Tropez.*[7] *Marceline and Jean-Pierre are alone. Behind them, the sea.*

JEAN-PIERRE: I'm going to change places . . . because this annoys me . . . I can't talk to you and see the sea at the same time, and if it doesn't bother you, I like to see the water, I mean the bottom of the sea, you're beautiful . . . there's a tragic side . . .

MARCELINE: You're kidding . . .

JEAN-PIERRE: It suits your face . . .

MARCELINE: You're saying that to make me happy . . .

JEAN-PIERRE: You always think I'm a bastard with you . . . that I'm always trying to . . . You were saying a while ago that I wanted to win you back . . . that I spend my time trying to seduce you . . . I mean, it's absurd . . .

MARCELINE: You spend your time trying to seduce others . . .

JEAN-PIERRE: No, no . . .

MARCELINE: Oh, yes you do.

JEAN-PIERRE: No, it's just that I . . . that I . . . I mean, yes . . . no . . . no . . . You don't seem to understand that we're not all on the same rhythm . . . for a month and a half you've been working . . . you've been sweating it out in Paris . . . a shitty month of August . . . miserable . . . and me, for a month and a half I've been living a totally different lifestyle . . .

MARCELINE: And how have you been living?

JEAN-PIERRE: Differently . . . A young man's vacation, you know . . .

MARCELINE: I understand that perfectly, but . . .

JEAN-PIERRE: No, you don't understand anything . . . because you don't understand that I was fed up . . . completely fed up . . . uh . . . I was fed up with you . . .

MARCELINE: Yeah, but I was fed up with—

JEAN-PIERRE: I was fed up with you . . . with the shitty life we were both leading . . .

MARCELINE: I had hoped in coming here . . . hoped to be able to really talk to you . . . to talk to you about myself . . .

JEAN-PIERRE: But that's it, exactly . . .

MARCELINE: But you don't accept me as I am . . . you don't accept how I am . . . You allow me nothing . . . you spend all your indulgence on yourself . . .

JEAN-PIERRE: But you expect me to be . . . I mean, I don't know . . . When I'm not there . . . you dream of me . . . but I think you're really dreaming about somebody else . . . you know . . . I'm sick of it . . . sick of you . . . sick of you . . . Ever since I've been living with you it's been the same thing . . . we just look at each other . . . with the result being that I haven't done a thing for two years . . . I'm bored to death . . . I don't see the world anymore . . . I don't see things . . . I've become incapable of seeing them . . . completely perverted . . . I want to look at them . . . I want to be young, and when you're like you are now, you prevent me from being . . . You're not always like that, but for a while now you've been more and more . . . I don't know if it's because you feel closed in . . . I don't know if it's because you feel me sliding away . . . I can't stand it . . . Have you noticed?

MARCELINE: I don't know what you expect of me . . . don't understand . . . I search . . . I search . . . I can't find any explanation that fits . . . and then when you talk to me, things go from bad to worse . . . uh . . . as though whatever I thought didn't exist any more . . . you know . . . I mean, like, two days ago I was drunk . . . drunk because of you, in fact . . . I had been drinking because of you . . .

JEAN-PIERRE: Oh, I know, but . . .

MARCELINE: When you came back to that room you were horrible to me . . . you . . . I don't know . . . you said things that I've never heard from a man before . . . But there was also a time, Jean-Pierre, where you spent your time challenging me . . . running after girls . . .

JEAN-PIERRE: But I don't challenge you anymore . . .

MARCELINE: Did you love me?

JEAN-PIERRE: Yeah, there was . . . there was a . . .

MARCELINE: Do you think you still love me?

JEAN-PIERRE: I don't know . . . Anyway, it's no use.

▶ ———————————————————————————————

## Milly

*A corner of Fountainebleau forest: a rockbound clearing. Angélo, his friend Jacques Mothet, and Jacques's wife, Maxie, and several children are finishing a picnic. Joyful atmosphere.*

A LITTLE GIRL: No, we don't want to go look for mushrooms!

OTHER GIRLS: No, I don't want to go look for mushrooms! We don't like mushrooms! Besides, I said something! Ouah!

ANGÉLO (singing): I know the way to annoy people.

A LITTLE GIRL: You know the way to annoy people?

*Angélo and Jacques go over to the rocks. Following Jacques, Angélo attempts to scale them. His efforts are clumsy, his feet unsure. Jacques encourages him with words and gestures.*

JACQUES: There! Like that . . . maybe you're a bit small . . . Go on! go on! Put your foot there! . . . put your foot on the thing, Angélo! . . . Angélo! . . . put your foot there as soon as you . . .

*Maxie, Jacques's wife, intervenes off-screen.*

MAXIE: Tell him to take it Dulfer style . . .

JACQUES: Huh?

MAXIE (off-screen): He should take it Dulfer style . . .

JACQUES: That's it! Okay, Angélo . . . you put your foot there and there immediately, you see . . . right away you're going to put it on the other . . . push it, your foot . . . push it . . . ah! . . . ah! Angélo! There . . . go ahead, put your foot there, the other foot . . . no, no! He's putting it higher!

MAXIE: Not so high!

JACQUES: He's putting it higher . . . idiot! idiot! . . . lower! lower, here, your foot! . . . on the divide . . . there . . . look here . . . Angélo! Look how stupid he is . . . that's it . . . now put your foot there . . . the step! the step, Angélo!

MAXIE (off-screen): Angélo! That's it! . . . on the divide . . . Angélo! Look how stupid . . . now put your foot there . . .

*Angélo, not without difficulty, finally makes it to the top of the rock. He is only half-satisfied.*

ANGÉLO: No . . . I could never do it because you were always bitching down there.

JACQUES: But I'm bitching because you're stupid . . . otherwise I wouldn't bitch . . . You've got . . . you have . . . you've got much more strength in your arms than I do . . .

*Saying this, Jacques slaps Angélo's arm lightly, and Angélo staggers as they go down toward the clearing and approach the foot of the rocks.*

JACQUES: You know, you've got one thing: you don't know where you're putting your feet, you don't know how to use your feet. You know how to use your arms, you don't know how to use your feet . . .

*The children in turn try to climb the rocks. One boy comes down by rappelling.*

JACQUES: Okay, who's next?

*Carine, Jacques's daughter, steps up.*

CARINE: My turn.

*We find Carine clinging to the face of the rock, rope in hand. Her father, up above, guides her descent.*

JACQUES: Carine! Take your foot out of there and you grab the rope behind you . . . Take your hand out of there . . . and take your rope and push yourself! And let yourself go! You take that rope . . . push yourself away from the rock, yes, yes! away from the rock! . . . from the rock . . . Don't be afraid . . . go on!
MAXIE *(off-screen):* Your father is there, honey . . . There's nothing to be afraid of . . .
JACQUES: Push yourself away from the rock!
ANGÉLO *(off-screen):* Go on . . . knock . . . Mothet!
JACQUES: Push away from the rock! Ah, now there . . . she must have it.
MAXIE *(off-screen):* She's got it . . .
ANGÉLO: She's got it, Mothet.
JACQUES: Okay, go on . . . take your hand out of there . . . that's it! Go on . . . push yourself away! push away! Jump a little . . . move away from the rock . . . let go with your hands . . .
VOICE *(off-screen):* She's got it . . . she's got it in back there, the rope!
JACQUES: What a goof! Put your hand in back of you . . . put your hand back . . . grab the rope . . . no! . . . the rope behind you! . . . grab the rope behind you! . . . right there . . . closer! . . . on that side . . . Ah!

*Jacques kicks Carine's hand lightly on the side where the rope is hanging.*

MAXIE: Now, don't go brutalizing the kid . . . there . . .
JACQUES: Go on, go ahead, go ahead . . . go on, let go, let yourself slip a bit, let yourself slip a little, that's it! with your other hand . . . Carine, your other hand, behind you . . . take that rope there . . . not that one!
VOICE *(off-screen):* No! that one . . . Carine!

*A hand holds up the rope, but Carine remains riveted to her rock, slightly dazed . . .*

JACQUES: Oh! What do you do with kids like that?

*Jacques, disappointed, gives up the struggle. Carine ends up grabbing hold of the famous rope and tries to use it to help her descend. But she maneuvers badly and slips toward the ground all of a sudden, amid great laughter.*

CARINE: I'm going to take a nap.

*Everyone has regrouped in the clearing. The children have formed a choir and are singing. The voices of the adults mingle with those of the children.*

So pretty and sweet, gorse flowers they're called
tell me where you see them
—where do you see them?—
In the town of the millers' wives
That is called the Land of Love
—the Land of Love—
On the edge of the clear-watered spring
Gorse flowers ever singing
—ever singing—
And the little white collars
Of the whole Breton countryside
—Breton countryside—

*As they sing, they offer each other fruit. Angélo, squatting near the children, seizes a bunch of grapes with his mouth. On this image, in close-up, we leave the Milly clearing.*

▶ ─────────────────────────────────────────

**Truth in Question**

*We hear for a moment more the song of the Milly picnickers, as the beam of a projector lamp appears on the screen, shining across the room plunged in obscurity. Then the song ends, the beam goes out, and light returns to the room, revealing the characters of* Chronicle of a Summer, *who have just seen the projection of certain sequences of their film, alongside Edgar Morin and Jean Rouch. Close-ups of different people as they respond.*

ROUCH: You've just seen yourselves on the screen . . . Edgar and I would like to know your opinions. First the children: Véro, do you like what you saw?
VÉRONIQUE: Oh well, it's not as good as Chaplin, but you know . . .
MORIN: So what's your impression, in the end?
VÉRONIQUE: I don't know . . . explain it to me!

MORIN: There's nothing to explain. Some people say it's not true, others say it's true.

VÉRONIQUE: Say what's not true? I mean, you can't lie in front of a camera . . .

JACQUES: In fact, most every time anybody wanted to express themselves, they often spoke in generalities, and in life you don't just speak in generalities.

MORIN: An example . . . an example . . . an example!

JACQUES: The discussion between Angélo and Landry is a discussion with lots of generalities.

NADINE: On the contrary, it's fantastic when he says to Landry, I like you a lot; it's because there was a contact . . . You know . . . they have the same problems, Angélo and . . .

MARCELINE: You cannot say they have the same problems, it's not true.

NADINE: There's a human contact between the two of them. You might say they discovered each other . . .

MARCELINE: They got along very well.

GABILLON: It's a meeting of two sensibilities.

MORIN: For me, it's the scene with the most . . . excuse me . . . it's the truest scene we did, because there's a friendship which forms right there, before our eyes.

JACQUES: You say there's empathy between Angélo and Landry, that's obvious; that's not what I'm saying: it's that all that isn't natural, it's not natural and it's artificial, you know . . .

ANGÉLO: I don't agree, because when there was the scene with Landry, I didn't know Landry, I didn't know a thing about him. And then it turned out that when I talked with him, I didn't see the cameras anymore, I didn't see them anymore, the cameras. It was only the problem that concerned me.

JEAN-PIERRE: If you examine everything we saw there, I mean, I find this film infinitely irksome because a part of what we saw is totally boring, and what isn't boring, is undeniably so at the price of a great deal of immodesty.

MARILOU: It seems to me that in the end, to have a tiny spark of truth the character usually has to be . . . I mean, it's not a rule . . . alone and on the verge of a nervous breakdown. I mean when he's talking about something that has touched him profoundly.

MAXIE: By that system you could only get scenes that were artificial or scenes that would be . . . but, and not only would they be, but they are, straight out, that are shameless. I agree with him; they are immodest. And at the beginning, when you asked whether we now wanted to get to know these people, well, for me, there's a certain number of people here, please excuse me, whom I have absolutely no desire to meet after this film, and among others, I confess that Marilou . . . it would really embarrass me . . . it would embarrass me because she told us too many things, she revealed too much of herself.

MME GABILLON: I think Marilou was really extraordinary, and all I want right now is to get to know her.

MORIN: Maxie's suggestions sounded monstrous to me, and really, for me, hers are reactions which are against the emergence of truth in the world, in social life, in people's lives or in life among people.

RÉGIS: Marilou, confronted by the camera, no longer acts. She plays a role not of inhibition but rather of self-searching. For Marceline, it's exactly the same thing; she speaks to herself, and it's in this sense that it embarrasses us, because we feel that it concerns her alone, and yet it is because of this that we are extremely, even completely, taken in.

JEAN-PIERRE: If the sequence of Marceline is much more perfect than the others . . . you say that it is truer than truth . . . it's because she is acting.

MARCELINE: They were extremely intimate memories, the most pervasive memories I have, but if you will, when I said those words, I was recalling things . . . at the moment I said them, I said them with feelings, but I was absolutely not involved with those feelings between shootings, or else I should have been . . . like Marilou said a minute ago, and that's why I don't agree with her at all . . . on the verge of a nervous breakdown, and that wasn't the case.

RÉGIS: What is really beautiful in this film is that we go from a naturalness that, in the end, is quite false, for example, a conversation in the street that means absolutely nothing, to a close-up of Marilou that never quite makes it, and that is extremely beautiful and that is no doubt much more true, and it's this transition from one to the other that gives all the interest to this film.

▶━━━━━━━━━━━━━━━━━━━━━━━━━━━━━━━━━━━━━━━━

### Self-Criticism

*In the hall of the Musée de l'Homme, Edgar Morin and Jean Rouch are alone. They walk up and down among the glass cases.*

ROUCH: So, Edgar, what do you think of this screening?

MORIN: Well, I think it's interesting because, all things considered, everything that has been said can be summed up in two things: either the characters are reproached for not being real enough, for example, Jacques reproaches Angélo for being sort of an actor when he's with Landry, or else they are reproached for being too real, like when Maxie, Jacques's wife, reproaches Marilou for laying herself bare before the camera. What does this mean? This means that we arrive at a certain degree where we investigate a truth which is not the truth of everyday relations . . . We've gone beyond that. As soon as people are a little more sincere then they are in real life, others say either, "You're a ham, an actor," or else they say, "You're an exhibitionist."

ROUCH *(off-screen):* Yeah . . .

*They have stopped walking and face each other. The camera frames Morin alone, then they start walking again.*

MORIN: So that's the fundamental problem, because us, what we wanted . . . if people think that these are actors or exhibitionists, then our film is a failure. And at the same time, I can say that I know, that I feel that they are neither actors nor exhibitionists.

ROUCH: Only one can't be sure of that.

MORIN: For whom?

ROUCH: They themselves can't know. You understand when, for example, Marceline says she was acting on the Place de la Concorde . . . we were witnesses?

MORIN: Yes.

ROUCH: She wasn't acting!

MORIN: If she was acting, you could say it was the most authentic part of herself when she was talking about her father . . . It's not an act, you know, you can't call that an act . . .

ROUCH: Of course.

MORIN: That is to say, this film, as opposed to ordinary cinema, reintroduces us to life. People approach the film as they do everyday life, that is, they aren't guided, because we have not guided the spectator . . . we have not told him, "So and so is kind, so and so is nasty, so and so is a nice guy, so and so is intelligent." And so, confronted with these people that they could meet in real life, they are disarmed, they feel that they themselves are implicated, they feel concerned, and they try to resist that.

ROUCH: Yeah, right.

MORIN: There are others who are moved by this. What struck me is that there are people who, for example, were very affected by Marilou, others who are very moved by Marceline, others by Jean-Pierre, others by Angélo . . . I mean that to some degree, I think that at least some of what we wanted to do is going to get across.

ROUCH: And you, are you moved?

MORIN: Me, well, I mean . . . the number of times we've seen the film ends up attenuating the emotions, but me . . . in the end I am very moved. I'm affected right now in another way. At the beginning, if you will, I thought that everyone would be moved by this film, and to see now that people that I like very much, like Marilou and Marceline, are criticized, well, that upsets me, that bothers me. I believed the viewer would like the characters that I liked.

*Both of them walk away toward the end of the hall, turning their backs to the camera, which stays immobile. Only their voices stay close. Soon they appear to be very far away.*

ROUCH: In other words, we wanted to make a film of love, and we end up at a sort of film of indifference, or in any case in which . . . no, not indifference . . .
MORIN: No, people do react . . .
ROUCH: . . . by reaction, and by reaction that is not necessarily a sympathetic reaction.
MORIN: That's the difficulty of communicating something. We are in the know . . .[8]

*The Champs-Elysées. Edgar Morin, on the edge of the sidewalk, waves his hand and walks up toward l'Étoile. Over images of passersby who walk past him and hide him, we hear the attentive voices of Marceline and Nadine, as though echoing . . .*

Are you happy?
Are you happy, sir?
Are you happy, ma'am?
Are you happy? . . . Happy?

▶───────────────────────────────────────

**End Titles**

Participants in the film: Marceline, Marilou, Angélo, Jean-Pierre
Workers: Jacques, Jean
Students: Régis, Céline, Jean-Marc, Nadine, Landry, Raymond
Employees: Jacques, Simone
Artists: Henri, Maddie, Catherine
A cover girl: Sophie
and various unknown people encountered in Paris

Photography: Roger Morillère, Raoul Coutard, Jean-Jacques Tarbès, Michel Brault
Assistants: Claude Beausoleil and Louis Boucher
Lighting: Moineau and Crétaux
Sound: Guy Rophé, Michel Fano, Barthélémy
Production Director: André Heinrich
Production Secretary: Annette Blamont
Editors: Jean Ravel, Nina Baratier, Françoise Colin

This film was made with the assistance of the Comité du Film Ethnographique, Musée de l'Homme, and with the help of the Kinotechnique team of André Coutant.

Laboratory: Eclair
Mix: Simo-Jean Neny
Production: Argos Films (Anatole Dauman and Philippe Lifchitz)

A film by Jean Rouch and Edgar Morin
Film Control Visa 23.792

◆───────────────────────────────────────────

## TRANSLATORS' NOTES

1. The English-subtitled print of the film translates *"cinéma-vérité"* as "filming the truth." The essays by Morin and Rouch (here and elsewhere in this book) place this term in the kind of perspective necessary to understand the nature of their experiment.
2. Angélo wanted to meet Landry after he saw the rushes of some of the Saint Tropez sequences in which Landry appeared as the "African explorer of France on vacation." Portions of these sequences appear later in the film.
3. The Buttes Chaumont is a beautiful park on a hill in the north of Paris.
4. Gouvernement Provisoire de la République Algérienne.
5. The bracketed section here is dialogue that is included in the French book but does not appear in the English-subtitled print of the film in U.S. distribution.
6. This scene is extended in the English-subtitled print of the film in U.S. distribution. Sophie continues to tell Landry and followers how people like to have their picture taken with Saint Tropez models to show their friends. One of the followers argues back that this is an overly general view and that many people do not think this way. Sophie protests, "Only a minority . . ." at which point the follower agrees, "The masses have not really advanced very far . . ."
7. In the French text, the following note appears: "This scene is not included in some copies of the film in distribution but is normally part of the film." The scene is cut from English-subtitled prints in U.S. distribution.
8. *Nous sommes dans le bain*. The idiom means to have one's hands in things, to be implicated, to be complicit. The English-subtitled print translates this phrase as "We're in for trouble," thus closing the film on a considerably less nuanced note.

# EDGAR MORIN
# AND JEAN ROUCH

## The Point of View of the "Characters"

We presented the principal participants of *Chronicle of a Summer* with the following questionnaire:

1. What were your feelings during the making of the film? Did you feel that you were interpreting a role? Were you bothered by the presence of the camera? by the method of the "authors"? Or, on the contrary, did you have the feeling of surrendering yourself totally and sincerely?

2. Do you think that some other method of inquiry, of "attack," might have achieved a greater degree of truth? What, for example?

3. Does the definitive representation of you in the film seem true to who you really are and to what your real preoccupations are? If not, how does it differ?

4. Do you think that some of the scenes that were shot but that don't appear in the public version of the film could give a more exact image of you?

5. Is there anything in what you did or said in front of the camera that you disavow, that does not correspond to what you judge to be your truth? What? Why?

6. On the other hand, is there anything that you did not show or say in front of the camera, something that is important to you, which you think is essential for someone to know you, and that you would have liked to express? If so, what?

7. Do you know the other participants in the film? Does the image it gives of them conform to the one you had and have of them yourself? Is it rather more real, less real, or simply different? In what way?

8. Did the fact that you participated in this film modify your way of living, your way of thinking, your idea of yourself? How so?

9. Do you regret this experience? Are you happy with it? Does it seem to have been useful to you?

10. What, in your opinion, is the true contribution of this film?

11. To the question "Are you happy?" what would you respond today?

The responses we received to these questions from Jacques Gabillon, Landry, Mme Gabillon, Angélo, and Marceline follow.

▶ _____

### Jacques Gabillon

1. Favorable sentiment; excitement at the prospect of participating in something new, if not of escaping daily mediocrity for a while. Rediscovering Edgar Morin, making new acquaintances.

No discomfort in front of the camera; however, felt the impression of finding myself "brutalized" by the leader of the game (here I rejoin the criticism of a certain conception of modesty). In any case, there intervenes, along with dignity, the internal freedom to reject or accept. As for me, I could not give myself over completely; more precisely, I did not attempt to break out of the particular frame that Morin had placed me in. Why?

Edgar Morin had solicited me personally. Since he addressed (my wife) Simone as well, the method of "attack" no longer involved merely the worker living in the new apartment, but the couple.

And this brings me to the following question:

2. To my understanding, it is now less a matter of method of "attack" than of its objective: since I am no longer individually solicited, I must keep in mind conjugal relations. This is why I could not "give" what was expected of me.

3. I think the personal truth of the characters is found to be limited, in that, with cutting and editing, the directors were able to bend the meaning of the whole with regard to the particular truth . . . Whatever it may be, it must not be forgotten that the characters clarify each other, one after the other, and that as a last resort, the truth is only really achieved by means of cinematographic vision. But there also lies the force of impact.

4. There are scenes that were filmed that do not figure in the screened version of the film. There are also scenes that could have been filmed.

In the first case, it was only a matter of useless chatter to cover up uneasiness. As for what could have been done, it would have required that the camera penetrate into my little world of anachronistic bureaucracy at SNCF, with its grotesque silhouettes and general grayness. The camera would have had to tune in to capture the aftereffects of the ordeal of deportation with the subsequent decline, and not the militant who never much existed, and finally to throw a violent light on what had inevitably remained in the shadow, understanding that the camera will more quickly uncover a wound than evoke the humiliation or simple paltriness of daily life. Moreover, in that moment of refuge in the apartment, with the friendly presence of the old collected books and records, after our Spanish vacation (which left us, after all, with more than just photos), the singular duality of the character that is me could have revealed its fundamental truth, no doubt inadequate at the present moment, that is to say, the moment in question.

5. Nothing to be disavowed, as far as the part of the filming that was used is concerned, this being pertinent only as a prefatory comment.

6. What is essentially lacking to a full understanding of me is as much the result of a certain dissimulation of my personality. It's why I don't assume what I really am, what's deep within me. Here enters the "pathology" of the wounded idealist, of the former concentration camp internee, coming to grips with the reality of a society to which he is poorly adapted, a society that, in fact, repudiates him and has, up till now, assailed his greatly diminished vitality. What is pathetic in my adventure is that for long years, the scream that was tearing me apart never left my throat. I no longer had the energy to scream.

7. I only knew Edgar Morin, his insatiable curiosity, his interest in my situation. Did he want to attack my inhibition or provoke some brutal change in this condition that I endure with such difficulty? An "old accomplice," as I've already said somewhere, in the course of a presentation. However, I did not know the other collaborators in the film, people from his circle or those who evolved around the group. Ecclecticism in the choice of the collaborators? In the choice of "patients"? Not so much. Under varied social trappings lies a common way of reacting to life. Angélo, the worker breaking the proletariat, is the counterpart of the others. On Marceline's shelves I noticed, unsurprisingly, many of the titles that figure in Morin's library or in my own collection of books, which marks my first years of reading. But could we do otherwise? It is a question here of wheedling an acceptance to participate in an operation that was,

after all, delicate, but where that acceptance was the natural result of long conversations in the past and of friendship.

I knew nothing about Jean Rouch until after the film was made. Jean Rouch is essentially a temperament that revealed itself under the African sun, among the blacks. You have to have seen him working, at ease with everyone, knowing how to gain confidence with a direct approach, a simple friendly gesture, toward the patient that he is about to "operate on." I am sorry that the camera was never turned toward him, to capture the instants when, sitting cross-legged on the floor at my house, he played to gain my son's confidence. *Chronicle of a Summer* being a team effort, the camera could have given us some other quality images, notably those that would have shown Jean Rouch at work with his operative grin!

8. Participating in the film did not change my way of thinking, even less my way of living. It did, however, constitute a landmark in my life where, even now, more trust has entered it.

I mean, it's amusing: a certain shade of me is shown by the screen, with my accent with muffled southern intonation that I never suspected. And that intimate mobility of the face with its southern fluency, while I always thought of myself as a northerner!

9. I am highly satisfied with the experience; the usefulness of the film, which is really pertinent to a period that is troubled and alarming on many counts.

10. This experience may not always have attained its ambitions, but the partial truth—those instants of truth captured in Marilou's shattered self, Marceline's secret complexion liberated by memories—all of this cannot leave you insensitive. Sometimes it's unbearable, but often thrilling. And then it's also the film of life in the Parisian melting pot, with its "aggressions" against everyday life: rapid "unscrewing" to him who doesn't recognize it in time!

11. To this question I had answered "more or less happy." What else could I reply? Because in the meantime nothing has really changed.

▶————————————————————————

## Landry

1. A feeling of unsettledness, a certain fear of not being able to stay myself until the end. I was not at all bothered by the camera because, first of all, this was my second experience of *"cinéma-vérité"*; and then when you're

wrapped up in something, really wrapped up, cameras, technicians, all that stuff becomes a part of some other universe than your own.

I worked with Rouch because I like what he does. When I start working with him, I know in advance that there will be a camera hidden somewhere, but I also know that Jean is ready to spend ten reels on me if I want to talk to him about my mother for those ten reels.

Surrendering myself entirely? I don't know if I surrender myself entirely, but what I know is that at the moment I say everything I have to say, without deceit, out of honesty to Jean, who allows me the most total freedom.

2. I think that this form of cinema demands of us who wish in some way "to offer our truth," a certain portion of honesty. First of all toward our director and then toward the public, who must not see us as exhibitionists. And then for me, I'm not used to mincing words; I say what I've got on my mind; I'm like that, take it or leave it. So for me all methods of attack are worthwhile, on the condition that they leave the individual complete freedom of expression and of manifestation of his personality.

3. *Chronicle of a Summer:* It's me during that summer of 1960, discovering the Riviera, which I had only heard of through the scandals of Mme Carmen Tessier; it's me seeing for the first time the running of the bulls at Bayonne; it's me surprised to see the slightly too scant attire of girls on vacation, which is barely different from the attire of our African women before the era of civilization; it's me discussing with Angélo, making the statements I always make whenever anyone asks me if I have complexes. Of course, you can't call the first things I've cited "preoccupations," but my discussion on the terrace, and my discussion with Angélo, are my preoccupations because they are permanent states in me.

4. As far as I'm concerned, I think that everything important I had to say in this film is there, since it was not really a question of me. I only had to serve as a catalyst to Angélo, and if, in the end, Angélo and I got around to the problem of inferiority complexes, it's simply because we felt so close to each other that he had a need to know who I really was and what I was thinking. But I would have liked them to keep certain sections where Raymond and I talk about what we think of marriage between blacks and whites, because I think white women are often asked what they think of mixed marriages, but young Africans are not often asked what they think about it. Mixed marriage is a danger of which certain of us are conscious. There are a lot of blacks who do not set their sights on a white woman,

blacks who are ill at ease going out with a white woman, in the interest of that white woman herself; certain blacks who seek a white woman's pure, true friendship, in no way connected with any sexual need. Now the young African student goes to look for his bride in Africa. I mean all these problems that have arisen since black Africa's accession to independence; certain realities that escape a large part of the white masses.

5. My own truth is one, and not double; when I have the chance to say it, I say it, and I will not renounce it because it shocks or because people might think it debatable or false. From the moment when I figure I'm being honest with myself, to hell with "What will they say?"!

6. I would really have liked to say more about mixed marriage and the worker situation in my country; to express myself more fully on the problem of the Congo; also to express myself more fully on this delicate problem they call the "skin complex." But I think that would have required a whole film just about me, while *Chronicle of a Summer* is a film on the life of people in general.

7. I'm going to take the participants of the film in order and classify them as to whether they were close to me:

Marilou: The friendship between me and Marilou was born, I think, without even the directors knowing about it. The first evening I saw her, Marilou gave me the impression of a lost girl who was actually looking for herself. She was tense, nervous, in her every gesture and movement. I think she was very impressed by my "kindness," and we got along from that very evening. Afterward I often went to see her at Cahiers du Cinéma; she even helped me out of my bad period. Then I went on vacation. When I came back I found Marilou distinctly more radiant than she had been that first evening. So we went out for a drink in a café near the Champs-Elysées. Marilou talked to me as though I were a brother, a relative, and told me that she was now better than before and that she had found happiness. Since then Marilou and I have remained friends, and I often go to see her at her job. I saw her two sequences with Morin a long time after they were shot (because we were not allowed to see the rushes), and absolutely nothing surprised me. Without pretending to have been a determining factor in Marilou's life, I do think I helped her a bit.

Next comes Angélo. My friendship with Angélo was born in front of the camera; it is nonetheless real and sincere. And just as Angélo currently has a photo enlargement of the two of us next to his phone at home, I have one too, covering a full page of my photo album. You have to see Angélo to really recognize that he is in real life just what he was trying to be in the film. Angélo truly did not like the situation he was put in at Renault, and he'll say so to anyone who cares to listen. But besides that, he is a good guy, extremely sensitive. It's very easy to communicate with him, and he is very sensitive to the friendship felt toward him; it bursts out on the screen, I think.

Marceline: She aroused different sentiments in me. Emotion when I learned for the first time that she was a deportee. And then she impressed me so much by the way she reclimbed that moral slope. I would have been marked by that for the rest of my life. And then, finally, pity, because it must be said that all that self-assurance, that trust Marceline had in the future, was all conditioned by her happiness with Jean-Pierre; a happiness that was falling apart in spite of all the directors' efforts to permit these two young people to get back together. But the drama of Marceline and Jean-Pierre was beyond me, and as I never had the chance to communicate with either of them, I never really felt close to them as I did with Marilou and Angélo.

8. This film changed nothing in my way of life, because I am, if you will, as much a "spectator" in this film as anyone else.

9. I in no way regret this experience, and I would start it all over if I had it to do again. I am pleased with it because it allowed me to discover two friends who are still friends, and God only knows that you can't buy real friends at the flea market.

11. I will not really be happy until the moment when I will have consolidated all these little transitory satisfactions that I have at the present moment.

▶

### Simone Gabillon

1. A very happy sensation. The daily routine was broken. No doubt at the beginning the camera was a bit intimidating, but mostly because of the heat of the lights. In the end I got used to it. On top of that, I had total confidence in Edgar Morin, who was interviewing me. I didn't have the impression of being misguided by the game leader, because at no time did I have the feeling of being asked indiscreet questions.

2. For me, attaining the truth is not all that easy. It would have been necessary to dig around in the past. No doubt—my husband being a former deportee—it would have been interesting to learn the repercussions of de-

portation on the life of a couple, and in particular on the life of a young woman who was not prepared to confront existence. To dig into the past, it was not just recollecting the housing shortage—the first difficulty of all young people in our day—but remembering those long years in which Jacques, out of work, was on the edge of madness.

3. The image of me that this film gives strikes me as superficial. However, curiously enough, this film helped me to know myself. My excessive nervousness, almost unbearable, was laid bare, along with a certain grin that accompanies a pretty disagreeable voice. To be fair, on the subject of my voice, I was obliged to raise it to the maximum, upon the request of the soundman, which was no doubt some disadvantage for me.

4. The other scenes filmed in our house were uninteresting because they did not reflect our way of life.

5. When I defended Marilou, I had only seen one sequence of the film. It is certain that my judgment would have been more colored had I seen the entire film.

6. My two quite different attitudes, at the office and at home: at the office, where I am really myself, relaxed, gay, very much at ease in my work; at the house, curiously different, feeling almost guilty for having lived a life with no great history until the moment of my marriage, almost guilty for not having a tragic past, in the face of my husband and the majority of his friends, who are almost all former deportees or resisters.

7. I did not know any of the participants in the film. However, the image it gives of them seems very real to me. Marceline, in particular, even though she claims that she is acting in the scene where she walks alone in Paris. It doesn't matter whether she is acting at that precise moment; we are sure that she has repeated those words to herself so many times that the images she evokes are a part of herself.

8. The film changed nothing in my way of living and thinking.

9. I have no regret. I was happy at the time of the filming because the ambience was so friendly.

10. I wonder if each viewer felt the same feeling I did when I saw the film the other evening at the Agriculteurs. None of the characters in the film

(except probably the artist-painter couple) found an equilibrium during this period, which was troubled in every way (memories of the last war, the war in Algeria, the events in the Congo). Each person feels more or less responsible. Racism is profoundly foreign to all of the participants of the film who were questioned about it, and that is very comforting. I do regret not having participated in the Saint Tropez rendezvous, specifically in the dialogue around the table.

In other respects (again, not counting the artist-painter couple and, I must say, me), no one likes his work, each one does it like forced labor. All of them claim to submit to it completely . . . since they've got to live.

11. I can't add anything to answer this question.

▶────────────────────────────────────────────

## Angélo

First of all, to give an account of the film and of my behavior, I need to recapitulate the basics.

I was a worker at Renault, as a machinist, spending lots of time on the problems of the worker and of management exploitation. One day a workmate, Jacques, who had a number of outside contacts, particularly in the literary world, came to see me, saying he was in touch with some people who would like to make a film about the life and the world of workers, where we would be able to express our way of thinking.

We had had this idea much earlier but had never been able to realize it, for the sole reason that we did not have the necessary money for such an enterprise.

So we made an appointment for one weekday when I was to meet Edgar Morin and Jean Rouch. We went to the home of Marceline, an actress in *Chronicle,* and there I was surprised: cameras and spotlights were trained on us. Then we sat down at a table that was covered with things that would have cost us a month's salary to provide.

Then some guys waved some gadgets around our faces and in back of our heads; I think these gadgets were for checking the intensity of the lighting. I felt like I had become another man, a sort of "Robespierre of the Machines," the rare beast that is shown to the public. I don't mean that I was forced, but it seemed like another world; it was something quite new to me.

The first question we were asked: If you had a film to make, what subject would you choose?

One of us replied: Me, I'd like to do a film on the lives of workers, and, in particular, to denounce the methods of management and the so-called defenders of the proletariat: the unions.

Then we discussed problems of the shop. We were not really in form after our day's work, and we were very impressed by this cinematographic domain, which we knew nothing about. Then we said good night, and I was convinced that one day the public would be shown what work in the twentieth century is like.

A few days later, Marceline came to my house with a tape recorder, to interview me on my "private life." "Do you love your fiancée?" "Do you sleep with her?" "Have you ever cheated on her?" These are the beginnings of the mirror-film. What was the connection with the worker problem? These questions left me perplexed.

Then there was the problem of vacation. Theoretically they were supposed to come film a day in my life, the life of a worker on vacation. And yet only a segment on Saint Tropez was filmed. Saint Tropez, a snobbish city par excellence, too pretentious for a worker. Once again, what was the connection with the basis of the film?

After vacation, Morin wrote to me to say that they were back in Paris, working on the film.

First of all, there was the Renault period, filmed at the company, then to my house, and the scene in my home. This sequence, I think, shows a bit of the worker's life. Then there was the contact with the students, where I met the greater part of the actors in the film.

For me personally, the scene with Landry and me on the Renault problem was very dissatisfying, in the sense that there was a bad reaction among the workers at Renault. What I meant to say was not really that the guys are poor slobs, but that this sort of evolution forces them to the point where they want to possess that excess of material things. For example, it is known that before the war about 40 percent of the people had their own cars. Whereas in the modern world, 80 percent of the people have a car, of which 40 percent are the real bourgeoisie, and 40 percent are the proletariat. In the 40 percent of the proletariat there are 20 percent who are really able to have their car, and the other 20 percent are obliged to make concessions.

In addition, I would add that Renault is a special factory; it's a factory of guarantees, a so-called serious factory. You know that a Renault worker can buy things outside, with all those guarantees. All he has to do is show his company card for all credit doors to be opened to him. And then we remember the sixty-day layoff, which was in fact nothing more than a filtration of the proletariat bourgeoisie. That's what I meant to say on television about the worker problem.

If someone were to ask me today, "If you could make a film, what subject would you choose?" I would take the subject proposed by a friend, with the difference that I would try to see to it that we were the ones who took charge of the operation, and not the sociologists. I would try to make a film for the workers and not for the intellectuals.

I think it would take too long to explain how I would go about it, but I could always give concrete guidelines. For example, put tape recorders around among the shop mates, record the most important problems, like strikes, discussions between delegates and workers, and the management's rebuffs.

This film changed nothing in my way of looking at things. I am not any happier than I was before. I think I never will be, because evolution creates division.

▶ _____

## Marceline

I lived the period of shooting *Chronicle of a Summer* as though it was both an adventure and a slightly crazy experience—but without ever forgetting that it was also a cinematographic experiment.

I thus gave myself over to this experiment that interested me for its slightly mad side, without knowing in the beginning where all this might lead and where I myself might end up. Being part of the technical crew from the start, I must say that a wonderful climate of camaraderie and friendship sprang up very quickly.

Not a fictional film, *Chronicle of a Summer* is called *"cinéma-vérité."* Yet nonetheless you have to start with the principle that it is first and foremost a cinematographic work.

There is no question here of raising the quarrel over *"cinéma-vérité,"* even though this was the source of much confusion and interminable polemic, nor of judging the value or the ideology of the film by posing the problem of possible methods of approach, of interviewing, et cetera. Given that I participated in this film, it would never occur to me to judge it in this fashion.

What is unquestionable, whether or not it succeeded, is the new tone; it's the fact that this film opens up directions for research that cannot be neglected in the domain of filmed investigations, for example: Mario Ruspoli's *Les inconnus de la terre,* prizewinner at the last Tours festival, or even another possible method for actors to try (of the Godard type, for example).

In any case, in a certain way this film will draw a following; it's an interesting experiment, even if you don't think the authors have gotten the essence out of the twenty-two hours that were filmed.

I am thinking of one scene in particular, of Jean-Pierre and me, which we filmed in Saint Tropez (it is going to be reedited into the distribution version) with all the desired distance (I admit to having had Antonionian reminiscences while we were filming). I must say that the choice of passages from this sequence, which lasts almost half an hour, is outside the context of the filming. Jean-Pierre appears as a hard, cynical person, and I seem like the "poor little victim," whereas the whole sequence is quite different, where I am far from being a saint.

Overall the present editing choice does not seem the best to me. They'll say they wanted to even out the sad, happy, nice, tragic parts. In any case, what's sure is that they did not always use the best things.

Coming back to me more specifically, I feel that I was freer than the other actors, and as far as I'm concerned, Edgar Morin has very little to do with it. After being intimidated the first time I was filmed, I controlled myself, completely dominating my personality, dramatizing with words, with my face, my tone, with gestures. Being particularly aware that the camera was there, that the technicians, the lights were there . . . et cetera, there was a certain directing of me by me, since there was no other direction of the actors. I thought that was the only way to act other than discourse, because the cinema is not a lecture, and I was doing a film.

During the filming of the sequence on deportation, I acted without being involved, having gotten control of the character. There too I had cinematographic fantasies; certain lines from *Hiroshima, mon amour* came to me, and I pushed them away. And if the technicians cried upon listening to the sound track, I didn't, and I recall asking Edgar several times, "Is this okay? Shall I go on like this?"

Is this quackery, playacting on my part, lies, because I was acting? Do I say this after the fact because I want to become, as we suggested, an actress? Is it also a reaction of self-defense?

I put myself in the situation, I dramatized myself, I chose a character that I then interpreted within the limits of the film, a character who is both an aspect of the reality of Marceline and also a dramatized character created by Marceline. So, too, the couple Jean-Pierre/Marceline is an aspect of the reality of the couple Jean-Pierre/Marceline, a mixture of reality. Let's also say it's a character among all the facets of characters that each one of us carries within.

Is this falsification? In the name of *cinéma-vérité*, perhaps, but isn't *cinéma-vérité* in its simplistic interpretation a myth?

My truth is not in this film even if the memories of deportation I evoked are real. In fact, this is where all the ambiguity of *cinéma-vérité* lies. Even if I thought about this scene long before filming it, and it was just a matter of finding the "tone" for me, my truth is there in this sequence, because what I say is what I really lived.

The problem of the truth of beings is much more complex, ambiguous, diffuse, uncapturable.

The same thing holds for Jean-Pierre, whose character has nothing to do with what he really is, nor even with his real preoccupations. He is interpreting a character; it's something else, it's not him.

The viewer may believe, after seeing the film, that we have separated, which is false, and I must add that neither the film nor what we said to each other in the film has entered our private life at any level. We both have preoccupations that were not touched upon in this film, and that we don't need to touch upon.

There is not especially, to answer the questionnaire directly, any truth about me lingering around somewhere that I would have liked to express in the film. The film is what it is. In some other context, it is possible that I would have played some other character of Marceline. In fact, Edgar Morin said about me in an interview "that I first chose a light and freethinking character for myself, and then later changed the register." That is entirely correct.

I don't really feel involved or wrapped up in this film, so that at the level of truth I didn't really learn anything about myself. I feel very distant from the character in the film, and even though that all may seem true, it is nonetheless not my reality. However, I don't think that this is important. The viewers may feel involved with one or another of the characters or find symbols, myths, and other things. At this level it's another problem. For the viewer, whether or not I am Marceline is not important, what's important is that Marceline or some other character provides something that touches him, that involves him. What is true is that through this film I met people who interested me and also perhaps found a career. It may also have been useful to me in that it may have helped to change my professional orientation.

Can one be happy in a country where police terror, torture, racism, and arbitrariness reign? I am all too familiar with racism, having suffered it myself, and I know that there is no basic difference in the way that Algerians are treated in France compared with my Jewish situation during the war, except maybe a difference in degree, which lies in the absence of crematoriums, that's all. At that time the French people, the German people, remained silent, not interfering except for a handful of people. Today as well, France remains silent except for a handful of people.

# IV   Works by Jean Rouch

**COMPILED BY STEVEN FELD**

## *Annotated Filmography*

This comprehensive listing of films by Jean Rouch draws from several sources. For the pre-1981 films, original synopses were written by Jean Rouch and first appeared in the catalog *Jean Rouch: Une rétrospective*, published in 1981 in Paris by the Ministère des Affaires Etrangères-Animation Audiovisuelle and the Service d'Etude, de Réalisation et de Diffusion de Documents Audio-Visuels of the Centre National de la Recherche Scientifique. Anny Ewing and I translated these synopses, and Jay Ruby embellished some of them with material from various sources, principally Mick Eaton's book *Anthropology–Reality–Cinema: The Films of Jean Rouch*, published by the British Film Institute in 1979. This portion of the filmography was then compiled by Jay Ruby and published as "A Filmography of Jean Rouch, 1946–1981," *Visual Anthropology* 2, nos. 3–4 (1989): 333–65.

Information on the films after 1980 comes from the document *Rouch films depuis 1980* provided by Françoise Foucault of the Comité du Film Ethnographique, Musée de l'Homme, with original comments and synopses by Jean Rouch. These were translated by Catherine Maziére and me and appended to the prior composite document. The entire filmography was then checked and completely revised for technical details (dates, running times); it was also updated to conform with the most recent Films Rouch database, also provided by Françoise Foucault of the Comité du Film Ethnographique, Musée de l'Homme.

The following abbreviations are used throughout the filmography.

CFE       Comité du Film Ethnographique
CNRS     Centre National de la Recherche Scientifique
FEMIS    École Nationale Supérieure des Métiers de l'Image et du Son

| GREC | Groupe de Recherche et d'Essai Cinématographique |
| IFAN | Institut Français d'Afrique Noire |
| INA | Institut National de l'Audiovisuel |
| KWK | Kinowerke Italy |
| NAV | Nippon Audio-Visual |
| NFI | Netherlands Film |
| SCOA | Société Commerciale de l'Ouest Africain |
| SERDDAV | Service d'Etude, de Realisation et de Diffusion de Documents Audio-Visuels |

Les Films de la Pléiade, the producer of many of the films, is now Les Films du Jeudi.

Unless otherwise stated, Rouch was the director of each film, and all films are in 16 mm with sound and in color. For distribution information, contact the Comité du Film Ethnographique, Musée de l'Homme, Palais de Chaillot, Place du Trocadéro, 75116 Paris, France. The primary North American distributor of Rouch's films is Documentary Educational Resources, 101 Morse Street, Watertown, Massachusetts 02172.

▶──────────────────────────────────

**1946**

*La chevelure magique* (Magical Hair)
  With Pierre Ponty and Jean Sauvy. Black and white.
  This film has been lost.

▶──────────────────────────────────

**1946–1947**

*Au pays des mages noirs* (In the Land of the Black Magi)
  Produced by Actualités Françaises. With Pierre Ponty and Jean Sauvy.
  Black and white. 12 minutes. Blown up to 35 mm.
  Synopsis: Hippopotamus hunting with a harpoon by the Sorko of Niger. In the village of Firgoun, in sheds shaped like amphorae, the fishermen build a large hunting canoe with strips of wood sewn together. Shots of daily life in the village. Making harpoons and propitiatory sacrifices to the spirit of the water. In the marshes on the edge of the river, the fishermen approach and harpoon a hippopotamus. The hippopotamus, covered with harpoons, cannot get out of the marshes. One of the fishermen kills it with a blow from a lance. They haul its body onto dry land to butcher it and divide the meat into portions. Possession dances with details of the dance steps; a woman is possessed by the spirits of the water. In the evening, some Hauka arrive. They are the powerful spirits of the villages and countryside of Niger.

**1947**

*Chasse traditionelle à Bangawi* (Bangawi Traditional Hunt)
  Black and white. 12 minutes.

Rouch's own cut of *Au pays des mages noirs.*

*Chasse à l'hippopotame* (Hippopotamus Hunt)
  With Pierre Ponty and Jean Sauvy. 50 minutes.
  Techniques of the hippopotamus hunt.

**1948**

*La circoncision* (Circumcision)
  Produced by CNRS and Secrétariat d'Etat à la Cooperation. 15 minutes.
  Awarded Prix du Reportage, Misguich Festival of the Short Subject, 1949.
  Circumcision rites of thirty Songhay children from the village of Hombori, Mali.
The boys are taken into the bush, prepared, and circumcised. After the circumcision
they are cared for, and in the evening, they make their first appearance and sing the
first song of the circumcised.

*Hombori*
  16 minutes.
  This film has been lost.

*Initiation à la danse des possédés* (Initiation into Possession Dance)
  Produced by CNRS. 22 minutes.
  Awarded first prize, Biarritz Festival, 1949.
  A woman is initiated into ritual possession dances among the Songhay of Firgoun,
Niger. The musicians arrive. The first dance. The dancing lesson: learning the main
steps. Dance of departure of the initiated, and group dance.

*Les magiciens de Wanzerbé* (The Magicians of Wanzerbé)
  Produced by CNRS and Secrétariat d'Etat à la Cooperation. In collaboration
with Marcel Griaule and Roger Rosfelder.
  Black and white. 33 minutes.
  Screened at the first ethnographic film conference, Musée de l'Homme.
  Principal rituals of Songhay magicians who are descendants of emperor Sonny
Ali, from the village of Wanzerbé, Niger. The Wanzerbé market, children's games,
Mossi the magician, dance of the magicians, sacrifice made to the village mountain
spirit.

▶

*Les fils de l'eau* (The Sons of the Water)

    Produced by Les Films de la Pléiade. 69 minutes. Blown up to 35 mm.

    A long work built up from excerpts from *Les hommes qui font la pluie, La circoncision, Cimitière dans la falaise, Bataille sur le grand fleuve,* and *Les gens du mil.*

▶

*Cimetière dans la falaise* (Cemetery in the Cliff)

    Produced by CNRS and Secrétariat d'Etat à la Cooperation. With Roger Rosfelder. Commentary by Marcel Griaule and Germaine Dieterlen. 18 minutes.

    *Synopsis:* Funeral rituals among the Dogon on the cliffs of Bandiagara, Mali. Dogon country: a cliff, waterfalls, cricks in the rocks, onion gardens, millet field. The farmers and their wives come back from working in the fields. The rainy season: wintry sky. The goat herders gather their flocks. The women grind the millet. It is raining. The streams are swollen with water. A man drowns.

    Sacrifice to the spirit of the water: at dawn two priests go to the edge of the stream. They undress and put on leather trunks. Holding a chicken, one of them speaks to the spirit of the water, asking him to give back the body of the dead man, while the other taps on a rock with a *tata* iron. Sacrifice of the chicken above the water of the stream. Its body is grilled over a wood fire.

    Return of the cadaver: The recovered corpse is carried on a man's back, at a running pace along the cliff toward the village of Idyeli at sunset. Funeral: The next morning, at dawn, the cadaver, attached to a stretcher, is brought out of the mortuary house, saluted by drums and bells and the cries of wailing women. On the village square, a mock combat to prevent the body from entering. The body enters the square, following a winding path, symbol of its resurrection. It is placed on the "stone of the brave." The women greet the body with upside-down gourds; the men take up the stretcher and carry the cadaver to the end of the village, at the foot of the cliff.

    Putting the body in the cemetery: Some men climb up to the cave, which dominates the village of Idyeli from above 100 meters, so as to hoist the cadaver up there. The cadaver is removed from its stretcher. It is wrapped in the blanket of the dead. They attach it to a thick rope. The men haul it up. It rises slowly toward the sky and the cemetery in the cliff. The condolences: In the village, all the women salute the dead man as he disappears. They cry. They scrape the earth with broken gourds ("the broken egg of the world"). They give the ritual condolences to the mother of the dead man, who is singing the praises of her departed son. Conclusion: In the cemetery cave, the men replace the stones that close the opening. All around them are the skeletons of the other dead men. Countryside, waterfall (a symbol of life, which is always reborn from death).

**1951**

*Les gens du mil* (The People of the Millet)
Assistant: Roger Rosfelder. 45 minutes.

*Les hommes qui font la pluie,* or *Yenendi, les faiseurs de pluie* (The Men Who
Make the Rain, or Yenendi: The Rainmakers)
Produced by Institut Français d'Afrique Noire. With Roger Rosfelder. 28 minutes.
*Synopsis:* Rain rituals with possession dances among the Songhay and Zarma
of Simiri, Zermaganda, Niger. Dry Season: The village of Simiri; water carriers,
the rainbow tree. Possession of the faithful making their way to the spirits' hut
on the seventh day of the seventh month of the dry season. All of the inhabitants
of the village go to the spirits' hut to celebrate the Yenendi, the festival of the rain.
Preparation by the musicians: under the shelter, gourd drummers. The chief of the
village, old Wadi Sorko, prepares his violin. Dance of the "spirit" horse (possession
dance).

Arrival of the spirits: Start of the possession dances, which permit the spirits to
speak through the voices of the dancers they have chosen. These are Moussa, spirit
of the wind; Naiberi, goddess of the cemeteries; Sadara, the rainbow; Tyirey, master
of the lightning; Hausakoy, master of the thunderbolt; and Dongo, master of the
thunder and the rain. They fall down before the hut. They back out, dressed in
their ritual costumes and carrying their ritual objects.

They go back to the hut to talk with the men about the next rainy season.
Bargaining: the men want a lot of rain and very little thunder. The gods want a
lot of thunder and very little rain because they are angry. They are appeased with
gifts.

Making rain: The priests and the faithful go behind the hut. A ditch is dug, running east to west (it represents the land of Simiri). The *hampi* (ritual jug) is placed
at the top of this ditch. It is filled with water and millet (first fruits of the last harvest): it represents the spirit of the thunder, and the priests and spectators place one
finger on the edge of the jug; this is the sermon of the rain. Dongo pours out the jug
of the sky: the year's rain falls on the land of Simiri. According to the pattern created by the streams of water and the distribution of the grains, the men learn whether
the season will be good and the crops abundant.

The men turn their backs. A black goat and a chicken are sacrificed above the
hole of the *hampi.*

Rainbow cult: The priests sacrifice a multicolored ram (with brown, black, and
white patches) to the tree and to the stones of the rainbow, which divert the waters
from the cloud to fill the wells. The blood is poured over the tree. The festival is
finished. Priests and faithful go home.

The first rain: The rainy season begins. Clouds appear. The sky is completely
black on the eastern side. The herds are brought in. Dust storm, tornado, lightning, rain.

▶

## 1952

*Bataille sur le grand fleuve* (Battle on the Great River)
Produced by Institut Français d'Afrique Noire and Centre National du Cinéma. With Roger Rosfelder. 33 minutes.
*Synopsis:* The Sorko hunt the hippopotamus with harpoon on the Niger River (around Ayorou and Firgoun, Niger). The fishermen build a large canoe out of planks sewn together. Harpoons with floats indicate where the beast has dived.

Ceremony to question the spirit of the river on the possibility and success of the hunt. Possession, dance: dance of a woman possessed by the spirit of the river, dance of the Haukas, spirits of force. Final three preparations before departure: the fisherman wash themselves with magic water in order to have courage.

February–March: Going back up the Niger with eight small canoes and one large one; the hippopotamuses have taken refuge in the tall grass marshes. First success: a two-ton female is killed.

April: The water level in the river has gone down; the beasts have abandoned the high grasses and have gone back up the rapids. New departure of the fishermen, who attach straw bumpers to the front of the canoes to break on the waves. Attack: a young hippopotamus is captured alive. New attack on an old hippopotamus; alone and ferocious, riddled with harpoons, he manages to escape after smashing up the large canoe.

Repairing the large canoe. Two fishermen leave again in pursuit of the hippopotamus; they catch a manatee.

The old hippopotamus has gone back down the Labbezenga rapids. In spite of the harpoons implanted in his body, he again manages to escape and completely demolishes the large canoe. It is the season of mists on the river; the hippopotamus is still impossible to find, vanished into the marshes of the north. Return of the fishermen, who have turned their clothes inside out as a sign of defeat.

▶

## 1953–1956

*Mammy Water* (Mamy Wata)
Produced by Films de la Pléiade and CNRS. 20 minutes.
Editing and sound track completed in 1966.
Daily life of the Fanti fishermen of Ghana, and rituals for the opening of the fishing season at Shama, Ghana.

▶

## 1955

*Les maîtres fous* (The Mad Masters)
Produced by Films de la Pléiade. Sound by Damouré Zika. Edited by Suzanne Baron. 24 minutes.

Prize for best short film, Venice, 1957.

*Synopsis:* Annual major ceremonies of the Hauka, spirits of power in Accra, Ghana. Titles and explanatory text concerning the basis of Hampi possession states. Urban life in Ghana and principal activities of Nigerian migrants. Amusements of migrants of all nationalities.

Headquarters of Hauka: the buying of salt in Accra. Departure for the annual grand ceremony in some trucks carrying some slogans. Arrival at the ritual arena of Mountyéba.

The arena: British pavilion displaying the Union Jack; wooden copy of statue of the governor. Presentation of a newcomer, which opens the first "possession."

Public confessions: each accuses himself, and the priest Mountyéba recites the slogans of Hauka. The guiltiest must make a sacrifice of chickens and sheep. The punished are sent to the bush. The priest Mountyéba sacrifices some eggs on "the stairs and the balconies" of the "secretary general." It is raining; at the sound of a violin, the initiates await the one who brings the sacrificial dog from the bush (all food is forbidden).

Beginning of the possession: dribbling, hands trembling, panting, the first possessed arrives, "Corp'ral Gardi" (the corporal of the guard). Then the other possessed arrive: Gerba "Conductor"; "Madam Lokotoro" (Madam Doctor); the "Ordinance Lieutenant" (eyes bulging, panting); "Madam Salma" (wife of Captain Salama, commander of Niamey club).

Inspection of the governor's statue: after different ceremonial greetings of all the Hauka, there is the inspection. Then the last possessed arrive: "General Furious"; the soldier, "Tiémoko"; then the "Secretary-General"; and the "truck driver." Finally, the "Sorry Commander" who almost set himself on fire with a torch.

Sacrifice of the dog: roundtable conference and gathering around the concrete altar; sacrifice; the Hauka lick the blood. Dismemberment, new conference, cutting up of the dog by the "Governor," the dog boiled in the cooking pot.

Consumption: the Hauka leave the broth boiling and eat it; they prepare some pieces for the absent ones. When the crisis state is over, the possessed lift themselves up and leave. Night falls on the arena of Mountyéba.

The next day: streets of Accra, headquarters of the initiated. The possessed sitting-up (like a wake) return to their usual jobs: "Madam Doctor" is a saleswoman in a shop; the "Corporal of the Guard" makes gravel; the "Lieutenant" is a pickpocket; the "General" is a simple soldier. The "Governor" and the "Conductor" work for the water department. While mastering the Hauka cult, they have resolved, through violent crises, their adjustment to today's world.

▶

## 1956

*Baby Ghana*
   Produced by CNRS. 12 minutes.
   The independence of Ghana.

*Jaguar*

Produced by Films de la Pléiade. Commentary and dialogue by Damouré Zika, Lam Ibrahima Dia, Illo Gaoudel, Amadou Koffo. Sound by Damouré Zika. Edited by Josée Matarassa, Liliane Korb, Jean-Pierre Lacam. Music by Enos Amelodon (guitar), Tallou Mouzourane (piano), Amisata Gaoudelize (chant), Yankori (violin), Ama (flute), Djenne Molo Kari (harp).

Cast: Damouré Zika (Damouré), Lam Ibrahima Dia (Lam), Illo Gaoudel (Illo), Douma Besso (the miner), Amadou Koffo, Jean Rouch (narrator). 92 minutes.

*Synopsis:* The migration of three young men from Niger to Ghana and their return. The journey of Lam, Illo, and Damouré to Ghana, where they find their fortune and the largest market in Africa. But they finally return to their country.

Introduction: presentation of the three heroes: Lam, a Peul herdsman, guards his cattle in the Niger bush. Illo, a Sorko fisherman, pulls up his wicker traps in the river and goes back to the fishing camp. Damouré, the young "gallant," gallops through the streets of the village on his horse, Tarzan. All of them are descendants of the warriors of yesterday.

The departure: every Sunday the market is opened in Ayorou. Arrival of Illo the fisherman in his canoe and Lam the herdsman with his cattle. Damouré in his "office" under a tree, since he knows how to read and write. They decide to leave on a trip and prepare themselves. During a marabou festival, Lam and Illo pray that God will give them a good journey. During a possession dance, Damouré asks the spirits to protect their voyage.

The voyage: three friends leave on foot. The vegetation changes a bit: the farther south they go, the more different the trees are. A stop in the land of the Somba, who live naked. Crossing the mountains of Togo. Discovery of the sea. Smuggled across the frontier. Then, separation of the three heroes.

Illo, the fisherman, stays on the coast. He will throw his nets with the Ewe fisherman. Then he will become a clothing retailer. As soon as he has a bit of money, he will leave for Accra.

Damouré, the gallant, walks along a paved road: he is hitchhiking to Accra. Discovery of the big city. He looks for people from his village whom he discovers at the timber market where everyone sells wood. He becomes a laborer there.

Lam, the herdsman, meets another herdsman who is going to the Kumasi market. Lam discovers the largest African market. He becomes a perfume merchant with a friend who has a shop there.

The beginning of success: Illo, the fisherman, discovers some friends who are dockers in the port of Accra. Damouré becomes a clerk for the wood merchant, then a foreman. Now Damouré is a "jaguar," a young man in style. Lam, the herdsman, has become a peddler and sells perfumes and cloths. In a gold mine he runs into Douma, an old friend from Niger, and makes him his partner.

Amusements: on Sundays, Damouré lives the life of Accra: races, dances in the streets, dances of the Hauka, general election of Kwame Nkrumah.

The meeting: Illo and Damouré take the train to Kumasi. They find Lam and Douma in their open-air shop. The shop, *Petit à petit l'oiseau fait son bonnet,* is a great success. They get rich. One evening it begins to rain. They decide to go back home.

The return: The four friends and their baggage leave in a truck. Once they arrive in the village, they distribute in one day what they earned over several months. They have nothing left, but they are the kings of their village.

Village life resumed: Douma, the miner, has become a farmer again. The herdsman, Lam, watches over his flock. Illo, the fisherman, hunts the hippopotamus. Damouré the gallant tries to seduce all the girls in the village.

▶ ─────────────────────────────────────────

## 1956–1957

*Moro Naba*
Produced by CNRS and the Institut Français d'Afrique Noir. Edited by Jean Ravel. 27 minutes.

Prize, Florence Festival, 1960. 28 minutes.

Funeral rituals for the traditional leader Moro Naba of the Mossi at Ougadougou, Upper Volta (now Burkina Faso). Election ceremonies for his successor. Preparing the feast for the end of mourning. Ceremony in the palace, the people of Ougadougou, the warriors in traditional dress. Presentation of the new leader.

▶ ─────────────────────────────────────────

## 1957–1964

*La chasse au lion à l'arc* (The Lion Hunters)
Begun in 1957 and completed in 1964. Produced by Les Films de la Pléiade/ Pierre Braunberger. Assistants: Damouré Zika, Lam Ibrahima Dia, Tallou Mouzourane. Sound by Idrissa Meiga, Moussa Amidou. Edited by Josée Matarasso, Dov Hoenig. Cast: *les chasseurs à l'arc* (the bow and arrow hunters) Tahirou Koro, Wangari Moussa, Issiaka Moussa, Yoya Koro, Belebia Hamadou, Ausseini Dembo, Sidiko Koro, and the apprentice, Ali. 90 minutes.

Golden Lion Prize at the 26th Venice Film Festival, 1965.

*Synopsis:* Between 1957 and 1964, hunters from the Yatakala region undertook seven hunting expeditions employing traditional bows and poisoned arrows. The film follows the technical and religious aspects of that hunt, which today has disappeared: the construction of the bows and arrows, preparation of the poison, tracking, arrow-making rituals, the death of the prey, cutting up the meat, and the telling of the story to the children. On the boundary between Niger, Mali, and Upper Volta (Burkina Faso) live the Gow—the last hunters of lions with bows and arrows. It is a "nowhere" land—"the bush that is farther than far"—beyond the sedentary villages, where the great Peul or Bella herdsmen wander around scattered ponds.

The cattle and the lions live in peculiar contact: the best pastures are precisely the lion's bush, where each night the wild beasts contend with the herds for the capture of the weaker animals. Natural selection, which the lion sometimes overdoes by killing for the pleasure of killing. So the herdsmen call upon the Gow hunters.

During the five years from 1957 to 1962, we followed the hunting campaigns of the Gow group from the village of Yatakala, led by the chief of hunters, Tahirou Koro.

Preparation of the bows, the arrows, and the arrow poison, *nadji boto,* the technique and the magic of the hunt are intimately mixed.

Tracking the lions from camp to camp. Failure of the first campaign: the bush is "spoiled," and a diviner reads in the earth that one of the hunters is allied with the lions.

New hunting campaigns where the death of a hyena is a bad sign of new spells to combat.

A young lion caught in a trap is put to death: the hunter who will shoot it knows that, in return, he will lose one of his own sons.

Discovery of the trail of a killer lion, "the American," who springs all of the traps of the hunters, who then kill two of his females. The first dies ritually, calmed by the praises of the hunter chief until the moment when she "vomits her death."

But the second, "Fitili's lion," counterattacks and dangerously wounds a Peul herdsman before being paralyzed by the poison. So the victorious hunters, "tired but happy," return to their village, where they divide up the lion meat. And in the evening they tell their sons the marvelous story of *gawey, gawey,* the lion hunt.

▶ ———————————————————————————————————————

## 1958

*Sakpata*

Produced by CNRS/CFE. With Gilbert Rouget. 25 minutes. Released in 1963.

The initiation of three new "horsemen" in a Vaudoun d'Allada monastery in southern Benin.

*Moi, un Noir* (Me, a Black)

Produced by Films de la Pléiade. Sound by André Lubin. Edited by Marie-Josèphe Yoyotte and Catherine Dourgnon. Orchestra music by Yopi Joseph Degré. Songs by Miryam Touré, N'Daye Yéro, Amadou Demba. French commentary by Oumarou Ganda. Adviser: Lam Ibrahima Dia. Director of production: Roger Felytoux.

Cast: Oumarou Ganda (E. G. Robinson), Petit Tourè, Alassane Meiga, Amadou Demba, Seydou Guede, Karidyo Faoudou, Mlle Gambi. 73 minutes.

Prix Delluc, 1959.

*Synopsis:* The lives of young Nigerian émigrés in Treichville on the Ivory Coast. Introduction: Presentation of the particular context in which the film was shot (a film biography). Night falls on Treichville; bridge in Abidjan at night.

Presentation of the hero: Edward G. Robinson, a young Nigerian, walks down the roads from the plateau and enumerates his misfortunes. No job, no place to live. He crosses the lagoon in a small motorboat and gets off at Treichville.

Presentation of this neighborhood to the theme of a modern African song; Robinson enters his home in the "Nigerian Community."

The week: Different activities of Nigerians in Abidjan. Unskilled laborers, porters, dock workers, and "coaxers"—men who coax passengers into trucks. Robinson's two best friends, Tarzan and Eddie Constantine, are a taxi driver and a peddler–cloth merchant, respectively. Robinson and his friend Eddie are looking for work as occasional laborers. Robinson keeps his eye on the hiring at the entrance to the port where once in a while he works all day loading sacks of coffee. At noon he has lunch at the Hotel des Bozeri, sleeps in the street, and returns to his work, reminded of his military campaigns. In the evening he goes back to the "Nigerian Fraternity," where they gamble away the day's wages at cards. He tells stories about the granddaughters of the chief of the Nigerian community, and goes to the Ambiance bar to find Tarzan in his boxing workout.

Saturday: In the afternoon no one works. Robinson meets "Little Jules," and they go to the beach in Tarzan's taxi with two young Nigerian women, Dorothy Lamour and Jeanne Tarzan. Beach games, picnic, swimming in the lagoon. Robinson, sitting next to Dorothy Lamour, dreams about becoming a boxing champion, but it is only a dream. In the evening, Robinson and "Little Jules" and Eddie Constantine are the sole spectators at a real boxing match. Upon leaving, Robinson is invited to the Esperance dance hall by Tarzan. He drinks beer and would like to pick up girls, but they ask him for money, and he doesn't have any. He goes home alone and unhappy.

Sunday: In the morning, Eddie Constantine goes to the cathedral exit to meet some girls, then goes to the hairstylist "Cha-Cha-Cha." This Sunday is both an election day and a Muslim holiday. Robinson goes to pray in the street near the Treichville mosque. Everyone but him is well dressed. He walks through a political demonstration, which he does not take part in. He doesn't vote, either. In the early afternoon Eddie Constantine goes to the stadium to see a soccer match. Here again he is much more interested in the young female spectators than in the sport. Then Tarzan, Robinson, and Eddie go to the Goumbé, Abidjan's dance club. Procession in the street accompanied by singing, drums, and trumpets. Then the start of the dance: a young novice champion, dressed cowboy style; bicycle dances (rodeo). When night falls, a dance contest: Eddie Constantine and Nathalie are the best dancers and are proclaimed "King and Queen of the Royal Goumbé." Robinson flirts with Dorothy Lamour, but an Italian sailor steals her away from him. Robinson, sad and solitary, gets drunk on beer. When he can no longer pay his tab, he is kicked out of the Mexico Saloon. He dreams that Dorothy Lamour is his wife and that they are happy in their house.

Conclusion: At dawn, Robinson gets up and decides to go see Dorothy Lamour. But the Italian sailor opens the door when he knocks. Fistfight. Robinson leaves. It is raining. He goes to find his friends at the entrance to the port. He learns that Eddie Constantine is in prison because he got into a fight with a policeman. He works in the rain and in the evening goes to the prison with Tarzan and "Little Jules." Eddie Constantine will be in for at least three months. The three friends go back down to the edge of the lagoon, which reminds them of their Niger homeland. Robinson becomes more and more bitter. Heading back to Treichville, on the banks of the lagoon, he recalls his military life and the war in Indochina, and philosophizing all the while, he crosses the new bridge, telling "Little Jules" that maybe the future will be better.

**1959**

*La pyramide humaine* (The Human Pyramid)

Produced by Films de la Pléiade. Cinematography by Louis Mialle. Sound by Michel Fano. Edited by Marie-Josèphe Yoyotte, Geneviève Bastide.

Cast: Nadine, Denise, Alain, Jean-Claude, Elola, Nathalie, Dominique, Landry. 90 minutes. Released in April 1961.

*Synopsis:* The problems of interracial relations in a school in Abidjan, Ivory Coast. Introduction: a young white woman and black man are walking along the Champs Elysées. This film is the story of their friendship.

Presentation of the place: Abidjan. The director gathers together a group of high school students, Africans and Europeans, boys and girls, and distributes roles: the racists and the nonracists. Nadine is the new European student in the Abidjan high school. Presentation of her friends, one of whom is Denise, a young African and leader of the black group in the class. Alain, a young European who has a scooter, seems the closest to her. The white group and the black group each lead separate lives. Alain takes Nadine to the swimming pool; he comes to see her with Jean-Claude, another European. She is astonished to hear that they never go out with the blacks. They decide to talk to their white friends about it. In the evening, next to the swimming pool, a general discussion among the core members of the white group. Two racists are violently opposed to any attempt at making friends with them, but the majority are favorable to the idea. Coming out of the next class, Jean-Claude tells his African friends about this decision. Meeting of the black group of the class. In spite of the reticence of the two black racists, Denise and her friends Elola, Raymond, and Baka are ready to try the experiment.

Beginning of the friendship between blacks and whites: Denise comes to see Nadine at home. Raymond and Jean-Claude play the guitar. The white group rapidly forms a little gang. They go to the stadium together and, through Denise as intermediary, learn to know the problems of racism. The Africans take the Europeans to a Goumbé (club for young Abidjan dancers), and for the first time, boys and girls, Africans and Europeans, dance in the streets, led by the "Goumbé Queen," Nathalie.

Their feelings: Some of the boys, black and white, fall in love with Nadine. Baka takes her out in a canoe; Alain takes her to visit his grounded ship (a cargo boat, half smashed by the bar). Jean-Claude takes her to the abandoned house, where he has hidden a piano. During a surprise party organized at Nadine's house, Jean-Claude and Alain have a fight. Raymond, a black, proposes a walk around town with Nadine. He tells her about his childhood. They both fall asleep at the foot of the tree. A division becomes evident in the group. Raymond insists to Denise that Nadine loves him and wants to supplant Baka. Alain, more simply, turns to the young black dancer Nathalie. Denise wants to avoid any dramas and one day, coming out of school, reproaches Nadine for her coquetry. Exams bring back calm.

The drama: Screening of the film for the young actors-improvisers. They decide to give a dramatic ending to the story. The group meets for a picnic on the wrecked boat. Order has apparently returned, but Alain, trying to show off, dares to swim around the shipwreck in a raging sea. He dives. He almost succeeds but then disappears into an enormous wave. Despair overcomes the group. Nadine cries for her departed young friend. The group gathers in Nadine's garden. An argument breaks out between the blacks and whites; the group splits up. The school year is finished. Nadine goes back to France. When she goes to say goodbye to Denise, Denise reproaches her sadly for her coquettish attitude. At the airport the group nonetheless comes to say good-bye to Nadine. She leaves in tears. Jean-Claude, the only white, stays beside the blacks. He makes up with his old friend Raymond, who gives him a ride home on his bicycle. We then see the principal actors, among them Alain, the "dead man," on the Champs Elysées in Paris. Thanks to this film, they have become friends and no longer have racial complexes.

▶ ────────────────────────────────────────────────

## 1960

*Chronique d'un été* (Chronicle of a Summer)

In collaboration with Edgar Morin. Produced by Argos Films/A. Dauman. Cinematography by Roger Morillère, Raoul Coutard, Jean-Jacques Tarbès, Michel Brault. Edited by Jean Ravel, Nina Baratier, Françoise Colin. Director of production: André Heinrich.

Cast: Marceline Loridan, Marilou Parolini, Angélo, Jean-Pierre; the workers, Jacques and Jean; the students, Régis, Céline, Jean-Marie, Nadine Ballot, Modeste Landry, and Raymond; the employees, Jacques and Simone; the artists, Henry, Madi, and Catherine; the cover girl, Sophie. Black and white. 90 minutes.

Festival prizes: Cannes, Venice, Mannheim, 1961.

*Synopsis:* A film experiment in Parisian sociology, or a sociological inquiry into Paris. Shot during the summer of 1960 with the prototype for the Coutant-Mathot KMT 16 mm camera, utilizing for the first time the Pilotone system to film synchronously with a Nagra neopilot perfectone magnetic recorder. This film, produced in collaboration with Edgar Morin, is an attempt at cinematographic investigation using an entirely new technique of synchronous sound (direct cinema) on young French people in the summer of 1960. This was the moment when it was thought that the war in Algeria was going to end. It was prolonged, and the incidents in the Congo added the problems of independence in the African states to the problems of the Maghreb states.

Over several months the film follows both the investigation itself and the evolution of the principal characters. These are Marceline (former deportee), doing socioeconomic research; her friend Jean-Pierre, a student of philosophy; Marilou, of Italian origin, a secretary at Cahiers du Cinéma; Angélo and his friend Jacques, workers at Renault; an SNCF employee; a discouraged former militant, and his wife; and Landry, a student from the Ivory Coast, coming from high school in Villeneuve-sur-Lot.

Around this group we discover other Parisians, unknown people met in the streets: Nadine, a high school friend of Landry, Raymond, a student from Ivory Coast at a commercial school, a happy artist-painter couple, a cover girl, a saleswoman in a fashion shop, the daughters of Edgar Morin, and the two authors of the film.

At the beginning, the question asked is "How do you live?" but other, more essential questions quickly appear: political despair, solitude, the battle against boredom. Vacation arrives, the factories empty, the beaches fill up. Algeria will be for some other year.

All of the protagonists attend the first screening of the film. They discuss, accept, or reject it. In the end, the two authors find themselves alone in the face of this cruel but fascinating experiment in *cinéma-vérité*.

*Hampi*
Produced by CNRS/CFE. 25 minutes.
Festival prize, Florence, 1962.
The display of a ritual vase at the Niamey Museum, Niger.

▶ ——————————————————————————————

## 1961

*Les ballets du Niger* (Ballets of Niger)
Black and white. 20 minutes.
A visit by the Nigerian ballet company to the Théâtre des Nations in Paris; an interview with Hamani Diori, the president of Niger, at intermission.

*Niger, jeune république* (Niger, Young Republic)
Produced by ONF, Quebec, Canada. Directed by Claude Jutra; Rouch acted as adviser. Assistants: Roger Morillière and Susanne Vianes. 58 minutes.
Made to commemorate the first anniversary of the independence of Niger. Versions in the Zarma and Hausa languages were made for distribution in Niger.

▶ ——————————————————————————————

## 1962

*La punition* (The Punishment)
Produced by Films de la Pléiade. Cinematography by Michel Brault, Roger Morillère, Georges Dufault. Sound by Roger Morillère. Editing by Annie Tresgot. Music by Johann Sebastian Bach.
Cast: Nadine Ballot (Nadine), Jean-Claude Darnal (a student), Jean-Marie Simon (an engineer), Modeste Landry (a black from Abidjan). Black and white. 58 minutes. Released in 1962 for broadcast on ORTF TV.
A Parisian examination of commedia dell'arte filmed with the techniques of direct cinema. The film follows the encounters of Nadine as she leaves her Parisian school.

*Abidjan, port de pêche* (Abidjan, Fishing Port)
Produced by CNRS/CFE. 25 minutes.
The relationship between industrial and traditional fishing in the Ivory Coast.

*Le cocotier* (The Coconut Palm)
Produced by CNRS/CFE. 21 minutes.

Agricultural research on coconut palms in the Ivory Coast at the experimental research station at Port Bouët.

*Fêtes de l'indépendance du Niger* (Celebrations of the Independence of Niger)
Produced by CNRS/CFE and IFAN, Niger. 27 minutes.
Independence celebrations in the Republic of Niger in 1961–1962.

*L'Afrique et la recherche scientifique* (Africa and Scientific Research)
Produced by CNRS for UNESCO. 32 minutes.
An overview of French scientific research in Africa in the fields of hydrology, botany, biology, and agriculture, including palm oil, coconut, and industrial fisheries.

▶

## 1963

*Le palmier à huile* (Palm Oil)
Produced by CNRS/CFE and IFAN. 23 minutes.
Agricultural research on the cultivation of palm oil in the Ivory Coast.

*Rose et Landry* (Rose and Landry)
Produced by ONF, Quebec, and the Canadian Film Board. Cinematography by Georges Dufault. Sound by Marcel Carrière. Edited by Jean-Jacques Godbout. Director of production: Fernand Dansereau.
Cast: Modeste Landry, Rose Bamba, George Neyra. Black and white.
28 minutes.
Two prizes at the Venice Festival, 1963.
Rose and Landry discuss the contrast between ancestral traditions and Western civilization.

*Le mil* (Millet)
Produced by CNRS/CFE. Assistants: Roger Rosfelder, Louis Civatte, and Moustapha Alassane. 28 minutes.
Traditional millet agriculture in Niger and problems in agronomic research.

*Monsieur Albert, prophète,* or *Albert Atcho* (Mr. Albert, Prophet, or Albert Atcho)
Produced by Argos Films and CNRS. Edited by Jean Ravel. 26 minutes.
Life in a community of Harrist followers of the prophet Alberto Atcho in the village of Bregbo in the Ivory Coast.

▶

## 1964

*Les veuves de quinze ans* (The Fifteen-Year-Old Widows)
A sketch for *The Adolescents* or *La fleur de l'age* (The Age of Awakening)
Alternative title: *Marie-France et Véronique* (Marie-France and Véronique)

Produced by Films de la Pléiade. Cinematography by Jacques Lang. Sound by Michel Fano. Edited by Claudine Bouché. 25 minutes.

A coproduction of France, Canada, Japan, and Italy.

One of four film sketches on the problems of adolescents facing the adult world in the 1960s. The three other sketches were directed by Michel Brault, Hiroshi Teshigahara, and Gian Vittorio Baldi.

▶ _____

**1965**

*La Goumbé des jeunes noceurs* (The Goumbé of the Young Revelers)

Produced by CNRS and Films de la Pléiade. 30 minutes.

*Synopsis:* La Goumbé is a voluntary association of young people from Upper Volta who work in Abidjan, Ivory Coast. The film shows the members of the association at their work, then at a reunion that ends on a dance floor in Treichville. The young people who come to work in Abidjan often form spontaneous associations for mutual help and entertainment, which are called "Goumbés" in Ivory Coast, after the name of a square drum that serves as the rhythmic base to their dance. During a general meeting, the secretary of the association reads the statutes, and it is these statutes that serve as both the backdrop and the commentary of the film.

Thus the professional activities of the principal members of the office are exposed: the president is the head of the valets at the Hotel Ivory, the vice president is a clerk for the express transport services, the high commissioner is a guard in the port, and so on.

Next, the association is composed of musicians and dancers. The tambourine player is a tailor, the singer-composer is a button sewer in a clothing-manufacturing business, and the leading lady, Nathalie, is a mother and homemaker. A section of young soccer players, "the alliance," is associated with the Goumbé and plays every Sunday morning. Every week the dancers practice to invent new dance steps. Once a month, the musicians must compose new songs for the Goumbé. Also every month, a parade of the Goumbé takes place in the streets of Treichville.

Twice a week, the members meet to pay their dues and eventually to decide the allocation of the funds, be it for the purchase of new instruments, or to come to the aid of a member in need.

The grand reunion takes place on Saturday evenings and Sunday afternoons in a street of Treichville. Chairs and benches block off the street; an electronic sound system permits the singer Sibiki to make himself heard and to present successive dancers. All the members of the association are dressed the same way: white shirt and black pants, and the dances begin. In the beginning the dancers follow the rhythm of the drums, and then, when they are inspired, they become the leaders of the orchestra, which follows their dance step.

*Gare du nord* (North Train Station)

Produced by Les Films de Losange. Cinematography by Étienne Becker. Edited by Jacqueline Raynal.

Cast: Nadine Ballot (Odile), Barbet Schroeder (Jean-Pierre), Gilles Qucant (the desperate one). 20 minutes.

This film was shot in real time: a young woman argues with her husband about the sadness in their lives and decides to leave him. In the street, she encounters a stranger who invites her to run away with him, but she refuses. He commits suicide. One of six sketches for the film *Paris vu par . . . ;* the other sketches are directed by Jean-Daniel Pollet, Jean Douchet, Jean-Luc Godard, Eric Rohmer, and Claude Charbrol.

*Batteries Dogon, éléments pour une étude des rythmes,* or *Tambours de pierre* (Dogon Drums, Elements of a Study in Rhythm, or Stone Drums)

Produced by CNRS/CFE. Codirector: Gilbert Rouget. With Germaine Dieterlen. 26 minutes.

The young goat herders from the cliff of Bandiagara practice on the stone drums of their ancestors. An ethnomusicological film experiment describing the subtle plays of the right and left hand of Dogon drummers.

*Sigui 66: Année zéro* (Sigui 66: Year Zero)

With Germaine Dieterlen. 15 minutes. Double System sound.

*Synopsis:* The head Hogon of Arou, religious chief of all the Dogon of the Bandiagara Cliffs, Mali, announces the beginning of the Sigui ceremonies for the next year. At the village of Yougo, where the ceremonies will begin, the old ones discuss the forewarning signs and the messages that they will send to the young people on the plain and to those who work in Ghana and the Ivory Coast. Thus we begin a series of eight documents (1966–1973) that concentrate on the sixty-year-cycle Sigui ceremonies among the Dogon. The film summarizes the myth that gave birth to the Sigui: the little natural children of the Pale Fox, God's first creation, who then revolted against him, live in the caves and grottoes. When God sends down the anvil of the first blacksmith and the science of agriculture, the anvil falls to earth, hollowing out an enormous lake, and then bounces back to wedge itself in the Mandingo mountains, where it now stands in the form of a stone needle. One of the little dwarfs from the grotto on which the anvil fell dies shortly thereafter. This calls for the first Sigui, the ritual for the first dead man during which the sacred language, *sigi so,* is spoken for the first time. The Dogon, having come from the Mandingo mountains to the Bandiagara cliff in the fifteenth century, have "transported" their ritual landscape with them. At Yougo Dogorou, a needle of stone is called "the anvil," and in the caves located beneath, little effigies represent the dwarfs and the first Sigui.

Similar to those at Songo, the paintings under the great cliff overhangs represent the Pale Fox and his children. Near Sangha, in the shelter of a rock overhang, an ancient construction near the "sleeping millstones" has a triangular opening: it is here that the Dogon watch the rising of Sirius and his "companion." When the time comes, that is, every sixty years, they commemorate what happened here, with the ancestor teaching men the ritual language of the Sigui: *sigi so.*

In 1966 the Hogon of Arou, chief religious figure of the Dogon, who does not have the right to leave his sanctuary, confirms to us that the Sigui will indeed take place the following year: they have already brought him the millet beer.

Now the Sigui can begin its seven-year circumnavigation, which we follow with aerial views: the anvil of Yougo, the sacred village of Tyogou, the cave of Bongo, the village of Amani at the foot of the perpendicular cliff, the spring of Idyeli and its nearby dune, the plateau village of Yame, and finally the circumcision huts at Songo. There, facing the wind that brought the Sigui on its wings, a painting represents the entire Sigui cycle. It will be recommemorated in sixty years, in 2027.

▶ ─────────────────────────────────────────────

**1967**

*Daouda Sorko*
    Produced by CNRS/CFE. 15 minutes.
    Daouda Sorko, fisherman from the village of Simiri, Niger, is a high priest of the cult of Dongo, the thunder spirit. Daouda recounts the myth to Damouré Zika of the origin of the seven *Torou* spirits, the principal deities of Songhay mythology, and in particular the way in which Dongo has become the most feared divinity, the master of the sky, responsible for thunder and rain.

*Faran Maka fonda* (Faran Maka's Path)
    Produced by CNRS/CFE. 90 minutes.
    Damouré Zika joins Daouda Sorko on the initiation path of the Sorko fisherman from the Niger River.

*Sigui no. 1: L'enclume de Yougo* (The Anvil of Yougo)
    Produced by CNRS/CFE. Codirectors: Gilbert Rouget and Germaine Dieterlen. 38 minutes.
    *Synopsis:* The first year of the sixty-year-cycle ceremony of Sigui among the Dogon of the Bandiagara cliffs. After having prepared the beer, the costumes, and ornaments, the men shave and put on the ritual costumes of Sigui and enter the public square dancing. Afterward they will "carry the Sigui" to the other villages. The film is a journal of the discovery of the Sigui by Germaine Dieterlen, Gilbert Rouget, and me. We only know about this ceremony through the investigations of Marcel Griaule, carried out between 1921 and 1936, that is, twenty years after the celebration of the Sigui at the beginning of the century. One year before the Sigui, we went to see the village of Yougo Dogorou: the village was completely empty. The men had gone to work in Ivory Coast; only the women and children were there. Under a *toguna,* a men's shelter, the old men welcome us, receive the message from the Hogon of Arou, and give us authorization to come back the following year.
    In January 1967, when we return, the village is overcrowded. The men and boys

are shaved; the young girls and young women have taken their jewels to the black-smith, who has set up his forge in a grotto so that he can remake the jewelry to fit the men who are supposed to wear it. On the little public square, the drum begins to sound; the three calls of the drum summon the dancers. They are wearing black trousers and high white headpieces; they hold in one hand the *dono* (a cup-shaped staff-seat), in the other hand a flyswatter and a gourd for drinking the millet beer. Some of them carry the Sigui "satchels" that we saw painted on the cliff overhangs at Songo. They enter into the square by strict order of age. Those who participated in the 1907 Sigui are at the head—the old men we had seen a year earlier dance just like all the rest—and then, behind them, the entire generation of old men, young men, boys, and little tots. The procession performs the dance of the serpent. The front of the procession turns back on itself until the entire square is filled. From time to time an old man shouts the words of the Sigui in the secret language, *sigi so*. Then the men raise their staffs and cry out the call of the fox. Along the narrow little streets of the village, they go to visit the terraces of the old *olubaru*. The new *olubaru* are there, wearing cross-chestbands made of cowrie shells. Their hair is adorned with pearls, and their cane seats are decorated with carving. Behind them, a woman wearing a cloth over her head holds the gourd of the *Yasigine:* she represents the twin sister of the fox, the sister of the *Sigui.* They will dance all day long. The next day the dances start up again in the afternoon, following the same scenario.

They have to pass under a wall of thorns that the old men hold above them. It's a veritable rite of passage. The third day, in the morning, the dancers gather again on the public square, then they leave along the steep roads of the cliff, in a procession to carry the Sigui to the next village, Yougo Na.

The Sigui has begun. It will not return to this place until seven years later.

*Yenendi de Boukoki* (Rain Dance at Boukoki)
    Produced by CNRS/CFE. 25 minutes.
    Rituals of rainmaking in the seventh month of the dry season at Boukoki, Niger.

▶ ───────────────────────────────────────────

## 1968

*Yenendi de Ganghel* (Rain Dance at Ganghel)
    Produced by CNRS/CFE. 35 minutes.
    In August, lightning struck a small fishing village near Niamey. The Zima priests and Sorko fisherman then organized a Yenendi, a ceremony of purification.

*Sigui (68) no. 2: Les danseurs de Tyogou* (The Dancers of Tyogou)
    Produced by CNRS/CFE. With Germaine Dieterlen. 26 minutes.
    *Synopsis:* The second year of the sixty-year cycle of Sigui ceremonies among the Dogon of the Bandiagara cliffs. At Tyogou, a mountainside village, the men prepare the hats and costumes of the Sigui. Then they go in procession toward the sites of the ancient villages to dance again at the village square and drink millet beer. The following day, they decorate the cave of the masks, where the new large mask will be placed at the conclusion of the ceremony. Tyogou faces the spike of the Yougo,

which dominates the gardens surrounding a semipermanent lake. For several days the visitors bring bundles of wood to Tyogou, for the preparation of millet beer. Beneath the *toguna,* the men's shelter, which overlooks the gardens, the final preparations are being made: the men and youths embroider the Sigui headpieces, they finish carving the cane-seats and paint them red (with sorrel dye or with *koranic* ink), and then they are shaved. Here all the men will wear chestbands with cowrie shells, which they have just finished decorating. In the afternoon, after three calls of the drum, all the men gather near this *toguna.* They go single file, preceded by the old men and the musicians, to scale the cliff that faces the village, to the site of the original village of Tyogou. There, on the site of the ancient village, they sing the songs of the Sigui. Then, by strict order of age, they enter the square, doing the dance of the serpent. On the square there are large vessels filled with millet beer. When the square is full, when the men have punctuated the cries of *sigi so* with the cry of the fox, they sit down on their cane-seats and drink beer. After this ceremonial drinking bout, the men dance in pairs, face-to-face. The old men separate rivals so as to avoid introducing an element of competition into this ritual. The dance is the essential element of this year's ritual.

The next morning, we visit the cave of the masks. We have not seen a mask in Yougo. Here the mask is in front of the cavern: it is carved in the form of the great serpent whose tail is adorned with a bird's head. It is sitting on the ground: it is unpainted. In the cave we see the three previous masks: the one from 1908, the one for 1848, and the one for 1788. The chief of the masks explains the origin of these masks to Amadigné.

In the afternoon, there is a gathering near the *toguna* of Upper Tyogou, with the *olubaru* coming behind the first old men. Then, after crossing the village, the procession penetrates into the square, where, for one last time, the dances of the serpent, the face-to-face dances, and the collective dances take place.

On the third day, the Sigui will leave for the village of Koundou.

*Un lion nommé "l'Américain"* (A Lion Named "the American")
Produced by CNRS/CFE. 20 minutes.
In the course of projecting *The Lion Hunters,* a film made about them, the bow lion hunters decide to clear the shame of the lion called "the American," who escaped them in 1965. They relocate his trail (he has a characteristic wound of the paw, caused by a trap). But he is more cunning than the hunters, and it is his female that is killed. The hunters and the director eat the meat of the lion. The radio announces the student revolution of May 1968; the director abandons the chase to return to Paris. Several weeks later, the lion is shamefully killed with a rifle.

▶────────────────────────────────────────

## 1968–1969

*Petit à Petit* (Little by Little)
Produced by Films de la Pléiade in collaboration with CNRS and CFE. Scenario improvised by the actors during the filming. Jean Rouch was assisted in direction

and cinematography by Philippe Luzuy. Sound by Moussa Amidou. Edited by Josée Matarosso, Dominique Villain.

Cast: Damouré Zika, Lam Ibrahima Dia, Illo Gaoudel, Safi Faye, Ariane Brunneton, Mustafa Alassane, Marie Idrissa, Alborah Maiga, Jacques Chaboud, Michel Delahaye, Sylvie Pierre, Patricia Finally, Zomo and his brothers, Philippe Luzuy, Tallou Mouzourane. Photographs by Daphné. 90 minutes in 16 mm and 35 mm blowup. Another version of 250 minutes also exists in 16 mm.

*Synopsis:* A fable produced as a sequel of *Jaguar,* which relates the curious and singular adventures of Damouré and Lam, two businessmen of contemporary Africa, in search of their role model. In the village of Ayorou on the banks of the Niger, Damouré, a jovial and malicious man, runs an import-export business called "Petit à Petit." His town partners are Lam, an ex-herdsman with a taciturn nature who cruises the bush in a Land Rover to keep watch on his flocks, and Illo, the fisherman. Having learned that they are going to build a seven-story building in Niamey, the capital of Niger, Damouré calls a meeting of his associates. They decide that they have to go one better: they'll build an even higher building. Damouré flies to Paris to find out how people live in multistory buildings. Perplexed, skeptical, and amused in turn, he discovers the curious ways of living, being, and thinking of the Parisian tribe. He regularly sends "Parisian postcards" to his associates in Niger, until the day when they receive a postcard that states that the Parisians eat only unslaughtered chickens—an unthinkable act in Moslem lands—and they suspect that Damouré has gone crazy and send Lam on a mission to bring him home. After having studied multistory houses of France, Italy, and the United States, Lam, too, falls into the trap of the capital. Faced with the difficulty of getting around in Paris, and since Lam is afraid of the metro, they decide to buy "a car that does not exist, but that is reminiscent of the Land Rover"—a Bugatti convertible.

In this contraption, on the Champs Elysées, they seduce Safi, a Senegalese cover girl and courtesan ("I sell it, my ass!" says she), who introduces them to Ariane, a dancer in a nightclub. On a boat ride on the Seine, Lam hires Philippe, a "bum" who is full of energy. The team is complete for returning to Niger.

In Ayorou the building slowly rises. Safi runs a seamstress shop. Ariane is a typist for Petit à Petit. Philippe, the bum, is a herdsman-cowboy, jack-of-all-trades. Damouré is religiously married to Ariane and Safi, who become wives number seven and eight, his favorites.

But soon enough, after the marvel of discovery, and weighed down by heat and boredom, Ariane notices that Marie, the Nigerian typist who earns one-fifth of what she earns, is incurably jealous. Safi is disappointed by her clients, who don't like the new fashions, "à la Sénégalese." Philippe, the bum, who thought he'd find real freedom on the banks of the Niger River, never worked so much in his life and detests the local food.

All three of them leave the country, thus awakening the consciousness of its directors. Damouré and Lam abandon the company and suggest to Illo that they create the "old asses" company.

Rediscovering horse, slingshot, and canoe, Damouré, Lam, and Illo retire to a straw hut on the edge of the river to think about what the "modern, new civilization" should be: a civilization that could not be inspired by the grotesque model they discovered in Paris.

*Sigui (69) no. 3: La caverne de Bongo* (Bongo Cave)

Produced by CNRS/CFE. With Germaine Dieterlen. 38 minutes.

*Synopsis:* The third year of the sixty-year Sigui cycle among the Dogon of the Bandiagara cliffs. The *olubaru* complete their retreat in the cave of Bongo. Around old Anaï, oldest member of the ceremony, who attends his third Sigui, the men shave and divide the salt and the sesame. They adorn the altar that will be the center of the ceremony in red and white. Then, outfitted in cowrie shell cross-chestbands, they make a tour of the fields before drinking the communal beer. Bongo is a plateau village above the plain of Gondo and the mountainside village of Banani. The Sigui has already arrived in Banani; five days later it will be in Bongo. The man responsible for the Sigui is the oldest man in Bongo, Anaï Dolo, who, we learn with surprise, is going to "see" his third Sigui. In 1849 he was in his mother's belly and was born a couple of months after the Sigui of 1849. In 1909 the old men placed him among those who had already seen the Sigui, since he was born just after the Sigui of 1849 and was able to drink the millet beer that had been kept for newborns. In 1969 he is thus 120 years old; he is almost blind, half-deaf, and he stays just in front of his house where the men are preparing their cane-seats, shaving, and sewing their Sigui costumes.

In a cavern on the other side of the little valley that goes toward Dyamini, the *olubaru* are on a retreat. They have been there for several weeks: someone from the village brings them food and millet beer. Since morning they have been aided by the *kabaga,* their assistants who carve the bullroarers (strips of wood that hum when spun, whose voice is said to be the "word" of the ancestors). Facing them, in the middle of the field, the old men prepare a mound that represents the altar of Dionou Serou, man's first ancestor, who died and returned to life in the form of a serpent. It is a simple mound of earth, rough-cast in clay and decorated with red and white tiles that represent the scales of the mythical serpent. It is topped with a piece of wood bearing seven notches, and this is crowned with a tuft of red fibers, which also represents the serpent being reborn.

In the evening the big new mask, which has now been painted, is placed in the cave of the circumcision. At sunset, the *olubaru* make the bullroarers roar and at night, the old men from the four villages that make up the agglomeration of Bongo carry in the four great masks, which they put down before the entrance of the cavern. The next day, when the sun rises, all the men in the village can see these great black, red, and white masks, symbols of the dead serpent; and the red and white masks, symbol of the serpent restored to life.

The men abandon their old clothes and don their Sigui costumes: black trousers gathered at the ankles, cowrie shell bands, earrings, rings, and necklaces from their wives or sisters. In their right hands they hold a flyswatter, in the left a gourd with which they drink the Sigui beer, and a cane-seat. When the men are dressed, they walk all around the field, then sit for a moment on their cane-seats, then get up again: they come to line up just in front of the cave, forming four lines, which represent the four generations to come from the men of the four villages of Bongo. The millet beer is distributed, starting with the oldest—it is the ritual communion of all the men in the village. The men of the four villages march all around the field of lineage, in strict order of age, singing the songs of the Sigui, encouraged by the shouters among the old men, who speak in *sigi so.* They dance until evening, under the enchanted eyes of the old men who danced the same dances here sixty years ago. At sunset, the old men and the *olubaru* go back toward the cave. The drums have gathered around the altar of the dead ancestor in the middle of the field of lineage, and big brothers and parents take the youngest boys in their arms to give them a walk around the altar: thus they too will have danced the Sigui. In a nearby cave, they burn the clothes that the men wore before donning their Sigui clothes—the sixty-year clothes.

Three days later, the Sigui that came from Banai will leave for Sangha.

*Porto Novo: La danse des reines* (Porto Novo: The Dance of the Queens)
    Produced by CNRS/CFE. With Gilbert Rouget. 31 minutes.
    Ritual dancing of the queens at the royal palace in Porto Novo, Dahomey. The technique of synchronous slow-motion filming permits a detailed analysis of the relationship between the dance and the music.

▶ ———————————————————————————————

## 1970

*Sigui (70) no. 4: Les clameurs d'Amani* (The Clamor of Amani)
    Produced by CNRS/CFE. With Germaine Dieterlen. 36 minutes.
    *Synopsis:* Fourth year of the sixty-year-cycle Sigui ceremony among the Dogon of the Bandiagara cliffs. Questioned by the chief of Bongo, the Pale Fox gives the route of the Sigui to Amani. Preceded by the elders and their drums, the men of Sigui begin their sinuous itinerary across the village before entering the ritual place. In March 1969, the Dogon of Bongo ask us to go through a divination before continuing. We consult the Pale Fox, who at night prints with his paws the news of the following day: "Yes, we may go on to Amani, but we will have great difficulty."
    Amani is thirty kilometers from Bongo, in the plain, and it turns out that we have to retrace our route, from which all the bridges have been removed. In Amani, everything is ready when we arrive: the men and little boys are shaved, and the old men are trying to find the route of the Sigui though the village, the route that the Sigui followed sixty years earlier. Since then, men have built houses, and they have to tear down walls so that the Sigui can take the same path. One old man confides in Amadigné that unlike what we have seen in the other villages, in Amani there are no cowrie shell chestbands, except for the *olubaru.* All the men simply wear women's loincloths, crossed over their chests, black cotton trousers, women's jewelry, and women's scarves holding down their high white headdresses.
    The Sigui arrives, following a complicated itinerary that winds around the place where the first men who lived on the cliff would have come out. Then it goes up on the upper public square. The mask that was prepared the year before is there. The paint is already peeling; it is placed near the *toguna,* in a place forbidden to everyone who is not participating in the Sigui. At the foot of the *toguna,* an old man exchanges long rejoinders with another old man, in the ritual tongue, *sigi so,* and begins to tell the myth of the creation of the world.

On the next day, all the men gather on the public square at the eastern end of the village. In procession, they visit all the houses of the dead (former dignitaries) and climb up on the terraces and dance. Then, toward the end of the morning, they come back to the upper public square to sing the songs of the Sigui and to hear the "criers" in the ritual language of *sigi so.*

In the afternoon, once the village is in the shadow of the cliff, everyone gathers on the other public square. One of the oldest men makes all the men sit on their cane-seats and tells them the story of the creation of the world in *sigi so.* From time to time the men punctuate his speech with long fox cries. These criers are essential because they represent the creation of the world and the rebirth of the newly dead. Next, still led by the same old man, the men dance and sing (in everyday language) the songs of the Sigui. The next day, in long lines, the men of Amani go to "carry" the Sigui to another village at the foot of the cliff. The mask that was painted last year is leaning against a rock. On top of the mask is a chicken that has been sacrificed.

The old men climb up a rock facing the village and begin an interminable dialogue in *sigi so* with the old men of the other village, who will transmit the word.

*Yenendi de Yantala* (Rain Dance at Yantala)
Produced by CNRS/CFE. 68 minutes.
In May 1969 at Yantala, a district of Niamey, the priests call upon Dongo and his brothers to ask them to make more rain and less thunder than in preceding years. The spirits are reticent about appearing (several possessions fail) and reserved in their response. The year will be a bad one.

*Yenendi de Simiri* (Rain Dance at Simiri)
Produced by CNRS/CFE. 30 minutes.
After three years of drought, the peasants of the Simiri region, Niger, interrogate the deities of the sky responsible for the causes of their misfortune. The deities respond evasively and accuse them of abandoning their old customs.

▶————————————————————————————————————————

## 1971

*Architectes Ayorou* (The Architects of Ayorou)
Produced by CNRS/CFE. 30 minutes.
For several years, the young people of these villages have constructed a new habitat on the island, appealing to mutual aid; they utilize ancient techniques of "banco" masonry and waterproof coatings, while they are inspired by the architecture of the modern cities.

*Sigui (71) no. 5: La dune d'Idyeli* (The Dune of Idyeli)
Produced by CNRS/CFE. With Germaine Dieterlen. 54 minutes.
*Synopsis:* The fifth year of the sixty-year cycle of Sigui ceremonies among the Dogon of the Bandiagara cliffs. The night before the festival, all the men climb on a dune facing the cliff. They bury themselves in all kinds of burrows, and without drinking or eating, they stay there until the beginning of the afternoon of the next

day. Then they descend and purify themselves at the village spring, put on women's clothes, and, doing the serpent's dance, enter the village square, where large jars of communal beer await them. The third day they carry the Sigui to the plateau villages. Idyeli is located near a permanent spring at the base of the cliff and at the foot of the dune that borders the plain of Gondo. The men devote themselves to the same preparations of costumes and staffs as in the other village. In the evening all the men leave the village, and the bullroarers sound. The next morning the village is empty. They are all on top of the dune facing the village. When we climb up there we see nothing. They are all buried in the burrows they have dug for themselves. They are like infants in the placenta of their mother. They will stay there for almost fifteen hours without drinking or eating.

Around four in the afternoon, when the sun begins to go down, an old man comes from the village. The *olubaru* take up their bullroarers and, in broad daylight, spin them around. The bullroarers have three voices, and the language of the bullroarers tells the men to come out of their holes: this is birth.

In a long single file, by strict order of age and accompanied by the bullroarers up to the entrance, the Sigui procession goes toward the permanent spring. There the newborns wash themselves. After washing, their wives help them to redon their women's clothes. They put on makeup, wear bracelets and necklaces, and by strict order of age, they enter into the public square doing the dance of the serpent and, in the evening, drink the communal beer.

The next morning, the young children begin to play the drum. The young girls and the women bring out big jugs of millet beer to refill the ones that will be used this day. Around four o'clock, when the village is in the shadow of the cliff, the procession enters the village, dances, and drinks the beer. The next afternoon, the Sigui will leave Idyeli and go back up to the plateau for good, without returning to the villages of the plain.

*Tourou et Bitti: Les tambours d'avant* (Tourou and Bitti: The Drums of the Past)
    Produced by CNRS/CFE. Assisted by Lam Ibrahima Dia and Tallou Mouzourane. Sound by Moussa Amidou. 12 minutes.
    *Synopsis:* The drums of the past. This shooting script was planned to show the most important moment of a possession ritual, during the course of which men from the village of Simiri demand that the spirits of the wilderness protect the coming harvests from locusts. The orchestra is composed of archaic drums, *tourou* and *bitti,* which are played on that occasion.
    On March 15, 1971, the fisherman Sorko Daouda asked me to come to Simiri, in the Zermaganda, to film a possession dance in which the black spirits of the bush were to be asked to protect the future crops against locusts.
    Despite the efforts of the priest, Zima Sido, the father of Daouda, and despite the use of the ancient drums *tourou* and *bitti,* there was no possession in the first three days.
    At the end of the fourth day, nothing had happened, and the director decided to film a few scenes of this beautiful music, which is threatened with extinction.
    We see the outside of the priest Zima's terrain, then the sacrificial goat; then we penetrate into the dance arena where old Sambou is dancing without great conviction. The camera follows him and approaches the orchestra. Suddenly the

drums stop beating. But the director continues filming. The lute resumes its solo; its player has "seen the spirit." Immediately Sambou enters into trance. He is possessed by the spirit Kure ("the butcher," "the hyena"). Then it is old Tusinyé Wasi's turn. She is possessed by the spirit Hadyo. Next we see the priests consulting the spirits, and the demand for a sacrifice. The film ends with a general view of the terrain, already invaded by darkness.

Upon seeing this film again, it seemed that the filming itself unleashed and accelerated the possession. And I would not be surprised to learn from the priests of Simiri, when I next show them this film, that it was my ciné-trance that played the role of the essential catalyst that evening.

▶────────────────────────────────────

**1972**

*Funérailles à Bongo: Le vieil Anaï, 1848–1971* (Funeral at Bongo: Old Anaï, 1848–1971)

Produced by SERDDAV–CNRS/CFE. Codirector: Germaine Dieterlen. 70 minutes.

*Synopsis:* The oldest member of the village of Bongo, Mali, who died at the age of 122, was the head of the mask society. The men arrive from the neighboring village to devote their attention to sham fights with flintlock rifles, lances, and bows. The large Bongo mask, prepared during the 1969 Sigui, was set up in front of the cave of the masks. After having recited the ritual mottoes of old Anaï, the men and women from Bongo dance and weep. When the Sigui took place in Bongo in 1969, the oldest man who presided at the ceremony, Anaï Dolo, was attending his third Sigui: he was 120 years old. A year later we went to see him at the entrance of his house. He was sitting on planks of acacia wood. He never went out of this yard; he always stayed in the same temperature. He had rediscovered the placenta, the belly of his mother. Everyone who went into the house greeted him and told him what they had come for.

The introduction of the film is a sequence filmed in 1970. Anaï Dolo died the following year.

Upon our return in 1972, one of the great trees in the field had fallen because when an old man dies, a great tree falls all by itself. His grandson counts the knots on a rope calendar that mark five-day weeks. Six lunar months have passed since his death. The funeral may begin. Anaï's house is decorated with cloth hangings, the large cloths in which the cadavers of the lineage chiefs are wrapped when they are taken to the funerary cave. Two flags of Mali and one French flag float above the terrace. In the middle is a statue that represents Anaï Dolo dressed in his festive clothes. He himself will preside over the funeral. The Mali and French flags recall that Anaï Dolo was wounded during the conquest of 1895. In the morning, his sons and nephews recount what happened in the war against the French, how Anaï Dolo was wounded by the French on the bank of the river Gona. The grandson of Anaï repairs the old flintlock that Anaï used during the war. On the first day, in the field just at the foot of the terrace where the effigy of Anaï Dolo stands, the men of Bongo and hunters and warriors from other villages will reenact the old war: with flintlocks and gunpowder that they made themselves, they act out the attacks. The family of Anaï Dolo represents the Dogon. His grandson shoots off the rifle and falls to the ground: Anaï is wounded. A nephew, armed with a dagger and gun and wearing a jacket adorned with magic charms against war weapons, dances. All around him the other Dogon represent the French army. After several volleys of shots, the Dogon are defeated. The men in the center cover themselves with dust, and everyone, men and women, gathers around them to sing the songs of courage, courage of the conquerors and courage of the conquered. Then everyone regroups on the village square, before the statue of Anaï Dolo.

During the days that follow, they will wash out the impurity of death. The women in the family are shaved; the statue of Anaï is brought down from his terrace. The great Sigui mask, which has been brought out in front of the cave of the masks, is taken back inside. The *pey* cloths are taken down from the terraces. The funeral gifts brought by relatives and friends from other villages are divided up: cotton, millet grain, tamarind fruit. The storehouses are filled, and what is left is shared. Then the women go to wash all the covers: "to wash the impurity of death."

In the evening the old men gather on the public square and recite, in the darkness, the *tegué*: the mottoes of the ancestors. They tell of the creation of the world, the animals of the bush, the histories of the villages, the history of the Dogon, the list of the principal altars of the Dogon, and they tell of the working life of Anaï Dolo.

Then they must ask the Pale Fox, on the divination tables, whether the time has come for the dances in the public square: When may they return to work in the bush? Will the next market be favorable? When can the men dance and drink on the public square?

The next day, the seers, who are Anaï's grandsons, receive favorable responses to all of the questions that were asked. The following day, gunshots resound in the streets of the village, and the men gather and begin a long combat with rifle shots against death. The horn blowers call them to the western gate. The next day, on the terrace of the hunters' altar, another statue has been taken down. This statue represents the first ancestor, Dyongou Sérou, wrapped in *pey* cloth and lying on a bier made of horns, recalling the bier of antelope horns that was used in the burial of the first dead man. The women weep for this ancestor from the beginning of the world, and the men shoot off their guns in his honor. On the public square, a cow has been sacrificed to recall the price that God demanded of men when he tricked them and introduced death into their world. The statue of Dyongou Serou, carried on its bier, enters the public square and dances the dance of death. The men and women dance the dances of burial. The young men, armed with rifles, go up in the western mountains and fire off gunshots to chase death away. They leap around the cow and fire hails of shots. When the shot is good, the women applaud them, crying out "you-you," and when it does not go off, the women make fun of them. One of the old men, a grandson of Anaï, takes up a bow and shoots at a target. In doing this, he is shooting the sun, shooting the fox, shooting to make life be reborn. After one last volley of shots, the warriors go to visit every part of the village and then gather one last time to sing a song of courage. The next morning, the great-grandson of Anaï Dolo climbs up on the cliff; he is the one who will be the *nani*, Anaï Dolo's correspondent. He is the one who will be entrusted with the rituals that must accompany his dead grandfather up to the moment when he reaches the home of the dead, in the land of Banga.

*Sigui (72) no. 6: Les pagnes de Yamé* (The Loincloths of Yamé)
    Produced by CNRS/CFE. With Germaine Dieterlen. 50 minutes.
    *Synopsis:* The sixth year of the sixty-year Sigui cycle among the Dogon of the Bandiagara cliffs. Presentation of the village; preparation of wooden cross-seats. In the bush, the men put on their clothes, then enter the village to drink millet beer. The dignitaries symbolically carry the Sigui toward the west, where it will remain for the following year. Yamé is a typical plateau village because of its three *toguna* (men's huts). Near the *toguna* of the rising sun, in a straw hut, the dignitaries end their retreat. This hut will be burned during the night. Near the *toguna* of the setting sun, all the men gather at the eastern entrance to the village: they undress, shave themselves, and dress in their wives' clothing. Often their trousers are covered by women's skirts; they wear jewelry; they are "mothers," and it is the year of mothering. Only the *olubaru* wear cowrie-adorned chestbands and carry highly decorated seat-staves. An old man accompanied by drums goes to look for the procession, which stops at the entrance to the village, and the oldest man tells the myth in *sigi so*. The men are turned toward the east, the priest makes them turn to the west, and then they turn back to the east. This means that the Sigui has arrived at its limit. It should continue to the west, but the entire zone that would now be entered is Islamized. It is thus the real end of the Sigui. The procession is organized in strict order by age, and the men file into the village, up to the *toguna* of the setting sun. They dance, sit on their cane-seats, and drink the beer. The old men thank those who have given their participation in support of the Sigui. Before leaving, the men go to place their cane-seats on the wooden roof of the men's hut. The next day, in the afternoon, the drum calls the men. They arrive slowly and dance in front of the *toguna* of the west. They sit not on their cane-seats but directly on the ground. They drink millet beer in their gourds and prepare to leave. They go in small groups, to "carry" the Sigui to a few villages where all the inhabitants are not Islamized.

*Horendi*
    Produced by CNRS/CFE. 72 minutes.
    An analytic essay about the relationship between dance and music at the center of a possession ceremony (certain sequences are made in synchronous slow-motion sound). Two women possessed by Kirey, a lightning divinity, are present during the seven days of initiation.

▶ ────────────────────────────────────────────

## 1973

*L'enterrement du Hogon* (The Burial of Hogon)
    Produced by CNRS/CFE. 18 minutes.
    The Hogon of Sanga, Mali, masterful high priest of the community of Ogal, who died during the night, is ritually interred. The front of his house is decorated with the coverings of the dead, and all of the men of the village conduct a sham fight.

The totemic priests, shrouded in burial coverings, make a tour of the village altar; then, after having sprinkled the cadaver with millet grains, it is given to the grave-digger, who carries it in a dancing procession toward the village graveyard.

*Le foot-girafe* (The Foot Giraffe)
    Produced by SCOA. 20 minutes.
    An advertising film for the Peugeot 403 featuring a football match between a giraffe and the car.

*Rhythme de travail* (Work Rhythms)
    Produced by CNRS/CFE. 12 minutes.
    Extracts from three films: some young women pound millet while improvising a song (from *Architects of Ayourou*); Simiri, during the rainy season, a farmer weeds his field while singing; at the end of a possession ritual, an expert dances for his own pleasure (from *Yenendi de Yantala*).

*Tanda singui* (To Fix the Shed)
    Produced by CNRS/CFE. 90 minutes.
    The inhabitants of the lower section of Yantala open a new sanctuary dedicated to Dongo, the thunder spirit. It is the prisoner of Dongo, Zatao, who plants the ritual posts for the new shed and gives the men advice for the new rainy season.

*VW Voyou*
    Produced by SCOA. 25 minutes.
    A SCOA advertising film with Damouré Zika and Lam Ibrahima Dia. The adventures of a VW that is a phantom, able to go everywhere and anywhere at once.

▶━━━━━━━━━━━━━━━━━━━━━━━━━━━━━━━━━━

## 1974

*Le Dama d'Ambara* (The *Dama* for Ambara)
    Produced by SERDDAV–CNRS/CFE. Codirector: Germaine Dieterlen.
60 minutes.
    *Synopsis:* In 1972 Ambara Dolo died. He had been a collaborator in the missions of Marcel Griaule and Germaine Dieterlen since 1931. Two years later his *Dama* took place. *Dama* is the festival that takes place every five years to celebrate the end of mourning for those who have died during that period. The film follows the three main days of this ceremony. The commentary carefully follows the text of Griaule's thesis. In the course of the festival, the men of the society of the masks abandon the five-year-old masks and make new ones.
    The new masks of upper Ogol come out of the bush, file into the village, and enter the hut of the masks. On the second day, the masks of lower Ogol come out in turn. They are joined by the masks of upper Ogol, and one after the other, they leap across a rocky chasm. The oldest men carry the cane seats on which the dead men sat to drink the communal beer for the Sigui in 1909 and 1969.
    On the third day, the masks go up to the terrace of the dead and dance there, to

charm the wandering souls. The masks lead the souls into the public square, where they dance out the myth and the creation of the world.

In the evening, the masks go back into the huts, where they rest near the paintings that represent them. The "charmed" souls leave the village for the home of the dead.

*Cocorico, Monsieur Poulet* (Cockadoodledoo, Mister Chicken)

A Franco-Niger Film, realized with the technical assistance of CNRS/IRSH, Niamey; CNRS/CFE; Musée de l'Homme, Paris; and SCC, Paris. A DALAROU Production (Damouré, Lam, Rouch). Cinematography by Jean Rouch. Sound by Moussa Amidou, Hama Soumana. Editing by Christine Lefort. Music by Tallou Mouzourane. Administrator: Idissa Meiga.

Cast: Damouré Zika, Lam Ibrahima Dia, Tallou Mouzourane, Caludine, Baba Nore, Moussa Illo, the girls d'Abada Goungou, the Niger River, Dyama, Mariama, Bana, Hima Do, and the Citroën 2 CV Cocorico. 90 minutes.

*Synopsis:* The adventures of three friends conducting their business in the Nigerian bush with their old automobile. Featuring the same team and made in the same spirit as *Jaguar* and *Petit à Petit,* this film is an attempt at collective improvisation on a Nigerian fable. The actors in the film started from a true fact: at the time of the shooting, Lam is indeed an itinerant chicken merchant who breezes through the bush markets around Naimey, in Niger, in an old delivery van, accompanied by a single assistant.

The invitation of a third person (Damouré) who, to kill time, wants to go around with his friends, brings trouble to an organization that is already precariously balanced. And if, as often happens in Africa, the catastrophes are attributed to a "she-devil," it is some imaginary being who will finally be the only one able to remedy the evil that has been wrought. With deliberation the authors decided to introduce this element of the imaginary into these scenes of daily life. If the film happens to depict, at the same time, a community of marginal outsiders, it is not by sheer chance. The young intellectuals of the rich countries are no longer the only ones to have a monopoly on restlessness.

*La 504 et les foudroyeurs* (The Peugeot 504 and the Lightning Bolts)

Produced by SCOA. 10 minutes.

A SCOA advertising film with Lam and Tallou and a Peugeot 504 in the Bandiagara Cliffs.

*Hommage à Marcel Mauss: Taro Okamoto* (Homage to Marcel Mauss: Taro Okamoto)

Produced by CNRS/CFE. 40 minutes.

A ciné-portrait of an anthropological artist. One of the most celebrated artists in Japan, Okamoto studied with Mauss at the School of Advanced Studies in Paris from 1930 to 1939. He tells of the influence the old master had on his art and on the way in which he thinks and lives.

*Pam Kuso Kar (Briser les poteries de Pam)* (Breaking Pam's Vases)

Produced by CNRS/CFE. 13 minutes.

In February 1974, Pam Sambo Zima, the oldest of the priests of possession in Niamey, Niger, died at the age of seventy-plus years. In his backyard, the followers from the possession cult symbolically break the dead priest's ritual vases and cry for the deceased while dividing up the clothes of the divinities.

*Sigui (73) no. 7: L'auvent de la circoncision* (The Circumcision Shelter)
   Produced by CNRS/CFE. With Germaine Dieterlen. 18 minutes.
   *Synopsis:* This film, shot in 1974, is a reconstruction of a simple ceremony of closure that took place in 1973 when it was forbidden to film in Mali. The ritual signaled the seventh and final year of the sixty-year cycle of Sigui ceremonies. The seventh year of the Sigui should theoretically take place in the circumcision shelter in the village of Songo. But as a result of the influence of Islam, the Sigui cannot go beyond the village of Bandiagara. In 1973 it was not possible for us to go back to the cliff of Bandiagara because of the drought. In 1974 we asked three Dogons to reenact the Songo ceremony for this film.
   The three *olubaru* of the village left for Songo carrying millet beer. They arrived at night before the grand pavilion and sacrificed a goat there. They sprinkled its blood on the altar of the ancestors. In the morning, they climbed up on the shelter and "refreshed" the paintings—that is to say, they caressed them, and they told us what these paintings represent. They went to see the *sistrums* (a type of noise-maker), which were brandished by the young infants who had just been ritually circumcised. Then they visited the paintings of the great shelter: the one representing *nommo,* the spirit of the sacrificial water, those representing the serpents, the little Pale Fox, the Sigui satchels (bags of words), and those representing the stars. Having said good-bye to the great sign that dominates the shelter of Songo, they left, singing the songs of the Sigui. Then they went directly, on foot, without stopping in any villages, to take a bit of beer to the village of Yougo. There, they said to the old men, "Here is the last of the Sigui beer. The Sigui is over."

*Toboy Tobaye (Lapin, petit lapin)* (Toboy Tobaye [Rabbit, Little Rabbit])
   Produced by CNRS/CFE. 13 minutes.
   Dances of today and yesterday by children disguised as rabbits during the nights of Ramadan (Niger).

▶

## 1975

*Babatou, les trois conseils* (Babatou, Three Pieces of Advice)
   Produced by CNRS/CFE. Scenario: Bouhou Hama. Cinematography by Jean Rouch. Sound by Moussa Amidou. Editing by Chrishne Lefort. Music by Dyeliba Badye and Daouda Kante.
   Cast: Damouré Zika, Lam Ibrahima Dia, Tallou Mouzourane, Dyama Djingareye, Baba More, Moussa Illo. 90 minutes.
   *Synopsis:* A "ciné-history" about the slave wars of Babatou, conqueror of the Songhay from Gurunsi-land, during the course of the last century. "It was a hundred years ago, which is not like today." Damouré and Lam, two friends who live on the Isle of Firgoun, in the Niger River, are a hunter and a herdsman. Damouré,

while training young men to hunt, wants also to prepare them for their future activity as warriors. A peaceful soul, Lam thinks only of his cattle until the day when his wife criticizes him for not going off to make war. His son, Moussa, age seven, also pushes his father to leave: "My friends make fun of me!" Lam decides to leave for the south, to the land of Gurunsi, home of Babatou.

Covered with magic charms, armed with lances, arrows, and sabers, and accompanied by their two servants, with Tallou in the lead, Damouré and Lam leave the Niger. Once they arrive in the camp of Babatou, they volunteer for the next expedition, led by the warrior Gazari. They lay siege to a village. Tallou is wounded; the chief of the village is killed. Gazari suffers an arrow in the eye and dies. Damouré, who fought with the daughter of the chief, burns the village and brings back all the captives. In Babatou's camp there is great joy over the victory and sorrow over the death of Gazari. The strongest captives are enrolled in Babatou's army; the others are sent back or sold. Dyama, the daughter of the chief, becomes Damouré's concubine. After the ritual burial of Gazari the warrior, Damouré becomes the warrior chief.

After three years, Lam allows himself to be caught up in this cruel game and lays hold of his own captive, Maryama. Dyama gives Damouré a son. Maryama is ready to do the same when an old soothsayer, returning from the seventh year campaign, comes to ask who would be willing to give up a captive in return for three pieces of advice. Amid jeers from the other warriors, Lam gives him Maryama. In exchange he receives three maxims: "Never go past a village at sunset; never cross a flooded river; if you get angry in the evening, wait until morning to act."

At the moment when Maryama wants to kill herself for Lam, we learn that the old soothsayer has liberated her. Maryama is free, but Lam has lost her forever. He decides to go back to the country with nothing.

On the way, he meets Moustapha, who does not want to stop at a village at sunset. He is devoured by a lion during the night, and Lam inherits his riches and captives.

Damouré rejoins Lam. But while crossing a flooded river he drowns, despite Lam's warnings. Lam has lost his friend and inherited all of his goods. He gives Dyama to Tallou.

One evening the caravan arrives at the Isle of Firgoun. Lam and Tallou scout ahead and discover a man sleeping at the side of Lam's wife. Lam is ready to kill him, but he remembers the third piece of advice. He will act tomorrow.

The next day is the triumphal entry into the village, despite the tears of Damouré's widow. Lam goes toward his house, and his wife says to him: "You don't recognize your own son. It's been eight years since you left." Lam says, "God is great—it's the third piece of advice." So he leads his son into the village square to give an account of Damouré's death to the notaries, and already Lam encourages his son to take his place and leave to make war.

Suddenly Lam thinks of his tranquillity of yesterday, of his character, which has become so nasty, of all the goods he doesn't know what to do with, of his son to whom he could not tell the truth, and of Damouré, his best friend, who is dead.

*Jomo et ses frères* (Jomo and His Brothers)
Produced by CFE. Super-8 mm. Blown up to 16 mm. 20 minutes.

Rouch's only film shot in Super-8, edited and enlarged in 16 mm by Vincent Blanchet. Damouré Zika's ten children call their family "Populist China" and refer to their father as "Mao." Their house, situated in the neighborhood of the Gawey fishermen, is named "la familiale Jomo," the name taken from Jomo Kenyatta. They have a rock band called "Gawey Youth," which simulates musical instruments with diverse materials. They dance and sing their "Gawey Youth" hit parade.

▶

## 1976

*Faba Tondi*
20 minutes.
At the entrance to the village of Simiri in Zermaganda, a buried stone protects the village: *Faba Tondi* (the stone of protection). Daouda Sorko, priest and guardian of the stone, recounts how his great-grandfather had used this protection against Tuareg warriors. Responding to his call, Dongo, the thunder spirit, killed four Tuaregs with lightning.

*Médecines et médecins* (Medicine and Doctors)
Produced by SERDDAV–CNRS/CFE and Institut de Recherches en Sciences Humaines de Niamey. Codirector: Inoussa Ousseini. 15 minutes.
Retired Niger nurses practice surgery in marketplaces and call on local healers for postoperative care.

▶

## 1977

*Ciné-portrait de Margaret Mead* (Ciné-portrait of Margaret Mead)
Produced by CFE and American Museum of Natural History. Sound by John Marshall. 35 minutes.
Upon the occasion of the first Margaret Mead Film Festival, an encounter with Margaret in her office, and in the workroom in the museum, where she speaks about her hopes for today's anthropology.

*Hommage à Marcel Mauss: Germaine Dieterlen* (Homage to Marcel Mauss: Germaine Dieterlen)
Produced by CNRS/CFE. 20 minutes.
Upon the occasion of a colloquium held in Mali, Germaine Dieterlen recalls the facade of the paintings on the Songo sheds that display the grand myths of the creation of the world among the Dogon. Then, in the refuge cave where the first inhabitants of the village of Bongo established themselves, she provokes a discussion on the architectural remains of ancient human establishments.

*Hommage à Marcel Mauss: Paul Lévy* (Homage to Marcel Mauss: Paul Lévy)
Produced by CNRS/CFE. 20 minutes.
Sociologist and theologian Paul Lévy discusses his memories of Marcel Mauss.

*Ispahan: Lettre Persane (La Mosquée du Chah à Ispahan)* (Ispahan: A Persian Letter [The Chah Mosque at Ispahan])

Produced by CNRS/CFE. 35 minutes.

A ciné-portrait of Iranian filmmaker Farrokh Gaffary, who discusses the dynamic architecture of the Chah mosque and the ambiguous rapport of Islam with filmic representation, with sex, and with death.

*Makwayela*

Produced by CNRS/CFE. With Jacques d'Arthuys. 20 minutes.

This is a teaching film created as an example of a "shot sequence" (an unbroken take edited in the camera) with the students from the Institute of Cinéma in Mozambique. The workers from a bottle factory have formed a mixed chorus that sings and dances about their work in the gold mines of South Africa. In the Barakalo language (a secret language of the miners), they denounce imperialism and apartheid.

*Le griot Badye* (Badye, the Storyteller)

Produced by CNRS/CFE. Coproducer: Inoussa Ousseini. 15 minutes.

A traditional singer employing birdsong as a source for the music he uses to accompany his storytelling.

▶ ────────────────────────────────

## 1979

*Simiri Siddo Kuma*

Produced by CNRS/CFE. 30 minutes.

Preparations for the funeral of Zima Siddo, who was responsible for the rituals of possession in the Simiri region of Niger. The spirits themselves nominate his successor, Daouda Sorko.

▶ ────────────────────────────────

## 1980

*Captain Mori*

Produced by NAV/CFE. Sound by John Marshall. 40 minutes.

A portrait of a Japanese merchant marine captain who opened the first commercial line between Japan and South Africa. Evokes the racism of this period; discussion of his meeting with Laurence Van Der Post.

*Ciné-Mafia*

Produced by CFE. Codirected with Groupe Cinéma of the University of Leyden. 35 minutes.

A ciné-meeting of Joris Ivens, Henri Storck, and Jean Rouch in the same village where Ivens shot his first fiction film, *The Breakers,* in 1921.

▶

**1981**

*Sigui synthese: Les cérémonies soixantenaires du Sigui* (Sigui Synthesis: The Sixty-Year Cycle of Sigui Ceremonies)
   Produced by CFE/NAV. 120 minutes.
   Every sixty years the Dogon of the Bandiagara cliffs commemorate the invention of the word, language, and thus of death. In 1931 Marcel Griaule learned that proceeding from one village to the next, a Sigui ritual had taken place in 1909–1914. He reconstructed these extraordinary ceremonies in a first study of them based on the memory of the participants. Twelve years after the death of Marcel Griaule, we filmed this unique seven-year adventure, discovering from one year to the next the themes that are staged in space and time by an "invisible author." This film is an essay of synthesis from the seven previous *Sigui* films.

*Ciné portrait de Raymond Depardon* (Ciné-portrait of Raymond Depardon)
   Produced by CFE. 10 minutes.
   A fortuitous meeting, late one afternoon, in the garden of the Tuileries, of one or two cameras, a tape recorder, and three cameramen/directors, Raymond Depardon, Jean Rouch, and Philippe Costantini. Directed by André Lenôtre. Set by Aristide Mayol.

▶

**1984**

*Dionysos*
   Produced by Les Films de Jeudi. 16 mm and 35 mm. 104 minutes.
   Five professors wait for a mysterious candidate, Hugh Gray, in the courtyard of the Sorbonne. He must defend his paradoxical thesis on "the necessity of the cult of nature in industrial societies." During the defense, beautiful young naked women appear as a bacchanalian choir facing the group of professors. After having taken the jury on a voyage outside of time and space, the candidate is proclaimed doctor of letters. Hugh Gray: Dionysius will transform a factory into the pleasure workshop whose workers will build a new prototype of the car "the perfumed panther." At the end of the construction, the workers will take off their everyday work-clothes, and the Dionysian feast will begin.

▶

**1986**

*Enigma*
   Produced by KWK–CNRS/CFE. 90 minutes.
   A benefactor invites a famous forger to his villa in Turin to ask him to execute a painting De Chirico had not completed during his brief stay in Turin in 1911. Walking in the city in search of inspiration, the forger has several meetings. He

encounters a group of children who want to go to Egypt in an abandoned submarine on the river of Po. Then he meets a philosopher contemplating the world and reading Nietzsche at the summit of the "Mole Antonelliana." Finally he meets an ambiguous and enigmatic young woman.

▶

## 1987

*Folie ordinaire d'une fille de Cham* (Ordinary Folly of a Girl of Cham)
    Produced by CNRS/CFE. Cocollaborators: Philippe Constantini and Daniel Mesguich. 75 minutes.
    Essay of ciné-theater based on a play by the Antillian author Julius Amedee Laou with the actresses Jenny Alpha and Sylvue Laporte. The play has been created and staged by Daniel Mesguich. The action takes place in a room at the Hospital Sainte Anne (a psychiatric hospital). A psychiatrist and his interns discover the fantastic delirium of an Antillian woman who has been held there since 1929, and of a nurse-aide that she thinks is her daughter.

*Bateau Givre (Épisode de brise glace)* (Frozen/Iced Boat)
    Produced by CFE/Svenska Filminstitutet. 16 mm and 35 mm. 35 minutes.
    Filmed on the Swedish icebreaker *Frej,* whose mission is to accompany the boats that are prisoners of the ice blocks on the high seas. Shows the daily work on the boat by its crew as Rouch plays with the unaccustomed light and the sounds, such as the buzzing of instruments, and water rubbing against the blade on the ice.

▶

## 1988

*Bac ou mariage* (Diploma or Marriage)
    Produced by FEMIS/INA/CNRS. Cocollaborator: Philippe Dussart. 70 minutes.
    At the end of the school year, Soukey learns that her father wants to marry her to one of his old and very rich friends, "Uncle Medal," in order to solve his own family financial problems. With her friends she decides to have Uncle Medal seduced. Meanwhile she falls in love with Madou, a young recent university graduate. Suddenly the radio announces that old Uncle Medal has been arrested for corruption ("rapid enrichment"). Everything returns to normal.

*Couleur du temps: Berlin Août 1945* (Color of Time: Berlin, August 1945)
    Produced by CFE. 10 minutes.
    In August 1945 Lieutenant Jean Rouch, commander of the section for Special Forces tank division, discovers Berlin and writes "Color of Time: August 1945," a text published by the revue *Fontaine* in Paris in 1945. It is his first film scenario, filmed now, forty-three years later, using the original text as the narration for the film.

## 1989

*Promenade inspirée* (An Inspired Promenade)
Produced by CNRS/CFE. 40 minutes.
In the Museum of the Maeght Foundation in St. Paul de Vence, Rouch discovers, with his camera, one of the most beautiful collections of African art and improvises a very personal commentary on the topic.

## 1990

*Liberté, Égalité, Fraternité . . . et puis après* (Liberty, Equality, Fraternity . . . and Then After)
Produced by Mission du Bicentenaire de la Révolution-Sodaperaga/CFE. 60 minutes.
Napoleon Bonaparte, one year after having been named general, imprisoned the Haitian brigade general Toussaint-Louverture. Enclosed in a fort, he will die in 1803 without having been judged. To commemorate the revolution, the Haitians are going to try to reconcile the victim and the executioner by a great voudou ritual in front of Les Invalides.

*Beau Navire*
Produced by CFE. 5 minutes.
A personal cinematographic evocation of the Eiffel Tower by Rouch, following a poem by Charles Baudelaire.

## 1992

*Damouré parle du SIDA* (Damouré Speaks about AIDS)
Produced by Sodaperaga. 10 minutes.
When the male nurse Damouré Zika talks about AIDS with his two friends Lam and Tallou, under the admiring eye of his own wife Lobo, who is a nurse's aide, it is because he believes that AIDS is a "disease of love that can only be conquered by love." And this right to love has only one passport for the moment: the condom, on whose use he gives an incredible demonstration.

*Madame l'eau*
Produced by NFI/Sodaperaga/BBC TV/CFE. 120 minutes.
The farmers Damouré, Lam, and Tallou are ruined by drought. They meet a Dutchman who introduces them to the windmill. They decide to construct a Dutch windmill on the banks of the Niger to irrigate their fields. This film is above all the story of the meeting of a Dutchman and three Nigerians, between whites and blacks, between North and South, the simple and the sophisticated, in short the history of the birth of a friendship to whose depth Rouch brings his ciné-eye.

▶

**1994–1996**

*Portrait de Germaine* (A Portrait of Germaine)
   Produced by CFE. 35 minutes. Double system sound.
   Portrait of the anthropologist Germaine Dieterlen.

▶

**1997**

*Moi fatigué debout, moi couché* (Tired Standing Up and Lying Down)
   Produced by CFE.
   Berlin Film Festival (1997), Montreal Film Festival, Festival du film
d'Environment Paris (1997). 90 minutes.
   If you dream under an *accacia albida* tree that is struck by lightning but remains
alive, your dreams will become reality, and as BouBou Hama says, "The double of
yesterday meets tomorrow." And in this country of backwardness and "nowhere,"
this is the daily rule of the game of four old friends, Damouré, Lam, Tallou, and
Rouch. With the help of Dongo, god of thunder, of Harakoy Dikko, the spirit of
water, and their accomplice Gaoberi, "I'm tired standing up and lying down," the
tree that speaks everything is possible. Time and space no longer exist; only dream
dictates the rules of the game: a cruel game of catastrophes, of drought, floods,
magic spells, and "who loses, wins." And the artisan of this adventure, the tree
lying down, stands up, the story changes title just like the film, we are tired lying
down, or standing up. So let's meet again in our next film, *The Incredible Cow.*

*En une poignée de mains amies* (In One Shake of a Friend's Hands)
   Produced by CNRS/CFE.
   Locarno Film Festival (1997), Rome Festival (1997). 35 minutes.
   Enjoying an old port wine together, I was talking with Manoël about the bridges
of Douro, and immediately we were of the same opinion: of all these bridges, the
great work of art in the capital of modern architecture is the bridge that Gustave
Eiffel had done before building his tower of Paris. In less than five minutes, the
project was constructed: Manoël was writing a poem that we will film with our
friends Bernard, Jérôme, and François. And our dreams of childhood were made in
less than a week by going back and forth to the banks of Douro, on foot, then by
car, then in a helicopter, back to where we were following these marvelous clouds,
with Manoël and me screaming stanzas of a poem inspired by the wind, the water,
and friendship.

*Faire–part* (Announcement)
   Produced by GREC-CNRS/FEMIS.
   Venice Film Festival (1997). 18 minutes.
   This film, made in one afternoon, is an "inspired promenade," that is to say, the
discovery of an exhibition where I improvise text and commentary. We decided
with the technical team (cameraman and soundman) to shoot this promenade in

five shot sequences of ten minutes apiece. No additional lighting was to be used. The five successive sequences follow the chronological order of the history of cinema as conceived by Henri Langlois thirty years ago. Two weeks later, the Musée was devastated by a fire at Palais de Chaillot. It is thus the final witnesssing, full of emotion and passion, of the last masterwork of Henri Langlois.

▶

## 1998

*Ciné-poèmes sur Paris* (Ciné-poems on Paris)
 Produced by CNRS. With Sandro Franchina. 18 minutes.
 In 1997 Jean Michel Arnold proposed that Sandro Franchina and I shoot his ciné-poems in Paris. After days and seasons passed, three films were made on the poems Paul Fort wrote from 1901 to 1902: *Nocturnes: The Park, Love in Luxembourg: Sunset in Summer,* and *Sentimental Paris, or The Novel of When We Were Twenty: Bullier.* There will be nothing following, but simply this ending, on Saturday, February 21, 1998.

▶

## 1999

*Premier matin du monde* (First Morning of the World)
 Produced by CFE. 10 minutes.
 Currently being completed.

*La vache merveilleuse* (The Incredible Cow)
 Produced by CFE.
 Currently in production.

Editing has not yet been completed for the following films:
*La royale Goumbé,* 1957
*Festival à Dakar,* 1963
*Urbanisme Africain,* 1963
*Tambours et violins de chasseurs,* 1964
*Jackville,* 1964
*Alpha Noir,* 1965
*Yenendi de Gamkallé,* 1966
*Koli Koli,* 1966
*Yenendi de Kongou,* 1967
*Yenendi de Kirkissey,* 1967
*Yenendi de Goudel,* 1967
*Yenendi de Gourbi Beri,* 1967
*Sécheresse à Simiri,* 1967–1973
*La révolution poétique,* 1968
*Wanzerbé,* 1968
*Pierres chantantes d'Ayorou,* 1968

*Yenendi de Karey Gorou,* 1969
*Taway Nya-La Mère,* 1970
*Initiation des femmes,* 1975
*Souma Kouma,* 1975
*Fêtes des Gandyibi à Simiri,* 1977
*Siddo Kuma,* 1978
*Le renard pâle,* 1984
*Sonchamp,* 1981
*Hassan Fathi,* 1983
*Cousins cousines,* 1985

# Selective Bibliography

**1943**

"Aperçu sur l'animisme Songhay." *Notes Africaines* (IFAN) 39: 4–8.

**1945**

"Cultes des génies chez les Songhay." *Journal de la Société des Africanistes* 15: 15–32.

**1947**

"Les pierres chantantes d'Ayorou." *Notes Africaines* (IFAN) 43: 4–6.
"Pierres taillées de grosses dimensions en pays Kouranko." *Notes Africaines* (IFAN) 43: 7–8.
*Le petit Dan* (in collaboration with Jean Sauvy and Pierre Ponty). Paris: Editions AMG.

**1948**

"'Banghawi,' chasse à l'hippopotame au harpon par les pêcheurs Sorko du Moyen Niger." *Bulletin de l'IFAN* 10: 361–77.
"Vers une littérature africaine." *Présence Africaine* 6: 144–46.

**1949**

"Les gravures rupestres de Kourki." *Bulletin de l'IFAN* 11: 340–53.
"'Surf riding' en Côte d'Afrique." *Notes Africaines* (IFAN) 44: 50–52.
"Chevauchée des génies, cultes de possession au Niger." *Plaisir de France* mimeograph.
"Les rapides de Boussa." *Notes Africaines* (IFAN) 43: 89–98.
"La mort de Mungo Park." *Notes Africaines* (IFAN) 44: 121–24.

**1950**

"Hypothèse sur la mort de Mungo Park." *Notes Africaines* (IFAN) 45: 15–20.
"La danse: 'Le monde noir.'" *Présence Africaine* 8: 219–26.
"Les Sorkawa, pêcheurs itinérants du Moyen Niger." *Africa* 21: 5–21.
"Les magiciens de Wanzerbé." *Caliban* 15: 1–7.
"Toponymie légendaire du 'W' du Niger." *Notes Africaines* (IFAN) 45: 50–52.

**1951**

"Les pêcheurs du Niger: Techniques de pêche, organisation économique et problèmes de migrations." *Bulletin de l'IFAN* 72–79: 17–20.

## 1952

"Cinéma d'exploration et ethnographie." *Les Beaux Arts* (Bruxelles), 1–7.
"L'âme noire." *Ode* (Paris), 69–91.

## 1953

"Contribution à l'histoire des Songhay." In *Mémoires* 29: 137–259. Dakar: IFAN.
"Rites de pluie chez les Songhay." *Bulletin de l'IFAN* 15: 1655–89.
"Renaissance du film ethnographique." *Le cinéma éducatif et culturel* 5: 23–25.

## 1954

*Les Songhay.* Paris: Presses Universitaires de France.
*Le Niger en Pirogue.* Paris: Fernand Nathan.
*Notes sur les migrations en Gold Coast.* Niamey: IFAN.
*Notes on Migrations into the Gold Coast.* Labour Départment, Accra.
*Projet d'enquête systématique sur les migrations en Afrique Occidentale.* Colloque de Bukavu.

## 1955

"A propros des films ethnographiques." *Positif,* 144–49.
*Catalogue des films ethnographiques français.* Cahiers du centre de documentation. Paris: UNESCO.

## 1956

"Migrations au Ghana, Gold Coast, enquêtes 1953–1955." *Journal de la Société des Africanistes* 26, nos. 1–2: 33–196.

## 1957

*Rapport sur les migrations nigériennes vers la basse Côte d'Ivoire.* Niamey: IFAN.
*Rapport sur les activités de la mission migration.* London/Bukavu/Lagos: CCTA/CSA.
"Notes sur les prostituées 'Toutou' de Treichville et d'Adjamé" (with Edmond Bernus). *Études Eburnéennes* 5: 231–42.

## 1958

"Contribution à l'étude du site rupestre de Tessalit." *Notes Africaines* (IFAN) 79: 72–77.
"Les 'marchés des voleurs' d'Abidjan" (with Edmond Bernus). *Mental Disorder and Mental Health Meeting,* CCTA Bukavu, Rwanda.
"L'Africain devant le film ethnographique." *Le cinéma et l'Afrique au sud du Sahara* (Bruxelles), 92–94.

## 1959

"Découverte de l'Afrique." *Explorations* (Paris), 15–88.

## 1960

*La religion et la magie Songhay.* Paris: Presses Universitaires de France.
*Projet de création d'un centre de films africains.* Niamey: IFAN.
"Problèmes relatifs à l'étude des migrations traditionnelles et des migrations actuelles en Afrique occidentale." *Bulletin de l'IFAN* (series B) 22, nos. 3–4: 369–78.
"Je recherche la vérité des comportements et des mentalités." *Lettres Françaises* 812 (February).
"Comment vivent ensemble." *Cinéma 60* 51 (November–December).

## 1961

"Second Generation Migrants in Ghana and the Ivory Coast." *International African Institute Special Studies* (London), 300–304.
"Restes anciens et gravures rupestres d'Aribinda." *Études Voltaïques* (Ouagadougou), 61–69.
"Migrations en Afrique Occidentale, premier rapport de l'enquête 'migration.'" *Colloque de Niamey,* CCTA/CSA, London.

"Situation et tendances actuelles du cinéma africain." Paris: UNESCO.
"A proposito di un certo film africano." *Filmcritica* 111 (July).

## 1962

"Musée et moyens audio-visuels." *Colloque ICOM*, Neuchâtel, Switzerland.
"Enregistrement sonore des traditions orales." *International Congress of Africanists*, Accra.
"The Awakening African Cinéma." *UNESCO Courier* (March), 11–15.
"Cinéma-vérité: Rouch répond." *Contre champ* 3 (March).

## 1963

"Introduction à l'étude de la communauté de Bregbo." *Journal des Africanistes* 33: 129–203.

## 1964

Preface to *"Malettes cinématographiques" sur l'Afrique.* UNESCO Courier.
"Nouvelles techniques cinématographiques et cinéma d'enquêtes." Venice: Cini Foundation.

## 1965

"Textes rituels Songhay." In *Textes sacrés d'Afrique Noire,* ed. G. Dieterlen, 44–56. Paris: Gallimard.
"Cantiques Harris." In *Textes sacrés d'Afrique Noire,* ed. G. Dieterlen, 98–106. Paris: Gallimard.

## 1966

*Catalogue de films sur l'Afrique noire—Analyse et présentation de 600 films sur l'Afrique— Introduction au cinéma africain* (with M. Salzmann). Paris: UNESCO.
*Catalogue de 100 films d'intérêt ethnographique* (with M. Gessain and M. Salzmann). Paris: CNRS.
"Les problèmes sonores du film ethnographique." *Colloque de Budapest sur la "colonne sonore" dans le cinéma d'aujourd'hui.* Paris: UNESCO.
"Le cinéma d'inspiration africaine." *Fonction et signification de l'art négro-africain dans la vie du peuple et pour le peuple.* Colloque de Dakar, 30 March–8 April 1966.
"Anthropologie et impérialisme." *Les Temps Modernes* 193–94: 299–300.
"De *Jaguar* à *Petit à petit.*" *Cahiers du Cinéma* 200–201: 58–59.

## 1968

"Les films ethnographiques." In *Ethnologie générale: Collection de la Pléiade,* 429–71. Paris: Gallimard.

## 1969

"Utilisation des techniques audio-visuelles pour la collecte et l'étude des traditions orales en Afrique." *Colloque UNESCO.* Porto-Novo.
"L'affaire Langlois." *Cahiers du Cinéma* 199 (October).

## 1970

*Catalogue de films ethnographiques sur la religion du Pacifique.* Paris: UNESCO.

## 1971

"Les Aventures d'un Nègre-blanc." *Image et Son* 249: 55–83.
"L'ethnologie au service du rêve poétique." *Le Devoir* (Montréal), 18 September.
"Essai sur les avatars de la personne du possédé, du magicien, du sorcier, du cinéaste et de l'ethnographe." In *La notion de personne en Afrique noire,* Colloques internationaux du CNRS 544, 528–44. Paris: CNRS.

## 1972

"La chasse au lion à l'arc." *Image et Son* 259 (March).
"Cinq regards sur Dziga Vertov." Préface to *Dziga Vertov,* by G. Sadoul. Paris: Éditions Champ Libre.

## 1974

"The Camera and Man." *Studies in the Anthropology of Visual Communication* 1, no. 1: 37–44.

## 1975

"Tradition orale dans la vallée du Niger, l'empire du Mali." In *Bamako 1, Colloque de 1975.* Paris: Foundation SCOA.

"The Situation and Tendencies of the Cinema in Africa." *Studies in the Anthropology of Visual Communication* 2, no. 1: 51–58, and 2, no. 2: 112–21.

"En diable." In *Prophétisme et thérapeutique: Albert Atcho et la communauté Bregbo,* 11–26. Paris: Hermann.

"Le calendrier mythique chez les Songhay-Zarma (Niger)." In *Systèmes de Pensée en Afrique Noire,* vol. 1, 52–62. Paris: CNRS.

"Mettre en circulation des objets inquiétants." *Nouvelle critique* 82 (March).

"Majorité du film ethnographique." *Courier du CNRS.*

## 1976

"Sacrifice et transfert des âmes chez les Songhay du Niger." In *Systèmes de Pensée en Afrique Noire,* vol. 2, 55–64. Paris: CNRS.

## 1978

"Le Renard fou et le Maître pâle." In *Système de signes: Textes réunis en hommage à Germaine Dieterlen,* 3–24. Paris: Hermann.

"Une confrontation unique: Histoire des Yanomami et du cinéma." *Le photographe* 3 (March).

"A proposito di 'Les funérailles du vieil Anaï.'" *Filmcritica* 298 (September).

"On the Vicissitudes of the Self: The Possessed Dancer, the Magician, the Sorcerer, the Filmmaker, and the Ethnographer." *Studies in the Anthropology of Visual Communication* 5, no. 1: 2–8.

## 1979

"La caméra et les hommes." In *Pour une anthropologie visuelle,* ed. Claudine de France, 53–71. Paris: Mouton.

## 1981

"Cinémappemonde." *Le Monde,* 9 April.

"Cinema ed ethnografia." *Filmcritica* 313 (March–April).

## 1982

"Le temps de l'anthropologie visuelle." *Film Échange* 18 (spring).

## 1983

*Le mythe de Dongo* (with Damouré Zika and Dioulé Laya). Niamey: Editions du CELHTO.

## 1985

"L'itinéraire initiatique." *Rencontres de l'audiovisuel scientifique.* Paris (November).

## 1987

*Filmer chez les Dogon: Trois générations d'anthropologie visuelle.* Paris: Archives du CIFE.

## 1988

"Our Totemic Ancestors and Crazed Masters." In *Cinematographic Theory and New Dimensions in Ethnographic Film,* ed. Paul Hockings and Yasuhiro Omuri, Senri Ethnological Series 24, 225–38. Osaka: National Museum of Ethnology.

"L'oeil mécanique." *Gradhiva* 4.
"L'insolence des dieux." *Le tour du monde en 60 jours*. Dieppe.

## 1989

*La religion et la magie songhay*. 2d enlarged and revised edition. Bruxelles: Editions de l'Université de Bruxelles.
*Pour une anthropologie enthousiaste: Titres d'honneur pour Marcel Griaule*. Paris.
"Le vrai et le faux." *Traverse* 47 (November).

## 1990

*Les "pères fondateurs" du film ethnographique: Des "Ancêtres Totémiques" aux chercheurs de demain*. Paris: Intermédia.
"Les cavaliers aux vautours: Les conquêtes des Zerma dans le Gurunsi, 1856–1900." *Journal des Africanistes* 60, no. 2: 5–36.
"Le 'Dit' de Théodore Monod." Preface to a biography of Théodore Monod. Paris.
"Les échos fertiles: Le double de demain a rencontré hier." Paris.
"Un train entre en gare de la Ciotat . . ." Preface for a biography of Michel Simon. Paris.

## 1991

"Les mille et une nuits d'Henry Langlois." Preface for *Catalogue du Musée Langlois*. Paris.

## 1994

"L'imagination au pouvoir!" Preface to *Le roi d'Afrique*, by Jean Yves Loude. Paris: Actes Sud.

## 1995

"L'autre et le sacré: Jeu sacré, jeu politique." *L'autre et le sacré: Surrealisme, cinéma, ethnologie*. Paris: L'Harmattan.

# Publication Information

The University of Minnesota Press gratefully acknowledges permission to reprint the following material in this book. The original French publications of essays and articles are copyrighted by Jean Rouch and appear here with his permission.

Portions of the Editor's Introduction were previously published in "Themes in the Cinema of Jean Rouch," *Visual Anthropology* 2, nos. 3–4 (1989): 223–47.

Translation of "The Camera and Man" by Steven Feld and Marielle Delorme originally appeared in *Studies in the Anthropology of Visual Communication* 1, no. 1 (1974): 37–44. Reprinted with permission from the Society for the Anthropology of Visual Communication. The original French text appeared in manuscript form in 1973 as "La caméra et les hommes."

Translation of "The Situation and Tendencies of the Cinema in Africa" by Steven Feld and Marielle Delorme originally appeared in *Studies in the Anthropology of Visual Communication* 2, no. 1 (1975): 51–58, and 2, no. 2 (1975): 112–21. Reprinted with permission from the Society for the Anthropology of Visual Communication. The original French essay was published as "Situation et tendances du cinéma en Afrique," in the catalog *Films Ethnographiques sur l'Afrique noire* (Paris: UNESCO, 1967), 374–408.

Translation of "On the Vicissitudes of the Self: The Possessed Dancer, the Magician, the Sorcerer, the Filmmaker, and the Ethnographer" by Steven Feld and Shari Robertson originally appeared in *Studies in the Anthro-*

*pology of Visual Communication* 5, no. 1 (1978): 2–8. Reprinted with permission from the Society for the Anthropology of Visual Communication. The original French essay was published as "Essai sur les avatars de la personne du possédé, du magicien, du sorcier, du cinéaste et de l'ethnographe," in *La Notion de Personne en Afrique Noire* (Paris: CNRS 544, 1973), 529–44.

"The Mad Fox and the Pale Master" originally appeared as "Le renard fou et le maître pâle," in *Systèmes des signes: Textes réunis en hommage à Germaine Dieterlen* (Paris: Hermann, 1978), 3–24. This translation by Steven Feld and Catherine Maziére appears here for the first time.

An earlier version of "A Life on the Edge of Film and Anthropology: Jean Rouch with Lucien Taylor" originally appeared in *Visual Anthropology Review* 7, no. 1 (1991): 92–102. Copyright 1991 Lucien Taylor. Reprinted with permission from Lucien Taylor and Jean Rouch.

Translation of "Ciné-Anthropology: Jean Rouch with Enrico Fulchignoni" by Anny Ewing and Steven Feld originally appeared as "Conversation between Jean Rouch and Professor Enrico Fulchignoni" in *Visual Anthropology* 2 (1989): 265–300. Reprinted with permission from Taylor and Francis Social Science Journals. The original French version of this interview appeared as "Entretien de Jean Rouch avec le Professeur Enrico Fulchignoni," in *Jean Rouch: Une rétrospective* (Paris: SERDDAV, 1981), 7–29.

An earlier version of "*Les maîtres fous, The Lion Hunters,* and *Jaguar*: Jean Rouch with John Marshall and John W. Adams" originally appeared as "Jean Rouch Talks about His Films to John Marshall and John W. Adams," *American Anthropologist* 80, no. 4 (1978): 1005–22. Copyright 1978 John Marshall. Reprinted with permission from John Marshall, John W. Adams, and Jean Rouch.

"The Politics of Visual Anthropology: Jean Rouch with Dan Georgakas, Udayan Gupta, and Judy Janda" originally appeared as "The Politics of Visual Anthropology: An Interview with Jean Rouch, by Dan Georgakas, Udayan Gupta, and Judy Janda," *Cineaste* 8, no. 4 (1978): 17–24. Reprinted with permission from *Cineaste* and Jean Rouch.

Translations of "Chronicle of a Film" by Edgar Morin, "The Cinema of the Future?" by Jean Rouch, and "*Chronicle of a Summer:* The Film" by

Anny Ewing and Steven Feld originally appeared in *Studies in Visual Communication* 11, no. 1 (1985): 2–78. Reprinted with permission from the Annenberg School of Communication. The original French versions appeared in the book *Chronique d'un été* (Paris: Interspectacles, Domaine Cinema, 1962).

A portion of the translation of "Annotated Filmography" by Anny Ewing and Steven Feld originally appeared in *Visual Anthropology* 2, nos. 3–4 (1989): 333–65. This version was substantially based on materials originally in *Jean Rouch: Une rétrospective* (Paris: SERDDAV, 1981), 34–44. Annotations have been updated and revised here with the collaboration of Françoise Foucault of the Comité du Film Ethnographique, Musée de l'Homme, Paris, and translation assistance from Catherine Maziére.

"Selective Bibliography" merges information from *Bibliographie sélective de Jean Rouch,* prepared by the Comité du Film Ethnographique; the bibliography compiled by Paul Stoller and published in his book *The Cinematic Griot* (Chicago: University of Chicago Press, 1992), 223–25; and additional sources.

# Index

**JEAN ROUCH** is a renowned ethnographer and filmmaker. Born in 1917 in Paris, he studied civil engineering before turning to film and anthropology in response to his experiences in West Africa during World War II. Since then he has made more than one hundred short and feature-length films in Africa and Europe. These films provocatively mix documentary, ethnographic, and fiction formats and are equally acknowledged for their technical innovations and compelling approach to everyday lives and to rituals.

Rouch has been the recipient of numerous awards, and his honors include the International Critics Prize at Cannes for the film *Chronicle of a Summer* in 1961. A founder and director of the Comité du Film Ethnographique at the Musée de l'Homme in Paris, he has also served as a director of research in the Centre National de la Research Scientifique and as president of the Cinémathèque Française. He is the author of the acclaimed book *La religion et la magie Songhay*.

**STEVEN FELD** is professor of music and anthropology at Columbia University. His books include *Sound and Sentiment: Birds, Weeping, Poetics, and Song in Kaluli Expression; Music Grooves* (coauthored with Charles Keil); *Senses of Place* (coedited with Keith Basso); and a trilingual dictionary of the Bosavi language of Papua New Guinea (coauthored with Bambi B. Schieffelin). His sound recordings include the CDs *Voices of the Rainforest; Bosavi: Rainforest Music from Papua New Guinea; Bright Balkan Morning;* and *Bells and Winter Festivals of Greek Macedonia.*

# COMPUTER PROGRAMMING FUNDAMENTALS WITH APPLICATIONS IN VISUAL BASIC® 6.0

## Mitchell C. Kerman
## Ronald L. Brown

**ADDISON-WESLEY**

An imprint of Addison Wesley Longman, Inc.

Reading, Massachusetts • Menlo Park, California • New York
Harlow, England • Don Mills, Ontario • Sydney • Mexico City
Madrid • Amsterdam

Senior Acquisitions Editor: Susan Hartman
Senior Production Editor: Amy Rose
Editorial Assistant: Lisa Kalner
Composition: Delgado Design, Inc.
Text Design: Delgado Design, Inc.
Project Management: Diane Freed Publishing Services, Inc.
Copyeditor: Roberta Lewis
Proofreader: Trillium Project Management
Art Source: Delgado Design, Inc.
Design Editor: Lynne Reed
Cover Design: Dede Cummings

Access the latest information about Addison-Wesley books from our World Wide Web site:
http://www.awlonline.com

Many of the designations used by manufacturers and sellers to distinguish their products are
claimed as trademarks. Where those designations appear in this book, and Addison-Wesley was
aware of a trademark claim, the designations have been printed in initial caps or all caps.

The programs and applications presented in this book have been included for their instructional
value. They have been tested with care, but are not guaranteed for any particular purpose. The
publisher does not offer any warranties or representations, nor does it accept any liabilities with
respect to the programs or applications.

This book was composed on a Macintosh G3 computer. The software applications used were
QuarkXpress, Abobe Illustrator, and Adobe Photoshop. The text fonts are ITC Garamond,
Gill Sans, and Courier.

**Library of Congress Cataloging-in-Publication Data**
Kerman, Mitchell C.
        Computer programming fundamentals with applications in visual
basic 6.0  /  by Mitchell C. Kerman & Ronald L. Brown.
             p. cm.
        Includes bibliographical references (p.
        ISBN 0-201-61268-2
        1.    Computer programming. 2. Microsoft Visual BASIC. I. Brown,
Ronald L.  II. Title.
        QA76.6 .K465 2000
        005.26'8—dc21                                                99-16971
                                                                             CIP

1 2 3 4 5 6 7 8 9 10-CRW-02010099

To my parents, Arnold and Joy, and brothers, Scott
and Andrew, for not unplugging a 15-year-old's computer
(even when he was late for dinner), and to my wife, Janet, and
children, Charles and Jessica, who don't unplug a 30-year-old's
computer (when he is still late for dinner…).

**M.C.K.**


To my wife, Darlene, and children, Kaity
and Gregory, for their patience, love, and
encouragement in making this book a reality.

**R.L.B.**

# Contents

# Preface

This book is geared toward the undergraduate level and assumes students have no knowledge of computer programming. The intent of the book is for students to attain a solid foundation in computer programming fundamentals and to exercise these fundamental skills using Visual Basic 6.0. In this manner, a student can master one programming language (such as Visual Basic) and then easily learn another. Our students, for instance, are introduced to Visual Basic as their first programming language and then learn Java as a second language. Additionally, the text is fully class-tested and has been used in draft form for almost two years. We are quite proud of the fact that many students new to computer programming have become competent programmers through the use of this text.

## WHY VISUAL BASIC?

Visual Basic is today's most widely used object-oriented programming language. Over three million developers use Visual Basic. Fifty-five percent of developers use Visual Basic as their primary development tool compared to nineteen percent who use C++ and five percent who use Java. The remaining developers use one or another of the less popular programming languages (See Microsoft Corporation, "Microsoft Visual Basic Advances RAD Industry Leadership Position," Internet copy, *http://www.microsoft.com/corpinfo/press/1998/Jan98/vb5mompr.htm*, 15 May 1998.) Visual Basic is also the underlying macro engine for all Microsoft products. Thus, Visual Basic is an important tool in a programmer's toolbox, and students should be introduced to the features that it offers.

## PURPOSE OF THIS BOOK

Few current Visual Basic texts adequately address problem solving and general programming methodology. Many texts focus on the nuances and language-specific features of Visual Basic. These texts tend to be lengthy and can often intimidate students. Our text is intended to rectify this situation by developing problem-solving skills, establishing a foundation of solid programming techniques, and promoting an understanding of the common control structures available in most high-level languages. We introduce control structures in general terms and then describe the Visual Basic implementation. Although our text is concise in comparison to others on the market, it is a complete introduction to programming fundamentals. We stress programming in general first and then use Visual Basic as the language to demonstrate sound programming practices. Advanced, language-specific features of Visual Basic are introduced after problem-solving skills are developed and programming fundamentals are mastered.

As a language for advanced programmers, Visual Basic offers many outstanding features. As an introductory programming language, however, Visual Basic has a few challenges that we feel need to be addressed from a programming fundamentals point of view. First, there is the overhead involved with learning Visual Basic's integrated development environment (IDE), which is required before a student can learn and practice computer programming skills using Visual Basic. Second, beginners often become confused as to the difference between the controls in the user interface they design and the programs they write to work with these controls. Finally, Visual Basic is a very forgiving language; programs will successfully execute even when poor programming practices are employed. Although this relieves some of the programming burdens for advanced programmers, it nurtures many bad programming habits for the novice, causing problems later on if used in other, less forgiving programming languages (such as C++ and Java).

This text rises to each of these challenges. We provide a quick but thorough introduction to the Visual Basic IDE in Chapter 2 and introduce more advanced IDE concepts later in the text. Our intent is for the student to start programming right away, and we introduce the first program in Chapter 2. The difference between a program and a user interface is emphasized throughout the text to avoid confusion between the two. Finally, our text promotes proper programming practices by identifying the possible programming pitfalls, showing examples of them, and presenting ways to avoid them.

## PEDAGOGICAL FEATURES

This text offers numerous features to aid instructors and enhance student learning:

**Chapter Objectives.** Each chapter begins with a list of chapter objectives, indicating the concepts that the student will learn and the tasks that will be performed by the conclusion of the chapter.

> **Chapter Objectives**
>
> In this chapter, you will:
> - Learn about the history of modern computers
> - Become acquainted with the different types of computer systems
> - Learn the difference between hardware and software

**Definition Boxes.** Definition boxes define the most important terms within the chapter and compare and contrast key terms.

```
If condition Then
    [statements]
End If
```

**Syntax Boxes.** Boxed inserts highlight important concepts and Visual Basic syntax, allowing students to quickly locate key information within the text.

**Programming Keys.** Programming Keys provide tips and warnings to aid the beginning programmer.

**Code Callouts.** Important points and key concepts in program source code are explained in code callout areas in the margins of the text.

$$((A \land B) \lor A) \land ((A \land B) \lor C) =$$ ◄— First parenthetical expression reduces to A

$$A \land ((A \land B) \lor C) =$$ ◄— Expand the second parenthetical expression

> **GUI Design Tips**
>
> A GUI should lead the user through the data entry process. The TabIndex property specifies an order for the different control objects on a form. A TabIndex of 0 indicates the first control object, 1 indicates the second, and so on.

**GUI Design Tips.** Graphical User Interface (GUI) design tips are presented throughout the text, providing guidelines for and enhancing student understanding of proper GUI design.

**Real-World Examples.** The examples in the text are taken from real-world problems in business, math, science, engineering, and operations research. The exercises and programming projects at the end of each chapter are geared toward these real-world problems as well.

**Case Studies.** Case studies appear throughout the text, providing the student with insight as to how the concepts presented apply to real-world situations.

> **CASE STUDY**
> **Good Look Cosmetics Company**
>
> Jean is a sales representative for the GoodLook Cosmetics Company. Each month, she is required to report sales figures for the different types of cosmetics. She simply multiplies the sales price by the quantity sold for each item and then sums these products. Since there is an exceptionally large number of items, hand calculations are both time-consuming and error-prone.

> **Summary**
>
> **Key Terms**
> **breakpoint**—a temporary stopping point during the execution of code for debugging purposes at design time
> **bug**—an error in a computer program
> **bullet-proofing**—error-proofing a computer program
>
> **Keywords**
>
> | Methods: | Statements: |
> | --- | --- |
> | Clear | Exit Function |
> | | Exit Sub |
> | Objects: | GoTo |
> | Err | On Error |
> | | Resume |
> | Properties: | Resume Next |
> | Number | |
>
> **Key Concepts**
> - Bullet-proofing, or error-proofing, programs is a fundamental concept in computer science. The possibility of unanticipated inputs causing a catastrophic failure in real-world applications necessitates the error-proofing of code.

**Chapter Summaries.** Each chapter concludes with a summary that provides the student with an indispensable study aid. The summary is divided into several sections appropriate for that chapter. The sections of a chapter summary include:

1) *Key Terms.* The key terms section provides a glossary of those terms presented in the chapter.

2) *Keywords.* The Visual Basic keywords introduced in the chapter are listed in the keywords section according to their applicability.

3) *Key Concepts.* The key concepts section summarizes all of the concepts and Visual Basic syntax introduced in the chapter.

**Review Questions.**  Each chapter contains review questions, allowing students to test their recall and understanding of the material presented.

**Chapter Problems.**  Each chapter contains problems to test student mastery of the material.

**Programming Projects.**  Programming projects allow students to combine material previously learned with the new concepts presented in the chapter.

**Chapter Supplements.**  Chapter supplements provide additional topics for instructors and additional information for more advanced students. The supplements cover the more advanced areas of computer science and extra features of Visual Basic. The information within a chapter supplement directly relates to the material presented in its associated chapter. The chapter supplements also enhance the flexibility of the text and diversify its application.

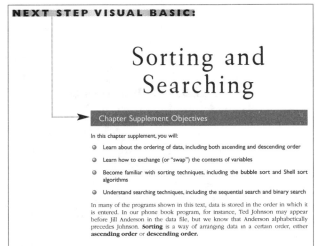

**NEXT STEP VISUAL BASIC:**

# Sorting and Searching

**Chapter Supplement Objectives**

In this chapter supplement, you will:

- Learn about the ordering of data, including both ascending and descending order
- Learn how to exchange (or "swap") the contents of variables
- Become familiar with sorting techniques, including the bubble sort and Shell sort algorithms
- Understand searching techniques, including the sequential search and binary search

In many of the programs shown in this text, data is stored in the order in which it is entered. In our phone book program, for instance, Ted Johnson may appear before Jill Anderson in the data file, but we know that Anderson alphabetically precedes Johnson. **Sorting** is a way of arranging data in a certain order, either **ascending order** or **descending order**.

**Online Supplements.**  A Web site provides an instructor's manual containing the answers to the review questions, chapter problems, and programming projects. This manual is for instructors only. It is available through your Addison-Wesley sales representative or by sending an e-mail message to aw.cse@awl.com.

**CD-ROM.**  The enclosed CD-ROM contains the Visual Basic 6.0 Working Model and coded examples from the text. The Working Model allows students to run all of the examples in this text and make their own projects, but it will not compile programs into stand-alone executable modules.

## STYLE CONVENTIONS

This book uses the following style conventions:

```
Visual Basic statements and program text appear in monospace
font. Words that the reader types also appear in this font.
```

```
Statements containing generic names that may be changed by the
programmer are italicized.
```

➥ This arrow indicates that the line of code continues on the next line in the text, but it should appear as one continuous line on the screen.

➥ This arrow indicates that the program code continues on the next page of the text.

Names of keys appear in all capital letters (e.g., ENTER key).

*Italics are used for emphasis and for variables within equations.*

## TO THE STUDENT

Welcome and congratulations on your decision to learn computer programming. We designed this text for you. Programming fundamentals are stressed in the initial chapters to prepare you for Visual Basic's advanced features that are covered in the later chapters. The chapters are organized so that they introduce specific concepts and build upon these concepts as you progress. Access to a computer with Visual Basic 6.0 installed is desirable so that you will be able to try examples presented in the text. Working through examples and getting the intended results from the computer is without question the best method of reinforcing the programming techniques presented. If you are not math savvy, don't worry: the most advanced mathematics in the text requires only a knowledge of basic algebra. Overall, we encourage you to experiment with Visual Basic; experimentation and discovery make up a major part of the learning process.

The CD-ROM packaged with the text contains the Visual Basic 6.0 Working Model, a student version of Visual Basic. You can install this version on your home computer so you can work on your programs both at home and in your school's computer lab.

Finally, we envy you, the student: you are about to embark on an enjoyable and rewarding journey into the world of computer programming. Bon voyage!

## TO THE INSTRUCTOR

We wrote this text to fill a very large void in the available literature. Few books using Visual Basic are truly introductory programming texts. Most of these books tend to be trade books or books for advanced programmers.

During the course of our writing, we noticed the dissension in the industrial and academic communities regarding the preferred methodology for teaching an introductory programming class. There are essentially two schools of thought. The first school believes in a fundamentals-first approach, introducing constants, variables, decision structures, and loops before advancing on to object-oriented programming. The second school believes in introducing objects as a fundamental structure. To answer this diversity, we designed our text with flexibility of presentation to accommodate both schools. The main flow of the text follows that of the first school, but objects and object-oriented programming may be introduced earlier by covering Chapter 8 Supplement along with Chapter 4.

This text contains enough material for a two-semester sequence of introductory and advanced programming in Visual Basic. The chapters and chapter supplements cover the following topics:

- Chapter 1 introduces computer history and the evolution of computer programming languages. For computer science or engineering students, Chapter 1 Supplement describes computer arithmetic and number systems, including binary, octal, and hexadecimal number systems.

- Chapter 2 describes the VB development environment and guides students through writing their first program. Chapter 2 Supplement explains how to customize the Visual Basic development environment.

- Chapter 3 introduces the program development cycle, flowcharts, pseudocode, and algorithm design.

- Chapter 4 describes the elements of programming, such as constants, variables, and strings.

- Chapter 5 introduces flow control structures, including decision structures and loops. Chapter 5 Supplement provides an early introduction to sequential file input and output prior to the more in-depth coverage of these topics found in Chapter 9. This provides instructors with a means of using examples and assigning programming projects that work with data files.

- Chapter 6 describes structured programming concepts, and Chapter 6 Supplement introduces recursion concepts.

- Chapter 7 teaches error trapping and debugging methods.
- Chapter 8 covers advanced data structures. This chapter introduces arrays, user-defined data types (records), stacks, queues, deques, pointers, and linked lists. Chapter 8 Supplement introduces object-oriented programming.
- File input and output methods appear in Chapter 9. Sorting and searching are covered in Chapter 9 Supplement.
- Advanced Visual Basic programming appears in Chapter 10. This chapter describes the use of several Visual Basic controls not introduced in earlier chapters. Topics such as graphics, random numbers, simulation, and Internet programming are also covered. Chapter 10 Supplement describes the Visual Basic Package and Deployment Wizard. This supplement explains how to package a program for use by others and shows an example.
- Chapter 11 introduces Visual Basic for Applications (VBA) programming.
- Chapter 12 describes database fundamentals and database programming.

## RECOMMENDED COVERAGE

The recommended coverage of the text depends upon the length of the class and the type of students being taught. We split our recommendations according to both of these criteria. Note that an S after a number indicates a chapter supplement (i.e., 1S denotes Chapter 1 Supplement). We recommend covering the chapters in the order listed. Later chapters build upon the concepts presented in earlier chapters.

*Computer Science and Engineering Students:*

> First Semester: Chapters 1, 1S, 2, 2S, 3, 4, 5, 5S, 6, 7, 8
> Second Semester: Chapters 6S, 8S, 9, 9S, 10, 10S, 11, 12
> *Note:* Object-oriented programming may be introduced earlier by covering 8S along with 4.

*Business and Other Majors:*

> First Semester: Chapters 1, 2, 2S, 3, 4, 5, 5S, 6, 7, 8
> Second Semester: Chapters 8S, 9, 9S, 10, 10S, 11, 12
> *Note:* Object-oriented programming may be introduced earlier by covering 8S along with 4.

## ACKNOWLEDGMENTS

As with any undertaking of this magnitude, there are always many people to thank upon its completion. First, we would like to thank the good people at Addison Wesley Longman (AWL) for giving us the opportunity to write this book. Many heartfelt thanks go to Senior Acquisitions Editor Susan Hartman and Editorial Assistant Lisa Kalner. The production staff is truly superb, and we could not have written this text without their help. We appreciate the outstanding work of our production manager, Amy Rose; book project manager, Diane Freed; copyeditor, Roberta Lewis; proofreader, Brooke Albright; and designers, artists, and compositors, Lisa Delgado and Ed Smith. Additionally, we extend thanks to Claire Collins, Julie Dunn, and Karen Wernholm, all formerly of AWL.

Our reviewers provided excellent recommendations for improving the text. You have our sincere appreciation:

> Carol Barner, Glendale Community College
>
> Peter Casey, Central Oregon Community College
>
> Kamesh Casukhela, Ohio State University at Lima
>
> Gary Farrar, Columbia College of Missouri
>
> Dana Johnson, North Dakota State University

Greg Jolda, University of Southern Maine

Don Kussee, Utah Valley State College

Frank Lanzer, University of Maryland, University College

Jim Prater, University of Alabama

Robert Rea, Wright State University

We are also grateful to several colleagues at Naval Postgraduate School for their recommendations, encouragement, and support during the production of this text. We extend our thanks to Professors Gordon Bradley, Arnie Buss, Sam Buttrey, Dick Franke, Bob Koyak, Alan Washburn, and Kevin Wood. Additionally, Mitchell Kerman extends a very special thanks to Professors Gerald Brown and Robert Dell for teaching him the art and joy of writing and to Lieutenant Colonel David Olwell for teaching both him and Ron the business of writing.

# Computer Basics

## Chapter Objectives

In this chapter, you will:

- Learn about the history of modern computers

- Become acquainted with the different types of computer systems

- Learn the difference between hardware and software

- Become familiar with the microcomputer hardware block diagram and the six components of a typical microcomputer system

- Learn about the different types of computer memory

- Gain an understanding of binary numbers and learn related terminology

- Learn the differences between machine language, low-level languages, and high-level languages

- Learn the difference between compilers and interpreters

## A BRIEF HISTORY OF COMPUTERS

In the early days of man, fingers were used for counting; that's why we use the base 10 number system known as decimal. Eventually, man discovered that he could use other objects, such as pebbles and sticks, to aid him in counting. In the stone age, wolf bones were used as tally sticks. These are the oldest known computing devices.

Many consider the first true computing devices to be the ancient counting tables and tablets known as abaci. The word **abacus** (plural *abaci*) is derived from the Greek *abax*, meaning table or board covered with dust. Evidence of these devices exists as early as about 3000 B.C. in the Tigris–Euphrates Valley and as late as about

5 B.C. in Egypt. The early abacus consisted of grooves carved into a stone or clay tablet. Pebbles were slid along these grooves from one side of the tablet to the other to represent numbers. This early abacus allowed for easier counting and aided in simple calculations like addition and subtraction. Somewhat later, around A.D.12, the modern abacus first appeared in China. This abacus consisted of a wood frame containing several columns of beads threaded on strings or wires. This modern abacus was an extremely useful computing tool, and it is still used in certain parts of the world today.

Many other devices besides the abacus have been used as computational tools over the years. The following time-line presents a brief history of computing devices that lead to the development of modern-day computers:

## 1600s

**Around 1600**—John Napier, the inventor of logarithms, invents a hand-held device to assist with multiplication and division operations. The device is known as Napier's Rods or Napier's Bones.

**1622**—Using Napier's logarithms as the basis, William Oughtred invents the slide rule. Oughtred's slide rule was circular in shape.

**1623**—William Schickard creates the first mechanical calculator. Blaise Pascal, the creator of the famous triangle, invents a mechanical adding machine with an automatic carry function (Figure 1.1).

**1673**—Gottfried Leibniz builds a multiplication machine.

## 1800s

**1820**—Thomas de Colmar invents the Arithometer.

**1822**—Charles Babbage, a British mathematician and engineer, designs the Difference Engine (Figure 1.2).

**1833**—Charles Babbage designs the Analytical Engine. Although the mechanical version of his design was never built, it contained all of the components of the modern computer. It had units for input, output, memory, arithmetic, logic, and

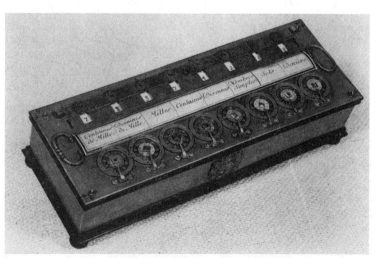

**Figure 1.1** Pascal's adding machine
Reproduced by permission from IBM. Copyright 1999 by International Business Machines Corporation.

**Figure 1.2** Babbage's Difference Engine
Reproduced by permission from IBM. Copyright 1999 by
International Business Machines Corporation.

control. The design used punched cards to communicate algorithms to the engine, and numbers were stored on toothed wheels that served as memory. Babbage's design had a great influence on the development of computers, and he is known as the "Father of the Computer."

**1854**—George Boole, a self-taught British mathematician, invents a system for symbolic and logical reasoning. This system becomes known as Boolean algebra and is the basis for computer design.

**1890**—The first punched cards were used to read information into a computing machine.

## 1920s

**1924**—The Forms Tabulating Company, started in 1896, becomes the C-T-R (Calculating-Tabulating-Recording) Company in 1914. In 1924, C-T-R Company changes its name to International Business Machines (IBM).

**1925**—Vannevar Bush invents the large-scale differential analyzer.

## 1930s

**1935**—Konrad Zuse develops the Z-1 computer.

**1936**—John Vincent Atanasoff, a mathematician and physicist at Iowa State University, and John Berry, Atanasoff's graduate assistant, develop the first electronic digital special-purpose computer known as the Atanasoff–Berry computer. This computer uses vacuum tubes instead of the less efficient relays for storage and arithmetic functions.

**1937**—Alan Turing, a British mathematician, develops the theoretical "Turing machine," laying the foundation for the development of general-purpose programmable computers. Turing is also famous for breaking the German "Enigma" code during World War II, thereby allowing Allied forces to decipher secret German messages.

**1939**—Bell Labs develops the Complex Number Calculator.

## 1940s

**1943**—The Colossus Mark I decrypting computer is built.

**1944**—The Harvard Mark I computer is developed.

**1945**—Grace M. Hopper finds a moth fused to a wire of the Mark I computer causing the machine to malfunction. She originates the term "debugging" for finding and removing errors.

**1946**—Two electrical engineers, John Mauchley and J. Presper Eckert, build ENIAC (Electrical Numerical Integrator and Calculator), the first large-scale fully electronic general-purpose digital computer, at the University of Pennsylvania. ENIAC uses 18,000 vacuum tubes for storage and computation, weighs 30 tons, and occupies an area of 1,500 square feet. ENIAC can perform 300 multiplications of two 10-digit numbers per second, as opposed to the Mark I, which performs only one multiplication every three seconds. ENIAC is shown in Figure 1.3.

**1947**—Three physicists, John Bardeen, Walter Brattain, and William Shockley, invent the transistor at Bell Labs. The transistor replaces the vacuum tube and revolutionizes computer design since it is smaller, lighter, cooler, and more reliable. Additionally, the first stored-program computer, the Manchester Baby, is developed this same year.

**Figure 1.3** ENIAC
Reprinted with permission of Unisys Corporation.

## 1950s

**1951**—The UNIVAC (Universal Automatic Computer) is delivered to the Census Bureau.

**1953**—IBM develops its first computer, the IBM 701 EDPM.

**1957**—John Backus and team members develop the FORTRAN (FORmula TRANslation) programming language, a compiled language useful in the scientific and academic communities.

**Late 1950s**—Grace M. Hopper pioneers the development and use of COBOL (COmmon Business Oriented Language), a programming language for the business community using English-like phrases. The LISP (LISt Processor) language is also developed.

## 1960s

**1960**—The ALGOL (ALGOrithmic Language) programming language is created.

**1964**—John G. Kemeny and Thomas E. Kurtz, two professors of mathematics at Dartmouth College, develop the BASIC (Beginners All-purpose Symbolic Instruction Code) language. The first computer "mouse" and "windows" are also developed this year. Additionally, IBM introduces the System 360 (Figure 1.4), its first "family of computers."

**1967**—The first computers using integrated circuits are built.

**1968**—Intel Corporation is created.

**1969**—Work begins on ARPAnet, a precursor of the modern-day Internet.

**Figure 1.4** IBM System 360
Reproduced by permission from IBM. Copyright 1999 by International Business Machines Corporation.

## 1970s

**1971**—Intel Corporation develops the first microprocessor. The floppy disk is also created this year.

**1973**—Ethernet, the first local area network (LAN), is developed.

**1974**—The Scelbi and the Mark-8, the first "personal computers," are introduced.

**1975**—Paul Allen and Bill Gates found Microsoft Corporation. Stephen Wozniak and Stephen Jobs found Apple Computer Corporation and sell the Apple I in kit form. IBM mass-produces its first personal computer, the IBM 5100. The MITS Altair 8800 personal computer is also introduced.

**1976**—Apple Computer Corporation introduces the Apple II.

**1977**—Radio Shack introduces the TRS-80.

**1978**—Dan Bricklin and Dan Fylstra write Visicalc, the first spreadsheet program, and found Software Arts.

## 1980s

**1981**—IBM introduces the IBM PC personal computer (Figure 1.5). Microsoft releases MS-DOS version 1.0.

**1984**—The Apple Macintosh (Figure 1.6) debuts.

**1985**—Microsoft releases their first version of Windows™, Intel creates the 80386 microprocessor.

**1989**—Intel introduces the 80486 microprocessor.

**Figure 1.5** IBM PC
Reproduced by permission from IBM. Copyright 1999 by International Business Machines Corporation.

## 1990s

**1992**—Intel introduces the Pentium microprocessor.

**1996**—Intel introduces the Pentium Pro microprocessor.

**1997**—Intel introduces the Pentium II microprocessor.

**1999**—Intel introduces the Pentium III microprocessor.

Based upon the above time-line, it is generally accepted that there have been four generations of electronic computers:

| | | |
|---|---|---|
| **1940 to 1950** | First generation | Computers use vacuum tubes |
| **1950 to 1964** | Second generation | Computers use transistors |
| **1964 to 1971** | Third generation | Computers use integrated circuits |
| **1971 to present** | Fourth generation | Computers use microprocessors |

## TYPES OF COMPUTERS

Computers are categorized according to power, size, and cost. Computer power does not refer to power in the electrical sense, but rather to other factors affecting the machine's computational capability, such as speed and storage capacity. **Mainframes** are large, powerful computers that cost hundreds of thousands, if not millions, of dollars. They perform calculations very quickly and have massive amounts of storage capacity. **Minicomputers** are smaller than mainframes, with costs ranging from tens to hundreds of thousands of dollars. They are typically not as fast as mainframes and have smaller storage capacities. **Microcomputers**, the smallest of the computer families, are the computers that are most commonly purchased by the general public and are usually referred to as **personal computers** (PCs). Microcomputer costs usually range from hundreds to thousands of dollars. With advancing technology, the power available in today's microcomputers rivals that of minicomputers and mainframes from just a few years ago.

**Figure 1.6** Apple Macintosh
Photo courtesy of Apple Computer, Inc.

This book introduces computer programming concepts using examples in the Visual Basic (VB) programming language. VB is produced by Microsoft Corporation and operates under the Microsoft Windows™ environment on IBM-compatible PCs. Thus, we focus our discussion on microcomputer systems, although the computer programming fundamentals presented in this text are applicable to programming any computer system, from a thousand-dollar PC to a multimillion-dollar mainframe.

## COMPONENTS OF A TYPICAL MICROCOMPUTER SYSTEM

### Key Terms

**computer hardware**—the physical components of a computer system

The **hardware**, or physical components, of a microcomputer system consists of six elements (Figure 1.7):

1. The **central processing unit** (**CPU**) is the "brain" of the computer. The CPU or **microprocessor** (often abbreviated μP) resides on the computer's **motherboard** (primary circuit board). A microprocessor is an integrated circuit (or chip) that performs the computer's main functions. The microprocessor contains a small amount of internal memory, or **registers**, as well as the **arithmetic logic unit** (ALU), which is responsible for performing all mathematical and logical operations.

2. A monitor is a **display device** that allows you to see information. The monitor is also referred to as the display or CRT (**cathode ray tube**).

3. The CPU receives information from **input devices**. The most common of these are the keyboard and mouse. Other input devices include game controllers, microphones, scanners, and digital cameras.

4. The CPU sends information to **output devices**. A common output device is a printer, which allows the computer to print information on paper, producing a hard copy. A monitor is the most common output device; without it, it would be difficult to interact with the computer. Speakers are another common output device. They allow you to hear sounds and music produced by the computer, provided that a sound card is installed.

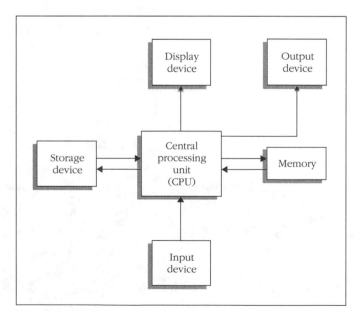

**Figure I.7** Hardware of a typical microcomputer system

**5.** Just like humans, computers store information in memory. The two types of computer memory are **read-only memory** (**ROM**) and **random access memory** (**RAM**). As the name implies, ROM is read-only; this is permanent memory where the computer's instruction set resides. No instructions can be added or written to ROM. Furthermore, ROM is not erased when the computer is shut down; instead, it is permanently retained, or **hardwired**, in the computer. Thus, ROM is also known as *nonvolatile memory*. RAM, on the other hand, is used as temporary memory or workspace by the computer's software programs. Unlike ROM, RAM is *volatile memory* that is erased when the computer is shut down.

**6.** Since RAM is erased when power is removed, we need a place to keep our programs. **Storage devices** allow programs to be saved for easy retrieval at some other time. Storage devices may be classified as either removable or nonremovable media. Hard disks are nonremovable media with massive amounts of storage space available. Floppy disks are removable media with significantly less storage capacity than hard disks. Recent advances in technology have made the distinction between floppy disks and hard disks less clear. Zip™ disks, for instance, are removable media that can store the equivalent of about 70 floppy disks. CD-ROM (compact disc read-only memory) drives are removable media, read-only storage devices that allow you to install programs from a CD (compact disc), run programs on CD, or listen to music CDs. Recordable CD (CD-R) and re-recordable CD (CD-RW) drives are also available. The most recent technology is the DVD (digital video disc), which is expected to replace CD-ROM drives due to its incredible storage capacity.

In contrast to computer hardware, computer **software** consists of the applications or programs that you buy or write to work on the computer. A few typical software applications include word processors, spreadsheets, databases, programming languages, and games. **Operating systems** software allows you to easily operate your computer. The operating system controls how the CPU interacts with all of the other components in the computer system. Windows 98™, for example, is an operating system that provides an easy **graphical user interface** (**GUI**).

### Key Terms

**computer software**—the computer programs or applications that run on a computer

## THE BINARY NUMBER SYSTEM

Although there are numerous computer languages, internally computers only understand the base-2 number system known as the **binary system**. People, unlike computers, use the **decimal system**, or base-10 system. That system comes more naturally to us since we first learned to count using our ten fingers. The binary system, by contrast, consists of only two digits, 0 and 1. In computer terms, these two digits translate to a switch being either open or closed. When a switch is open (binary value of 0), it does not allow electrical current flow, so the switch is "off" and no signal is present. When the switch is closed (binary value of 1), however, it allows electrical current flow, so the switch is "on" and a signal is present.

$1001\ 1100_2$ is an example of a binary number. For clarity, we subscript the number with a 2 to indicate that this number is a binary number rather than 10,011,100 (ten million, eleven thousand, one hundred) in decimal. Each 0 or 1 in this number is called a **bit**, meaning **b**inary dig**it**. Computers group and store information in a series of eight bits, called a **byte**. Using a food consumption analogy, computer programmers humorously say that when you take half a byte, you get a

**nibble**, or four bits. But this analogy doesn't apply when you combine two bytes to get a **word**.

Storage and memory capacities are measured in bytes. Common units include the **kilobyte**, **megabyte**, and **gigabyte**. A kilobyte (KB) is 1,024 ($2^{10}$), or approximately 1,000 bytes. Similarly, a megabyte (MB) is 1,048,576 ($2^{20}$) bytes, and a gigabyte (GB) is 1,073,741,824 ($2^{30}$) bytes.

As a programmer and computer user, you should be aware that not all numbers can be exactly represented on a computer. A computer uses a finite number of bits to store any number. The real number system, however, is continuous; between any two real numbers lies an infinite number of other real numbers. For instance, how many real numbers lie between 1.01 and 1.02? Well, start counting: 1.011, 1.0101, 1.01001, 1.010001, 1.0100001, and on and on. Unfortunately, since computers represent numbers in a finite number of bits, they can only represent a finite number (albeit a very large number) of real numbers. The main point here is that computers and mathematical operations performed on computers are subject to **round-off errors** due to their imprecise representation of numbers.

## THE EVOLUTION OF COMPUTER PROGRAMMING LANGUAGES

Since computers truly understand only binary, that is how people first programmed them. Programs written in binary code are called **machine language** programs. Programming in machine language was both time-consuming and error-prone, so programmers developed **assembly language**. In assembly language, programmers write code using **mnemonics,** or symbolic instructions that are easily memorized and understood by the programmer. For instance, to load the accumulator (an internal register in the microprocessor) with the contents of memory location 201, a programmer need only write LDA 201 rather than its machine language equivalent, 0010 0010 0000 0001. Once an assembly language program is complete, it is converted to machine language by an **assembler** so that it can be executed by the computer. Assembly language is a **low-level language** since there is a direct (usually one-to-one) correspondence between assembly language and machine language instructions.

As you can see, the idea is to make programming easier for us. Why should we have to translate our instructions into binary when the computer can do it for us? Computer programming languages evolved along this philosophy, and **high-level languages** use English-like phrases as programming constructs. Examples of such high-level languages include BASIC, C, FORTRAN, and Pascal. Furthermore, many high-level languages are **general-purpose languages** that may be used to solve various types of problems.

The underlying goal in developing high-level languages was to make programs independent of the machine architecture and easily transportable among different platforms. Unfortunately, most high-level languages failed miserably in this respect due to different implementations of the languages on the various machines. For instance, a Pascal program written on an IBM PC will probably not work on an Apple Macintosh without changing the original program, or **source code**. Java, a language developed by Sun Microsystems, is the first computer language designed to be truly platform-independent. A Java program works the same way and without modification on any machine that supports Java.

Most recent computer languages are object-oriented and allow for the creation and use of objects. These languages include C++, Java, Object Pascal, and Visual Basic. The object-oriented paradigm allows computer programs to more closely model the real world, and it has a wide range of applications. Some of its most popular uses include simulation and modeling.

High-level languages are either **compilers** or **interpreters**. The difference is in how the actual program is executed. Like an assembly language, a compiled language requires the source code to be translated to machine language by a compiler. In other words, your source code is translated into machine language and an executable module is created. This executable module is the actual program that is run by the computer. The computer will not see any changes that you make to the source code until you recompile your program into a new executable module. Languages such as C, FORTRAN, and Pascal are compilers. Interpreters, on the other hand, work much the same way as human interpreters. In order for you to understand a foreign language, an interpreter translates spoken words into your native language phrase by phrase or sentence by sentence. Thus, an interpreter on a computer reads the source code one line or statement at a time, translates the statement into machine language, and executes the machine language equivalent of the statement. The computer will immediately see any changes that you make to the source code once you reexecute the program. The disadvantage is that interpretive languages execute code more slowly (and often significantly more slowly) than compiled languages. BASIC and Java are examples of interpreters.

## FROM BASIC TO VISUAL BASIC

In 1964, John Kemeny and Thomas Kurtz, two Professors in the Dartmouth College Mathematics Department, developed the Beginner's All-purpose Symbolic Instruction Code (BASIC) as a tool to simplify programming for unsophisticated computer users. They designed BASIC as a stepping-stone for students to learn one of the more "advanced" programming languages, such as FORTRAN or ALGOL.

In the late 1970s, Bill Gates and Paul Allen, the two founders of Microsoft Corporation, created versions of BASIC for several different personal computer platforms, including Apple, Commodore, Atari, and IBM. The BASIC interpreter was the first product sold by Microsoft, and it opened up the world of computer programming to the personal computer market.

The BASIC language was always under the scrutiny of professional programmers and educators alike. Although it allowed anyone to learn how to program, the language had many "bad" features and encouraged "poor" programming habits. A sample BASIC program is shown in Figure 1.8. Although we have not yet introduced these programming concepts, we point out some flaws and limitations of the BASIC language as a precursor of the ideas to come:

1. In BASIC, line numbers must identify and begin each line, making it difficult to add lines to programs or make large changes. Additionally, the source code is not "free form," and the programmer has little control over the amount of "white space," or blank lines, in the code.

2. BASIC does not require that all variables be explicitly declared before use.

3. Only the first two characters of a variable name are significant in BASIC. Thus, long or descriptive variable names are difficult to implement. For example, BASIC sees the variables *day* and *date* as the same variable, *da*.

4. BASIC uses a GOTO statement to skip over lines of code. This is considered poor programming practice according to many professionals and educators.

5. BASIC has little support for structured or modular programming.

6. BASIC was designed before the popularity of object-oriented languages, so it does not support objects.

**Key Terms**

**compiler**—a computer program that translates high-level source code into machine language and creates an executable file

**interpreter**—a computer language that translates and executes the source code instruction by instruction

```
10 REM DECIMAL TO BINARY CONVERSION PROGRAM
20 CLS
30 PRINT "DECIMAL TO BINARY CONVERSION"
40 PRINT "---------------------------"
50 PRINT
60 INPUT "Please enter a DECIMAL number (-1 to QUIT): "; QUOTIENT
70 IF QUOTIENT < 0 THEN 190
80 RESULT$ = ""
90 REMAINDER = QUOTIENT MOD 2
100 QUOTIENT = QUOTIENT \ 2
110 RESULT$ = RIGHT$(STR$(REMAINDER), 1) + RESULTS
120 IF QUOTIENT > 0 THEN 90
130 PRINT
140 PRINT QUOTIENT; " = "; RESULT$; " in binary."
150 PRINT
160 PRINT "Press the SPACE BAR to continue"
170 IF INKEY$ <> " " THEN 170
180 GOTO 20
190 END
```

**Figure 1.8** Example BASIC program

All in all, BASIC is a poor language of choice for large programs. It is hard to read and trace code, even for the programmer who originally wrote it. Despite its drawbacks, we acknowledge the great impact that BASIC had on the evolution and popularity of personal computers. In fact, one of the authors is originally a self-taught BASIC programmer and is eternally grateful to Professors Kemeny and Kurtz.

With Microsoft's development of the Windows operating system in the late 1980s, it was only natural for them to revise programming languages to work under the Windows environment. Visual Basic 1.0 was released in 1991 and was followed by a new version each year for the next two years: Visual Basic 2.0 in 1992 and Visual Basic 3.0 in 1993. Version 4.0 was released in 1996, soon to be followed by version 5.0 in 1997. The most recent update is Visual Basic 6.0, which was released in September 1998. Visual Basic (VB) is a key product for Microsoft, and Microsoft has incorporated it as the underlying macro engine in all of its office products. Thus, learning VB will allow you to write a macro in any Microsoft Office application.

VB is more powerful and vastly different from its predecessor, BASIC. The main difference is the speed at which Windows programs can be written in VB. Microsoft specifically designed VB as a rapid application development (RAD) tool that is visually oriented for the Windows environment.

There are four different editions of VB 6.0: Learning, Professional, and Enterprise Editions, and the Visual Basic 6.0 Working Model. Differences between the editions are in the functionality and limitations imposed. All editions require the Windows 95/98/NT operating system. Any edition of VB 6.0 can be used with this textbook. Previous releases may also be used, but the figures in the book may not exactly match the computer screen.

The Visual Basic 6.0 Working Model is a "student version" of Visual Basic and is packaged on a CD-ROM with this textbook. The Working Model allows the student to learn computer programming and write code in Visual Basic, but it does have some major reductions in functionality. For example, the student can write and execute VB code in the Working Model, but the Working Model will not compile code into an executable module.

# Summary

## Key Terms

**abacus**—an ancient counting device still used in some parts of the world today; derived from the Greek abax, meaning table or board covered with dust. Plural is *abaci*

**arithmetic logic unit (ALU)**—the part of a computer responsible for performing all mathematical and logical operations

**assembler**—a program that converts assembly language into machine language

**assembly language**—a low-level language that uses mnemonic instructions

**binary system**—the base-2 number system consisting of the digits 0 and 1

**bit**—a binary digit; a 0 or 1

**byte**—a group of eight bits

**cathode ray tube (CRT)**—see display device

**central processing unit (CPU)**—the "brain" of the computer. In a microcomputer, the CPU is a microprocessor

**compiler**—a computer program that translates high-level source code into machine language and creates an executable file

**decimal system**—the base-10 number system consisting of the digits 0 through 9

**display device**—a specific type of output device that allows the operator to visually see information. Also called the display, monitor, or cathode ray tube (CRT).

**general-purpose language**—a computer language that may be used to solve various types of problems

**gigabyte (GB)**—1,073,741,824 ($2^{30}$) bytes

**graphical user interface (GUI)**—a user-friendly interface composed of both pictures (or icons) and words

**hardware**—the physical components of a computer system

**hardwire**—to permanently place or write into the computer hardware

**high-level language**—a computer language that uses English-like phrases as instructions

**input device**—a device from which the CPU receives information

**interpreter**—a computer language that translates and executes the source code instruction by instruction

**kilobyte (KB)**—1,024 ($2^{10}$) bytes

**low-level language**—a language in which there is a direct (usually one-to-one) correspondence between its instructions and the related machine language instructions

**machine language**—the native binary language of a computer

**mainframe**—a large, powerful, high-speed computer with massive amounts of storage capacity which costs hundreds of thousands to millions of dollars

**megabyte (MB)**—1,048,576 ($2^{20}$) bytes

**memory**—physical locations or addresses where a computer stores information

**microcomputer**—the type of computer that is most commonly purchased by the general public and referred to as a personal computer (PC). Costs usually range from hundreds to thousands of dollars

**microprocessor** (µP)—an integrated circuit that performs the computer's main functions. The microprocessor contains registers and the arithmetic logic unit

**minicomputer**—a computer that is typically not as fast as a mainframe and has a smaller storage capacity with a cost ranging from tens to hundreds of thousands of dollars

**mnemonics**—symbolic assembly language instructions that are easily memorized and understood by a programmer

**monitor**—see display device

**motherboard**—the primary circuit board in a microcomputer

**nibble**—half of a byte; a group of four bits

**operating system**—software that controls how the CPU interacts with all of the other components in the computer system

**output device**—a device to which the CPU sends information

**personal computer**—a microcomputer

**random access memory** (**RAM**)—volatile memory used as workspace by the computer's software programs; this memory is erased when the computer is turned off

**read-only memory** (**ROM**)—nonvolatile memory that contains the computer's permanent instruction set. This type of memory is read-only; data cannot be temporarily stored in this memory

**register**—a memory location internal to a microprocessor

**round-off error**—an error due to the imprecise representation of numbers on a computer

**software**—computer programs or applications

**source code**—a program as written in its original language

**storage device**—a device that allow programs and data files to be saved on storage media for easy retrieval at some later time

**word**—two bytes; a group of 16 bits

## Key Concepts

- There are four generations of electronic computers characterized by the main components of the computers. These generations are divided into vacuum tube, transistor, integrated circuit, and microprocessor-based machines.

- The three different types of computer systems include mainframes, minicomputers, and microcomputers. The differences between these systems are in regard to power, size, and cost.

- Although the focus of this text is on programming microcomputer systems, the programming fundamentals presented are applicable to programming any computer system.

- Hardware consists of the physical components of the computer system. A typical microcomputer system classifies the hardware components into six categories.

- Computer programs and applications that run on a computer are software. The operating system is the most important software package on a computer; it controls the interaction of all computer components.

- The two types of computer memory include random access memory (RAM) and read-only memory (ROM). RAM is volatile memory used as workspace by a computer's software. This memory is erased when the computer is turned off.

ROM is nonvolatile, read-only memory that contains the computer's permanent instruction set.

● People use the decimal number system, the base-10 system. Internally, computers only understand binary or base-2 numbers. The binary number system contains only two digits, 0 and 1.

● Not all numbers can be exactly represented on a computer since numbers are stored using a finite number of bits. This limitation results in round-off errors.

● Computer programming languages evolved from machine language to low-level languages to the high-level languages of today.

● High-level languages can either be interpreters or compilers. A compiler converts the entire source code into an executable module, whereas an interpreter executes the source code line by line.

● Visual Basic is an advanced, Windows-based programming language that evolved from BASIC.

## Review Questions

1. Who is considered to be the "Father of the Computer?"
2. Which mathematician created a system of algebraic logic?
3. Name the three different types of computer systems and explain the differences among them.
4. What is the difference between hardware and software? Give examples of each.
5. Draw a hardware block diagram for a typical microcomputer system.
6. What is the binary number system? Why is it important to understand this number system?
7. What is machine language? Why were low-level and high-level languages developed?

## Chapter 1 Problems

1. Name the four generations of electronic computers and their respective years of inclusion.
2. State the six elements of microcomputer system hardware and the purpose of each element. Give examples of each element.
3. What are RAM and ROM? What are the differences between them?
4. Define the following terms:
   a. bit
   b. byte
   c. nibble
   d. word
   e. kilobyte (KB)
   f. megabyte (MB)
   g. gigabyte (GB)
5. What is the difference between a high-level language and a low-level language? Give examples of each.
6. What is the difference between a compiler and an interpreter? Give example languages for each.

# Computer Arithmetic and Number Systems

## Chapter Supplement Objectives

In this chapter supplement, you will:

- Learn to translate binary numbers to decimal and vice versa

- Perform binary addition and subtraction

- Find the two's complement of a binary number and use it to perform binary subtraction

- Gain an understanding of the octal and hexadecimal number systems

- Learn how to convert numbers between binary, octal, decimal, and hexadecimal

- Perform octal and hexadecimal addition and subtraction

### A Look Back at the Decimal Number System

Chapter 1 introduces binary numbers with $1001\ 1100_2$ as an example binary number. So, what does $1001\ 1100_2$ translate to in decimal? Let's examine a decimal number first. For example, look at the number 1,425. Notice that we do not subscript 1,425 as $1,425_{10}$ since decimal is our natural number system and the base 10 is implied. We all know that this number is one thousand, four hundred and twenty-five, but what do the digits and their locations in respect to each other represent? If you think back to when you were introduced to numbers and the decimal number system, your teacher told you that the five is in the one's place, the two is in the ten's place, the four is in the hundred's place, and the one is in the thousand's place. Then, mathematically, to get this number from the digits, we perform the following operations:

$$(1 \times 1{,}000) + (4 \times 100) + (2 \times 10) + (5 \times 1) = 1{,}425$$

Now, 1, 10, 100, and 1000 are all powers of 10, so we can rewrite the above as:

$$(1 \times 10^3) + (4 \times 10^2) + (2 \times 10^1) + (5 \times 10^0) = 1{,}425$$

Notice that the power of 10 starts at zero with the rightmost digit and increments by one as we proceed from right to left.

## The Binary Number System

This same idea applies to the binary number system, except that powers of 2 are used instead of powers of 10. So, we translate $1001\ 1100_2$ to decimal as follows:

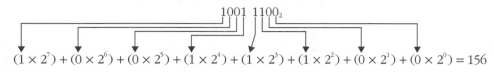

$$1001\ 1100_2$$

$$(1 \times 2^7) + (0 \times 2^6) + (0 \times 2^5) + (1 \times 2^4) + (1 \times 2^3) + (1 \times 2^2) + (0 \times 2^1) + (0 \times 2^0) = 156$$

Figure 1.9 summarizes a method of translating binary numbers to decimal.

How about converting decimal numbers into binary? For example, how do you convert 156 back to its binary equivalent? Well, instead of multiplying by powers of

---

We can explicitly write the decimal equivalent of each bit of the binary number $1001\ 1100_2$:

| 128 | 64 | 32 | 16 | 8 | 4 | 2 | 1 | Value |
|---|---|---|---|---|---|---|---|---|
| $2^7$ | $2^6$ | $2^5$ | $2^4$ | $2^3$ | $2^2$ | $2^1$ | $2^0$ | |
| 1 | 0 | 0 | 1 | 1 | 1 | 0 | 0 | Bit |

Then, to translate $1001\ 1100_2$ to decimal, we perform the following operations:

$$(1 \times 2^7) + (0 \times 2^6) + (0 \times 2^5) + (1 \times 2^4) + (1 \times 2^3) + (1 \times 2^2) + (0 \times 2^1) + (0 \times 2^0) =$$

$$(1 \times 128) + (0 \times 64) + (0 \times 32) + (1 \times 16) + (1 \times 8) + (1 \times 4) + (0 \times 2) + (0 \times 1) =$$

$$128 + 0 + 0 + 16 + 8 + 4 + 0 + 0 = 156$$

As illustrated by the flow chart below, the following algorithm can be used for converting from binary to decimal:

1. Set RESULT = the leftmost bit in the binary number

2. If there is another bit to the right, multiply RESULT by 2 and then add the next bit to RESULT

3. Continue step 2 until there are no more bits to the right

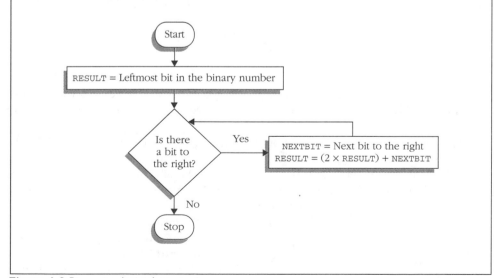

**Figure 1.9** Binary to decimal conversion

Our familiar example of 1001 1100₂ is used to demonstrate:

$$①①①① \; 1 \; 1 \; 0 \; 0_2$$

Iteration 1: RESULT = 1

Iteration 2: RESULT = (1 × 2) + 0 = 2

Iteration 3: RESULT = (2 × 2) + 0 = 4

Iteration 4: RESULT = (4 × 2) + 1 = 9
Iteration 5: RESULT = (9 × 2) + 1 = 19
Iteration 6: RESULT = (19 × 2) + 1 = 39
Iteration 7: RESULT = (39 × 2) + 0 = 78
Iteration 8: RESULT = (78 × 2) + 0 = 156

The algorithm has performed the following operations:

2 (2 (2 (2 (2 (2 (2 (1) + 0) + 0) + 1) + 1) + 1) + 0) + 0 = 156

Notice that this is mathematically equivalent to our original equation:

$(1 \times 2^7) + (0 \times 2^6) + (0 \times 2^5) + (1 \times 2^4) + (1 \times 2^3) + (1 \times 2^2) + (0 \times 2^1) + (0 \times 2^0) =$

2 (2 (2 (2 (2 (2 (2 (1) + 0) + 0) + 1) + 1) + 1) + 0) + 0 = 156

**Figure 1.9** Binary to decimal conversion (continued)

the base number, we use successive divisions. Again, think back to your earlier learning of arithmetic and use long division with remainders at each step, as follows:

$156 \div 2 = 78 \; r \; 0$

$78 \div 2 = 39 \; r \; 0$

$39 \div 2 = 19 \; r \; 1$

$19 \div 2 = 9 \; r \; 1$

$9 \div 2 = 4 \; r \; 1$

$4 \div 2 = 2 \; r \; 0$

$2 \div 2 = 1 \; r \; 0$

$1 \div 2 = 0 \; r \; 1$

So, where is our binary equivalent of 156? Look at the remainders. Do you notice anything? If you write down the remainders in reverse order, you get 1001 1100, or the binary equivalent of 156.

How do you know when to stop performing the successive divisions? In the first division (156 ÷ 2 = 78 r 0), the base number 2 is the divisor, 156 is the dividend, 78 is the quotient, and 0 is the remainder. We stop the successive divisions when the quotient is 0. If we were to continue the successive divisions, we would just get 0 ÷ 2 = 0 r 0 for all further divisions, and the end result would be the same. The **least significant bit** (**LSB**) is the rightmost bit in a binary number since it is associated with the lowest value ($2^0$, or the "one's position"). It is given by the remainder from the first division. The **most significant bit** (**MSB**) is the leftmost bit in a binary number; it is associated with the highest value and is equivalent to the remainder from the last division. Therefore, we reverse the order of the remainders to get our final answer. Figure 1.10 summarizes the method of converting decimal numbers into binary.

## Binary Arithmetic

Now that you know about the binary number system and conversions between binary and decimal, how does the computer perform math? The answer is: The computer performs math exclusively in binary. The rules for binary addition are as follows:

$$0 + 0 = 0$$

$$0 + 1 = 1 + 0 = 1$$

$$1 + 1 = 10_2$$

The last addition "carries" a 1 to the two's place. This is just like addition in the decimal system. You proceed from right to left, or from the least significant digit to the

An algorithm for converting a decimal number to binary:

**1.** Clear the RESULT variable.

**2.** Let DIVIDEND = the decimal number to be converted.

**3.** Let DIVISOR = the base number (= 2 for binary).

**4.** QUOTIENT = DIVIDEND/DIVISOR, where QUOTIENT is an integer value.

**5.** REMAINDER = DIVIDEND − (QUOTIENT × DIVISOR)

**6.** DIVIDEND = QUOTIENT

**7.** RESULT = REMAINDER with the old value of RESULT appended on the right. (This reverses the order of the remainders.)

**8.** Repeat steps 4 through 7 until QUOTIENT = 0.

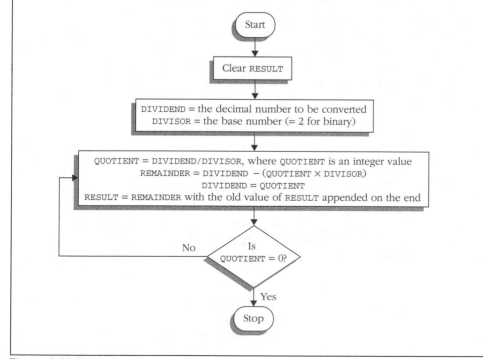

**Figure 1.10** Decimal to binary conversion

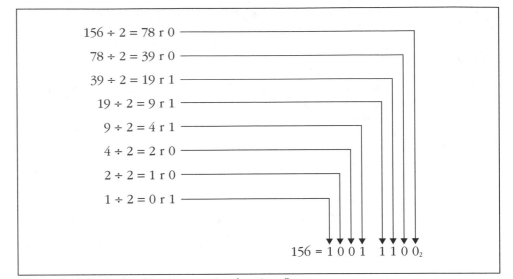

$156 \div 2 = 78 \text{ r } 0$

$78 \div 2 = 39 \text{ r } 0$

$39 \div 2 = 19 \text{ r } 1$

$19 \div 2 = 9 \text{ r } 1$

$9 \div 2 = 4 \text{ r } 1$

$4 \div 2 = 2 \text{ r } 0$

$2 \div 2 = 1 \text{ r } 0$

$1 \div 2 = 0 \text{ r } 1$

$156 = 1001\ 1100_2$

**Figure 1.10** Decimal to binary conversion (continued)

most significant digit, adding the corresponding digits and "carrying" any excess tens over to the next addition operation. When you add 17 to 15, for example, you first add the 7 and 5, giving you 12. You then "carry" the 1 to the ten's place and add the three 1s, giving you a 3. The result is 32. Use this same reasoning to add the following two binary numbers:

$$1011\ 1000_2$$

$$+\ 1011\ 0111_2$$

Did you get $1\ 0110\ 1111_2$? Did you correctly reason that $1 + 1$ plus a "carried" $1 = 11_2$?

How about subtraction? Again, think of the decimal system first; you proceed from right to left and subtract corresponding digits. When the subtrahend is larger than the digit from which it is being subtracted, you "borrow" a ten from the next digit to the left. When you subtract 65 from 256, for instance, you first subtract 5 from 6. The result is 1. Next, you need to subtract 6 from 5, but 6 is larger than 5. So, you "borrow" a ten from the 2 on the left. The 2 becomes a 1, and 6 is subtracted from 15, giving you a 9. Finally, nothing (or 0) is subtracted from the 1, and the result is 191. Use this same method to perform the following binary subtraction:

$$1011\ 1000_2$$

$$-\ 1011\ 0111_2$$

Did you get $0000\ 0001_2$? Did you correctly reason that you need to "borrow" from the 1 in the eight's position (the fourth bit from the right)? Did you perform the sequential "borrowing" operation correctly?

The subtraction method described above is not really how computers perform subtraction. The only mathematical operation most computers can really perform is binary addition. So, how do computers subtract numbers? Well, if you were to rewrite $256 - 65$ as an addition, it is equivalent to $256 + (-65)$. That's right, computers perform subtraction by simply adding a negative number.

How do we represent the negative of a binary number? Without getting into too much detail about computer representation of numbers, the computer equivalent of the negative of a binary number is the **two's complement** of the number. Once the two's complement has been determined, the desired subtraction can then be completed by adding the negative (or two's complement) of the number. To illustrate, consider the following example:

Subtract 36 from 163 in binary.

*Step 1.* Write the numbers in binary

$$1010\ 0011_2 \qquad \text{163 in binary}$$
$$\underline{-\ 0010\ 0100_2} \qquad \text{36 in binary}$$

*Step 2.* Find the one's complement of the subtrahend. For a binary number, the **one's complement** is found by reversing all of the bits: each 0 becomes a 1 and each 1 becomes a 0.

$$0010\ 0100_2 \longrightarrow 1101\ 1011_2$$

36 in binary $\longrightarrow$ one's complement of 36 in binary

*Step 3.* Find the two's complement of the subtrahend by simply adding a 1 to the one's complement.

$$1101\ 1011_2 \longrightarrow 1101\ 1100_2$$

one's complement of 36 in binary $\longrightarrow$ two's complement of 36 in binary

*Step 4.* Complete the subtraction by *adding* the two's complement of the subtrahend to the first term.

$$1010\ 0011_2 \qquad \text{(163 in binary)}$$
$$\underline{+\ 1101\ 1100_2} \qquad \text{(two's complement of 36 in binary)}$$
$$\boxed{1}\ 0111\ 1111_2$$

When added together, the two binary numbers give us $0111\ 1111_2$, or 127. So what happened to the "carried" 1 from the leftmost addition? Stated very simply, we ignore it. If you don't ignore it, your answer is a number larger than 163, which does not make sense for a subtraction operation. The basic rule for binary subtraction is that your answer should always have the same number of bits as your original values.

## Octal and Hexadecimal Number Systems

Working with binary numbers can be quite tedious since large decimal numbers are very lengthy when represented in binary. Therefore, computer programmers use two other number systems, **octal** (base 8) and **hexadecimal** (base 16), or *hex* for short. Binary numbers have two digits, 0 and 1; octal numbers have eight digits, 0 through 7; and hexadecimal numbers have sixteen digits. With only ten digits in the decimal system, 0 through 9, how do we represent sixteen different digits in hexadecimal? The answer is to use a combination of numbers and letters. Hexadecimal digits consist of the numbers 0 through 9 and the letters A through F, where A represents 10 and F represents 15. As you may have surmised, for any base $n$, there are $n$ digits, 0 through the digit or letter representing the value $n - 1$. Similar to subscripting a binary number with 2, octal numbers are commonly subscripted with an 8, and hexadecimal numbers are subscripted with either a 16 or the letter H. Octal–decimal and hexadecimal–decimal conversions follow rules similar to binary–decimal conversions. Examples are shown in Figure 1.11.

Binary–octal, binary–hexadecimal, and octal–hexadecimal conversions are simple since both 8 and 16 are multiples of 2. It is just a matter of regrouping the bits. One octal digit can be represented with three bits. To convert binary to octal, start from the right-hand side and group the bits in threes, and then write the octal equivalent of each group of bits. Using our example of $1001\ 1100_2$:

**1.** Regroup the bits in threes: $10\!01\ 1\!100$        $010\ 011\ 100$
**2.** Write the octal equivalent:                                2    3    4

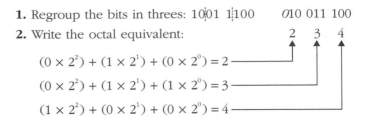

$$(0 \times 2^2) + (1 \times 2^1) + (0 \times 2^0) = 2$$
$$(0 \times 2^2) + (1 \times 2^1) + (1 \times 2^0) = 3$$
$$(1 \times 2^2) + (0 \times 2^1) + (0 \times 2^0) = 4$$

Thus, $1001\ 1100_2 = 234_8$. Notice that the leading zero is implied when we regroup the bits. In other words, any bit to the left of the MSB in a binary number is inherently a zero. To convert back from octal to binary, simply write each octal digit in binary form using three bits per octal digit.

The same method can be used to convert between binary and hexadecimal, only the bits must be grouped in fours (which is why binary numbers are commonly written as nibbles). Using our example on the next page:

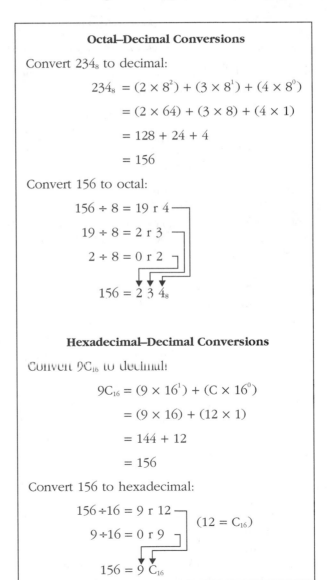

**Octal–Decimal Conversions**

Convert $234_8$ to decimal:

$$234_8 = (2 \times 8^2) + (3 \times 8^1) + (4 \times 8^0)$$
$$= (2 \times 64) + (3 \times 8) + (4 \times 1)$$
$$= 128 + 24 + 4$$
$$= 156$$

Convert 156 to octal:

$$156 \div 8 = 19 \text{ r } 4$$
$$19 \div 8 = 2 \text{ r } 3$$
$$2 \div 8 = 0 \text{ r } 2$$
$$156 = 2\ 3\ 4_8$$

**Hexadecimal–Decimal Conversions**

Convert $9C_{16}$ to decimal:

$$9C_{16} = (9 \times 16^1) + (C \times 16^0)$$
$$= (9 \times 16) + (12 \times 1)$$
$$= 144 + 12$$
$$= 156$$

Convert 156 to hexadecimal:

$$156 \div 16 = 9 \text{ r } 12 \qquad (12 = C_{16})$$
$$9 \div 16 = 0 \text{ r } 9$$
$$156 = 9\ C_{16}$$

**Figure 1.11** Octal–decimal and hexadecimal–decimal conversions

**1.** Regroup the bits in fours:                                        1001 1100

**2.** Write the hexadecimal equivalent:                          9      C

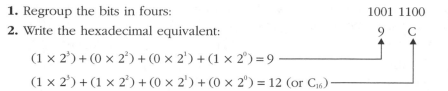

$$(1 \times 2^3) + (0 \times 2^2) + (0 \times 2^1) + (1 \times 2^0) = 9$$
$$(1 \times 2^3) + (1 \times 2^2) + (0 \times 2^1) + (0 \times 2^0) = 12 \text{ (or } C_{16})$$

Thus, $1001\ 1100_2 = 9C_{16}$. Again, converting back from hexadecimal to binary is simply a matter of writing each hexadecimal digit in binary form using four bits per hexadecimal digit.

To convert between octal and hexadecimal, translate the number to binary first and then convert the binary number into the desired base. To convert $74_8$ to hexadecimal, for instance:

**1.** Write $74_8$ in binary:                          111 100

**2.** Regroup the bits in fours:                      111 100        0011 1100

**3.** Write the hexadecimal equivalent:                          3      C

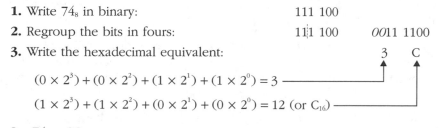

$$(0 \times 2^3) + (0 \times 2^2) + (1 \times 2^1) + (1 \times 2^0) = 3$$
$$(1 \times 2^3) + (1 \times 2^2) + (0 \times 2^1) + (0 \times 2^0) = 12 \text{ (or } C_{16})$$

So, $74_8 = 3C_{16}$.

Addition and subtraction in octal and hexadecimal are performed in the same manner as their decimal counterparts. Remember to "carry" or "borrow" eights and sixteens instead of tens. Examples of addition and subtraction in octal and hexadecimal are shown in Figure 1.12. Many scientific calculators can perform conversions and mathematics in binary, octal, decimal, and hexadecimal.

## Summary

### Key Terms

**hexadecimal**—the base-16 number system consisting of the digits 0 through 9 and A through F

**least significant bit (LSB)**—the rightmost bit in a binary number; the bit that is associated with the lowest value ($2^0$, or the one's position)

**Octal**

$$654_8$$
$$+\ 307_8$$
$$\overline{1163_8}$$

$$654_8$$
$$-\ 307_8$$
$$\overline{345_8}$$

**Hexadecimal**

$$1AC_{16}$$
$$+\ \ C7_{16}$$
$$\overline{273_{16}}$$

$$1AC_{16}$$
$$-\ \ C7_{16}$$
$$\overline{E5_{16}}$$

**Figure 1.12** Examples of addition and subtraction in octal and hexadecimal

**most significant bit (MSB)**—the leftmost bit in a binary number; the bit that is associated with the highest value

**octal**—the base-8 number system consisting of the digits 0 through 7

**one's complement**—the binary number resulting from reversing (or complementing) each bit of a binary number

**two's complement**—the binary number resulting from adding one to the one's complement; the computer representation of the negative of a binary number

## Key Concepts

- The binary system is the base-2 number system; octal refers to the base-8 system, decimal to the base-10 system, and hexadecimal to the base-16 number system.

- The rules for decimal arithmetic have counterparts in other number bases, such as the rules for "carrying" and "borrowing" values.

- The two's complement of a binary number is useful for performing binary subtraction. The two's complement is essentially the negative of a binary value. It is formed by adding one to the one's complement, where the one's complement results from reversing the bits of a binary number.

- Conversions from base $n$ to decimal are performed by multiplying each digit in the base-$n$ number by $n^p$, where p represents the position of the digit, and then summing the results. The rightmost digit is in position 0. This is the same as performing successive multiplications by $n$. Starting with the leftmost digit in the base-$n$ number, multiply the value by $n$ and then add the next digit to the right. Continue this process until there are no more digits.

- Decimal to base-$n$ conversions are performed using successive divisions. Using long division (with quotients and remainders), divide the original decimal number by $n$. Then, continue to divide the quotients by $n$ until the quotient is zero. Reversing the order of the remainders yields the decimal value expressed as a base-$n$ number.

- Binary–octal–hexadecimal conversions are performed by regrouping the bits.

## Review Questions

1. Describe how to convert between binary and decimal.
2. What is the one's complement of a binary number?
3. What is the two's complement of a binary number? What purpose does it serve?
4. What are octal and hexadecimal numbers? What are the digits used in each system?
5. Describe how to convert between binary and octal, binary and hexadecimal, and octal and hexadecimal.
6. Describe how to convert between octal and decimal and between decimal and hexadecimal.

## Chapter I Supplement Problems

1. Convert the following binary numbers to decimal by multiplying each bit by its respective decimal value and summing the results.
   a. $0011_2$
   b. $0011\ 0011_2$

c.  $1010\ 1001_2$

d.  $0110\ 1000_2$

e.  $1100\ 1001\ 0011_2$

f.  $0111\ 1100\ 1001\ 0011_2$

2. Convert the binary numbers in Problem 1 to decimal using the algorithm in Figure 1.9.

3. Convert the following decimal numbers to binary.

a.  13

b.  42

c.  125

d.  255

e.  300

4. What decimal values can be represented using one bit? one nibble? one byte? one word?

5. Perform the following binary additions.

a.  $0100\ 1101_2 + 1010\ 0011_2$

b.  $0101\ 1101_2 + 0000\ 0011_2$

c.  $1000\ 1101_2 + 0011\ 1111_2$

d.  $1111\ 1111_2 + 0000\ 0001_2$

e.  $1111\ 1111_2 + 1111\ 1111_2$

6. Perform the following binary subtractions using the "borrowing" method.

a.  $0110\ 0010_2 - 0001\ 0011_2$

b.  $1110\ 0011_2 - 0000\ 0011_2$

c.  $0010\ 0110_2 - 0001\ 0011_2$

d.  $1000\ 1111_2 - 0001\ 0101_2$

e.  $1110\ 0000_2 - 0110\ 0011_2$

7. Perform the binary subtractions of Problem 6 using the two's complement method.

8. Convert the following binary numbers to octal and hexadecimal

a.  $1110_2$

b.  $1110\ 1001_2$

c.  $1111\ 1101\ 0110_2$

d.  $0011\ 1001\ 1111\ 0010_2$

9. For each of the problems shown below, perform the required operation in decimal. Then, convert the decimal numbers to binary, octal, and hexadecimal and perform the same mathematical operation in the different bases. Convert your results back to decimal to check your answers.

a.  221 + 187

b.  221 − 187

c.  162 − 137

d.  162 + 137

e.  198 − 77

f.  198 + 77

g.  240 − 18

h.  240 + 18

# 2

# The Visual Basic Development Environment

## Chapter Objectives

In this chapter, you will:

- Become familiar with the operation of a graphical user interface (GUI), including the use of the mouse and icons

- Learn the necessity of an easy, yet functional user interface

- Become familiar with the Visual Basic (VB) integrated development environment, including the menus and windows

- Become familiar with the "elementary" VB controls

- Learn how to create a simple user interface

- Gain an understanding of the relationship between VB projects and forms

- Learn about the different VB file types

- Learn about the VB editor and how to save, print, compile, and execute a program

- Become familiar with the VB help facility and online documentation

This chapter describes the Visual Basic (VB) program development philosophy and introduces the VB screen layout and "elementary" controls. It is designed to quickly familiarize you with the VB development environment.

## THE VISUAL BASIC PHILOSOPHY

The Microsoft Windows operating system provides the user with a simple **graphical user interface (GUI)**. In this GUI, a user controls the operations of the computer by moving a **pointer** and selecting **icons**. An icon is a button with a picture, and it may represent either a **program (application)** or **folder** (directory location). For instance, the ⬛ icon is associated with Microsoft Word word-processing software, and the ⬛ icon represents a folder containing personal files. The user controls the pointer by physically moving an input device, such as a **mouse**. An icon is "activated" by positioning the pointer above the icon and then clicking the left mouse button twice (i.e., **double-clicking** the left mouse button).

In such a graphical operating environment, it is desirable to include a graphical, point-and-click interface in applications software as well. Before object-oriented programming and the Windows graphical user interface, creating such user interfaces required a great deal of programming effort. To simplify this lengthy programming chore, VB provides the programmer with a **toolbox** of user interface controls that can be used to quickly design interfaces with point-and-click, drag-and-drop ease. To create a user interface, the programmer needs only to select the desired controls from the toolbox and place them in the program. To make this task easily achievable, Microsoft designed VB as a language for **rapid application development (RAD)** under the Windows operating system.

So, why do we place so much interest in a program's user interface? Well, the importance of a simple and appealing user interface should not be underestimated. Extremely useful and effective programs have failed miserably in the commercial market because of their complicated user interfaces. The bottom line is this: *Programs should make things easy for the user, not the other way around.* In other words, *a programmer should take whatever steps are necessary to ensure that a program suits the customer's needs, not only in terms of functionality but also in terms of ease of use.* Therefore, a constant dialog between the programmer and customer is essential. VB provides a perfect vehicle for this task. It allows a programmer to easily design a user interface that satisfies the customer's requirements. Any modifications can be made "on the fly" until the customer is satisfied with the user interface.

## USING VISUAL BASIC

### Key Term

control—an object in the user interface of a VB program or any object that may appear in the VB Toolbox window

This section provides a rudimentary introduction to Visual Basic. As you'll soon see, VB programs display a Windows-type screen known as a **form**. The boxes, buttons, sliders, and other such **objects** that are typically found on such forms are referred to as **controls**. We'll describe the VB opening screen, menus, toolbars, and windows and then introduce the five "elementary" VB controls that comprise a simple user interface. We also show how to place, move, and size controls in a user interface.

In the next section, you will create your first Visual Basic program. In the process, you will learn about the VB editor and how to save, print, compile, and run (or execute) your programs.

Finally, the last section of this chapter describes the VB help facility and online documentation.

## THE VISUAL BASIC OPENING SCREEN

When you start VB, the Microsoft Visual Basic "splash page" appears. This "splash page" simply announces that VB is starting. Next, the New Project window shown in Figure 2.1 appears on the screen. From this window, you may choose to create a new project (under the New tab) or work on an existing project that is listed under the Existing or Recent tabs. A new project may be one of several different types. Standard executable files, ActiveX executables, ActiveX **dynamic link libraries** (**DLL**s), ActiveX controls, and Add-Ins are a few of the most common project types.

For the most part, we use standard executable files. In a later chapter, you will learn how to create ActiveX controls (see Chapter 10). Unless stated otherwise, a new project will be initiated by selecting "Standard EXE" (standard executable file) and clicking the Open button in the New Project window.

## VISUAL BASIC SCREEN LAYOUT

Figure 2.2 shows the typical VB **integrated development environment** (**IDE**) screen layout. Like most other Windows applications, this screen contains a menu bar and a toolbar. Additionally, it contains five smaller windows: the Project Explorer window, Form window, Properties window, Form Layout window, and Toolbox window.

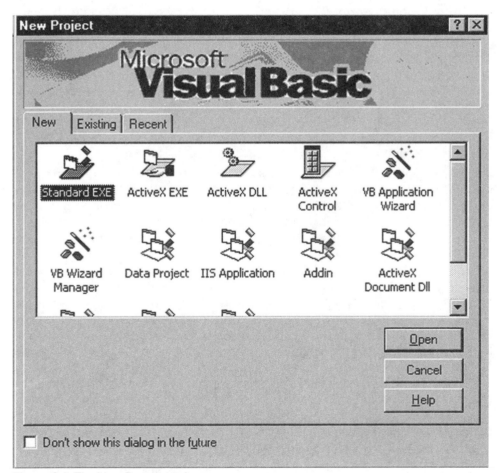

**Figure 2.1** The New Project window

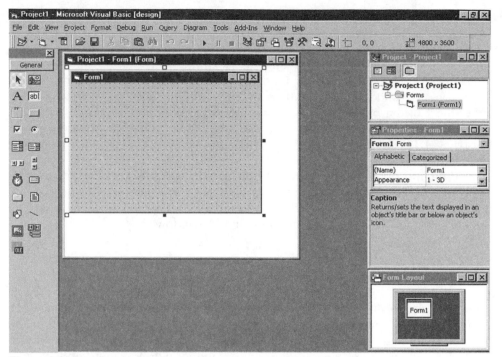

**Figure 2.2** Visual Basic screen layout

The VB **menu bar** appears in Figure 2.3. This is a typical drop-down menu; that is, when a menu item is selected, all of the options available for that menu item appear on a drop-down list. An example of the drop-down list for the View option of the menu bar can be seen in Figure 2.3. Positioning the pointer over the desired menu option and pressing the left mouse button activates the drop-down menu. To select an option from the drop-down menu, position the pointer over the desired menu option and press the left mouse button (i.e., left-click on the option).

You'll notice, in Figure 2.3, that there are many menu headings on the menu bar. Rather than describe each menu heading and all of the related tasks and options in detail, we introduce them as necessary in the text. When a reference to a menu and subsequent menu option is required, we will use the following naming convention: Menu Heading/Option. You should select the Menu Heading from the Menu bar and then select the Option from the associated drop-down menu. We encourage you to experiment with these menus as a way of increasing your familiarity with the VB user interface. You cannot physically damage your computer by experimenting with VB.

As with most applications, the **toolbar** contains icons that provide a shortcut means of performing various tasks found on the menu bar. The ✄ icon, for instance, which means "Cut," can also be found in the Edit menu. To display the meaning of a toolbar icon, simply position the pointer on the icon and leave it there. After a few seconds, a description of the icon's function will appear. Once again, we encourage you to experiment with the toolbar so that you can become familiar with each icon.

Figure 2.4 shows the standard toolbar and the associated icon descriptions. This toolbar can be customized to suit your needs by right-clicking in an empty area of the toolbar and selecting the Customize option. Additionally, right-clicking the toolbar provides access to the Debug, Edit, and Form Editor toolbars.

If the standard toolbar is not visible, select View/Toolbars/Standard from the menu. The View/Toolbars menu allows you to select the toolbars to be displayed and to customize them to suit your personal preferences.

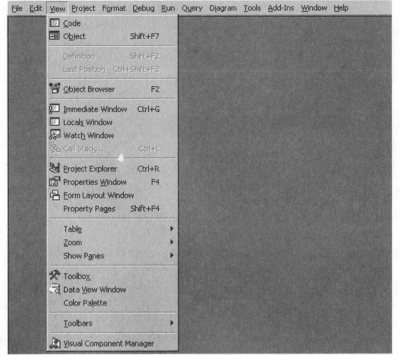

**Figure 2.3** Visual Basic menu bar and drop-down menus

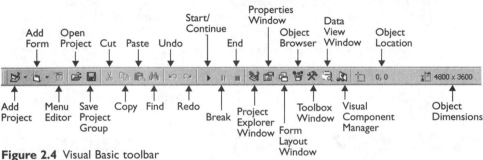

**Figure 2.4** Visual Basic toolbar

On the standard toolbar, the object location and dimensions indicators show the position of the current object relative to the upper left-hand corner of the form and the size of the object (width × height), respectively. The default unit of measurement in VB is **twips**, of which there are approximately 1,440 per **logical inch.** (A logical inch is the length of a screen item measuring one inch when printed.) This ensures that the placement and proportional sizes of screen elements are the same on all display systems.

The **Project Explorer window** displays a hierarchical list of all open **projects** and the items contained in these projects. Each project is a different VB program. So, VB allows a programmer to simultaneously have multiple programs open in the IDE. Figure 2.5 shows a Project Explorer window with an open project named `Project1`, which itself contains a form named `Form1`. If the Project Explorer window does not appear on your screen, you can display it by selecting View/Project Explorer, pressing the CTRL key and R key (CTRL+R), or left-clicking on its icon in the toolbar.

A form is the default container for VB controls. Essentially, it comprises the user interface of your program. The currently selected form (highlighted in the Project Explorer window) is displayed in the **Form window**. From this window, the form can be edited, resized, and have VB control objects placed on it. Figure 2.6 shows a sample Form window containing a blank form named `Form1`. If the Form window

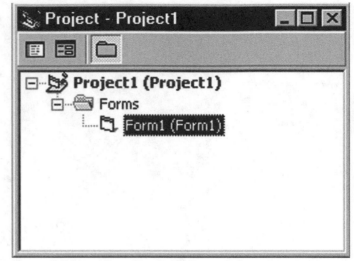

**Figure 2.5** Visual Basic Project Explorer window

does not appear on your screen, double-click on the form name or select the desired form and left-click on the View Object icon in the Project Explorer window.

All controls in VB are objects, so VB is an **object-oriented language**. All objects have various **properties** associated with them. A form, for instance, is an object in VB and has certain properties, such as a name, height, and width. When a new control object is created, VB automatically assigns **default settings** to each of its properties. As you design your program (i.e., at **design time**), the **Properties window** allows you to change a control's properties from their default settings. Changing a property is as simple as clicking on the property that you'd like to change and replacing the current setting with the desired setting.

Figure 2.7 shows an example Properties window for a form named Form1. If the Properties window does not appear on your computer screen, it may be dis-

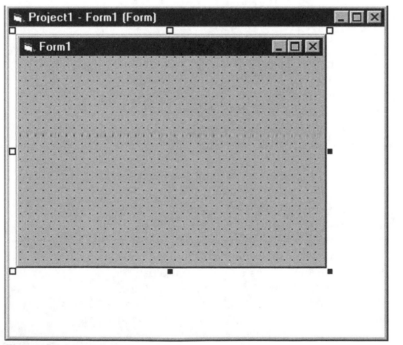

**Figure 2.6** Visual Basic Form window

**Figure 2.7** Visual Basic Properties window

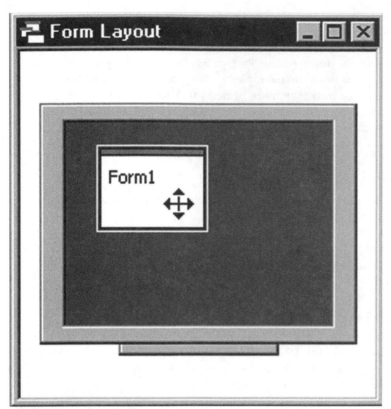

**Figure 2.8** Visual Basic Form layout window

**Figure 2.9**
Visual Basic
Toolbox window

played by selecting View/Properties Window, pressing the F4 key or CTRL+W, or left-clicking on its icon in the toolbar.

The **Form Layout window** allows you to visually position your forms at design time. When you move the pointer over a form in this window, the pointer changes to a pair of arrows. Hold down the left mouse button and move the mouse to reposition the form on the screen. This operation is referred to as **dragging**. The form does not reposition itself in the IDE, but it will appear in this location when your program executes (i.e., at **run time**).

A sample Form Layout window is shown in Figure 2.8. If the Form Layout window does not appear on the computer screen, it may be displayed by selecting View/Form Layout Window or by left-clicking on its icon in the toolbar.

As shown in Figure 2.9, the **Toolbox window** displays all standard VB controls and any other controls that you have added to your project. Again, each of these controls is an object that has properties associated with it. If the Toolbox window does not appear on the screen, select View/Toolbox or left-click on its icon in the toolbar to display it.

Now that you've been introduced to the VB user interface and the concept of VB controls, let's look more closely at five "elementary" VB controls that you'll be using throughout this text.

## Key Terms

**design time**—the time when the program and user interface are being written in the VB integrated development environment
**run time**—the time when the program is executing or running

## ELEMENTARY VISUAL BASIC CONTROLS

The "elementary" VB controls are not described as elementary because they are easier to use than other controls, but rather because they are generally used in more complex combinations to form a simple user interface for a program. The elementary controls include labels, text boxes, picture boxes, command buttons, and forms.

Of these five control objects, the **form** is the only object that does not appear in the Toolbox. To insert a new form in your project, select Project/Add Form or click the Add Form button on the toolbar. Similarly, to remove a form from your project, select the form in the Project Explorer window and then select Project/Remove Form. Most of the examples in this text use projects consisting of only one form. Creation of more complex projects that require the use of multiple forms is discussed in Chapter 10. For now, our discussion concentrates on the four other elementary controls.

## LABEL

A **label** is a control used in a program to display text that the user will be unable to change. You can follow the steps listed below to practice using the label control:

1. Start a new project by selecting File/New Project or pressing CTRL+N. Select Standard EXE for a standard executable file and click the OK button.

2. Place a label on your form. This can be accomplished by double-clicking the label icon in the Toolbox.

3. Now, move this label by dragging it to a new location on the form: With the mouse over the label, click and hold the left mouse button and then move the mouse to reposition the label. When the label is in the desired location, release the mouse button.

4. Change the (Name) property of the label to lblMyLabel. In the Properties window, click on the (Name) property and then type lblMyLabel. Make sure that you are changing the properties of the label and not the form. Verify this by ensuring that Label1 Label appears in the box at the top of the Properties window.

5. Select the Caption property in the Properties window and type: This is my first label! The caption on the label changes as you type this text.

6. Select the AutoSize property. Click the arrow in the property box and select True from the drop-down menu. This tells VB to automatically size the label to fit your caption.

7. Change the background and foreground colors of the label. Select the BackColor property, click on the arrow in the box, and select the Palette tab. Click on the light yellow color. Next, select the ForeColor property and repeat the above steps, but select red instead of light yellow.

8. Change the label's font. Select the Font property and click on the ellipses (the three dots). From the Font menu, change the font to Arial, style to Bold Italic, and size to 20. Then, click the OK button.

9. Finally, add another label to the form. This time, single-click on the label control in the Toolbox. Next, go to an empty space on the form in the Form window and click and hold the left mouse button. Drag the mouse and then release the mouse button. The new label appears on your form in the exact size and position where you dragged the mouse.

10. Now let's run this very rudimentary program. This can be accomplished three ways—by clicking the Start icon in the toolbar, selecting Run/Start from the menu bar, or pressing the F5 key. VB should display a form similar to the one shown in Figure 2.10.

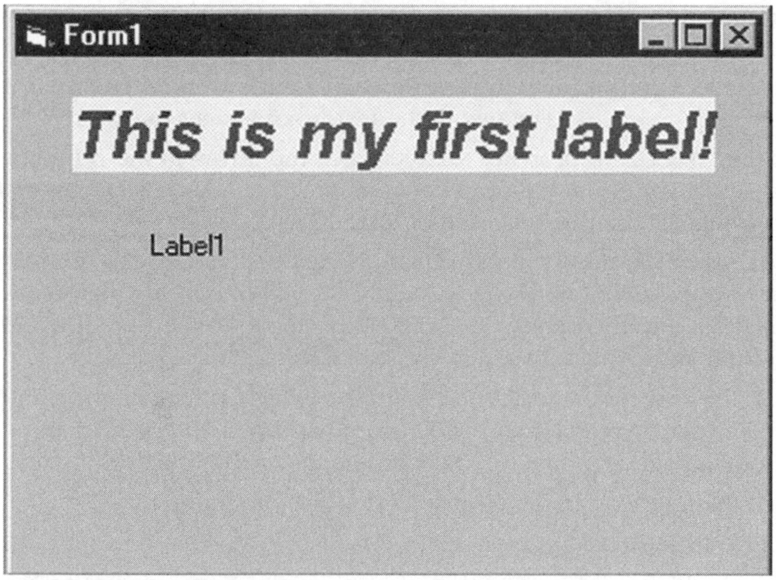

**Figure 2.10** Label control example

**11.** Stop the program by clicking the X in the upper right-hand corner of the form, clicking the End icon on the toolbar, or by selecting Run/End from the menu bar.

## TEXT BOX

A **text box** control, also called an edit field or edit control, contains text that is placed in the box either at design time or at run time. The Text property contains the text that is displayed in the text box, and the MultiLine property specifies whether or not the text box displays text on multiple lines. The Font property allows you to set the Font object properties for the text box control. If the Locked property is set to True, data in the text box cannot be altered by the user at run time. If you want to practice using the text box control, just follow these steps:

**1.** Start a new project by selecting File/New Project or pressing CTRL+N. Select Standard EXE for a standard executable file and click the OK button.

**2.** Place a text box on your form. This can be accomplished by double-clicking the text box icon in the Toolbox.

**3.** Resize the text box. Position the pointer on top of one of the "sizing handles" along the perimeter of the text box and click-and-drag using the left mouse button. When the text box is the desired size, release the mouse button.

**4.** Now, move this text box by dragging it to a new location on the form: With the mouse over the text box, click and hold the left mouse button and then move the mouse to reposition the text box. When the text box is in the desired location, release the mouse button.

**5.** Change the (Name) property of the text box to txtMyText. In the Properties window, click on the (Name) property and then type: txtMyText. Make sure that you are changing the properties of the text box and not the form. Verify this by ensuring that Text1 TextBox appears in the box at the top of the Properties window.

6. Select the Text property in the Properties window and type: This is a text box control. The text in the text box changes as you type.

7. Set the MultiLine property to True. Click the arrow in the property box and select True from the drop-down menu. This tells VB that the text box can contain more than one line of text.

8. Now, select the Text property again. Notice that it is now a drop-down window containing lines of text. Add a second line of text that reads Line two and then press CTRL+ENTER to move to the third line. Add a third line of text that says: And yet another line of text.

9. Press the F5 key to execute this interface (which is really a program with none of our own code) and experiment with the text box. The screen should appear as in Figure 2.11. Change some of the text in the text box.

10. Click the End icon in the toolbar to stop the program.

11. Change the Locked property to True.

12. Press the F5 key to execute this interface again. Now, attempt to change the text in the text box. Notice that it cannot be changed by the user while the interface is executing (i.e., at run time).

13. Click the End icon in the toolbar to stop the program.

Well, you just created a few simple forms (and VB programs) within minutes. Yes, it is really that easy to create a Windows-based user interface using VB. You are now familiar with several commonly used properties of both the label and text box controls. Rather than present detailed step-by-step outlines for each of the remaining elementary controls, we encourage you to experiment with the different controls and property settings. You can design some really creative interfaces. We briefly describe the remaining elementary controls below.

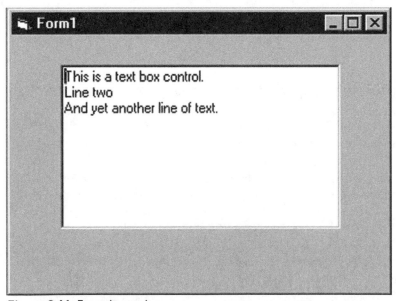

**Figure 2.11** Example text box

## PICTURE BOX

A **picture box** can display text or graphics (pictures). If a picture is to be displayed, the `Picture` property is used to specify the file name of the picture. Picture boxes are used solely for output; there is no way to extract data from the text or pictures displayed in a picture box.

## COMMAND BUTTON

A **command button** is used to begin, interrupt, or end a process. Command buttons are typically used to execute a portion of code or an entire program. In other words, the user expects something to happen when a command button is clicked. When a command button is clicked with the mouse, it appears to be "pushed in." So, command buttons are also referred to as push buttons.

Command buttons can be assigned **shortcut key combinations**. This is a way of making a combination of keyboard keys equivalent to clicking the command button with the mouse. For example, try the following:

1. Start a new project by selecting File/New Project or pressing CTRL+N.
2. Place a command button on the blank form (Form1).
3. Change the (`Name`) property to cmdMyButton.
4. Change the `Caption` property to &Click Me.

Notice that the caption of cmdMyButton reads Click Me and not &Click Me. The ampersand (&) in front of a character in the Caption property denotes the shortcut key combination. This character is underlined in the caption that appears on the command button to indicate the availability of a shortcut key to the user. At run time, the shortcut key combination is activated by holding down the ALT key and then pressing the key associated with the underlined character. In this case, hold down the ALT key and then press the C key (denoted ALT+C) on the keyboard (at run time). This result is comparable to clicking the cmdMyButton command button, except that the button does not appear to be "pushed in" as it does when it is clicked. To place an ampersand in the caption of a command button, use the double ampersand (&&). For instance, setting the Caption property of cmdMyButton to This && That displays the caption This & That on the button, and no shortcut key is assigned to the button.

## PLACING, MOVING, AND SIZING CONTROLS

As described in the label and text box control examples above, there are two methods of placing a control on a form, either double-clicking or clicking-and-dragging. These methods work for all Toolbox controls.

What if you want to change the position of a control object? To reposition a control object, simply click-and-drag the object to the desired position on the form. When the control is in the desired location, release the mouse button. While repositioning a control, the object location (relative to the top left-hand corner of the form) appears underneath the mouse pointer after a short pause in mouse movement. The default unit of measurement is twips (1 inch = 1,440 twips).

A control object is resized by selecting the object (clicking on the object) and then dragging a sizing handle until the object reaches the desired size. Figure 2.12 displays an example of a text box with sizing handles. While resizing a control, the

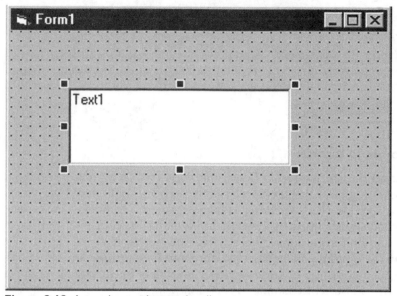

**Figure 2.12** A text box with sizing handles

object dimensions appear underneath the mouse pointer after a short pause in mouse movement. As with the location information, the default unit of measurement for size is twips.

## ACCESSING ADDITIONAL TOOLBOX CONTROLS

By default, Visual Basic has the most commonly used controls preloaded in the Toolbox. There are additional (more advanced) controls that are available to the programmer simply by adding them to the Toolbox. To add additional controls, right-click in an empty area of the Toolbox and select Components from the pop-up menu. The Components window (Figure 2.13) opens and you can select the controls that you want to add to the Toolbox. Click on the box adjacent to the desired controls. A check mark will appear in the box to·indicate the control that will be added to the Toolbox. Make sure a check mark appears in the box next to the components that you want to add and then click the OK button. We will use several of these controls in later chapters.

## CONTROL NAMING CONVENTIONS

Throughout this text, we use a prescript consisting of three lowercase characters as the naming convention for all VB control objects. For instance, all label names are prescripted with lbl, and a label that identifies the date is named lblDate rather than just Date. Similarly, text boxes are prescripted with txt, picture boxes with pic, and command buttons with cmd. This allows a programmer to easily identify the type of control object based solely upon the name.

## CHANGING THE INTEGRATED DEVELOPMENT ENVIRONMENT

Visual Basic allows you to modify the IDE by changing environment options. Select Tools/Options from the menu bar and the Options window shown in Figure 2.14

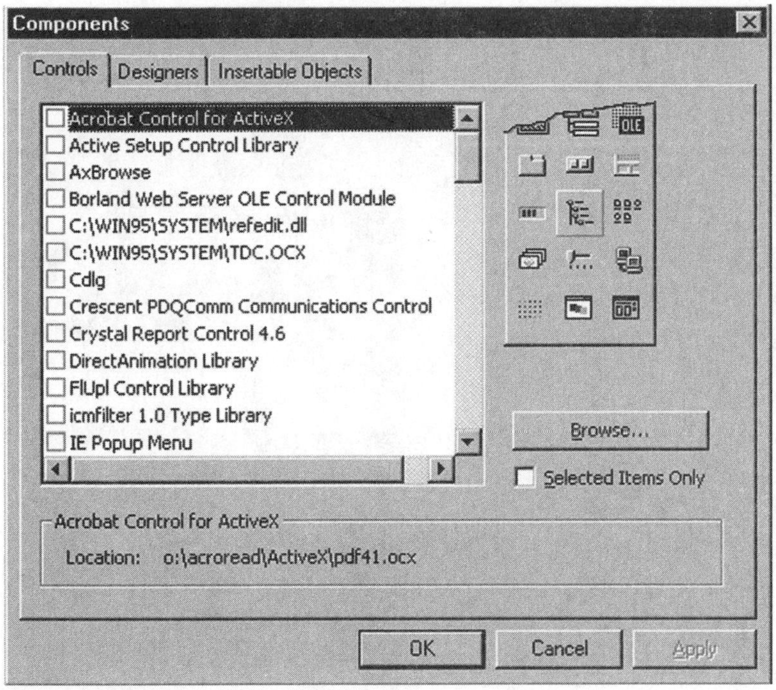

**Figure 2.13** The Components window

appears on your screen. From this window, you can select tabs and options to modify the VB editor or working environment. Specific options are discussed in later sections of the text as they arise. Additionally, Chapter 2 Supplement describes how to customize the VB IDE and explains the Option window tabs and settings in detail.

## YOUR FIRST PROGRAM

Of course, this text would be incomplete without a VB version of the infamous "Hello, World!" program. This section provides the instructions necessary for you to create your first VB program, and it helps you to practice working with the VB interface and controls. Once again, learning comes through experimentation, so feel free to experiment with VB. You cannot physically damage your computer by programming, experimenting, or playing with VB.

Figure 2.15 displays the form we will use in our program. Notice that the form contains a command button and a picture box. In the beginning chapters of this text, we provide programming examples by displaying the form in a figure. Accompanying the figure is a table that lists object types and property settings that were changed from the default settings. The table below shows the object types and property settings applicable to this program:

| Object | Property | Setting |
| --- | --- | --- |
| Form | Name | frmMyProgram |
| | Caption | My First Program |
| Command Button | Name | cmdDisplay |
| | Caption | Display Message |
| Picture Box | Name | picOutput |

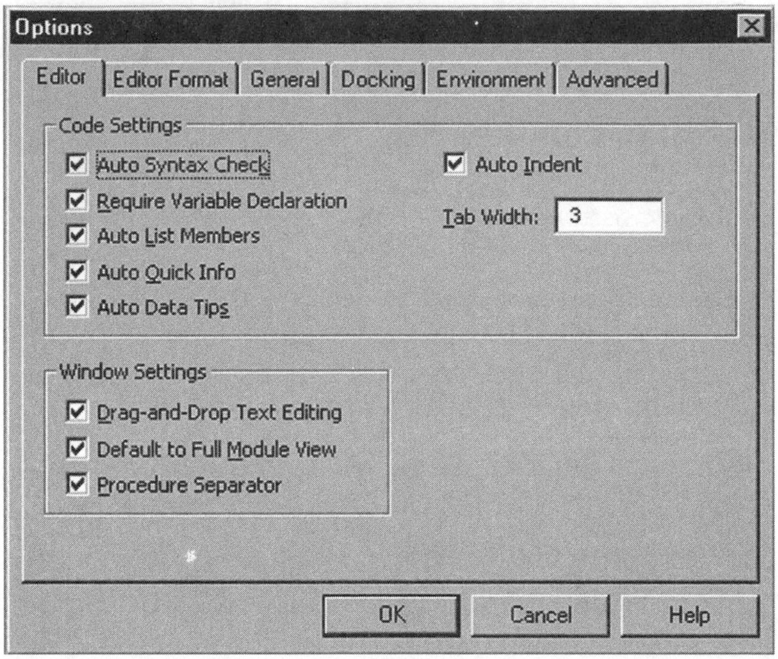

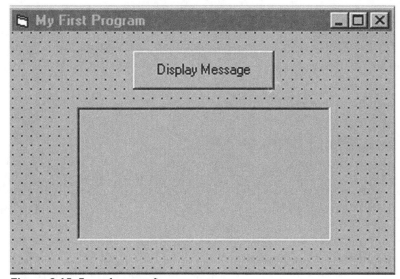

**Figure 2.14** Visual Basic options window

**Figure 2.15** Form for your first program

Place a command button and a picture box on the form and then modify the object property settings to match those listed in the previous table. When complete, your form should resemble Figure 2.15.

In later chapters, we assume that you have more mastery of the VB interface. In these later chapters, we show the form (or a sample program execution) in a figure accompanied by a listing of the program code. You then determine what control objects and property settings are required by examining the form and reading the code. In those instances where property settings in the code are unclear, we also give a table that specifies the desired settings.

```
Option Explicit
Private Sub cmdDisplay_Click ()
'My first program: "Hello, World, from Visual Basic!"
    picOutput.Cls
    picOutput.Print "Hello, World, from Visual Basic!"
End Sub
```

**Figure 2.16** Source code for your first program

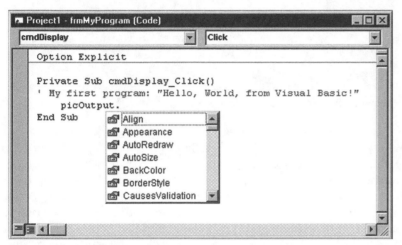

**Figure 2.17** Visual Basic auto code-completion feature

## DESIGNING THE USER INTERFACE

If we wish to write a VB program, we proceed in stages, as with all programming. Designing the user interface is the initial task. You place the objects on the form, and then you must specify the appropriate object properties. This means that you must assign descriptive names and informative captions to your program's control objects. To illustrate, the default name and caption for the first command button on a form is Command1. This name is uninformative for other programmers, and the caption provides the user with no insight as to the purpose of the button. So your assignment of a descriptive name and caption to your program's control objects will greatly enhance the program's usability.

## WRITING THE SOURCE CODE

After you design the form and change the default property settings, it is time to write the source code. Double-click the command button on the form. A code window opens, and VB automatically places the code headings in the window. Do not worry about the meaning of these headings right now; we explain them more fully in later chapters. Type in the code listed in Figure 2.16 so that your code window matches it.

As you type in the code, notice that a pop-up menu appears when you type the period (dot separator) following picOutput (Figure 2.17). This pop-up menu lists the available **methods** and properties of the picture box object named

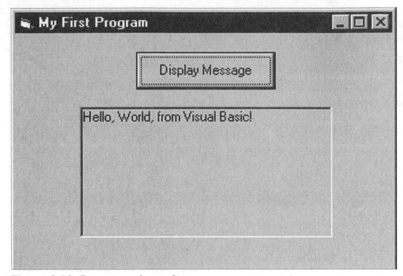

**Figure 2.18** Execution of your first program

`picOutput`. You may select the desired method or property from this pop-up menu by using the mouse or cursor keys. Alternatively, you can begin to type in the desired method or property name, and VB will automatically scroll in the pop-up menu to the method or property name matching the characters that you've typed. VB will automatically complete the method or property name for you in the code when you press a nonalphanumeric key (a key other than a number or a letter such as the TAB key or space bar). Or it will automatically complete the name when you double-click on the name in the pop-up menu.

For instance, type `picOutput.` and then select Cls from the pop-up menu. Press the ENTER key to have VB automatically complete the line of code.   This feature is the **auto code-completion feature** of VB, and it can save you from doing a lot of typing. However, if you prefer VB not to pop-up a menu of object "members" as you type in code, select Tools/Options, uncheck the box next to Auto List Members under the Editor tab of the Options window (Figure 2.14), and then click the OK button.

Once you finish typing in the code, run your program by clicking the Start button on the toolbar, selecting Run/Start from the menu bar, or by pressing F5. When you click the Display Message button, you should see the message appear in the picture box as in Figure 2.18.

## VISUAL BASIC FILE TYPES

As with any work that you do on a computer, we recommend that you intermittently save your work in case of a power outage or in the unlikely event that your computer crashes. Of course, you should always save a finished copy of your programs so that you may modify them at a later date. A VB project is composed of several different file types; the two main VB file types are **project files** and **form files**. A VB project may contain multiple forms, but we rarely use more than one form in this text. As previously mentioned, Chapter 10 addresses the use of multiple forms in VB programs.

The project file tells VB which forms are associated with a specific project. The form file lists the objects on the form, the object property settings, and the

Versions of VB prior to VB 6.0 recorded both the form file names and their paths, or locations, inside of the project files. Problems arose when students edited projects on multiple machines. For instance, a student might edit his project and then save it on his account on the school's computer. He might then copy all of his files to a floppy disk and bring it home. When he tried to open the project on his floppy disk with his home computer, VB would inform him that it could not find the associated form files (since VB was looking for the files in the same directory location as on the school's computer).

If you are working with VB 5.0 or earlier and you are editing projects on multiple machines, we recommend saving your projects on floppy disk. This way, the path information that is saved along with the form file name is the path of the floppy disk (normally a:\).

```
Type=Exe
Form=HelloWorld.Frm
Reference=*\G[00020430-0000-0000-C000-
000000000046]#2.0#0#..\..\..\..\WIN95\SYSTEM\STDOL
E2.TLB#OLE Automation
IconForm="frmMyProgram"
Startup="frmMyProgram"
Command32=""
Name="Project1"
HelpContextID="0"
CompatibleMode="0"
MajorVer=1
MinorVer=0
RevisionVer=0
AutoIncrementVer=0
ServerSupportFiles=0
VersionCompanyName="NPS"
CompilationType=0
OptimizationType=0
FavorPentiumPro(tm)=0
CodeViewDebugInfo=0
NoAliasing=0
BoundsCheck=0
OverflowCheck=0
FlPointCheck=0
FDIVCheck=0
UnroundedFP=0
StartMode=0
Unattended=0
Retained=0
ThreadPerObject=0
MaxNumberOfThreads=1
```

**Figure 2.19** Sample project file

```
VERSION 5.00
Begin VB.Form frmMyProgram
   Caption              =      "My First Program"
   ClientHeight         =      3195
   ClientLeft           =      60
   ClientTop            =      345
   ClientWidth          =      4680
   LinkTopic            =      "Form1"
   ScaleHeight          =      3195
   ScaleWidth           =      4680
   StartUpPosition      =      3   'Windows Default
   Begin VB.PictureBox picOutput
     Height         =      1815
     Left           =      413
     ScaleHeight    =      1755
     ScaleWidth     =      3795
     TabIndex       =      1
     Top            =      1080
     Width          =      3855
   End
   Begin VB.CommandButton cmdDisplay
     Caption        =      "Display Message"
     Height         =      495
     Left           =      1493
     TabIndex       =      0
     Top            =      360
     Width          =      1695
   End
End
Attribute VB_Name = "frmMyProgram"
Attribute VB_GlobalNameSpace = False
Attribute VB_Creatable = False
Attribute VB_PredeclaredId = True
Attribute VB_Exposed = False
Option Explicit

Private Sub cmdDisplay_Click ()
'  My first program: "Hello, World, from Visual Basic!"
     picOutput.Cls
     picOutput.Print "Hello, World, from Visual Basic!"
End Sub
```

**Figure 2.20** Sample form file

source code associated with the form. *The important point to remember is that you must save both a project file and a form file.* To save the form file, select File/Save *formName* from the menu bar or press CTRL+S. To save the project file, click the Save Project button on the toolbar or select File/Save Project from the menu. Figures 2.19 (on previous page) and 2.20 show the contents of the "Hello, World" project and form files, respectively.

Another common file type is a **code module** (*.BAS, or Basic file). Code modules are extremely useful since they allow the same code to be used in different projects. To add a code module to a project, select Project/Add Module from the menu. You'll be given a choice of creating a new code module or selecting an existing one. If you create a new code module, change its name by editing the (Name) property in the Properties window. Also, do not forget to save your new code module after you enter source code in the module's code window. To save the code module, select File/Save *moduleName* from the menu or press CTRL+S. To remove a code module from a project, left-click on the module name in the Project Explorer window and select Project/Remove *moduleName* from the menu. Alternately, you can right-click on the module name in the Project Explorer window to open a pop-up menu. This pop-up menu provides options to save or remove the code module.

Finally, **class modules** (*.CLS) allow the programmer to define new object **classes** in a separate file. These modules allow for easy reuse of the same code. The same objects and classes that a programmer defines in one project can be used in a different project simply by adding the class module. The procedures to add, save, and remove class modules parallel those of code modules.

Visual Basic offers flexible code printing capabilities. You can print out or obtain a **hard copy** of the source code for the current module or the entire project. Additionally, you can print the form images (Figure 2.15) or the form file (Figure 2.20). If you do not have a printer connected to your computer, VB offers the option of printing to a file. To obtain a hard copy, select File/Print from the menu or press CTRL+P. The Print dialog box (Print window) shown in Figure 2.21 opens on the screen, and you can select what you want to print.

A compiled program is an **executable module** (*.EXE file) that can be run without starting VB. You can compile your program by selecting File/Make *projectName.exe* from the menu bar. The Make Project dialog box shown in Figure 2.22 opens on the screen. The Options button in this dialog box allows you to set advanced compiler options. To run (or execute) a compiled program, first find the associated *.EXE file using Windows Explorer (a file utility included with Windows 95/98). Then, double-click the program icon, and the program executes.

> **Key Term**
>
> **executable module**—also called a program file or EXE file—a file that may be executed by the computer

## VISUAL BASIC HELP AND ONLINE DOCUMENTATION

Microsoft substantially revised the help facility and online documentation with the release of Visual Basic 6.0. The Microsoft Developers' Network (MSDN) Library Visual Studio 6.0 release (a two-CD set) is included with the Professional and Enterprise editions of VB 6.0. The VisualStudio 6.0 family of development products includes Visual Basic, Visual C++, Visual FoxPro, Visual InterDev, Visual J++, and Visual SourceSafe. The MSDN Library includes documentation for all of these products, and the VB help facility and documentation are integrated in this two CD volume. Figure 2.23 displays an example of the online help and documentation.

**Figure 2.21** Print window

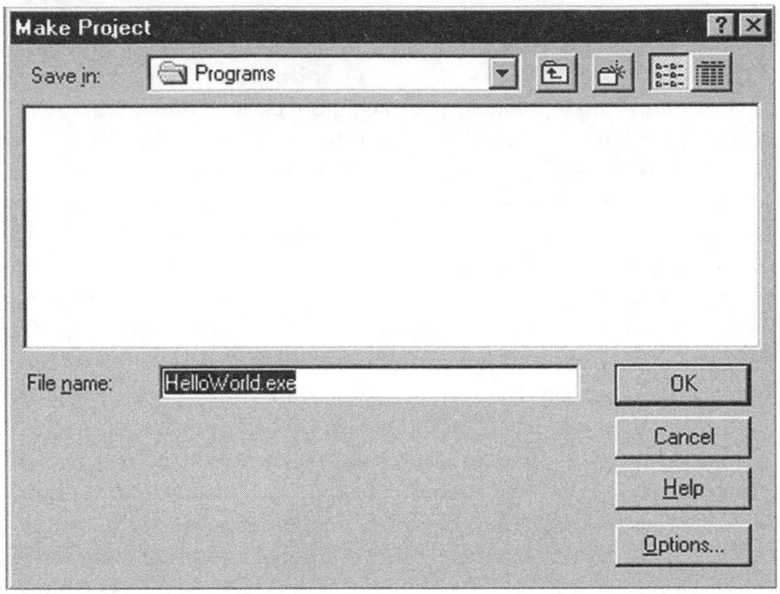

**Figure 2.22** Make Project window

**Figure 2.23** Visual Basic online help and documentation

Online documentation for VB 6.0 includes the *Visual Basic Programmer's Guide*, *Component Tools Guide*, and *Data Access Guide*. The *Visual Basic Programmer's Guide* is a comprehensive programming manual using Visual Basic. The *Component Tools Guide* provides complete documentation on the creation and use of ActiveX-based components. Finally, details concerning database programming and data access programming in VB are located in the *Data Access Guide*.

When searching the documentation, you can limit the scope of the search by selecting an Active Subset. Therefore, you should change the Active Subset to Visual Basic Documentation before performing a search. The VB 6.0 online documentation provides an easily accessible reference for additional information and advanced topics.

# Summary

## Key Terms

**auto code-completion feature**—a feature of the VB editor in which a pop-up menu appears listing applicable properties and methods of an object; this feature allows the programmer to quickly complete a line of code

**class**—refers to an object's type

**class module**—a file that defines a new object class

**code module**—a generic file that contains VB code

**command button**—a VB control used to begin, interrupt, or end a process

**control**—an object in a user interface; any object that may appear in the VB Toolbox window

**default setting**—the setting automatically assigned to a property of an object by VB

**design time**—the time when the program and user interface are being written in the VB IDE

**double-click**—the act of rapidly clicking a mouse button twice (typically the left mouse button)

**dragging**—the act of repositioning an object on the display by clicking the left mouse button on the object and holding the button while moving the mouse. The object then moves in accordance with the mouse movements

**dynamic link library** (**DLL**)—a library file that may be added (or linked) to a program to provide additional functionality

**executable module**—a file that may be executed by the computer; a program file

**folder**—a directory location on a storage device

**form**—the default container for VB controls; a window or dialog box that appears in a program

**form file**—a VB file that lists the objects, property settings, and program code associated with the form

**Form Layout window**—a VB window that allows the programmer to visually position forms on the display at design time

**Form window**—a VB window that displays the currently selected form

**graphical user interface** (**GUI**)—refers to a user interface that contains icons and is controlled via a pointing device such as a mouse

**hard copy**—a printed or paper copy; a print out

**icon**—a button that contains a picture

**integrated development environment** (**IDE**)—in VB, a working environment that integrates all phases of the programming process, including editing, testing, and debugging

**label**—a VB control used to display text that the user is not allowed to change

**logical inch**—the length of a screen item measuring one inch when printed; one logical inch contains approximately 1,440 twips

**menu bar**—a group of words or headings typically located at the top of the screen. When one of these words is clicked with the mouse, an associated drop-down menu opens

**method**—a subprogram associated with an object. In general, a method alters an object's properties

**mouse**—a hand-operated input device used to control the pointer location on the display. The mouse typically contains a mechanical ball to control the pointer position and left and right buttons to allow the user to make selections

**object**—an item that has associated properties and methods

**object-oriented language**—refers to a computer programming language that supports objects

**picture box**—a VB control that may display text or graphics

**pointer**—a position indicator on the display typically in the form of an arrow. Pointers are necessary in GUIs

**program** (or **application**)—a file that may be executed (or run) by the computer to perform a specific task

**project**—a program in VB. A project may contain one or more forms

**Project Explorer window**—a VB window that displays a hierarchical list of all open projects and the items contained in these projects

**project file**—a VB file that associates a project with its form file(s)

**Properties window**—a VB window that allows the programmer to change control property settings at design time

**property**—an attribute of an object

**rapid application development** (**RAD**)—refers to the program development philosophy for which VB was created; the process of designing, coding, testing, correcting, and distributing applications programs quickly

**run time**—the time when the program is executing or running

**shortcut key combination**—a "hot key" combination that performs a specific task when the associated keys are pressed together

**text box**—a VB control that contains text that may be entered at design time or possibly at run time; an edit field or edit control

**toolbar**—a group of icons typically located below the menu bar. Many of these icons provide menu shortcuts by performing the same tasks as the menu items

**toolbox**—see Toolbox window

**Toolbox window**—a VB window that displays all standard VB controls and any other controls added to an open project

**twip**—the default unit of screen measurement in VB; there are approximately 1,440 twips in one logical inch

## Keywords

*Properties:*

| | |
|---|---|
| AutoSize | Locked |
| BackColor | MultiLine |
| Caption | Name |
| Font | Picture |
| ForeColor | Text |

## Key Concepts

- The Microsoft Windows operating system is a GUI, and programs designed for this environment are usually graphical in nature. VB is one of Microsoft's RAD tools for Windows-based programs.

- VB provides an integrated development environment (IDE) for the programmer. This environment consists of a menu bar, toolbar, Project Explorer window, Form window, Properties window, Form Layout window, and Toolbox window.

- VB has five elementary controls that can be used to create a simple user interface. These controls include labels, text boxes, picture boxes, command buttons, and forms. With the exception of forms, all of these controls are located in the VB Toolbox.

- There are two main file types in VB: project files and form files. Each VB project is a separate program, and a project may contain multiple forms. The project file indicates which forms are associated with the project, while a form file lists the objects, property settings, and code associated with the form.

- The version of the "Hello, World!" program shown in the text introduced the steps required to save, print, compile, and execute a program in VB.

- The VB help facility and online documentation consists of a two-CD set containing the MSDN Library for Visual Studio 6.0.

## Review Questions

1. What is a GUI? Give an example of one.
2. Why is the user interface of an application so important?
3. Name and describe the seven major parts of the VB IDE.
4. Name and describe the five elementary VB controls. Why do we call these controls elementary?
5. How are controls placed on a form? How are they moved? How are they resized?
6. How do you change the VB IDE options?
7. What is the difference between a project file and a form file?
8. Where can you look for additional information about VB?

## Chapter 2 Problems

1. What is a shortcut key combination? How does the programmer assign a shortcut key and on which control is it used? How is the shortcut key combination activated?
2. What is the purpose of the control naming conventions?
3. Create the following user interface in VB:

| Object | Property | Setting |
|---|---|---|
| Form | Name | frmLabels |
|  | Caption | Label Example |
| Label | Name | lblLastName |
|  | Caption | *your last name* |
| Label | Name | lblFirstName |
|  | Caption | *your first name* |

4. Design a user interface with red, white, and blue labels. Each label caption should name its color in black text.
5. What is the purpose of the MultiLine property in a text box?

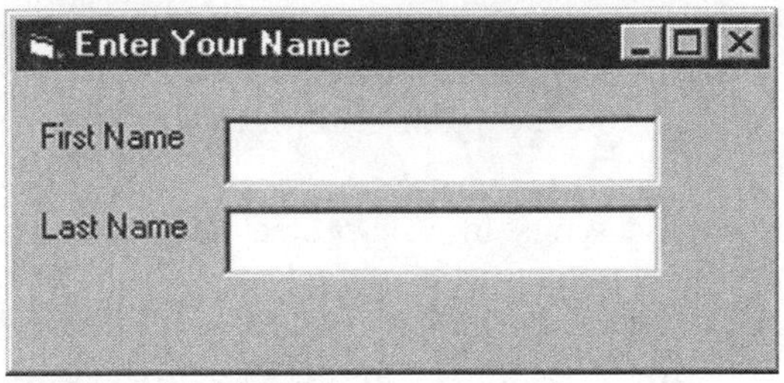

**Figure 2.24** Name entry user interface

6. Create the user interface shown in Figure 2.24.

| Object | Property | Setting |
|--------|----------|---------|
| Form | Name | frmNameExample |
| | Caption | Enter Your Name |
| Label | Name | lblFirstName |
| | Caption | First Name |
| Label | Name | lblLastName |
| Caption | Last Name | |
| Text Box | Name | txtFirstName |
| | Caption | *blank* |
| Text Box | Name | txtLastName |
| | Caption | *blank* |

7. Design a user interface with two command buttons. The first command button says "Yes" and the second command button says "No."

8. Modify the "Hello, World!" program to display the text "Hello, *your name*." when the Display Message button is clicked.

9. Modify the "Hello, World!" program. Change the command button name to cmdDontClick and the caption to read Don't Click Me. The program should display the text "Please follow directions. Don't click the button!" when the button is clicked.

10. Modify the "Hello, World!" program to display a message of your own choosing.

# Customizing the Visual Basic Integrated Development Environment

In this chapter supplement, you will:

- Become familiar with the Visual Basic Integrated Development Environment (IDE) options

- Learn to customize the Visual Basic IDE to suit your personal preferences

Chapter 2 introduces the method of modifying the operation of the VB Integrated Development Environment (IDE) by changing environment settings in the Options window. This Supplement describes the IDE Options window and settings in detail.

To open the Options window, select Tools/Options from the menu bar. We now describe each of the tabs and options in detail:

## Editor Tab

The Editor tab appears in Figure 2.14. This tab specifies the Code window and Project window settings.

### Code Settings

**Auto Syntax Check**—VB automatically verifies for correct syntax after each line of code is entered.

**Require Variable Declaration**—Explicit variable declarations are required in program modules. This adds the Option Explicit statement to the (General Declarations) section of any new module.

**Auto List Members**—Enables the auto code-completion feature of the editor.

**Auto Quick Info**—Enables the display of information about functions and their parameters.

**Auto Data Tips**—Enables the display of variable values or object properties over which the cursor is placed while in Break mode in the Code window. The display is limited to variables and objects that are in the current scope. Also available for the Immediate window while in Break mode.

**Auto Indent**—Automatically indents a new line to the starting position of the previous line of code.

**Tab Width**—Sets the tab width from 1 to 32 spaces. The default tab width is 4 spaces.

### Window Settings

**Drag-and-Drop Text Editing**—Allows the drag-and-drop of elements from the Code window into the Immediate or Watch windows.

**Default to Full Module View**—Sets the default view for new modules to a single scrollable list vice one subprogram at a time.

**Procedure Separator**—A separator bar appears at the end of each subprogram in the Code window.

### Editor Format Tab

The Editor Format tab appears in Figure 2.25. This tab specifies the appearance of the VB code.

### Code Colors

Sets the foreground and background colors used for each type of text.

**Text List**—Lists the text items that have customizable colors.

**Foreground**—Specifies the foreground color for the text selected in the Color Text List.

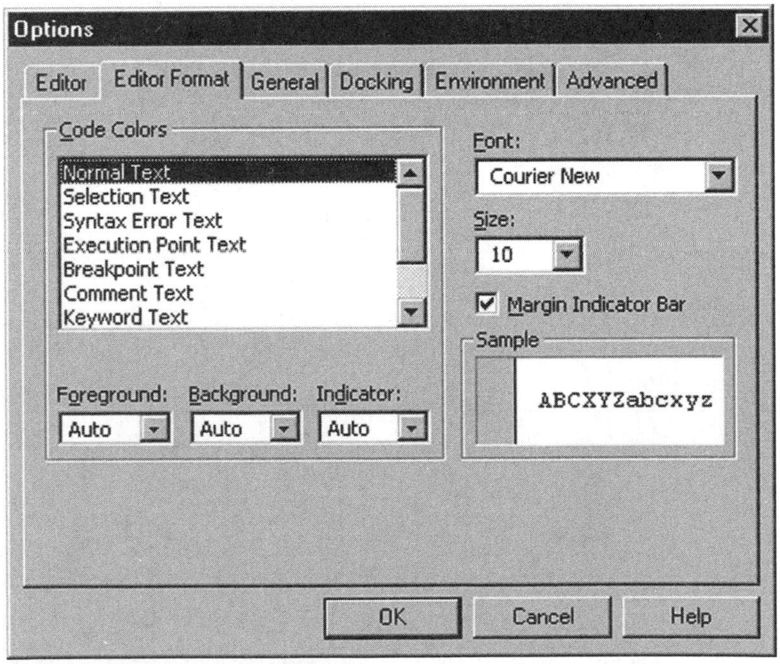

**Figure 2.25** Editor Format tab

**Background**—Specifies the background color for text selected in the Color Text List.

**Indicator**—Specifies the margin indicator color.

## Font
Specifies the font used for all code.

## Size
Specifies the size of the font used for all code.

## Margin Indicator Bar
Toggles the visibility of the margin indicator bar.

## Sample
Displays sample text for the current font, size, and color settings.

## General Tab
Specifies the form grid settings, the error trapping, and compile settings for the current VB project. This tab is shown in Figure 2.26.

## Form Grid Settings
Determines the appearance of the form grid at design time.

**Show Grid**—Displays the grid at design time.

**Grid Units**—Displays the grid units used for the form. The default is twips.

**Width**—Sets the width of grid cells on a form.

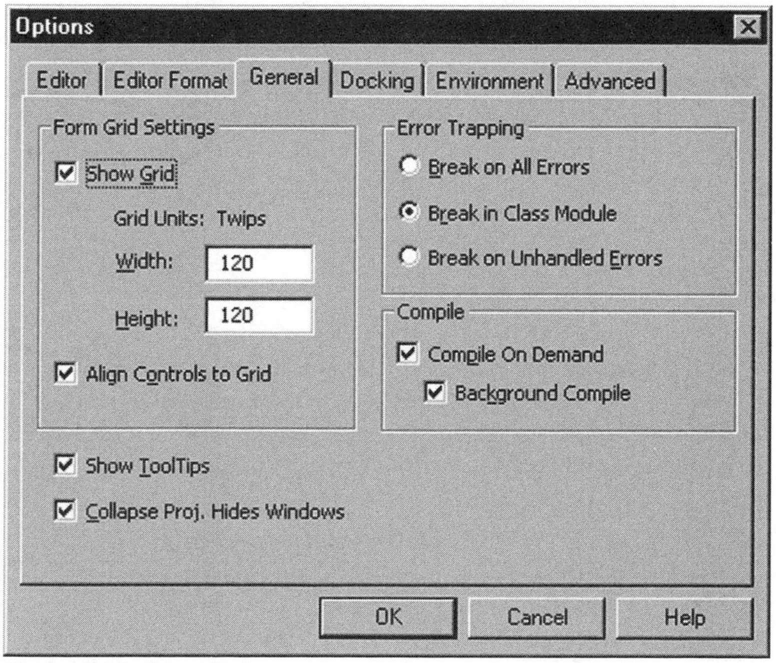

**Figure 2.26** General tab

**Height**—Sets the height of grid cells on a form.

**Align Controls to Grid**—Automatically positions (or "snaps") the outer edges of controls on grid lines.

### Show ToolTips
Displays ToolTips for the toolbar and Toolbox items.

### Collapse Proj. Hides Windows
Determines whether the windows are hidden when a project is collapsed in the Project Explorer.

### Error Trapping
Determines how errors are handled and sets the default state of error trapping for all subsequent instances of VB. To set the error trapping option for only the current session of VB without changing the default for future sessions, use the Toggle command on the Code window's shortcut menu.

**Break on All Errors**—Any error causes the program to enter Break mode, whether or not an error-handler is active or the code is in a class module.

**Break in Class Module**—Any unhandled error produced in a class module causes the project to enter Break mode at the line of code that produced the error.

**Break on Unhandled Errors**—If an error-handler is active, the error is trapped without entering Break mode. If there is no active error-handler, the error causes the program to enter Break mode. An unhandled error in a class module, however, causes the project to enter Break mode on the line of code that invoked the offending procedure of the class.

### Compile
Determines how a project compiles.

**Compile on Demand**—Determines whether a project is fully compiled before it starts, or whether code is compiled as needed, allowing the application to start sooner. If Start With Full Compile is chosen on the Run menu, VB ignores the Compile on Demand setting and performs a full compile.

**Background Compile**—Determines whether idle time during execution is used to finish compiling a program in the background. Background Compile can improve run time execution speed, but this feature is not available unless Compile on Demand is also selected.

## Docking Tab
The Docking tab is shown in Figure 2.27. This tab sets the docking state of the windows. A **docked window** attaches or anchors itself to other docked windows or to the main window in **multiple document interface** (**MDI**) mode. A docked window always "snaps" to a specific location on the screen. An undocked window, on the other hand, remains in the position where it is left on the screen.

### Dockable
Select the dockable windows by setting the appropriate check boxes. Any, all, or none of the windows in the list may be selected.

## Environment Tab

The Environment tab appears in Figure 2.28. This tab specifies the attributes of the VB development environment. All changes are effective every time VB is loaded.

### When Visual Basic Starts

**Prompt for Project**—Requests a project to open when VB starts.

**Create Default Project**—Creates a default executable (EXE) project that opens each time VB starts.

### When a Program Starts

**Save Changes**—Automatically saves the changes when a project is run. If the project has not previously been saved, the Save As common dialog box appears so that a name and location for the project may be specified.

**Prompt To Save Changes**—Displays a dialog box prompting to save the changes for a project when it is run. Selecting Yes opens the Save As common dialog box so that a name and location for the project may be specified. Selecting No causes VB to run the project using the memory image but does not save any changes.

**Don't Save Changes**—When a project is run, VB runs the memory image of the project but does not save any changes.

### Show Templates For

Specifies which templates are visible in the Add *item* dialog box when an item is added to a project. If cleared, a blank form appears when the Add *item* command is selected. Any, all, or none of the following *item* check boxes (listed on the next page) may be selected:

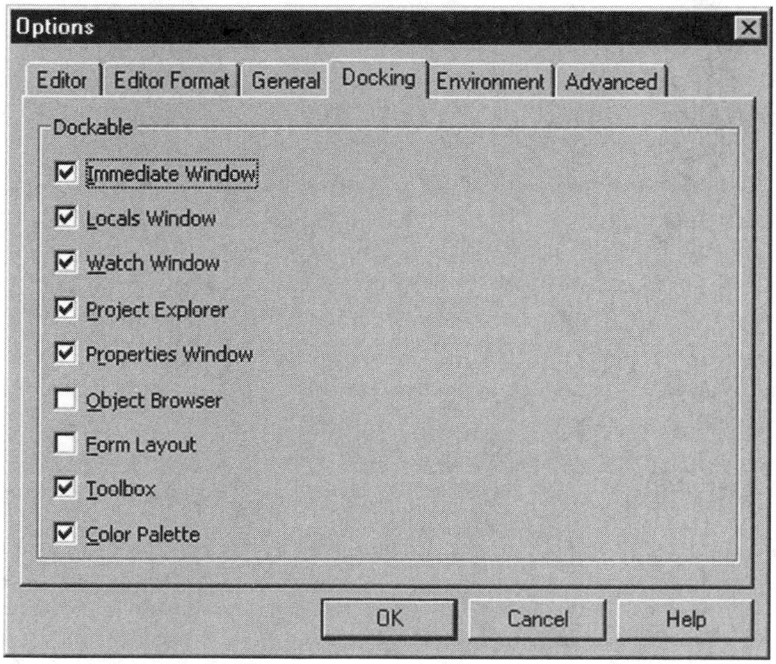

**Figure 2.27** Docking tab

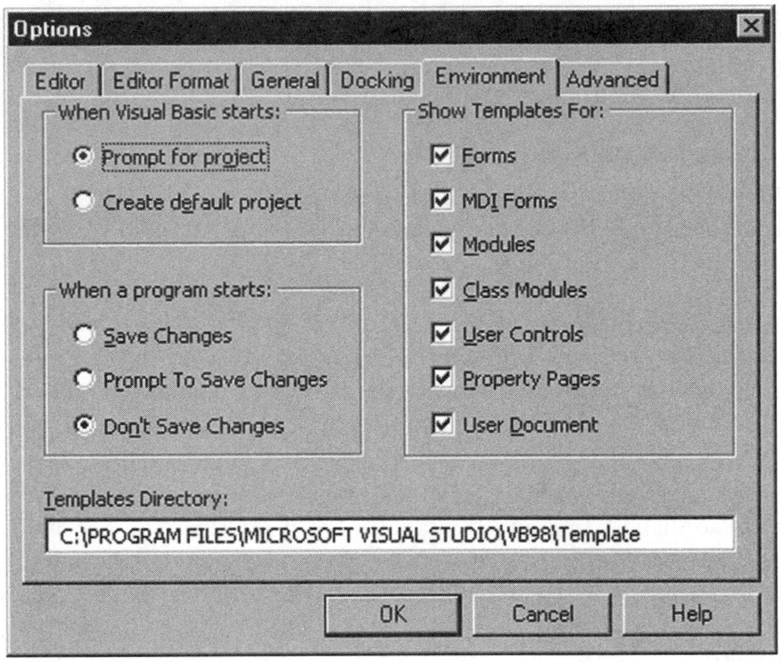

**Figure 2.28** Environment tab

Forms

MDI Forms

Modules

Class Modules

User Controls

Property Pages

User Documents

### Templates Directory
Specifies the location of the template files.

### Advanced Tab
Specifies the settings for various advanced features as they apply to the current VB project. This tab appears in Figure 2.29.

### Background Project Load
Determines whether code is loaded in the background, returning control to the developer more quickly.

### Notify When Changing Shared Project Items
Determines whether the programmer is notified when a shared project item, such as a form or module, is changed and a save operation is attempted. Several projects can share the same items. Shared items are loaded into memory and each project has its own copy. If a shared item in one project is changed, the other projects retain the copy of the item that was initially loaded. The last project saved determines the contents of the shared file. When this option is selected, all copies of the item may be synchronized before the item is saved, thus ensuring that no changes to the item are lost.

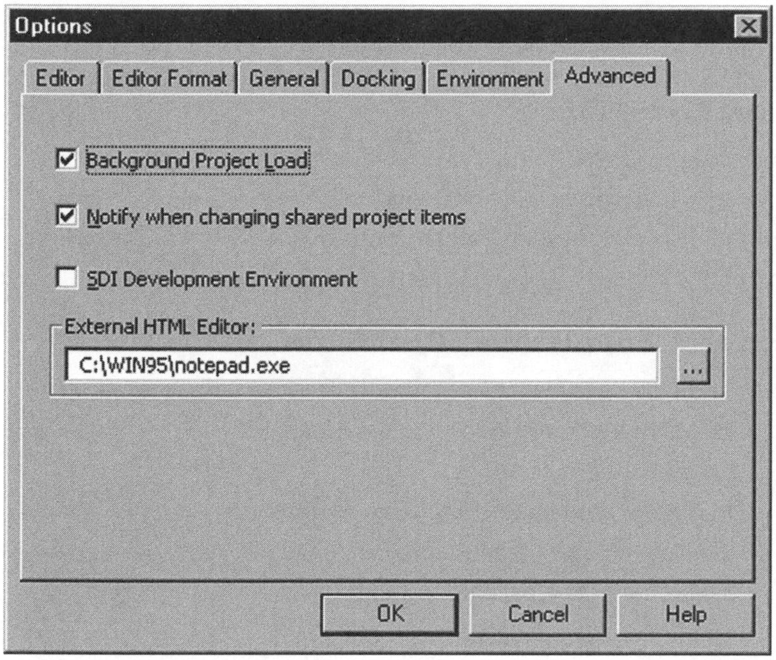

**Figure 2.29** Advanced tab

### SDI Development Environment

Changes the development environment from a multiple document interface (MDI) to a **single document interface** (**SDI**). When this option is selected, the SDI appears every time VB starts.

## Summary

### Key Terms

**docked window**—a window that attaches or anchors itself to other windows. A docked window always "snaps" to a specific location on the screen

**multiple document interface (MDI)**—a user interface that consists of parent and child windows, where a parent window may contain several child windows. The user may work on several files simultaneously in this type of interface

**single document interface (SDI)**—a user interface in which the user may work on only one file at a time

### Key Concepts

- The VB IDE options are changed through the Options window. To open the Options window, select Tools/Options from the VB Menu bar.

- The Options window contains six tabs: Editor, Editor Format, General, Docking, Environment, and Advanced. The Editor tab specifies the Code window and Project window settings, and the Editor Format tab controls the appearance of the VB code. The General tab specifies the form grid settings, the error trapping, and compile settings for the current VB project. The Docking tab sets the docking state of the windows. The Environment tab specifies the attributes of the VB development environment. Lastly, the Advanced tab sets various advanced features for the current VB project.

## Review Questions

1. What is the purpose of the Options window?
2. How do you open the Options window?
3. Name the six tabs in the Options window and state the purpose of each tab.

## Chapter 2 Supplement Problems

1. Name the editor tab that allows you to:
   a. Enable background project compilation
   b. Change the editor font
   c. Disable the auto-code completion feature
   d. Auto-save changes when a project runs
   e. Change the editor background color
   f. Default to full module view
   g. Specify the dockable windows
   h. Set error trapping options
   i. Enable background project loading
   j. Change the editor foreground color
2. What is a dockable window? an undockable window?

# Planning Your Program

**3**

Now we turn to planning your program, to solve the many problems of business, science, and engineering.

Many of these problems will require you to analyze a given set of inputs in order to determine the solution to the problem. **Problem solving** is the process of taking a set of inputs, doing some calculations with these inputs, and then acquiring a result. Oftentimes, the most difficult aspect of problem solving is the transformation of the inputs into the desired result. If the result is incorrect (i.e., cannot be verified by hand calculation or simply does not make sense), the problem solving process must be repeated until the correct result is achieved.

The problem solving process involves a series of steps, or a method, for converting the inputs for a specific problem into a meaningful output. This solution method is an **algorithm**—a "recipe" for problem solving. Erroneous results usually indicate an incorrect algorithm that must subsequently be corrected. Figure 3.1 shows a diagram of the problem solving process.

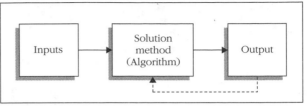

**Figure 3.1** The problem solving process

Now let's think about how we solve problems. Suppose that you are in charge of planning a graduation party. How would you do it? Well, there is a certain logical ordering of the tasks that must be performed to hold such an event. You must first send out the invitations and determine the number of people who will attend. Then, you need to assign specific people to bring certain items, such as plates, cups, drinks, and food. Next, you need to find a place to hold the party. You may also want to hire a disc jockey (DJ) or find a band to play music at the party. This sequence of necessary events continues. In your mind or on paper, you are creating a "laundry list" of the things that need to be done to have a successful graduation party. In essence, you are creating an algorithm to plan a party.

## PLANNING: THE FIRST STEP

Planning is the crucial first step in any problem solving process. Like an architect who develops blueprints for a building before it is constructed, you should plan a solution method before you attempt to solve a problem. In terms of computer programming, you should create an algorithm before you sit in front of a computer and start writing code. Two popular tools that programmers use to develop algorithms and plan programs are flowcharts and pseudocode.

### FLOWCHARTS

**Flowcharts** are diagrams that show the "flow" of program events through time. Commonly, we use specific shapes to represent different processes performed by the computer. For instance, a diamond represents a decision structure and a parallelogram denotes an input or output operation. Lines with arrows, called **flowlines**, connect the different shapes to show the sequence of events as the program progresses from start to finish. There are many symbols used in flowcharts, the most common of which are described in Figure 3.2.

You have already seen examples of flowcharts. Chapter 1 Supplement contains flowcharts for converting between binary and decimal numbers. A flowchart for a simple "cash register" program is shown in Figure 3.3. This program allows a user to enter the prices for any number of products purchased and then computes the tax and total for the transaction.

Flowcharts are not as popular today as they were many years ago in the early days of computer science. Their popularity has diminished because they require a large investment of time to produce and they are not easy to change or correct. Assume, for example, that you want to modify the cash register program to track the total number of customers, the total of all purchases, and the total taxes collected over a day. This modification could not be accomplished without rewriting (or redrawing) the entire flowchart as shown in Figure 3.4.

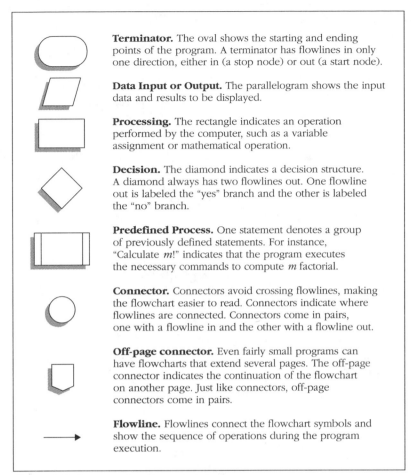

**Terminator.** The oval shows the starting and ending points of the program. A terminator has flowlines in only one direction, either in (a stop node) or out (a start node).

**Data Input or Output.** The parallelogram shows the input data and results to be displayed.

**Processing.** The rectangle indicates an operation performed by the computer, such as a variable assignment or mathematical operation.

**Decision.** The diamond indicates a decision structure. A diamond always has two flowlines out. One flowline out is labeled the "yes" branch and the other is labeled the "no" branch.

**Predefined Process.** One statement denotes a group of previously defined statements. For instance, "Calculate *m*!" indicates that the program executes the necessary commands to compute *m* factorial.

**Connector.** Connectors avoid crossing flowlines, making the flowchart easier to read. Connectors indicate where flowlines are connected. Connectors come in pairs, one with a flowline in and the other with a flowline out.

**Off-page connector.** Even fairly small programs can have flowcharts that extend several pages. The off-page connector indicates the continuation of the flowchart on another page. Just like connectors, off-page connectors come in pairs.

**Flowline.** Flowlines connect the flowchart symbols and show the sequence of operations during the program execution.

**Figure 3.2** Common flowchart symbols

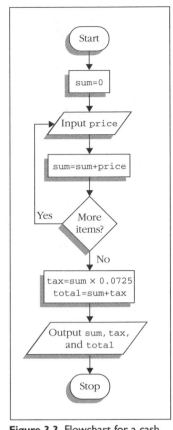

**Figure 3.3** Flowchart for a cash register program

## PSEUDOCODE

**Pseudocode**, as the name implies, is "false" code. Pseudocode is similar to a high-level language in that it uses English-like phrases as statements. Each programmer uses his or her own pseudocode; consequently, there is no standard pseudocode.

Pseudocode has several advantages in comparison to flowcharts and has become the most widely used program planning technique. First, unlike flowcharts, pseudocode does not require a large amount of time to write. A programmer can simply focus on developing an efficient algorithm rather than worrying about creating a "clean" flowchart. Figure 3.5 contains an example of pseudocode for the cash register program.

Since pseudocode is like high-level code, it is easier to convert to actual program code. Additionally, pseudocode is very easy to modify. The pseudocode for the cash register program in Figure 3.5 is easily converted into the pseudocode for the modified version of this program shown in Figure 3.6. Notice that the original pseudocode from Figure 3.5 is contained within the modified pseudocode in Figure 3.6.

### Key Term

**pseudocode**—"false" code consisting of English-like phrases used to develop or describe an algorithm

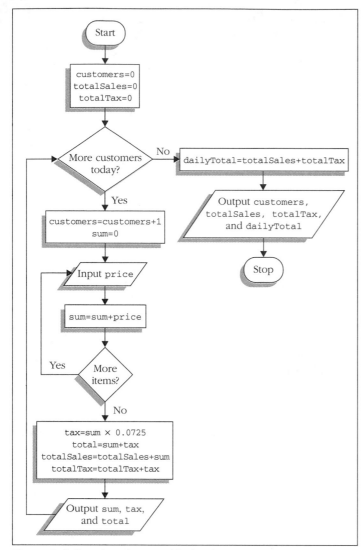

**Figure 3.4** Flowchart for a modified cash register program

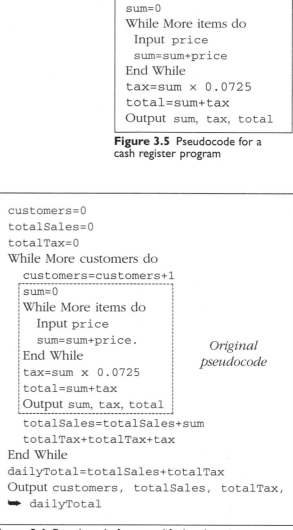

**Figure 3.5** Pseudocode for a cash register program

```
customers=0
totalSales=0
totalTax=0
While More customers do
    customers=customers+1
    sum=0
    While More items do
        Input price
        sum=sum+price.
    End While
    tax=sum x 0.0725
    total=sum+tax
    Output sum, tax, total
    totalSales=totalSales+sum
    totalTax+totalTax+tax
End While
dailyTotal=totalSales+totalTax
Output customers, totalSales, totalTax,
➥ dailyTotal
```

*Original pseudocode*

**Figure 3.6** Pseudocode for a modified cash register program

## THE PROGRAM DEVELOPMENT CYCLE

Program development is a lengthy and time consuming process. To ensure that the final version of a program works correctly and is as error-free as possible, programmers use a **program development cycle**. The program development cycle consists of six basic steps. These are illustrated in Figure 3.7 and described below.

1. **Analyze the problem.** Clearly define the problem to ensure that it is fully understood. Determine the inputs and the required output.

2. **Design the solution algorithm.** Determine the relationship between the inputs and output. Write an algorithm to solve the problem and use a simple test case to validate your algorithm.

3. **Design the user interface.** Determine what you want a user of your program to see. Determine the screen layout. Where will the user input data? Where and how (in what format) will the output be displayed? Is there a way to make data entry easier for the user? As dis-

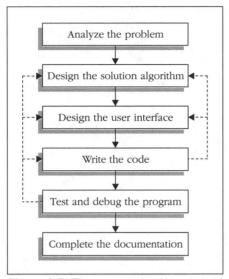

**Figure 3.7** The program development cycle

cussed in Chapter 2, designing a user interface is relatively easy in VB.

4. **Write the code.** Translate the algorithm into a computer programming language. In this text, we translate our algorithms into VB.

5. **Test and debug the program.** Testing is a means of finding errors in a program, and debugging is the process of correcting those errors. As we discussed in Chapter 1, a **bug** refers to an error in a program. (This term originated with Rear Admiral Grace M. Hopper of the United States Navy. In 1945, she found that a moth fused to a wire on the Mark I computer caused the machine to malfunction.) Thus, in order to get a program to work, you first have to **debug**, or get all of the bugs out.

6. **Complete the documentation.** Documentation consists of all materials that describe the program, its purpose, and how it operates. Documentation may be *internal* or *external*. **Internal documentation** consists of comments that are placed inside the program code. This allows someone unfamiliar with the program to read the code and understand what it does. **External documentation** includes flowcharts, pseudocode, program purpose statements, assumptions, design requirements, and input/output requirements. Commercial programs often contain user's manuals as documentation. The primary purpose of documentation is to allow someone other than the programmer to use the program and to modify the code if necessary.

## CASE STUDY
### The Knapsack Problem

Debra is packing her knapsack for a hiking trip on Saturday. A list of the possible items that she can pack appears on the next page. This list indicates the weight of each item, the value or relative worth of each item, and the number of each item available. The value of an item is rated on a scale from 1 to 10, where 10 is the most valuable and 1 is the least valuable. Debra expects to hike 5 miles, and she does not want the weight of her backpack to exceed 10 pounds. Which items and how many of each should Debra pack?

| Item | Value (points) | Weight (lbs.) | Number available |
|---|---|---|---|
| Binoculars | 2 | 2.00 | 2 |
| Compass | 4 | 0.10 | 2 |
| Extra clothing | 3 | 4.00 | 1 |
| First aid kit | 4 | 0.25 | 1 |
| Flashlight | 4 | 0.25 | 2 |
| Insect repellant | 3 | 0.25 | 1 |
| Map | 5 | 0.10 | 1 |
| Matches & fire starters | 6 | 0.10 | 1 |
| Pocketknife | 5 | 0.25 | 1 |
| Rain gear | 4 | 1.00 | 1 |
| Sun protection | 5 | 0.10 | 1 |
| Trail food | 6 | 0.50 | 1 |
| Water | 10 | 2.00 | 2 |

If we restate this problem somewhat, Debra desires to maximize the value of the items in her backpack so that the total weight of the backpack does not exceed 10 pounds. Debra cannot take all items since the total weight is going to be 15.25 pounds.

To solve this problem, Debra uses the ratio of an item's value to its weight (points/pound ratio). After calculating this ratio for each item, Debra acts in a "greedy" fashion and packs those items that give her the most points per pound. Thus, Debra's solution algorithm is called a greedy algorithm, and her solution appears below:

| Item | Number taken | Value subtotal | Weight subtotal |
|---|---|---|---|
| Binoculars | 1 | 2 | 2.00 |
| Compass | 2 | 8 | 0.20 |
| Extra clothing | 0 | 0 | 0.00 |
| First aid kit | 1 | 4 | 0.25 |
| Flashlight | 2 | 8 | 0.50 |
| Insect repellant | 1 | 3 | 0.25 |
| Map | 1 | 5 | 0.10 |
| Matches & fire starters | 1 | 6 | 0.10 |
| Pocketknife | 1 | 5 | 0.25 |
| Rain gear | 1 | 4 | 1.00 |
| Sun protection | 1 | 5 | 0.10 |
| Trail food | 1 | 6 | 0.50 |
| Water | 2 | 20 | 4.00 |
| | 15 | 76 | 9.25 |

Debra packs 15 items with a total weight of 9.25 pounds and total value of 76 points.

# Summary

## Key Terms

**algorithm**—a series of steps, or a method, for converting the inputs for a specific problem into a meaningful output; a "recipe" for problem solving

**bug**—an error in a computer program

**debug**—the process of removing errors from a computer program

**external documentation**—any paper documents that describe a program, including flowcharts, pseudocode, program purpose statements, assumptions, design requirements, input/output requirements, and user's manuals

**flowchart**—a diagram that shows the "flow" of program events through time with specific shapes representing different processes performed by the computer

**flowline**—a line with an arrow that connects flowchart symbols to show the sequence of events during program execution

**greedy algorithm**—an iterative algorithm that operates in a greedy fashion by choosing the item of greatest value in each step

**internal documentation**—comments that are written inside of the program source code

**problem solving**—the process of taking a set of inputs, doing some calculations with these inputs, and then acquiring a result

**program development cycle**—a series of six basic steps in the process of developing a computer program

**pseudocode**—"false" code consisting of English-like phrases used to develop or describe an algorithm

## Key Concepts

- The problem solving process involves a sequence of steps to arrive at a result from a set of inputs.

- An algorithm is a solution method and identifies the steps necessary to solve a particular problem.

- Programmers commonly use flowcharts and pseudocode to formalize solution algorithms. Even though flowcharts contain standard symbols to represent different computer operations, there is no such standard for pseudocode; each programmer develops his or her own pseudocode. Despite this lack of standardization, pseudocode is more frequently used than flowcharts since it is less time-intensive and easier to modify.

- Programmers follow a six-step program development cycle to ensure that a program is as error-free as possible. The last step of this cycle is to complete the program documentation, which consists of both internal and external documentation. Adequate documentation allows someone other than the programmer to use or modify the program.

## Review Questions

1. What is the problem solving process?
2. What is an algorithm?
3. Name the two tools commonly used by programmers to develop algorithms.

4. Name and describe the meaning of five different flowchart symbols.

5. What are the advantages of pseudocode over flowcharts?

6. State and describe the six steps of the program development cycle.

## Chapter 3 Problems

1. Create a flowchart for an algorithm to make a peanut butter and jelly sandwich.

2. From Problem 1, assume that you have two predefined processes named `MakeHalf` and `PutTogether`. `MakeHalf` can make half of the sandwich by inputting the slice of bread and either peanut butter or jelly. For instance, `MakeHalf (slice1, jelly)` puts jelly on slice1 of the bread. `PutTogether (slice1, slice2)` puts the two slices of bread together to create a whole sandwich. Rewrite your flowchart from Problem 1 to use these two predefined processes.

3. Write the pseudocode for Problems 1 and 2.

4. Create a flowchart for a program that determines the largest of three numbers using the following simple two-step method: (1) Compare the first number with the second number and select the larger of the two; (2) Compare the number chosen in step 1 with the third number and select the larger.

5. Write the pseudocode for Problem 4.

6. Develop a flowchart for a program that adds a series of user-entered numbers. The program should display the sum and terminate when the user enters 0.

7. Write the pseudocode for Problem 6.

8. Develop a flowchart for the game of High-Low. The first player enters a number between 0 and 100. The second player then tries to guess the first player's number. If the number is lower than the guess, the computer responds "lower." Similarly, the computer responds "higher" if the number is higher than the guess. The game ends when the second player correctly guesses the first player's number. The program should track the number of guesses and display this information before it terminates.

9. Write the pseudocode for Problem 8.

10. Given the amount of time it takes an automobile to travel a certain distance, we can compute the vehicle's average velocity using the following formula:

$$average\ velocity = distance \div time$$

Create a flowchart for a program that computes the average velocity of a vehicle.

11. In Problem 10, it does not make sense to have a negative distance or non-positive time. Modify your flowchart from Problem 10 to "bullet-proof" your program and prevent invalid entries for *distance* and *time*.

12. Write the pseudocode for Problems 10 and 11. Did it take you longer to write the flowcharts or the pseudocode? Which was easier to modify when converting your answer from Problem 10 into an answer for Problem 11?

13. The current inventory policy of the Ace Widget Shop is to place an order for 100 widgets with a widget supplier whenever the daily ending inventory reaches 30, provided that there are no outstanding orders that have not yet been received. Create a flowchart for a program that helps the

Ace Widget Shop determine whether or not to place an order based on the following variables: beginning inventory, sales, ending inventory, reorder point, quantity delivered, and projected delivery date of last order placed.

**14.** Write the pseudocode for Problem 13.

**15.** Develop a flowchart for the dealer of a game of Blackjack in which the dealer must continue to draw cards until the dealer's hand contains five cards or 16 or more points.

**16.** Write the pseudocode for Problem 15.

**17.** For any positive integer m, m! is read "m factorial" and is defined as:

$$m! = (m)(m-1) \cdots (2)(1), \text{ and } 0! = 1$$

Write a flowchart for a program that computes $m!$ for any positive integer $m$.

**18.** Write the pseudocode for Problem 17.

**19.** A permutation of size k is any *ordered* sequence of $k$ objects taken from a set of $n$ distinct objects, where $n \geq k$. The number of permutations of size $k$ that can be constructed from the $n$ objects is given by:

$$_nP_k = \frac{n!}{(n-k)!}$$

A combination of size $k$ is any *unordered* subset of $k$ objects taken from a set of $n$ distinct objects, where $n \geq k$. The number of combinations of size $k$ that can be formed from $n$ distinct objects is given by:

$$_nC_k = \binom{n}{k} = \frac{n!}{k!(n-k)!}$$

Create a flowchart for a program that computes the number of permutations and combinations for given $n$ and $k$ values. You may use a predefined process to compute factorials.

**20.** Write the pseudocode for Problem 19.

# 4

# Elements of Programming

## Chapter Objectives

In this chapter, you will:

- ○ Learn about variables and data types

- ○ Learn how to declare, initialize, and use variables

- ○ Learn about constants, including the difference between hard-coded and named constants

- ○ Learn about arithmetic operators, precedence rules, and common math functions

- ○ Learn about string variables, the concatenation operator, and common string functions

- ○ Understand the concepts of scope and lifetime

- ○ Discover the advantages and disadvantages of global variables

- ○ Learn how to comment code and improve program readability

- ○ Become familiar with methods of interactive input and output

**S**everal elements of programming are common to all computer languages. These include variables, constants, data types, scope and lifetime, and comments. We'll discuss each of these, with special reference to Visual Basic.

## VARIABLES

In mathematics, a **variable** is a quantity that can assume any value. A variable is easily recorded on paper by simply writing down its value, which can be of any size. On a computer, however, variables are stored in memory. As we've seen,

## Key Term

**variable**—a quantity that can assume any value; a computer variable is a named memory location that stores a value

memory requires physical resources. Thus, a computer variable is a named location in memory where values are stored. These values can be changed throughout a program's execution. Because a computer's physical resources are limited, the memory allocated for storing a variable should be conserved to the maximum extent possible. This optimization of memory space also has the effect of limiting the size of the values that the variable can assume, or the **range** of the variable. How do we limit a variable's range? We assign a **data type** to a variable. This assignment limits the amount of memory that the variable consumes and informs the compiler how much memory should be reserved for the variable. Variables can assume any value within the limits of their assigned data types.

The type of information contained by a computer variable differs from the information contained by a mathematical variable. Whereas mathematical variables contain only **numeric data** (numbers), computer variables may contain either numeric data or **character data** (letters and symbols as well as numbers). **Alphanumeric data** is a subset of character data and refers to data containing numbers and letters. So, the two types of data that can be stored in computer variables include numbers and characters.

These two types of data are treated differently when stored by the computer. A **string** is a group of characters that is stored by the computer as a **string variable**. Since storage of character data is comparatively simple, a string variable is the only data type necessary for storing character data. Numeric variables, on the other hand, require more than one data type since numbers come in more than one flavor. Numbers can be either integers or real-numbers. **Integers** are numbers with no fractional components; **real-numbers (floating-point numbers)** have fractional components. Generally, integers require less memory to store than real numbers. Thus, it makes sense to use different data types to conserve memory if we know that a variable will contain only integer values.

For example, if you are certain that a value will be an integer ranging from 0 to 255, you can assign the variable the `Byte` data type. From our discussion of bits, bytes, and binary numbers in Chapter 1 Supplement, it follows that the binary representation of 255 is $1111\ 1111_2$. As you can see, there are eight digits (or bits) in the binary representation of 255. Since there are eight bits in a byte, there is simply no reason to use more memory space than a byte to store this value.

The VB data types, memory requirements, and associated variable ranges appear in Figure 4.1. Several of these data types are common to many high-level languages, but they may differ in terms of memory requirements and the range of values that may be stored. To obtain specific information on each of these data types, you can refer to the documentation that accompanies your compiler.

## NAMING, DECLARING, AND USING VARIABLES

In most languages, variable names must begin with a letter and be followed by any number of alphanumeric characters. For instance, A5 is a valid variable name, but 5A is not. Additionally, some languages are **case-sensitive.** That means that lowercase letters and uppercase letters are considered to be different. For example, the variables A5 and a5 would be considered different variables. Whether or not the language is case-sensitive, variable names should be chosen so that the name is **self-commenting**, or describes its contents. Someone reading your program really has no idea what a variable named A5 contains unless your code is carefully traced. Compare it with a variable named todaysDate, which is self-explanatory.

Variable names in VB must begin with a letter and may be followed by alphanumeric characters or the underscore (_) character. The maximum size allowed for a variable name is 255 characters. VB is not case sensitive; the VB editor automatically

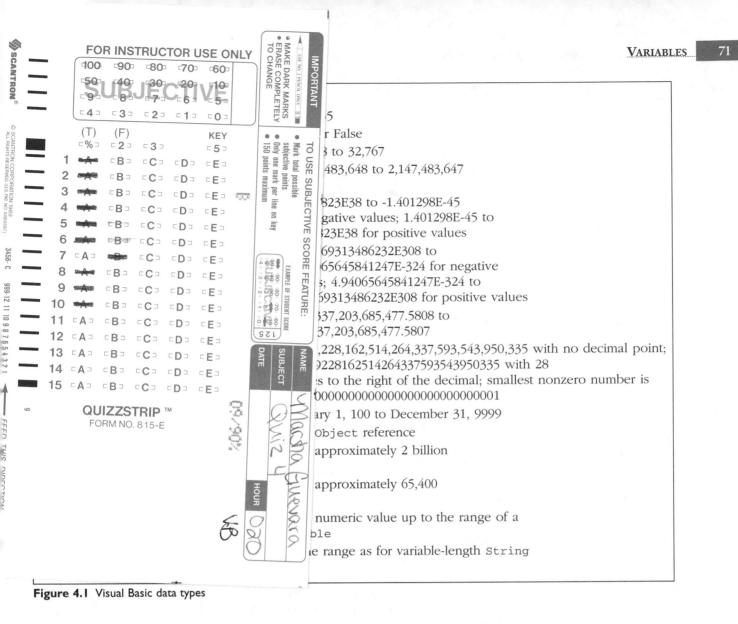

**Figure 4.1** Visual Basic data types

changes variable names to the same case. For example, if you name a variable `todaysDate` and then name another variable `todaysDATE`, the VB editor automatically changes this second variable to `todaysDate`, the same as the first variable name. The naming convention used throughout this text is to employ lowercase letters to begin a variable name, and an uppercase letter to distinguish second and subsequent words contained in a variable name. Thus, `todaysDate`, `totalSales`, `dailyTotal`, and `costOfGoodsSold` are examples of variable names that satisfy this text's programming standards.

A variable is assigned a data type by **declaring** the variable as a particular data type in your program. VB, like some other languages, does not require that you explicitly declare variables. However, *we highly recommend that you always explicitly declare all of your variables*. Declaring a variable serves several purposes:

1. It allows other programmers reading your code to easily determine the type of data stored in the variables and the ranges of the variables.

2. It provides greater control over the memory required by your program. Unless otherwise specified, VB assumes a variable is of the `Variant` data type and 16 or more bytes will be reserved for its storage. You can save considerable memory by explicitly assigning a specific data type to each of your variables.

**3.** It avoids confusion between variables of the same name in different sections of your code.

**4.** It encourages use of self-commenting variable names.

**5.** It gets you in the habit of declaring variables before their use, making it easier to transition to other computer languages.

VB can be set up to ensure that you explicitly declare all of your variables by selecting Tools/Option and looking under the Editor tab. Make sure that there is a check mark in the Require Variable Declaration check box. If you prefer to manually inform VB that you would like it to check for explicit variable declarations, simply type Option Explicit on a single line at the top of your code before all procedures. Since this code is placed outside of all procedures, it is located in the (General) object, (Declarations) section [or (Declarations) procedure] of your code.

## CODE VIEWS

How can you view the code you've written in VB? VB offers two different code "views," a full module view and a procedure view. The full module view displays all of the code in the current module. The two buttons at the bottom left-hand corner of the Code window allow you to switch between the procedure view and full module view. The full module view is the default view, and a solid line separates the different procedures of your code. These default options may be changed in Tools/Options under the Window Settings frame of the Editor tab.

The procedure view displays only one procedure at a time in the Code window. The two drop-down list boxes at the top of the code window allow you to select the object and procedure displayed. Alternately, you can use the PAGE UP and PAGE DOWN keys to scroll through the different objects and procedures.

## DECLARING VARIABLES

### Key Term

keyword—a reserved word or symbol recognized as part of a programming language

The Dim, or dimension, statement is used to declare variables in VB. This **keyword** tells the VB compiler the size, or dimension, of the variable, and the compiler then knows the amount of memory space to reserve for the variable. The general form of the Dim statement is shown below. The portion in brackets is optional; it illustrates how to declare several variables on the same line. Be sure to include As with each variable name for which you are specifying a data type; otherwise, the default type, Variant, will be assigned.

```
Dim variableName As DataType [, variableName As DataType, …]
```

```
Private Sub cmd1_Click()

Dim var1 As Integer                   ' One variable declaration on a line.

Dim var2 As Single, var3 As Single    ' Multiple variable declarations on
                                      ' the same line.

Dim var4, var5, var6 As Double        ' DON'T FALL INTO THIS TRAP.
                                      ' Only var6 is declared as a double-
                                      ' precision real number. var4 and
                                      ' var5 are of the Variant data type
                                      ' (the default data type).

End Sub
```

**Figure 4.2** Using the Dim statement

Figure 4.2 shows a **code segment**, or portion of source code, that uses the Dim statement to declare several variables. In Figure 4.2, the first statement declares one integer variable, var1. The second statement declares two single-precision variables, var2 and var3. The third statement declares only var6 as a double-precision variable. var4 and var5 are assigned the default data type, Variant. An alternate method of declaring variables in VB is to use variable type-declaration characters. A **type-declaration character** is a character appended to the end of a variable name that specifies the variable's data type. Type-declaration characters are described in Figure 4.3. Someone unfamiliar with VB would have a difficult time understanding your source code if you used type-declaration characters. Therefore, we prefer the use of Dim statements to declare variables rather than type-declaration characters since the Dim statements make for more readable source code.

## VARIANT DATA TYPE

The VB default data type is the Variant data type. This data type can store data that can be contained in any one of the other built-in data types. *We do not recommend using the Variant data type except for advanced programming.* However, it is important that you are aware of this data type. The following code segment illustrates our reasoning:

```
Private Sub cmdExample_Click()
    Dim num1, num2 As Integer
    num1 = 7
    num2 = 3
End Sub
```

Only num2 is dimensioned as an Integer. num1 is dimensioned as a Variant since no data type is specified using the As keyword.

In the above code segment, num2 is dimensioned as an Integer, but num1 is dimensioned as a Variant since no data type is specified using the As keyword. Both variables are assigned integer values. In some rare instances, this "flaw" can cause problems in the execution of your code. Similarly, in Figure 4.2, only var6 is declared as a double-precision real number. var4 and var5 are dimensioned as Variant since the keyword As is not specified with them.

To assign values, VB uses the equals operator (=) with an optional Let keyword. For instance, the following **code fragment**, or incomplete portion of source code, increments the count variable by one:

```
Let count = count + 1
```

These two lines of code are equivalent.

Again, the Let keyword is optional so it is usually omitted. The following line of code is equivalent to the one above:

```
count = count + 1
```

| Character | Data Type |
|-----------|-----------|
| % | Integer |
| & | Long |
| ! | Single |
| # | Double |
| @ | Currency |
| $ | String |
| There are no type-declaration characters for Boolean, Byte, Date, Object, and Variant data types. | |

**Figure 4.3** Visual Basic type-declaration characters

### USING = IN CODE

From the previous statements, notice that the = operator means "is assigned" rather than "is equal to" as in mathematics. If you were to give this "equation" to a mathematician, you would be told that it does not make sense. We could subtract the count variable from each side and end up with 0=1, which is simply incorrect. In computer science, however, this is a perfectly valid statement. It is interpreted as "assign the value of count plus one to the count variable." *The rule for variable assignments is that the result from the expression on the right-hand side of the = operator is stored in the variable that appears on the left-hand side.* Thus, to assign a value of one to the count variable, we write count = 1, but never 1 = count since we cannot assign the value of count to 1, a numeric constant. In assignment statements, it is best to think of the = operator as an arrow pointing toward the left (←) to mean "is assigned to." In fact, many programmers use ← in their pseudocode rather than = to avoid confusion.

To check your understanding of variable declaration and use, examine the program in Figure 4.4; it declares and uses variables. Can you tell what this code does? What is the output? Compare your answer to the actual program output shown to the right in Figure 4.4.

### INITIALIZING VARIABLES

In Figure 4.4, notice that the variable num is assigned the value 5 immediately after it is declared. So, we say num is initialized to 5. After any variable is declared, it must then be **initialized**, that is, assigned an initial value. The default initial value in VB is zero for numeric variables, False for boolean variables, and the **null string** (the string containing no characters) for string variables. Although VB automatically initializes variables to these default values in the variable declarations, most other high-level languages do not. In most other languages, after a variable is declared, it contains whatever "junk" value is residing in its assigned memory location. If there is no initialization, in other high-level languages some unspecified previous value will be used. Even in VB, some problems can arise. In the code in Figure 4.4,

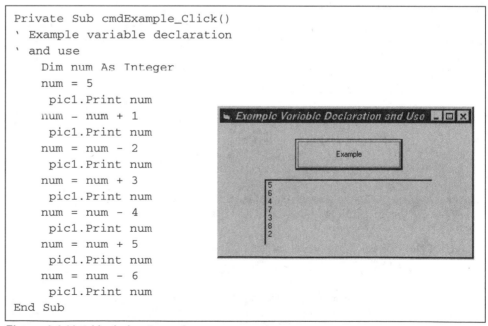

```
Private Sub cmdExample_Click()
' Example variable declaration
' and use
    Dim num As Integer
    num = 5
     pic1.Print num
    num = num + 1
     pic1.Print num
    num = num - 2
     pic1.Print num
    num = num + 3
     pic1.Print num
    num = num - 4
     pic1.Print num
    num = num + 5
     pic1.Print num
    num = num - 6
     pic1.Print num
End Sub
```

**Figure 4.4** Variable declaration and program execution

for example, if we omit the line num = 5, the output is still predictable in VB since num is initialized to zero by default. However, the output of the code no longer matches that of Figure 4.4, and it is not the desired output. So, our code now has a **logic error** due to the omission of the variable initialization. In other languages, the output is unpredictable due to this type of logic error. Thus, we emphasize: *Initialize all variables after declaring them.*

## CONSTANTS

A **constant** is a named item that retains a constant value throughout the execution of a program. It may be defined by any mathematical or string expression. At **compile time** (during program compilation), the compiler simply replaces the constant name with its associated value. A **numeric constant** refers to a number, or numeric literal, and a **string constant** is a string literal. The number 7, for example, is a numeric constant, and "days per week" is a string constant. Numeric and string constants that are used explicitly within the source code in lieu of named constants are said to be **hard-coded** into the program. Named constants are easily changed when necessary by simply editing the line of source code that specifies the value for the constant. Hard-coded constants are not as easily changed; a programmer must change every line of source code in which the constant is used in order to modify the program. Therefore, it is best to use named constants within your code to allow for easy future modifications.

### DEFINING CONSTANTS

In VB, the Const statement is used to define constants. The general form of the Const statement appears below. As shown in the square brackets, specifying a data type for a constant is optional.

```
Const constantName [As DataType] = Expression
```

Figure 4.5 shows the use of the Const statement and exemplifies the difference between named constants and hard-coded constants. Which method is easier to read? Which is more descriptive and self-commenting? If the constants are used throughout your code, which method is easier to change?

## MATHEMATICAL CALCULATIONS

Just as there are arithmetic **symbols** that denote specific operations to be performed in mathematics, there are equivalent **operators** to denote these operations on a computer. Addition, for instance, is denoted by the plus sign (+) in mathematics and on a computer. Multiplication, however, is denoted by the times symbol (×) in mathematics and by an asterisk (*) on a computer. Additionally, exponentiation is denoted by a superscript in mathematics, but the exponentiation operator on a computer depends upon the computer language or software package. The most common computer exponentiation operators are the caret symbol (^) and the double asterisk (**). Figure 4.6 displays the VB arithmetic operators and their mathematical equivalents.

```
Private Sub cmdExample_click()
'Example Use of Constants
'-----------------------------------
'This program demonstrates the difference between
'hard-coded and named constants
'Calculate the number of seconds in a year
Const SecondsPerMinute = 60    '60 seconds/minute
Const MinutesPerHour = 60      '60 minutes/hour
Const HoursPerDay = 24         '24 hours/day
Const DaysPerWeek = 7          '7 days/week
Const WeeksPerYear = 52        '52 weeks/year
Dim result As Long             'Store the number of seconds
                               'per year in result

'Using named constants
result = SecondsPerMinute * MinutesPerHour
result = result * HoursPerDay
result = result * DaysPerWeek
result = result * WeeksPerYear
pic1.Cls
pic1.Print "Using the named constants:"
pic1.Print Result; "seconds in a year"
pic1.Print
'Using hard-coded constants
result = 60 * 60
result = result * 24
result = result * 7
result = result * 52
pic1.Print "Using the hard-coded constants:"
pic1.Print result; "seconds in a year"
pic1.Print
End Sub
```

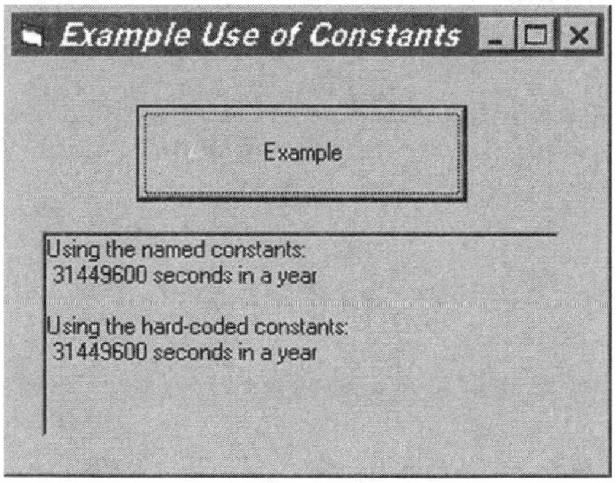

**Figure 4.5** Use of constants

**Integer division** and **modulo division** may perhaps be mathematical operations that you are not familiar with. Integer division, denoted by a backward slash (\) in VB, is used to divide two numbers and return only the integer part of the quotient; any fractional portion is simply truncated or ignored. For example, the result of 5\2 is 2. While 5 divided by 2 equals 2.5, it is only the integer part of the

| Mathematics | Math Example | Visual Basic | Visual Basic Example |
|---|---|---|---|
| Exponentiation | $5^2$ | ^ (caret) | 5^2 |
| Negation, − | −5 | − (minus sign) | −5 |
| Multiplication, × | 5×2 | * (asterisk) | 5*2 |
| Division, ÷ | 5÷2 | / (forward slash) | 5/2 |
| Addition,+ | 5+2 | + (plus sign) | 5+2 |
| Subtraction, − | 5−2 | − (minus sign) | 5−2 |
| Integer division | | \ (backward slash) | 5\2 |
| Modulo division | | Mod | 5 Mod 2 |

**Figure 4.6** Visual Basic arithmetic operators

quotient, 2, that is the result of integer division. The fractional part of the quotient is ignored. Modulo division, denoted by the Mod operator in VB, is used to divide two numbers and return only the integer portion of the remainder. For example, 5 Mod 1.7 equals 1 as does 5 Mod 2. 5 divided by 1.7 equals 2 with a remainder of 1.6. The integer part of the remainder, 1, is the result of modulo division.

## ORDER OF OPERATIONS

Mathematical operations are not evaluated from left to right. Instead, mathematical operators follow certain **precedence rules**, or an **order of operations**, that are listed in Figure 4.7. For instance, we evaluate $10 - 3 \times 2$ as 4. Multiplication has a higher precedence than subtraction, so we first multiply 3 by 2, resulting in 6. The 6 is then subtracted from 10, and the final answer is 4. As in mathematics, parentheses may be used to override the order of operations. Evaluation of $(10 - 3) \times 2$ yields 14 since we must evaluate 10 minus 3 first.

1. Exponentiation (^)
2. Negation (−)
3. Multiplication and division (*, /)
4. Integer division (\)
5. Modulo division (Mod)
6. Addition and subtraction (+, −)
7. String concatenation (&)

When multiplication and division occur together in an expression, each operation is evaluated as it occurs from left to right.

Likewise, when addition and subtraction occur together in an expression, each operation is evaluated in order of appearance from left to right.

The string concatenation operator (&) is not an arithmetic operator; it is performed at the end, after all the arithmetic operators.

Parenthetical expressions may be used to override predefined precedence rules.

**Figure 4.7** Visual Basic arithmetic operator precedence rules (order of operations)

## MATHEMATICAL FUNCTIONS

VB has many built-in mathematical functions. Figure 4.8 describes the most commonly used VB math functions as well as built-in functions for formatting numeric output.

The following code segment illustrates the use of the Format function described in Figure 4.8:

```
Private Sub cmdFormatEx_Click()
    Dim proportion As Single, sales As Single
    proportion = 0.8725
    sales = 5798.6125
    pctOutput.Print Format(proportion, "Percent"); " of
    ➡ inventory sold."
    pctOutput.Print Format(sales, "Currency"); " in total
    ➡ sales."
End Sub
```

The output of this code is shown below:

```
87.25% of inventory sold.
$5,798.61 in total sales.
```

### PROGRAMMING KEY: VB 6.0 FEATURES

VB 6.0 contains several new variations of the Format function and an additional function to format data. These functions are summarized below:

| Function | Description |
|---|---|
| FormatCurrency | Returns an expression formatted as a currency value along with the default currency symbol. |
| FormatDateTime | Returns an expression formatted as a date or time. |
| FormatNumber | Returns an expression formatted as a number. |
| FormatPercent | Returns an expression formatted as a percentage with a trailing % character. |
| Round | Returns a numeric expression rounded to a specified number of decimal places. |

## MIXED-MODE ARITHMETIC

**Mixed-mode arithmetic** is arithmetic that uses variables of different data types. VB is very forgiving and will allow mixed-mode arithmetic operations. However, this practice should be avoided in order to prevent unanticipated results. For example, the following VB code compiles with no errors:

```
Private Sub cmdExample_Click()
    Dim num1 As Single, num2 As Integer, result as Integer
    num1 = 7.2
    num2 = 3
    result = num1 * num2
End Sub
```

num1 * num2 **is a** ➡
mixed-mode operation.

In the above program, num1 is a single-precision real number and num2 is an integer. So, num1 * num2 is a mixed-mode operation. VB automatically converts the variable data types as required to perform the necessary operations. In this

## Math Functions

| | |
|---|---|
| Abs(x) | Returns the absolute value of *x*. |
| Atn(x) | Returns the angle corresponding to the arctangent of *x* in radians. |
| Cos(x) | Returns the cosine of angle *x*, where *x* is in radians. |
| Exp(x) | Returns the value $e^x$ where *e* is approximately 2.718282. |
| Fix(x) | Returns the integer part of *x*. If *x* is negative, it returns the next integer greater than or equal to *x*. |
| Int(x) | Returns the integer part of *x*. If *x* is negative, it returns the next integer less than or equal to *x*. |
| Log(x) | Returns the natural logarithm of *x*. |
| Rnd(x) | Returns a random number. See Visual Basic online help for a description of the result based upon values of *x*. |
| Sgn(x) | Returns a 1 if *x* is positive. -1 if *x* is negative, and 0 if *x* is zero. |
| Sin(x) | Returns the sine of angle *x*, where *x* is in radians. |
| Sqr(x) | Returns the square root of *x*. |
| Tan(x) | Returns the tangent of angle *x*, where *x* is in radians. |
| Format(x, fmt) | Returns the number *x* in numeric format fmt. |

## Numeric Formats

Predefined numeric format names include:

| Format name (fmt) | Description |
|---|---|
| General Number | Display number as is, with no thousand separators. |
| Currency | Display number with thousand separator, if appropriate; display two digits to the right of the decimal separator. Note that output is based on system locale settings. |
| Fixed | Display at least one digit to the left and two digits to the right of the decimal separator. |
| Standard | Display number with thousands separator, at least one digit to the left and two digits to the right of the decimal separator. |
| Percent | Display number multiplied by 100 with a percent sign (%) appended to the right; always display two digits to the right of the decimal separator. |
| Scientific | Use standard scientific notation. |
| Yes/No | Display No if number is 0; otherwise, display Yes. |
| True/False | Display False if number is 0; otherwise, display True. |
| On/Off | Display Off if number is 0; otherwise, display On. |

**Figure 4.8** Visual Basic math functions and numeric formats

example, num2 is **promoted** to a single-precision real number to perform the num1 * num2 calculation, and then the result of this calculation, 21.6, is converted to the integer value 22 and stored in the integer variable result. If such mixed-mode arithmetic is attempted in other languages, data type conversions may not be performed automatically and an error will result. To get in the habit of avoiding mixed-mode arithmetic, *we recommend that you explicitly convert to the necessary data types.*

Figure 4.9 lists the data type conversion functions available in VB. Rewriting the previous example to include explicit data type conversions yields:

```
Private Sub cmdExample_Click()
    Dim num1 As Single, num2 As Integer, result As Integer
    num1 = 7.2
    num2 = 3
    result = CInt(num1 * CSng(num2))
End Sub
```

The CInt and CSng functions explicitly convert variable data types in this code, avoiding mixed-mode arithmetic.

| | |
|---|---|
| `Asc(x)` | Returns the ASCII value of character $x$. |
| `CBool(x)` | Returns $x$ as a `Boolean` data type. |
| `CByte(x)` | Returns $x$ as a `Byte` data type. |
| `CCur(x)` | Returns $x$ as a `Currency` data type. |
| `CDate(x)` | Returns $x$ as a `Date` data type. |
| `CDbl(x)` | Returns $x$ as a `Double` data type. |
| `Chr(x)` | Returns the character associated with ASCII value $x$. |
| `CInt(x)` | Returns $x$ as an `Integer` data type. |
| `CLng(x)` | Returns $x$ as a `Long` data type. |
| `CSng(x)` | Returns $x$ as a `Single` data type. |
| `CStr(x)` | Returns $x$ as a `String` data type. |
| `CVar(x)` | Returns $x$ as a `Variant` data type. |
| `Hex(x)` | Returns a string representing the hexadecimal value of $x$. |
| `Oct(x)` | Returns a string representing the octal value of $x$. |
| `Str(x)` | Returns the string representing of number $x$. |
| `Val(x)` | Returns the number contained in string $x$. |

**Figure 4.9** Visual Basic data type conversion functions

## STRINGS

A string is a group of characters. String literals are denoted by quotes. The following code fragment assigns a value (a string literal) to a string variable.

```
Dim today As String
today = "Tuesday"
```

### STRING CONCATENATION

The **concatenation** operation is the only string operation in VB. Concatenation combines strings in the prescribed left to right order. Both the plus sign (+) and the ampersand (&) are valid concatenation operators. Since the plus sign performs different operations depending upon the context in which it is used, it is called an **overloaded operator**. To avoid confusion and promote program readability, *we recommend using the ampersand (&) as the exclusive string concatenation operator.*

An example code fragment demonstrating string concatenation is shown below.

```
Dim weekendDays as String
weekendDays = "Saturday" & " and " & "Sunday"
```

Upon execution of this code, the variable `weekendDays` contains the string `Saturday and Sunday`.

### SPECIAL CHARACTERS IN STRINGS

In the example above, you may have noticed that the quotes are not part of the string. What if you want to define a string that contains the quote characters? The following code fragment *does not work:*

This line of code does ➝
not work. It generates a syntax error.

```
weekendDays = ""Saturday and Sunday""
```

This code fragment generates a **syntax error**, or an error in grammar or punctuation. VB does not understand the structure of this statement. Fortunately, there is a way to include special characters and symbols that are not readily available on your keyboard in your strings.

Every character in the computer has an associated **ASCII** (American Standard Code for Information Interchange) value. Windows cannot display all ASCII (pronounced *ask-ee*) characters, so it uses the more limited **ANSI** (American National Standards Institute) character set. For the most part, ASCII and ANSI (pronounced *ann-see*) character values are equivalent. VB has two built-in functions to work with ASCII characters.

| | |
|---|---|
| `Chr(n)` | Returns the character whose ASCII value is `n`. |
| `Asc(chr)` | Returns the ASCII value of the character `chr`. |

For example, `Chr(65)` returns the character `A`, and conversely, `Asc("A")` returns the value 65. So, the ASCII value for a capital `A` is 65. Appendix A contains a table of ASCII (ANSI) character values. The ASCII value for a quote character is 34. We can now fix our code fragment as follows:

```
weekendDays = Chr(34) & "Saturday and Sunday" & Chr(34)
```

## STRING FUNCTIONS

VB has numerous built-in string functions, making it one of the best languages for working with strings. Figure 4.10 describes some of VB's most useful built-in string functions.

## FIXED-LENGTH STRINGS

Finally, if it is desirable for a string to always be a certain length, we can declare it as a **fixed-length string**. Fixed-length strings may be used when you know the maximum length of the data to be contained in the string. The general syntax for dimensioning a fixed length string is as follows:

```
Dim stringName As String * StringLength
```

| | |
|---|---|
| `LCase(x)` | Returns the string *x* converted to lowercase. |
| `Left(x, n)` | Returns the leftmost *n* character of string *x*. |
| `LTrim(x)` | Returns the string *x* without leading spaces. |
| `Mid(x, s, n)` | Returns the middle *n* characters of string *x* starting at character number *s*. |
| `Right(x, n)` | Returns the rightmost *n* characters of string *x*. |
| `RTrim(x)` | Returns the string *x* without trailing spaces. |
| `Trim(x)` | Returns the string *x* without leading and trailing spaces. |
| `UCase(x)` | Returns the string *x* converted to uppercase. |
| `Len(x)` | Returns the number of characters in string *x* or number of bytes required to store variable *x*. |

**Figure 4.10** Common Visual Basic string functions

**PROGRAMMING KEY: TIP**

In order to use the quote character or a nonkeyboard character in a string, you must first find the character's ASCII value (see Appendix A). Then, use the string concatenation operator (&) and the `Chr` function with the character's ASCII value to add this character to your string.

Note that the variable *stringName* will *always* be of the fixed-length *StringLength*. For example, examine the code fragment below:

```
Dim str1 As String * 15
Dim str2 As String * 15
str1 = "Visual Basic"      pads w/ blanks
str2 = "Visual Basic!!!!!"   loses 2 !
```

What are the contents of `str1` and `str2`? `str1` contains `Visual Basic` with three trailing spaces and `str2` contains `Visual Basic!!!` (Note the *three* trailing exclamation points). Both strings have a fixed-length of 15 characters. If a string of less than 15 characters is assigned to one of these variables, VB automatically adds trailing spaces to fill the variable. Similarly, if a string of more than 15 characters is assigned, VB automatically truncates the string at 15 characters.

## SCOPE AND LIFETIME

### Key Terms

**scope**—an object's availability, or visibility, to specific parts of a program
**lifetime**—the length of an object's existence in the computer's memory space

The **scope** of an object refers to its availability, or visibility, to specific parts of a program. The **lifetime** of an object refers to how long the object exists in the computer's memory space. Scope and lifetime are important programming concepts.

A variable's scope, for example, may be either local or global. A variable with a local scope is called a **local variable**; similarly, a variable with a global scope is called a **global variable**. Local variables are available for use only within the procedure in which they are declared. The variable is allocated memory space (or created) when the procedure begins, and it is de-allocated (or destroyed) when the procedure ends. Global variables, however, are available to all parts of the program. They are created when the program begins and removed from memory when the program ends.

In VB, there are two different types of global variables, form-level variables and public variables. **Form-level (or module-level) variables** are global only to the form in which they are declared. In other words, a form-level variable may be used anywhere in the form. A form-level variable is declared by placing the variable declaration at the top of the source code (outside of all procedures) in the (General) object, (Declarations) section. The `Private` keyword is equivalent to the `Dim` keyword since form-level variables are private to the form in which they are declared. The following code, for example, declares and uses a form-level variable.

```
Option Explicit
Private number As Integer    ' Form-level variable

Private Sub cmdClear_Click()
    number = 0
End Sub

Private Sub cmdIncrement_Click()
    number = number + 1
    picOutput.Print number
End Sub
```

Pressing the cmdClear button initializes the `number` variable to 0. Pressing cmdIncrement increments the value of `number` by one and displays the result in the picOutput picture box.

Since a VB program may have multiple forms, there is a way to declare a variable global (and therefore available) to all forms in the project. Such variables are called **public variables**. To declare a public variable, place the variable declaration in a standard code module and use the `Public` (or `Global`) keyword in place of `Dim`. A standard code module contains code that is accessible to all of the parts of a project. To create a standard code module, select Project/Add Module from the menu bar.

Local variables are also called **dynamic variables** since they are created and destroyed dynamically during the program execution. Thus, local variables generally have a short lifetime, and their values are not retained after they are destroyed. What if we want to keep a local variable and its value after the procedure ends? We could use a form-level variable, but these variables are usually used to share data among different procedures. Microsoft's solution to this problem is to use **static variables**. These variables are declared at the procedure level by using the `Static` keyword rather than `Dim`; the variables are retained in memory even after the procedure ends. Furthermore, static variables are not automatically re-initialized when the procedure is invoked again. Static variables are ideal for counters or toggling the visibility property of controls. An example is shown below:

```
Option Explicit
Private Sub cmdToggle_Click()
' Toggle the visibility of the output picture box
    Static vis As Boolean    ' Static variable
    vis = Not (vis)
    picOutput.Visible = vis
End Sub


Private Sub cmdIncrement_Click()
' Increment number and display the result
    Static number As Integer ' Static variable
                             ' NOTE: VB automatically
                               initializes number to 0
    number = number + 1
    picOutput.Print number
End Sub
```

The cmdIncrement button works the same as in the previous example, except that we use a static variable rather than a form-level variable. The cmdToggle button toggles the `Visible` property of the picture box picOutput.

## PROGRAMMING KEY: TIPS

We do not recommend the use of global (form-level or public) variables except for advanced programming. The use of global variables is typically considered "bad technique" in introductory programming courses; there are several disadvantages in their use. First, global variables often confuse novice programmers when there are both global and local variables of the same name. It is also extremely easy for a new programmer to assume that a global variable has a certain value based upon a previous operation, when, in fact, the variable was changed to an unexpected value by some other code. Finally, global variables do not promote modular design and the reusability of code, topics which are discussed in later chapters.

Despite their disadvantages, global variables are useful in certain situations. Since all VB code is contained in subprograms (or procedures), global variables avoid the passing of multiple parameters between procedures. Additionally, VB is event-driven, and using global variables eliminates the need to create and initialize local variables at the beginning of each event. This allows the code to execute faster (although the saved microseconds are usually undetectable by the user), and it saves the programmer from typing a lot of `Dim` statements at the beginning of each event-handler. Finally, using global variables may provide "cleaner" (more understandable) code in some situations.

## PROGRAM READABILITY

Programming is the ultimate means of self-expression on a computer. Like an artist who completes a beautiful painting, programmers often feel pride and accomplishment in their work. Computer programming can also give feelings of great power; the computer dances at your command. An artist's painting, however, is worthless unless other people have the opportunity to enjoy it. Like the artist conveying thoughts through canvas, a programmer communicates ideas through source code. Remember, a program is not only a means of informing the computer of your desires, but it also communicates your ideas to other people. Programmers clarify and explain source code by using comments. Just as a cookbook describes the details of a recipe with comments, you should add comments to your program.

*prologs*

Comments at the beginning of your source code should include the program title, program purpose or description, programmer's name, program version number, date programmed, and date last modified. Not every line of source code needs to be commented. In fact, comments should be used sparingly in your source code. Remember, the idea is to make your source code self-commenting by using descriptive names for objects, variables, constants, functions, and procedures. Comments should be placed at the beginning of each function and procedure to describe its purpose, required parameters, and output. Furthermore, it is better to place comments before a large block of code to describe what it does rather than comment each line of the code.

The use of indented code and added white space (blank lines) can play a major role in enhancing your program's readability. Indenting code within control structures by two or three spaces is usually sufficient. The examples in this text use indentation and white space to enhance readability. You should adopt a method of indentation and white space that is most comfortable for you and best suited to your programming style.

### COMMENT KEYWORDS

The `Rem`, or remark, statement is used to comment VB code. Everything appearing on the same line after the `Rem` keyword is considered a comment and ignored by VB. Alternately, an apostrophe (') may be used in place of the `Rem` keyword. The syntax for comments follows:

```
Rem comment
```

or

```
' comment
```

If the `Rem` keyword follows other statements on a line, it must be separated from the statements by a colon (:). However, when you use an apostrophe, the colon is not required after other statements. For instance, the following lines of code are equivalent:

```
startNum = 1: Rem Define the starting value
startNum = 1 'Define the starting value
```

The colon (:) may also be used to separate several statements on the same line. However, we do not recommend combining several statements on one line since it reduces program readability.

## LINE CONTINUATION CHARACTER

VB has a line-continuation character to further promote program readability. Eventually, some lines of your code may exceed 80 characters, especially when you start nesting (or embedding) multiple control structures. When you print your source code, the printer just prints the remaining code on the very next line, and it does not indent. To overcome this problem, use the line-continuation character. The underscore (_) is the VB line-continuation character, and it is used by simply placing a space and an underscore at the end of the line of code and continuing the code on the next line. Note that a space should be placed before the line continuation character so VB does not consider it part of something else (a variable, constant, etc.). Additionally, the line-continuation character may be used to extend comments over several lines. For example:

```
Rem This comment extends over multiple lines, _
    but the Rem statement only appears on _
    the first line.
```

## INTERACTIVE INPUT AND OUTPUT

Chapter 2 introduced the elementary VB controls, such as command buttons, text boxes, and picture boxes. These controls constitute the primary method of interactive input and output (I/O) used in this text. Text boxes may be used for both input and output, but we use them only for input. Picture boxes are exclusively for output.

## TEXT BOXES

VB is an **object-oriented language**. All of the controls (such as text boxes, picture boxes, etc.) are objects, and objects have associated **methods** that act on them. VB, like most object-oriented languages, uses the dot separator to separate the object name from methods and object properties. A text box named txt1, for example, has a Text property that contains the string that is in the text box. To clear the contents of txt1 in a program, we write the following line of code:

```
txt1.Text = ""
```
no space

The above line of code assigns the null string or empty string to the Text property of text box txt1. The null string is a quote character immediately followed by another quote character (nothing is in between the quotes). This method may be used to clear or reassign the values of text boxes in your programs.

## PICTURE BOXES

A picture box has methods that perform tasks associated with clearing the box and displaying messages in the box. Two of the most important methods are:

```
picBox.Cls                    Clear picBox
picBox.Print expression       Print expression in picBox
```

The example program in Figure 4.11 computes the square root of a number. A text box (txtInputNumber) allows the user to input a number. The user must press the Compute Square Root command button (cmdCompute) in order for the program to perform the calculation and display the output. The output is displayed in a picture box (picOutput).

## INPUT BOXES AND MESSAGE BOXES

Input boxes are another means of interactive user input, and message boxes allow for interactive output. Input and message boxes are not predesigned on the form by the programmer at **design time**, but they open separate windows when the code is encountered at **run time**. A simplified syntax for using input and message boxes appears below. Consult the VB online help for more information.

```
Dim varName As String
varName = Str(InputBox(prompt, title))

        Displays an input box with the given title and
        prompt. User input is assigned to the string
        variable varName.

MsgBox message, 0, title

        Displays a message box with the given title and
        message.
```

```
Private Sub cmdCompute_Click()
' Compute the square root of a number input by user
    Dim number As Double
    number = CDbl(Val(txtInputNumber.Text))
    picOutput.Cls
    picOutput.Print "The square root of"; number; "is";
    ➡ Sqr(number)
End Sub
```

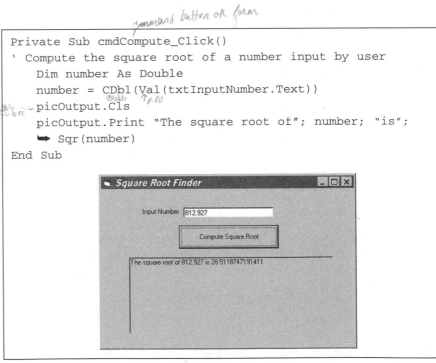

**Figure 4.11** Square root finder and program execution

The program in Figure 4.12 performs the same task as the program in Figure 4.11, but it uses input and message boxes. Note that the text box and picture box are no longer needed on the form; the only object on the form is a command button (cmdCompute).

## YOUR SECOND PROGRAM

For your second program, we show you how to create a temperature conversion program. The purpose of the program is to convert between temperatures measured in Fahrenheit and Celsius. The relationship between temperatures in Fahrenheit (°F) and Celsius (°C) is as follows:

$$F = 32 + (9/5)(C)$$

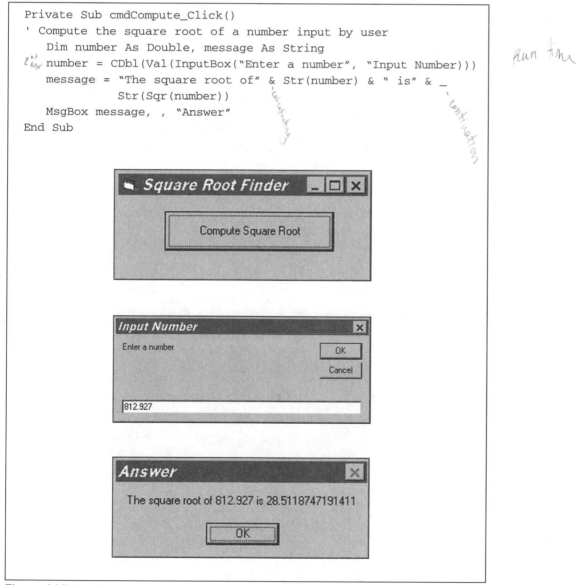

```
Private Sub cmdCompute_Click()
' Compute the square root of a number input by user
    Dim number As Double, message As String
    number = CDbl(Val(InputBox("Enter a number", "Input Number)))
    message = "The square root of" & Str(number) & " is" & _
            Str(Sqr(number))
    MsgBox message, , "Answer"
End Sub
```

**Figure 4.12** Modified square root finder and program execution

Figure 4.13 displays the form we will use in this program. This form contains one label, one text box, two command buttons, and one picture box. Modify the property settings to match those listed in the table below:

| Object | Property | Setting |
| --- | --- | --- |
| Form | Caption | Temperature Conversion |
| | Name | frmTempConv |
| Label | AutoSize | True |
| | Caption | Temperature |
| | Name | lblTemp |
| Text Box | Name | txtTemp |
| | Text | *Empty* (Null String) |
| Command Button | Caption | Convert Fahrenheit to Celsius |
| | Name | cmdFtoC |
| Command Button | Caption | Convert Celsius to Fahrenheit |
| | Name | cmdCtoF |
| Picture Box | Name | picOutput |

Now, open a Code window and type in the code shown in Figure 4.14. After you type in the code, run your program by clicking the Start button, selecting Run/Start from the menu bar, or pressing F5. Enter the number 25 in the text box and click the Convert Celsius to Fahrenheit button. The program informs you that 25°C is 77°F. Now type 77 in the text box and click the Convert Fahrenheit to Celsius button. Make sure that the program tells you the answer is 25°C as shown in Figure 4.15.

Finally, convert any temperature that you desire. When you are done, click the End button to stop the program.

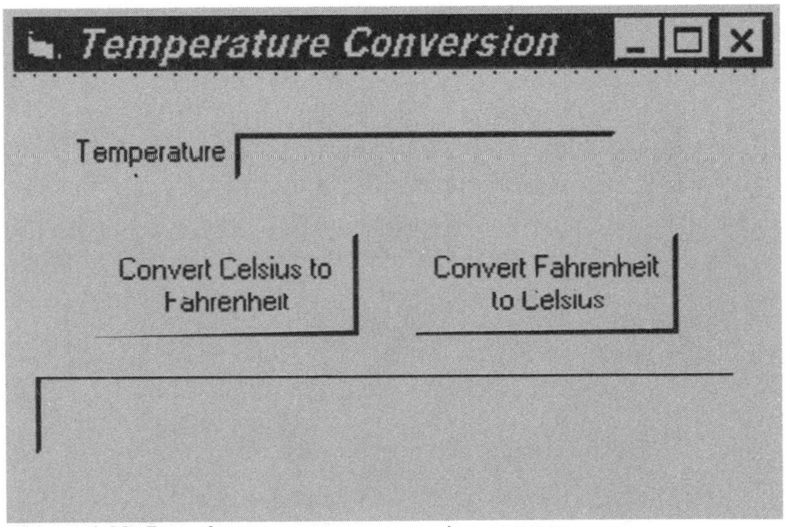

**Figure 4.13** Form for temperature conversion program

```
'  Temperature Conversion Program
'  ------------------------------------------------
'  Convert between temperatures in Fahrenheit and Celsius
'
'  Applicable formulae:
'
'    F = 32 + (9/5)C
'    C = (5/9)(F-32)

Option Explicit

Private Sub cmdCtoF_Click()
' Convert Celsius to Fahrenheit

    Dim celsius As Single, fahrenheit As Single
    Dim degree As String

    degree = Chr(176)  ' Degree symbol
    celsius = CSng(Val(txtTemp.Text))
    fahrenheit = Csng(32) + (9 / 5) * celsius

    picOutput.Cls
    picOutput.Print Trim(Str(celsius)) & degree & "C is " & Trim(Str(fahrenheit)) & degree & "F"

End Sub

Private Sub cmdFtoC_Click()
' Convert Fahrenheit to Celsius

    Dim celsius As Single, fahrenheit As Single
    Dim degree As String

    degree = Chr(176)  ' Degree symbol
    fahrenheit = CSng(Val(TxtTemp.Text))
    celsius = (5/9) * (fahrenheit - CSng(32))

    picOutput.Cls
    picOutput.Print Trim(Str(fahrenheit)) & degree & "F is " & Trim(Str(celsius)) & degree & "C"

End Sub
```

**Figure 4.14** Source code for temperature conversion program

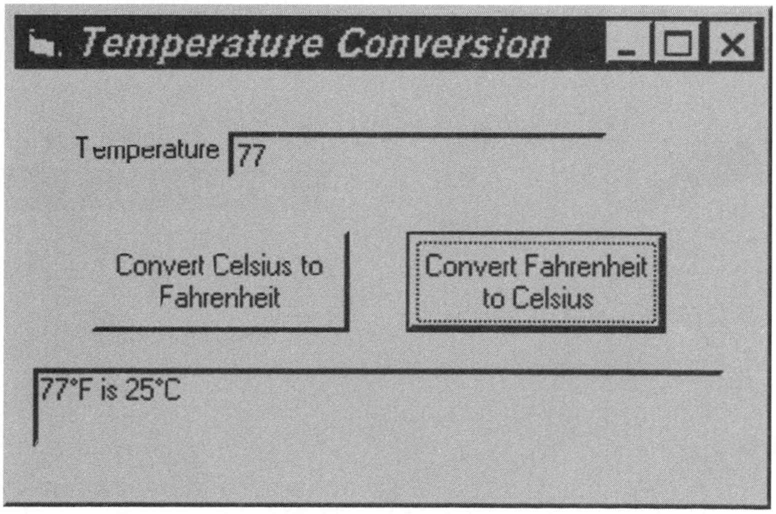

**Figure 4.15** Answer to temperature conversion problem

· · · · · · · · · · · · · · · · · · · · · · · · · · · · · · ·
C A S E   S T U D Y
## The Global Variable Trap

Comments are intentionally omitted from the following code. This code contains a logic error. Can you find it?

```
Option Explicit
Dim number As Integer

Private Sub cmdDisplay_Click()
    Call DisplayValue
End Sub

Private Sub cmdIncrement_Click()
    number = number + 1
End Sub

Private Sub cmdReset_Click()
    number = 0
End Sub

Private Sub cmdLocal_Click()
    Dim number As Integer
    number = -1
    Call DisplayValue
End Sub

Private Sub DisplayValue()
    picOutput.Print number
End Sub
```

This code contains a global variable named number. The event handler for the cmdLocal command button contains a local variable also named number. This event handler calls the DisplayValue procedure. However, DisplayValue prints the value of the global variable number, not the local variable, in the picture box. In summary, the value of the local variable number is never displayed in the picture box. This illustrates a common mistake made by novice programmers.

## Summary

### Key Terms

**alphanumeric data**—a subset of character data that consists of letters and numbers

**ANSI**—American National Standards Institute

**ASCII**—American Standard Code for Information Interchange

**case-sensitive**—a program's ability to recognize a difference between uppercase and lowercase letters

**character data**—data consisting of letters, numbers, symbols, or any combination thereof

**code fragment**—an incomplete portion of source code

**code segment**—a portion of source code

**compile time**—the time when a program's source code is translated into machine language and an executable file is created

**concatenation**—an operation that combines strings in a prescribed left to right order

**constant**—a named item that retains the same value throughout the execution of a program

**data type**—a keyword that describes the size of a variable and the range of values that it may contain

**declare**—the process of associating a variable with a data type and reserving memory space for the variable

**design time**—the time when the program and user interface are being written

**dynamic variable**—a variable that is created and destroyed dynamically during program execution; a local variable

**fixed-length string**—a string that contains a constant or fixed number of characters

**floating-point numbers**—see real numbers

**form-level variable** (or **module-level variable**)—a variable that is available to all parts of the form in which it is declared; a variable that is global to a form or module

**global variable**—a variable that is available to all parts of a program; a variable with global scope

**hard-coded**—refers to numeric constants and string constants that appear in a program's source code

**initialization**—the process of assigning an initial value to a variable

**integer**—a number with no fractional component

**integer division**—a division operation that returns only the integer part of the quotient; any fractional portion of the quotient is simply truncated or ignored

**keyword**—a reserved word or symbol recognized as part of a programming language

**lifetime**—the length of an object's existence in the computer's memory space

**local variable**—a variable that is available for use only within the procedure in which it is declared; a variable with local scope

**logic error**—an error in the logic of a program or algorithm

**method**—a subprogram that is associated with an object. Typically, a method alters the properties of its associated object

**mixed-mode arithmetic**—arithmetic that uses variables of different data types

**modulo division**—a division operation that returns only the integer portion of the remainder; any fractional portion of the remainder is simply truncated or ignored

**null string**—a string containing no characters; the empty string

**numeric constant**—a number; a numeric literal

**numeric data**—data consisting of numbers

**object-oriented language**—a computer language that contains object data types

**operator**—a symbol that denotes a mathematical or string operation

**order of operations**—see precedence rules

**overloaded operator**—an operator that performs different operations depending upon the context in which it is used

**precedence rules (order of operations)**—a designated order of carrying out operations to evaluate an expression

**promote**—the act of changing a variable's data type to one that requires more memory space

**public variable**—a variable that is available to all parts of a VB project

**range**—the bounds or limits of a variable's possible values

**real number (floating-point number)**—a number with a fractional component

**run time**—the time when the program is executing or running

**scope**—an object's availability, or visibility, to specific parts of a program

**self-commenting**—the name of a program element describes its contents or purpose

**static variable**—in VB, a variable whose value is retained in memory even after the procedure in which it is declared ends. A static variable is not automatically re-initialized when the procedure is invoked again

**string**—a group of characters

**string constant**—a string literal

**string variable**—a variable that contains character data

**syntax error**—an error in the grammar or punctuation of the source code

**type-declaration character**—a character appended to the end of a variable name that specifies the variable's data type

**variable**—a quantity that can assume any value; a named memory location that stores a value

**variant**—the default VB data type; a data type able to store data that can be contained in any one of the other built-in VB data types

## Keywords

| *Data Types:* | Atn | FormatDateTime |
|---|---|---|
| Boolean | CBool | FormatNumber |
| Byte | CByte | FormatPercent |
| Currency | CCur | Hex |
| Date | CDate | Int |
| Decimal | CDbl | LCase |
| Double | Chr | Left |
| Integer | CInt | Len |
| Long | CLng | Log |
| Object | Cos | LTrim |
| Single | CSng | Mid |
| String | CStr | Oct |
| Variant | CVar | Right |
| | Exp | Rnd |
| *Functions:* | Fix | Round |
| Abs | Format | RTrim |
| Asc | FormatCurrency | Sgn |

| | Methods: | Operators: | Properties: | Statements: |
|---|---|---|---|---|
| Sin | | | | |
| Sqr | Cls | - | TabIndex | ' |
| Str | Print | * | Text | As |
| Tan | | / | | Const |
| Trim | | \ | | Dim |
| UCase | | ^ | | Global |
| Val | | + | | Private |
| | | = | | Public |
| | | Mod | | Rem |
| | | | | Static |

## Key Concepts

● There are several elements of programming that are common to all computer languages; these include variables, constants, data types, scope and lifetime, and comments.

● A variable's value can change throughout program execution. A variable can contain either numeric or alphanumeric data.

● Variables are assigned data types to limit the amount of memory they require and inform the computer and other programmers of the type of data they store. The Dim statement is used to declare variables:

```
Dim variableName As DataType [, variableName As DataType, …]
```

● Although VB assigns default values to declared variables, the programmer should explicitly initialize the variables to the desired values. Initialization is done using the assignment operator (=). In a variable assignment, the variable name must appear on the left-hand side of the = operator:

```
variableName = expression
```

● A constant maintains the same value throughout the program. There are two types of constants, named constants and hard-coded (or literal) constants. The Const statement allows the programmer to define named constants. Named constants are preferred since they are typically self-commenting and easier to change. The general syntax follows:

```
Const constantName [As DataType] = Expression
```

● Arithmetic and string operators provide a method of performing computations. All computations are performed in strict adherence to the operator precedence rules.

● There are many common VB math and string functions. The Format function allows a programmer to format numeric output. Data type conversion functions explicitly convert a variable of one type to another type.

● Every character in the computer has an associated ASCII (or ANSI) value. The Asc function returns the ASCII value of a character. The Chr function returns the character associated with a particular ASCII value.

● A fixed-length string is a string that contains a constant or fixed number of characters. To dimension a fixed-length string, use:

```
Dim stringName As String * StringLength
```

● Scope refers to the visibility of an object, whereas lifetime is the duration of an object's existence in the computer's memory space. For example, a variable's scope may be either local or global.

● Local variables are dynamic variables since they are created and destroyed dynamically during program execution. Static variables have a longer lifetime than dynamic variables, and they are retained in memory even after the procedure in which they are declared ends.

● Comments and white space can greatly improve the readability of code. The Rem, or remark, statement is used to comment code, and the apostrophe (') is equivalent to the remark statement. The syntax follows:

```
Rem comment
' comment
```

● The underscore (_) is the VB line-continuation character, and it may be used to extend code or comments over more than one line.

● Text boxes and picture boxes are the primary means of interactive input and output in VB.

To clear a text box, use:

```
txtBox.Text = ""
```

Methods for clearing and printing a picture box include:

```
picBox.Cls              Clear picBox
picBox.Print expression    Print expression in picBox
```

● Input boxes and message boxes may also be used for input and output, respectively.

To read data from an input box into *varName*:

```
varName = Str(InputBox(prompt, title))
```

To output *message* to a message box titled *title*:

```
MsgBox message, 0, title
```

## Review Questions

1. What is a variable? How is it different from a constant?
2. Why should you assign a data type to a variable?
3. What statement is used to declare variables? to declare constants?
4. Why is it important to initialize variables?
5. What data types can contain numeric data? alphanumeric data?

6. How is the = operator used in a variable assignment statement? Give an example.

7. What is the difference between hard-coded and named constants? In what instance(s) is each preferred and why?

8. What arithmetic operator is used to perform exponentiation? multiplication? division?

9. What are scope and lifetime? How do they apply to variables?

10. State the advantages and disadvantages of global variables.

11. What can a programmer do to improve the readability of his code?

12. Why is it important to comment your code? What VB statements are used to comment code?

13. How do you clear a picture box? a text box?

14. What are input boxes and message boxes?

## Chapter 4 Problems

1. Change the program in Figure 4.11 to find the cube root of a number that the user enters. Use a text box for input and a picture box for output.

2. Repeat Problem 1 using an input box for input and a message box for output.

3. Modify the program in Figure 4.14 to use an input box to input the temperature and a message box to display the result.

4. Write a program that allows the user to enter his or her first and last names in two separate text boxes. The program then outputs the last name, a comma, and the first name all on one line in a picture box.

5. Write a program that allows the user to enter his or her first, middle, and last names in three separate text boxes. The program then outputs the user's initials in a picture box.

6. Write a program that computes a vehicle's average velocity using the formula shown below (*distance* and *time* are user inputs).

   *average velocity = distance ÷ time*

7. *The Car Chase Problem.* A speeding car is traveling at $x$ miles per hour. A police car in pursuit of the speeder is traveling at $y$ miles per hour, where $y > x$. If the police car is initially a distance $d$ away from the speeder, how long does it take the police car to catch the speeder and how far must the police car travel to do so? Write a VB program to solve this problem, where $x, y,$ and $d$ are user inputs. Remember to account for both cases: The speeder can be traveling either toward or away from the police car.

8. The speed of light, c, is approximately $3 \times 10^8$ meters per second. Write a program that prompts the user to input time in seconds and displays the distance that light travels in that time period.

9. Use your program from Problem 8 to find the approximate distance of a light-year, the distance that light travels in one year. Modify your program from Problem 8 to display the distance in feet, meters, kilometers, and miles. Remember that there are 3.28 feet per meter and 1.61 kilometers per mile.

10. The quadratic formula can solve for the roots of a quadratic equation of the form $ax^2 + bx + c = 0$. The quadratic formula is shown as:

$$x = \frac{-b \pm \sqrt{b^2 - 4ac}}{2a}$$

Write a program that allows the user to input values for $a$, $b$, and $c$, and then displays the two roots of $x$. Do not worry about imaginary roots; assume the value of $a$ is always nonzero.

11. The normal distribution, or Gaussian distribution, is the most important continuous probability distribution in all of statistics. The probability density function (pdf) of the normal random variable $X$, with mean $\mu$ and standard deviation $\sigma$, gives the probability that $X$ is equal to some value $x$, and is defined by:

$$N(x, \mu, \sigma) = \frac{1}{\sigma\sqrt{(2\pi)}} e^{-(1/2)[(x-\mu)/\sigma]^2}$$

for $-\infty < x < +\infty$, where $-\infty < \mu < +\infty$ and $\sigma > 0$. $\pi$ is approximately 3.14159 and $e$ is approximately 2.71828.

Write a program that displays the probability density for user-entered values of $x$, $\mu$, and $\sigma$.

12. A cumulative distribution function (cdf) for a random variable $X$ gives the probability that $X$ is less than or equal to some value x. The cdf for the exponential distribution is defined below:

$$P(X \leq x, \lambda) = \begin{cases} 1 - e^{-\lambda x} & x \geq 0 \\ 0, & x < 0 \end{cases}$$

Write a program that displays the cumulative probability of the exponential distribution for user-entered values of $x$ and $\lambda$.

### Programming Projects

1. Modify Chapter 4, Problem 12 to solve for $x$, the point where the exponential cdf equals a value of $y$. The user inputs the values of $y$ and $\lambda$, and your program solves for $x$.

2. Sam has a three-year auto loan at an 8.5% annual interest rate. His monthly payment is $250. He has made payments on the loan for the past 18 months, and he wants to know the payoff balance. Write a program to determine the payoff balance of Sam's auto loan. The applicable formula appears below:

$$B = P\left[\frac{1 - (1+i)^{k-n}}{i}\right]$$

where

$B$ = payoff balance
$P$ = monthly payment
$i$ = monthly interest rate
$k$ = number of payments already made
$n$ = total number of monthly payments

# 5

# Flow Control

## Chapter Objectives

In this chapter, you will:

- Learn about flow control structures and the two main categories of these structures

- Learn the comparison operators, including both relational and logical operators

- Become familiar with the precedence rules for relational and logical operators

- Learn DeMorgan's laws and understand how they relate to both computer science and mathematics

- Gain an understanding of logical expressions and learn how to expand and reduce them

- Use truth tables to evaluate and compare logical expressions

- Learn decision structures, including `If`-blocks and `Select-Case` blocks, and the appropriate situations for their use

- See how to convert an `If`-block into a `Select-Case` block and vice versa

- Learn the operation and use of repetition structures, including `For-Next` loops and `Do` loops, and discover the major differences between these structures

- Learn how to convert a `Do While-Loop` into a `Do-Loop Until` and vice versa

- Understand sequential and nested control structures

- Learn about accumulator and flag variables

- Learn how to use `End` and `Stop` statements to end program execution

- Learn about programming style and programming standards

So far, we have seen that a computer executes program code sequentially from the beginning of the program to the end. Oftentimes, a programmer wants the computer to repeat a group of program statements or execute specific code based upon the presence (or absence) of certain conditions. These types of operations require programming constructs formally known as **control structures**. Control structures control the flow of program execution; they include both decision and repetition structures. But in order to understand these structures we will first discuss comparison operators; an understanding of these will provide a basis for our later discussion of control structures.

## COMPARISON OPERATORS

**Comparison operators** consist of both relational operators and logical operators. We'll take up each of these in turn.

### RELATIONAL OPERATORS

**Key Term**

**expression**—a combination of keywords, operators, variables, and constants that yields a string, number, or object

For any two expressions *A* and *B* of the same type, one of three conditions must exist: Either $A < B$, $A = B$, or $A > B$. An **expression** is a combination of keywords, operators, variables, and constants that yields a string, number, or object. **Relational operators** are used to compare expressions. As is done in mathematics, relational operators can be combined in computer programming to test whether $A \leq B$, $A \geq B$, or $A \neq B$.

Figure 5.1 shows the VB relational operators and their mathematical counterparts. These relational operators are common to most high-level languages. Like the plus sign (+), the equals sign (=) is an overloaded operator in VB; it is used for assignment statements and for comparisons of equality.

A relational operator that compares two expressions forms a **logical expression** (or **boolean expression**); this is an expression that evaluates to be either True or False. The result of a logical expression that contains numeric expressions is self-explanatory. For instance, the logical expression $5 < 2$ is false, whereas $5 > 2$ is true. String expressions are evaluated according to the ASCII values of their characters. For example, since "A" has ASCII value 65 and "a" has ASCII value 97, the following string expression is evaluated to be True.

```
"America" < "america"      is True
```

Another example is shown below. This time the logical expression is evaluated to be False. Can you see why?

```
"America" < "AMERICA"      is False
```

**PROGRAMMING KEY: WARNING**

Be careful when using relational operators with string expressions since they are evaluated according to their ASCII values; results of these logical expressions are not intuitive.

| Relational operator | Visual Basic | Mathematics |
|---|---|---|
| Less than | < | $<$ |
| Less than or equal to | <= | $\leq$ |
| Greater than | > | $>$ |
| Greater than or equal to | >= | $\geq$ |
| Equal to | = | $=$ |
| Not equal to | <> | $\neq$ |

**Figure 5.1** Visual Basic relational operators

## LOGICAL OPERATORS

**Logical operators** are used to combine logical (boolean) expressions. The three primary logical operators are AND, OR, and NOT. All other logical operators can be derived from these primary logical operators, but are beyond the scope of this text. The results of combining logical expressions with logical operators are commonly displayed in **truth tables**, as in Figure 5.2.

As shown in Figure 5.2, the AND operator performs a **logical conjunction** of two expressions; the result is True only if *both* expressions evaluate to True. The OR operator performs a **logical disjunction** of two expressions; the result is True if *either or both* expressions evaluate to True. Finally, the NOT operator performs a **logical negation** of an expression; the result is the opposite of the expression evaluation.

> ## Key Term
>
> **truth table**—a table that displays the evaluation of a logical expression according to the values of the variables

## RELATIONAL AND LOGICAL OPERATOR PRECEDENCE

In VB, all relational operators have equal precedence and are evaluated from left to right, in the order in which they appear. For the logical operators, NOT has the highest precedence, followed by AND, and then OR. When an expression contains operators of more than one type, mathematical operators are evaluated first, relational operators are evaluated next, and logical operators are evaluated last. Again, parentheses may be used to override operator precedence or improve program readability. Figure 5.3 shows an example.

> ### PROGRAMMING KEY: WARNING
>
> In mathematics, we can write expressions such as $5 < x < 6$. While this expression is legal in mathematics, it is not legal in modern programming languages such as VB. This mathematical expression actually consists of two logical expressions: $5 < x$ and $x < 6$. Therefore, the AND operator may be used to create an equivalent expression as shown below:
>
> | **Mathematics** | **Visual Basic** |
> |---|---|
> | $5 < x < 6$ | (5 < x) AND (x < 6) |

## LOGICAL EXPRESSIONS

Besides using parentheses, we can call on certain rules ("laws") when we work with logical expressions.

| A | B | A AND B | A OR B | NOT A | NOT B |
|---|---|---|---|---|---|
| FALSE | FALSE | FALSE | FALSE | TRUE | TRUE |
| FALSE | TRUE | FALSE | TRUE | TRUE | FALSE |
| TRUE | FALSE | FALSE | TRUE | FALSE | TRUE |
| TRUE | TRUE | TRUE | TRUE | FALSE | FALSE |

**Figure 5.2** Truth table for AND, OR, and NOT logical operators.

> ### PROGRAMMING KEY: TIPS
>
> When operators of different types are used in the same expression, use parentheses to improve program readability.

Which of the following logical expressions is easier to read and evaluate? Does this logical expression evaluate to True or False?

**Without parentheses:**

3 * 5 > 8 * 2 Or 6 * 7 < 100 − 5 ^ 2

**With parentheses:**

((3 * 5) > (8 * 2)) Or ((6 * 7) < (100 − (5 ^ 2)))

**Answers:** With parentheses; True

**Figure 5.3** Parentheses improve program readability

## DeMorgan's Laws

DeMorgan's laws concern the negation of logical expressions and logical operators. These laws are used to reduce or expand logical expressions into equivalent logical expressions. DeMorgan's laws have many applications in mathematics, probability, and computer science. In fact, a direct parallel can be drawn between these laws in set theory and computer science, as displayed in Figure 5.4.

### Expanding and Reducing Logical Expressions

Many texts use a shorthand notation when writing logical expressions. In this section, we use the customary shorthand notation to display examples of the expansion and reduction of logical expressions. The AND operator is typically replaced by $\wedge$, and the OR operator by $\vee$. The NOT operator is indicated by either a tilde (~) preceding the logical expression or a line above the logical expression. We use the tilde (~) as the NOT operator. So, the expression A AND (NOT B) translates to $A \wedge (\sim B)$ in our shorthand notation. To determine which of these operators is acted upon first, recall the precedence rules for logical operators. In the preceding example, the parentheses are not really necessary in either notation since NOT has a higher precedence than AND, but they are added for clarity.

The expansion of a logical expression is relatively straightforward. An example follows:

$$A \wedge (B \vee C) = (A \wedge B) \vee (A \wedge C)$$

Figure 5.5 uses a truth table to confirm the equality of these two expressions. The True and False values for A, B, C are all entered in the table. Then the values of the expressions are entered. The two columns (the fifth and last columns) that are the same throughout indicate that the expressions are equivalent.

To reduce the logical expression on the right-hand side of the equal sign back to its original form, we can simply "factor out" the A from each "term." Alternatively, we can continue to expand this expression and then logically reduce terms as shown next.

| Set theory | Computer science |
|---|---|
| NOT(A∩B)=NOT(A)∪NOT(B) | NOT(A AND B)=NOT(A) OR NOT(B) |
| NOT(A∪B)=NOT(A)∩NOT(B) | NOT(A OR B)=NOT(A) AND NOT(B) |

**Figure 5.4** DeMorgan's laws

| A ∧ (B ∨ C) = (A ∧ B) ∨ (A ∧ C) | | | | | | | |
|---|---|---|---|---|---|---|---|
| A | B | C | B OR C | A AND (B OR C) | A AND B | A AND C | (A AND B) OR (A AND C) |
| FALSE | FALSE | FALSE | FALSE | FALSE | FALSE | FALSE | FALSE |
| FALSE | FALSE | TRUE | TRUE | FALSE | FALSE | FALSE | FALSE |
| FALSE | TRUE | FALSE | TRUE | FALSE | FALSE | FALSE | FALSE |
| FALSE | TRUE | TRUE | TRUE | FALSE | FALSE | FALSE | FALSE |
| TRUE | FALSE | FALSE | FALSE | FALSE | FALSE | FALSE | FALSE |
| TRUE | FALSE | TRUE | TRUE | TRUE | FALSE | TRUE | TRUE |
| TRUE | TRUE | FALSE | TRUE | TRUE | TRUE | FALSE | TRUE |
| TRUE | TRUE | TRUE | TRUE | TRUE | TRUE | TRUE | TRUE |

Equivalent expressions

**Figure 5.5** Using a truth table to confirm equality of logical expressions

$(A \land B) \lor (A \land C) =$

$((A \land B) \lor A) \land ((A \land B) \lor C) =$ ← First parenthetical expression reduces to A

$A \land ((A \land B) \lor C) =$ ← Expand the second parenthetical expression

$A \land ((A \lor C) \land (B \lor C)) =$ ← Expand this expression about A

$(A \land (A \lor C)) \land (A \land (B \lor C)) =$ ← First parenthetical expression reduces to A

$A \land (A \land (B \lor C)) =$ ← A ∧ A evaluates to A, so we get the following

$A \land (B \lor C)$

Logical reduction is important in producing tighter or more compact code. We'll employ logical reduction of expressions further in our discussion of decision structures.

## PROGRAMMING KEY: TIPS

How can we reduce the following logical expression:  (x = 10) OR (x > 10)?

The equivalent logical expression is simply x >= 10. The main point here is that the <=, >=, and <> operators are all combinations of two separate operators. The following table shows long logical expressions and their equivalent short expressions:

| Long expression | Equivalent short expression |
|---|---|
| (x = 10) OR (x > 10) | x >= 10 |
| (x = 10) OR (x < 10) | x <= 10 |
| (x < 10) OR (x > 10) | x <> 10 |

## DECISION STRUCTURES

VB contains two decision structures: If-blocks and Select-Case blocks.

### IF-BLOCKS

If-blocks in VB are very similar to subjunctive statements in English. For instance, consider the following subjunctive (if...then) statement:

*If my average golf score is 10 or more strokes less than yours, then*
*I will give you a 5 stroke handicap on our next game.*

This statement can be directly translated into VB code as shown in the following code fragment:

```
difference = yourAverageScore - myAverageScore
If difference >= 10 Then
   handicap = 5
End If
```

If-blocks form the primary decision structure in VB and most other high-level languages. The general form for a *simple* If statement is shown below. This structure is called an If-Then statement.

```
If condition Then
    [statements]
End If
```

All of the statements between the Then and End If keywords are executed only when *condition* is true, and *condition* must form a logical expression. An If-Then structure that contains no statements to be executed when *condition* is true is called an empty If-block and serves no practical purpose. Therefore, empty If-blocks should be removed from the source code.

Sometimes decisions are more complex than can be expressed by a simple If-Then statement. Consider modifying our earlier statement:

*If my average golf score is 10 or more strokes less than yours, then*
*I will give you a 5 stroke handicap on our next game. Otherwise,*
*I will give you a two stroke handicap.*

To translate this statement we need a more advanced structure, an If-Then-Else structure with the following simplified form:

```
If condition Then
    [statements1]
Else
    [statements2]
End If
```

The code in *statements1* is executed only when *condition* is true; *statements2* is executed only when *condition* is false. So, our modified code follows:

```
difference = yourAverageScore - myAverageScore
If difference >= 10 Then
   handicap = 5
Else
   handicap = 2
End If
```

In the above code, notice that the opposing player is always given a minimum handicap of two strokes; the handicap is given even when the opposing player is a better golfer. We now modify the subjunctive statement one last time to introduce the ElseIf statement.

> *If my average golf score is 10 or more strokes less than yours, then I will give you a five stroke handicap on our next game. If it is between 7 and 9 strokes less than yours, then I will give you a three stroke handicap. If it is between 4 and 6 strokes less than yours, then I will give you a two stroke handicap. Otherwise, I will give you no handicap on our next game.*

Because we have several conditions, we must now use the general form of the If-Then-Else statement shown below:

```
If condition1 Then
    [statements1]
ElseIf condition2 Then
    [statements2]
         .
         .
         .
ElseIf conditionN Then
    [statementsN]
Else
    [statementsX]
End If
```

An If-block may have any number of ElseIf statements. In evaluating the If-block, statements1 executes when condition1 is true; statements2 executes when condition1 is false and condition2 is true; statementsN executes when conditionN is true and all other preceding conditions (condition1 through condition{N-1}) are false; finally, statementsX executes only if all conditions (condition1 through conditionN) are false.

In the modified code fragment below, only one assignment statement for handicap is executed depending upon the value of difference. Trace this code to be sure that you understand what happens when the value of difference is 15, 8, 4, and 1.

```
difference = yourAverageScore - myAverageScore
If difference >= 10 Then
   handicap = 5
ElseIf difference >= 7 Then
   handicap = 3
ElseIf difference >= 4 Then
   handicap = 2
Else
   handicap = 0
End If
```

**PROGRAMMING KEY: TIPS**

In any If-block, at most one set of statements is executed; the only statements executed in an If-block are those statements that follow the first condition that is evaluated to be true. So, the order of the conditions is important and must follow logically.

........................................
### Key Terms
_____

**sequential statements**—statements or constructs that follow each other in sequence; in general, sequential statements consist of a sequential grouping of the same programming construct in the source code
........................................

The previous code fragment and If-blocks that contain ElseIf statements can also be written as **sequential** If-Then **statements**. Again, the order of the conditions is important and must be logically correct.

```
handicap = 0
difference = yourAverageScore - myAverageScore
If difference >= 4 Then
   handicap = 2
End If
If difference >= 7 Then
   handicap = 3
End If
If difference >= 10 Then
   handicap = 5
End If
```

### COMPARISON OF CODE STRUCTURES

Both of the two previous code fragments are correct, and they perform the same operation. Notice, however, that there is a difference in the number of statements executed. When the value of difference is greater than or equal to 10, for example, the If-Then-Else structure only performs one comparison and two assignment operations (including assigning the value to difference), whereas the sequential If-block performs three comparisons and five assignments. In this case, the sequential If-block performs almost three times as many operations as the If-Then-Else structure. The difference in the execution speed of each block of code may be negligible when this code is executed once or only a few times. However, if the code must be repeated a large number of times, the If-Then-Else structure will execute substantially faster. Such factors are important in **code** (or **algorithm**) **optimization**.

In general, why does a programmer choose one structure over another? As we have seen, one factor is code optimization. The main reason, however, is the programmer's own preferred **programming style**. Use whichever style you prefer, but remain consistent in style throughout your source code. Additionally, in all of the above code fragments, notice how indentation improves the readability of the code. Keeping the If and End If keywords aligned is a common practice that is used to improve code readability.

### NESTED IF-BLOCKS

........................................
### Key Term
_____

**nested statements**—statements or constructs that appear within other statements or constructs; in general, a nested statement refers to a construct that appears in the same type of programming construct
........................................

Many programmers use **nested statements**; for instance, If-blocks may be contained within other If-blocks. An example nested If-block structure follows:

```
If condition1 Then
    If condition2 Then
        [statements1]
    Else
        [statements2]
    End If
End If
```

This nested If-block is equivalent to the following un-nested If-block, statements1 executes when both condition1 and condition2 are true; statements2 executes when condition1 is true and condition2 is false.

```
If condition1 AND condition2 Then
    [statements1]
ElseIf condition1 AND NOT(condition2) Then
    [statements2]
End If
```

Finally, the above un-nested If-block may be simplified as follows:

```
If condition1 AND condition2 Then
    [statements1]
ElseIf condition1 Then
    [statements2]
End If
```

As shown above, the AND NOT(condition2) clause can be removed from the ElseIf statement. Why? Simply stated, this clause is redundant. Remember that conditions are checked sequentially in If-blocks. If statements1 is not executed, then either or both condition1 and condition2 must be false. When condition1 is true, condition2 must be false in order for statements1 not to be executed. Thus, we need only check if condition1 is true in the ElseIf statement since condition2 is known to be false based upon the order of the conditions.

Once again, nesting or un-nesting If-blocks is simply a matter of programming style. Use whichever method is most comfortable for you and easier for you to understand.

As a final note concerning If-blocks, we previously discussed reducing and expanding logical statements. You should keep this idea in mind when writing If-blocks. Reduce or expand the logical statements as necessary so that your If-blocks are readable and easy to understand. If-blocks containing conditions that are difficult to understand should be adequately commented.

## PROGRAMMING KEY: TIPS

Novice programmers often write unnecessary If-blocks, and there are some programming shortcuts that may be used. The following code fragment is an unnecessary If-block:

```
If A > B Then
    C = True
End If
```

The boolean variable C is assigned the value True if the value of variable A is greater than the value of variable B. This code fragment may be written as a single line of code that performs this same operation:

```
C = (A > B)
```

In summary, assigning values to boolean variables usually does not require an If-block.

## SELECT-CASE BLOCKS

VB has an alternate decision structure called the Select-Case block. Any If-block may be written as a Select-Case block and vice versa. Additionally, many other high-level languages have control structures equivalent to the VB `Select-Case` block. The general form of the `Select-Case` block follows:

```
Select Case testexpression
    Case expressionlist1
        statements1
    Case expressionlist2
        statements2
            .

            .

            .

    Case expressionlistN
        statementsN
    Case Else
        statementsX
End Select
```

Notice in the general form of the `Select-Case` block just shown that there are several `Case` statements. A `Select-Case` block may have any number of `Case` statements. The *testexpression* in the first line is the expression that is compared to each *expressionlist*, where an *expressionlist* is a delimited list of one or more of the following forms: *expression*, *expression* To *expression*, Is *relationaloperator expression*. The `To` keyword is used to specify a range of values, where the smaller value appears to the left of the `To`. The `Is` keyword is used with relational operators to specify a range of values, and if not supplied by the programmer, the `Is` keyword is automatically inserted by the VB editor. A *relationaloperator* is any one of the relational operators previously discussed (`<`, `>`, `<=`, and so forth).

The execution of a `Select-Case` block parallels that of the `If-Then-Else` structure. If *testexpression* matches any `Case` *expressionlist* expression, the statements following that `Case` statement are executed up to the next `Case` statement, or for the last `Case` statement, up to the `End Select` statement. Control then passes to the statement following `End Select`. If *testexpression* matches an *expressionlist* expression in more than one `Case` statement, only the statements following the first match are executed.

The `Case Else` statement contains *statementsX*, or the statements to be executed if no match is found between *testexpression* and *expressionlist* in any of the other `Case` statements. Although a `Case Else` statement is not required in the `Select-Case` structure, using one allows your code to handle unforeseen *testexpression* values. If *testexpression* does not match any *expressionlist* expression and there is no `Case Else` statement, execution of the code continues after the `End Select` statement.

A `Case` statement may have multiple expressions that form its *expressionlist* by delimiting, or separating, the expressions with a comma (`,`). The following `Case` statement, for instance, constitutes a valid line of code:

```
Case 1, 5 To 7, 3 * 4, Is > 5 * 5
```

The above `Case` statement matches any *testexpression* whose value equals 1 or 12, is between 5 and 7, or is greater than 25. Note that ranges and multiple expressions may also be specified for strings. In the following example, the `Case` statement matches any *testexpression* string that is exactly equal to `Basic` or that falls between `Beginner` and `Computer` in alphabetic (ASCII) order.

```
Case "Basic", "Beginner" To "Computer"
```

Select-Case blocks can be nested in the same manner as If-blocks. Each nested Select Case statement must have a matching End Select statement.

### CONVERTING TO A SELECT-CASE BLOCK

Finally, we conclude our discussion of decision structures by converting an If-Then-Else structure to an equivalent Select-Case block. The following code fragment implements the last golf handicap example as a Select-Case block rather than an If-block:

```
difference = yourAverageScore - myAverageScore
Select Case difference
  Case Is >= 10
     handicap = 5
  Case 9, 7, 8
     handicap = 3
  Case 4 To 6
     handicap = 2
  Case Else
     handicap = 0
End Select
```

# REPETITION STRUCTURES

Oftentimes, an algorithm requires repeating a group of statements; this repetition is commonly called looping by programmers. **Loops** allow for the repetition of code. A loop is a control structure used to repeat a group of statements until a certain condition is met. Consider, for example, the following problem:

*What is the sum of the integers from 1 to 100?*

This problem is rather easy and quick to solve on a computer by using a loop, whereas it may take you a great deal of time to solve by hand. Fortunately for us, the great mathematician Carl Friedrich Gauss recognized that the sum of the integers from 1 to $n$ is given by:

$$\sum_{i=1}^{n} i = \frac{n(n+1)}{2}$$

In the equality above, the $\Sigma$ (sigma) denotes summation. So, the variable $i$ is summed from 1 to $n$. The formula on the right-hand side of the equality allows us to quickly obtain the answer of 5,050 for $n = 100$.

VB, like most other high-level languages, has two different loop structures, For-Next loops and Do loops.

## FOR-NEXT LOOPS

For-Next loops are a **determinate** (or **definite**) **loop structure**. They can only be used when the programmer knows or can calculate the exact number of times that the loop must execute. A simplified form of the For-Next loop follows:

```
For counter = start To end
    [statements]
Next [counter]
```

The variable *counter*, the **loop counter**, may be of any numeric data type. The expressions *start* and *end* specify the starting and ending values of *counter*, where the value of *start* must be less than or equal to the value of *end* in order for the statements inside of the loop to execute. The Next statement increments the value of *counter* by 1 and then returns control to the top of the loop. Note that *counter* is optional in the Next statement.

Figure 5.6 displays a flowchart of the simplified For-Next loop execution cycle.

The number of times that this simplified For-Next loop executes the statements inside the loop (the **body of the loop** or **body**) is shown below:

```
(end - start) + 1,   where start ≤ end
0,                   where start > end
```

A For-Next loop that contains no statements between the For and Next keywords (i.e., no statements in the body of the loop) is an **empty loop**. Empty loops are commonly used to create **time delays** during program execution.

The code fragment below implements a simple For-Next loop to compute the sum of the integers from 1 to 100:

```
Dim sum As Integer, counter As Integer
sum = 0
For counter = 1 To 100
   sum = sum + counter
Next counter
```

After executing the above For-Next loop, the variable sum contains the sum of the integers from 1 to 100, or 5,050.

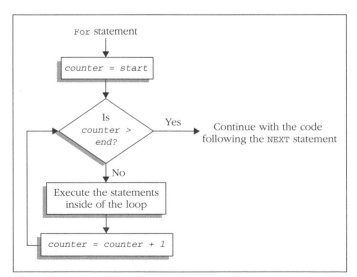

**Figure 5.6** Execution of the simplified For-Next loop

Suppose we modify the problem as follows:

*What is the sum of the odd integers from 1 to 100?*

This problem requires that the loop structure use an increment, or **step value**, of 2 instead of 1, and the general form of the `For-Next` loop must be used:

```
For counter = start To end Step stepvalue
    [statements]
Next [counter]
```

The only difference between the general form and the simple form of the `For-Next` loop is that an increment value (`stepvalue`) is specified for the loop `counter` in the general form. This loop executes exactly the same way as the simple form, except that the `Next` statement increments `counter` by `stepvalue` and then returns control to the top of the loop. Figure 5.7 displays a flowchart of the general `For-Next` loop execution cycle.

Note that a `stepvalue` of zero will cause an **infinite loop** or **endless loop** (a loop that never terminates) when `start` ≤ `end`, but causes the loop not to execute at all when `start` > `end`. If the computer is stuck in an infinite loop, press CTRL+BREAK to stop the execution of the program. For a nonzero `stepvalue`, the statements inside the general `For-Next` loop are executed the following number of times:

```
(end - start)\stepvalue + 1, where start ≤ end, stepvalue > 0
                    or       start ≥ end, stepvalue < 0
0,                           otherwise
```

Just as in VB code, we use the backward slash (\) to indicate integer division.

The following code fragment sums the odd integers from 1 to 100:

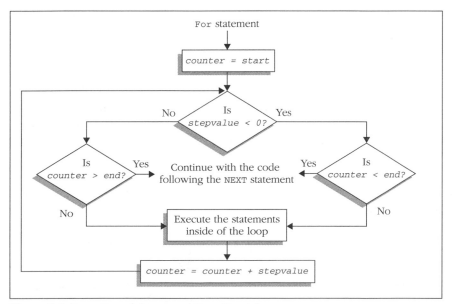

**Figure 5.7** Execution of the general `For-Next` loop

```
Dim sum As Integer, counter As Integer
sum = 0
For counter = 1 To 100 Step 2
  sum = sum + counter
Next counter
```

After executing the above code, the variable sum contains the sum of the odd integers from 1 to 100, or 2,500.

Just like If-blocks, For-Next loops can be nested. Each loop must have a unique variable name for its loop counter. The following example uses nested For-Next loops to display a multiplication table up to 12×12. Picture box picOutput displays the table.

```
' Display a 12 x 12 multiplication table
For i = 1 To 12
  For j = 1 To 12
    picOutput.Print i * j;
  Next j
  picOutput.Print
Next i
```

The semicolon (;) after the first Print statement informs VB to keep printing on the same line, or not to print a carriage return (and line feed). The second Print statement (outside of the For j loop) forces VB to print a carriage return.

Note that if you omit *counter* in a Next statement, execution continues as if *counter* was included in the statement. If a Next *counter* statement is encountered before its corresponding For statement, an error occurs. Additionally, the first Next statement encountered must correspond to the last For statement or an error results. The following example shows the previous code with the i and j variables swapped in the Next statements:

```
' ERROR in code:  i and j variables swapped in _
                  Next statements
For i = 1 To 12
  For j = 1 To 12
    pctOutput.Print i * j;
  Next i
  pctOutput.Print
Next j
```

The order of the Next statements is incorrect: Next i precedes Next j. Thus, this example is both logically and syntactically incorrect.

## Do Loops

Do loops allow for **indeterminate** (or **indefinite**) **loop structures** in which the programmer does not know the exact number of times to execute the loop. Additionally, Do loops can be used in place of For-Next loops as determinate loop structures.

There are two common Do loop structures in VB. The Do While-Loop is equivalent to While loops in other high-level languages, and the Do-Loop Until is comparable to Repeat-Until loops. The general form of each of these loop structures appears below:

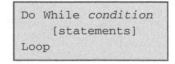

```
Do While condition
      [statements]
Loop
```

```
Do
      [statements]
Loop Until condition
```

condition is a logical expression. The Do While-Loop repeats the statements inside the loop as long as *condition* is true (while *condition* is True), whereas the `Do-Loop Until` repeats the statements as long as *condition* is False (until *condition* becomes True). Figure 5.8 contains execution flowcharts of both `Do` loop structures. Unlike the `For-Next` loop, the programmer must explicitly change the value of *condition*, the **control expression**, within the statements in the loop; otherwise, an infinite loop results, and CTRL+BREAK must be pressed to stop the execution of the code.

## COMPARING DO WHILE-LOOP AND DO-LOOP UNTIL

Along with the terminating conditions, there is another major difference between the two `Do` loop structures. A `Do-Loop Until` executes the body of the loop at least once, whereas the `Do While-Loop` may never execute its body. Thus, every `Do-Loop Until` can be easily translated into a `Do While-Loop`, but translating in the reverse direction may require a little more work. The fact that the body of a `Do While-Loop` may never execute can be easily overcome by using an `If`-block as a redundant check of the condition in the `Do-Loop Until` structure. Notice that we call this `If`-block a redundant check. You should be aware of code optimization opportunities. There are situations in which one `Do` loop structure is more appropriate than the other. In general, if the loop must execute at least once, a `Do-Loop Until` is appropriate; otherwise, use a `Do While-Loop`.

## COMPARATIVE EXAMPLE OF DO LOOPS

As an example use of `Do` loops, we show the code to sum the integers from 1 to 100 using each `Do` loop structure:

```
' Using a Do While-Loop
sum = 0
count = 1
Do While count <= 100
   sum = sum + count
   count = count + 1
Loop
```

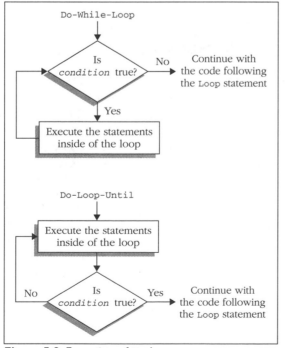

**Figure 5.8** Execution of Do loops

```
' Using a Do-Loop Until
sum = 0
count = 1
Do
   sum = sum + count
   count = count + 1
Loop Until count > 100
```

Notice that there are few changes between the two code fragments. In fact, only the loop structure changes and the end condition logically reverses. In this case, any loop structure (`For-Next` or `Do` loop) is appropriate for this problem. Again, it is a matter of programming style.

The variable `sum` is an **accumulator** since it sums, or accumulates, the final answer. A **flag** is a logical variable that indicates a condition. The code fragment below uses the flag variable `correct` to loop until the user enters either `Yes` or `No`:

```
Dim answer As String, correct As Boolean
Do
   answer = CStr(InputBox("Yes or No", "Enter Your Answer"))
   answer = Trim(UCase(answer))
   correct = (Answer = "YES" Or Answer = "NO")
Loop Until correct
```

### OTHER DO LOOPS

VB also has `Do Until-Loop` and `Do-Loop While` structures available, but these are nonstandard loops; there are no equivalent loop structures for these forms in most other high-level languages. The reason is that these loop forms are redundant. For instance, a `Do Until-Loop` can be written as a standard `Do While-Loop` by negating the logical condition; likewise, we negate the logical condition in converting a `Do-Loop While` into a standard `Do-Loop Until`. Therefore, *we recommend negating the logical condition in order to use either a* `Do While-Loop` *or* `Do-Loop Until` *as appropriate.*

## ENDING A PROGRAM

Ending a program is usually not of great concern since VB is designed for the Windows operating system. The user can minimize the program window or close the window at any time to end the program. As the programmer, you may desire to end the program automatically once it completes a certain task. You might also include a command button that ends the program when it is clicked.

The `End` statement ends a VB program. Additionally, the `Stop` statement suspends execution. Unlike `End`, `Stop` does not close any files or clear variables, unless it is in a compiled executable (.EXE) file. At design time, the `Stop` statement is a useful debugging tool to temporarily halt program execution. The programmer may continue program execution by selecting Run/Continue, pressing the F5 key, or clicking the Continue button on the toolbar. In an executable file, `End` and `Stop` are equivalent.

The following code segment ends the program when the command button cmdEnd is clicked:

```
Private Sub cmdEnd_Click()
    End
End Sub
```

### Key Terms

**accumulator**—a variable that sums values within a loop structure

**flag**—a variable (typically, a boolean variable) that indicates the presence (or absence) of a condition

## PROGRAMMING STYLE

We mention programming style several times throughout this chapter and indicate that you have a choice among different styles. Often, this is not the case when programming in an academic or commercial environment. Many companies and institutions adopt a set of **programming standards** so that all of their programmers follow the same programming style. Remember, you are not only programming for yourself, but for other people as well. An institution may desire to modify your code long after you have left. The *Visual Basic Programming Standards* from the Naval Postgraduate School appear in Appendix B as an example.

---

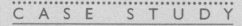

## C A S E   S T U D Y
## GoodLook Cosmetics Company

Jean is a sales representative for the GoodLook Cosmetics Company. Each month, she is required to report sales figures for the different types of cosmetics. She simply multiplies the sales price by the quantity sold for each item and then sums these products. Since there is an exceptionally large number of items, hand calculations are both time-consuming and error-prone. Jean needs a program that allows her to enter the sales price and quantity sold for each item and then performs the calculations automatically.

Help Jean by writing a VB program to perform the required operations. First develop an algorithm and then code your algorithm in VB. Compare your answer against Jean's program below:

```
' GoodLook Cosmetics Company
' Monthly Sales Computer
Option Explicit

Const PMESSAGE =   "Enter the product price. " & _
                   "Enter a non-positive value to stop."
Const QMESSAGE =   "Enter the quantity sold for the item
                     ➡ priced at "


Private Sub cmdEnter_Click()
' Enter data and compute the total sales

    Dim price As Single, quantity As Integer
    Dim count As Integer, totalSales As Single
    Dim message As String

    count = 0
    totalSales = 0#
    Do
        count = count + 1
        price = CSng(Val(InputBox(PMESSAGE, "Enter Price for
          ➡ Item " & _ Trim(CStr(count)))))
        If (price > 0) Then
                                                        ➡
```

```
            Do
                message = QMESSAGE & Format(price, "currency")
                quantity = CInt(Val(InputBox(message, "Enter
            ➥ Quantity")))
                If (quantity <= 0) Then
                    MsgBox "Quantity sold must be a positive
                    ➥ integer!", , _
                    "QUANTITY ERROR"
                End If
            Loop Until (quantity > 0)
            totalSales = totalSales + (price * quantity)
        End If
    Loop Until (price <= 0)

    picOutput.Cls
    picOutput.Print Trim(CStr(count - 1)) & " items
    ➥ entered."
    picOutput.Print "Total Sales: "; Format(totalSales,
    ➥ "currency")
End Sub
```

## Summary

### Key Terms

**accumulator**—a variable that sums values within a loop structure

**body of the loop** (or **body**)—the statements inside of a loop structure

**boolean expression**—see logical expression

**code** (or **algorithm**) **optimization**—the process of writing compact code (or algorithms) that executes quickly

**comparison operator**—a relational or logical operator

**control expression**—a boolean expression that controls the operation of a Do loop

**control structure**—a program construct that controls the flow of program execution

**control variable**—a variable that is tested for the ending condition in a For-Next loop

**determinate** (or **definite**) **loop structure** a loop structure in which the programmer knows or can calculate the exact number of times that the body of the loop will execute; a For-Next loop structure

**empty If-block**—an If-block that contains no statements to be executed when the controlling expression is true; empty If-blocks serve no practical purpose and should be removed from the source code

**empty loop**—a loop structure that contains no statements in its body

**expression**—a combination of keywords, operators, variables, and constants that yields a string, number, or object

**flag**—a variable that indicates the presence (or absence) of a condition; typically a boolean variable

**indeterminate** (or **indefinite**) **loop structure**—a loop structure in which the programmer does not necessarily know or cannot calculate the exact number of times that the body of the loop will execute; a Do loop structure

**infinite loop** (or **endless loop**)—a loop structure that never terminates

**logical conjunction**—a combination of logical expressions where the result is true only if *both* expressions evaluate to True

**logical disjunction**—a combination of logical expressions where the result is true if *either or both* expressions evaluate to True

**logical expression** (**boolean expression**)—an expression that evaluates to be either True or False

**logical negation**—a logical expression where the result is the opposite of the expression evaluation

**logical operator**—an operator used to combine logical (or boolean) expressions

**loop**—a control structure used to repeat a group of statements until a certain condition is present (or absent)

**loop counter**—the loop control variable in a For-Next loop

**nested statements**—statements or constructs that appear within other statements or constructs; generally refers to a programming construct that contains the same type of programming construct within its executable statements

**programming standards**—a set of rules regarding programming style

**programming style**—refers to a programmer's choice of constructs and use of nesting, white space, and comments

**relational operator**—an operator used to compare expressions

**sequential statements**—statements or constructs that follow each other in sequence; generally refers to a sequential grouping of the same programming construct in the source code

**step value**—the increment value of the control variable in a loop structure

**time delay**—statements that cause a program to wait for a specific length of time before executing the remainder of the code; generally refers to an empty loop

**truth table**—a table that displays the evaluation of a logical expression according to the values of the variables

## Keywords

| *Operators:* | Do While |
| --- | --- |
| < | Else |
| <= | ElseIf |
| <> | End If |
| = | End Select |
| > | For |
| >= | If |
| And | Is |
| Not | Loop |
| Or | Loop Until |
| | Loop While |
| *Statements:* | Next |
| Case | Select Case |
| Case Else | Step |
| Do | Then |
| Do Until | To |

## Key Concepts

- Flow control structures include decision and repetition structures. A decision structure allows the execution of specific code based upon the presence or absence of certain conditions. Repetition structures provide an easy means of repeating a group of statements.

- Flow control structures generally require the use of relational and logical operators.

- Relational operators are used to compare expressions. In VB, the relational operators include less than (<), less than or equal to (<=), greater than (>), greater than or equal to (>=), equal to (=), and not equal to (<>).

- The comparison of two expressions with a relational operator forms a logical (or boolean) expression. Logical expressions are combined using logical operators, such as AND, OR, and NOT.

- A VB expression may combine the three different types of operators: mathematical, relational, and logical. Precedence rules are rules that specify the order of evaluation of the operators in expressions. In VB, mathematical operators are evaluated first, relational operators are evaluated next, and logical operators are evaluated last. Additionally, all relational operators have equal precedence and are evaluated in the order in which they appear from left to right. NOT has the highest precedence among the logical operators, followed by AND, and then OR. Parentheses can be used to override these precedence rules. Using parentheses in an expression that contains operators of different types greatly enhances program readability.

- DeMorgan's laws concern the negation of logical expressions and logical operators and have various applications in mathematics, probability, and computer science. These laws may be used to reduce or expand logical expressions into equivalent expressions. We can show the equivalence among logical expressions algebraically (by using algebraic logic) or by using a truth table.

- The two decision structures in VB include the If-block and Select-Case block. Generally, an If-block is used when checking a single or a few conditions and a Select-Case block is used for checking multiple conditions or a range of values. Every If-block can be converted into a Select-Case block, and every Select-Case block can be written as an If-block.

  The general syntax of an If-block follows:

  ```
  If condition1 Then
      [statements1]
  ElseIf condition2 Then
      [statements2]

          .

          .

          .

  ElseIf conditionN Then
      [statementsN]
  Else
      [statementsX]
  End If
  ```

  The syntax for a Select-Case block appears below:

  ```
  Select Case testexpression
      Case expressionlist1
  ```

```
            statements1
        Case expressionlist2
            statements2
                .
                .
                .
        Case expressionlistN
            statementsN
        Case Else
            statementsX
    End Select
```

● The two repetition or loop structures in VB include `For-Next` loops and Do loops. `For-Next` loops are determinate loops; the programmer knows or can calculate the exact number of times that a loop of this type executes. A `Do` loop, on the other hand, can be either determinate or indeterminate; the programmer does not necessarily know the number of times that this loop executes. Therefore, every `For-Next` loop can be written as a `Do` loop, but every `Do` loop cannot be written as a `For-Next` loop.

The general form of the `For-Next` loop follows:

```
    For counter = start To end Step stepvalue
        [statements]
    Next [counter]
```

● There are two common `Do` loop structures, the `Do While-Loop` and the `Do-Loop Until`. A `Do-Loop Until` executes the statements within the loop at least once, whereas the `Do While-Loop` may never execute its statements. If we precede the `Do-Loop Until` with an `If`-block, we can convert every `Do While-Loop` into a `Do-Loop Until`. Converting a `Do-Loop Until` into a `Do While-Loop` requires less work and is relatively straightforward.

The general form of the `Do While-Loop` is:

```
    Do While condition
        [statements]
    Loop
```

The general syntax of the `Do-Loop Until` is:

```
    Do
        [statements]
    Loop Until condition
```

● Oftentimes, control structures are nested, or one control structure is contained within another. For example, one `If`-block may be inside of another `If`-block. Indenting nested control structures and statements within control structures improves program readability.

● An accumulator variable sums, or accumulates, the numbers inside of a loop to eventually arrive at a final answer. A flag variable is a logical (boolean) variable that is used to indicate a condition.

● Both the `End` and `Stop` statements halt program execution. In a compiled program, these two statements are equivalent. At design time, however, there is a difference between them. While the End statement ends a program, the Stop statement merely suspends program execution. The Stop statement does not close any files or clear variables, and it provides a useful debugging tool. The programmer may continue program execution by selecting Run/Continue, pressing the F5 key, or clicking the Continue button on the toolbar.

- Programming standards are a set of standards adopted by a company or institution so that all programmers follow the same programming style.

## Review Questions

1. What are the two categories of flow control structures?
2. Name and give an example use of three relational operators.
3. Name the three logical operators.
4. What are precedence rules and why are they important?
5. State DeMorgan's laws.
6. Name some methods of showing equivalence among logical expressions.
7. Describe the syntax and operation of the general If-block and Select-Case block.
8. When should you use an If-block instead of a Select-Case block? a Select-Case block instead of an If-block?
9. Can every If-block be written as a Select-Case block and vice versa? Explain.
10. Describe the syntax and operation of the For-Next loop, Do While-Loop, and Do-Loop Until.
11. Can every For-Next loop be written as a Do loop structure? Why or why not?
12. Can every Do loop be written as a For-Next loop? Why or why not?
13. Can every Do While-Loop be written as a Do-Loop Until? Why or why not?
14. Can every Do-Loop Until be written as a Do While-Loop? Why or why not?
15. What is a nested control structure?
16. What is an accumulator variable? a flag variable?
17. Describe the difference between the End and Stop statements. What do these statements do?
18. What are programming standards?

## Chapter 5 Problems

1. Modify the average velocity program from Chapter 4, Problem 6 to check the user's input. If the user enters a negative distance or nonpositive time, display the appropriate error message and end the program.
2. Modify the average velocity program from Chapter 4, Problem 6 to validate the user's input. Force the user to input a nonnegative distance and positive time by using loops.
3. Modify the quadratic formula solver from Chapter 4, Problem 10 to check the user's input. If the roots are imaginary or the value of $a$ is zero, display the appropriate message and end the program.

4. Modify the quadratic formula solver from Chapter 4, Problem 10 to validate the user's input. Force the user to enter a nonzero value of $a$. If the roots are imaginary, display a message indicating so.

5. Write a program that allows the user to input a string in a text box and prints the string in reverse order in a picture box.

6. A palindrome is a word or phrase that is the same forwards and backwards. For example, "mom" and "dad" are palindromes. Write a program that determines whether a user-entered string is a palindrome. Make sure that your program is not case sensitive. For instance, "Mom" and "MOm" and all other permutations of upper- and lowercase letters should still be recognized as palindromes by your program.

7. Write a program that converts a user-entered decimal number to its binary equivalent.

8. Write a program that converts a user-entered binary number to its decimal equivalent.

9. Our calendar, the Gregorian calendar, was introduced in 1582. Write a program that determines the day of the week for any date after 1582. Your program should:

   a.  Request the month and year as numeric inputs.

   b.  Determine the number of days in the month and request the day as a numeric input. Ensure that the user input is valid. All years divisible by 4 are leap years, with the exception of those years divisible by 100 and not by 400. The years 1600 and 2000 are leap years, for instance, but 1700, 1800, and 1900 are not. If you are clever, this condition can be tested using a single If statement.

   c.  Use the following algorithm to determine the day of the week:

   (1) Treat January and February as the 13th and 14th months of the previous year, respectively. Thus, 1/10/1998 is treated as 13/10/1997. Similarly, 2/10/1998 becomes 14/10/1997.

   (2) Let m, d, and y denote the month, day, and year, respectively. Compute w, where

   w = d + 2*m + Int((3/5)*(m+1)) + y + Int(y/4) − Int(y/100) + Int(y/400) + 2

   (3) The remainder of w divided by 7 denotes the day of the week, where 0 is Saturday, 1 is Sunday, 2 is Monday, and so on.

10. Modify the program from Problem 9 to print a monthly calendar. The user should input the month and year as numeric inputs, and the program should output a calendar for that month and year.

11. Write a program that adds 20 nonzero numbers entered by the user and displays their sum.

12. Modify the program from Problem 11 to add any quantity of nonzero numbers entered by the user. The input loop ends and the program displays the sum when the user enters a zero.

13. Given the rational function

$$f(x) = \frac{8x}{3x^2 + 5x + 2}$$

Write a program that computes the values of $f(x)$ when x varies between −5 and 5 with an increment of 0.5. Display $x$ and corresponding $f(x)$ values in a table within a picture box.

**14.** Modify the program from Problem 13 to prompt the user for an $x$ value and output the corresponding $f(x)$ value. The program ends when the user inputs a value of 100,000 for $x$.

**15.** Write a VB program that implements the Cash Register Program from Chapter 3.

**16.** Write a VB program that implements the Modified Cash Register Program from Chapter 3.

**17.** Write a program that determines the number of each type of coin to give in change for a user-entered amount. If the user enters $5.88, for instance, your program should output "3 Quarters, 1 Dime, and 3 Pennies." (Do not be concerned with the dollar amount.) The program should consider only quarters, dimes, nickels, and pennies. The objective of the program is to give change in the minimum number of coins possible.

**18.** Write a program that determines the minimum number of each type of coin required to give change in any amount between 1¢ and 99¢. The program should consider only quarters, dimes, nickels, and pennies.

## Programming Projects

**1.** A tickertape program is a program that scrolls a message across the screen, similar to the old-fashioned stock exchange tickertape machines. Write a tickertape program. The program should allow the user to enter a message and then scroll this message in a label on the form. The program should include command buttons to start and stop the tickertape.

**2.** Write a program that mimics the operation of a typewriter. The program should allow the user to enter a message, and then the program "types" this message in a picture box.

# An Introduction to Sequential File Input and Output

## Supplement Objectives

In this chapter supplement, you will:

- Discover the need for data files

- Learn a simplified syntax to read and write comma-separated data from and to sequential files, respectively

- Learn how to write formatted text to a sequential file

### Key Term

**file input and output (file I/O)**—the part of computer programming concerned with storing information to and retrieving information from data files

Some computer programs are not very effective unless they have the ability to store and retrieve data. Consider a **Personal Information Manager** (**PIM**) program that requires you to retype the names, addresses, and telephone numbers of all of your contacts each time the program starts. This program is not very useful. A better means of data storage and retrieval is needed. Thus, we turn our attention to file input and storage for programs. **File input and output** (**file I/O**) is that part of computer programming concerned with storing information to and retrieving information from data files.

This section presents an overview of sequential file input and output; however, Chapter 9 provides more detailed information regarding the nuances of file handling in VB. The examples presented here provide programming templates for students who require a means of data storage and retrieval at this stage in their learning process.

### Sequential Files

A **sequential file** is a file that is accessed in order, or sequentially, from the beginning of the file to the end of the file. The word "**access**" refers to both reading from the file and writing to the file. Before we can access a file, the file must be **opened**. Similarly, when we have completed our operations with the file, the file should be **closed**. For example, the code fragment below writes Marshall Bishop's height and weight data to the file named Bishop.dat:

```
Dim lastName As String, firstName As String
Dim height As Single  ' in inches
Dim weight As Single  ' in pounds
```

```
lastName = "Bishop"
firstName = "Marshall"
height = 71.25
weight = 201.5

Open "C:\Bishop.dat" For Output As #1
Write #1, lastName, firstName, height, weight
Close #1
```

After this code executes, the file Bishop.dat contains:

```
"Bishop","Marshall",71.25,201.5
```

## Key Term

**comma-separated data file**—a data file in which the different pieces of information are separated by commas

Notice that the `Write #` statement automatically encloses strings in quotation marks and separates the data with commas, creating a **comma-separated data file**.

### Syntax—Writing Data

The simplified syntax shown below allows data to be written to a sequential file:

```
Open filename For Output As #n
Write #n, data
Close #n
```

`filename` is any valid file name, `data` is any valid variable or expression, and n is the **file number**, an integer value between 1 and 511.

As an example of file input, the following code uses the `Input #` statement to read the name, height, and weight data from Bishop.dat and then displays this information in the picOutput picture box:

```
Dim lastName As String, firstName As String
Dim height As Single   ' in inches
Dim weight As Single   ' in pounds

Open "C:\Bishop.dat" For Input As #1
Input #1, lastName, firstName, height, weight
Close #1

picOutput.Print "Name: ", firstName & " " & lastName
picOutput.Print "Height: ", CStr(height) & " inches"
picOutput.Print "Weight: ", CStr(weight) & " pounds"
```

### Syntax—Reading Data

The simplified syntax below reads data from a sequential file:

```
Open filename For Input As #n
Input #n, data
Close #n
```

`filename` is any valid file name and n is the file number. `data` must be a variable for file input operations, whereas it may be any valid expression in the case of file output.

Lastly, the `Print #` statement may be used to write formatted text to a file rather than comma-separated data. The following code illustrates by writing formatted text to the Report.dat file:

```
Dim lastName As String, firstName As String
Dim height As Single   ' in inches
Dim weight As Single   ' in pounds

lastName = "Bishop"
firstName = "Marshall"
height = 71.25
weight = 201.5

Open "C:\Report.dat" For Output As #1
Print #1, "Name: ", firstName & " " & lastName
Print #1, "Height: ", CStr(height) & " inches"
Print #1, "Weight: ", CStr(weight) & " pounds"
Close #1
```

After the above code executes, Report.dat contains:

```
Name:          Marshall Bishop
Height:        71.25 inches
Weight:        201.5 pounds
```

### Syntax—Formatted Text

The simplified syntax below writes formatted text to a sequential file:

```
Open filename For Output As #n
Print #n, data
Close #n
```

*filename* is any valid file name, *data* is any valid variable or expression, and *n* is the file number.

## Summary

### Key Terms

**access**—to read from or write to a data file

**close**—to end the access of a data file and disassociate it with a file number

**comma-separated data file**—a data file in which the different pieces of information are separated by commas

**file input and output (file I/O)**—the part of computer programming concerned with storing information to and retrieving information from data files

**file number**—an integer value between 1 and 511 that is associated with a data file

**open**—to prepare a data file for access and associate it with a file number

**Personal Information Manager (PIM)**—a program that maintains the user's personal information, such as contacts, appointments, and expenses

**sequential file**—a file that is accessed in order, or sequentially, from the beginning of the file to the end of the file

## Keywords

*Statements:*
Close #
For Input As
For Output As
Input #
Open
Print #
Write #

## Key Concepts

⬤ Data files provide a means of data storage and retrieval.

⬤ A sequential file is a type of data file that is accessed sequentially, from the beginning of the file to the end of the file.

⬤ Before a file can be accessed, it must be opened using the Open statement. When file operations are completed, all open data files should be closed using the Close statement.

⬤ The Write # statement writes comma-separated data to a sequential file:

```
Open filename For Output As #n
Write #n, data
Close #n
```

⬤ The Input # statement reads data from a file:

```
Open filename For Input As #n
Input #n, data
Close #n
```

⬤ The Print # statement writes formatted text to a data file:

```
Open filename For Output As #n
Print #n, data
Close #n
```

## Review Questions

**1.** Why do some computer programs require data files? Give some examples.

**2.** Write the code necessary to create a comma-separated data file named Andrews.dat whose contents are as follows:

```
"Andrews","Timothy"
"1234 Whitecloud Lane"
"Anytown","USA","00905"
```

**3.** Write the code to read the data from the Andrews.dat file as shown in Review Question 2 and display the data in a picture box.

**4.** Write the code to output the data in Review Question 2 as formatted text to a data file.

## Chapter 5 Supplement Problems

1. Write a program that outputs 10 user-entered numbers to a sequential file.

2. Write a program that reads 10 numbers from a sequential file and displays the numbers and their sum in a picture box.

3. Write a program that reads 10 numbers from a sequential file and outputs these numbers and their sum to another sequential file as formatted text.

4. Write a program that outputs your name and birth date to a sequential file.

5. Write a program that reads your name and birth date from a sequential file and displays this information in a picture box.

6. Write a program that outputs your name and birth date to a sequential file as formatted text.

7. Write a program that outputs a user-entered name and address to a sequential file.

8. Write a program that reads a name and address from a sequential file and displays this information in a picture box.

9. Write a program that outputs a user-entered name and address to a sequential file as formatted text.

10. Modify the program from Chapter 5, Problem 10 to output a monthly calendar to a sequential file as formatted text.

11. Modify the program from Chapter 5, Problem 13 to output a table of $x$ and $f(x)$ values to a sequential file as formatted text.

## Programming Projects

1. Write a program that finds the sum and average of the numbers in a user-specified data file. The first line of the data file contains the number of data items within the file, and this information is not considered part of the data (i.e., it should be excluded from the sum and average calculations).

2. Modify Chapter 5, Project 2 to read the contents of a user-specified data file and "type" this information in a picture box.

# Structured Programming

**6**

If you own a stereo system, you are probably familiar with the concept of **components**. A typical stereo system, for instance, has a receiver, a tape deck, a CD changer, and speakers. Manufacturers know that if they provide each of these components separately, it allows consumers to mix and match the components as they desire. Component stereo systems are also a more attractive alternative than integrated systems (one-piece systems) since they can be upgraded by simply purchasing a new component. For example, a 3-CD changer in a component system can be easily replaced by a 50-CD changer. Additionally, as technology improves and new components become available, they can be added to the system.

# MODULAR PROGRAMMING

A stereo system component is analogous to a **module** in the world of computer programming. **Modular programming** refers to computer programming in a modular, or component-based, design that utilizes **subprograms.** The subprograms are components of the program; they are designed to perform a specific task. Programs that are written using a modular design are called **structured programs**. These programs normally contain statements that execute sequentially and oftentimes use decision and repetition structures.

Modular programming has several advantages. First, it allows the programmer to logically organize a program by dividing the problem into smaller subproblems. Repeatedly using this "divide and conquer" technique to solve a problem is called **stepwise refinement** and is part of the **top-down design** programming methodology. For instance, a programmer may write a program using three subprograms: one subprogram contains the input routine, another performs calculations, and a final subprogram displays the output. As the programmer continues to refine the problem further he or she might further subdivide the larger tasks into smaller ones, thus achieving stepwise refinement.

Another advantage of modular programming is that it enhances the readability of the code and is easier for the programmer to debug. Additionally, like the components in a stereo system, a module can be replaced (or upgraded) to improve the program. Finally, modular programming allows for the reuse of code. **Code reuse** is an important factor in computer programming. Once a programmer designs a subprogram to perform a certain task in one program, it is best not to recreate the subprogram to perform the same task in a different program. A better option would be to simply reuse the existing code. Any reuse of code relies on adequate documentation. The documentation must specify the required subprogram inputs and the type of output. As we emphasized earlier, good, specific documentation is again essential.

# SUBPROGRAMS: PROCEDURES AND FUNCTIONS

Procedures and functions comprise the two types of subprograms. You have already seen examples of both in VB. The following code is modified from the Square Root Finder example of Chapter 4. This code presents an example of a subprogram for our discussion.

## AN EXAMPLE OF A SUBPROGRAM

```
1    Private Sub cmdSquareRoot_Click()
2    ' Compute and display the square root of _
3       a user-entered number
4
5       Dim number As Double, sqrRt As Double
6
7       number = CDbl(txtInput.Text)
8       sqrRt = Sqr(number)
9
10      picOutput.Cls
11      picOutput.Print "The square root of ";
        ➥ Trim(Str(number)); _
```

```
12                      " is "; Trim(Str(sqrRt)); "."

13

14    End Sub
```

The line numbers in the above code are not part of the program and are added just for reference. This program has three objects on the form: a text box (txtInput), a command button (cmdSquareRoot), and a picture box (picOutput). As described in the comments, this program simply computes and displays the square root of a number that the user enters in txtInput when cmdSquareRoot is clicked.

Remember, VB is an object-oriented language designed for the Windows operating system. **Events** (key presses, mouse clicks, and so forth) occur in Windows, and we write **event handlers** to manage these events. Line 1 is the heading of the Click event handler for the cmdSquareRoot object. In other words, when the mouse pointer is on the cmdSquareRoot command button and the left mouse button is clicked, the cmdSquareRoot method is **invoked** (called or executed). Notice two other items on line 1. The Sub (meaning *subprogram*) indicates that this event handler is a procedure in VB. In other words, all event handlers in VB are procedures, and you have been writing subprograms all along! Also, Private indicates the scope of this procedure; this procedure is only available to the form in which it is defined. On line 14, the End Sub indicates the end of the procedure.

This example program also contains **function calls**. Line 7 invokes the built-in data type conversion function CDbl. Line 8 calls Sqr, the built-in math function that finds the square root of a number. Lines 11 and 12 call the built-in string function Trim and data type conversion function Str.

Do you notice any similarity between procedures and functions just by examining the previous example program? In the procedure declaration on line 1, the Click event has parentheses following it; it is written as Click(). Similarly, all of the built-in functions have parentheses that contain items following their names. *Parentheses enclose the information passed to subprograms.*

## ARGUMENTS AND PARAMETERS

Let's look at another example. This time, a procedure called Adder is created to sum together two numbers.

```
Private Sub Adder(num1 As Double, num2 As Double, sum As
➥ Double)
' Add num1 and num2 and store the result in sum
    sum = num1 + num2
End Sub
```

num1, num2, and sum are the **parameters** of the Adder procedure. Parameters are merely placeholders for the information passed to a subprogram when it is invoked. The parameter list specified in the Adder procedure contains three elements, thereby informing the VB compiler that the Adder procedure requires three double-precision numbers to be passed to it.

A simple **driver program**, or test program, for the Adder procedure appears below. This program has two text boxes (txtNum1 and txtNum2), a command button (cmdAdd), and a picture box (picOutput).

```
Private Sub cmdAdd_Click()
'Driver program for Adder procedure
```

```
'Add two user-entered numbers
    Dim firstNum As Double, secondNum As Double
    Dim result As Double

    firstNum = CDbl(txtNum1.Text)
    secondNum = CDbl(txtNum2.Text)

    Call Adder(firstNum, secondNum, result)

    picOutput.Cls
    picOutput.Print "Sum = "; result
End Sub
```

## Key Terms

**argument**—a piece of information passed to a subprogram *(original program)*
**parameter**—a placeholder for the information passed to a <u>subprogram</u> when it is invoked; each argument has a corresponding parameter

*(handwritten margin note: calling program / being called)*

In VB, the `Adder` procedure is invoked using the `Call` statement which is discussed in the next section. The variables `firstNum`, `secondNum`, and `result` are the **arguments** of the `Adder` procedure; these variables contain the information (values) that are **passed** to the procedure. Note that arguments can be any VB expression.

Finally, there are several important points concerning subprogram arguments and parameters. For their effective use, you should observe each of the following conditions.

1. The number of arguments must equal the number of parameters.
2. Order is important. The first argument corresponds to the first parameter, the second argument to the second parameter, and so on.
3. The data type of each argument must match the data type of its corresponding parameter.
4. Names are not important. The name of an argument does not have to correspond to the name of its parameter.
5. Recognize the manner in which data is passed, either by reference or by value.

These topics are discussed in a later section.

## DEFINING AND USING SUBPROGRAMS

A subprogram is either a procedure or a function. Procedures and functions that are not built into VB are called **user-defined subprograms** because the programmer (the user of the compiler) must define them. Next, we will discuss how to define and use a procedure; following that we will discuss how to define and use a function.

### PROCEDURES

As shown in the example in the previous section, the general form for defining a procedure is:

```
Private Sub ProcedureName(parameter1 As Type1,
➥ parameter2 As Type2, ...)
    [statements]
End Sub
```

A procedure is invoked using the `Call` statement. The syntax of the `Call` statement follows:

```
Call ProcedureName(argument1, argument2, ...)
```

## PROGRAMMING KEY: TIPS

The `Call` keyword is optional, but the syntax of a VB procedure call changes when the `Call` keyword is not used. The following syntax performs the same procedure call as the `Call` statement above:

```
ProcedureName argument1, argument2, ...
```

In this syntax, notice the absence of parentheses surrounding the arguments. A common mistake is to use parentheses, and this can lead to logic errors (see the *Warning* in the next section). Additionally, this syntax makes it more difficult for a programmer to distinguish between a procedure call and a function call. Therefore, *we highly recommend that you use the `Call` statement for procedure calls.*

## FUNCTIONS

Functions are somewhat different from procedures. A **function** may take any number of arguments, but it always returns a single value to the **calling routine**, the part of the program that invoked the function. A **procedure**, on the other hand, does not necessarily return a value or may return multiple values. *The general rule is to use a function if you need to return exactly one value to the calling routine.*

Our previous `Adder` procedure, therefore, is better written as a function:

```
Private Function Adder(num1 As Double, num2 As Double)
➥ As Double
'Add num1 and num2 and return the result
   Adder = num1 + num2
End Function
```

A driver program for the `Adder` function follows:

```
Private Sub cmdAdd_Click()
'Driver program for Adder function
'Add two user-entered numbers
   Dim firstNum As Double, secondNum As Double

   firstNum = CDbl(txtNum1.Text)
   secondNum = CDbl(txtNum2.Text)

   picOutput.Cls
   picOutput.Print "Sum = "; Adder(firstNum, secondNum)
End Sub
```

From this example, we see the general form of a user-defined function:

```
Private Function FunctionName(param1 as Type1, ...)
➥ As FunctionType
    [statements]
    FunctionName = ReturnValue
End Function
```

Notice that the function is defined with a specific data type (*FunctionType*); this is the data type of the value that the function returns to the calling routine. In order for the function to return a value to the calling routine, the value must be assigned to the function name as shown in the line preceding the `End Function` statement.

Unlike a procedure invocation, a function invocation does not require a `Call` statement. A function is invoked simply by writing the function name along with the required arguments. Remember that a function returns a single value, and your program should do something with this value (such as store it in a variable or print it). The general form of a function invocation where the returned value is assigned to a variable follows:

```
variableName = FunctionName(argument1, argument2, ...)
```

## CREATING A SUBPROGRAM IN VB

To create a subprogram, you can either manually type the subprogram heading in the Code window or use the menu bar. With the Code window active, select Tools/Add Procedure from the menu bar to open the Add Procedure window shown in Figure 6.1. Then, type in the desired subprogram name and select the subprogram type and scope. Finally, click the OK button, and VB creates the subprogram heading for you.

## PARAMETER PASSING

### Key Terms

**pass by reference**—a type of parameter passing in which the memory location (address) of the argument is passed to the subprogram instead of the argument's value, allowing the subprogram to access the actual variable and modify its contents; this is the default method of parameter passing in VB

**pass by value**—a type of parameter passing in which the value of the argument is passed to the subprogram, allowing the subprogram to access a copy of the variable; pass by value preserves the contents of the original variable

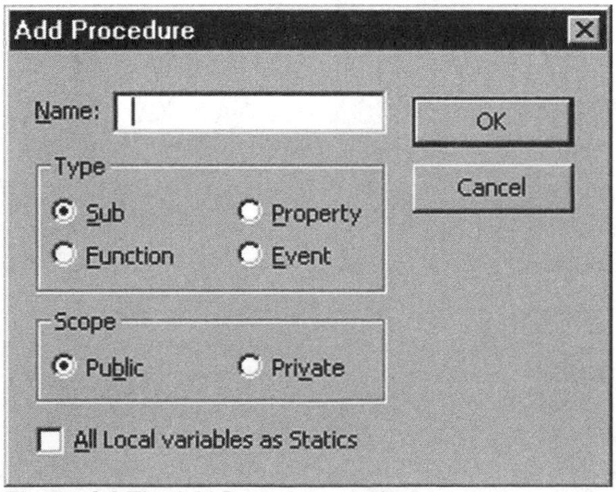

Parameters can be **passed** either **by reference** or **by value**. Passing a parameter by reference actually passes the memory location (address) of the argument to the

**Figure 6.1** The Add Procedure window

subprogram instead of the argument's value. This allows the subprogram to access the actual variable. As a result, the variable's value can be changed by the subprogram. Passing by reference is the default method of parameter passing in VB. That is, unless otherwise specified, VB passes parameters by reference. Passing a parameter by value, on the other hand, passes the value of the argument to the subprogram. This allows the subprogram to access a copy of the variable, and the variable's actual value cannot be changed by the subprogram to which it is passed. The following examples illustrate these points:

*Default = reference*

```vb
Private Sub cmdTest_Click()
' Driver program for MyProcedure
   Dim value As Integer

   value = 5

   picOutput.Print "Start driver program: Value = "; value
   Call MyProcedure (value)
   picOutput.Print "End driver program:   Value = "; value
End Sub

Private Sub MyProcedure(number As Integer)
   picOutput.Print "Start MyProcedure: Number = "; number
   number = 2 * number
   picOutput.Print "End MyProcedure:   Number = "; number
End Sub
```

The above program passes parameters by reference. The output from this program follows:

```
Start driver program: Value = 5
Start MyProcedure: Number = 5
End MyProcedure:   Number = 10
End driver program:   Value = 10
```

Now, we modify this program by adding the ByVal keyword before the number parameter in MyProcedure. The new program follows:

```vb
Private Sub cmdTest_Click()
' Driver program for MyProcedure
   Dim value As Integer

   value = 5

   picOutput.Print "Start driver program: Value = "; value
   Call MyProcedure (Value)
   picOutput.Print "End driver program:   Value = "; value
End Sub

Private Sub MyProcedure(ByVal number As Integer)
   picOutput.Print "Start MyProcedure: Number = "; number
   number = 2 * number
   picOutput.Print "End MyProcedure:   Number = "; number
End Sub
```

← Notice that this program is identical to the previous one except that the ByVal keyword precedes the parameter name in this version.

This program passes parameters by value and its output follows:

```
Start driver program: Value = 5
Start MyProcedure: Number = 5
End MyProcedure:    Number = 10
End driver program:   Value = 5
```

The `ByVal` keyword must precede each parameter that is passed by value. Since passing parameters by reference is the default method in VB, the `ByRef` keyword is optional.

VB also provides a way to force arguments to be passed by value even when their associated parameters are by reference in the subprogram heading. Enclosing an argument in parentheses forces VB to pass the argument by value. The following code illustrates this technique:

```
Private Sub cmdTest_Click()
    Dim num1 As Double, num2 As Double

    num1 = CDbl(5)
    num2 = CDbl(10)

    Call DoubleEm((num1), num2)

    picOutput.Cls
    picOutput.Print "num1 ="; num1
    picOutput.Print "num2 ="; num2
End Sub

Private Sub DoubleEm(val1 As Double, val2 As Double)
    val1 = CDbl(2) * val1
    val2 = CDbl(2) * val2
End Sub
```

num1 is passed by value since ➡️ it is enclosed in parentheses.

In the above code, the argument `num1` is passed by value and `num2` is passed by reference. The output of this code follows:

```
num1 = 5
num2 = 20
```

## PROGRAMMING KEY: WARNING

By modifying the example above, we also illustrate the reason for using the `Call` statement to invoke procedures. In the following code, can you tell whether `DoubleIt (number)` is a procedure call or a function call (with an insignificant return value) just by looking at the `cmdTest_Click` event handler? The answer is "no."

```
Private Sub cmdTest_Click()
    Dim number As Double

    number = CDbl(5)

    DoubleIt (number)
```

```
        picOutput.Cls
        picOutput.Print "number ="; number
End Sub

Private Sub DoubleIt(value As Double)
    value = CDbl(2) * value
End Sub
```

In this code, `DoubleIt (number)` is a procedure call since `DoubleIt` is a procedure. The argument `number` is passed by value since it is enclosed in parentheses. Therefore, the `DoubleIt` procedure cannot modify the original value of `number`, and the output of this program is `number = 5`.

As written, this program does not perform its intended function (i.e., double the value of `number` and output the result). Placing a `Call` statement in front of `DoubleIt` `(number)` corrects the problem. In summary, a *missing* `Call` *statement can cause your program to behave unexpectedly.*

## EVENTS AND EVENT HANDLERS

We have already mentioned that event handlers are subprograms in VB, and a user action (such as a key press or a mouse click) constitutes an event in the Windows operating system. There are also event handlers that are invoked upon the initiation or termination of a program.

### EVENT HANDLERS FOR FORM EVENTS

The `Load` event for a form occurs when a form is loaded or placed on the screen. Typically, this event procedure contains initialization code for the form. Module-level variables, for instance, may be initialized in the `Form_Load` event handler. For a startup form (the first form in a program), this event occurs when the program starts. The `Initialize` event may also be used to initialize variables and objects on the form, but this event occurs prior to placing the form on the screen and before the `Load` event. The `Unload` event occurs when a form is about to be removed from the screen, and the `Terminate` event occurs when the form is removed from the screen after the `Unload` event. The following code confirms the sequence of these events:

```
Private Sub Form_Initialize()
    MsgBox "Form_Initialize event", , "INITIALIZE"
End Sub

Private Sub Form_Load()
    MsgBox "Form_Load event", , "LOAD"
End Sub

Private Sub Form_Terminate()
    MsgBox "Form_Terminate event", , "TERMINATE"
End Sub
```

```
Private Sub Form_Unload(Cancel As Integer)
    MsgBox "Form_Unload event", , "UNLOAD"
End Sub
```

The Form_Unload event handler has one integer parameter, Cancel. Setting Cancel to any nonzero value prevents the form from being removed from the screen (and prevents the Terminate event from occurring).

## EVENT HANDLERS FOR FOCUS EVENTS

In the Windows environment, only one object can receive input (a mouse click or a key press) at any instant in time. The currently active object that can receive input said to "have the **focus**." A form that has the focus, for instance, has a highlighted caption or title bar. The user can change the focus to another object by clicking on the object or by pressing the TAB key to alternate between objects. Additionally, program code can change the focus through the SetFocus method. The two associated events are the GotFocus and LostFocus events. GotFocus occurs when an object receives the focus, and LostFocus occurs when an object loses the focus. The following example illustrates these events using two picture boxes, picOut1 and picOut2.

```
Private Sub picOut1_GotFocus()
    picOut1.Cls
    picOut1.Print "Got Focus"
End Sub

Private Sub picOut1_LostFocus()
    picOut1.Cls
    picOut1.Print "Lost Focus"
End Sub

Private Sub picOut2_GotFocus()
    picOut2.Cls
    picOut2.Print "Got Focus"
End Sub

Private Sub picOut2_LostFocus()
    picOut2.Cls
    picOut2.Print "Lost Focus"
End Sub
```

## EVENT HANDLERS FOR MOUSE EVENTS

Programmers often desire to track mouse events in the Windows environment. The MouseDown event occurs when the user presses a mouse button, the MouseUp event occurs when the user releases a mouse button, and the MouseMove event occurs when the user moves the mouse. The event handlers for each of these events contain four parameters: button, shift, x, and y. The button parameter is an integer that identifies which mouse button is pressed or released. This is a bit field with bits corresponding to the left button (bit 0), right button (bit 1), and middle button (bit 2). In the MouseUp and MouseDown events, only one of these bits is set, indicating the button that caused the event. Any combination of these bits may be set in the

MouseMove event since a combination of buttons may be activated. Similar to the button parameter, shift identifies the state of the SHIFT, CTRL, and ALT keys. shift is a bit field with bits corresponding to the SHIFT key (bit 0), CTRL key (bit 1), and ALT key (bit 2). Again, any combination of these bits may be set since more than one of these keys may be pressed at the same time. Finally, the x and y parameters indicate the horizontal and vertical position of the mouse pointer within the object, respectively. The code below provides an interactive view of mouse events in the picOutput picture box:

```
Private Sub picOutput_MouseDown(button As Integer,
   shift As Integer, x As Single, y As Single)
   Call Display(button, shift, x, y)
   picOutput.Print "MouseDown event"
End Sub

Private Sub picOutput_MouseMove(button As Integer,
   shift As Integer, x As Single, y As Single)
   Call Display(button, shift, x, y)
   picOutput.Print "MouseMove event"
End Sub

Private Sub picOutput_MouseUp(button As Integer,
   shift As Integer, x As Single, y As Single)
   Call Display(button, shift, x, y)
   picOutput.Print "MouseUp event"
End Sub

Private Sub Display(button As Integer, shift As Integer,
   x As Single, y As Single)
   picOutput.Cls
   picOutput.Print "button: ";

   Select Case button
      Case vbLeftbutton
         picOutput.Print "Left"
      Case vbRightbutton
         picOutput.Print "Right"
      Case vbMiddlebutton
         picOutput.Print "Middle"
      Case Else
         picOutput.Print
   End Select

   picOutput.Print "shift: ";
   If shift And vbShiftMask Then
      picOutput.Print "SHIFT";
      If shift > vbShiftMask Then
         picOutput.Print "+";
      End If
   End If

   If shift And vbCtrlMask Then
      picOutput.Print "CTRL";
```

```
              If shift > (vbCtrlMask + vbShiftMask) Then
                  picOutput.Print "+";
              End If
          End If

          If shift And vbAltMask Then
              picOutput.Print "ALT"
          Else
              picOutput.Print
          End If

          picOutput.Print "X: "; x
          picOutput.Print "Y: "; y
      End Sub
```

# Summary

## Key Terms

**argument**—a piece of information passed to a subprogram

**calling routine**—the part of the program (or the routine) from which the currently executing subprogram was invoked

**code reuse**—use of the same source code (or the same modules) in different programs; a benefit of modular programming

**component**—a part of a system

**driver program**—a program designed to test the operation of a subprogram

**event**—an action that occurs and is detected by the computer, such as a key press or a mouse click

**event handler**—a subprogram that is automatically invoked when an event occurs

**focus**—the currently active object on the display that can receive input. The currently active object is said to "have the focus"

**function**—a type of subprogram that returns a single value to the calling routine; usually, a function performs a computation

**function call**—a function invocation

**invoke**—to call a subprogram with the arguments having corresponding parameters and begin the subprogram execution

**modular programming**—computer programming in a modular or component-based design that utilizes subprograms

**module**—a part of a computer program that usually occupies its own file (as a code module in VB)

**parameter**—a placeholder for the information passed to a subprogram when it is invoked

**pass**—to send information to a subprogram by relating arguments to corresponding parameters

**pass by reference**—a type of parameter passing in which the memory location (address) of the argument is passed to the subprogram instead of the argument's value, allowing the subprogram to access the actual variable and modify its contents. This is the default method of parameter passing in VB

**pass by value**—a type of parameter passing where the value of the argument is passed to the subprogram, allowing the subprogram to access a copy of the variable and preserve the contents of the original variable

**procedure**—a type of subprogram that may return any number of values (including no value) to the calling routine; a subprogram that performs a specific task

**stepwise refinement**—a solution method that involves dividing a large problem into smaller subproblems and solving each subproblem to ultimately yield a solution to the large problem

**structured program**—a program that is written using a modular design

**subprogram**—a component of a program designed to perform a specific computation or complete a certain task; a procedure or a function

**top-down design**—a programming methodology that involves the process of stepwise refinement

**user-defined subprogram**—a subprogram that is written by the programmer and not built into the VB language

## Keywords

| *Events:* | *Methods:* | *Statements:* |
|---|---|---|
| GotFocus | SetFocus | ByRef |
| Initialize | | ByVal |
| Load | | Call |
| LostFocus | | End Function |
| MouseDown | | End Sub |
| MouseMove | | Private Function |
| MouseUp | | Private Sub |
| Terminate | | |
| Unload | | |

## Key Concepts

- Modular programming is programming in a component-based design through the use of subprograms. This technique provides an inherently logical organization of large programs, enhances the readability of code, allows easier debugging, and promotes code reuse.

- A subprogram is either a procedure or a function.

- Parameters are placeholders for the information passed to a subprogram, while arguments contain the actual data passed to the subprogram. The number, order, and data types of the arguments must correspond to the parameters of the subprogram, but the names of the arguments and parameters are unimportant.

- A procedure performs some operation and may return any number of values (or even no value) to the calling routine.

  The following general syntax defines a procedure:

```
Private Sub ProcedureName(parameter1 As Type1,
  parameter2 As Type2, ...)
    [statements]
End Sub
```

Either syntax below may be used to invoke a procedure, but we highly recommend using the Call statement:

```
Call ProcedureName(argument1, argument2, ...)
{Recommended syntax}
```

or

```
ProcedureName argument1, argument2, ...
```

● A function is usually associated with a calculation and returns only one value to the calling routine.

The following general syntax defines a function:

```
Private Function FunctionName(param1 as Type1, ...)
➥ As FunctionType
    [statements]
    FunctionName = ReturnValue
End Function
```

A function is invoked by writing the function name along with the required arguments. The general form of a function invocation where the returned value is assigned to a variable follows:

```
variableName = FunctionName(argument1, argument2, ...)
```

● Passing a parameter by reference means that the memory location of the argument is passed to the subprogram rather than its value, allowing the subprogram to access and change the value of the actual variable. Passing by reference is the default method of parameter passing in VB.

● Passing a parameter by value passes the value of the argument to the subprogram, and the subprogram cannot change the value of the original variable in the calling routine. The ByVal keyword must precede each parameter that is passed by value in the subprogram definition. Additionally, surrounding an argument with parentheses in a subprogram invocation forces the argument to be passed by value, regardless of the subprogram definition.

● In the Windows operating system, the object that can receive input at a given instant in time is said to "have the focus." The GotFocus and LostFocus events in VB may be used to perform an operation when an object receives or loses the focus, respectively. VB also has events associated with forms (load, unload, initialize, and terminate) and the mouse (pressing buttons, releasing buttons, and moving).

## Review Questions

1. What is modular programming? Describe some of its advantages.
2. Name the two different types of subprograms.
3. Define arguments and parameters and describe the relationship between them.
4. Write the general syntax for a procedure definition and a function definition. Highlight the differences in the syntax.

**5.** Write the general syntax for a procedure invocation and a function invocation. Highlight the differences in the syntax.

**6.** When should you use a function as opposed to a procedure?

**7.** What does it mean to pass a parameter by reference? by value? How do you accomplish this in VB?

**8.** What is "focus" in the Windows operating system?

**9.** Describe some of the VB events for a form, focus, and the mouse.

## Chapter 6 Problems

**1.** Write a program that allows the user to input first and last names in two separate text boxes and then displays the last name, a comma, and then the first name in a picture box. Use a subprogram to display the output.

**2.** Write a program that allows the user to input first and last names in two separate text boxes and then displays the names with the letters in reverse order. Use a subprogram to reverse the letters in the names, and use another subprogram to display the output. The program should automatically capitalize the first letter of each name. For instance, Tom Smith should be displayed as Mot Htims.

**3.** Write a program that reads the account name, account balance, total deposits, and total withdrawals from a data file named Checkbook.dat and then computes the new balance. Use three subprograms: one to read the data file, a second to compute the new account balance, and a third to display the output. Sample data appears below:

```
Ima Richman
815.34
312.00
400.00
```

Your program output should be similar to the output shown below:

```
Account Name:       Ima Richman
-------------------------------------
Previous Balance:   815.34
Total Deposits:     312.00
Total Withdrawals:  400.00
-------------------------------------
New Balance:        727.34
```

**4.** Write a program that reads a name, address, and phone number from a data file named Address.dat and then displays the data in a picture box. Use two subprograms: one reads the data from the file, and another displays the data. Sample data appears below:

```
John Doe
1234 Sunshine Drive
Nowhere, AZ 85200
(602) 511-1221
```

**5.** Write two VB functions: DecToHex converts a decimal number to its hexadecimal equivalent, and HexToDec converts a hexadecimal number to its decimal equivalent. Write a simple driver program to test these functions.

6. Modify the quadratic formula solver program from Chapter 4, Problem 10. Use subprograms to perform the input, calculations, and output.

7. The gamma function is defined as follows:

$$\Gamma(n) \quad = (n - 1)!$$
$$\Gamma(1/2) = \sqrt{\pi}$$

Write a program that finds the value of the gamma function for a user-entered value of $n$, where $n$ is an integer or an integer plus 0.5 such that $n \geq 1$.

8. A continuous random variable $x$ has a gamma distribution, with parameters $\alpha > 0$ and $\beta > 0$, if its probability density function (pdf) is given by:

$$f(x) = \frac{1}{\beta^{\alpha} \Gamma(\alpha)} x^{\alpha - 1} e^{-x/\beta}$$

for $x > 0$. If $x \leq 0$, then $f(x) = 0$.

Write a program that finds the value of the gamma density function for user-entered values of $x$, $\alpha$, and $\beta$.

9. Write a program that displays your name, course title, date, and school name in a picture box as soon as the program starts (without any user action).

10. Write a program that displays the message "HOORAY! I was tired of the left mouse button." in a picture box when the user clicks the right mouse button inside the picture box.

## Programming Projects

1. The Lanchester equations can be used to compute force sizes as functions of time in a battle:

$a$ = rate at which one $Y$ using aimed fire causes $X$ casualties (units are $X$ casualties per $Y$ firer per time period)
$b$ = rate at which one $X$ using aimed fire causes $Y$ casualties (units are $Y$ casualties per $X$ firer per time period)

Equations for force size as a function of time:

Let $m = (a/b)^{(1/2)}$, $n = (1/m)$, $r = (ab)^{(1/2)}$

$$X(t) = (1/2)(X_0 - mY_0)e^{rt} + (1/2)(X_0 + mY_0)e^{-rt}$$
$$Y(t) = (1/2)(Y_0 - nX_0)e^{rt} + (1/2)(Y_0 + nX_0)e^{-rt}$$

where

$X_0$ = initial force size of $X$
$Y_0$ = initial force size of $Y$
$X(t)$ = force size of $X$ at time $t$
$Y(t)$ = force size of $Y$ at time $t$

Write a program that uses the Lanchester equations to compute force sizes as functions of time. The program should interactively request input from the user and display the results in a picture box. (*Hint:* If you are clever, you can implement the Lanchester equations using only one function.)

**2.** The officer and enlisted ranks in the United States Navy are shown in the accompanying table along with their associated titles. Write a program that allows the user to input a rank and outputs the associated title. Be sure to use subprograms.

| Officer | | Enlisted | |
|---|---|---|---|
| Officer Rank | Title | Enlisted Rank | Title |
| O-1 | Ensign | E-1 | Seaman Recruit |
| O-2 | Lieutenant Junior Grade | E-2 | Seaman Apprentice |
| O-3 | Lieutenant | E-3 | Seaman |
| O-4 | Lieutenant Commander | E-4 | Petty Officer Third Class |
| O-5 | Commander | E-5 | Petty Officer Second Class |
| O-6 | Captain | E-6 | Petty Officer First Class |
| O-7 | Rear Admiral Lower Half | E-7 | Chief Petty Officer |
| O-8 | Rear Admiral Upper Half | E-8 | Senior Chief Petty Officer |
| O-9 | Vice Admiral | E-9 | Master Chief Petty Officer |
| O-10 | Admiral | | |

# Recursion

## Supplement Objectives

In this chapter supplement, you will:

● Become familiar with a recursive function from mathematics

● Learn how to write recursive subprograms and understand their operation

### Mathematical Recursion

In mathematics, a **recursive function** is a function whose name appears on both the left- and right-hand sides of the function equation. Thus, recursion provides a method of solving a complex problem by first solving a set of simpler subproblems. Some problems naturally lend themselves to a recursive solution. The factorial function ($n!$), for instance, may be defined recursively:

$$n! = \begin{cases} n \times (n-1)! & \text{for an integer } n \geq 1 \\ 1 & \text{for } n = 0 \end{cases}$$

Using the above definition, we can find 5! as follows:

$$5! = 5 \times 4!$$
$$4! = 4 \times 3!$$
$$3! = 3 \times 2!$$
$$2! = 2 \times 1!$$
$$1! = 1 \times 0!$$
$$0! = 1$$

Then, through backward substitution, we find the value of 5!:

$$5! = 5 \times 4 \times 3 \times 2 \times 1 \times 1 = 120$$

Thus, recursion forms an implicit loop structure.
Note that we can define the factorial function nonrecursively as well:

$$n! = \begin{cases} n \times (n-1) \times \cdots \times 1 & \text{for an integer } n \geq 1 \\ 1 & \text{for } n = 0 \end{cases}$$

From the above definition, we immediately find the result of 5!:

$$5! = 5 \times 4 \times 3 \times 2 \times 1 = 120$$

This definition of the factorial function may be easily implemented in VB using an explicit loop structure formed by an `If`-statement and a `For-Next` loop. This is left as an exercise for the reader.

## RECURSIVE SUBPROGRAMS

To implement the recursive definition in VB, we need to use a **recursive subprogram**, or a subprogram that calls itself. A recursive subprogram repeatedly calls itself, each time with a simpler situation, until it reaches the trivial case. Once the trivial case is reached, the recursion stops. A recursive function that computes *n*! is shown below. The trivial case occurs when n = 0, then `Factorial = 1`.

```
Private Function Factorial(ByVal n As Long) As Long
' Compute n! recursively

   If n < 0 Then
      picOutput.Print "ERROR: Invalid Argument in Factorial
      ➥ Function"
   ElseIf n = 0 Then
      Factorial = 1
   Else
      Factorial = n * Factorial(n - 1)
   End If
End Function
```

For values of n greater than 12, the long–integer data type is **overflowed** in the above function. This error occurs regardless of whether the function is written recursively or not. One way to prevent this error is to use the double-precision data type:

```
Private Function Factorial(ByVal n As Double) As Double
' Compute n! recursively
' Use double-precision numbers to prevent overflow errors

   n = CDbl(Int(n))
   If n < 0 Then
      picOutput.Print  "ERROR: Invalid Argument in Factorial
      ➥ Function"
   ElseIf n = 0 Then
      Factorial = 1
   Else
      Factorial = n * Factorial(n - 1)
   End If
End Function
```

In this function, the double-precision data type is overflowed for values of n greater than 170, a value about 14 times higher than the previous function.

Notice that the parameter n is preceded by the `ByVal` keyword in both versions of the `Factorial` function above. In other words, this function passes parameters by value. Removing the `ByVal` keyword from either version of this function does not cause the function to perform incorrectly. In many cases, however, a recursive subprogram that passes parameters by reference rather than by value will not operate correctly. Recall that passing parameters by reference allows the values of the original variables in the calling routine to be altered, and this is usually not desirable in a recursive subprogram.

The following example demonstrates the difference between passing parameters by value and by reference in a recursive subprogram:

```
Option Explicit

Private Sub RecursionTest(ByVal number As Integer)
    If (number <= 0) Then
        ' Trivial case -- end the recursion
    Else
        picOutput.Print number;
        number = number - 1
        Call RecursionTest(number)
        If (number < 3) Then
            Call RecursionTest(number)
        End If
    End If
End Sub

Private Sub cmdExample_Click()
    picOutput.Cls
    Call RecursionTest(5)
End Sub
```

This code outputs 5 4 3 2 1 1 2 1 1 when the cmdExample button is clicked. Now, let's remove the ByVal keyword in front of the number parameter. This modified version of the code passes number by reference. The output of the code is now 5 4 3 2 1, and the recursion does not work as desired.

In many languages, a common problem with recursive subprograms is the **stack overflow** error. The stack data structure is discussed in a later chapter. Each microprocessor has an internal stack structure, and compilers may reserve extra memory to function as a stack and store information during program execution. During program execution, these structures may become overflowed with information. However, we have not encountered any stack overflow problems when using recursive subprograms in VB 6.0.

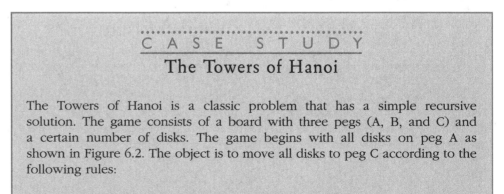

C A S E    S T U D Y
# The Towers of Hanoi

The Towers of Hanoi is a classic problem that has a simple recursive solution. The game consists of a board with three pegs (A, B, and C) and a certain number of disks. The game begins with all disks on peg A as shown in Figure 6.2. The object is to move all disks to peg C according to the following rules:

**1.** One disk is moved at a time.
**2.** A disk can only be placed on top of one that is larger in size.

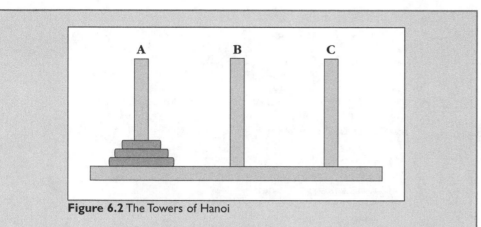

**Figure 6.2** The Towers of Hanoi

Now, take a few minutes and try to develop an algorithm to solve this problem. Think about this problem for one disk, two disks, and three disks. Do you see any patterns?

For one disk, the solution is trivial: Move the disk from peg A to peg C. How about for two disks? Move the first disk from peg A to peg B. Then, move the second disk from peg A to peg C. Finally, move the first disk from peg B to peg C. Note that the first and last steps repeat the solution for the one-disk case. Now, how about for three disks? Obviously the solution is longer, but it contains the solution to the two-disk case: Use the two-disk solution to move two disks from peg A to peg B. Then, move the third disk from peg A to peg C. Finally, use the two-disk solution to move two disks from peg B to peg C. Again, notice the references to the previous solution. The general solution algorithm follows:

**1.** Use the ($n$–1)-disk solution to move ($n$–1) disks from peg A to peg B.

**2.** Move disk $n$ from peg A to peg C.

**3.** Use the ($n$–1)-disk solution to move ($n$–1) disks from peg B to peg C.

This algorithm is implemented in the VB program below:

```
' Towers of Hanoi
' ----------------
' This program solves the Towers of Hanoi problem
' for 1 or more disks

Option Explicit

Private Sub cmdSolve_Click()
' Find a solution to the Towers of Hanoi problem by
' calling a recursive procedure

    Dim numDisks As Integer

    picOutput.Cls
    numDisks = CInt(Val(txtNumDisks.Text))
    If numDisks > 0 Then
        Call MoveDisk(numDisks, "A", "C", "B")
    Else
        picOutput.Print "Number of disks must be greater
    ➥ than 0."
```

```
      End If
   End Sub

   Private Sub MoveDisk(ByVal numDisks As Integer, ByVal
   ➡ startPeg As String, _
                       ByVal endPeg As String, ByVal
                       ➡ sparePeg As String)
   ' A recursive procedure to move disks

      Dim move As String

      If numDisks = 1 Then
         move = "Move a disk from " & startPeg & " to "
         ➡ & endPeg
         picOutput.Print move
      Else
         Call MoveDisk(numDisks - 1, startPeg, sparePeg,
         ➡ endPeg)
         move = "Move a disk from " & startPeg & " to "
         ➡ & endPeg
         picOutput.Print move
         Call MoveDisk(numDisks - 1, sparePeg, endPeg,
         ➡ startPeg)
      End If
   End Sub
```

This code outputs the following solution for the three-disk case:

```
Move a disk from A to C
Move a disk from A to B
Move a disk from C to B
Move a disk from A to C
Move a disk from B to A
Move a disk from B to C
Move a disk from A to C
```

The program gives this solution for the four-disk case:

```
Move a disk from A to B
Move a disk from A to C
Move a disk from B to C
Move a disk from A to B
Move a disk from C to A
Move a disk from C to B
Move a disk from A to B
Move a disk from A to C
Move a disk from B to C
Move a disk from B to A
Move a disk from C to A
Move a disk from B to C
Move a disk from A to B
Move a disk from A to C
Move a disk from B to C
```

Notice that for $n$ disks, the solution contains $2^n-1$ moves. Legend has it that the 64-disk Towers of Hanoi problem was given to monks in an ancient monastery. When all 64 disks were in order on peg C, the world was to come to an end. Applying some mathematics, the 64-disk solution requires on the order of $1.84 \times 10^{19}$ moves. At a phenomenal rate of moving one disk per second, it would still require 584.9 billion years to solve the 64-disk problem by hand.

## Summary

### Key Terms

**overflow**—a run-time error that occurs when a variable's value exceeds the limit specified by its data type

**recursive function**—a function whose name appears on both the left and right-hand sides of the function equation; a function that contains itself in its definition

**recursive subprogram**—a subprogram that invokes itself

**stack overflow**—a run-time error caused by the stored stack data exceeding the amount of memory space reserved for the stack structure

### Key Concepts

- A recursive function in mathematics is a function whose name appears on both the left and right-hand sides of the function equation. That is, the function contains itself in its definition.

- Recursion forms an implicit loop structure and provides a method of solving a complex problem by solving a set of simpler subproblems.

### Review Questions

1. In mathematics, what is a recursive function?
2. What is a recursive subprogram and how is it used in programming? Give an example.

### Chapter 6 Supplement Problems

1. Modify your program from Chapter 6, Problem 7 to implement the gamma function as a recursive function in VB. The recursive definition of the gamma function follows:

$$\Gamma(n)=(n-1)\Gamma(n-1)$$
$$\Gamma(1/2)=\sqrt{\pi}$$

2. Bill works at Crazy Computer Corp. and is leaving on Christmas vacation at the end of the day. He usually receives quite a bit of e-mail, so he programmed his e-mail system to reply to all incoming messages with the following message:

```
I am on vacation. Merry Christmas and Happy New Year!
I'll talk to you after the New Year.
-- Bill
```

During lunch, Bill told Mary about his clever e-mail setup. Without telling Bill, Mary programmed her e-mail system in a similar fashion, and then she left on vacation. Bill sent a message of holiday cheer to all employees of the company, and then he left on vacation. What is the problem here?

3. Write a program that uses a recursive subprogram to print the following output in a picture box:

```
abracadabra
abracadabr
abracadab
abracada
abracad
abraca
abrac
abra
abr
ab
a
```

4. Modify the program from Problem 3 to print a similar output for any user-entered word or phrase.

5. Write a program that uses a recursive function to sum the integers from 1 to $n$, where $n$ is a user-specified integer greater than or equal to one.

## Programming Projects

1. Write a program that uses a recursive subprogram to reverse the order of the characters in a user-entered word or phrase. Display the result in a picture box.

2. The Fibonacci numbers are defined by the sequence $a_{n+1} = a_n + a_{n-1}$, where $a_1 = 1$ and $a_2 = 1$. Write a program that uses a recursive subprogram to find $a_n$, the $n^{th}$ Fibonacci number, for $n > 2$.

# 7

# Error Trapping and Debugging

N ow that you are familiar with the basics of programming, we turn to the important topic of how to best handle errors in a program. First, you want to bullet proof your program. **Bullet-proofing** a program means to make the program as error-proof as possible. When the user enters an unexpected value, for instance, the program should not **crash** (end program execution and deliver a **fatal error** message). Simple programming errors can be catastrophic in real-world applications. Imagine, for example, a U.S. Navy fighter aircraft uncontrollably flipping upside-down when it crosses the equator due to a flaw in its navigation software. The necessity of bullet-proofing programs thus becomes apparent.

## BUILT-IN ERROR TRAPPING

To completely bullet-proof a program, a programmer must think of every possible contingency that may occur during the program's execution, such as erroneous input values, non-existent input files, or illegal file names. For large programs, this task is daunting. Commercial programs, for instance, usually undergo months of testing, yet they are still error-prone. Serious errors may even crash an entire computer system, requiring the user to **reboot**, or restart, the machine.

Fortunately, the VB designers at Microsoft created a method to **trap**, or catch, common errors that occur during program execution (**run-time errors**). The Err object contains information about the most recent run-time error encountered. The Number property of Err identifies the error by a specific code number; these code numbers and their associated error messages are shown in Figure 7.1 and Appendix C.

It is generally desirable to retain control over a program's execution rather than having it end abruptly when VB encounters a run-time error. **Error-handling routines**, or **error-handlers**, tell the computer what operations to perform when an error is encountered. In VB, the On Error statement is used to enable or disable an error-handling routine, and it specifies the location of the routine within a subprogram. The general form of the On Error statement is shown in the sample subprogram structure below:

```
Private Sub cmdExample_Click()
' General form of the On Error statement and placement of the
' error-handling routine

    On Error GoTo ErrorHandler      ' Enable error-trapping routine

    [subprogram code]

    Exit Sub

ErrorHandler:

    [error-handling routine] - subroutine code

    Resume

End Sub
```

The statement On Error GoTo ErrorHandler activates error trapping. If an error occurs during the execution of the subprogram code, the program will jump to the error-handling routine (i.e., GoTo ErrorHandler). Once the error-handling routine is complete, the Resume statement instructs the program to return to its previous location and re-execute the code that caused the error. The Exit Sub statement exits from the procedure and prevents the error-handling routine from executing when no error occurs. The Err object's properties are reset to zero or zero-length

| Code | Message | Code | Message |
|------|---------|------|---------|
| 3 | Return without GoSub | 371 | The specified object can't be used as an owner form for Show |
| 5 | Invalid procedure call | 380 | Invalid property value |
| 6 | Overflow | 381 | Invalid property-array index |
| 7 | Out of memory | 382 | Property Set can't be executed at run time |
| 9 | Subscript out of range | 383 | Property Set can't be used with a read-only property |
| 10 | This array is fixed or temporarily locked | 385 | Need property-array index |
| 11 | Division by zero | 387 | Property Set not permitted |
| 13 | Type mismatch | 393 | Property Get can't be executed at run time |
| 14 | Out of string space | 394 | Property Get can't be executed on write-only property |
| 16 | Expression too complex | 400 | Form already displayed; can't show modally |
| 17 | Can't perform requested operation | 402 | Code must close topmost modal form first |
| 18 | User interrupt occurred | 419 | Permission to use object denied |
| 20 | Resume without error | 422 | Property not found |
| 28 | Out of stack space | 423 | Property or method not found |
| 35 | Sub, Function, or Property not defined | 424 | Object required |
| 47 | Too many DLL application clients | 425 | Invalid object use |
| 48 | Error in loading DLL | 429 | ActiveX component can't create object or return reference to this object |
| 49 | Bad DLL calling convention | 430 | Class doesn't support Automation |
| 51 | Internal error | 432 | File name or class name not found during Automation operation |
| 52 | Bad file name or number | 438 | Object doesn't support this property or method |
| 53 | File not found | 440 | Automation error |
| 54 | Bad file mode | 442 | Connection to type library or object library for remote process has been lost |
| 55 | File already open | 443 | Automation object doesn't have a default value |
| 57 | Device I/O error | 445 | Object doesn't support this action |
| 58 | File already exists | 446 | Object doesn't support named arguments |
| 59 | Bad record length | 447 | Object doesn't support current locale setting |
| 61 | Disk full | 448 | Named argument not found |
| 62 | Input past end of file | 449 | Argument not optional or invalid property assignment |
| 63 | Bad record number | 450 | Wrong number of arguments or invalid property assignment |
| 67 | Too many files | 451 | Object not a collection |
| 68 | Device unavailable | 452 | Invalid ordinal |
| 70 | Permission denied | 453 | Specified DLL function not found |
| 71 | Disk not ready | 454 | Code resource not found |
| 74 | Can't rename with different drive | 455 | Code resource lock error |
| 75 | Path/File access error | 457 | This key already associated with an element of this collection |
| 76 | Path not found | 458 | Variable uses a type not supported in Visual Basic |
| 91 | Object variable or With block variable not set | 459 | This component doesn't support the set of events |
| 92 | For loop not initiated | 460 | Invalid Clipboard format |
| 93 | Invalid pattern string | 461 | Specified format doesn't match format of data |
| 94 | Invalid use of Null | 480 | Can't create AutoRedraw image |
| 97 | Can't call Friend procedure on an object that is not an instance of the defining class | 481 | Invalid picture |
| 98 | A property or method call cannot include a reference to a private object, either as an argument or as a return value | 482 | Printer error |
| | | 483 | Printer driver does not support specified property |
| 298 | System DLL could not be loaded | 484 | Problem getting printer information from the system. Make sure the printer is set up correctly |
| 320 | Can't use character device names in specified file names | 485 | Invalid picture type |
| 321 | Invalid file format | 486 | Can't print form image to this type of printer |
| 322 | Can't create necessary temporary file | 520 | Can't empty Clipboard |
| 325 | Invalid format in resource file | 521 | Can't open Clipboard |
| 327 | Data value named not found | 735 | Can't save file to TEMP directory |
| 328 | Illegal parameter; can't write arrays | 744 | Search text not found |
| 335 | Could not access system registry | 746 | Replacements too long |
| 336 | ActiveX component not correctly registered | 31001 | Out of memory |
| 337 | ActiveX component not found | 31004 | No object |
| 338 | ActiveX component did not run correctly | 31018 | Class is not set |
| 360 | Object already loaded | 31027 | Unable to activate object |
| 361 | Can't load or unload this object | 31032 | Unable to create embedded object |
| 363 | ActiveX control specified not found | 31036 | Error saving to file |
| 364 | Object was unloaded | 31037 | Error loading from file |
| 365 | Unable to unload within this context | | |
| 368 | The specified file is out of date. This program requires a later version | | |

**Figure 7.1** Visual Basic trappable errors

strings (null strings) after any form of the `Resume` or `On Error` statement and after an `Exit Sub` or `Exit Function`. The `Clear` method can be used to explicitly reset `Err` by issuing the command `Err.Clear`.

In the general form shown previously, `ErrorHandler` is a **line label**. A line label can be any word of at most 40 characters, and it should be descriptive and self-commenting. Hence, we use `ErrorHandler` since it meets these requirements. A line label must begin at the left margin and end with a colon. The line label specified by an `On Error` statement must appear within the same subprogram as the `On Error` statement, but the error-handling routine can call another subprogram. Thus, each subprogram that requires error trapping must have its own `On Error` statement and error-handling routine. If the `On Error` statement is not used, any run-time error that occurs is fatal: An error message will be displayed and execution stops.

There are several variations of the `On Error` and `Resume` statements. If `Resume` is replaced by `Resume Next` in the general form previously seen, the program executes the error-handling routine and then jumps to the next line following the one that caused the error. Similarly, `On Error Resume Next` specifies that when a run-time error occurs, program execution continues with the statement immediately following the statement containing the error. Finally, `On Error GoTo 0` disables any previously enabled error-handler in the current subprogram. off

The following function incorporates VB's built-in error trapping to prevent uncontrolled program termination from occurring if the function attempts division by zero:

```
Private Function AveVelocity(distance As Double, time As
➥ Double) As Double
' Calculate average velocity
' Use built-in error trapping to check for division by 0
   On Error GoTo ErrorHandler

   AveVelocity = distance / time

   Exit Function

ErrorHandler:               built in value/number
   Select Case Err.Number
      Case 11
         MsgBox "time = 0! -> Division by 0 error", ,
         ➥ "ERROR"
      Case Else
         MsgBox CStr(Err.Description), , "RUN-TIME ERROR"
   End Select
   AveVelocity = 0#
   Resume Next
End Function
```

The error-handler executes ➡ when a run-time error occurs. For a division-by-0 error, `Err.Number` equals 11.

## THE GoTo STATEMENT

The `GoTo` statement performs an **unconditional branch** to a specified line label or **line number**. A line number is similar to a line label, except it uses numbers instead of letters. You have already seen the `GoTo` statement used in the previous section. Early versions of BASIC did not contain many of the structured control statements found in VB. As a result, programmers were forced to use a `GoTo` statement for branching (jumping) operations. This was the biggest complaint by programmers about BASIC. `GoTo` statements make the code hard to read, the program logic more difficult to comprehend, documentation harder to write, and debugging code a nightmare. With the exception of its use in the `On Error` statement described in the previous section, `GoTo` statements should be avoided; structured control statements should be used whenever possible. In fact, the `GoTo` statement is unnecessary since any program can be written using sequential statements, loops, and decision structures.

## TYPES OF PROGRAMMING ERRORS

Run-time errors occur at **run time**, or during program execution. A run-time error is often the result of the user entering invalid input, such as a nonexistent file name. As discussed previously, the programmer should account for these types of errors by writing error-handlers or by using the built-in error-trapping routines.

### SYNTAX ERRORS AND LOGIC ERRORS

Additionally, there are two types of errors that a programmer can make when writing a computer program (at **design time**): syntax errors and logic errors. **Syntax errors** are errors in the **syntax**, or structure (spelling, grammar, or punctuation), of the program. The following code segment contains a syntax error. Can you find it?

```
Private Sub cmdExample_Click()
' Example code containing a syntax error

    Dim thisValue As Integer

    thiValue = 10
    picOutput.Print thisValue
End Sub
```

**Key Terms**

**design time**—the time when the programmer designs the user interface and writes the source code
**run time**—the period of time during program execution
**syntax**—refers to the structure of the code, whereas **semantics** is concerned with its meaning

In the above code segment, the variable `thisValue` is misspelled in the assignment statement. An undeclared variable named `thiValue` is assigned the value of 10 instead of the intended variable named `thisValue`. Instead of being assigned a value of 10 as was intended, `thisValue` retains a value of 0 (the VB default value). Thus, this code always outputs a 0.

Spelling errors of this type are typical syntax errors. Fortunately, VB automatically finds errors like this if you require explicit variable declarations (i.e., `Option Explicit`); this alone is a compelling reason for requiring explicit variable declarations in VB. To ensure that automatic syntax checking is enabled in the VB editor environment, make sure that there is a check mark in the check box called Auto Syntax Check in the Tools/Options menu under the Editor tab.

**Logic errors** are the second type of programming error, and they deal with the **semantics**, or meaning, of the code. Computers follow the precise instructions of the programmer; they do *exactly* what they are told to do. However, sometimes what we (as programmers) think we told the computer to do differs from what we actually told it to do. For example, examine the code segment below. Can you find the logic error?

```
Private Sub cmdExample_Click()
' Example code containing a logic error

    Dim number As Single
```

```
        number = CSng(10)

        Do
           picOutput.Print number
           number = number - 3 / 4
        Loop Until number = CSng(10)
    End Sub
```

The above code segment contains a logic error in the `Loop Until` statement. The variable `number` never equals 0; therefore, we created an endless (infinite) loop, or a logic error. To stop the execution of this endless loop in VB, hold down the CTRL (control) key and press the BREAK key (CTRL+BREAK). To correct this error, replace the `Loop Until` statement with the following line:

```
        Loop Until number <= CSng(10)
```

As with this simple example, typical logic errors include endless loops and errors in mathematical formulae.

A **bug** in a computer program may be either a syntax error or a logic error. It is the programmer's responsibility to debug a program, thus eliminating all syntax and logic errors. Syntax errors are more readily apparent to the programmer and often easier to fix than logic errors. Furthermore, the VB editor assists the programmer in finding syntax errors. Logic errors are not as evident, and sometimes, there is no easy way to fix a logic error without recoding part of the program. The next two sections discuss debugging methods; the first section is language-independent, whereas the second section is VB-specific.

## Key Terms

**syntax error**—an error in the structure (spelling, grammar, or punctuation) of a computer program
**logic error**—an error in the logic or meaning of the code

## STANDARD DEBUGGING TECHNIQUES

Finding errors in a program has come to be called **debugging** (see Chapter 1). The two standard debugging techniques include the data dump and hand-execution of code. These are standard techniques because they work regardless of the computer language being used.

### DATA DUMP

The simplest debugging technique is the data dump. When a program is not working as expected, the programmer strategically adds lines of code to output the values of selected variables (either to the screen or to an output file). The output of these variables is called a **data dump**. By tracing through the data dump, a programmer can pinpoint problems in the code (provided that the data dump includes the problematic variables and portions of source code). For instance, consider the logic error example in the previous section. This code already performs a data dump since the value of the variable `number` is output during each iteration of the `Do` loop. In this case, the programmer is fortunate and can easily spot the mistake.

### HAND-EXECUTION OF CODE

The second standard debugging technique, is **hand-execution** of code—an invaluable programming skill. Here you, the programmer, act as the computer. You manually execute (trace) the source code with a pencil and paper. The pencil and paper act as the computer's memory space, and you act as the microprocessor, sequentially executing each line of code and performing the necessary operations. This technique is essentially a manual version of the data dump. So, why would a programmer trace code rather than perform a data dump? First, tracing a program by hand does not require a computer. You can debug a program anywhere with just a hardcopy of the code, pencil, and paper. Secondly, programmers often locate logic errors faster by tracing through their code rather than performing simple data dumps. We demonstrate tracing code by using a modified version of the logic error example from the previous section:

```
Private Sub cmdExample_Click()
' Example of tracing code
' This code contains an infinite loop

    Dim number As Integer

    number = 5
    Do
       picOutput.Print number
       number = number - 2
    Loop Until number = 0
End Sub
```

The hand-executed results are as follows:

| Iteration | number | picOutput |
|-----------|--------|-----------|
| 0 | 5 | Empty |
| 1 | 3 | 5 |
| 2 | 1 | 5 |
|   |   | 3 |
| 3 | −1 | 5 |
|   |   | 3 |
|   |   | 1 |

At this point, the programmer sees the value of number is −1 and realizes that an infinite loop was created. This is a rather simple example; hand-execution of code is usually more involved and may take longer to locate the error. Try hand-executing the original (unmodified) version of this code, for instance. It takes many more iterations before the value of number becomes negative. Again, the good news concerning hand-execution is that you may find your errors after tracing just a small portion of the code.

## THE VISUAL BASIC DEBUGGER

The Visual Basic development environment contains a built-in debugger to assist the programmer in tracing code and locating errors. The debugger commands are available through the Debug menu or the Debug toolbar. To activate the Debug toolbar, click the right mouse button (right-click) on the menu bar to view the toolbar menu, and then left-click on Debug. Figure 7.2 displays the Debug toolbar and explains the icons.

The VB debugger provides a semi-automatic method of locating errors. It enables a programmer to simply **watch** specific variables or expressions without requiring a program modification that executes a data dump. Additionally, the debugger can be used to stop the program execution at designated **breakpoints** or execute the program code step by step (that is, to **step** into the program). Note that the debugger is a design time utility; none of the debugger commands may be used at run time in an executable module.

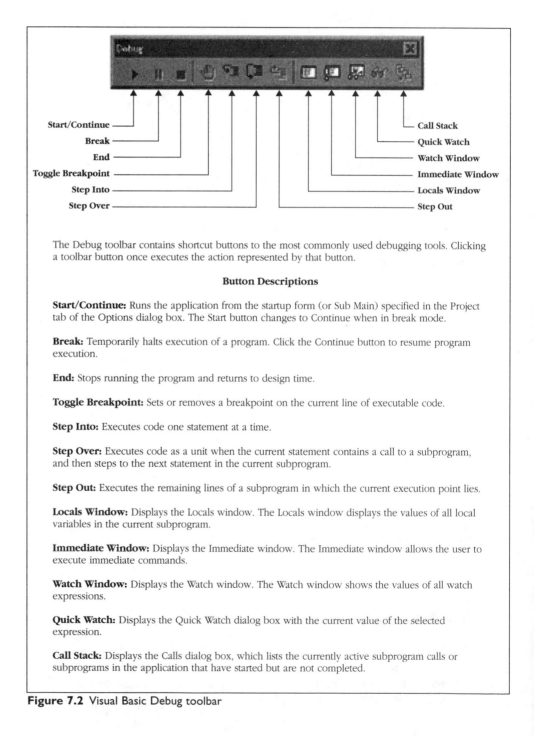

The Debug toolbar contains shortcut buttons to the most commonly used debugging tools. Clicking a toolbar button once executes the action represented by that button.

### Button Descriptions

**Start/Continue:** Runs the application from the startup form (or Sub Main) specified in the Project tab of the Options dialog box. The Start button changes to Continue when in break mode.

**Break:** Temporarily halts execution of a program. Click the Continue button to resume program execution.

**End:** Stops running the program and returns to design time.

**Toggle Breakpoint:** Sets or removes a breakpoint on the current line of executable code.

**Step Into:** Executes code one statement at a time.

**Step Over:** Executes code as a unit when the current statement contains a call to a subprogram, and then steps to the next statement in the current subprogram.

**Step Out:** Executes the remaining lines of a subprogram in which the current execution point lies.

**Locals Window:** Displays the Locals window. The Locals window displays the values of all local variables in the current subprogram.

**Immediate Window:** Displays the Immediate window. The Immediate window allows the user to execute immediate commands.

**Watch Window:** Displays the Watch window. The Watch window shows the values of all watch expressions.

**Quick Watch:** Displays the Quick Watch dialog box with the current value of the selected expression.

**Call Stack:** Displays the Calls dialog box, which lists the currently active subprogram calls or subprograms in the application that have started but are not completed.

**Figure 7.2** Visual Basic Debug toolbar

## DEBUGGER OPERATION

Breakpoints, stepping, and watches are pictured in Figure 7.2 and are briefly described in the following paragraphs. For more detailed information, consult the VB documentation or online help.

Breakpoints are toggled on and off at specific lines of code designated by the programmer. Breakpoints can be set only on executable lines of code. Blank lines, declaration statements, and comments cannot have breakpoints. When a breakpoint is encountered, program execution is temporarily halted until the programmer selects Continue from the Run menu, presses F5, or left-clicks on the Continue button (Run button). While the program is halted, the programmer has the ability to immediately execute commands in the Immediate window. For instance, the programmer can change or print the values of expressions in the Immediate window.

The VB debugger has three different stepping operations. The Step Into option executes code one statement at a time. For example, if the statement is a call to a subprogram, the next statement displayed is the first statement in the subprogram. The Step Over option executes a subprogram call as a single unit, and then steps to the next statement in the current subprogram. Thus, the next statement displayed is the next statement in the current subprogram regardless of whether the current statement is a call to another subprogram (i.e., execution of the subprogram that was called is transparent). Finally, the Step Out option executes the remaining lines of a subprogram in which the current execution point lies. The next statement displayed is the statement following the subprogram call.

A **watch expression** is a user-defined expression that allows the programmer to observe its behavior. Watch expressions appear in the Watch window, and their values are automatically updated in break mode. Furthermore, the Locals window automatically displays the values of all declared variables in the current subprogram (all local variables).

## VB DEBUGGER EXAMPLE

To practice using the VB debugger, follow the steps outlined below:

1. The **Fibonacci numbers** are defined by the sequence $a_{n+1} = a_n + a_{n-1}$, where $a_1 = 1$ and $a_2 = 1$. The program below displays the Fibonacci numbers whose values are less than 50,000 and the square of each of these numbers. Enter this VB program on your computer. The program requires one command button (cmdFibonacci) and one picture box (picOutput).

```
' Fibonacci numbers and their squares
Option Explicit

Private Sub cmdFibonacci_Click()
' Show the Fibonacci numbers less than 50000

    Dim num1 As Long, num2 As Long, sum As Long

    num1 = 1
    num2 = 1

    picOutput.Cls
    picOutput.Print "Fibonacci #", "Squared Value"
    picOutput.Print num1, Square(num1)
```

```
        Do
            picOutput.Print num2, Square(num2)
            sum = num1 + num2
            num1 = num2
            num2 = sum
        Loop Until num2 > 50000
    End Sub

    Private Function Square(number As Long) As Double
    ' Compute the square of number

        Square = CDbl(number) * CDbl(number)
    End Function
```

2. Set the AutoRedraw property of the picOutput picture box to True. This maintains the output in the picture box even when its window is inactive.

3. Add a breakpoint to the first line following the Do statement. Move the cursor to this line and then select Debug/Toggle Breakpoint, press the F9 key, or click the Toggle Breakpoint button on the Debug toolbar. Notice that the VB editor highlights the line and places a circle next to it (Figure 7.3).

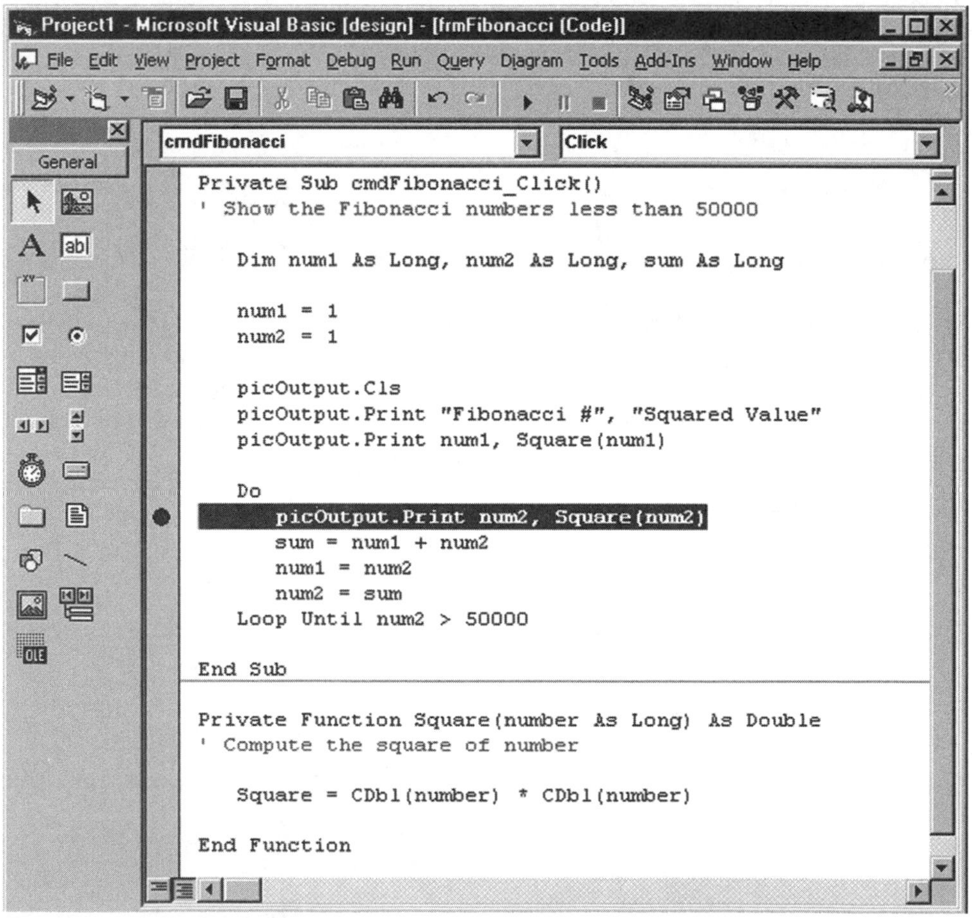

**Figure 7.3** Add a breakpoint

**4.** Run the program: Select Run/Start, press the F5 key, or click the Start button on the Standard or Debug toolbar. Click the cmdFibonacci command button. Notice that VB halts the program execution and displays the Code window shown in Figure 7.4. The next line to be executed is highlighted in yellow and a yellow pointer (**the instruction pointer**) appears in the left margin.

**5.** Open the Immediate window: Select View/Immediate Window or press CTRL+G on the keyboard. Type print num1, num2, sum in the Immediate window and then press the ENTER key. This command is immediately executed by VB, and you now see the current values of the variables as shown in Figure 7.5. Thus, the Immediate window allows you to dynamically interact with VB during the debugging process.

**6.** Open the Locals window: Select View/Locals Window from the menu bar. Notice that the Locals window contains the same information that we just displayed in the Immediate window. The screen should be similar to Figure 7.6.

**7.** The values of local variables can be changed using either the Locals window or the Immediate window. Click on the 1 under the Value column for num1 in the Locals window. Now, type 5 and press the ENTER key. Notice that the value of num1 changes to 5. Verify this change by typing print num1 in the Immediate window and pressing the ENTER key.

```
Project1 - Microsoft Visual Basic [break] - [frmFibonacci (Code)]

File  Edit  View  Project  Format  Debug  Run  Query  Diagram  Tools  Add-Ins  Window  Help

[cmdFibonacci]                        [Click]

Private Sub cmdFibonacci_Click()
' Show the Fibonacci numbers less than 50000

    Dim num1 As Long, num2 As Long, sum As Long

    num1 = 1
    num2 = 1

    picOutput.Cls
    picOutput.Print "Fibonacci #", "Squared Value"
    picOutput.Print num1, Square(num1)

    Do
        picOutput.Print num2, Square(num2)
        sum = num1 + num2
        num1 = num2
        num2 = sum
    Loop Until num2 > 50000

End Sub

Private Function Square(number As Long) As Double
' Compute the square of number

    Square = CDbl(number) * CDbl(number)

End Function
```

**Figure 7.4** Execution halts at the breakpoint

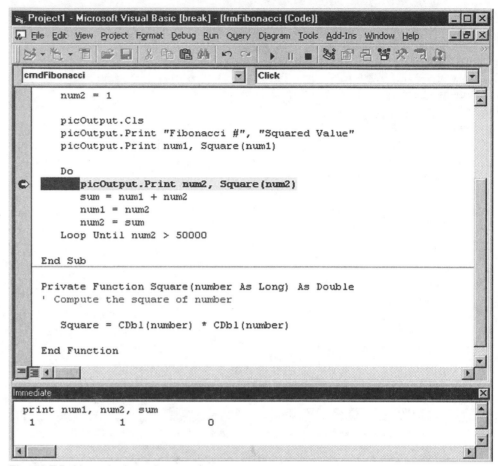

```
Project1 - Microsoft Visual Basic [break] - [frmFibonacci (Code)]

File  Edit  View  Project  Format  Debug  Run  Query  Diagram  Tools  Add-Ins  Window  Help

cmdFibonacci                          Click

        num2 = 1

        picOutput.Cls
        picOutput.Print "Fibonacci #", "Squared Value"
        picOutput.Print num1, Square(num1)

        Do
            picOutput.Print num2, Square(num2)
            sum = num1 + num2
            num1 = num2
            num2 = sum
        Loop Until num2 > 50000

    End Sub

    Private Function Square(number As Long) As Double
    ' Compute the square of number

        Square = CDbl(number) * CDbl(number)

    End Function
```

```
Immediate

print num1, num2, sum
 1              1              0
```

**Figure 7.5** Using the Immediate window

**8.** Change the value of num1 back to 1: In the Immediate window, type num1 = 1 and press the ENTER key. Notice that the value of num1 changes in the Locals window. The screen should now look similar to Figure 7.7.

**9.** Select Debug/Step Into, press F8, or click the Step Into button on the Debug toolbar. Notice that the instruction pointer moves to the next instruction to be executed.

**10.** Press F8 seven more times to return to the first statement inside the Do loop.

**11.** Now, select Debug/Step Over, press Shift+F8, or click the Step Over button on the Debug toolbar. Notice that VB executes the Square function and the instruction pointer steps "over" the function code.

**12.** Press F8 four times to return to the first statement inside the Do loop.

**13.** Select Run/Continue, press F5, or click the Continue button on the Standard or Debug toolbar. VB executes the loop until it reaches the same breakpoint during the next iteration.

**14.** Remove the breakpoint: Select Debug/Toggle Breakpoint, press the F9 key, or click the Toggle Breakpoint button on the Debug toolbar.

**15.** Step out of the current subprogram and end the program execution: select Debug/Step Out, press CTRL+SHIFT+F8, or click the Step Out button on the Debug toolbar. Alternately, you could continue program execution through the end of the code by repeating step 13.

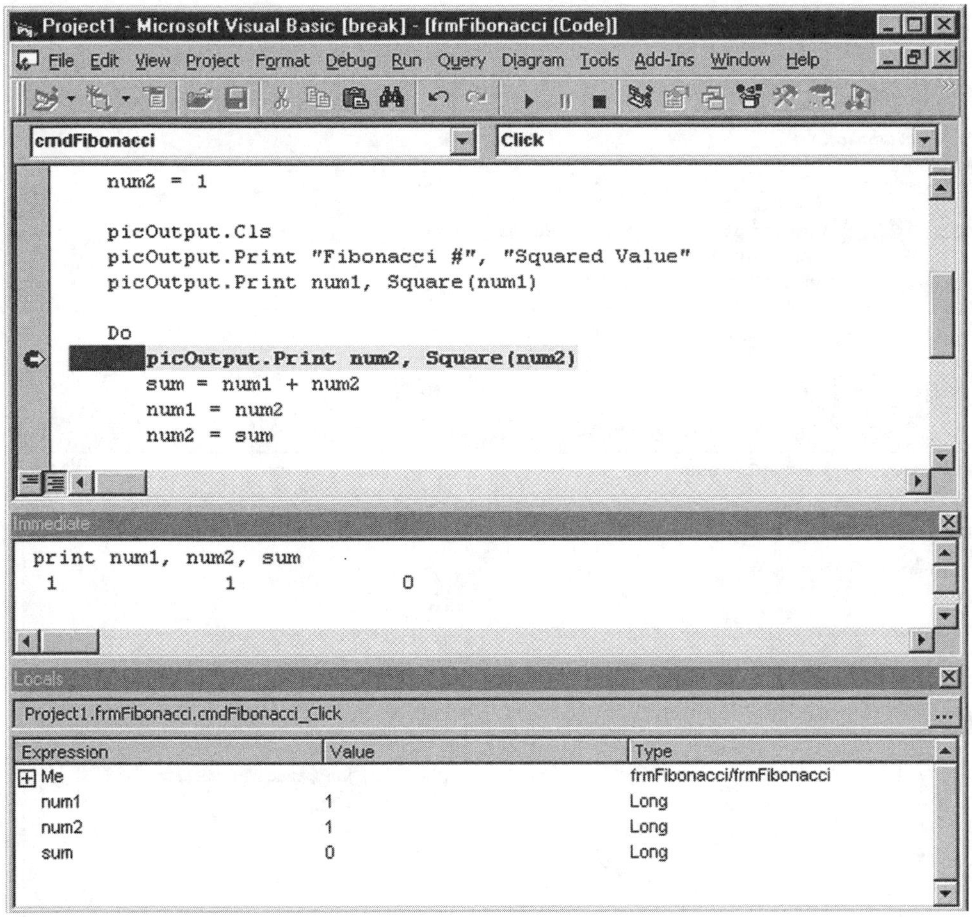

**Figure 7.6** Using the Locals window

**16.** View the results of your program by clicking the program name on the Windows taskbar.

**17.** Close the program by selecting Run/End or clicking the End button on the Standard or Debug toolbar.

**18.** Now, let's add a watch to our program. Select Debug/Add Watch from the menu bar and the Add Watch window shown in Figure 7.8 opens.

**19.** Type num1 as the Expression and select Break When Value Changes in the Watch Type frame. Click the OK button.

**20.** Run the program: Select Run/Start, press the F5 key, or click the Start button on the Standard or Debug toolbar. Click the cmdFibonacci command button. Notice that the program now halts when the value of num1 changes.

**21.** If the Watch window does not appear on your screen, select View/Watch Window or click the Watch Window icon on the Debug toolbar.

**22.** The value of num1 is shown in the Watch window. Like the Locals window, variable values may be altered in the Watch window. The screen should now appear as in Figure 7.9.

**23.** Select Run/Continue, press F5, or click the Continue button on the Standard or Debug toolbar. Notice that the value of num1 changes in the Watch window.

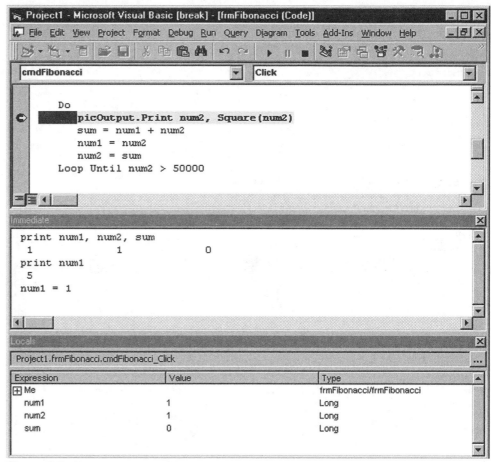

**Figure 7.7** Changing variable values

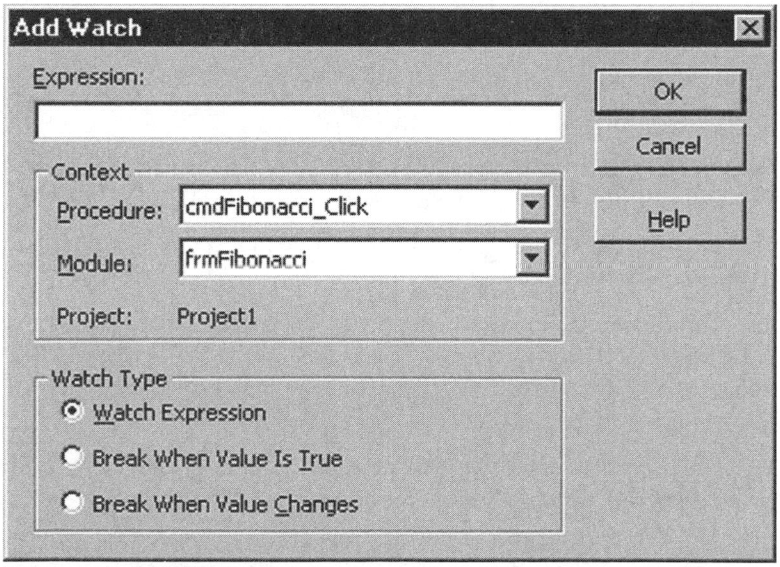

**Figure 7.8** Add Watch window

**24.** Remove the watch: Select Debug/Edit Watch or press CTRL+W. The Edit
Watch window shown in Figure 7.10 appears on the screen. Click the
Delete button to remove the watch.

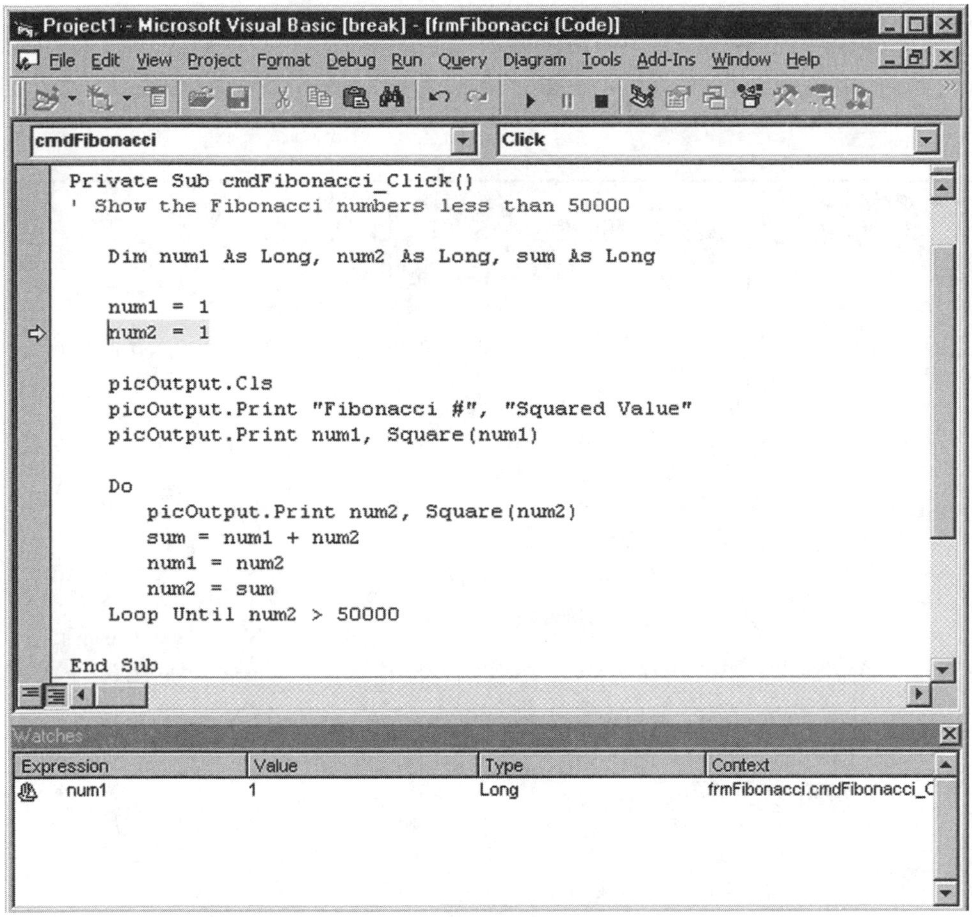

```
 Project1 - Microsoft Visual Basic [break] - [frmFibonacci (Code)]        _ □ X

 File  Edit  View  Project  Format  Debug  Run  Query  Diagram  Tools  Add-Ins  Window  Help    _ 8 X

 [toolbar]

 cmdFibonacci            ▼   Click                                    ▼

    Private Sub cmdFibonacci_Click()
    ' Show the Fibonacci numbers less than 50000

       Dim num1 As Long, num2 As Long, sum As Long

       num1 = 1
 ⇨     num2 = 1

       picOutput.Cls
       picOutput.Print "Fibonacci #", "Squared Value"
       picOutput.Print num1, Square(num1)

       Do
          picOutput.Print num2, Square(num2)
          sum = num1 + num2
          num1 = num2
          num2 = sum
       Loop Until num2 > 50000

    End Sub
```

| Watches | | | | X |
|---|---|---|---|---|
| Expression | Value | Type | Context | |
| ⚭  num1 | 1 | Long | frmFibonacci.cmdFibonacci_C | |

**Figure 7.9**  Using the Watch window

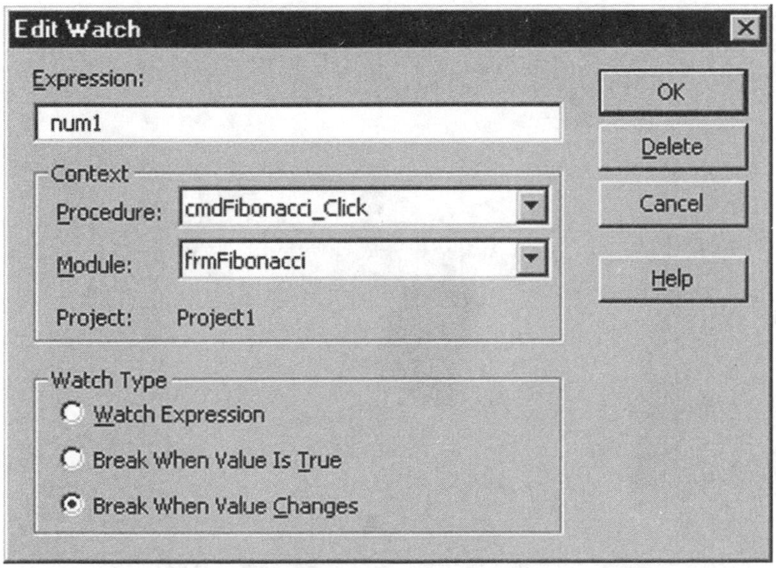

```
 Edit Watch                                                   X

    Expression:                                        ┌─────────┐
    ┌──────────────────────────────────────────┐      │   OK    │
    │ num1                                       │      └─────────┘
    └──────────────────────────────────────────┘      ┌─────────┐
    ┌─ Context ──────────────────────────────┐        │ Delete  │
    │                                          │       └─────────┘
    │  Procedure: [cmdFibonacci_Click    ▼]   │        ┌─────────┐
    │                                          │        │ Cancel  │
    │  Module:    [frmFibonacci          ▼]   │        └─────────┘
    │                                          │        ┌─────────┐
    │  Project:    Project1                    │        │  Help   │
    └──────────────────────────────────────────┘       └─────────┘
    ┌─ Watch Type ───────────────────────────┐
    │  ○ Watch Expression                     │
    │  ○ Break When Value Is True             │
    │  ⦿ Break When Value Changes             │
    └──────────────────────────────────────────┘
```

**Figure 7.10**  Edit Watch window

**25.** Select Run/Continue, press F5, or click the Continue button on the Standard or Debug toolbar to complete program execution.

26. View the results of your program by clicking the program name on the Windows taskbar.

27. Close the program by selecting Run/End or clicking the End button on the Standard or Debug toolbar.

---

## CASE STUDY
### A Failed Space Mission

On July 22, 1962, the Mariner 1 spacecraft was launched from Cape Canaveral, Florida to perform a Venus flyby and become the first spacecraft to successfully encounter another planet. Mariner 1 veered off course and the guidance system was directing it towards a crash, possibly in the North Atlantic shipping lanes or an inhabited area. The spacecraft was destroyed by the Range Safety Officer 293 seconds after launch. Several days later, the cause was isolated to the flight control computer generating incorrect steering commands due to a flaw in the programming. The Mariner 1 loss was attributed to the omission of a hyphen in coded computer instructions.

On August 27, 1962, the Mariner 2, a backup for the Mariner 1 mission, was successfully launched. Mariner 2 became the first spacecraft to encounter another planet, and it is responsible for many scientific discoveries concerning Venus.

The Mariner spacecraft is pictured in Figure 7.11.
(Reference: *New York Times,* July 28, 1962, p. 1, col. 4.)

---

## CASE STUDY:
### The Y2K Problem

The **Y2K (Year 2000) problem** stems from the use of a two-digit field to represent the year on a computer, either in the software or hardware. For instance, 1900 would be represented by 00 and 1999 by 99. Computer soft-

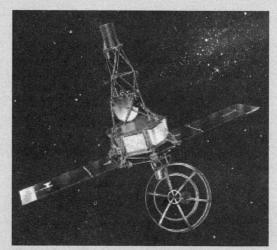

**Figure 7.11** The Mariner spacecraft
Photo courtesy of National Aeronautics and Space Administration (NASA).

ware and hardware that contain this problem are unable to address dates after December 31, 1999. Many appliances and other household devices rely upon computer technology and are susceptible to this flaw. Older mainframes and personal computers, especially those built prior to 1997, are most likely to be afflicted.

To what can we attribute the cause of this problem? Essentially, the cause of this bug was the shortsightedness of hardware and software engineers. Many years ago, computer memory was expensive. To conserve memory space, programmers and engineers shortened the year to two digits. This effectively halved the memory space required to store the year, but created a problem (the Y2K bug) in the long run.

# Summary

## Key Terms

**breakpoint**—a temporary stopping point during the execution of code for debugging purposes at design time

**bug**—an error in a computer program

**bullet-proofing**—error-proofing a computer program

**crash**—to end program execution due to a fatal error

**data dump**—a debugging method in which variable values are output to the screen or a data file

**debugging**—the process of finding and removing errors from a computer program

**design time**—the time when the programmer designs the user interface and writes the source code

**error-handling routine** (or **error-handler**)—instructions that are executed when a run-time error occurs

**fatal error**—an unrecoverable error that causes a computer program to halt execution

**Fibonacci numbers**—the numbers defined by the sequence $a_{n+1} = a_n + a_{n-1}$, where $a_1 = 1$ and $a_2 = 1$

**hand-execution (tracing)**—the process of a programmer acting as the computer and manually executing the source code with pencil and paper

**instruction pointer**—in a microprocessor, a register that contains the address of the next instruction to be executed. A pointer to the next instruction to be executed

**line label**—a word of at most 40 characters used to name a line of source code. The line label must begin at the left margin and end with a colon (:)

**line number**—a number used to label a line of code

**logic error**—an error in the logic or meaning of the code

**reboot**—to restart the computer system

**run time**—the time when the program is executing

**run-time error**—an error that occurs during program execution

**semantics**—meaning

**step**—to execute program code instruction-by-instruction for debugging purposes at design time

**syntax**—structure

**syntax error**—an error in the structure (spelling, grammar, or punctuation) of a computer program

**trap**—catch

**unconditional branch**—a "jump" over some program instructions regardless of condition as executed by the GoTo statement

**watch**—in the VB debugger, a method of examining the values of specific variables and expressions

**watch expression**—an expression that allows the programmer to observe its value for debugging purposes at design time

**Y2K (Year 2000) problem**—a problem in computer hardware or software due to representing the year as a two-digit field. Computers afflicted with this problem are unable to address dates after December 31, 1999

## Keywords

| | |
|---|---|
| *Methods:* | *Statements:* |
| Clear | Exit Function |
| | Exit Sub |
| *Objects:* | GoTo |
| Err | On Error |
| | Resume |
| *Properties:* | Resume Next |
| Number | |

## Key Concepts

● Bullet-proofing, or error-proofing, programs is a fundamental concept in computer science. The possibility of unanticipated inputs causing a catastrophic failure in real-world applications necessitates the error-proofing of code.

● There are three different types of program errors: run-time errors, syntax errors, and logic errors.

● Run-time errors are errors that occur during program execution and are often the result of invalid input from the user. Such errors include division-by-zero and data-type-mismatch errors.

● In VB, the Err object contains information about the most recent run-time error encountered.

● VB offers the programmer the ability to write error-handlers that utilize built-in error-trapping routines to provide control of program termination if a run-time error is encountered. The general form of a subprogram containing an error-handler appears below:

```
Private Sub cmdExample_Click()
' General form of the On Error statement and placement of the
' error-handling routine

  On Error GoTo ErrorHandler      ' Enable error-trapping
➥ routine

  [subprogram code]
```

```
    Exit Sub

    ErrorHandler:

      [error-handling routine]

    End Sub
```

- VB's built-in error-trapping requires the use of the GoTo statement to perform an unconditional branch. Unconditional branches are neither highly encouraged nor desired by advanced programmers. They make the code harder to read, program logic more difficult to follow, documentation harder to write, and debugging very difficult.

- GoTo statements should only be used in built-in error-trapping routines and should not appear anywhere else in the code.

- Syntax errors are errors in the code structure (spelling, grammar, or punctuation). VB can assist a programmer with identifying these errors through its automatic syntax checking and by requiring the use of explicit variable declarations.

- Logic errors are errors in the semantics, or meaning, of the code. These errors are often the most difficult to identify and debug. Common logic errors include infinite loops and incorrect mathematical formulae.

- Standard debugging techniques work regardless of the computer language being used. The two standard debugging techniques include the data dump and hand-execution of code.

- The data dump requires the programmer to add additional code to output values of important variables and other information during program execution.

- Hand-executing (or tracing) code is performed by the programmer using a pencil and paper; this is an invaluable computer programming skill.

- VB contains a built-in debugger to assist the programmer in finding and correcting errors at design time. This debugger allows the programmer to step through code, add breakpoints and watches, and examine and modify variable values.

## Review Questions

1. Why is it important for a programmer to "bullet-proof" a program? Give an example.

2. Describe the difference between a run-time error, syntax error, and logic error and give an example of each error. What features does VB offer to help prevent each of these errors?

3. What is the purpose of the Err object in VB?

4. What is an error-handler? Write the general syntax for an error-handling routine in a subprogram structure.

5. What does the GoTo statement do? What disadvantages does this statement have that make it unattractive?

6. Explain the differences between the data dump and hand-execution debugging techniques? State some advantages of hand-executing or tracing code.

7. Describe the contents of the Debug toolbar.

8. What is a breakpoint? a watch?

9. What is displayed and what operations can be performed in the Locals window? in the Immediate window? in the Watch window?

10. Describe the difference between the Step Into, Step Over, and Step Out commands in the VB Debugger.

## Chapter 7 Problems

1. Hand-execute the following code. What is the output?

```
Option Explicit

Private Sub cmdProblem1_Click()
' Chapter 7, Problem 1

    Dim num1 As Double, num2 As Double

    num1 = 5#
    num2 = 10#

    Call Confuse1(num1, num2)
    Call Confuse2(num2, num1)
    Call Output(num1, num2)
End Sub

Private Sub Confuse1(ByVal x As Double, y As Double)
' Confuse me once

    x = x - 1 / 4
    y = y * 2 + 5
End Sub

Private Sub Confuse2(val1 As Double, ByVal val2 As Double)
' Confuse me twice, but be nice!

    val1 = val1 / 5
    val2 = val2 - 3
End Sub

Private Sub Output(num1 As Double, num2 As Double)
' Output variable values

    picOutput.Print num1, num2
End Sub
```

2. Type in the code from Problem 1. Trace the code by using a data dump to the screen. What is the output of the code? Check your answer to Problem 1.

3. Now, use the VB debugger to trace the code from Problem 1. Add watches and breakpoints as necessary. Practice using the Step Into, Step Over, and Step Out commands. What is the difference between these commands?

4. Hand-execute the following code. What is the output?

```
Option Explicit

Private Sub cmdProblem4_Click()
' Chapter 7, Problem 4

    Dim first As String, last As String
    Dim target As String, pos As Integer

    first = "Humpty"
    last = "D"

    If Len(first) > Len(last) Then
        target = first
    Else
        target = last
    End If

    pos = 1
    Do
        picOutput.Print Mid(first, pos, 1);
        picOutput.Print Mid(last, pos, 1);
        pos = pos + 1
    Loop Until pos > Len(target)
End Sub
```

**5.** Type in the code from Problem 4. Trace the code by using a data dump to the screen. What is the output of the code? Check your answer to Problem 4.

**6.** Use the VB debugger to trace the code from Problem 4. Add watches and breakpoints as necessary.

**7.** Write a function named `AveScore` that returns the average exam score. The parameters include `totalOfScores` and `numberOfStudents`. Be sure to use built-in error-trapping. Write a driver program to test your function using the following test cases:

| totalOfScores | numberOfStudents |
|---|---|
| 500 | 5 |
| 603 | 7 |
| 0 | 0 |

**8.** Find all errors in the following code:

```
Private Sub cmdProblem8_Click()
' Chapter 7, Problem 8

    Dim count1 As Integer, count2 As Integer
    Dim count3 As Integer

    For count1 = 1 To 10
        count3 = 1
        For count2 = 1 To 20
            Do While count3 + count2 > 0
                picOutput.Print coun3
                count3 = count3 + 1
            Loop
```

```
                count1 = count1 + 2
           Next count1
       Next count2
    End Sub
```

**9.** Find all errors in the following code:

```
Option Explicit

Private Sub cmdProblem9_Click()
' Chapter 7, Problem 9

    Dim a, b, c As Single
    Dim check As Boolean

    a = CSng(Val(txtValueA.Text))
    b = CStr(Val(txtValueB.Text))
    c = Chr(txtValueC.Text)

    check = a < b
    If check Then
        If a < b < c Then
            picOutput.Print "c is largest"
        Else
            picOutput.Print "b is largest"
        End If
    Else
        If a > c Then
            picOutput.Print "c is largest"
        Else
            pictOutput.Print "a is largest"
        End If
    End If
End Sub
```

**10.** Find all errors in the following code:

```
Option Exp

Private Sub cmdProblem10_Click()
' Chapter 7, Problem 10

    For counter = 1 To 50
        picOutput.print counter, counter ** 2
        counter = counter + 1
    Next counter

    For counter = 100 To 1
        picOutput.Print counter, counter \ 2
    Next counter
End Function
```

# Advanced Data Structures

## Chapter Objectives

In this chapter, you will:

- Learn the difference between static and dynamic data structures

- Become familiar with array data structures

- Learn how to create records and user-defined data types

- Become acquainted with the operation of stacks, queues, deques, and lists and how to write VB code to implement these data structures

- Be introduced to pointers and linked lists and how to implement them in VB

*→ holds multiple data items*

**A** **data structure** is, as its name implies, a structure that contains data. In computer science, entire classes are devoted to data structures and numerous texts have been written concerning the best methods to organize and store data. This chapter introduces many of the advanced data structures common to most high-level languages.

## STATIC VS. DYNAMIC DATA STRUCTURES

First, a data structure may be either static or dynamic. A **static data structure** has a fixed type and size; it cannot be changed unless a programmer modifies the source code. A **dynamic data structure**, on the other hand, can change size (and sometimes type) during program execution (i.e., dynamically). Some data structures are inherently dynamic and are created and destroyed only at run time. Finally, some data structures may be declared as either static or dynamic structures.

*dynamic = run time*

# ARRAYS

**Key Terms**

**static data structure**—a data structure of a fixed type and size; it cannot be changed unless a programmer modifies the source code

**dynamic data structure**—a data structure that can change size (and sometimes type) during program execution

Consider the following problem: A computer programming class consisting of 10 students takes an exam. The instructor wants to write a computer program that outputs the average exam score and a phrase describing each student's score relative to the class average (for example, "Above Average," "Average," or "Below Average"). Using the programming techniques presented thus far, you might write a program similar to the one that follows.

```
Option Explicit
Private Sub Compare(num As Integer, score As Single,
➥ average As Single)
' Compare student score to the average score
    picOutput.Print "Student "; Trim(CStr(num)); ": ";
    If score < average Then
        picOutput.Print "Below Average"
    ElseIf score = average Then
        picOutput.Print "Average"
    Else
        picOutput.Print "Above Average"
    End If
End Sub

Private Sub cmdClassAverage_Click()
' Find the class average and compare student scores
    Dim student1 As Single, student2 As Single,
    ➥ student3 As Single
    Dim student4 As Single, student5 As Single,
    ➥ student6 As Single
    Dim student7 As Single, student8 As Single,
    ➥ student9 As Single
    Dim student10 As Single, aveScore As Single

    student1 = CSng(txtStudent1.Text)
    student2 = CSng(txtStudent2.Text)
    student3 = CSng(txtStudent3.Text)
    student4 = CSng(txtStudent4.Text)
    student5 = CSng(txtStudent5.Text)
    student6 = CSng(txtStudent6.Text)
    student7 = CSng(txtStudent7.Text)
    student8 = CSng(txtStudent8.Text)
    student9 = CSng(txtStudent9.Text)
    student10 = CSng(txtStudent10.Text)

    aveScore = (student1 + student2 + student3 + student4
    ➥ + student5 + _
        student6 + student7 + student8 + student9
        ➥ + student10) / CSng(10)

    picOutput.Cls
    picOutput.Print "Average Score: "; aveScore
    picOutput.Print

    Call Compare(1, student1, aveScore)
```

```
        Call Compare(2, student2, aveScore)
        Call Compare(3, student3, aveScore)
        Call Compare(4, student4, aveScore)
        Call Compare(5, student5, aveScore)
        Call Compare(6, student6, aveScore)
        Call Compare(7, student7, aveScore)
        Call Compare(8, student8, aveScore)
        Call Compare(9, student9, aveScore)
        Call Compare(10, student10, aveScore)
    End Sub
```

Notice that a separate variable must be declared for each student's exam score as well as a variable for the average score. As illustrated by the form in Figure 8.1, 10 separate text boxes are needed to input the student exam scores.

This programming technique works fine for a small class of 10 students, but what happens when the class size is larger (say, 50 or 100 students)? As you can imagine, writing the variable declarations and mathematical formula (not to mention designing the user interface) would become quite tedious. Fortunately, there is a better (shorter, simpler, and faster) way to write this program using the array data structure.

*element = cell*

An **array** is a set of sequentially indexed elements of the same intrinsic data type. Each **element** of an array has a unique identifying index number. Figure 8.2 depicts the physical structure of an array.

In VB, a Dim statement is used to declare a **static array** as follows:

*— stays until program terminates*

```
Dim arrayName(start To stop) As DataType
```

In this statement, *start* is the starting array index value and *stop* is the final index value. *start* and *stop* must be integer values with *start* less than or equal to *stop*. *arrayName* is any valid variable name, and *DataType* is any built-in or user-defined data type.

### Key Terms

**array**—a set of sequentially indexed elements of the same intrinsic data type
**element**—a single location within an array; each element has a unique identifying index number, and each element acts as a separate variable that can be accessed using this index value

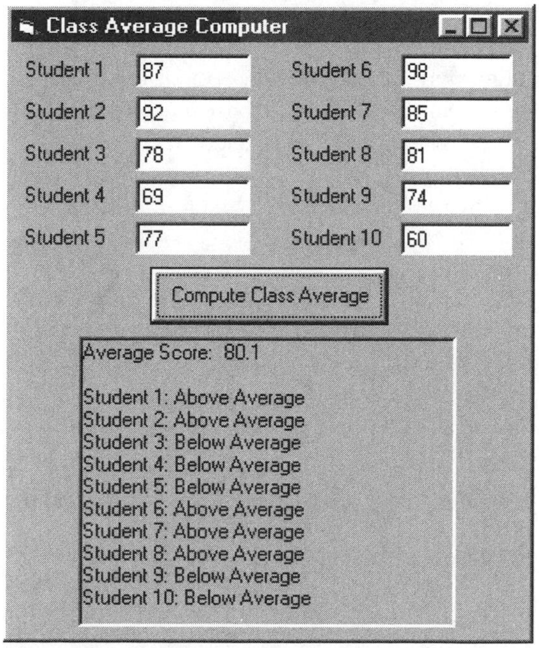

**Figure 8.1** Class Average computer

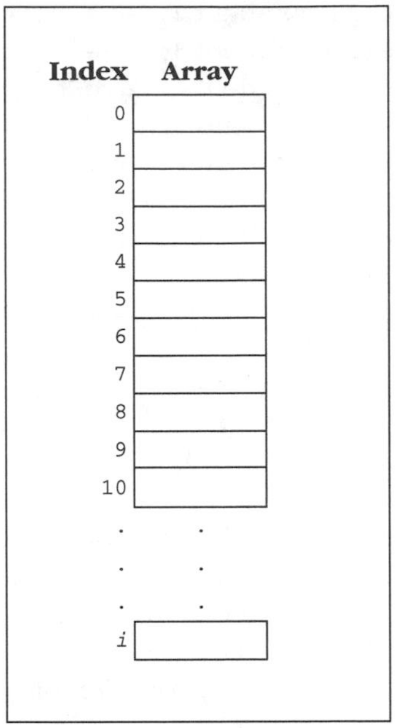

**Figure 8.2** Physical diagram of an array structure

## THE OPTION BASE STATEMENT

When *start*, the lower bound of an array, is not explicitly stated, it is controlled by the `Option Base` statement. The default value of *start* is zero if it is unspecified and no `Option Base` statement is present. Thus, the statement `Dim myArray(9) As Integer` has 10 integer array elements, at indices 0 through 9, when the `Option Base` statement is absent. The general syntax of the `Option Base` statement follows:

```
Option Base { 0 | 1 }
```

In the above syntax, the {0 | 1} indicates that either a 0 or a 1 must follow the `Option Base` statement. Thus, the two possible statements are `Option Base 0` and `Option Base 1`. Since the default base is 0, the `Option Base` statement is required to start array indices at 1. If it is used, it can appear only once in a module and must precede all array declarations containing dimensions. The following code illustrates the use of the `Option Base` statement:

```
Option Explicit
Option Base 1

Private Sub cmdArrayExample_Click()
' An example array declaration using the Option Base
  statement

  Dim myArray(5) As Integer

  Dim counter As Integer

  For counter = 1 To 5          ' The Option Base 1
    statement
```

`Option Base 1` informs VB that 1 is the starting index value for all arrays with unspecified lower bounds in their declarations. So, `myArray` contains five elements, having index values 1 through 5.

* remember
Subscript = index

```
        myArray(counter) = counter   ' makes 0 an invalid
        ➡ index
    Next counter

End Sub
```

In the above code, `myArray` has only five index values, 1 through 5. The starting index value is 1, and 0 is an invalid index due to the `Option Base 1` statement.

## ACCESSING AN ARRAY ELEMENT

Each element of an array acts as a separate variable that can be accessed using its unique index value. To access a specific array element, use the form *arrayName(indexValue)* as in the above code. The following statement, for example, assigns the value 10 to the fifth element of `myArray`:

```
        myArray(5) = 10
```

◀—— Assign the integer value 10 to the fifth element of `myArray`.

As demonstrated by the following code, our earlier Class Average program can be simplified by using an array variable.

```
Option Explicit

Private Sub Compare(num As Integer, score As Single,
➡ average As Single)
' Compare student score to the average score
    picOutput.Print "Student "; Trim(CStr(num)); ": ";
    If score < average Then
        picOutput.Print "Below Average"
    ElseIf score = average Then
        picOutput.Print "Average"
    Else
        picOutput.Print "Above Average"
    End If
End Sub

Private Sub cmdClassAverage_Click()
' Enter student scores, compute class average, and
' compare student scores
    Dim student(1 To 10) As Single   ' Student scores array
    Dim sumScores As Single          ' Sum of all student
    ➡ scores
    Dim aveScore As Single           ' Class average
    Dim count As Integer             ' Loop counter

    sumScores = CSng(0)
    For count = 1 To 10
        student(count) = CSng(InputBox("Enter exam score for
        ➡ student " & _
                        Trim(CStr(count)), "Enter Score"))
        sumScores = sumScores + student(count)
    Next count
```

➡

```
                        aveScore = sumScores / CSng(10)

                        picOutput.Cls
                        picOutput.Print "Average Score: "; aveScore
                        picOutput.Print

                        For count = 1 To 10
                            Call Compare(count, student(count), aveScore)
                        Next count
                    End Sub
```

## ARRAY STRUCTURES AND NOTATION

Arrays may be classified by their index structures. An array with one index is a **one-dimensional array**. The mathematical equivalent of this array is a vector. A **two-dimensional array** is an array with two separate indices, and a matrix is its mathematical equivalent. Finally, a **multidimensional array** (or *n*-dimensional array) is an array with more than two indices. Figure 8.3 displays physical examples of these array structures.

✱ AKA vector

✱ myArray (rows, columns, depth)

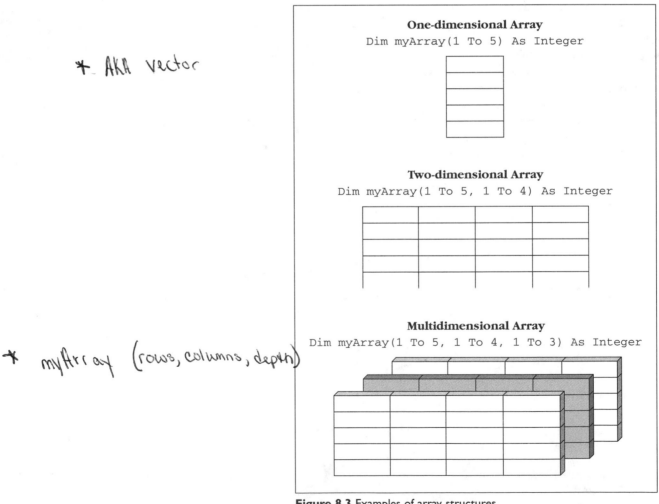

**Figure 8.3** Examples of array structures

The notation for arrays in most programming languages directly parallels mathematical notation. For example, an element of a vector is commonly denoted by $x_i$, where $x$ is the variable representing the vector and $i$ is the index value. Since we cannot easily write a subscript in a program, we use parentheses instead; the $x_i$ element of a vector corresponds to the x(i) element of an array.

## DYNAMIC ARRAYS

Now, let's modify the Class Average program to allow for an unknown number of students in the class. One way to overcome this problem is to use a static array whose length is the maximum possible class size and use another variable to specify the exact number of students in the class. However, this method wastes memory space for any class smaller in size than the maximum, and it requires modifying the source code if the maximum class size increases. A better solution is to use a **dynamic array**.

To declare a dynamic array, use the Dim statement with empty parentheses after the variable name. After declaring a dynamic array, the ReDim statement is used within a subprogram to define the number of dimensions and elements in the array. In VB, the ReDim statement can only change the data type of Variant arrays. Additionally, using the ReDim statement on a static array generates an error. The syntax of the ReDim statement follows:

```
ReDim arrayName(subscripts) As DataType
```

The ReDim statement re-initializes the array (clears all of its contents). To keep the data already in the array and prevent re-initialization, the Preserve keyword must follow the ReDim keyword. The syntax is as follows:

```
ReDim Preserve arrayName(subscripts) As DataType
```

— keeps initial data
(no re-initializing)

The Preserve keyword does not allow the number of dimensions of the array to be changed, but will allow the last dimension to be resized. When resizing the last dimension, only the upper bound can be changed; resizing the lower bound causes an error. If the last dimension is decreased, the data in the eliminated elements is lost.

There are two useful array-related functions. The LBound and UBound functions return long integer values corresponding to the smallest and largest index values for a specified dimension of an array variable, respectively. The general syntax is as follows:

```
LBound(arrayName [, dimensionNumber])
UBound(arrayName [, dimensionNumber])
```

In the following modification of the previous example, a dynamic array is used to allow for any number of students:

```
Option Explicit

Private Sub Compare(num As Integer, score As Single,
➥ average As Single)
' Compare student score to the average score
```

➥

```
            picOutput.Print "Student "; Trim(CStr(num)); ": ";
            If score < average Then
                picOutput.Print "Below Average"
            ElseIf score = average Then
                picOutput.Print "Average"
            Else
                picOutput.Print "Above Average"
            End If
    End Sub

    Private Sub cmdClassAverage_Click()
    ' Enter number of students and student scores, compute
        ➥ class average, and
    ' compare student scores
        Dim student() As Single          ' Dynamic array of
            ➥ student scores
        Dim numStudents As Integer       ' Number of students
            ➥ in class
        Dim sumScores As Single          ' Sum of all student
            ➥ scores
        Dim aveScore As Single           ' Class average
        Dim count As Integer             ' Loop counter

        numStudents = CInt(txtNumber.Text)

        If numStudents > 0 Then

            ReDim student(1 To numStudents) As Single
            sumScores = CSng(0)
            For count = 1 To numStudents
              student(count) = CSng(InputBox("Enter exam score
                ➥ for student " & _
                              Trim(CStr(count)), "Enter Score"))
              sumScores = sumScores + student(count)
            Next count

            aveScore = sumScores / CSng(numStudents)

            picOutput.Cls
            picOutput.Print "Average Score: "; aveScore
            picOutput.Print

            For count = 1 To numStudents
                Call Compare(count, student(count), aveScore)
            Next count

        End If
    End Sub
```

*leave element (index) blank to pass entire array* ← **ARRAYS AS ARGUMENTS AND PARAMETERS**

Both of the previous code examples pass an array element as an argument of the `Compare` procedure. To demonstrate using entire arrays as arguments and parameters of subprograms, we now modify the Compare procedure so that it performs the loop from the calling routine:

```
Private Sub Compare(number As Integer, score() As Single,
➡ average As Single)
' Compare each student score to the average score
    Dim count As Integer   ' Loop counter

    For count = 1 To number
        picOutput.Print "Student "; Trim(CStr(count)); ": ";
        If score(count) < average Then
            picOutput.Print "Below Average"
        ElseIf score(count) = average Then
            picOutput.Print "Average"
        Else
            picOutput.Print "Above Average"
        End If
    Next count
End Sub
```

We must also modify the calling routine [cmdClassAverage_Click()]. We replace the loop

```
For count = 1 To numStudents
    Call Compare(count, student(count), aveScore)
Next count
```

with the following line:

```
Call Compare(numStudents, student(), aveScore)
```

In summary, to pass an array variable as an argument of a subprogram, simply write the array variable name followed by empty parentheses in the argument list. To denote an array parameter in a subprogram definition, write the parameter name followed by empty parentheses in the parameter list.

## PROGRAMMING KEY: WARNING

Array variables can only be passed by reference. We can simulate passing arrays by value simply by making a local copy of the array within the subprogram:

```
Private Sub Example(inArray() As Integer)
' Simulate passing an array by value
    Dim copyArray() As Integer
    Dim lower As Long, upper As Long
    Dim counter As Integer

    lower = LBound(inArray)
    upper = UBound(inArray)
    ReDim copyArray(lower To upper) As Integer

    For counter = lower To upper
        copyArray(counter) = inArray(counter)   ' Copy the
        ➡ array
```

```
                                                             ' element-by
                                                          ➥  -element

        Next counter
              .
              .
              .
        End Sub
```

## PROGRAMMING KEY: VB 6.0 FEATURES

Previous versions of Visual Basic required copying arrays element by element (as in the previous *Warning* box). VB 6.0 allows dynamic arrays to appear on the left side of an assignment statement, but static arrays can only appear on the right side of an assignment. Thus, VB 6.0 provides a method to easily copy a static array into a dynamic array. Rewriting the code from the previous *Warning* box, we simulate passing an array by value in VB 6.0 as follows:

```
Private Sub Example(inArray() As Integer)
' Simulate passing an array by value
    Dim copyArray() As Integer
    Dim lower As Long, upper As Long

    lower = LBound(inArray)
    upper = UBound(inArray)
    ReDim copyArray(lower To upper) As Integer

    copyArray = inArray    ' This assignment only works in
    ➥ VB 6.0
              .
              .
              .
    End Sub
```

Additionally, VB 6.0 allows functions and properties procedures to return arrays.

### GUI Design Tips

Arrays are capable of storing large quantities of information. When working with large arrays, it is often easier for a user to enter data into a data file rather than text boxes or input boxes in the user interface. The data file can then be used as an input file for the program. Chapter 5 Supplement and Chapter 9 discuss file input and output in VB.

## CASE STUDY
## Using Arrays

The Del Presto Company manufactures toasters, blenders, and cutting boards. Each toaster sold yields the Del Presto Company a profit of $12, each blender gives a $20 profit, and each cutting board gives a $7 profit. Ruth, the company's accountant, has the sales data for the past three months. She wants to figure out the monthly profit for each of the past three months, the total profit over the past three months, and the average monthly profit. Ruth does this same computation every quarter (i.e., every three months). Can you write a VB program to help Ruth?

Arrays are very helpful in a program of this nature. There are three different products and three sales figures per product, giving a total of nine sales figures. Rather than creating nine text boxes on a form, Ruth uses an input file named `DelPresto.DAT` to enhance the flexibility of the program. Ruth's input file contains the three product names, profit per product sold, and three months of sales figures per product. So, if Del Presto Company changes its products, Ruth can modify the input file rather than the program. Ruth's VB program appears below:

```
' Del Presto Company
' Quarterly Profit Computer
' -------------------------

' Input File Name: C:\DelPresto.DAT
' Input File Format:

'          product1, product2, product3  {Strings}
'          profit1, profit2, profit3     {Single precision}

' SALES: {Integers}
'                 Products
'           -------------->
'           | prod1/month1, prod2/month1, prod3/month1
'   Month   | prod1/month2, prod2/month2, prod3/month2
'           | prod1/month3, prod2/month3, prod3/month3
'           V

' Example Input File:

'   "Toasters","Blenders","Cutting Boards"
'   12.00,20.00,7.00
'   500,300,150
'   620,125,480
'   370,165,400

Option Explicit
Const MONTHS = 3     ' 3 months of data per quarter
Const PRODS = 3      ' 3 products

Private Sub cmdCompute_Click()
' Compute quarterly profit using the
' monthly sales data in the input file

    Dim products(1 To PRODS) As String
    Dim profit(1 To PRODS) As Single
    Dim sales(1 To MONTHS, 1 To PRODS) As Integer
    Dim item As Integer, mnth As Integer
    Dim subtotal As Single, total As Single

    On Error GoTo ErrorHandler
    Call OpenFile

    picOutput.Cls     ' Clear the picture box

    ' Input the product names
    picOutput.Print "PRODUCTS:"
    picOutput.Print "--------"
    For item = 1 To PRODS
```

```
          Input #1, products(item)
          picOutput.Print products(item),
     Next item
     picOutput.Print

     ' Input the profit per product
     picOutput.Print
     picOutput.Print "PROFIT PER PRODUCT:"
     picOutput.Print "------------------"
     For item = 1 To PRODS
          Input #1, profit(item)
          picOutput.Print Format(profit(item), "currency"),
     Next item
     picOutput.Print

     ' Input the sales data for each product and month
     ' Compute monthly profits and total profit
     picOutput.Print
     total = 0#
     For mnth = 1 To MONTHS
          subtotal = 0#
          For item = 1 To PRODS
               Input #1, sales(mnth, item)
               subtotal = subtotal + (profit(item) *
               ➥ CSng(sales(mnth, item)))
          Next item
          picOutput.Print "Month " & CStr(mnth) & ": "; _
                    Format(subtotal, "currency")
          total = total + subtotal
     Next mnth
     picOutput.Print "Total Profit:    "; Format(total,
     ➥ "currency")

     ' Compute average monthly profit
     If (MONTHS > 0) Then
          picOutput.Print "Average Profit: "; Format
          ➥ (total / MONTHS, "currency")
     End If

     Call CloseFile
     Exit Sub

ErrorHandler:
     MsgBox CStr(Err.Description), , "RUN-TIME ERROR"
     Call CloseFile
End Sub

Private Sub OpenFile()
' Open the input file
     Open "C:\DelPresto.DAT" For Input As #1
End Sub

Private Sub CloseFile()
' Close the input file
     Close #1
End Sub
```

A sample `DelPresto.DAT` input file follows:

```
"Toasters","Blenders","Cutting Boards"
12.00,20.00,7.00
500,300,150
620,125,480
370,165,400
```

The output of Ruth's program for this input file appears below:

```
PRODUCTS:
---------

Toasters          Blenders          Cutting Boards

PROFIT PER PRODUCT:
-------------------

$12.00            $20.00            $7.00


Month 1: $13,050.00
Month 2: $13,300.00
Month 3: $10,540.00
Total Profit:    $36,890.00
Average Profit: $12,296.67
```

To test your understanding of arrays, try modifying Ruth's program to compute the total profit per item over the three months. In other words, compute the profits for toaster sales, blender sales, and cutting board sales. What is the total profit? Why?

## RECORDS AND USER-DEFINED DATA TYPES

Now that you've been introduced to arrays, the next step is to learn how to do something useful with them. Consider the design of a simple address book program. The variable declarations for this program appear below. For the sake of simplicity, we use static array variables.

```
Dim firstName(50) As String     ' First Name
Dim lastName(50) As String      ' Last Name
Dim address(50) As String       ' Street Address
Dim city(50) As String          ' City
Dim state(50) As String         ' State
Dim zipCode(50) As String       ' Zip Code
Dim phoneNumber(50) As String   ' Telephone Number
Dim number As Integer           ' Number of addresses in
➥ address book
```

Each of these variable declarations creates an array variable that will hold one of the different pieces of data required to form a complete address card (address and telephone number data). There is an array for the first name, last name, street address, and so on. Additionally, the `number` variable specifies the number of active address cards in our address book program, where the maximum allowable number of active addresses is 51 (assuming `Option Base 0`).

An address book program using these variable declarations as the underlying data structure relies heavily upon proper correspondence of the index values. In other words, the person with firstName(1) and lastName(1) lives at street address address(1) in city(1) and state(1). Furthermore, all other pertinent information for this individual is in the first element (index 1) of each of the remaining arrays. Arrays of this form are called **parallel arrays**. Unfortunately, if the data is sorted incorrectly or the index values somehow become misaligned (either through a programming error or file I/O error), all of the address book data is corrupted. In this case, the reliability of the entire data set is questionable. Records provide a safer and more reliable data structure than parallel arrays for implementing our address book program.

## RECORDS

A **record** encapsulates a group of related data. Each different piece of information in a record is called a **field**. The data set consisting of all records forms a **database**. In our address book example, each address card is a record. Each record has first name, last name, street address, city, state, zip code, and telephone number fields. The database consists of all address cards, or the entire address book.

## USER-DEFINED DATA TYPES

In VB, records are created using **user-defined data types**. The general syntax for declaring a user-defined data type is as follows:

```
Type RecordName
    fieldName1 (subscripts) as DataType1
    fieldName2 (subscripts) as DataType2
                    .
                    .
                    .
    fieldNameN (subscripts) as DataTypeN
End Type
```

The Type statement can be used only at the module level. Once a user-defined type is declared, a variable of that type can be declared anywhere within its scope by using the Dim, Private, Public, ReDim, or Static keywords. Notice that the fields of a user-defined type can be arrays.

The following type declaration, for instance, defines the StudentInfo data type. We also declare a static array students of type StudentInfo.

```
Private Type StudentInfo
    lastName As String
    firstName As String
    age As Integer
End Type

Dim students(25) As StudentInfo
```

To access a specific field of a record, separate the record variable from the field name with a period ("."). This **dot-separator** is also used to separate properties and methods from objects in VB. Thus, the form recordVariableName.fieldName accesses the *fieldName* field of record variable *recordVariableName*. Continuing the above code, we assign data to students(0), the first student record:

```
students(0).lastName = "Smith"
students(0).firstName = "John"
students(0).age = 19
```

Alternatively, we can use the With statement to access the fields of a record. Rewriting these assignment statements using the With statement yields:

```
With students(0)
    .lastName = "Smith"
    .firstName = "John"
    .age = 19
End With
```

The general syntax of the With statement is as follows:

```
With Object
    [statements]
End With
```

## USING RECORDS

To conclude this section, we illustrate the use of records in the address book program. Figure 8.4 displays the user interface, and the routine used to input the address book records is shown in the accompanying code. Additionally, Chapter 9 discusses the use of records for file input and output.

```
' Address Book Program
Option Explicit
Option Base 1
```

This code contains only the routine to add an address card to the address book. Also, this code uses global variables to simplify the implementation.

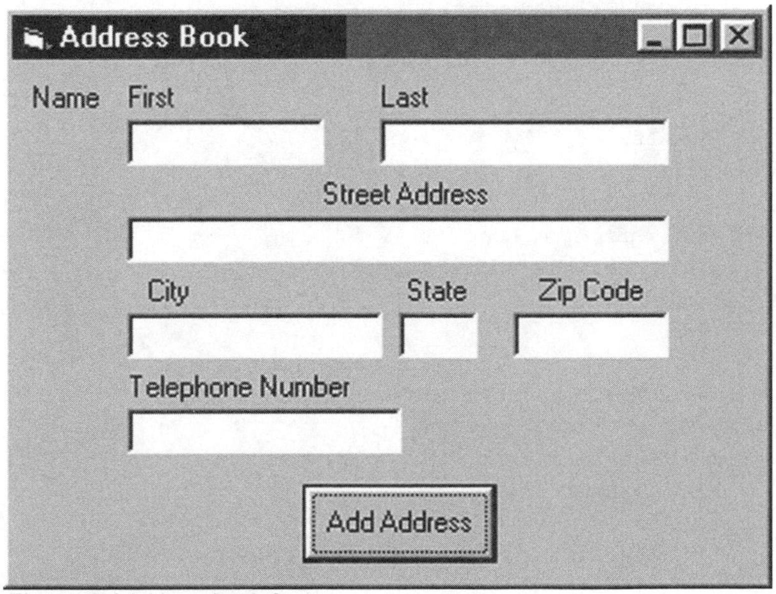

**Figure 8.4** Address book form

```
                    Const MAXSIZE = 50    ' Maximum number of address cards

                    ' User-defined data type
                    Private Type AddressCard
                        firstName As String       ' First Name
                        lastName As String        ' Last Name
                        address As String         ' Street Address
                        city As String            ' City
                        state As String           ' State
                        zipCode As String         ' Zip Code
                        phoneNumber As String     ' Telephone Number
                    End Type

                    ' GLOBAL VARIABLES
                    ' These global variables make the coding of this program
                    ' sufficiently easier. Suffice it to say, this is one
                       ➡ occasion where global variables are desirable.
                    Dim addressBook(MAXSIZE) As AddressCard ' Address book
                    ➡ data: array of AddressCard records
                    Dim number As Integer                   ' Number of
                    ➡ address cards in the database

                    Private Sub cmdAddAddress_Click()
                    ' Add address card
                        If number < MAXSIZE Then
                            number = number + 1
                            With addressBook(number)
                                .firstName = txtFirstName.Text
                                .lastName = txtLastName.Text
                                .address = txtAddress.Text
                                .city = txtCity.Text
                                .state = txtState.Text
                                .zipCode = txtZip.Text
                                .phoneNumber = txtPhoneNumber.Text
                            End With
                            Call ClearForm
                        Else
                            MsgBox "Unable to add new address card", , "ADDRESS
                            ➡ BOOK FULL"
                        End If
                    End Sub

                    Private Sub Form_Load()
                    ' Initialize the address book
                        number = 0
                    End Sub

                    Private Sub ClearForm()
                    ' Clear the text boxes
                        txtFirstName.Text = ""
                        txtLastName.Text = ""
                        txtAddress.Text = ""
                        txtCity.Text = ""
```

```
        txtState.Text = ""
        txtZip.Text = ""
        txtPhoneNumber.Text = ""
    End Sub
```

## STACKS, QUEUES, DEQUES, AND LISTS

A **list** is an ordered set of data to which data can be added or removed. Stacks, queues, and deques (pronounced "decks") are specific types of lists, each with its own convention for adding and removing data. This section introduces these concepts using a static array as the underlying data structure. While the static array structure works well for relatively small amounts of data, the next section introduces a better technique when working with large lists or lists of an unknown size. Additionally, the static array and related variables have global scope. Once again, the code in this section demonstrates instances where global variables are useful and can greatly reduce the length and complexity of the code.

### STACKS                                     *stacks = LIFO*

*\* built in RAM (temp)*
*\* can save to hard-drive*

A **stack** is similar to a stack of plates in a cafeteria. After dirty plates are washed, a cafeteria worker places the newly cleaned plates on top of the previously cleaned plates already in the stack. As customers enter, they remove plates from the top of this stack. In short, the last plate placed on top of the stack is the first one removed. Thus, stacks operate in a **last-in first-out**, or **LIFO**, manner. The process of adding data to a stack is called **pushing**, and removing data is referred to as **popping**. Again, imagine the cafeteria worker pushing the plates down onto the spring-ejector mechanism of the plate dispenser. Likewise, the ejector-mechanism pops a new plate up as plates are removed from the stack. Programmers commonly refer to the **top of the stack** and the **bottom of the stack**, where the top of the stack indicates the next data item to be removed and the bottom of the stack indicates the last item to be removed. Figure 8.5 shows a stack diagram example.

The code below implements a stack and demonstrates the `Push` and `Pop` routines. Figure 8.6 displays the output of this code.

```
' Stack Example
' -------------
' Implement a stack using a static array
```

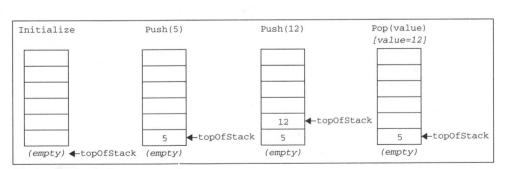

**Figure 8.5** Stack diagram example

```
Option Explicit

Const STACKSIZE = 50      ' Maximum Stack Size

Dim stack(1 To STACKSIZE) As Integer    ' A stack of
➥ integers
Dim topOfStack As Integer               ' Pointer to the top
➥ of the stack

Private Sub Initialize()
' Initialize the stack
   topOfStack = 0
End Sub

Private Function IsEmpty() As Boolean
' Returns True if the stack is empty
   IsEmpty = (topOfStack = 0)
End Function

Private Function IsFull() As Boolean
' Returns True if the stack is full
   IsFull = (topOfStack = STACKSIZE)
End Function

Private Sub Pop(value As Integer)
' Pop an integer value from the top of the stack
   If IsEmpty() Then
      MsgBox "Illegal Pop operation -- stack empty!", ,
      ➥ "ERROR"
   Else
      value = stack(topOfStack)
      topOfStack = topOfStack - 1
   End If
End Sub

Private Sub Push(value As Integer)
' Push an integer value onto the stack
   If IsFull() Then
      MsgBox "Illegal Push operation -- stack full!", ,
      ➥ "ERROR"
   Else
      topOfStack = topOfStack + 1
      stack(topOfStack) = value
   End If
End Sub

Private Sub cmdTestStack_Click()
' Test the stack
   Dim value As Integer, count As Integer

   Call Initialize
   picOutput.Cls
   For count = 1 To 10
      Call Push(count)
```

```
        picOutput.Print "Pushed:"; count
    Next count
    For count = 1 To 5
        Call Pop(value)
        picOutput.Print "Popped:"; value
    Next count
    For count = 30 To 33
        Call Push(count)
        picOutput.Print "Pushed:"; count
    Next count
    For count = 1 To 9
        Call Pop(value)
        picOutput.Print "Popped:"; value
    Next count
End Sub
```

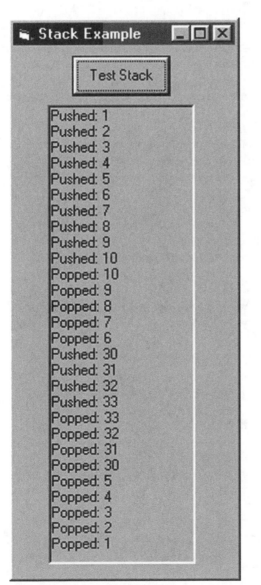

**Figure 8.6** Stack example

*handwritten note in margin:*
* add to top.
* remove from bottom

## QUEUES

A **queue** is the opposite of a stack. Whereas a stack can be thought of as a stack of plates in a cafeteria, a queue is the line of customers in the cafeteria. The first customer in line is the first customer served. Thus, queues operate in a **first-in first-out**, or **FIFO**, manner. To add data to the end of a queue, we **enqueue** the data. Conversely, we **dequeue** data to remove data from the front of the queue. Programmers refer to the **front** and **rear** of a queue, where the front indicates the next data item to be removed and the rear indicates the last data item to be removed. Figure 8.7 provides a queue diagram example.

The code below implements a queue with Enqueue and Dequeue routines, and Figure 8.8 displays the output.

*margin note:*
This code uses a static array to implement a circular queue. That is, the queue can "wrap around" the endpoints of the array. For a static array with 50 elements (from index values 1 to 50), for instance, front may be 45 and rear may be 10 when the queue contains 15 items. The LimitCheck procedure adjusts front and rear as necessary to implement the circular queue.

```vb
' Queue Example
' ------------
' Implement a circular queue using a static array

Option Explicit

Const QUEUESIZE = 50     ' Maximum Queue Size
Const STARTPOS = 1       ' Starting index

Dim queue(STARTPOS To QUEUESIZE) As Integer ' A queue of
➡ integers
Dim front As Integer, rear As Integer       ' Pointers to
➡ the front and rear of the queue
Dim numData As Integer                       ' Number of
➡ elements currently in the queue

Private Sub Dequeue(value As Integer)
'Remove an integer value from the front of the queue
    If IsEmpty() Then
        MsgBox "Illegal Dequeue operation -- queue empty!",
           ➡ , "ERROR"
    Else
        value = queue(front)
        front = front + 1
        Call LimitCheck(front)
        numData = numData - 1
    End If
End Sub
```

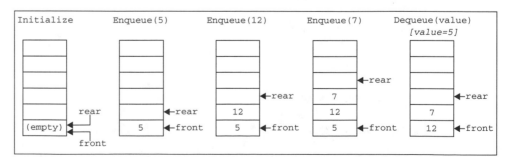

**Figure 8.7** Queue diagram example

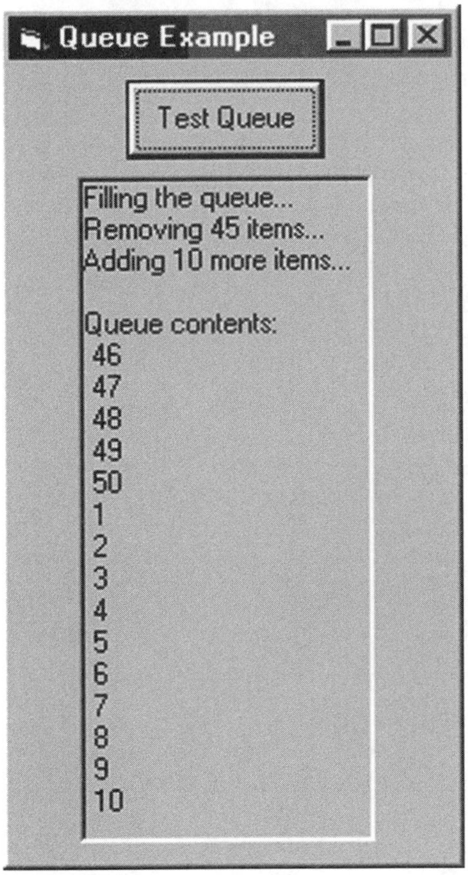

**Figure 8.8** Queue example

```
Private Sub Enqueue(value As Integer)
' Add an integer value to the rear of the queue
   If IsFull() Then
      MsgBox "Illegal Enqueue operation -- queue full!", ,
      ➥ "ERROR"
   Else
      queue(rear) = value
      rear = rear + 1
      Call LimitCheck(rear)
      numData = numData + 1
   End If
End Sub

Private Sub Initialize()
' Initialize the queue
   front = STARTPOS
   rear = STARTPOS
   numData = 0
End Sub

Private Function IsEmpty() As Boolean
' Returns True if the queue is empty
   IsEmpty = (numData = 0)
End Function
```

➥

```
          Private Function IsFull() As Boolean
          ' Returns True if the queue is full
              IsFull = (numData = QUEUESIZE)
          End Function

          Private Sub LimitCheck(position As Integer)
          ' Check if endpoints of the queue are exceeded and adjust
            ➡ the pointer accordingly
              If position < STARTPOS Then
                  position = QUEUESIZE
              ElseIf position > QUEUESIZE Then
                  position = STARTPOS
              End If
          End Sub

          Private Sub cmdTestQueue_Click()
          ' Test the queue

              Dim value As Integer, count As Integer

              Call Initialize

              picOutput.Cls
              picOutput.Print "Filling the queue..."
              For count = STARTPOS To QUEUESIZE
                  Call Enqueue(count)
              Next count

              picOutput.Print "Removing 45 items..."
              For count = 1 To 45
                  Call Dequeue(value)
              Next count

              picOutput.Print "Adding 10 more items..."
              For count = 1 To 10
                  Call Enqueue(count)
              Next count
              picOutput.Print

              picOutput.Print "Queue contents:"
              For count = 1 To numData
                  Call Dequeue(value)
                  picOutput.Print value
              Next count
          End Sub
```

## DEQUES

Finally, a **deque** (double-ended queue) is sort of a combination of a stack and a queue. Data may be added to or removed from either end of the deque. Notice that this is the first structure in which data may be added to the front; both stacks and queues add data to the rear. Deques commonly have AddFront, RemoveFront, AddRear, and RemoveRear procedures. Figure 8.9 shows a deque diagram example.

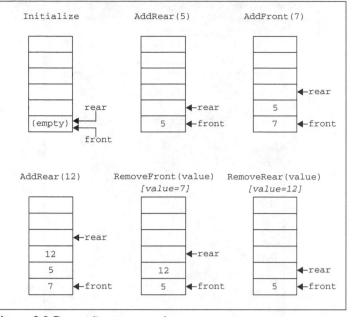

**Figure 8.9** Deque diagram example

A VB implementation of a deque appears below, and Figure 8.10 contains the output.

```
' Deque Example
' -------------
' Implement a circular deque using a static array

Option Explicit


Const DEQUESIZE = 50      ' Maximum Deque Size
Const STARTPOS = 1        ' Starting index


Dim deque(STARTPOS To DEQUESIZE) As Integer ' A deque of
➥ integers
Dim front As Integer, rear As Integer        ' Pointers to
➥ the front and rear of the deque
Dim numData As Integer                       ' Number of
➥ elements currently in the deque


Private Sub AddFront(value As Integer)
' Add an integer value to the front of the deque
    If IsFull() Then
        MsgBox "Illegal Add operation -- deque full!", ,
        ➥ "ERROR"
    Else
        front = front - 1
        Call LimitCheck(front)
        deque(front) = value
        numData = numData + 1
```

This code uses a static array to implement a circular deque. That is, the deque can "wrap around" the endpoints of the array. For a static array with 50 elements (from index values 1 to 50), for instance, `front` may be 45 and `rear` may be 10 when the queue contains 15 items. The `LimitCheck` procedure adjusts `front` and `rear` as necessary to implement the circular deque.

➡

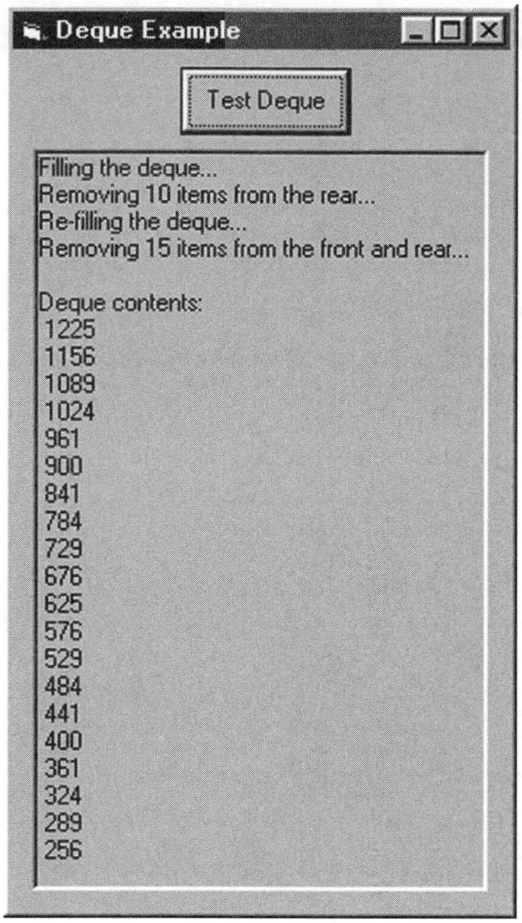

**Figure 8.10** Deque example

```
      End If
End Sub

Private Sub AddRear(value As Integer)
' Add an integer value to the rear of the deque
   If IsFull() Then
      MsgBox "Illegal Add operation -- deque full!", ,
      ➡ "ERROR"
   Else
      deque(rear) = value
      rear = rear + 1
      Call LimitCheck(rear)
      numData = numData + 1
   End If
End Sub

Private Sub Initialize()
' Initialize the deque
   front = STARTPOS
   rear = STARTPOS
   numData = 0
End Sub
```

```
Private Function IsEmpty() As Boolean
' Returns True if the deque is empty
    IsEmpty = (numData = 0)
End Function


Private Function IsFull() As Boolean
' Returns True if the deque is full
    IsFull = (numData = DEQUESIZE)
End Function


Private Sub LimitCheck(position As Integer)
' Check if deque endpoints are exceeded and adjust the
    ➥ pointers accordingly
    If position > DEQUESIZE Then
        position = STARTPOS
    ElseIf position < STARTPOS Then
        position = DEQUESIZE
    End If
End Sub


Private Sub RemoveFront(value As Integer)
' Remove an integer value from the front of the deque
    If IsEmpty() Then
        MsgBox "Illegal Remove operation -- deque empty!", ,
        ➥ "ERROR"
    Else
        value = deque(front)
        front = front + 1
        Call LimitCheck(front)
        numData = numData - 1
    End If
End Sub


Private Sub RemoveRear(value As Integer)
' Remove an integer value from the rear of the deque
    If IsEmpty() Then
        MsgBox "Illegal Remove operation -- deque empty!", ,
        ➥ "ERROR"
    Else
        rear = rear - 1
        Call LimitCheck(rear)
        value = deque(rear)
        numData = numData - 1
    End If
End Sub


Private Sub cmdTestDeque_Click()
' Test the deque

    Dim value As Integer, count As Integer

    Call Initialize
    picOutput.Cls                                    ➥
```

```
    ' Fill the deque
    picOutput.Print "Filling the deque..."
    For count = STARTPOS To DEQUESIZE
        Call AddFront(count ^ 2)
    Next count

    ' Remove 10 items from the rear
    picOutput.Print "Removing 10 items from the rear..."
    For count = 1 To 10
        Call RemoveRear(value)
    Next count

    ' Re-fill the deque
    picOutput.Print "Re-filling the deque..."
    For count = 1 To 10
        Call AddRear(count)
    Next count

    ' Remove 15 items each from the front and rear
    picOutput.Print "Removing 15 items from the front and
  ➡ rear..."
    For count = 1 To 15
        Call RemoveFront(value)
        Call RemoveRear(value)
    Next count

    ' Display deque contents
    picOutput.Print
    picOutput.Print "Deque contents:"
    For count = 1 To numData
        Call RemoveFront(value)
        picOutput.Print value
    Next count
End Sub
```

## POINTERS AND LINKED LISTS

A **pointer** is a variable that contains the memory address of another variable instead of the variable's value. In other words, a pointer is a variable that points to the memory location of another variable. Thus, pointers provide indirect references to variables.

The advantage of using pointers is that a programmer can create **linked lists** of data using dynamic memory allocation (dynamic variables). Data can be easily added to or removed from any part of a list by using pointers. Either of these operations is much more difficult to perform when using an array implementation. An example of a linked list appears in Figure 8.11.

Pointers are memory efficient because they use dynamic variables. This dynamic memory allocation, however, is also one of the disadvantages of using pointers. The programmer must ensure that all broken links (or unused dynamic variables) are removed from memory; otherwise, a **memory leak** occurs. Memory leaks are often difficult to debug, and severe memory leaks can cause the computer to crash.

Unfortunately, the VB language does not contain pointers, and linked lists must be implemented using other methods. For this reason, many advanced program-

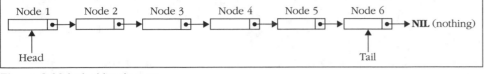

**Figure 8.11** Linked list diagram

mers feel that VB is not a "real" computer language. We point out, however, that no computer language is *the perfect language*, and many commercially available programs are written in VB. The authors believe that a little programming skill can overcome any "flaw" in a computer language.

## LINKED LIST EXAMPLE

We now show one method of creating linked lists using dynamic arrays. The following code, for instance, has been successfully used in an advanced computer simulation with no noticeable impact on execution speed. In this implementation, data is always added to the end of the list, but data can be removed from any part of the list. Figure 8.12 displays the output of this code. Objects can also be used to create linked lists in VB, as described in the supplement to this chapter, which introduces object-oriented programming.

```
' Linked List Example
' --------------------
' This program simulates pointers and creates a linked list
' using a dynamic array
'
' NOTE: The next field of RecordType is not really
➥ necessary, but we use it to simulate the actions of a
➥ pointer(i.e. ptr = linkedList(ptr).next).

Option Explicit
Option Base 0

Private Type RecordType
    name As String
    next As Integer
End Type

Dim linkedList() As RecordType   ' Dynamic array to simulate
➥ linked list
Dim numNodes As Integer          ' Number of nodes
➥ (data items) in the linked list

Private Sub Initialize()
' Initialize the linked list
    numNodes = 0
    ReDim linkedList(numNodes) As RecordType
End Sub
```

*must know address of last item at all times

*good for searching or sorting

```
Private Sub Add(data As String)
' Add a node to the linked list

    numNodes = numNodes + 1
    ReDim Preserve linkedList(numNodes) As RecordType

    linkedList(numNodes).name = data
    linkedList(numNodes).next = 0

    If numNodes > 1 Then
        linkedList(numNodes - 1).next = numNodes
    End If
End Sub

Private Sub FindData(data As String, position As Integer)
' Find the index position of the data string within the
    ➡ linked list

    Dim count As Integer ' Loop counter

    position = 0
    count = 0

    Do
        count = count + 1
        If linkedList(count).name = data Then
            position = count
        End If
    Loop Until (count = numNodes) Or (position > 0)
End Sub

Private Sub Reindex(position As Integer)
' Reindex the nodes and fix the last link

    Dim count As Integer ' Loop counter

    If numNodes > 1 Then
        If position <> numNodes Then
            For count = position To (numNodes - 1)
                linkedList(count).name = linkedList(count +
                    ➡ 1).name
            Next count
        End If
        linkedList(numNodes - 1).next = 0
    End If
End Sub

Private Sub Remove(data As String)
' Remove the node containing the data string from the
    ➡ linked list

    Dim position As Integer   ' List pointer
```

```
        If numNodes > 0 Then
            Call FindData(data, position)
            If position > 0 Then
                Call Reindex(position)
                numNodes = numNodes - 1
                ReDim Preserve linkedList(numNodes) As RecordType
            End If
        End If
End Sub


Private Sub DisplayList()
' Display the linked list

    Dim ptr As Integer    ' List pointer

    If numNodes > 0 Then
        ptr = 1
        Do
            picOutput.Print linkedList(ptr).name;
            ptr = linkedList(ptr).next
            If ptr <> 0 Then
                picOutput.Print " --> ";
            End If
        Loop Until ptr = 0
        picOutput.Print
    Else
        picOutput.Print "(Empty)"
    End If
End Sub


Private Sub cmdTest_Click()
' Test the linked list

    Call Initialize
    Call Add("Jack")
    Call Add("Bill")
    Call Add("Tom")
    Call Add("Harry")
    Call DisplayList
    Call Remove("Jack")
    Call DisplayList
    Call Remove("Harry")
    Call DisplayList
    Call Add("Sally")
    Call DisplayList
    Call Remove("Tom")
    Call DisplayList
    Call Add("Lucy")
    Call DisplayList
End Sub
```

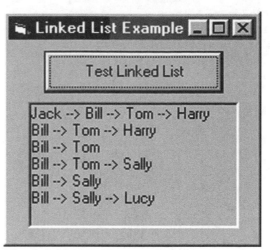

**Figure 8.12** Linked list example

# Summary

## Key Terms

**array**—a set of sequentially indexed elements of the same intrinsic data type

**bottom of stack**—a pointer indicating the last data item to be removed from a stack

**data structure**—a structure that contains data

**database**—the data set consisting of all records

**deque**—a list in which data can be added to or removed from either end; a double-ended queue

**dequeue**—the process of removing an item from the front of a queue

**dot-separator**—in VB, a period used to separate record variables from field names and objects from properties and methods

**dynamic array**—an array that can change size during program execution

**dynamic data structure**—a data structure that can change size (and sometimes type) during program execution (dynamically)

**element**—a single location within an array. Each element has a unique identifying index number, and each element acts as a separate variable that can be accessed using this index value

**enqueue**—the process of adding a new item to the rear of a queue

**field**—a single piece of information within a record

**first-in first-out (FIFO)**—the first item added is the first one removed (similar to the line of customers in a cafeteria)

**front**—a pointer to the beginning of a list structure

**last-in first-out (LIFO)**—the last item added is the first one removed (similar to a stack of plates in a cafeteria)

**linked list**—a list data structure in which data elements are linked together using pointers

**list**—an ordered set of data to which data can be added or removed

**memory leak**—a decrease in available system memory caused by a failure to remove unused dynamic variables from memory

**multidimensional (or *n*-dimensional) array**—an array with more than two indices

**one-dimensional array**—an array with one index. The equivalent of a vector in mathematics

**parallel arrays**—separate arrays in which the elements with corresponding index values contain related information

**pointer**—a variable that contains the memory address of another variable instead of the variable's value

**pop**—the process of removing an item from the top of a stack

**push**—the process of adding a new item to the top of a stack

**queue**—a list that operates in a FIFO manner

**rear**—a pointer to the end of a list structure

**record**—an object or user-defined data type that encapsulates a group of related data. A record contains information in one or more fields

**stack**—a list that operates in a LIFO manner

**static array**—an array of a fixed type and size (an array that is a static data structure)

**static data structure**—a data structure of a fixed type and size. A static data structure cannot be changed unless a programmer modifies the source code

**top of stack**—a pointer indicating the next data item to be removed from a stack

**two-dimensional array**—an array with two separate indices. The equivalent of a matrix in mathematics

**user-defined data type**—a data type defined by the programmer (the user of the compiler)

## Keywords

| *Compiler Directives:* | *Statements:* | ReDim |
|---|---|---|
| Option Base | Dim | Type |
| | Preserve | With |

## Key Concepts

- A data structure may be either static or dynamic. While a static data structure has a fixed type and size, a dynamic structure can change size (and sometimes type) during program execution.

- An array is a set of sequentially indexed elements having the same intrinsic data type. Arrays may be either static or dynamic data structures.

- A static array is declared using the following syntax:

  ```
  Dim arrayName(start To stop) As DataType
  ```

- To declare a dynamic array, use the syntax:

  ```
  Dim arrayName() As DataType
  ```

Then, use the `ReDim` statement within a subprogram to size the array:

```
ReDim arrayName(subscripts) As DataType
```

The `ReDim` statement re-initializes the array. To prevent re-initialization, use the `Preserve` keyword in the `ReDim` statement:

```
ReDim Preserve arrayName(subscripts) As DataType
```

- To access an array element, use the form `arrayName(indexValue)`. For instance, `myArray(5) = 10` assigns the value 10 to element 5 of the one-dimensional array `myArray`.

- To pass an array variable as an argument of a subprogram, simply write the array variable name followed by empty parentheses in the argument list. To denote an array parameter in a subprogram definition, write the parameter name followed by empty parentheses in the parameter list.

- A one-dimensional array is the computer representation of a vector in mathematics, and a two-dimensional array is the equivalent of a matrix. Arrays with more than two indices are called multidimensional (or $n$-dimensional) arrays.

- A record encapsulates a group of related data by containing a field for each piece of information. A database is the set of all records.

- Records are created in VB using user-defined data types. The general syntax for declaring a user-defined data type is:

```
Type RecordName
    fieldName1 (subscripts) as DataType1
    fieldName2 (subscripts) as DataType2
        .
        .
        .
    fieldNameN (subscripts) as DataTypeN
End Type
```

- The dot-separator is used to separate a record variable from a field name. The form `recordVariableName.fieldName` accesses the `fieldName` field of record variable `recordVariableName`.

- The `With` statement can access the fields of a record and object properties and methods. The general form of the With statement is:

```
With Object
    [statements]
End With
```

- There are several data structures in which information is added and removed in a specific order. A list is a set of ordered data; data may be added to or removed from any part of the list. Stacks, queues, and deques are specific types of lists.

- A stack operates like a stack of plates in a cafeteria; the last plate in is the first plate out. So, a stack is a last-in first-out, or LIFO, structure.

- A queue operates like the customers in a cafeteria; the first customer in line is the first one served. So, a queue operates in a first-in first-out, or FIFO, manner.

- A deque (double-ended queue) is a combination of a stack and a queue; data can be added to or removed from either end. Thus, of these three types of lists, the deque is the only one in which data can be added to the front.

- A pointer is a variable that contains the memory location of another variable. Therefore, a pointer is an indirect reference to a variable. Pointers are useful in creating linked lists of data, but VB does not contain pointers.

- Pointers and linked lists can be emulated in VB using dynamic arrays, or linked lists can be created directly using objects.

## Review Questions

1. What is the difference between a static data structure and a dynamic data structure?

2. Show an example VB declarations for a one-dimensional array, a two-dimensional array, a three-dimensional array, and a seven-dimensional array.

3. What is the mathematical equivalent of a one-dimensional array? a two-dimensional array?

4. Describe the use of arrays as arguments and parameters of subprograms.

5. How can you define your own data type in VB? Give an example.

6. Describe the operations of a list, stack, queue, and deque. Compare and contrast these data structures (i.e., what are their similarities and differences).

7. What is a pointer? Can you use pointers in VB?

8. What is a linked list? How can you create a linked list in VB?

## Chapter 8 Problems

1. Write a simple database program that contains the titles and authors of your textbooks. Your program should use two one-dimensional arrays, one for the book title and one for the author(s). Your program must allow the user to enter a book, remove a book, and find a book's record. Assume that the database can contain a maximum of 20 textbooks.

2. Modify the program from Problem 1 to use dynamic arrays. The database can contain any number of textbooks.

3. Write the program for Problem 1 using a user-defined data type (records) and a static array of records. Assume that the database can contain a maximum of 20 textbooks.

4. Modify the program from Problem 3 to use a dynamic array of records. The database can contain any number of textbooks.

5. Write a code module that implements a stack of single-precision values using a dynamic array. Also, write a test driver program for this code module.

6. Repeat Problem 5 for a queue.

7. Repeat Problem 5 for a deque.

## Programming Projects

1. *FlyHigh Airlines Reservation System*. FlyHigh Airlines accepts passenger reservations on a first-come first-served basis. A single aircraft can carry

40 passengers. Once the aircraft is full, prospective passengers are placed on stand-by (a waiting list). Write a program that accepts reservations and cancellations for a single aircraft. If the aircraft is full and a "ticketed" passenger cancels his reservations, the program should give the seat to the first person on the waiting list.

2. *The Eight Queens Problem.* A chessboard is an 8 × 8 board consisting of 64 squares. A Queen can move in any direction (horizontally, vertically, or diagonally) until it encounters another piece. The goal of the Eight Queens Problem is to place eight queens on a chessboard so that no Queen is in the path of another. Write a VB program that finds all solutions to the Eight Queens Problem. [*Hint:* Use recursion.]

3. *The Knight's Tour Problem.* In chess, a Knight moves by jumping two squares horizontally or vertically and then one square to the left or right. The goal of the Knight's Tour Problem is to find a path for a single Knight to visit every square on an empty $n \times n$ board. Write a VB program that finds a solution to the Knight's Tour Problem when the Knight starts in the upper left-hand corner of a 5 × 5 board. [*Hint:* Use recursion.]

4. Write a program that plays a game of Tic-Tac-Toe against the user.

5. Write a matrix algebra package. This package is a code module containing subprograms that add, multiply, scalar multiply, and invert matrices. Write a test driver program to aid in debugging your matrix algebra package.

# Object-Oriented Programming

## Chapter Supplement Objectives

In this chapter supplement, you will:

- Be introduced to object-oriented programming (OOP) concepts
- Learn how OOP is implemented in VB
- Learn how to create and use objects and classes in VB

**Object-oriented programming** (**OOP**) is itself a vast topic that requires at least a textbook to explain in detail. Rather than providing a comprehensive glossary of OOP terminology, this supplement introduces the main concepts of OOP and describes how they are implemented in VB.

## Overview of Object-Oriented Programming

So, what is all of the hype about OOP? Consider the example of a library. A library contains bookcases, bookcases have several shelves, and each shelf contains many books. Furthermore, each book has certain **properties**, such as a title, author, publisher, and so on. Since each of these items is an object in the real world, this problem nicely lends itself to OOP.

In Chapter 8, we learned about records and user-defined data types. Records could be used to contain the data for the books, shelves, bookcases, and the entire library. However, this would require using dynamic array structures of records within records. *As a rule of thumb, any time that a data structure requires records within records and must be dynamic in nature, it is far easier and makes more sense to use OOP.*

OOP has three main concepts: encapsulation, inheritance, and polymorphism. **Encapsulation** combines the data and behavior of an object into one package. Thus, an object contains properties as well as **methods** that use those properties. The advantage of encapsulation is that it provides a means of **data-hiding**, that is, the way in which the data is stored is hidden from the user of the object. The user can manipulate an object's properties only by passing messages to the object (using the object's methods). This stresses code reuse since the programmer only needs knowledge of the object's properties and methods rather than its specific data structure.

An object's type is called its **class**. Thus, when we create a new object type, we create a new class. Furthermore, when a new object of a specific class is created, it is **instantiated**; that is, it is a new **instance** of the object class. Therefore, an object's properties are also called its instance fields, member fields, or instance variables.

**Inheritance** *extends* an object class, and allows a *parent* and *child* relationship between objects. For instance, an employee database program may have an employee class and a manager class. The employee class contains employee information such as the name and social security number. Since a manager is simply a higher-level employee, the manager class must contain the manager's ID number as well as his or her employee information. Thus, a logical relationship exists between these classes: the manager class forms a *superset* of the employee class. The manager class (child class) inherits all of the properties and methods of the employee class (base class or parent class). Unfortunately, VB does not allow true inheritance. Instead, VB offers containment, where one object can contain another object of a different class. Note that this is not the same as inheritance: Containment forms a "has a" relationship between objects, whereas inheritance forms an "is a" relationship.

**Polymorphism** (literally "the ability to take on many forms") allows the same code to be used for objects of different classes. For instance, a SetEmployeeSSN method that sets the social security number of an employee object can also be used by objects of the manager class. VB, however, does not support polymorphism. Instead, VB allows for the creation of interfaces between objects. VB interfaces are beyond the scope of this text; consult the VB documentation for more information.

In VB, an object variable points to the memory locations of the object data. Object variables provide indirect references to data and are, in fact, pointers. Since pointers are dynamic in nature, objects are also dynamic data types. An object variable is declared using the Dim statement as follows:

```
Dim ObjectVariable As ObjectClass
```

This statement only declares an object variable; it does not create an instance of *ObjectClass*. In the above declaration, VB initializes *ObjectVariable* to Nothing by default. The Nothing keyword is used to disassociate an object variable from an actual object.

Much the same way that the Let keyword assigns an expression to a variable, the Set keyword associates an object variable with an actual object or Nothing. Unlike the Let keyword, however, the Set keyword is not optional. The syntax of the Set statement is as follows:

```
Set ObjectVariable = ObjectExpression
```

The following line of code, for instance, assigns Nothing to *ObjectVariable* and disassociates *ObjectVariable* with any object instance:

```
Set ObjectVariable = Nothing
```

Since an object variable declaration does not create a new instance, we must use the New keyword to create a new instance of *ObjectClass*. The following code assigns *ObjectVariable* to a new instance of *ObjectClass*:

```
Set ObjectVariable = New ObjectClass
```

Finally, the object variable declaration, object instantiation, and assignment statement in the previous lines of code can be combined into one line. The following code declares *ObjectVariable* as an instance of *ObjectClass* and initializes it to Nothing:

```
Dim ObjectVariable As New ObjectClass
```

Since object variables are pointers, comparing two object variables for equality means that the variables reference the same locations in memory. Since VB uses the Is operator rather than the = operator to compare object variables for equality, the following code is used to test whether or not two object variables reference the same data:

```
booleanVariable = ObjectVariable1 Is ObjectVariable2
```

If ObjectVariable1 and ObjectVariable2 reference the same memory location, then booleanVariable is True.

To make two object variables refer to the same data (ensuring that booleanVariable is True), use code of the form:

```
Set ObjectVariable2 = ObjectVariable1
```

Finally, to test whether an object variable is empty (does not refer to an object), use the following code:

```
booleanVariable = ObjectVariable Is Nothing
```

booleanVariable is True if ObjectVariable is not associated with an object.

To create a new class in VB, a **class module** must be created. On the menu bar, select Project/Add Class Module. A dialog box gives the option of using the VB Class Builder Wizard. We'll forego discussing it in favor of designing our own object-oriented code in VB.

## An Example Object-Oriented Program in VB

As an example of OOP in VB, we design a simple phone book program. We first create a new class module, change its name to PhoneInfo class, and then use the following code to add instance variables relating to each of its properties.

```
Option Explicit

' Instance Variables
Dim nameLast As String        ' Last name
Dim nameFirst As String       ' First name
Dim telephoneNum As String    ' Telephone number
Dim nextEntry As Object       ' Next entry in the phone book
```

The nextEntry instance variable allows us to create a linked list of objects. The Object class is the base class in VB; all objects in VB are children of the Object class.

First, we must write an event-handler that initializes the instance variables when a new object is instantiated. This event-handler is called Class_Initialize and has the following syntax:

```
Private Sub Class_Initialize()
    InstanceVariable = DefaultValue
End Sub
```

`Class_Initialize` is automatically executed when a new object is created. `Class_Initialize` for the `PhoneInfo` class follows:

```
Private Sub Class_Initialize()
' Initialize a new PhoneInfo object
   nameLast = ""
   nameFirst = ""
   telephoneNum = ""
   Set nextEntry = Nothing
End Sub
```

In order to prevent memory leaks, we must also write an event-handler that releases all object references when the object is destroyed. This event-handler is called `Class_Terminate`, and it executes automatically when an object is set to `Nothing`. In the general syntax shown below, *InstanceVariable* is an instance variable that references an object:

```
Private Sub Class_Terminate
    Set InstanceVariable = Nothing
End Sub
```

`Class_Terminate` for the `PhoneInfo` class follows:

```
Private Sub Class_Terminate()
' Terminate the PhoneInfo object
' Set all objects contained in this object to Nothing
   Set nextEntry = Nothing
End Sub
```

To make this class useful in a phone book program, our class must also contain methods that set and get values of the instance variables. These methods are essentially procedures that allow an object's properties to be modified or retrieved. A method that modifies or *sets* a property value is called a **setter method**. A method that retrieves or *gets* a property value is a **getter method**. A setter method is written using the `Property Set` statement if the object property refers to another object; otherwise, use the `Property Let` statement. Simply stated, use the `Property Set` statement if the `Set` keyword appears in the statements within the method. To write a getter method, use the `Property Get` statement. The general syntax for these methods appears below:

```
Property Set PropertyName(parameters, ObjectReference)
    [statements]
    Set InstanceVariable = ObjectReference
End Property

Property Let PropertyName(parameters, value)
    [statements]
    InstanceVariable = value
End Property

Property Get PropertyName(parameters) as DataType
    [statements]
    PropertyName = Expression
End Property
```

A getter method is invoked when VB encounters a statement of the form:

```
VariableName = ObjectVariable.PropertyName
```

Conversely, a setter method is invoked when VB encounters a statement of the form:

```
ObjectVariable.PropertyName = Expression
```

In addition to the code above, the setter and getter methods for the `PhoneInfo` class are as follows:

```
Property Let lastName(last As String)
' Set the last name
   nameLast = last
End Property

Property Get lastName() As String
' Get the last name
   lastName = nameLast
End Property

Property Let firstName(first As String)
' Set the first name
   nameFirst = first
End Property

Property Get firstName() As String
' Get the first name
   firstName = nameFirst
End Property

Property Let phoneNumber(phone As String)
' Set the telephone number
   telephoneNum = phone
End Property

Property Get phoneNumber() As String
' Get the telephone number
   phoneNumber = telephoneNum
End Property

Property Set nextPtr(nextEnt As Object)
' Set the next entry in the phone book
   Set nextEntry = nextEnt
End Property

Property Get nextPtr() As Object
' Get the next entry in the phone book
   Set nextPtr = nextEntry
End Property
```

Finally, a listing of the phone book program appears below. This program requires the PhoneInfo class created earlier in this supplement. Figure 8.13 shows the form for this program.

```
' Phone Book Program
' ------------------

' This program demonstrates the use of objects
' to create a simple phonebook in VB

Option Explicit

Dim PhoneList As PhoneInfo

Private Sub cmdAdd_Click()
' Add an entry to the phonebook
    Dim Pointer As PhoneInfo, Entry As PhoneInfo

    If txtLastName.Text <> "" Then

        Set Pointer = PhoneList
        Do While Not (Pointer.nextPtr Is Nothing)
            Set Pointer = Pointer.nextPtr
        Loop

        Set Entry = New PhoneInfo
        Entry.lastName = Trim(txtLastName.Text)
        Entry.firstName = Trim(txtFirstName.Text)
        Entry.phoneNumber = Trim(txtPhone.Text)
        Set Entry.nextPtr = Nothing

        Set Pointer.nextPtr = Entry

    End If
End Sub

Private Sub cmdFind_Click()
' Find an entry in the phonebook
    Dim Pointer As PhoneInfo
    Dim found As Boolean

    If txtLastName.Text <> "" Then

        Set Pointer = PhoneList
        found = False

        Do While Not (found) And Not (Pointer Is Nothing)
            Set Pointer = Pointer.nextPtr
            If Not (Pointer Is Nothing) Then
                found = (Pointer.lastName = _
                    Trim(txtLastName.Text)) And _
                        (Pointer.firstName =
                            Trim(txtFirstName.Text))
            End If
        Loop
```

```
            If found Then
                txtPhone.Text = Pointer.phoneNumber
            Else
                txtPhone.Text = "Unlisted"
            End If

    End If
End Sub

Private Sub cmdRemove_Click()
' Remove an entry from the phonebook
    Dim Pointer As PhoneInfo, LastPtr As PhoneInfo
    Dim found As Boolean

    If txtLastName.Text <> "" Then

        Set Pointer = PhoneList
        found = False

        Do While Not (found) And Not (Pointer Is Nothing)
            Set LastPtr = Pointer
            Set Pointer = Pointer.nextPtr
            If Not (Pointer Is Nothing) Then
                found = (Pointer.lastName =
            ➥ Trim(txtLastName.Text)) And _
                        (Pointer.firstName =
                    ➥ Trim(txtFirstName.Text))
            End If
        Loop

        If found Then
            Set LastPtr.nextPtr = Pointer.nextPtr
            Set Pointer = Nothing
        End If

    End If
End Sub

Private Sub Form_Load()
' Initialize the phonebook
' Create a header node for the linked list of objects
    Set PhoneList = New PhoneInfo
End Sub
```

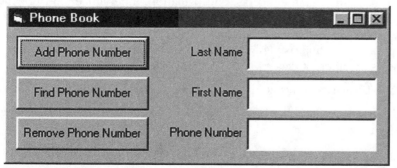

**Figure 8.13** Phone Book form

## Summary

### Key Terms

**class**—an object's type

**class module**—a VB code module that defines a new object class

**data-hiding**—the way in which the data is stored is hidden from the user of the object

**encapsulation**—the grouping of the data (properties) and behavior (methods) of an object into one package

**getter method**—a method that retrieves or gets a property value

**inheritance**—the extension of an object class by allowing a parent and child relationship between objects

**instance**—a new object of a specific class

**instantiate**—to create a new object of a specific class; to create a new object instance

**method**—a subprogram that is associated with an object. Typically, a method alters the properties of its associated object

**object-oriented programming (OOP)**—computer programming with object data types

**polymorphism**—allowing the same code to be used for objects of different classes. Literally, "the ability to take on many forms"

**property**—a value that is associated with an object

**setter method**—a method that modifies or sets a property value

### Keywords

| *Event-handlers:* | *Operators:* | Property Let |
|---|---|---|
| Class_Initialize | Is | Property Set |
| Class_Terminate | | Set |
| | *Statements:* | |
| *Objects:* | Let | |
| Nothing | New | |
| Object | Property Get | |

### Key Concepts

- Any time that a data structure must be dynamic and requires records within records, object-oriented programming (OOP) should be used.

- OOP has three main concepts: encapsulation, inheritance, and polymorphism. Encapsulation combines the data and behavior of an object into a single package. Inheritance extends an object class, allowing a parent and child relationship between objects. Polymorphism allows the same code to be used for objects of different classes.

- In VB, object variables are pointers to the memory locations of the object data.

- The Object class is the base class in VB; all objects in VB are children of the Object class.

- Object variables are dynamic variables. To declare a new object variable, use the syntax:

```
Dim ObjectVariable As ObjectClass
```

Before an object variable can be used, it must be instantiated using:

```
Set ObjectVariable = New ObjectClass
```

The object variable declaration and instantiation can be combined in the same line of code:

```
Dim ObjectVariable As New ObjectClass
```

- The Nothing keyword is used to disassociate an object variable from an actual object. The Set keyword associates an object variable with an actual object or Nothing. The general syntax for these operations follows:

```
Set ObjectVariable = Nothing
Set ObjectVariable = ObjectExpression
```

- The Is operator compares object variables for equality. The following code tests whether or not two object variables reference the same data:

```
booleanVariable = ObjectVariable1 Is ObjectVariable2
```

To test whether an object variable is empty, use:

```
booleanVariable = ObjectVariable Is Nothing
```

- A class module defines a new object class in VB. This module contains the object's instance variables, methods, and event-handlers.

- The Class_Initialize event-handler automatically executes when a new object is instantiated. In general, this event-handler is used to initialize the instance variables:

```
Private Sub Class_Initialize()
    InstanceVariable = DefaultValue
End Sub
```

- The Class_Terminate event-handler automatically executes when an object is set to Nothing. In general, this event-handler is used to prevent memory leaks by releasing all object references when an object is destroyed:

```
Private Sub Class_Terminate
    Set InstanceVariable = Nothing
End Sub
```

- Typically, a class module also contains methods to set and get the values of the instance variables, or setter and getter methods, respectively. The Property Get statement defines a getter method. Property Let and Property Set define setter methods. Property Set is used if the object property refers to another object (if the Set statement is used within the method). The general syntax is:

```
Property Set PropertyName(parameters, ObjectReference)
    [statements]
```

```
          Set InstanceVariable = ObjectReference
      End Property


      Property Let PropertyName(parameters, value)
          [statements]
          InstanceVariable = value
      End Property


      Property Get PropertyName(parameters) as DataType
          [statements]
          PropertyName = Expression
      End Property
```

A getter method is invoked when VB encounters a statement of the form:

```
      VariableName = ObjectVariable.PropertyName
```

A setter method is invoked when VB encounters a statement of the form:

```
      ObjectVariable.PropertyName = Expression
```

## Review Questions

1. What is object-oriented programming (OOP) and when is it useful? Give an example.
2. Define the terms encapsulation, inheritance, and polymorphism as they relate to OOP. How are these implemented in VB?
3. How can objects be used in VB to create linked lists of data? Give an example.

## Chapter 8 Supplement Problems

1. Write the program for Chapter 8, Problem 1 using objects.
2. Write a code module that implements a stack of single-precision values using objects. Also, write a test driver program for this code module.
3. Repeat Problem 2 for a queue.
4. Repeat Problem 2 for a deque.

## Programming Projects

1. Create a Matrix class. This class should contain methods that perform matrix operations, including matrix addition, multiplication, scalar multiplication, and inversion. Write a test driver program to aid in debugging your Matrix class.
2. Create a simple Statistics class. Class properties should include the sum of the observations, the sum of the squared observations, and the number of observations. There should be methods to add an observation, compute the mean, compute the variance, and compute the standard deviation.

# 9

# File Input and Output

A database-type program like the phone book program in the previous chapter is of little use unless it is capable of permanently storing data. Programs store data in and retrieve data from **data files**. VB, like many other languages, has two different types of data files available: sequential files and random-access files.

## SEQUENTIAL FILES

**Key Terms**

**sequential file**—a file that is accessed from the beginning of the file to the end of the file (in sequence)

The process of reading from or writing to a **sequential file** starts at the beginning of the file and continues until the end of the file is reached (i.e., in sequence, hence the name). This type of file consists of ASCII text and can be edited using any text editor or word processor that supports saving files in ASCII format. For instance, we can create a sequential file using the Windows 95/98 accessory named WordPad. Open WordPad (Start\Programs\Accessories) and type the following lines:

```
"Andrews","Lisa","670-7898"
"Kimball","Jeffrey","685-8765"
"McGuire","Jerry","685-5544"
"Mnemonic","Johnny","670-1234"
"Swan","Kristie","640-4511"
```

Now, click on File/Save As and a Save As dialog box appears. Type in `phone` as the file name, and select Text Document – MS-DOS Format from the "Save as type" list box as shown in Figure 9.1. Click on the Save button and WordPad saves the file named `phone.txt` as an ASCII text file.

You have just created a **comma-separated data file** (or **comma-delimited data file**). This means that commas separate the different pieces of information in the file. Additionally, notice that quotation marks surround each string in this file. *Although it is not required, we highly recommend using quotation marks to delimit strings in sequential files.* This avoids potential problems when a string contains a comma.

This data file also contains **control characters** (also called **hidden** or **escape characters**). If these control characters were visible, the `phone.txt` file would appear as follows:

```
"Andrews","Lisa","670-7898"<CR><LF>
"Kimball","Jeffrey","685-8765"<CR><LF>
"McGuire","Jerry","685-5544"<CR><LF>
"Mnemonic","Johnny","670-1234"<CR><LF>
"Swan","Kristie","640-4511"<CR><LF>
<EOF>
```

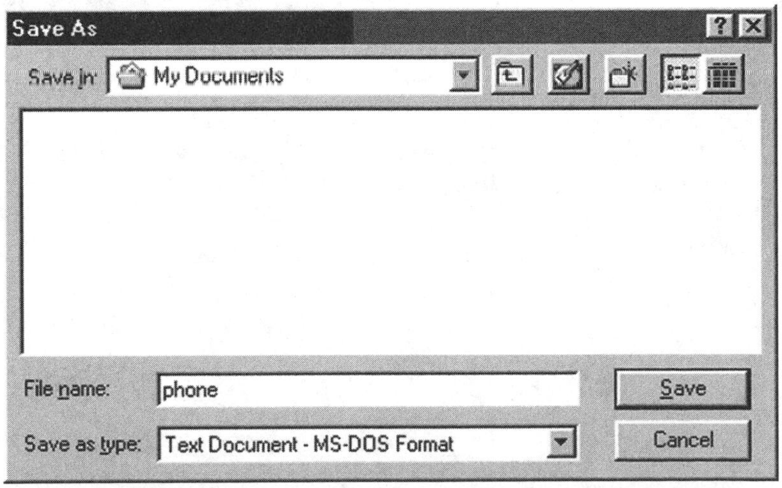


**Figure 9.1** Saving an ASCII file using Wordpad

Each pair of pointed brackets and sequence of letters (i.e., <letters>) designates a control character. <CR> is a carriage return (ASCII value 13) and <LF> is a line feed (ASCII value 10). In much the same way that a typewriter works, a carriage return forces the output to begin at the left margin and a line feed moves the output to the next blank line. For instance, move the cursor (the blinking position indicator) to the end of the first line of text and press the right arrow (→) key to move one space to the right. The control characters (<CR> and <LF>) force the cursor to move to the beginning of the next line. Now, press the down arrow key (↓) until the cursor will not move down any farther. <EOF> is the end-of-file marker that prevents the cursor from moving past the end of the written text.

Now that you know about the format of sequential files, we introduce the VB statements to work with these files. As with any other computer program, before you can work with a file, the file must be opened. The Open statement is used to open data files in VB. When opening a sequential file, we must tell VB whether this file is to be used for input or output. The general syntax of the Open statement for sequential files is as follows:

```
Open filename For { Input | Output | Append } As #n
```

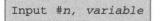

Here *filename* is any valid Windows 95/98 file name and can specify the **path** of the file, where the path indicates the disk drive and subdirectory where the file resides. *n* is the **file number**, which must be an integer value between 1 and 511. Thus, VB can have a maximum of 511 files open simultaneously. File numbers 1 though 255 are used for files that are not accessible to other applications, and file numbers 256 through 511 are reserved for files that are accessible from other applications.

When a file is opened for Input, the **file pointer** is reset to the beginning of the file. A file pointer is similar to the cursor in a text editor. That is, a cursor indicates the position within a file in a text editor, and the file pointer indicates the position in an open file. For an input file, the file pointer indicates the next data item to be read from the file. If a program tries to read more data items from a file than the number of items that actually exist, a run-time error occurs. This error is caused by the program attempting to move the file pointer past the end-of-file character, and an "attempt to read past end of file" error results. Furthermore, *filename* must already exist or it cannot be opened as an input file. If VB attempts to open a file that does not exist or cannot be located, a "file not found" error results.

When a file is opened for Output, VB creates a new file called *filename* and sets the file pointer to the *beginning* of the file. If *filename* already exists, VB overwrites it and any data that was in this file is lost. If *filename* does not exist, VB creates a new file with this name.

Finally, opening a file for Append is another form of output that creates a new file if *filename* does not exist. However, if *filename* already exists, VB sets the file pointer to the *end* of this file; any new data written to this file is added (appended) to the end of the file.

Once a sequential file is opened for Input using an Open statement, data can be read from the file using an Input # statement:

```
Input #n, variable
```

This statement reads the next piece of data indicated by the file pointer from the input file with file number *n*, stores this data in *variable*, and then moves the file pointer to the next item in the input file. Since commas delimit data in sequential files, the file pointer moves to the first data item following the next comma. If the

*append moves ptr to 1^st empty space in an existing file*

file pointer encounters a <CR><LF> sequence, it simply moves to the beginning of the next line. Additionally, the data type of *variable* should match the type of data that is being read from the input file. If the data file consists of strings, for example, the data should be read into string variables. Finally, multiple Input # statements can be combined into one statement. For example:

```
Input #1, variable1
Input #1, variable2
Input #1, variable3
```

is equivalent to:

```
Input #1, variable1, variable2, variable3
```

While the Input # statement reads data item by item, the Line Input # statement reads an entire line from a sequential file. This statement ignores the comma delimiters and reads a line until it reaches a <CR> or <CR><LF> sequence. Data read with the Line Input # statement must be stored in a string variable. The general syntax is as follows:

> Line Input #*n*, *stringVar*

Just as before, we can combine multiple statements into one statement.

```
Line Input #1, stringVar1
Line Input #1, stringVar2
Line Input #1, stringVar3
```

reads three lines from file number 1 and is equivalent to:

```
Line Input #1, stringVar1, stringVar2, stringVar3
```

To output data to a sequential file (a file opened for Output or Append), use the Write # statement:

> Write #*n*, *variableList*

In this statement, *variableList* is a list of variables separated by commas. The Write # statement automatically inserts commas between data items and quotation marks around strings as they are written to the output file, so the programmer does not have to put explicit delimiters in the output. The Write # statement also inserts a <CR><LF> sequence after it has written the final variable in *variableList* to the output file.

Oftentimes, a programmer may want to format an output file rather than create a comma-separated output file. A point-of-sale program, for example, may create a customer invoice as an output file. The Print # statement writes display-formatted data to a sequential file. This statement works the same way as the Print method of a picture box, but it redirects the output to a file. The general syntax is as follows:

> Print #*n*, *expression*

Finally, when a program is finished working with a file, the file should be closed. The `Close` statement ends the association of a file number with a file and returns these resources to the system. For an output file, the `Close` statement also writes the end-of-file character before it closes the file. The syntax of the `Close` statement follows:

| | |
|---|---|
| `Close #n` | Close file number *n* |
| `Close #n1, #n2, [#n3, ...]` | Close file numbers *n1, n2, ...* |
| `Close` | Close all files |

There are two important functions that work with sequential files: the `LOF` function and `EOF` function. The `LOF` (length of file) function returns a long integer representing the length of a file in bytes. The `EOF` (end of file) function returns an integer containing the boolean value True when the end of an input file is reached. This integer value is –1 for True and 0 for False. The `EOF` function can be used in an indefinite loop structure to read data from an input file until the end-of-file is reached. The general syntax of these functions follows:

```
LOF (filenumber)

EOF (filenumber)
```

The `Dir` function is another useful function for file input and output. This function returns a string representing the name of a file, directory, or folder that matches a specified pattern, file attribute, or volume label of a drive. The `Dir` function returns the null string if no match is found. The general syntax follows:

```
Dir (filename)
```

An example program that uses sequential files for input and output appears on the next page. This program uses the `phone.txt` file as an input file. Two output files are created: `names.txt` is a comma-separated data file consisting of all the names in `phone.txt` and `fonelist.txt` is the phone list as a display-formatted text file. Figure 9.2 displays the contents of `names.txt` and `fonelist.txt` upon completion of the program.

```
names.txt
"Andrews","Lisa"
"Kimball","Jeffrey"
"McGuire","Jerry"
"Mnemonic","Johnny"
"Swan","Kristie"

fonelist.txt
Last Name     First Name     Phone Number
---------     ----------     ------------
Andrews       Lisa           670-7898
Kimball       Jeffrey        685-8765
McGuire       Jerry          685-5544
Mnemonic      Johnny         670-1234
Swan          Kristie        640-4511
```

**Figure 9.2** Output file contents

**PROGRAMMING KEY: WARNING**

Errors in the formatting of input data files are often the cause of run-time file input/output errors. Extra blank lines preceding the end of file marker are a common cause of such run-time errors. Before you debug your program, make sure that the input file is in the required format.

```
' SEQUENTIAL FILE I/O EXAMPLE
Option Explicit
Private Sub cmdPhoneList_Click()
' Open "phone.txt" and create "names.txt" and "fonelist.txt"
' "names.txt" contains all of the names in "phone.txt"
' "fonelist.txt" is a display-formatted output file
    Dim lastName As String, firstName As String, phoneNum As
    ➥ String
    Open "c:\phone.txt" For Input As #1
    Open "c:\names.txt" For Output As #2
    Open "c:\fonelist.txt" For Output As #3
    Print #3, "Last Name", "First Name", "Phone Number"
    Print #3, "————-", "—————", "———————"
    Do While Not (EOF(1))
        Input #1, lastName, firstName, phoneNum
        Write #2, lastName, firstName
        Print #3, lastName, firstName, phoneNum
    Loop
    Close     ' Close all files
    MsgBox "Files created.", vbInformation, "STATUS"
End Sub
```

## C A S E   S T U D Y
## Character Pattern Matching

Frank's English teacher informed him that he used the transition "however" too many times in his essay. Frank realized that he has a problem with overusing the same words. Being a proficient VB programmer, Frank created a character pattern matching program to aid him in analyzing his future writing.

Frank's program prompts the user for an input file name and a character pattern. The program then counts the number of matching character patterns in the input file. Frank's program is extremely flexible. It can count the number of occurrences of a single character (such as a letter, space, or punctuation mark), a word, or an entire phrase. The VB code for Frank's program appears below:

```
' Character Pattern Counter
Option Explicit

Private Sub cmdCount_Click()
' Count the number of matching character patterns
' in the input file and display the results
    Dim count As Long

    Call OpenFile
    count = CountMatches()
    Call CloseFile
    Call DisplayResults(count)
End Sub


Private Function CountMatches() As Long
```

```
' Count the number of pattern matches in the input file
    Dim count As Long, position As Integer, length As
    ➡ Integer
    Dim pattern As String, lineData As String

    pattern = CStr(txtPattern.Text)
    length = Len(pattern)
    count = 0

    Do While Not (EOF(1))
        Line Input #1, lineData
        For position = 1 To (Len(lineData) - length + 1)
            If Mid(lineData, position, length) = pattern Then
                count = count + 1
            End If
        Next position
    Loop

    CountMatches = count
End Function

Private Sub DisplayResults(count As Long)
' Display the number of pattern matches
    picOutput.Cls
    picOutput.Print count; "match";
    If count <> 1 Then
        picOutput.Print "es";
    End If
    picOutput.Print "."
End Sub

Private Sub OpenFile()
' Open the input file
    Open txtInFile.Text For Input As #1
End Sub

Private Sub CloseFile()
' Close the input file
    Close #1
End Sub
```

## RANDOM-ACCESS FILES

Unlike sequential files, **random-access files** can access data in any order; data can be read from or written to any location in the file. To perform this task, VB must know the exact length of a record in the data file. *Therefore, we highly recommend using fixed-length strings in your user-defined types (record types) to reduce the record size and the size of the resulting random-access file.*

As with sequential files, the Open statement opens a random-access file. The difference, however, is that opening a random-access file allows both input and output operations on the same file, whereas an Open statement for a sequential file allows just one of these operations. Additionally, there are slight differences in the syntax since the record length must be specified for random-access files. The general syntax of the Open statement for random-access files is as follows:

*✱can be written or read sequentially*

```
Dim recorVar As RecordType

Open filename For Random As #n Len = Len(recordVar)
```

*filename* and *n* are as specified in the section on sequential files. *recordVar* is a variable of the user-defined type *RecordType*. The Len = Len(*recordVar*) statement at the end of the Open statement specifies the record length in the data file.

Since VB can read from and write to any location in a random-access file, we must specify a **record number** during input and output operations. VB then moves the file pointer to the beginning of that record and performs the desired operation. The first record in a random-access file is assigned record number 1. If no record number is specified during input or output operations, VB performs the operation in the current position of the file pointer.

The Get # statement reads data from a random-access file. The general syntax follows:

READS

```
Get #n, recordNum, recordVar
```

Once again, *n* is the file number and *recordVar* is a variable of the user-defined type *RecordType*. *recordNum* is a long integer value specifying the record number. The above statement moves the file pointer to the beginning of record number *recordNum*, reads the data in this record into *recordVar*, and then moves the file pointer to the beginning of the next record.

If we omit the record number in the Get # statement, we obtain the following line of code:

```
Get #n, , recordVar
```

Notice that the commas are still required to delimit the different parameters of the Get # statement. This statement simply reads the data from the current record (the record indicated by the file pointer) into *recordVar*, and then moves the file pointer to the beginning of the next record.

To write data to a random-access file, use the Put # statement. This statement's syntax and operation are similar to the Get # statement, except that data is written to the file rather than read from the file. The syntax follows:

WRITES

```
Put #n, recordNum, recordVar          record number specified
Put #n, , recordVar                   no record number specified
```

The Seek # statement moves the file pointer in a random-access file without performing an input or output operation. The statement below moves the file pointer to the beginning of record number *recordNum* in file *n*:

```
Seek #n, recordNum
```

VB also contains a Seek function. The code below returns a long integer value specifying the current record number (the record where the file pointer is currently positioned).

```
Seek (n)
```

On a final note, both the LOF and EOF functions work with random-access files as well as sequential files. The LOF function works in the same manner for random-access files as it does for sequential files. So, to determine the number of records in a random-access file, use code similar to the following:

```
Dim numRecords As Long, recordVar As RecordType
Open filename For Random As #1 Len = Len(recordVar)
numRecords = LOF(1) / Len(recordVar)
```

## PROGRAMMING KEY: TIPS

There is no way to reduce the size of a random-access file. Once a record is created in a random-access file, the record exists forever. However, this does not mean that the record cannot be cleared. Programmers usually devise some method to indicate cleared or empty records within a random-access file (see the example below). Additionally, a programmer may use a "clean-up" routine to remove all empty records from a file by copying the nonempty records to a new file, deleting the old file, and then renaming the new file to the name of the old file. This prevents random-access files from becoming exceptionally large.

We now show a simple address book program that uses a random-access file named Address.txt. Figure 9.3 displays the form for this program.

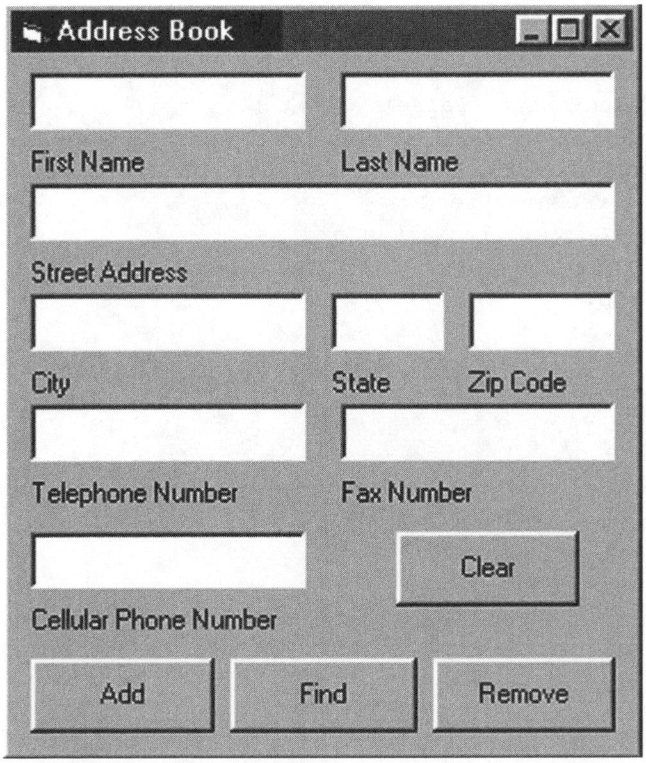

**Figure 9.3** Address book form

This address book program
uses (Empty) in the lastName field of
a record to designate a cleared record
within the random-access file. The
procedure for the Add command button
inserts a new record (new information)
into the first empty record, if one exists.
If no empty record exists, this procedure
inserts a new record at the end of the
random-access file.

```
' RANDOM-ACCESS FILE I/O EXAMPLE
' Address Book Program
Option Explicit

Private Type AddressCard
    firstName As String * 15
    lastName As String * 30
    street As String * 40
    city As String * 25
    state As String * 20
    zip As String * 10
    phone As String * 20
    fax As String * 20
    cellular As String * 20
End Type

Private Sub cmdAdd_Click()
' Add an address card to the data file
    Dim thisCard As AddressCard, aCard As AddressCard
    Dim foundEmpty As Boolean, recNum As Long

    thisCard.firstName = txtFirst.Text
    thisCard.lastName = txtLast.Text
    thisCard.street = txtAddress.Text
    thisCard.city = txtCity.Text
    thisCard.state = txtState.Text
    thisCard.zip = txtZip.Text
    thisCard.phone = txtPhone.Text
    thisCard.fax = txtFax.Text
    thisCard.cellular = txtCellular.Text

    Seek #1, 1
    foundEmpty = False
    recNum = 0
    Do While Not (EOF(1)) And Not (foundEmpty)
        recNum = recNum + 1
        Get #1, recNum, aCard
        foundEmpty = (Trim(aCard.lastName) = "(Empty)")
    Loop

    If Not (foundEmpty) Then
        recNum = recNum + 1
    End If

    Put #1, recNum, thisCard
    MsgBox "Address card added.", vbInformation, "ADD"
End Sub

Private Sub cmdClear_Click()
' Clear the form
    txtFirst.Text = ""
    txtLast.Text = ""
    txtAddress.Text = ""
    txtCity.Text = ""
```

```vb
        txtState.Text = ""
        txtZip.Text = ""
        txtPhone.Text = ""
        txtFax.Text = ""
        txtCellular.Text = ""
End Sub

Private Sub cmdFind_Click()
' Find an address card in the data file
    Dim aCard As AddressCard, recNum As Long

    recNum = FindCard()
    If recNum > 0 Then
        Get #1, recNum, aCard
        txtFirst.Text = aCard.firstName
        txtLast.Text = aCard.lastName
        txtAddress.Text = aCard.street
        txtCity.Text = aCard.city
        txtState.Text = aCard.state
        txtZip.Text = aCard.zip
        txtPhone.Text = aCard.phone
        txtFax.Text = aCard.fax
        txtCellular.Text = aCard.cellular
    Else
        MsgBox "Address card not found!", vbExclamation,
        ➥ "FIND"
    End If
End Sub

Private Sub cmdRemove_Click()
' Remove an address card from the data file
    Dim aCard As AddressCard, recNum As Long
    aCard.lastName = "(Empty)"
    recNum = FindCard()

    If recNum > 0 Then
        Put #1, recNum, aCard
        MsgBox "Address card removed.", vbExclamation,
        ➥ "REMOVE"
    Else
        MsgBox "Address card not found!", vbExclamation,
        ➥ "REMOVE"
    End If
End Sub

Private Function FindCard() As Long
' Return the record number of the address card matching
' the first and last names
    Dim aCard As AddressCard, found As Boolean, recNum As
    ➥ Long

    Seek #1, 1
    found = False
```

➥

```
            recNum = 0
            Do While Not (EOF(1)) And Not (found)
               recNum = recNum + 1
               Get #1, recNum, aCard
               found = (Trim(aCard.lastName) = Trim(txtLast.Text)
               ➥ And _
                        Trim(aCard.firstName) = Trim(txtFirst.Text))
         Loop

         If found Then
            FindCard = recNum
         Else
            FindCard = 0
         End If
      End Function

      Private Sub Form_Load()
      ' Open the data file
         Dim aCard As AddressCard
         Open "C:\Address.txt" For Random As #1 Len = Len(aCard)
      End Sub

      Private Sub Form_Unload(Cancel As Integer)
      ' Close the data file
         Close #1
      End Sub
```

## Summary

### Key Terms

**comma-separated data file** (or **comma-delimited data file**)—a data file in which commas separate the different pieces of information

**control** (**hidden,** or **escape**) **characters**—nonvisible characters that perform special functions, such as a carriage return or line feed

**data file**—a file that contains data

**file number**—in VB, an integer value between 1 and 511 that is associated with a specific file name

**file pointer**—a pointer that indicates the current read or write position in an open data file

**path**—a disk drive and subdirectory combination that indicates the location of a file

**random-access file**—a file that can be accessed in any order; data can be read from or written to any location in the file

**record number**—a number that references a specific record in a random-access file. The first record is associated with record number 1

**sequential file**—a file that is accessed from the beginning of the file to the end of the file (in sequence)

## Keywords

*Functions*:        Input
Dir               Input #
EOF               Len
Len               Line Input #
LOF               Open
Seek              Output
                  Print #
*Statements*:       Put #
Append            Random
Close             Seek #
Close #           Write #
Get #

## Key Concepts

● Data files allow programs a means of information storage and retrieval.

● Sequential files and random-access files are the two different types of data files available in VB. While sequential files must be accessed in order (from the beginning of the file to the end of the file), random-access files allow data to be accessed in any order.

● The most common sequential file format is the comma-separated (or comma-delimited) data file. This file format separates the data using commas, and strings are typically enclosed in quotation marks. A file of this type can be created using a simple text editor, such as WordPad.

● Before a data file can be accessed in a program, it must be opened. Similarly, when a program has completed all operations with a specified file, the file should be closed. VB has a distinct syntax for opening the different types of data files, but it uses the same statement to close all types of data files.

The general syntax to open a sequential file is:

```
Open filename For { Input | Output | Append } As #n
```

The general syntax to open a random-access file is:

```
Dim recorVar As RecordType
Open filename For Random As #n Len = Len(recordVar)
```

To close a specific file or files, use the `Close #` statement:

```
Close #n                    Close file number n
Close #n1, #n2, [#n3, ...]   Close file numbers n1, n2, ...
```

To close all data files, use:

```
Close
```

● VB contains statements to access data in both sequential and random-access files.

Statements for sequential file input include:

```
Input #n, variable
Line Input #n, stringVar
```

Statements for sequential file output include:

```
Write #n, variableList
Print #n, expression
```

Statements to work with random-access files include:

```
Get #n, recordNum, recordVar
Get #n, , recordVar

Put #n, recordNum, recordVar
Put #n, , recordVar
```

● VB has several functions that are useful for data file access. These functions include LOF, EOF, Dir, Seek, and Len.

## Review Questions

1. What is the purpose of a data file?
2. Name the two types of data files in VB. Describe the differences between these file types.
3. What is a comma-separated data file?  How can you create one?
4. Write the VB statement(s) necessary to:
   a. open a sequential file for input
   b. open a sequential file for output (by overwriting old data)
   c. open a sequential file for output (without overwriting old data)
   d. open a random-access file for input
   e. open a random-access file for output
5. File #1 is a sequential file open for input. In your code, you forget to close the file. The user enters a new file name and presses the Get Data command button. What happens when your code tries to re-open file #1?
6. What does the Close statement do?

## Chapter 9 Problems

1. Write a program that displays the contents of a file in a picture box (line by line). This program just "dumps" the data from the file onto the screen, so it is referred to as a "file dump" program.
2. Modify your code from Chapter 8, Problem 1 to save data to and load data from a user-specified sequential file.
3. Modify your code from Chapter 8, Problem 3 to save data to and load data from a user-specified random-access file.
4. Modify your code from Chapter 8 Supplement, Problem 1 to save data to and load data from a user-specified random-access file.
5. Modify the address book program in this chapter to use objects. Your program should store objects in the random-access file instead of records.

## Programming Projects

**1.** VB contains an end of file (EOF) function but no end of line (EOLN) function. This makes it difficult to read and interpret complicated data files (as in the case of Programming Project 2 below). Write a code module that contains ReadLine, ReadData, and EOLN functions. The ReadLine function reads the next line of data from the input file, ReadData returns the next piece of comma-separated data, and the EOLN function indicates whether or not more data exists on the current line.

**2.** Use the code module from Programming Project 1 above in a program that reads student names, course grades, and course credit hours from a sequential file and then computes grade point averages (GPAs) for the students. The student GPAs should be written to a text-formatted sequential file. A sample input file is as follows:

```
"Smith","John","A",4,"B",4,"B",4,"A",3
"Thomas","Mark","C",5,"A",5,"A",4
"Hoffman","Susan","B",3,"B",4,"C",3,"B",4,"B",3
```

Students can take different numbers of courses, but each student takes at least one course. The input file format is:

Last Name, First Name, Letter Grade, Credit Hours [Letter Grade, Credit Hours ...]

**3.** Write a program that allows the user to create an input file for Programming Project 2.

**4.** Write a word frequency counter program. This program accepts an ASCII text file for input and counts the number of occurrences of each word in the file. The results are stored in a user-designated output file. Your program should not be case-sensitive, and it should ignore punctuation marks. (In other words, make sure that your program does not count a punctuation mark as part of a word.)

A sample input file appears below:

```
The quick brown fox jumped over the lazy dog.
```

The output file associated with the above input file is as follows:

```
Word            Frequency
____            _____

the             2
quick           1
brown           1
fox             1
jumped          1
over            1
lazy            1
dog             1
```

# Sorting and Searching

## Chapter Supplement Objectives

In this chapter supplement, you will:

● Learn about the ordering of data, including both ascending and descending order

● Learn how to exchange (or "swap") the contents of variables

● Become familiar with sorting techniques, including the bubble sort and Shell sort algorithms

● Understand searching techniques, including the sequential search and binary search

## Key Terms

**sorting**—a method of arranging data

**searching**—in contrast to sorting, a method of locating a specific data item quickly

In many of the programs shown in this text, data is stored in the order in which it is entered. In our phone book program, for instance, Ted Johnson may appear before Jill Anderson in the data file, but we know that Anderson alphabetically precedes Johnson. **Sorting** is a way of arranging data in a certain order, either **ascending order** or **descending order.** When data is arranged in ascending order, a particular data item is preceded by a lower-valued data item. If arranged in descending order, the same data item would be preceded by a higher-valued data item. For instance, the digits 1 through 5 are arranged as:

> 1, 2, 3, 4, 5   in ascending order
>
> and
>
> 5, 4, 3, 2, 1   in descending order

Sorting is used to arrange data; in contrast,  **searching** is concerned with finding a specific data item quickly. This task is extremely fast when we have only 10 data items, but it can be considerably slower when there are 10,000 (or an exceptionally large number of) data items.

Sorting and searching techniques are advanced topics in computer science. Volumes of literature are devoted to these subjects, and most of these texts are primarily concerned with the efficiency (speed) of the algorithms involved. Since the computation of algorithm efficiency is beyond the scope of this text, we limit our discussion to a few of the most common sorting and searching algorithms.

### Sorting

We discuss two different sorting algorithms, the bubble sort and the Shell sort. Both of these sorting algorithms require exchanging the contents of variables. Let's think about how to exchange variable values, perhaps by using the following code:

```
Dim value1 As Integer, value2 As Integer
```

```
value1 = 5
value2 = 10

‘ Swap value1 and value2 ??? (Incorrect swap)
value1 = value2
value2 = value1
```

Do you see the problem? Both `value1` and `value2` contain the value 10 after this code executes, and the original contents of `value1` are lost. We need to temporarily store the contents of `value1` in another variable. We create a variable named `temp` for this purpose, and a correct method for swapping variable values appears below:

```
‘ Swap value1 and value2
temp = value1
value1 = value2
value2 = temp
```

The **bubble sort** compares adjacent data items and swaps them if they are out of order. This process is repeated for each pair of adjacent data items in the list. This sort continues to make **passes** through the list, comparing adjacent data items and swapping values as necessary, until all data items are in order. The methodology of this sorting technique follows:

1. Compare the first and second items. Swap values if they are out of order.
2. Compare the second and third items. Swap values if they are out of order.
3. Continue this process for all remaining pairs of data items in the list.
4. Repeat steps 1 through 3 until the data is ordered (no more swaps are required).

Essentially, small values "bubble" up to the top in an ascending bubble sort. In more general terms, we present the pseudocode for an ascending bubble sort on a list containing $N$ data items. Note that at most $N-1$ passes are necessary to sort a list using this technique. One additional pass is necessary to verify that the list has been sorted.

```
          Bubble Sort Pseudocode

Do
    sorted = True
    For i = 1 To N-1
        If data(i) > data(i+1) Then
            temp = data(i)
            data(i) = data(i+1)
            data(i+1) = temp
            sorted = False
        End If
    Next i
Loop Until sorted
```

The following program uses a bubble sort to sort an array of 10 user-entered integer values in ascending order. Figure 9.4 displays a sample execution of this program.

```
' Bubble Sort Example
' ─────────────────────

Option Explicit
Const N = 10

Private Sub cmdStart_Click()
    Dim data(1 To N) As Integer, sorted As Boolean, temp As
    ➥ Integer
    Dim i As Integer, passNum As Integer, message As String

    ' Enter data
    picOutput.Cls
    picOutput.Print "Original order of data:"
    picOutput.Print "──────────────────────────"
    For i = 1 To N
        message = "Enter value #" & Trim(Str(i)) & ":"
        data(i) = CInt(InputBox(message, "Enter Integer
        ➥ Value"))
        picOutput.Print data(i);
    Next i
    picOutput.Print
    picOutput.Print

    ' Sort the data
    passNum = 0
    Do
    passNum = passNum + 1
        sorted = True
        For i = 1 To N - 1
```

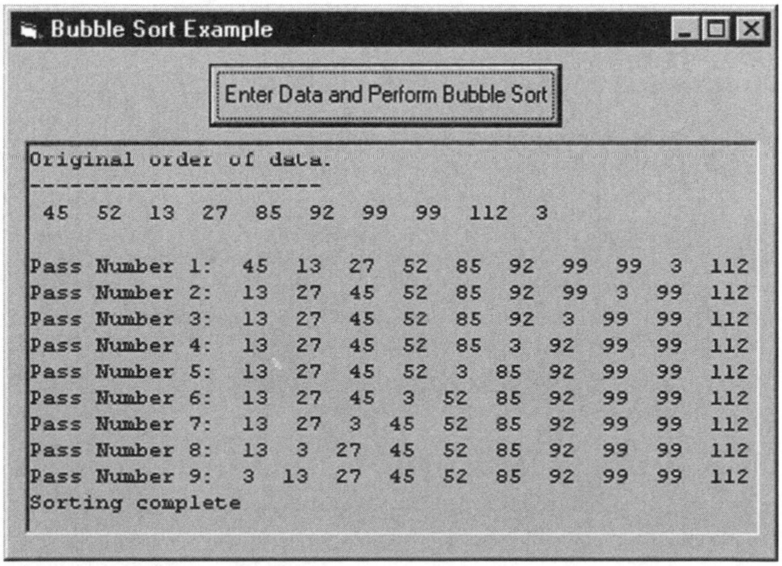

**Figure 9.4** Bubble sort example

```
        If data(i) > data(i + 1) Then
            temp = data(i)
            data(i) = data(i + 1)
            data(i + 1) = temp
            sorted = False
        End If
    Next i
    If Not (sorted) Then
        picOutput.Print "Pass Number ";
        ➥ Trim(Str(passNum)); ": ";
        For i = 1 To N
            picOutput.Print data(i);
        Next i
        picOutput.Print
    End If
    Loop Until sorted
    picOutput.Print "Sorting complete"
End Sub
```

The **Shell sort** is named after its creator, Donald L. Shell, and it is much more efficient than the bubble sort for sorting large lists. This algorithm compares distant data items first and works its way down toward comparing close data items. The **gap** is the interval that separates the data items being compared. Initially, the gap is one-half the number of data items in the list; it is successively halved until eventually each item in the list is compared with its neighbor as in the bubble sort. The Shell sort algorithm for a list containing $N$ items follows:

1. Set gap = N \ 2.
2. For each item $i$ in the list, where $i$ ranges from 1 to N – gap, compare item $i$ and item $i$ + gap. Swap the items if necessary.
3. Repeat step 2 until no swaps are made for this value of *gap*.
4. Set *gap* = *gap* \ 2.
5. Repeat the above steps until the value of *gap* is 0.

By translating the above algorithm into pseudocode, we obtain the pseudocode for an ascending Shell sort on a list containing $N$ items:

```
            Shell Sort Pseudocode

gap = N \ 2
Do
    Do
        gapDone = True
        For i = 1 To N - gap
            If data(i) > data(i + gap) Then
                temp = data(i)
                data(i) = data(i + gap)
                data(i + gap) = temp
                gapDone = False
            End If
        Next i
    Loop Until gapDone
    gap = gap \ 2
Loop Until gap = 0
```

We now rewrite the previous program using a Shell sort instead of a bubble sort. A sample program execution appears in Figure 9.5.

```
' Shell Sort Example
' _____

Option Explicit
Const N = 10

Private Sub cmdStart_Click()
    Dim data(1 To N) As Integer, gap As Integer, temp As
    ➡ Integer
    Dim gapDone As Boolean, i As Integer, message As String

    ' Enter data
    picOutput.Cls
    picOutput.Print "Original order of data:"
    picOutput.Print "————————————————————"
    For i = 1 To N
        message = "Enter value #" & Trim(Str(i)) & ":"
        data(i) = CInt(InputBox(message, "Enter Integer
        ➡ Value"))
        picOutput.Print data(i);
    Next i
    picOutput.Print
    picOutput.Print

    ' Sort the data
    gap = N \ 2
    Do
```

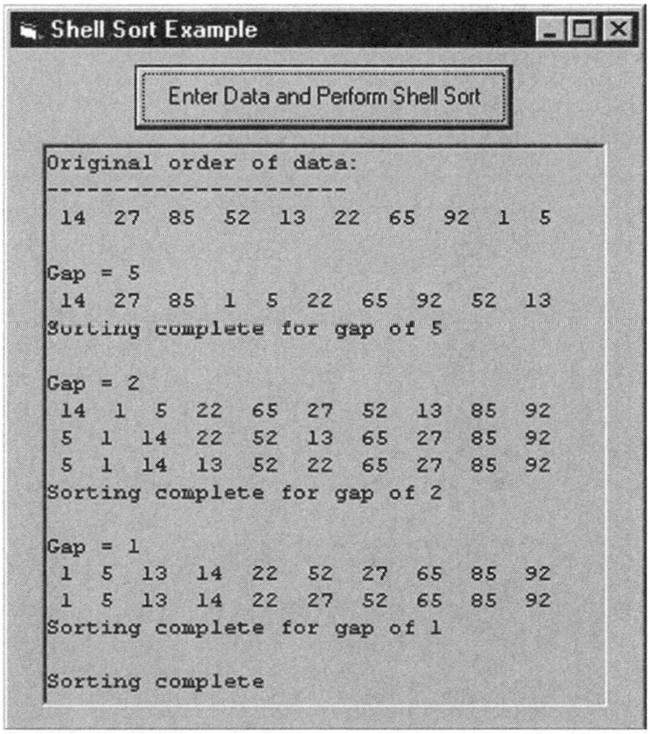

**Figure 9.5**  Shell sort example

```
        picOutput.Print "Gap ="; gap
        Do
            gapDone = True
            For i = 1 To N - gap
                If data(i) > data(i + gap) Then
                    temp = data(i)
                    data(i) = data(i + gap)
                    data(i + gap) = temp
                    gapDone = False
                End If
            Next i
            If Not (gapDone) Then
                For i = 1 To N
                    picOutput.Print data(i);
                Next i
            Else
                picOutput.Print "Sorting complete for gap of "
                ➥ & gap
            End If
            picOutput.Print
        Loop Until gapDone
        gap = gap \ 2
    Loop Until gap = 0
    picOutput.Print "Sorting complete"
End Sub
```

## Searching

We now present two searching algorithms, the sequential search and the binary search. The **sequential search**, as you might expect, starts at the beginning of the data and looks at each data item in sequence until it finds the **target data item**. Examples of a sequential search appear in the address book program in this chapter. The FindCard() function, for instance, sequentially searches the random-access file for the record that matches the first and last names. If a matching record is found, FindCard() returns the associated record number; otherwise, FindCard() returns a 0. A similar sequential search appears in the cmdAdd_Click() procedure. When a new address card is added, the program searches for the first empty record in the random-access file. Empty records are formed by removing address cards from the file. A new address card is stored in the first empty record found in the random-access file. If no empty record is found, then the new address card is appended to the end of the file.

Like the bubble sort, the sequential search is not very efficient for large amounts of data. Imagine searching sequentially through the phone book for the last name "Zugfield;" it could take a long time to find the desired piece of information. A **binary search** is more efficient than the sequential search for large data sets. However, *a binary search requires the data to be sorted in a specific order, whereas the sequential search does not.* Once again, there is little difference in the performance of these searches for small amounts of data.

To understand the binary search, think of the game of High-Low (Pick-A-Number). In this game, your friend picks a number from 1 to 100, for instance. Now, you try to guess the number that he picked. If the number that you pick is lower than his, he tells you "higher." Similarly, if your number is too high, your friend tells you "lower." After a few guesses, you can get upper and lower bounds on your friend's number until you finally "zero-in" on the correct number. The binary search operates much the same way. It continues to split the list of data items in half until it finds the target item or discovers that it is not contained in the data set.

The pseudocode for a binary search on a list of *N* data items sorted in ascending order appears below.

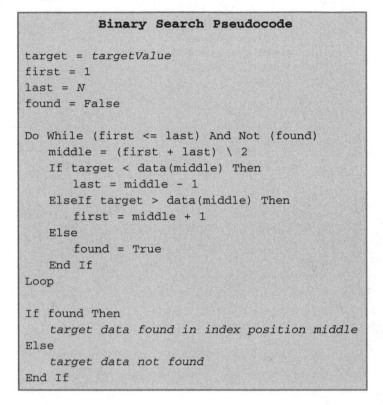

```
               Binary Search Pseudocode

target = targetValue
first = 1
last = N
found = False

Do While (first <= last) And Not (found)
    middle = (first + last) \ 2
    If target < data(middle) Then
        last = middle - 1
    ElseIf target > data(middle) Then
        first = middle + 1
    Else
        found = True
    End If
Loop

If found Then
    target data found in index position middle
Else
    target data not found
End If
```

## Summary

### Key Terms

**ascending order**—arrangement of data in order of increasing value

**binary search**—a search algorithm that iteratively splits the list of data items in half until it finds the target data item or discovers that it is not contained in the data set

**bubble sort**—a sorting algorithm that compares adjacent data items and swaps them if they are out of order

**descending order**—arrangement of data in order of decreasing value

**gap**—in a Shell sort, the interval that separates the data items being compared

**pass**—one complete iteration through all values

**searching**—a method of locating a specific data item quickly

**sequential search**—a search algorithm that starts at the beginning of the data and examines each item in sequence until it finds the target data item

**Shell sort**—a sorting algorithm created by Donald L. Shell that compares distant data items first and works its way down toward comparing close data items

**sorting**—a method of arranging data

**target data item**—the data item of interest in a search

## Key Concepts

● Sorting arranges data in a particular order. Data may be sorted in either ascending or descending order. Ascending order is the arrangement of data by increasing value, and descending order is the arrangement by decreasing value.

● Exchanging the values of variables is a key concept in sorting data. To exchange (or "swap") the contents of two variables, we must create a temporary variable (temp) to hold the value of one of the variables during the swap; otherwise, we lose a piece of data and get a redundant value. The proper method of swapping the contents of variables `value1` and `value2` follows:

```
temp = value1
value1 = value2
value2 = temp
```

● The bubble sort and Shell sort are two sorting algorithms. The bubble sort compares adjacent values and swaps data as necessary, allowing small values to "bubble up" to the top of an ascending list. The Shell sort begins by comparing distant items and works its way toward comparing close data items. While both the bubble sort and Shell sort work well for small amounts of data, the Shell sort is much more efficient for large lists.

● Searching is a method of locating a specific data item (the target data item) quickly.

● The sequential search and the binary search are two searching algorithms. The sequential search starts at the beginning of the data and looks at each item in sequence until it finds its target. The binary search attempts to locate the target data item by iteratively splitting the list in half. Therefore, the binary search requires the data to be sorted prior to the search. While there is little difference in the performance of these searches for small amounts of data, the binary search is much more efficient for large data sets.

## Review Questions

1. Write the following numbers in ascending order and descending order.

    88, 76, 94, 52, 37, 29, 100, 92, 67, 48

2. Write the VB code to swap the values of two integer variables, `variable1` and `variable2`.

3. Write the pseudocode for an ascending bubble sort on a list containing $N$ items.

4. Write the pseudocode for an ascending Shell sort on a list containing $N$ items.

5. Write the pseudocode for a sequential search on a list containing $N$ items.

6. Write the pseudocode for a binary search on a list containing $N$ items. Assume that the list is already sorted in ascending order.

## Chapter 9 Supplement Problems

1. Write a program that sorts a data file created with the address book program using a bubble sort.

2. Repeat Problem 1 using a Shell sort instead of a bubble sort.

3. Write a program that finds a specific record and prints an address label. The program should use a data file created with the address book program. Use a sequential search in this program.

4. Repeat Problem 3 by first sorting the data file using a Shell sort. Then, find the target record using a binary search.

## Programming Projects

1. Modify the code from Chapter 9, Programming Project 2 to write the text-formatted sequential file in descending order by GPA.

2. Assume that you have two different output files from Programming Project 1 above. Write a program that merges (combines) these files in descending order by GPA.

3. Modify the code from Chapter 9, Programming Project 4 to write the output file in alphabetical order of the words.

# 10

# Advanced Visual Basic

## Chapter Objectives

In this chapter, you will:

- Be introduced to additional Visual Basic controls

- Learn how to add components to the Toolbox

- Learn about the Menu Editor and how to create custom menus

- Learn the purpose and use of control arrays

- Gain an understanding of ActiveX technology and how to create an ActiveX control

- Learn about the collection data structure

- Learn about multiple forms programming and multiple document interface (MDI) forms

- Be introduced to random numbers and computer simulation

- Become familiar with Visual Basic's graphics capabilities and graphics programming

- Learn about object linking and embedding (OLE) and dynamic data exchange (DDE)

- Examine Visual Basic's Internet capabilities and Internet programming

- Acquire an understanding of compiler directives and conditional compilation

This chapter discusses more advanced topics in Visual Basic, including additional Visual Basic controls, control arrays, ActiveX controls, collections, multiple forms programming, multiple document interface (MDI) forms, random numbers, graphics, object linking and embedding (OLE), dynamic data exchange (DDE), Internet programming, and Visual Basic compiler directives.

# ADDITIONAL VISUAL BASIC CONTROLS

In Chapter 2, we introduced the elementary VB controls required to make a simple program. Although forms, text boxes, picture boxes, labels, and command buttons are sufficient controls for most programs, much of the power and appeal of VB comes from the ease with which a programmer can design complex user-interfaces by selecting specific controls and setting the appropriate properties.

This section introduces several additional VB control objects. We show simple applications of these objects and explain some of their properties; this section does not provide a comprehensive reference for these VB controls. The VB online help, books online, and *Visual Basic Programmer's Guide* provide more detail concerning these controls and they should be consulted as necessary.

## ☑ CHECK BOX

The check box control allows the user to select *one or more* items from a list of several alternatives. A check mark is placed in the box when it is selected, and the box is empty when it is not selected. The user may use either the mouse or the space bar to toggle the state of the check box.

The Caption property contains the text that appears to the right of the check box. The Value property describes the state of the check box. The Value property is 0 if the check box is cleared (no check mark), 1 if the check box is selected, and 2 if the check box is unavailable (not able to be checked or unchecked). An example program using check boxes follows, and a sample execution of this code appears in Figure 10.1. Note that the Name property for a check box control is prefaced with chk in the same manner used for other controls in Chapter 2 and Appendix B.

| Object | Property | Setting |
|---|---|---|
| Form | Name | frmCheckBox |
| | Caption | Credit Cards |
| CommandButton | Name | cmdEvaluate |
| | Caption | Evaluate Answer |
| PictureBox | Name | picOutput |
| Label | Name | lblQuestion |
| | AutoSize | True |
| | Caption | Which credit cards do you use? |
| CheckBox | Name | chkVisa |
| | Caption | Visa |
| CheckBox | Name | chkMaster |
| | Caption | Mastercard |
| CheckBox | Name | chkDiscover |
| | Caption | Discover Card |
| CheckBox | Name | chkAmEx |
| | Caption | American Express |

```
' Check Box Example
Option Explicit

Private Sub cmdEvaluate_Click()
' Evaluate user's answers
```

**Figure 10.1** Check box example

```
picOutput.Cls
picOutput.Print "You use the following credit cards:"

If chkVisa.Value = 1 Then
    picOutput.Print "Visa"
End If
If chkMaster.Value = 1 Then
    picOutput.Print "Mastercard"
End If
If chkDiscover.Value = 1 Then
    picOutput.Print "Discover Card"
End If
If chkAmEx.Value = 1 Then
    picOutput.Print "American Express"
End If
End Sub
```

**PROGRAMMING KEY: TIPS**

The = 1 in each of the If-statements in the Check Box Example may be omitted. VB evaluates a nonzero value as True and a zero value as False.

## OPTION BUTTON

In contrast to check boxes, which allow one or more items to be selected, option buttons allow the user to select a single item from a list of several alternatives. Option buttons are grouped by placing them inside a container object, such as a form, picture box, or frame. Furthermore, all option buttons within the same container act as a single group. To group option buttons within a picture box or frame, place the picture box or frame on the form first, and then place the option button controls inside.

When an option button is selected, all other option buttons in the group are automatically cleared. The Value property describes the state of the option button. It is set to True when the option button is selected and False when the option button is not selected. The Caption property contains the text that appears to the right of the option button. An example program containing option buttons follows, and Figure 10.2 shows a sample execution of this code.

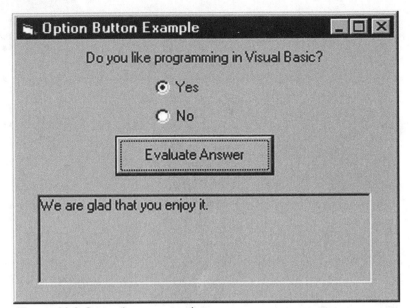

**Figure 10.2** Option button example

| Object | Property | Setting |
|--------|----------|---------|
| Form | Name | frmOptionButton |
| | Caption | Option Button Example |
| CommandButton | Name | cmdEvaluate |
| | Caption | Evaluate Answer |
| PictureBox | Name | picOutput |
| Label | Name | lblQuestion |
| | AutoSize | True |
| | Caption | Do you like programming in Visual Basic? |
| OptionButton | Name | optYes |
| | Caption | Yes |
| OptionButton | Name | optNo |
| | Caption | No |

```
' Option Button Example
Option Explicit

Private Sub cmdEvaluate_Click()

    picOutput.Cls

    If optYes.Value Then
        picOutput.Print "We are glad that you enjoy it."
    ElseIf optNo.Value Then
        picOutput.Print "Why not?  It's fun!"
    End If
End Sub
```

## FRAME

Frames, as mentioned above, provide an identifiable group of related controls and functionally subdivide a form. For example, option buttons can be grouped inside

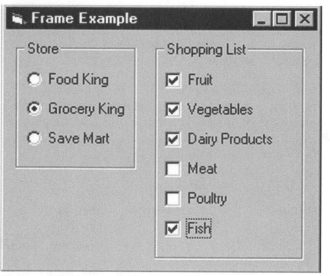

**Figure 10.3** Frame example

**GUI Design Tips**

Frames act as containers for other controls. To place controls inside of a frame, first insert the frame on the form, and then place the controls inside of the frame. Any number of check boxes may be selected within a frame, but only one option button may be selected within a frame.

of a frame, allowing only one of the option buttons in the frame to be selected. Once again, the `Caption` property contains descriptive text to identify the frame. Figure 10.3 displays a form containing two frames.

## LIST BOX

The list box control allows the user to select one or more items from a list. If the number of items in the list exceeds the number of items that can be displayed in the list box, a scroll bar is automatically added to the list box control.

At design time, items are added to the list box using the `List` property, which has a drop-down menu in which list items are located. To add multiple items to the

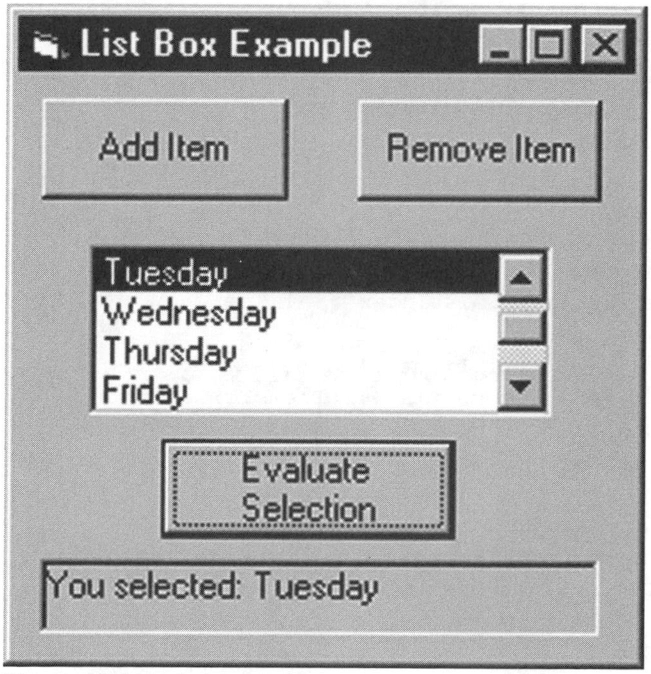


**Figure 10.4** List box example

**PROGRAMMING KEY: TIPS**

At run time, items can be added to a list box in alphabetical order by setting the `Sorted` property to True and omitting the index argument in the `AddItem` method. When the `Sorted` property is set to True, using the `AddItem` method with an index argument can lead to unpredictable results.

list box at design time, press CTRL+ENTER after each item (rather than just ENTER) to prevent the `List` property from closing the drop-down menu. At run time, items can be added to the list box using the `AddItem` method or removed from the list box using the `RemoveItem` method. The `List`, `ListCount`, and `ListIndex` properties allow the programmer to access items in the list. The first item in the list is associated with a `ListIndex` property value of 0, and `ListCount` contains the number of items in the list (i.e., `ListCount` is the largest `ListIndex` value plus 1). `ListIndex` contains the value −1 if no item is selected. The `MultiSelect` property specifies whether more than one item may be selected from the list. The `Sorted` property specifies whether or not the items are listed in alphabetical order. The following code shows an example use of the list box control. Figure 10.4 on the previous page shows the form for this example.

| Object | Property | Setting |
|---|---|---|
| Form | Name | frmListBox |
| | Caption | List Box Example |
| CommandButton | Name | cmdAdd |
| | Caption | Add Item |
| CommandButton | Name | cmdRemove |
| | Caption | Remove Item |
| CommandButton | Name | cmdEvaluate |
| | Caption | Evaluate Selection |
| PictureBox | Name | picOutput |
| ListBox | Name | lstItems |
| | List | Monday; Tuesday; Wednesday; Thursday; Friday; Saturday; Sunday |

The semicolons in the `List` ➞ property indicate that these items are separated on different lines in the list box (i.e., press CTRL+ENTER after entering each item).

```
' List Box Example
Option Explicit

Private Sub cmdAdd_Click()
' Add an item to the list
   Dim item As String
   item = CStr(InputBox("Item to add:", "ADD ITEM"))
   If item <> "" Then
      lstItems.AddItem (item)
   End If
End Sub

Private Sub cmdEvaluate_Click()
' Evaluate the selected item
   If lstItems.ListIndex > -1 Then
       picOutput.Cls
       picOutput.Print "You selected: ";
    ➥ lstItems.List(lstItems.ListIndex)
   End If
End Sub

Private Sub cmdRemove_Click()
' Remove the selected item from the list
   If lstItems.ListIndex > -1 Then
       lstItems.RemoveItem (lstItems.ListIndex)
   End If
End Sub
```

## COMBO BOX

The combo box is similar to a list box, and it can save space on a form. There are three different styles of combo boxes available: the drop-down combo box, simple combo box, and drop-down list. The desired type of combo box is specified at design time using the `Style` property.

The drop-down combo box (style 0) contains both a text box and a drop-down list. The user can either type an item in the text box or select one from the list. The simple combo box (style 1) includes a text box and a list that does not drop down (i.e., it is visible at all times). Finally, the drop-down list (style 2) contains only a list; there is no text box where a user can type data.

The combo box control has the same methods and properties as the list box control. In the following code, the previous example is modified to use a drop-down combo box instead of a list box. Figure 10.5 displays the form for this code.

| Object | Property | Setting |
|---|---|---|
| Form | Name | frmComboBox |
| | Caption | Combo Box Example |
| CommandButton | Name | cmdRemove |
| | Caption | Remove Item |
| CommandButton | Name | cmdEvaluate |
| | Caption | Evaluate Selection |
| PictureBox | Name | picOutput |
| ComboBox | Name | cboItems |
| | Style | 0 |
| | Text | Day of the Week |
| | List | Monday; Tuesday; Wednesday; Thursday; Friday; Saturday; Sunday |

The semicolons in the `List` property indicate that these items are separated on different lines in the combo box (i.e., press CTRL+ENTER after entering each item).

```
' Combo Box Example
' (uses a drop-down combo box [style 0])
Option Explicit

Private Sub cboItems_GotFocus()
' Clear picture box whenever combo box is selected
   picOutput.Cls
End Sub

Private Sub cboItems_KeyPress(KeyAscii As Integer)
' Add an item to the combo box
' NOTE: To add an item, type it in the text box and press
➥ ENTER
   If KeyAscii = 13 Then
      cboItems.AddItem (cboItems.Text)
```

The `cboItems_KeyPress` event handler adds the item typed in the combo box to the list when the user presses the ENTER key.

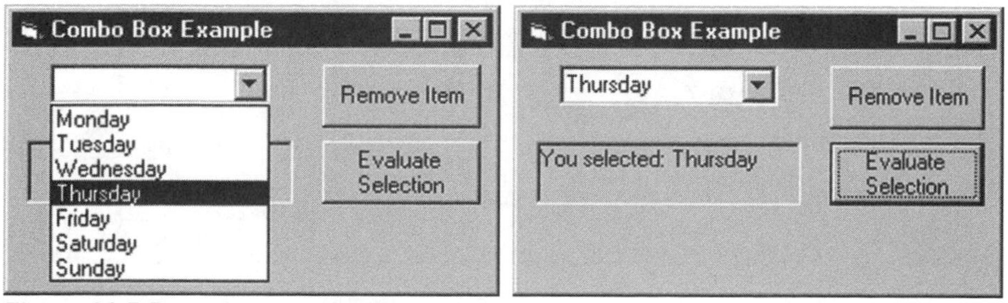

**Figure 10.5** Drop-down combo box example

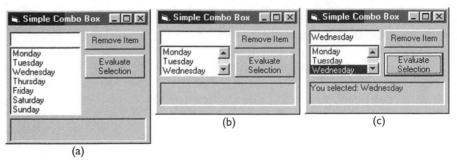

**Figure 10.6** Simple combo box example

```
        End If
End Sub

Private Sub cmdEvaluate_Click()
' Evaluate the selected item
    picOutput.Cls
    picOutput.Print "You selected: ";
    If cboItems.ListIndex > -1 Then
        picOutput.Print cboItems.List(cboItems.ListIndex)
    ElseIf cboItems.Text <> "" Then
        picOutput.Print cboItems.Text
        cboItems.AddItem (cboItems.Text)
    Else
        picOutput.Print "NOTHING"
    End If
End Sub

Private Sub cmdRemove_Click()
' Remove the selected item from the combo box
    If cboItems.ListIndex > -1 Then
        cboItems.RemoveItem (cboItems.ListIndex)
    End If
End Sub
```

This same code can be used with a simple combo box; the only change required is using a Style setting of 1 rather than 0. As illustrated by Figure 10.6(a), the entire list is displayed at all times, provided that the list box is made sufficiently large at design time. Otherwise, a vertical scroll bar is automatically inserted as in Figure 10.6(b). As seen in Figure 10.6(c), program execution produces a result similar to the drop-down combo box.

Like the other two combo box controls, the drop-down list box, illustrated in Figure 10.7(a), also displays a text box and a list of items from which the user can choose. However, the user is unable to type in the text box to add to the list, and the list itself is displayed only when the arrow to the right of the list box is clicked, as seen in Figure 10.7(b). This type of control is best suited for forms in which space is limited. Program execution [Figure 10.7(c)] produces a result similar to the other combo box controls.

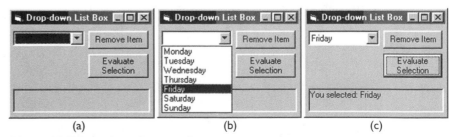

**Figure 10.7** Drop-down list example

## HORIZONTAL AND VERTICAL SCROLL BARS

Scroll bars provide a rapid means of navigating through long lists of items or large quantities of data. They are often used as input devices to indicate a desired speed or quantity level. Furthermore, scroll bars can be used to provide an analog representation of position.

The `Min` and `Max` properties of the scroll bar specify the appropriate range for the control. The `Value` property contains the current value (position) of the scroll bar. The `LargeChange` property specifies the amount that `Value` changes when the scroll bar is clicked. Similarly, the `SmallChange` property specifies the amount that `Value` changes when an arrow at the end of the scroll bar is clicked.

An example use of scroll bars follows, and Figure 10.8 displays the associated form.

| Object | Property | Setting |
| --- | --- | --- |
| Form | Name | frmAirplane |
|  | Caption | Scrolling Airplane |
| VScrollBar | Name | vsbY |
|  | LargeChange | 500 |
|  | SmallChange | 100 |
|  | Max | 2500 |
|  | Min | 100 |
|  | Value | 500 |
| HScrollBar | Name | hsbX |
|  | LargeChange | 500 |
|  | SmallChange | 100 |
|  | Max | 3000 |
|  | Min | 100 |
|  | Value | 500 |
| Label | Name | lblAirplane |
|  | AutoSize | True |
|  | Caption | Q |
|  | Font | Wingdings |

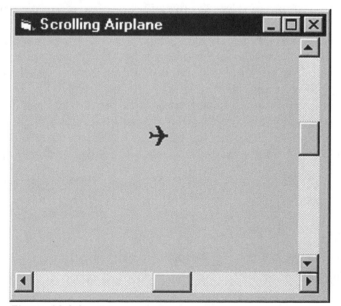

**Figure 10.8** Scroll bar example

```
' Scroll Bar Example
Option Explicit

Private Sub Form_Load()
' Set the starting position of the airplane
   hsbX.Value = hsbX.Min
   vsbY.Value = vsbY.Min
   lblAirplane.Left = hsbX.Value
   lblAirplane.Top = vsbY.Value
End Sub

Private Sub hsbX_Change()
' Change the X position of the airplane
   lblAirplane.Left = hsbX.Value
End Sub

Private Sub hsbX_Scroll()
' Change the X position of the airplane
   lblAirplane.Left = hsbX.Value
End Sub

Private Sub vsbY_Change()
' Change the Y position of the airplane
   lblAirplane.Top = vsbY.Value
End Sub

Private Sub vsbY_Scroll()
' Change the Y position of the airplane
   lblAirplane.Top = vsbY.Value
End Sub
```

## DRIVE, DIRECTORY, AND FILE LIST BOXES

The drive, directory, and file list boxes are list boxes that access the computer's disk drive information in order to display drive, directory folder, and file name information, respectively, at run time. These controls are most often used in combination to allow a user to select a specific file. Using the controls in combination requires that they first be synchronized in the program's code. For example, when the user selects a specific drive from the drive list box, the information in the directory and file list boxes should change accordingly.

Since these controls are list boxes, they have List, ListCount, and ListIndex properties. Additionally, the directory and file list boxes have Path properties that specify the location of files. The following code demonstrates the use of drive, directory, and file list boxes. Figure 10.9 shows the form for this program.

| Object | Property | Setting |
|---|---|---|
| Form | Name | frmFiles |
|  | Caption | Select a File |
| PictureBox | Name | picOutput |
| FileListBox | Name | filList |
| DirListBox | Name | dirList |
| DriveListBox | Name | drvList |

**Select a File**

```
c: [G283]                          ▼

C:\
Program Files
Microsoft Visual Studio
VB98

READMEDT.HTM
READMERP.HTM
READMEVB.HTM
REDIST.TXT
RICHTX32.oca
SCCVBUS.CHI
SCCVBUS.CHM
TABCTL32.oca
VB6.EXE

The current path is C:\Program Files\Microsoft Visual Studio\VB98
You selected file: VB6.EXE
```

**Figure 10.9** Drive directory and file list box example

```
' Drive, directory, and file list box example
Option Explicit

Private Sub dirList_Change()
' Change the directory
    filList.Path = dirList.Path
End Sub

Private Sub drvList_Change()
' Change the disk drive
    dirList.Path = drvList.Drive
    filList.Path = dirList.Path
End Sub

Private Sub filList_DblClick()
' Select a file (double-click on a file)
    picOutput.Cls
    picOutput.Print "The current path is "; filList.Path
    picOutput.Print "You selected file: "; filList.filename
End Sub
```

## TIMER

The timer control allows specific code to be executed at user-specified intervals by causing a Timer event to occur. The timer control is transparent to the user, and it is useful for background processing.

The length of time between triggering events is measured in milliseconds and set in the `Interval` property. For timer control `Timer1`, for instance, the `Timer1_Timer()` event is automatically triggered each time `Timer1.Interval` milliseconds elapse. The `Interval` property can range from 0 to 65,535 milliseconds (1 minute, 5.535 seconds). To begin timing, the `Enabled` property of the timer must be set to True. A timer control may be disabled by setting its `Enabled` property to False or setting its `Interval` to 0.

The code for a stopwatch program appears below, and Figure 10.10 shows a sample execution of this program.

| Object | Property | Setting |
|---|---|---|
| Form | Name | frmStopwatch |
| | Caption | Stopwatch |
| CommandButton | Name | cmdReset |
| | Caption | Reset |
| CommandButton | Name | cmdToggle |
| | Caption | Start |
| Timer | Name | tmrStopwatch |
| | Enabled | False |
| | Interval | 100 |
| Label | Name | lblOutput |
| | AutoSize | True |
| | Caption | 0.0 seconds |
| | Font | Tahoma (size 24) |
| Label | Name | lblStopwatch |
| | AutoSize | True |
| | Caption | 0.0 |
| | Visible | False |

```
' Timer Example
Option Explicit

Private Sub cmdReset_Click()
' Reset the stopwatch
    lblStopwatch.Caption = "0.0"
    lblOutput.Caption = Format(lblStopwatch.Caption,
➥ "##0.0") & " seconds"
End Sub


Private Sub cmdToggle_Click()
' Toggle the stopwatch on and off.  Update the command
➥ button caption to reflect the currently available option
    tmrStopwatch.Enabled = Not (tmrStopwatch.Enabled)
```

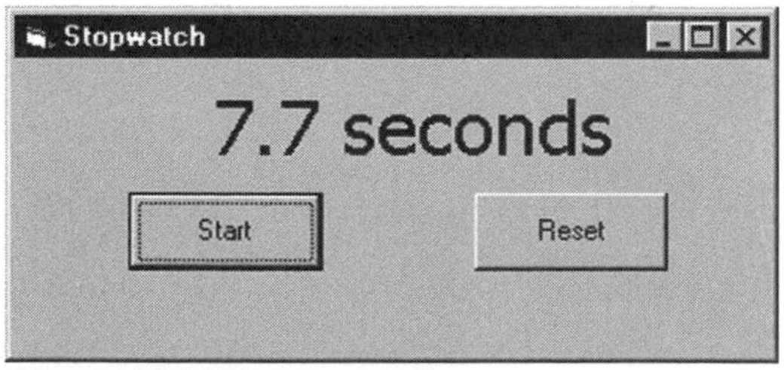

**Figure 10.10** Timer example

```
    If tmrStopwatch.Enabled Then
        cmdToggle.Caption = "Stop"
    Else
        cmdToggle.Caption = "Start"
    End If
End Sub

Private Sub Form_Load()
' Initialize the stopwatch
    Call cmdReset_Click
End Sub

Private Sub tmrStopwatch_Timer()
' Update the time
' NOTE: This event is triggered every
➥ tmrStopwatch.Interval
' milliseconds
    lblStopwatch.Caption =
    ➥ CStr(CSng(Val(lblStopwatch.Caption)) + 0.1)
    lblOutput.Caption = Format(lblStopwatch.Caption,
    ➥ "##0.0") & " seconds"
End Sub
```

## SHAPE AND LINE CONTROLS

Shape and line controls enable the programmer to place shapes and lines on VB
forms at design time. These controls can decorate or highlight specific parts of the
form. The shape control can be used to display a rectangle, square, oval, circle,
rounded rectangle, or rounded square. While similar to a frame control or picture
box control in its ability to display a variety of shapes, the shape control cannot be
used as a container. The line control can be used to generate horizontal, vertical, and
diagonal lines. Figure 10.11 displays a form with several shape and line controls.

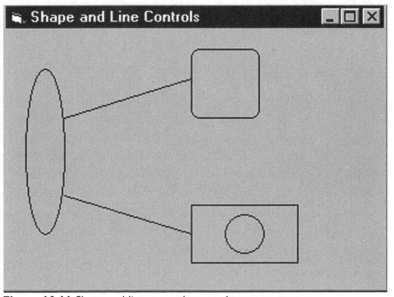

**Figure 10.11** Shape and line controls example

## IMAGE

The image control displays images or graphics on a form. It supports a variety of graphic file formats, including bitmap, icon, metafile, enhanced metafile, JPEG, and GIF files. While the image control uses fewer system resources and can display a picture faster than the picture box control, it offers only a few of the picture box's properties, events, and methods.

If the `Stretch` property is set to False (the default value), the image control is resized to fit the picture that it contains. When the `Stretch` property is set to True, however, the picture resizes to fit the image control. A picture can be assigned to an image control at design time or run time. At design time, simply specify the appropriate graphic file in the `Picture` property of the image control. To assign a picture file to an image control at run time, use the `LoadPicture` function. For instance, to display picture file *picfile* in the image control Image1 at run time, use a statement of the form:

```
Let Image1.Picture = LoadPicture (picfile)
```

Image controls also respond to click and mouse events; so, image boxes can be used as graphical command buttons. Figure 10.12 shows an example use of image controls.

## DATA

The data control provides access to data stored in database files, such as those files created with the Microsoft Access relational database program. This control allows the user to view and manipulate data in database files. In order to display and edit data, other controls such as text boxes must be bound to the data control. Chapter 12 introduces database concepts and details the use of the data control.

**Figure 10.12** Image Control Example
Pictured above (left to right): Charles and Jessica Kerman;
Kaity and Gregory Brown

# OLE

**OLE** is an acronym for object linking and embedding. The OLE container control enables objects and other applications to be inserted into VB programs. The OLE control may contain an **embedded object** or a **linked object**. An embedded object is an object that is created in another application and then placed in a VB program. All of the data associated with the embedded object is copied to and contained in the VB program. Conversely, a linked object is an object that is created in another application and then linked to a VB program. Unlike an embedded object, a linked object's data is actually stored in and managed by the application that created it; a placeholder only is inserted in the VB program. As a result, changes to the original data that are made using another application will be reflected in the object that is linked to VB. A later section in this chapter describes OLE in greater detail.

# COMMON DIALOG CONTROL

As the name implies, the common dialog control contains dialog boxes that are common to most Windows-based applications. When you save a text file in WordPad, for example, you use the Save As dialog box. When you save a workbook in Microsoft Excel, a similar Save As dialog box appears. The designers of Microsoft VB have made it easy for us. We do not have to "re-invent the wheel" each time we want a dialog box to appear when the user saves or opens a file. We simply need to invoke the common dialog box control for the desired task.

So where is this common dialog control icon? If the common dialog control icon does not appear in your toolbox, go to an empty place on the toolbox, click the right mouse button, and select Components from the pop-up menu. A large list of components appears. Click the box next to Microsoft Common Dialog Control, make sure that the box is checked, and click the OK button to make the common dialog control appear in the toolbox.

There are five common dialog boxes available: Open, Save As, Color, Font, and Print. The common dialog control has methods and properties but no events. Like the timer control, the common dialog control appears as an icon on a form and it is hidden from the user. To invoke the common dialog control, use a statement of the form:

```
CommonDialog1.Show{Open | Save | Color | Font |Print}
```

For instance, to invoke an Open dialog box, use the statement `CommonDialog1.ShowOpen`. The following program allows the user to select a file using a common dialog box and then displays the name of the selected file in a text box. A sample execution appears in Figure 10.13.

| Object | Property | Setting |
|---|---|---|
| Form | Name | frmCommonDialog |
| | Caption | Common Dialog Box Example |
| PictureBox | Name | picOutput |
| | AutoRedraw | True |
| CommonDialog | Name | dlgBox |

```
' Common Dialog Example
Option Explicit

Private Sub Form_Load()
```

### Key Terms

**embedded object**—an object that is created in some applications program and then placed in a VB program; in this case, the VB program contains a copy of the object, and any changes made to the object by the VB program only affect this copy

**linked object**—an object that is created in an application and then linked to a VB program; the VB program contains a reference to the original object, and any changes to the object affect the original version

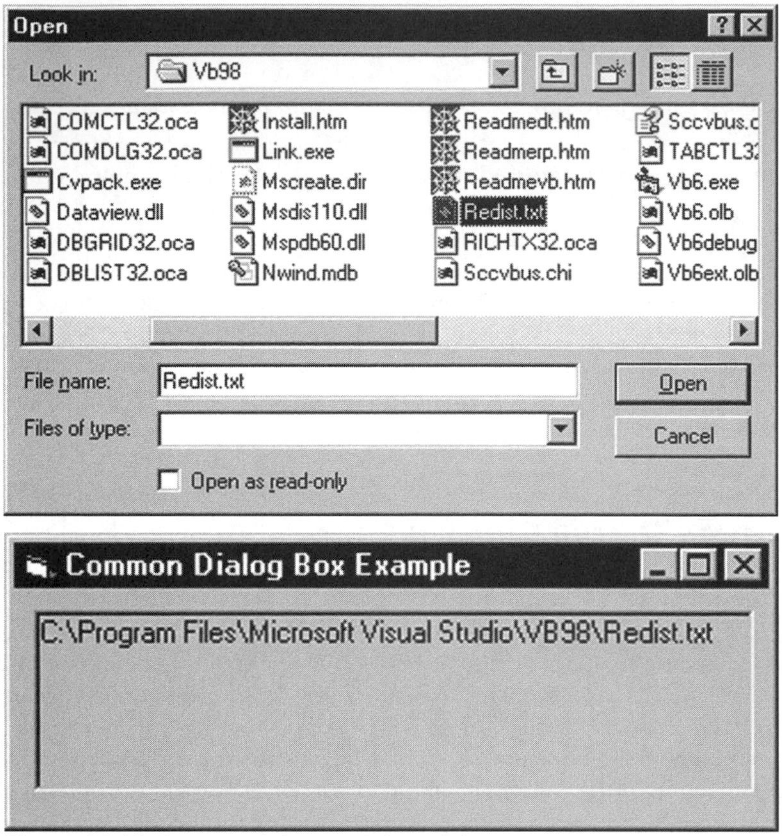

**Figure 10.13** Common dialog control example

```
' Use a common dialog box to select a file and then
' display the file name in the picture box
    frmCommonDialog.Visible = True
    dlgBox.ShowOpen
    picOutput.Print dlgBox.FileName
End Sub
```

## MENU CONTROL

The menu control enables a programmer to create custom menus in VB programs. This control does not appear as an icon in the toolbox. To create a custom menu on a VB form, select the form by clicking on it and then open the Menu Editor by clicking on Tools/Menu Editor from the VB menu bar. In order to create a new menu, two essential items must be provided: a menu caption and a menu name. With these properties specified, items such as commands, submenus, and separator bars can be added to the new menu. Figure 10.14 displays a sample of a Menu Editor dialog box and the resulting menus that are generated. Notice that the dialog box creates a File menu containing Open and Exit items followed by a Help menu containing "Help on Help" and "About Menu Controls" items.

As described in Chapter 2, the ampersand (&) placed before a letter in the caption denotes a shortcut key combination. The ampersand does not appear in the caption on the menu, but the letter following the ampersand is underlined and designated as the shortcut key. The shortcut key combination is activated by holding down the ALT key and then pressing the key associated with the underlined letter.

For instance, the mnuFile caption is &File, and this caption appears as <u>F</u>ile on the menu. To open the File menu, the user can either click on the word "File" or press the F key while holding down the ALT key (ALT+F). To place an ampersand in a caption, use the double ampersand (&&). So, a caption of This && That is displayed as This & That and no shortcut key is assigned.

The following steps create a menu system similar to the one shown in Figure 10.14.

1. Enter &File as the caption and mnuFile as the name for the first menu heading.

2. Click the Next button (or press the ENTER key).

3. To create a menu item under this menu heading, click the right arrow button to indent one level.

4. Enter Open as the menu item caption, mnuFileOpen as the menu item name, and specify Ctrl+O as the shortcut.

5. Click the Next button (or press the ENTER key).

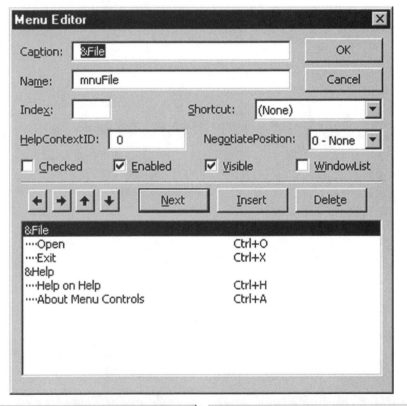

**Figure 10.14** Menu editor dialog box and resulting menus

6. Enter Exit as the menu item caption, mnuFileExit as the menu item name, and specify Ctrl+X as the shortcut.

7. Click the Next button (or press the ENTER key).

8. Click the left arrow button to outdent one level and make the next entry a second menu heading.

9. Enter &Help as the caption and mnuHelp as the name for the second menu heading.

10. Repeat steps 3 through 5 for the menu items of the second menu listed in the following table.

| Caption | Name | Shortcut |
|---|---|---|
| Help on Help | mnuHelpHelp | Ctrl+H |
| About Menu Controls | mnuHelpAbout | Ctrl+A |

The following example uses this menu control along with a common dialog control. Figure 10.15 displays the results of executing this code when the File/Open menu item is clicked and a file is then selected from the common dialog box.

| Object | Property | Setting |
|---|---|---|
| Form | Name | frmMenu |
| | Caption | Menu Control Example |
| PictureBox | Name | picOutput |
| | AutoRedraw | True |
| CommonDialog | Name | dlgBox |
| Menu | (as described above) | |

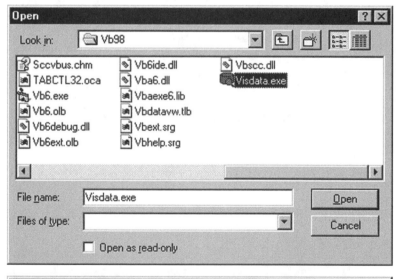

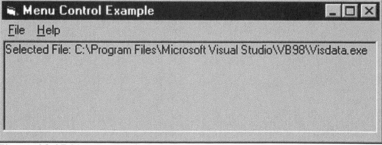

**Figure 10.15** Menu control example

```
' Menu Control Example
Option Explicit

Private Sub mnuHelpAbout_Click()
' Display About Information
   MsgBox "Menu Control Example", , "About Information"
End Sub

Private Sub mnuFileExit_Click()
' End the program
   End
End Sub

Private Sub mnuHelpHelp_Click()
' Display Help on Help
   MsgBox "No help available at this time.", , "Help on
   ➥ Help"
End Sub

Private Sub mnuFileOpen_Click()
' Select a file to open
   dlgBox.ShowOpen
   picOutput.Cls
   picOutput.Print "Selected File: "; dlgBox.FileName
End Sub
```

## CONTROL ARRAYS

While an array generally refers to an array of variables, a **control array** is an array of VB controls. A control array is created using the following procedure:

1. Place the desired type of control on the form. This will be the first control in the control array.

2. Set the default properties of the control, such as the control name, caption, and so on.

3. Select this first control (make sure it is highlighted), and then select Edit/Copy from the menu bar, press the Copy button on the toolbar, or click the control with the right mouse button and select Copy from the list of options that appears.

4. Select Edit/Paste from the menu bar, press the Paste button on the toolbar, or right click on the form and select Paste from the list of options that appears.

5. VB now asks if you desire to create a control array. Click the Yes button.

6. The first control is automatically assigned an Index of 0 and the second control (the copy) an Index value of 1. Each control in the control array is given a name of the form ControlName(*Index*).

7. Continue to paste controls on the form until the control array reaches the desired size.

The Index property of each control in a control array must be an integer value between 0 and 32,767. VB automatically increments the value of the Index property by one each time a new control is created in the control array, but this feature can be overridden by manually changing the Index values. Additionally, the first control in a control array is not required to have an Index value of 0, and the Index values need not be sequential (i.e., values can be skipped).

When an event occurs to an object in a control array, VB calls the control array's event procedure and automatically passes the appropriate Index value as an argument. Another advantage of using control arrays is that they can be easily used in loop and decision structures. The following code illustrates these points, and Figure 10.16 shows a sample execution.

| Object | Property | Setting |
|---|---|---|
| Form | Name | frmControlArray |
| | Caption | Yes or No |
| CommandButton | Name | cmdButton |
| | Caption | Yes |
| | Index | 0 |
| CommandButton | Name | cmdButton |
| | Caption | No |
| | Index | 1 |
| PictureBox | Name | picOutput |

```
' Control Array Example
Option Explicit

Private Sub cmdButton_Click(Index As Integer)
' Which button did the user press?
   picOutput.Cls
   If Index = 0 Then
      picOutput.Print "You pressed the Yes button."
   ElseIf Index = 1 Then
      picOutput.Print "You pressed the No button."
   End If
End Sub
```

The steps outlined above create a control array at design time. Control arrays can also be created (and destroyed) at run time (dynamically) by using Load and Unload statements to create and destroy elements of a control array, respectively. The following example, which creates an array of six option buttons, illustrates dynamic creation of control arrays. Notice that the initial form contains only a single option button, a label, and a picture box. The For-Next loop creates the remaining option buttons using the Load statement and then sets the Left, Top, Caption, and Visible properties for each control. Figure 10.17 displays a sample execution of this program ((a) shows view at design time; (b) shows view at run time).

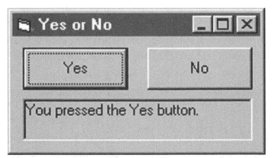

**Figure 10.16** Control array example using command buttons

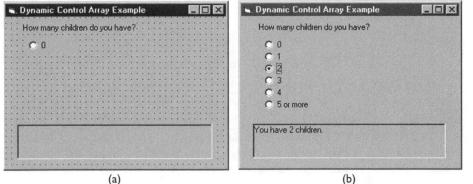

(a)                                (b)

**Figure 10.17** Dynamic control array example

| Object | Property | Setting |
|---|---|---|
| Form | Name | frmDynControlArray |
| | Caption | Dynamic Control Array Example |
| Label | Name | lblQuestion |
| | AutoSize | True |
| | Caption | How many children do you have? |
| OptionButton | Name | optChildren |
| | Caption | 0 |
| | Index | 0 |
| PictureBox | Name | picOutput |

```
' Dynamic Control Array Example
Option Explicit

Private Sub Form_Load()
' The first element (index 0) is already on the form
➥ [created at design time].
' Create the remaining elements of the control array.
   Dim count As Integer ' Loop counter

   For count = 1 To 5
      Load optChildren(count)
      optChildren(count).Left = optChildren(count - 1).Left
      optChildren(count).Top = optChildren(count - 1).
      ➥ Top + optChildren(count - 1).Height
      optChildren(count).Caption = CStr(count)
      optChildren(count).Visible = True
   Next count
   optChildren(5).Caption = "5 or more"
End Sub

Private Sub optChildren_Click(Index As Integer)
' Display the answer
   picOutput.Cls
   picOutput.Print "You have "; optChildren(Index).Caption;
   If Index = 1 Then
      picOutput.Print " child."
   Else
```

➡

```
                        picOutput.Print " children."
                End If
        End Sub
```

## ACTIVEX CONTROLS

ActiveX technology allows programmers to design and develop their own software components, such as VB controls. The ActiveX specification is part of Microsoft's component object model (COM), which allows user-developed and off-the-shelf software components to work together seamlessly. Microsoft has led the industry in component-based software design by providing this open, extensible standard for software interoperability. Component-based software development significantly reduces programming time and produces more robust applications.

ActiveX technology differs from object-oriented programming (OOP). While OOP allows for the creation of object-based software components, ActiveX technology allows the programmer to combine object-based components created using different tools and enables these objects to work together. For instance, you can use VB to construct a set of useful objects. These objects can be used and further extended by other developers. If you package your objects in an ActiveX component, however, they can be used and further extended with any programming tool that supports ActiveX technology.

VB allows a programmer to create several different ActiveX components, including ActiveX controls, executable (EXE) files, dynamic link libraries (DLLs), and documents. As a result, the programmer has the tools necessary for rapidly creating, debugging, and deploying a variety of software components.

This section introduces ActiveX controls by designing and implementing an example control in a VB program. We do not discuss ActiveX documents, EXE files, or DLLs; these items are left for the reader to explore further through experimentation and the VB documentation.

### AN ACTIVE CONTROL EXAMPLE

We now create an ActiveX control called NameBox. The purpose of the NameBox control is to encapsulate a first name, middle initial, and last name in one control object. Follow the steps below to create the control:

1. Start Visual Basic or select File/New Project from the VB menu bar.
2. Select ActiveX Control from the New Project window and click the OK button.
3. Design a user control similar to the one shown in Figure 10.18. Set the properties as follows:

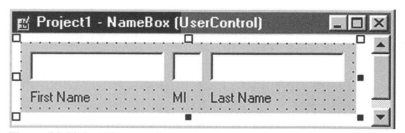

**Figure 10.18** ActiveX control example

| Object | Property | Setting |
|--------|----------|---------|
| UserControl | Name | NameBox |
| Label | Name | lblFirstName |
| | AutoSize | True |
| | Caption | First Name |
| Label | Name | lblMI |
| | AutoSize | True |
| | Caption | MI |
| Label | Name | lblLastName |
| | AutoSize | True |
| | Caption | Last Name |
| TextBox | Name | txtFirstName |
| | Text | *(Empty)* |
| TextBox | Name | txtMiddleInitial |
| | Text | *(Empty)* |
| TextBox | Name | txtLastName |
| | Text | *(Empty)* |

**4.** Select View/Code and enter the following code for this ActiveX control:

```
' NameBox control
' ---------------
' This code implements FirstName, MiddleInitial, and
➥ LastName properties for the NameBox control
Option Explicit

Private Sub UserControl_Initialize()
' Empty the text boxes to initialize the NameBox control
    txtLastName.Text = ""
    txtMI.Text = ""
    txtFirstName.Text = ""
End Sub

Public Property Get FirstName() As String
' Get the First Name
    FirstName = txtFirstName.Text
End Property

Public Property Let FirstName(ByVal first As String)
' Set the First Name
    txtFirstName.Text = first
End Property

Public Property Get MiddleInitial() As String
' Get the Middle Initial
    MiddleInitial = txtMI.Text
End Property

Public Property Let MiddleInitial(ByVal midinit As String)
' Set the Middle Initial
    txtMI.Text = midinit
End Property
```

```
Public Property Get LastName() As String
' Get the Last Name
    LastName = txtLastName.Text
End Property

Public Property Let LastName(ByVal last As String)
' Set the Last Name
    txtLastName.Text = last
End Property
```

**5.** Select File/Save UserControl1 As and save the control as `NameBox.ctl`.

**6.** Select File/Save Project As and save the project as `NameBox.vbp`.

**7.** Select File/Make NameBox.ocx to build the ActiveX control.

Congratulations, you have just created your first ActiveX control, the `NameBox` control.

## TESTING THE ACTUAL CONTROL

Now, let's test this control in a VB program:

**1.** Start Visual Basic or select File/New Project from the VB menu bar.

**2.** Select Standard EXE from the New Project window and click the OK button.

**3.** Select Project/Components from the menu bar, press CTRL+T, or right-click an empty spot in the Toolbox and select Components from the pop-up menu. The Components window now appears on the screen.

**4.** Click the Browse button to open the Add ActiveX Control window. Click on the NameBox.ocx file and then click the Open button. The `NameBox` control now appears in the Toolbox.

**5.** Design a form similar to the one shown in Figure 10.19. Set the properties as follows:

| Object | Property | Setting |
|---|---|---|
| Form | Name | frmActiveXExample |
| | Caption | ActiveX Control Example |
| NameBox | Name | nbxName |
| PictureBox | Name | picOutput |
| CommandButton | Name | cmdDisplay |
| | Caption | Display Name |

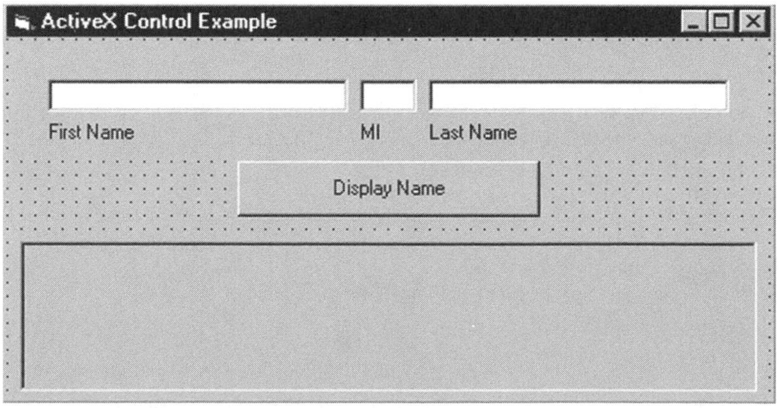

**Figure 10.19** ActiveX control example form

**6.** Select View/Code and enter the following code for this form:

```
' ActiveX Control Example
' ----------------------
' This program uses the NameBox control
Option Explicit

Private Sub cmdDisplay_Click()
' Display the name in the NameBox
    Dim first As String, midInit As String, last As String
    first = Trim(nbxName.FirstName)
    midInit = Trim(nbxName.MiddleInitial)
    last = Trim(nbxName.LastName)
    picOutput.Cls
    If last <> "" Then
       picOutput.Print "The name is ";
       If first <> "" Then
          picOutput.Print first & " ";
       End If
       If midInit <> "" Then
          picOutput.Print midInit & ". ";
       End If
       picOutput.Print last & "."
    Else
       picOutput.Print "You must enter a last name."
    End If
End Sub
```

Now, execute the program. Type your name in the text boxes and press the Display Name button. The program writes your name in the picture box. A sample execution is shown in Figure 10.20.

## COLLECTIONS

A **collection** is a data structure similar to an array, but it is always dynamic in nature. Collections generally group objects, but they can contain any object or data type. Essentially, a collection is an object that contains other objects. VB's collection data structure is somewhat unique; many other high-level languages do not

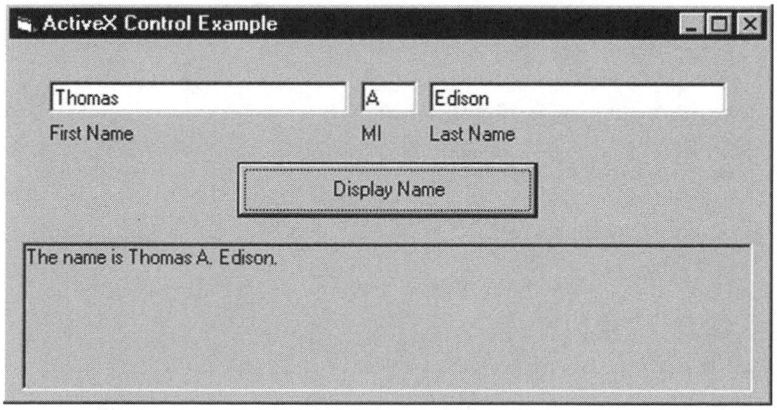

**Figure 10.20** ActiveX control example execution

offer an equivalent data structure. Thus, VB is an extremely flexible language with regard to objects and data structures.

The syntax to declare and instantiate a collection is as follows:

```
Dim CollectionName As New Collection
```

*CollectionName* is the name of the collection and must be a valid VB variable name.

As summarized below, a collection object has two properties and two methods.

---

**PROPERTIES**

*CollectionName*.Count
  The number of objects in *CollectionName*. This value is zero when *CollectionName* is empty and increments by one each time a new object is added to the collection.

*CollectionName*.Item (*n*)
  The object at index location *n* in collection *CollectionName*.

**METHODS**

*CollectionName*.Add *ObjectName*
  Adds object *ObjectName* to collection *CollectionName* in the next available index location.

*CollectionName*.Remove (*n*)
  Removes the object at index location *n* from collection *CollectionName*.

---

The following example implements a stack structure using a collection. A sample execution of this code appears in Figure 10.21.

```
' Collection Example
' ------------------
' Implement a stack structure using a collection
Option Explicit

Dim Stack As New Collection

Private Sub cmdExecute_Click()
    Dim value As Integer

    ' Push integer values onto the stack
    picOutput.Print "Pushing integers 1 through 10 onto the
    ➥ stack."
    For value = 1 To 10
        Call Push(value)
    Next value

    ' Pop values off of the stack
    picOutput.Print "Popping the first 5 values off of the
    ➥ stack:"
```

```
        For value = 1 To 5
            picOutput.Print Pop()
        Next value

        ' Push integer values onto the stack
        picOutput.Print "Pushing integers 100, 99, 98, and 97
    ➡ onto the stack" & _
                        " (in that order)."
        For value = 100 To 97 Step -1
            Call Push(value)
        Next value

        ' Pop values off of the stack
        picOutput.Print "Popping 2 values off of the stack:"
        For value = 1 To 2
            picOutput.Print Pop()
        Next value

        'Empty the stack
        picOutput.Print "Emptying the stack:"
        Do While (Stack.Count > 0)
            picOutput.Print Pop()
        Loop
End Sub

Private Function Pop() As Integer
' Pop an integer value off the top of the stack
    If (Stack.Count > 0) Then
```

Figure 10.21 Collection example

```
                                Pop = Stack.Item(Stack.Count)
                                Stack.Remove (Stack.Count)
                        Else
                                Pop = 0
                                MsgBox "Stack Empty!", vbExclamation, "ERROR"
                        End If
                End Function


                Private Sub Push(value As Integer)
                ' Push an integer value onto the stack
                ' NOTE: Maximum number of items able to be pushed onto the
        ➡ stack depends upon the memory space available in the
        ➡ computer
                        Stack.Add value
                End Sub


                Private Sub Form_Terminate()
                ' Release stack space to the system and terminate the form
                        Set Stack = Nothing
                End Sub
```

## PROGRAMMING KEY: TIPS

The For Each-Next structure repeats a group of statements for each element in an array or collection. The general syntax of this structure is as follows:

```
For Each element In groupName
        [statements]
Next element
```

In this syntax, element is a variable used to iterate through the elements of the array or collection named groupName. element must be of a specific object type, the generic object type Object, or Variant.

The following example stores the hexadecimal digits in a collection and then uses the For Each-Next statement to iterate through the collection and print the contents.

```
Option Explicit

Private Sub cmdExample_Click()
' Example use of the For Each-Next statement
    Dim hexDigits As New Collection
    Dim number As Integer
    Dim element As Variant

' Place the hexadecimal digits in the collection
    For number = 0 To 9
        hexDigits.Add number
    Next number
    For number = 65 To 70
        hexDigits.Add Chr(number)
    Next number

' Print the contents of the collection
```

```
        For Each element In hexDigits
            picOutput.Print element
        Next
End Sub
```

# MULTIPLE FORMS PROGRAMMING AND MULTIPLE DOCUMENT INTERFACE (MDI) FORMS

Programming with multiple forms in VB is simply a matter of setting the `Visible` properties and calling the `SetFocus` methods of the forms at appropriate times within the program code. The example provided below contains two forms, a main form and a sub form. The main form contains two command buttons that can show or hide the sub form, respectively. Similarly, the sub form contains one command button that toggles the visibility of the main form. Notice that the `Form_Unload()` procedure of the sub form makes the main form visible and gives it the focus. This ensures that the user exits the program from the main form. Figure 10.22 shows both the main and sub forms.

```
' Multiple Forms Programming Example
' Main Form code
Option Explicit

Private Sub cmdHideSubForm_Click()
' Hide the Sub Form
    frmMain.SetFocus
```

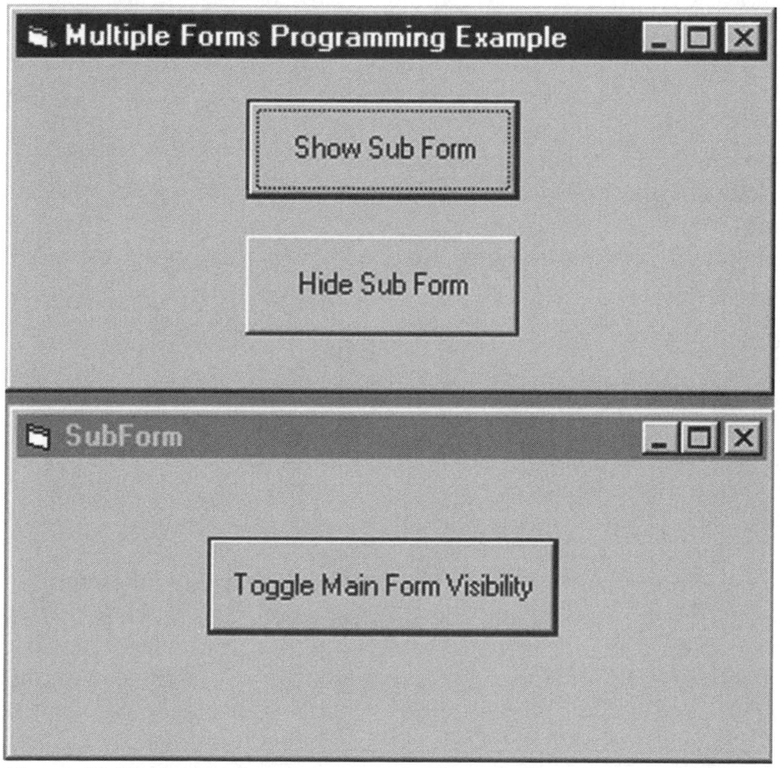

**Figure 10.22** Multiple forms programming example

```
                                    frmSub.Visible = False
                                End Sub

                                Private Sub cmdShowSubForm_Click()
                                ' Show the Sub Form
                                    frmSub.Visible = True
                                    frmSub.SetFocus
                                End Sub



                                ' Sub Form code
                                Option Explicit

                                Private Sub cmdToggle_Click()
                                ' Toggle visibility of Main Form
                                    frmMain.Visible = Not (frmMain.Visible)
                                    frmSub.SetFocus
                                End Sub

                                Private Sub Form_Unload(Cancel As Integer)
                                ' Make sure that the Main Form is visible
                                ' when the user closes the Sub Form
                                    frmMain.Visible = True
                                    frmMain.SetFocus
                                End Sub
```

A **multiple document interface** (**MDI**) is an application that allows multiple forms (or windows) to be open within a single container form (or window). The container form/window is referred to as the *parent*; it provides a workspace for all of the *child* forms/windows that are open in the application. Many Windows-based programs have MDI forms as their main form. Microsoft Word, for instance, allows several documents to be open at the same time; each document is displayed in a separate child window. Similarly, Microsoft Excel allows several workbooks to be open at the same time in different child windows.

A **single document interface** (**SDI**) is the opposite of an MDI. In an SDI application, only one file may be open at a time; the current file must be closed before another file may be opened. Notepad and WordPad are examples of SDI applications that are included with Microsoft Windows.

## MDI Versus SDI

MDI and SDI are two different styles of user interfaces. So, how does the programmer decide which interface to use? Quite simply, the choice between MDI and SDI depends upon the user's requirements. An MDI is best if the user needs to have several files open simultaneously. MDI is also more flexible than SDI since the user can control the number of open windows. The disadvantage, however, is that an MDI is slightly more complex and takes longer to program than an SDI.

Another consideration is that MDI forms are limited in terms of the controls that they can contain. MDI forms usually contain menu bars, toolbars, or picture boxes. The menu bar and toolbar typically have commands available to open, save, and close files. Remember that the MDI form is the parent form in your application, and it should control all of its child windows.

## MDI APPLICATION EXAMPLE

As an example MDI application, we create a `Notebook` program using the steps listed below.

1. Start Visual Basic or select File/New Project from the VB menu bar.
2. Select Standard EXE from the New Project window and click the OK button.
3. Select Project/Add MDI Form and open a new MDI form. Your project now contains two forms, `Form1` and `MDIForm1`.
4. Place three text boxes and two labels on `Form1` as shown in Figure 10.23. Set the properties as follows:

| Object | Property | Setting |
|--------|----------|---------|
| Form | Name | frmNotebook |
| | Caption | Notebook |
| | MDIChild | True |
| Label | Name | lblSubject |
| | AutoSize | True |
| | Caption | Subject |
| Label | Name | lblDate |
| | AutoSize | True |
| | Caption | Date |
| TextBox | Name | txtSubject |
| | Text | *(Empty)* |
| TextBox | Name | txtDate |
| | Text | *(Empty)* |
| TextBox | Name | txtNotes |
| | Text | *(Empty)* |

⟵ Make sure that you set the `MDIChild` property of `frmNotebook` (formerly `Form1`) to True. This property setting tells VB to display the form as an MDI child form.

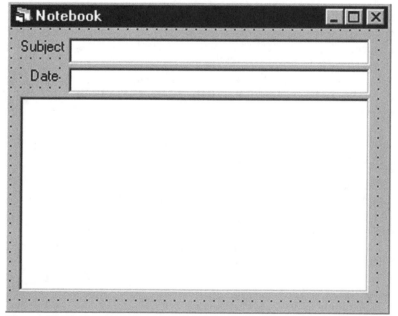

**Figure 10.23** Notebook form

**5.** Using the Menu Editor, create a menu on `MDIForm1`. The menu has one menu heading (one top-level heading) that says `File`. This heading contains two commands, `Open New Notebook` and `Exit`.

| Name | Caption | Top Level | Shortcut |
|------|---------|-----------|----------|
| mnuFile | &File | Yes | |
| mnuOpen | Open New Notebook | No | CTRL+O |
| mnuExit | Exit | No | CTRL+E |

**6.** Set the properties of `MDIForm1` as follows:

| Object | Property | Setting |
|--------|----------|---------|
| Form | Name | frmMDINotebook |
| | Caption | My Notebooks |

**7.** Place the following code in the code window for `frmMDINotebook` (previously `MDIForm1`):

```
' MDI Example
' ----------
' Notebook program
Option Explicit

Private Sub mnuExit_Click()
' Exit the program
    End
End Sub

Private Sub mnuOpen_Click()
' Open a new notebook
    Dim Notebook As New frmNotebook
    Notebook.Show
End Sub
```

**8.** Select Project/Properties to open the Project Properties menu. Under the General tab, select `frmMDINotebook` as the Startup Object and click the OK button.

Now, execute the program. You can use the menu to open multiple notebooks (multiple child windows) within the MDI form. A sample execution is shown in Figure 10.24.

## RANDOM NUMBERS

Random numbers play an important role in games and simulation. The `Randomize` statement and `Rnd` function are used to generate random numbers in VB. The `Timer` function is also related to random number generation.

The `Randomize` statement initializes the VB random number generator. The syntax follows:

```
Randomize [number]
```

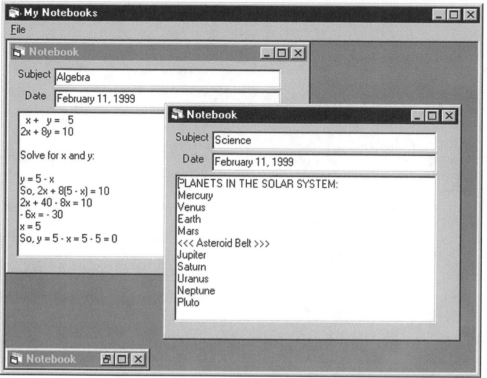

**Figure 10.24** MDI example

The *number* argument is any valid numeric expression, but it is optional. The Randomize statement uses *number* as the **seed value** for the Rnd function's random number generator. The seed value is simply an initial value used by VB to generate pseudorandom numbers. If *number* is omitted, a value generated by the Timer function is used as the seed value. The Timer function returns a single-precision value representing the number of seconds elapsed since midnight (according to the system clock).

The Rnd function returns a single-precision random number whose value is less than 1 but greater than or equal to zero. The syntax is shown below:

$$randomNumber = Rnd[(number)]$$

This statement assigns a single-precision random number generated by the Rnd function to the single-precision variable *randomNumber*. Once again, *number* is an optional argument (but the parentheses must be used if *number* is specified). The value of *number* determines how Rnd generates a random number. The following table summarizes the different cases:

| If *number* is | Rnd generates |
| --- | --- |
| Less than zero | The same number every time, using *number* as the seed |
| Greater than zero | The next random number in the sequence |
| Equal to zero | The most recently generated number |
| Not specified | The next random number in the sequence |

For any given seed value, the Rnd function generates the same sequence of numbers each time since it uses the previous number as a seed for the next number in the sequence. Before you call the Rnd function, the Randomize statement without an argument may be used to initialize the random number generator with a seed value based on the system timer.

To produce random integer values in a given range, use the following statement:

```
randomInteger = Int ((upperbound - lowerbound + 1)
                 * Rnd + lowerbound)
```

This statement assigns a random integer in the range of [*lowerbound, upperbound*] to the integer variable *randomInteger*, where *upperbound* and *lowerbound* specify the highest and lowest integer values in the range, respectively.

On a final note, to repeat sequences of random numbers, call Rnd with a negative argument immediately followed by Randomize with a numeric argument. Using Randomize with the same value for *number* does not repeat the previous sequence.

The following program demonstrates the use of random numbers in a **Monte Carlo simulation**. This program simulates tossing a die 1,000 times and repeats this experiment 10 times. The overall percentage of occurrences of each number is reported by the program. Figure 10.25 shows a sample execution of this code.

```
' Random Number Example
Option Explicit

Const TRIALS = 10    ' Number of trials
Const ITERS = 1000   ' Number of rolls (iterations) per
➡ trial
Const SIX = 6        ' Max die value

Private Sub cmdSimulate_Click()
' Simulate rolling a die 1000 times, repeat this
➡ experiment 10 times,
' and report the final results
    Dim die(1 To SIX, 1 To TRIALS) As Integer
```

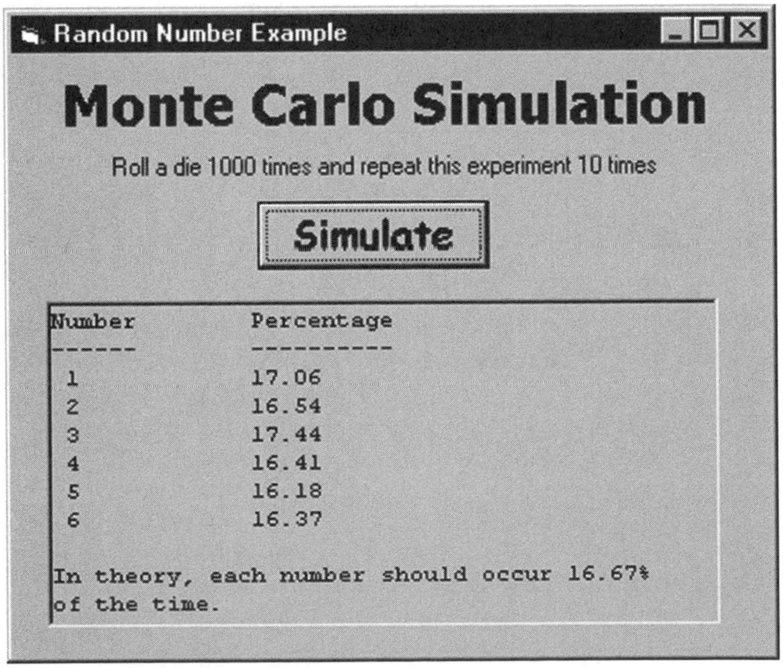

**Figure 10.25** Random number example

```
    Dim iteration As Integer, trial As Integer, roll As
➥ Integer
    Dim sum As Integer

    ' Initialize the array
    For trial = 1 To TRIALS
        For iteration = 1 To SIX
            die(iteration, trial) = 0
        Next iteration
    Next trial

    Randomize      ' Reset the random number seed based upon
➥ system timer

    For trial = 1 To TRIALS
        For iteration = 1 To ITERS
            roll = Int(SIX * Rnd + 1)     ' Roll the die
            die(roll, trial) = die(roll, trial) + 1
        Next iteration
    Next trial

    ' Output final results (overall % of time each number
➥ occurred)
    picOutput.Cls
    picOutput.Print "Number", "Percentage"
    picOutput.Print "------", "----------"
    For iteration = 1 To SIX
        picOutput.Print iteration,
        sum = 0
        For trial = 1 To TRIALS
            sum = sum + die(iteration, trial)
        Next trial
        picOutput.Print Format(sum / (TRIALS * ITERS) * 100,
➥ "##.00")
    Next iteration

    picOutput.Print
    picOutput.Print "In theory, each number should occur ";
    picOutput.Print Format((1 / SIX) * 100, "##.00") & "%"
    picOutput.Print "of the time."
End Sub
```

## GRAPHICS

VB has powerful graphics capabilities. In particular, three methods commonly used to generate graphics are the PSet, Line, and Circle methods. These methods are generally used in conjunction with picture box objects.

For a given VB object, the CurrentX and CurrentY properties contain the horizontal and vertical coordinates for the next printing or drawing method, respectively. These two properties are only available at run time. The CurrentX property is 0 at an object's left edge, and the CurrentY property is 0 at an object's top edge. The ScaleMode property specifies the unit of measure, and the default unit of measure is twips. A **twip** is a screen-independent unit used to ensure that placement and proportion of screen elements in an application are the same on all display systems. A twip is equivalent to 1/20 of a printer's point, and there are approximately 1,440 twips per inch (or 567 twips per centimeter).

The `Scale` method defines the coordinate system for an object. The general syntax is as follows:

```
Object.Scale (x1, y1) - (x2, y2)
```

In this syntax, *(x1, y1)* defines the coordinates of the upper-left corner of *Object*, and *(x2, y2)* defines the lower-right corner of *Object*.

The `PSet` method sets a specific point on an object to a specified color. The size of the point drawn depends on the setting of the object's `DrawWidth` property. When `DrawWidth` is 1, `PSet` sets a single pixel to the specified color. When `DrawWidth` is greater than 1, the point is centered on the given coordinates. Additionally, the manner in which the point is drawn depends on the setting of the `DrawMode` and `DrawStyle` properties. The general syntax follows:

```
Object.PSet [Step] (x, y), [color]
```

In the above syntax, *Object* is the name of the object for which the point color will be set. *x* and *y* are single-precision values specifying the horizontal (*x*-axis) and vertical (*y*-axis) coordinates of the point to set. `Step` is an optional keyword to inform VB that the coordinates are relative to the current graphics position given by the `CurrentX` and `CurrentY` properties. Finally, *color* is a long integer value indicating the desired color of the point. If it is omitted, the current color specified by the `ForeColor` property is used. The `RGB` function or `QBcolor` function may be used to specify colors in VB. To clear a single pixel with the `PSet` method, specify the coordinates of the pixel and use the `BackColor` property setting as the color argument. On a final note, when `PSet` executes, the `CurrentX` and `CurrentY` properties are set to *x* and *y*, respectively.

The `Line` method draws lines and rectangles on an object. The general syntax follows:

```
Object.Line [Step] (x1, y1) [Step] (x2, y2), [color], [B[F]]
```

*Object*, `Step`, and *color* are as previously described. `B` is an optional argument, and if included, causes a box to be drawn using the specified coordinates as opposite corners of the box. By default, the box is filled using the current `FillColor` and `FillStyle`. If `F` is also specified (i.e., BF), then the box is filled with the same color used to draw the box. *(x1, y1)* and *(x2, y2)* specify the starting and ending points of the line (or box), respectively. After this code executes, `CurrentX` and `CurrentY` contain the values of *x2* and *y2*, respectively.

The `Circle` method draws a circle, arc, or ellipse on an object. The general syntax is as follows:

```
Object.Circle [Step] (x, y), radius, [color, start, end, aspect]
```

*Object*, `Step`, and *color* are as previously described. The point (*x, y*) specifies the coordinates for the center of the circle, arc, or ellipse. *start* and *end* are single-precision values that indicate the starting and ending positions of an arc in radians. In any circle, there are $2\pi$ radians. The default value for *start* is 0 and *end* is $2\pi$, yielding an entire circle. *aspect* is a single-precision value indicating the aspect ratio of the circle. The default value is 1.0, which yields a perfect (nonelliptical) circle. An aspect value of greater than 1.0 produces a vertically oriented ellipse, while an aspect ratio of less than 1.0 produces a horizontally oriented ellipse.

The following program provides an example of graphics in VB. This program plots the values of $x$ squared for values of $x$ ranging from −10 to 10. A sample execution of this program appears in Figure 10.26.

```
' Graphics Example
' Draw the graph of x squared for x in [-10, 10]
Option Explicit

Private Sub cmdGraph_Click()
    Dim x As Single, y As Single, message As String

    ' Set the scale
    picOutput.Scale (-15, 120)-(15, -10)

    ' Center and print the title
    message = "Graph of x squared"
    picOutput.CurrentX = -(picOutput.TextWidth(message) / 2)
    picOutput.Print message

    ' Draw the x and y axes
    picOutput.Line (-10, 0)-(10, 0)
    picOutput.Line (0, 100)-(0, 0)

    ' Draw a hash mark at every unit on the x axis
    For x = -10 To 10
```

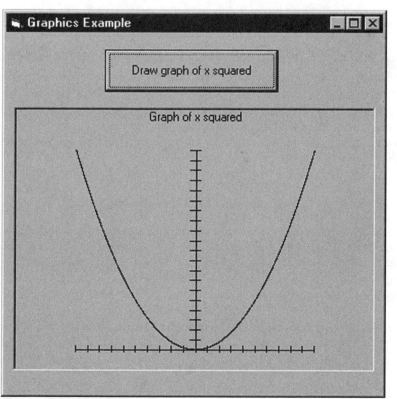

**Figure 10.26** Graphics example

```
                    picOutput.Line (x, 2)-(x, -2)
            Next x

            ' Draw a hash mark every 5 units on the y axis
            For y = 5 To 100 Step 5
                picOutput.Line (-0.5, y)-(0.5, y)
            Next y

            ' Plot the graph
            For x = -10 To 10 Step 0.01
                y = x ^ 2
                picOutput.PSet (x, y)
            Next x
        End Sub
```

## OBJECT LINKING AND EMBEDDING (OLE)

VB has two different types of **OLE** objects: OLE Automation objects and OLE container-control objects. **OLE Automation objects** are created exclusively at run time. **OLE container controls** are placed on the form at design time, and their properties can be set at design time or run time.

In Chapter 8, we discussed object-oriented programming and stated that all controls in VB are objects. Not only are controls objects, but other applications can be treated as VB objects as well. This is the theory behind OLE Automation objects.

The `CreateObject` function creates an OLE Automation object, and the `Set` statement is used to assign it to an object variable. The general syntax follows:

```
Dim ObjectVar As Object
Set ObjectVar = CreateObject(ClassName)
```

`ObjectVar` is the name of the object variable. The string `ClassName` specifies the type (or class) of object to create. It has the form `Application.ObjectType.Version`, where `Application` is the name of the application that supplies the object, `ObjectType` is the object's name as defined in the application's object library, and `Version` is the version number of the object or application.

Once the OLE Automation object is no longer needed, we clear the object variable and free system resources with a statement of the form:

```
Set ObjectVar = Nothing
```

Finally, an OLE Automation object is controlled by changing its properties and calling its methods. The properties and methods are different for different object classes. The following code, which creates and saves an Excel spreadsheet and a Word document, is used to illustrate. Both files (`Welcome.doc` and `Welcome.xls`) contain the statement "Welcome to OLE Automation controls!" after this code executes.

```
        ' OLE Automation Object Example
        Option Explicit

        Private Sub cmdOLEauto_Click()
            Dim ObjExcel As Object
            Dim ObjWord As Object
```

```
     ' Create a Microsoft Excel sheet
     Set ObjExcel = CreateObject("Excel.sheet")
     ObjExcel.Application.Visible = True
     ObjExcel.Application.Cells(3, 1).Font.Bold = True
     ObjExcel.Application.Cells(3, 1) = "Welcome to OLE
  ➥ Automation controls!"
     ObjExcel.Application.Save "C:\Welcome"
     ObjExcel.Application.Quit

     ' Create a Microsoft Word document
     Set ObjWord = CreateObject("Word.Basic")
     ObjWord.FileNewDefault
     ObjWord.Bold
     ObjWord.Insert "Welcome to OLE Automation controls!"
     ObjWord.FileSaveAs "C:\Welcome"
     ObjWord.FileClose

     Set ObjExcel = Nothing
     Set ObjWord = Nothing
  End Sub
```

The OLE container control allows objects from other applications to be linked or embedded in VB programs at design time. When this control is placed on a form, the Insert Object dialog window will open, offering the programmer a choice of objects from other applications to be placed on the form. As illustrated in Figure 10.27, the programmer can create a new object from a list of several applications (a) or select an existing file (b).

The OLE container control has many properties, and we briefly describe a few here. The AutoActivate property describes the activation method of the OLE object. For instance, the OLE object may be activated manually through code, automatically when the program starts, or manually by double-clicking the container control. The Class property contains the *ClassName* of the object as previously described. DisplayType describes whether the container control displays the contents of the object or an icon, and OLETypeAllowed indicates whether the container control can contain an embedded object, a linked object, or either type of object. SourceDoc contains the file name of the object, and SourceItem indicates the data within the file to be linked. Finally, UpdateOptions determines how an object is updated when linked data is modified.

## DYNAMIC DATA EXCHANGE (DDE)

Rather than link or embed objects that contain data in a VB program, a programmer may choose to transfer data between applications. **Dynamic data exchange (DDE)** provides a means of exchanging information between active applications. In order to exchange data between two applications, both applications must support DDE.

The LinkItem, LinkTopic, LinkTimeout, and LinkMode properties of an object are used to establish a DDE data link. These properties must be set for the *destination* object, or the object that requests (receives) the data and can be set at either design time or run time. LinkTopic specifies the *source* application and the topic (the fundamental data grouping used in the application). LinkItem indicates the data that is passed to the destination. Together, LinkTopic and LinkItem specify a complete data link. LinkTimeout contains the amount of time (in tenths of seconds) that a control waits for a response to a DDE message. LinkTimeout is set to 50 (or 5 seconds) by default. Lastly, the LinkMode property must be set to acti-

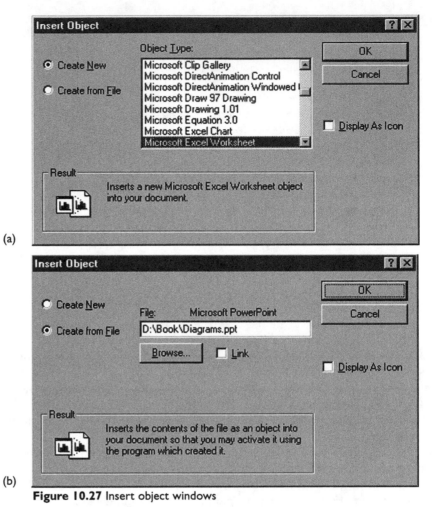

(a)

(b)

**Figure 10.27** Insert object windows

vate the conversation between the applications (activate the link). The `LinkMode` property settings are outlined in the table below:

**LinkMode**

| Setting | Description |
|---------|-------------|
| 0 | None (*Default*). No DDE. |
| 1 | Automatic. Destination control is updated when the linked data changes. |
| 2 | Manual. Destination control is updated only when the `LinkRequest` method is invoked. |
| 3 | Notify. A `LinkNotify` event occurs when the linked data changes. The destination control is updated only when the `LinkRequest` method is invoked. |

From the information in the above table, it is apparent that several events and methods are associated with DDE. These events and methods are summarized in the following tables:

| Event | Cause |
|-------|-------|
| `LinkOpen` | A DDE conversation is being initiated. |
| `LinkExecute` | A command string is sent from a destination application to a source application. |
| `LinkNotify` | `LinkMode` is 3 and the source changed the data associated with `LinkItem`. |

| | |
|---|---|
| LinkError | An error occurs during a DDE conversation. |
| LinkClose | A DDE conversation terminates. |

| Method | Operation |
|---|---|
| LinkExecute | Sends a command string from a destination application to a source application. |
| LinkPoke | Transfers the contents of a label, picture box, or text box to the source application. |
| LinkRequest | Requests that the source application update the contents of a label, picture box, or text box. |
| LinkSend | Transfers the contents of a picture box to the destination application. |

The following code provides a very basic example of DDE by establishing a DDE link between a text box (txtR1C1) in the program and cell R1C1 in a Microsoft Excel spreadsheet. The LinkMode property is set to 1 (Automatic). So, every time the value in cell R1C1 of the Microsoft Excel spreadsheet changes, the text box is automatically updated. Note that both this program and Microsoft Excel (with Sheet1 open) must be active in order to establish the DDE link. A sample execution appears in Figure 10.28.

| Object | Property | Setting |
|---|---|---|
| Form | Name | frmDDEExample |
| | Caption | DDE Example |
| Label | Name | lblR1C1 |
| | AutoSize | True |
| | Caption | R1C1 |
| TextBox | Name | txtR1C1 |
| | Text | (Empty) |

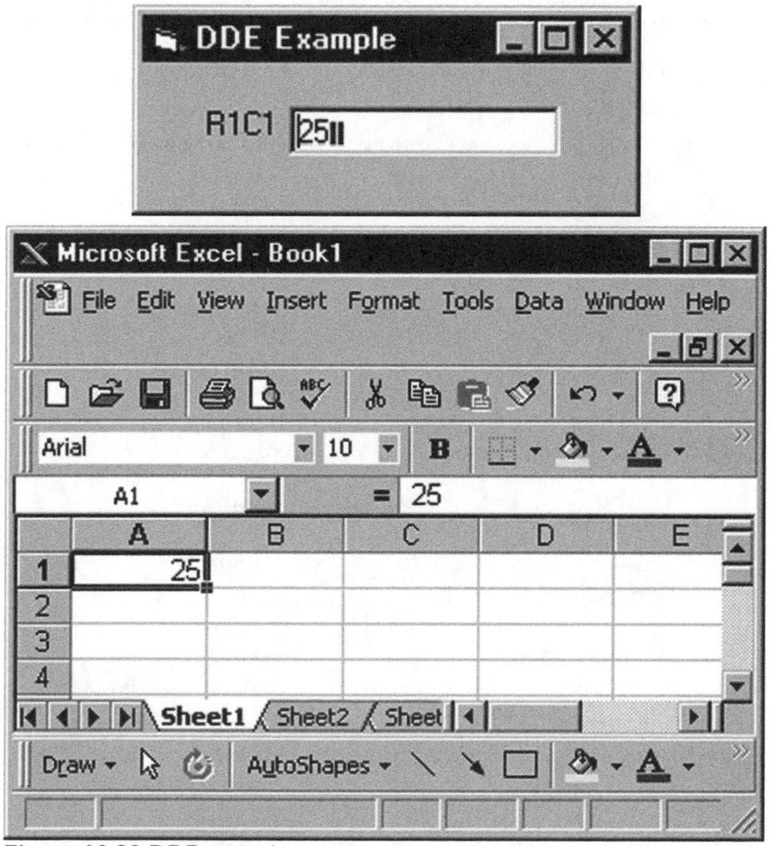

**Figure 10.28** DDE example

```
' Dynamic Data Exchange Example
' ----------------------------
' Establish an automatic link with R1C1 in Sheet1 of a
' Microsoft Excel spreadsheet
Option Explicit

Private Sub Form_Load()
' Establish an automatic DDE link
    txtR1C1.LinkTopic = "Excel|Sheet1"
    txtR1C1.LinkItem = "R1C1"
    txtR1C1.LinkMode = 1
End Sub
```

Microsoft Excel and Sheet1 ⟶ must open prior to executing this code

## INTERNET PROGRAMMING

VB has various controls available to access and make programs for the Internet. Like the common dialog control, these controls must be added to your toolbox as required. Right-click on an empty space in the toolbox and select Components from the pop-up menu. Under the Controls tab, check the box next to Microsoft Internet Controls and click the OK button. The WebBrowser and ShellFolderViewOC icons now appear in the toolbox.

VB does have other controls available that provide Internet access, such as the Microsoft Internet Transfer Control. Additionally, VB allows you to program for the Internet using ActiveX controls and VBSCRIPT. The Microsoft Internet Transfer Control, ActiveX controls for the Internet, and VBSCRIPT are beyond the scope of this text. We concentrate on the WebBrowser control and provide an example program.

The following code implements a simple Web browser in VB using the WebBrowser control. Figure 10.29 displays a sample execution of this program.

| Object | Property | Setting |
|---|---|---|
| Form | Name | frmBrowser |
| | Caption | A Simple Web Browser |
| Label | Name | lblURL |
| | AutoSize | True |
| | Caption | URL |
| Label | Name | lblTitle |
| | AutoSize | True |
| | Caption | Page Title: |
| Label | Name | lblLocation |
| | AutoSize | True |
| | Caption | (*Empty*) |
| | BackColor | Window Background |
| TextBox | Name | txtURL |
| | BackColor | Window Background |
| | Text | (*Empty*) |
| CommandButton | Name | cmdForward |
| | Caption | Forward |
| CommandButton | Name | cmdBack |
| | Caption | Back |
| CommandButton | Name | cmdHome |
| | Caption | Home |
| CommandButton | Name | cmdQuit |
| | Caption | Quit |
| WebBrowser | Name | webBrowser |

```
' A Simple Web Browser
Option Explicit

Private Sub cmdBack_Click()
' Go back to previous URL
   webBrowser.GoBack
End Sub

Private Sub cmdForward_Click()
' Go forward to next URL
   webBrowser.GoForward
End Sub

Private Sub cmdHome_Click()
' Go to home page
   webBrowser.GoHome
End Sub

Private Sub cmdQuit_Click()
' Quit the program
   End
End Sub

Private Sub Form_Load()
' Navigate to the default URL
   Call txtURL_KeyPress(13)
End Sub
```

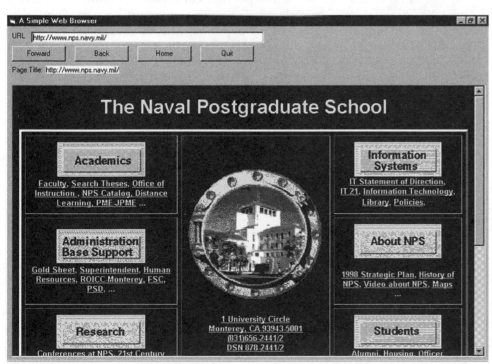

**Figure 10.29** Internet programming example

```
Private Sub Form_Resize()
' Resize the web browser
   webBrowser.Height = frmBrowser.ScaleHeight - 1500
   webBrowser.Width = frmBrowser.ScaleWidth - 200
End Sub

Private Sub txtURL_KeyPress(KeyAscii As Integer)
' Navigate to the user-entered URL when the user
' presses the ENTER key
   If KeyAscii = 13 Then
      webBrowser.Navigate (txtURL.Text)
   End If
End Sub

Private Sub webBrowser_NavigateComplete2(ByVal pDisp As
➡ Object, URL As Variant)
' Update the text box to display the current URL
' and display the Page Title
   txtURL.Text = webBrowser.LocationURL
   lblLocation.Caption = webBrowser.LocationName
End Sub
```

## VISUAL BASIC COMPILER DIRECTIVES

In previous chapters, we introduced the Option keyword and statements such as Option Explicit and Option Base 0. Statements of this type are called **compiler directives**. These statements are instructions for the VB compiler; they have no machine language equivalent, and thus, they are not compiled into machine code. In other words, these are **nonexecutable statements**.

Compiler directives may be used to perform **conditional compilation**, that is, to compile specific blocks of code when certain conditions are met. Conditional compilation is typically used to compile the same program for different computer platforms. Also, it may be used to prevent debugging code from appearing in an executable file. The code excluded during conditional compilation is completely omitted from the final executable file.

VB uses the pound sign (#) to designate compiler directives used for conditional compilation. Essentially, there are two different conditional compilation directives: #Const and #If-Then-#Else.

The #Const directive is used to define conditional compiler constants. The general syntax is as follows:

```
#Const CONSTANT_NAME = expression
```

CONSTANT_NAME is the name of the conditional compiler constant and must follow standard variable naming conventions. expression is any valid expression able to be evaluated at compile time. Constants defined using the #Const directive can only be used for conditional compilation. Conversely, using a standard constant defined with Const in expression causes an error to occur.

The #If-Then-#Else directive conditionally compiles selected blocks of VB code and operates in the same manner as a standard If-Then-Else statement. The general syntax follows:

```
#If condition1 Then
    [statements1]
[#ElseIf condition2 Then
    [statements2]]
        .

        .

        .
[#Else
    [statementsX]]
#End If
```

In the above syntax, the #ElseIf statement is optional, and any number of these statements may appear in the decision structure. The #Else statement is also optional, but only one of these statements may appear in the decision structure.

The following example uses conditional compilation for debugging purposes. Figure 10.30 displays a sample output.

```
'Conditional Compilation Example
Option Explicit

#Const DEBUGMODE = 2    ' 1 = Moderate debugging
                        ' 2 = Full debugging
                        ' otherwise, no debugging
```

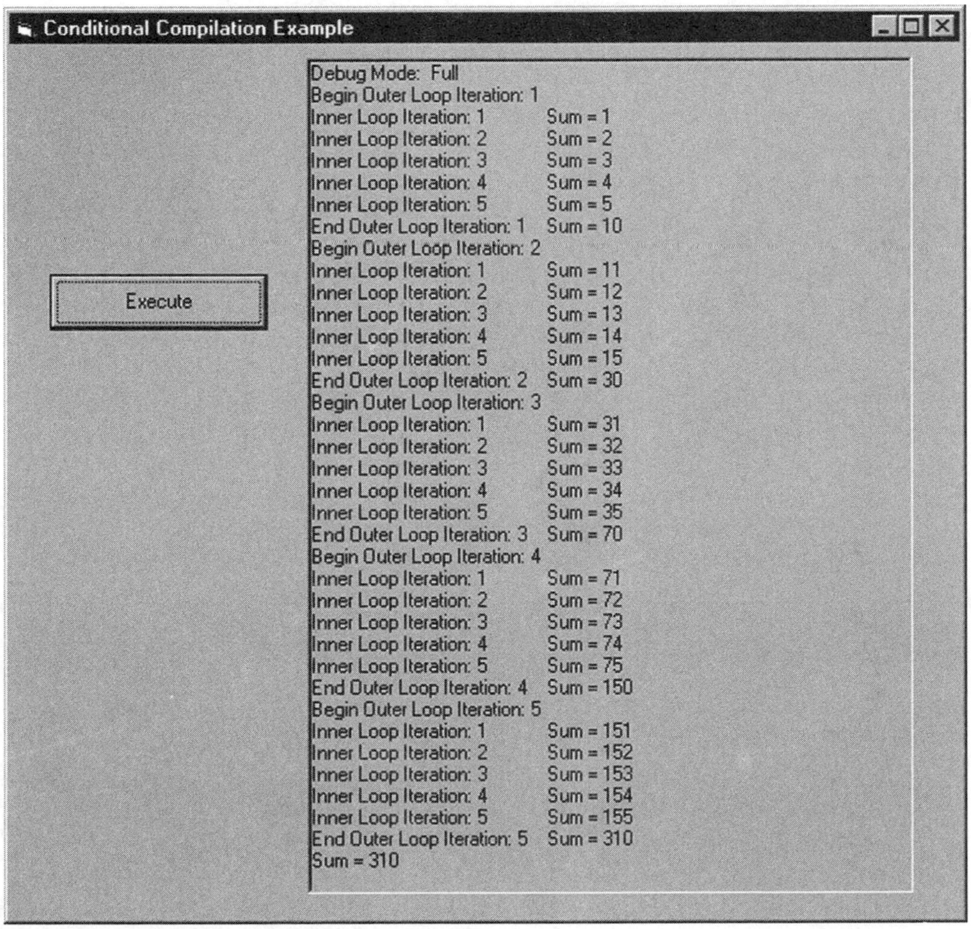

Figure 10.30 Conditional compilation example

```vb
Private Sub cmdExecute_Click()
' Execute loops
    Dim outer As Integer, inner As Integer
    Dim sum As Integer

    ' Display debug mode
    #If DEBUGMODE = 2 Then
        picOutput.Cls
        picOutput.Print "Debug Mode:   Full"
    #ElseIf DEBUGMODE = 1 Then
        picOutput.Cls
        picOutput.Print "Debug Mode:   Moderate"
    #End If

    sum = 0
    For outer = 1 To 5
        #If DEBUGMODE = 2 Then
            picOutput.Print "Begin Outer Loop Iteration:";
            ➥ outer
        #End If

        For inner = 1 To 5
            sum = sum + 1
            #If DEBUGMODE = 2 Then
                picOutput.Print "Inner Loop Iteration:";
                ➥ inner, "Sum ="; sum
            #End If
        Next inner

        sum = 2 * sum
        #If DEBUGMODE = 1 Or DEBUGMODE = 2 Then
            picOutput.Print "End Outer Loop Iteration:";
            ➥ outer, "Sum ="; sum
        #End If
    Next outer

    #If DEBUGMODE <> 1 And DEBUGMODE <> 2 Then
        picOutput.Cls
    #End If

    picOutput.Print "Sum ="; sum
End Sub
```

## CASE STUDY
### A Computerized Survey

Alan owns and operates EZ Online Inc., a small Internet service provider (ISP). Alan wants to collect customer data concerning Internet use. He wants to know the primary user's gender, yearly income, weekly Internet usage (in hours), and primary reasons for accessing the Internet. Alan decides to design a customer survey as a means of data collection. He wants to computerize this survey by writing it in VB and eventually put it on the Internet as a Web page. Can you help Alan design the initial survey program in VB?

The survey form for Alan's program appears in Figure 10.31.

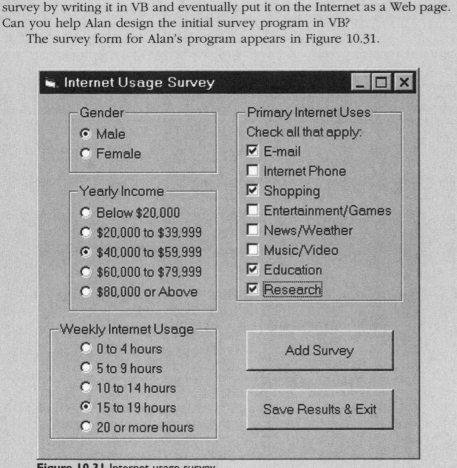

**Figure 10.31** Internet usage survey

The source code for Alan's survey program follows. The `cmdSave` command button writes text-formatted survey results to the `Internet.txt` file on the `C:` drive and exits the program.

```
' Internet Usage Survey
' ----------------------

Option Explicit

Dim gender(0 To 1) As Long
Dim income(0 To 4) As Long
Dim hourlyUsage(0 To 4) As Long
Dim uses(0 To 7) As Long
Dim surveyCount As Long

Private Sub cmdAdd_Click()
' Add survey results to total results and
' clear the survey form
    Dim index As Integer
```

```
        For index = 0 To 7
            If (index < 2) Then
                If optGender(index).Value Then
                    gender(index) = gender(index) + 1
                End If
            End If
            If (index < 5) Then
                If optIncome(index).Value Then
                    income(index) = income(index) + 1
                End If
                If optUsage(index).Value Then
                    hourlyUsage(index) = hourlyUsage(index) + 1
                End If
            End If
            If chkUse(index).Value = 1 Then
                uses(index) = uses(index) + 1
            End If
        Next index

        surveyCount = surveyCount + 1
        Call ClearSurvey
End Sub

Private Sub cmdSave_Click()
' Write the survey results to a text-formatted
' data file and exit the program
    Dim index As Integer

    Open "C:\Internet.txt" For Output As #1
    Print #1, "INTERNET SURVEY RESULTS"
    Print #1, "-----------------------"
    Print #1,

    Print #1, "Total Surveys: " & CStr(surveyCount)
    Print #1,

    Print #1, "GENDER"
    For index = 0 To 1
        Print #1, Trim(CStr(optGender(index).Caption)) & ":
        ➡ " & CStr(gender(index))
    Next index
    Print #1,

    Print #1, "INCOME"
    For index = 0 To 4
        Print #1, Trim(CStr(optIncome(index).Caption)) & ":
        ➡ " & CStr(income(index))
    Next index
    Print #1,

    Print #1, "HOURLY USAGE"
    For index = 0 To 4
```

```vb
            Print #1, Trim(CStr(optUsage(index).Caption)) & ": "
            ➡ & CStr(hourlyUsage(index))
    Next index
    Print #1,

    Print #1, "USES"
    For index = 0 To 7
        Print #1, Trim(CStr(chkUse(index).Caption)) & ": "
        ➡ & CStr(uses(index))
    Next index

    Close #1
    End
End Sub

Private Sub Form_Load()
' Clear the survey form and totals
    Call ClearSurvey
    Call ClearTotals
End Sub

Private Sub ClearSurvey()
' Clear the survey form
    Dim index As Integer

    optGender(0).Value = True
    optIncome(0).Value = True
    optUsage(0).Value = True

    For index = 0 To 7
        chkUse(index).Value = 0
    Next index
End Sub

Private Sub ClearTotals()
' Clear the total survey results
    Dim index As Integer

    For index = 0 To 7
        If (index < 2) Then
            gender(index) = 0
        End If
        If (index < 5) Then
            income(index) = 0
            hourlyUsage(index) = 0
        End If
        uses(index) = 0
    Next index

    surveyCount = 0
End Sub
```

A sample `Internet.txt` output file for four surveys appears below:

```
INTERNET SURVEY RESULTS
-----------------------


Total Surveys: 4

GENDER
Male: 2
Female: 2

INCOME
Below $20,000: 0
$20,000 to $39,999: 1
$40,000 to $59,999: 2
$60,000 to $79,999: 1
$80,000 or Above: 0

HOURLY USAGE
0 to 4 hours: 0
5 to 9 hours: 0
10 to 14 hours: 2
15 to 19 hours: 1
20 or more hours: 1

USES
E-mail: 4
Internet Phone: 1
Shopping: 2
Entertainment/Games: 1
News/Weather: 2
Music/Video: 1
Education: 2
Research: 1
```

# Summary

## Key Terms

**collection**   a VB data structure similar to a dynamic array that can contain any object or data type

**compiler directives**—compiler commands or instructions that are placed in a program's source code

**conditional compilation**—compilation of specific blocks of code when certain conditions are met

**control array**—an array of VB controls

**dynamic data exchange (DDE)**—a means of exchanging information between active applications

**embedded object**—an object that is created in an application and then placed in a VB program; a copy of the object is contained in the VB program

**linked object**—an object that is created in an application and then linked to a VB program; only a reference to the object is placed in the VB program

**Monte Carlo simulation**—a type of simulation named after casino-style gambling in Monte Carlo

**multiple document interface (MDI)**—an application that allows multiple forms (or windows) to be open within a single container form (or window)

**nonexecutable statements**—statements that are not compiled into machine code, such as comments and compiler directives

**OLE**—an acronym for object linking and embedding

**OLE Automation object**—an application that is created as a VB object at run time

**OLE container control**—a control that allows objects from other applications to be linked or embedded in VB programs at design time

**seed value**—an initial value used by the VB random number generator to produce pseudorandom numbers

**single document interface (SDI)**—an application in which only one file may be open at a time; the current file must be closed before another file may be opened

**twip**—a screen-independent unit used to ensure that placement and proportion of screen elements in an application are the same on all display systems; the equivalent to 1/20 of a printer's point; there are approximately 1,440 twips per inch or 567 twips per centimeter

## Keywords

*Compiler Directives:*
#Const
#If–Then–#Else

*Events:*
LinkClose
LinkError
LinkExecute
LinkNotify
LinkOpen
Timer

*Functions:*
CreateObject
LoadPicture
QBcolor
RGB
Rnd
Timer

*Methods:*
Add
AddItem
Circle
Line
LinkExecute
LinkPoke
LinkRequest
LinkSend
Pset
Remove

RemoveItem
Scale
SetFocus

*Properties:*
AutoActivate
BackColor
Caption
Class
Count
CurrentX
CurrentY
DisplayType
DrawMode
DrawStyle
DrawWidth
Enabled
FillColor
FillStyle
ForeColor
Index
Interval
Item (*n*)
LargeChange
Left
LinkItem
LinkMode
LinkTimeout
LinkTopic
List

ListCount
ListIndex
Max
MDIChild
Min
MultiSelect
Name
OLETypeAllowed
Path
Picture
ScaleMode
SmallChange
Sorted
SourceDoc
SourceItem
Stretch
Style
Top
UpdateOptions
Value
Visible

*Statements:*
For Each
Load
Next
Randomize
Set
Unload

## Key Concepts

- VB offers a programmer a variety of controls, and the default controls in the Toolbox represent only a small number of the components available. The Components window allows the programmer to access additional components, such as the common dialog control. To open this window, select Project/Components from the menu bar, press CTRL+T, or right-click an empty spot in the Toolbox and select Components from the pop-up window.

- The image control displays images or graphics on a form and supports a variety of graphic file formats, including bitmap, icon, metafile, enhanced metafile, JPEG, and GIF files. To assign a picture file to an image control at run time, use the LoadPicture function:

  ```
  Let Image1.Picture = LoadPicture (picfile)
  ```

- The common dialog control contains dialog boxes that are common to most Windows-based applications. To invoke the common dialog control, use a statement of the form:

  ```
  CommonDialog1.Show{Open | Save | Color | Font |Print}
  ```

- Although custom menus are VB controls, they are not accessed through either the Components window or default Toolbox. The Menu Editor allows the programmer to create a custom menu for a VB application. To initiate the Menu Editor, select Tools/Menu Editor from the menu bar or press CTRL+E.

- A control array is an array of VB control objects. Objects in a control array can be placed on the form at either design time or run time. At run time, the Load and Unload statements create and destroy elements of the control array, respectively. Each control in the control array has a unique Index value. These Index values need not start at zero nor be sequential. Control arrays are extremely useful in decision and repetition structures and when a group of controls are related.

- Component-based software development significantly reduces programming time and produces more robust applications. Microsoft's ActiveX technology is part of the Component Object Model (COM) and allows programmers to design and develop their own software components, such as VB controls. Using ActiveX technology, a programmer can rapidly create, debug, and deploy a variety of software components.

- A collection is a dynamic data structure similar to an array that groups objects. A collection may contain any number of objects or data types. VB is an extremely flexible language with regard to objects and data structures, as many other high-level languages do not offer a structure equivalent to the collection.

  To declare and instantiate a collection, use:

  ```
  Dim CollectionName As New Collection
  ```

  A collection object has two properties:

  ```
  CollectionName.Count
  CollectionName.Item (n)
  ```

  A collection object also has two methods:

  ```
  CollectionName.Add ObjectName
  CollectionName.Remove (n)
  ```

● The `For Each-Next` structure repeats a group of statements for each element in an array or collection:

```
For Each element In groupName
    [statements]
Next element
```

● Multiple document interface (MDI) and single document interface (SDI) are two different user-interface styles. An MDI application consists of a main form that may contain several child windows. An SDI application, on the other hand, contains only a main window; there are no child windows in an SDI application. If the user requires several files to be open simultaneously, an MDI is best. MDI is also more flexible than SDI since the user can control the number of open windows. However, an MDI is slightly more complex and takes longer to program than an SDI.

● VB offers powerful random number features. Random numbers are useful in computer simulations and games.

The `Randomize` statement initializes the VB random number generator:

```
Randomize [number]
```

The `Rnd` function returns a single-precision random number whose value is less than 1 but greater than or equal to zero:

```
randomNumber = Rnd[(number)]
```

To produce random integer values in a given range, use:

```
randomInteger = Int ((upperbound - lowerbound + 1) * Rnd
➡ + lowerbound)
```

● VB offers powerful graphics features. Graphics are useful in games, mathematics, engineering, and business programs. The default unit of screen measure is twips. A twip is a screen-independent unit used to ensure that placement and proportion of screen elements in an application are the same on all display systems. A twip is equivalent to 1/20 of a printer's point, and there are approximately 1,440 twips per inch (or 567 twips per centimeter).

The `Scale` method defines the coordinate system for an object:

```
Object.Scale (x1, y1) - (x2, y2)
```

The `PSet` method sets a specific point on an object to a specified color:

```
Object.PSet [Step] (x, y), [color]
```

The `Line` method draws lines and rectangles on an object:

```
Object.Line [Step] (x1, y1) [Step] (x2, y2), [color],
[B[F]]
```

The `Circle` method draws a circle, arc, or ellipse on an object:

```
Object.Circle [Step] (x, y), radius, [color, start, end,
➡ aspect]
```

● Both object linking and embedding (OLE) and dynamic data exchange (DDE) allow VB programs to access information from other applications. OLE allows other applications and their objects to be treated as objects in VB. For instance, a sheet from a Microsoft Excel workbook may be linked or embedded in a VB application. OLE does not require Microsoft Excel to be active when the VB application is executing. DDE allows information to be passed between active applications. When a DDE link is established between a VB program and a Microsoft Excel spreadsheet, both applications must be active.

● The CreateObject function creates an OLE Automation object, and the Set statement is used to assign it to an object variable:

```
Dim ObjectVar As Object
Set ObjectVar = CreateObject(ClassName)
```

Once the OLE Automation object is no longer needed, we clear the object variable and free system resources with a statement of the form:

```
Set ObjectVar = Nothing
```

● VB has various controls available to access and make programs for the Internet, such as the WebBrowser control.

● Conditional compilation compiles designated blocks of code only when certain conditions exist. Conditional compilation is typically used to compile the same program for different computer platforms. Also, it may be used to prevent debugging code from appearing in an executable file. The code excluded during conditional compilation is completely omitted from the final executable file.

The #Const directive is used to define conditional compiler constants:

```
#Const CONSTANT_NAME = expression
```

The #If-Then-#Else directive conditionally compiles selected blocks of VB code and operates in the same manner as a standard If-Then-Else statement:

```
#If condition1 Then
    [statements1]
[#ElseIf condition2 Then
    [statements2]]
        .
        .
        .
[#Else
    [statementsX]]
#End If
```

## Review Questions

1. Name and describe all controls in the VB default Toolbox. How do you add components to the VB Toolbox?

2. What tool must be used to create a custom menu in a VB program?

3. What is a control array? How is a control array useful?

4. What is ActiveX? Describe the steps necessary to create an ActiveX control.

5. What is a collection?

6. Define MDI and SDI. How do you determine which one to use?

7. Write the VB code to generate a random number between 1 and 10.

8. Describe OLE and DDE. How are they similar? How are they different?

9. What is conditional compilation? How is it useful?

10. State the two different conditional compilation directives.

## Chapter 10 Problems

1. Enhance the user interface in your program from Chapter 5, Problem 9. The new interface should include option buttons to select a month and combo boxes to select the day and year. Additionally, the option buttons should form a control array.

2. Implement a deque of integer values using a collection.

3. Modify your program from Problem 1 to use a multiple document interface (MDI). This allows several calendars to be open simultaneously in different child windows.

4. Simulate tossing a coin 1,000 times and count the number of occurrences of heads and tails. Repeat this experiment 10 times and report the percentage of occurrences for each of the two possible outcomes.

5. Simulate rolling a pair of dice 1,000 times and count the number of occurrences of the sum. For instance, if one die lands on 4 and the other lands on 3, the sum of the dice roll is 7 and your program should update the counter for "7." Repeat this experiment 10 times and report the percentage of occurrences of each sum.

6. Modify your program from Chapter 4, Problem 11 to graph the normal density function for a user-specified range of $x$ values, $\mu$, and $\sigma$.

7. Modify your program from Chapter 4, Problem 12 to graph the cumulative distribution function of the exponential distribution for a user-specified $\lambda$ and range of $x$ values.

8. Modify the dynamic data exchange (DDE) example to use `LinkMode 2` (Manual). You must write the appropriate event handlers and invoke the proper methods.

## Programming Projects

1. Design and program your own custom Web browser. Use conditional compilation to prevent debugging code from appearing in your executable file.

2. Convert the stopwatch program in this chapter (see the Timer control example) to an ActiveX control named Stopwatch. Test this control in a simple program.

# Package and Deployment Wizard

## Chapter Supplement Objectives

In this chapter supplement, you will:

- Learn the purpose of the VB Package and Deployment Wizard

- Learn how to use VB Add-Ins

- Walk through an example of packaging an application for distribution

Since programs created in VB run under the Windows operating system, they require several VB and Windows files, components, and libraries. Thus, a VB executable file created on one computer cannot simply be copied to another computer and expected to work. In most cases, the program does not execute on the second machine unless VB is installed. To overcome this problem, Microsoft includes the Package and Deployment Wizard in VB 6.0, replacing the similar Application Setup Wizard of VB 5.0.

### Using the Package and Deployment Wizard

The Package and Deployment Wizard allows you to create the necessary files and **distribution media** to install and execute your application on a machine that does not contain VB. Under the Package option, the Wizard creates cab files (.CAB) for your application and groups them into a **package**. A **cab file** is a file that contains application files in a compressed format. A package groups these cab files and all other files necessary to install your application. In the Deploy option, the Wizard automates the process of creating distribution media, such as floppy disks, a network drive, or a Web site, to deliver your packaged application.

We use the simple Web browser program of Chapter 10 (see Figure 10.29) to demonstrate the use of the Package and Deployment Wizard. Our program is named Browser and is located in the C:\Programs directory. Before we use this Wizard, we must first compile the program:

1. Start Visual Basic.

2. Enter the simple Web browser example associated with Figure 10.29 or select File/Open Project and load this project if it already exists.

## Key Term

**distribution media**—the media used to deliver packaged applications, such as floppy disks, CD-ROMs, network drives, or Web sites

3. Save the project and form files as `C:\Programs\Browser.vbp` and `C:\Programs\Browser.frm`, respectively.

4. Select File/Make Browser.exe to create the executable file. This file should be created in the `C:\Programs` directory.

## Using the Package and Deployment Wizard as a VB Add-In

The Package and Deployment Wizard can be run as either a stand-alone program or an Add-In within VB. The operation of the Wizard is the same regardless of how it is executed. To start the Wizard as a stand-alone program, click on the Windows 95/98 Start button and select Programs/Microsoft Visual Basic 6.0/Microsoft Visual Basic 6.0 Tools/Package & Deployment Wizard. We describe how to run the Wizard as a VB Add-In along with the example directions:

5. From the VB menu bar, select Add-Ins/Add-In Manager to open the Add-In Manager window.

6. Select the Package and Deployment Wizard from the list of Available Add-Ins and click on the Loaded/Unloaded check box in the Load Behavior frame. The window should now appear as in Figure 10.32.

7. Click on the OK button. The Package and Deployment Wizard is now an available Add-In.

8. Select Add-Ins/Package and Deployment Wizard to start the Wizard shown in Figure 10.33.

9. Click on the Package icon or press ALT+P.

10. The Package Type window opens. You can create either a **standard setup package** or a **dependency file**. A standard setup package creates the necessary package files and a `Setup.exe` program to install your application on a computer. A dependency file is a file that lists all components required by your program. Select Standard Setup Package as the package type. Click the Next button or press ALT+N.

11. The Package Folder window opens. In this window, you specify the location where your package files are created. Enter `C:\Programs\Package` as the package folder. Click the Next button or press ALT+N.

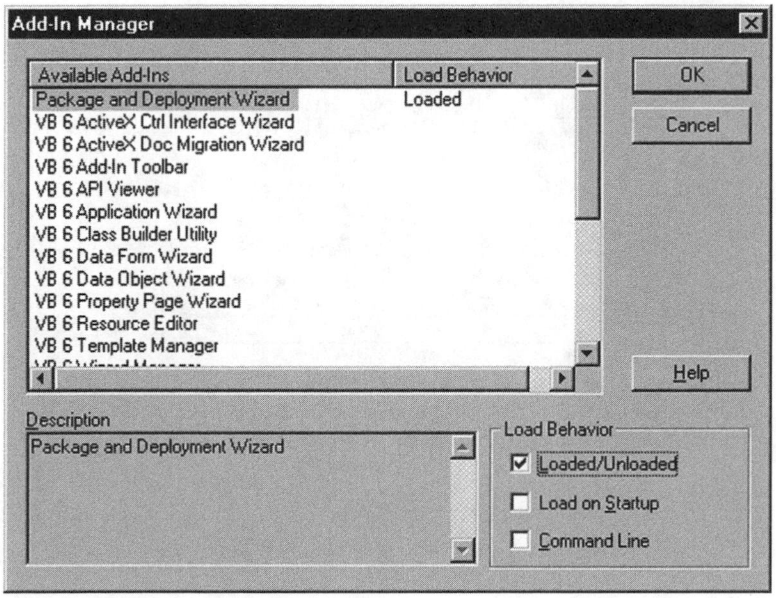

**Figure 10.32** Add-In manager

**Figure 10.33** VB 6.0 Package and Deployment Wizard

**12.** The Included Files window opens. As shown in Figure 10.34, this window lists all of the VB and Windows files required by your program. Review the files in the window and click the Next button or press ALT+N to continue.

**13.** The Cab Options window shown in Figure 10.35 appears on the screen. A cab file is a file that is part of a package and used to distribute an application. You can create one large cab file or multiple cab files for your package. If you are distributing your application on floppy disks, you should use multiple cab files with the file size (cab size) no larger than a single disk. Select the Multiple cabs option button with a Cab size of 1.44 MB. Click the Next button or press ALT+N.

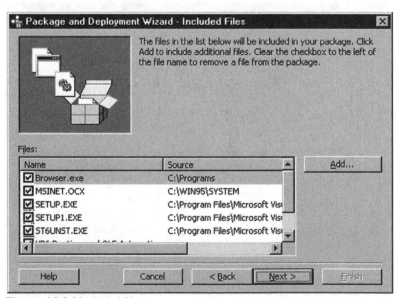

**Figure 10.34** Included files

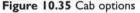

**Figure 10.35** Cab options

**14.** The Installation Title window opens. You can specify the title that you want to be displayed when the setup program is executed. Enter My Web Browser as the installation title. Click the Next button or press ALT+N.

**15.** The Start Menu Items window shown in Figure 10.36 appears on the screen. You can specify the Start menu groups and items that are created by the installation program. Click the Next button or press ALT+N to continue.

**16.** The Install Locations window opens. You can change the install location for each of the files listed in this window. Keep the default install locations settings and click the Next button or press ALT+N to continue.

**17.** The Shared Files window opens. In this window, you can select files to be installed as shared files. A **shared file** is a file that may be used by more than one application. A shared file is removed only when every application that uses it is removed. Do not select any files and click the Next button or press ALT+N to continue.

**Key Term**

**shared file**—a file that may be used by more than one application and is removed only when every application that uses it is removed

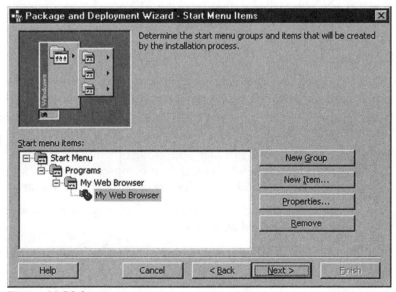

**Figure 10.36** Start menu items

18. The final window opens. In this window, you can specify a script name to save the settings necessary to build your package. Enter My Web Browser as the Script name and click the Finish button or press ALT+F to create the package.

19. The Packaging Report window opens. This window lists information concerning your packaged application. Review the information in this window and click the Close button.

You can now manually copy the cab files to the distribution media or use the Deploy option in the Package and Deployment Wizard to perform this task automatically. We leave the Deploy option to be explored by the reader.

20. Click the Close button to close the Package and Deployment Wizard.

Finally, executing the Setup.exe program located on the distribution media starts the application installation process.

## Summary

### Key Terms

**cab file**—a file used to distribute an application; it contains the application files in a compressed format

**dependency file**—a file that lists all other files and components required by an applications program

**distribution media**—the media used to deliver a packaged application, such as floppy disks, CD-ROMs, a network drive, or a Web site

**package**—a group of cab files and all other files necessary to install an application

**shared file**—a file that may be used by more than one application and is removed only when every application that uses it is removed

**standard setup package**—the necessary package files and a Setup.exe program to install an application on a computer

### Key Concepts

● The VB 6.0 Package and Deployment Wizard provides a means of distributing VB programs to other Windows-based computers that do not contain VB 6.0. This Wizard is necessary since VB programs depend upon other Windows and VB components.

● The Package option creates cab files and groups them into a package. A cab file is a file that contains application files in a compressed format, and a package is a group of cab files and other files necessary to install the application.

● The Deploy option automates the process of creating distribution media to deliver a previously packaged application.

● The Package and Deployment Wizard can be run as either a stand-alone program or a VB 6.0 Add-In.

## Review Questions

1. What does the VB 6.0 Package and Deployment Wizard do? Why is it necessary?
2. In what two ways can you execute the Package and Deployment Wizard?
3. How do you use an Add-In in VB?
4. What is a dependency file?
5. What is a shared file?
6. What files does the Package and Deployment Wizard create?
7. Summarize the steps necessary to package an application for distribution?

## Chapter 10 Supplement Problems

1. Package your program from Chapter 10, Problem 3. Deploy this package on 3½-inch floppy disks.
2. Package your program from Chapter 10, Problem 5. Deploy this package on a local or network drive.
3. Package your program from Chapter 10, Problem 7. Deploy this package using the distribution media of your choice.

## Programming Projects

1. Package and deploy your program from Chapter 10, Programming Project 1 on 3½-inch floppy disks.

# Visual Basic for Applications

## Chapter Objectives

In this chapter, you will:

○ Learn to create and use macros in Microsoft Office applications

○ Become familiar with Visual Basic for Applications and learn how to edit macro code

○ Learn how to create macro shortcuts, including toolbar buttons and shortcut keys

○ Learn how to use Visual Basic control objects in Microsoft Office applications

○ Develop an understanding of the differences between Visual Basic and Visual Basic for Applications

## Key Terms

**macro**—a set of actions or commands in an applications program, such as Microsoft Word or Microsoft Excel

**Visual Basic for Applications (VBA)**—a specialized version of Visual Basic built into Microsoft Office applications; the macro language for Microsoft applications

**A** macro is a set of actions or commands in an applications program. All Microsoft Office products, such as the Microsoft Word word processor and Microsoft Excel spreadsheet, use Visual Basic as the underlying macro language. Although similar, this macro language is not exactly the same as Visual Basic 6.0. Microsoft Office applications use a special version of Visual Basic called **Visual Basic for Applications (VBA)**. In fact, each Microsoft Office application has its own version of VBA since each application contains a different set of objects. Macros in a word processor, for instance, must be able to access text, whereas a macro in a spreadsheet must access specific cells.

The easiest way to learn how to program in VBA is to create a macro using an application's built-in macro recorder, view the resulting VBA code, and then modify the code as necessary. The next section shows how to create and run macros in both Microsoft Word and Microsoft Excel.

# USING MACROS

Microsoft Office applications allow the user to create macros by using a recording process similar to that of a cassette recorder. Just as a cassette recorder records everything you say, the macro recorder records everything you do in the application (including keystrokes, mouse clicks, menu selections, and so on). To create a new macro, select Tools/Macro/Record New Macro in a Microsoft Office application. The process of recording, viewing, and modifying macros in Microsoft Word and Microsoft Excel is illustrated in the following examples. This same process can be used to create macros in the other Microsoft Office applications as well.

## AN EXAMPLE MACRO IN MICROSOFT WORD

1. Open Microsoft Word and select Tools/Macro/Record New Macro from the menu. A window similar to the one shown in Figure 11.1 appears on your screen.

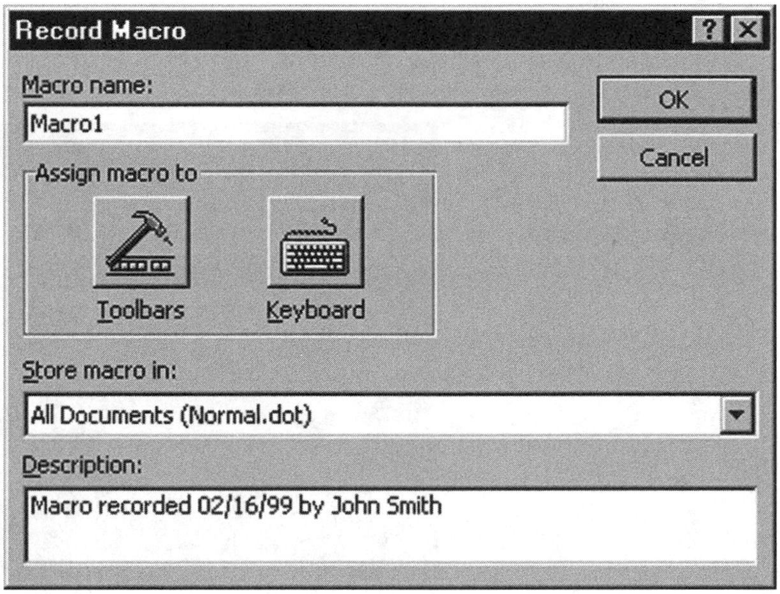

**Figure 11.1** Record Macro window

2. Change the macro name to myMacro and change the storage location to Document1. Click the OK button. Your screen should now look similar to Figure 11.2.

3. Notice the Stop Recording toolbar that appears on your screen. This toolbar contains buttons to both stop and pause recording. If this toolbar does not appear on your screen, select View/Toolbars/Stop Recording from the menu.

4. Hold down CTRL and press the HOME key (CTRL+HOME). This places the cursor at the beginning of the text document. Next, select the Times New Roman font and size 12 (if this font and size are already selected, select them again). Finally, type in the text exactly as shown on the screen in Figure 11.3.

5. Click the Stop Recording button (the solid square) on the Stop Recording toolbar.

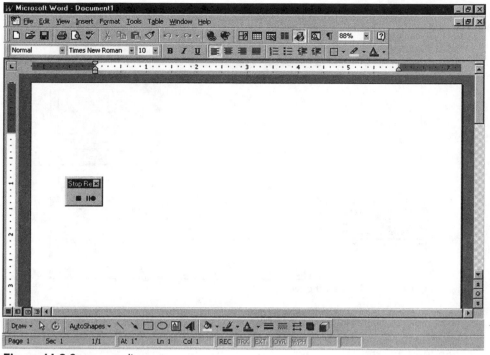

**Figure 11.2** Start recording a macro

6. Select Tools/Macro/Macros from the menu. The Macros window in Figure 11.4 appears on your screen.

7. Click on the Run button. Your Microsoft Word document should now resemble the one in Figure 11.5.

8. Again, select Tools/Macro/Macros from the menu. The Macros window in Figure 11.4 appears on your screen.

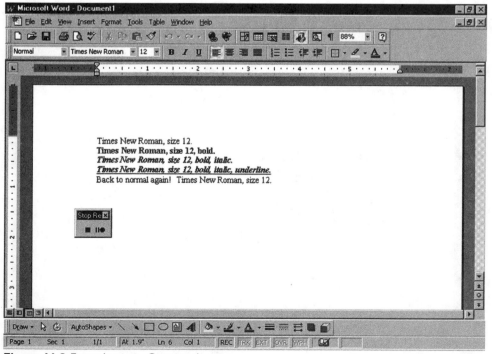

**Figure 11.3** Example text—Creating the macro

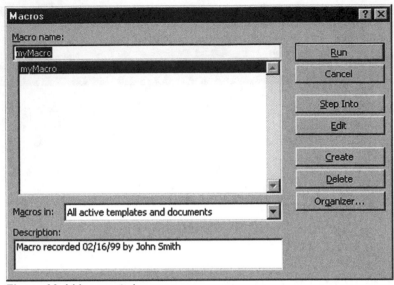

**Figure 11.4** Macros window

9. Click on the Edit button. The Microsoft Visual Basic for Applications window opens and the code for the macro appears in a code window. These windows are shown in Figure 11.6.

10. Now, let's modify the macro. Add the lines of code shown in Figure 11.7 and then exit the VBA window by clicking the close button (the X button) in the upper right-hand corner.

11. Run the macro again by selecting Tools/Macro/Macros and clicking the Run button. Your document should now resemble Figure 11.8.

12. Exit Microsoft Word by clicking the close button in the upper right-hand corner or by selecting File/Exit from the menu.

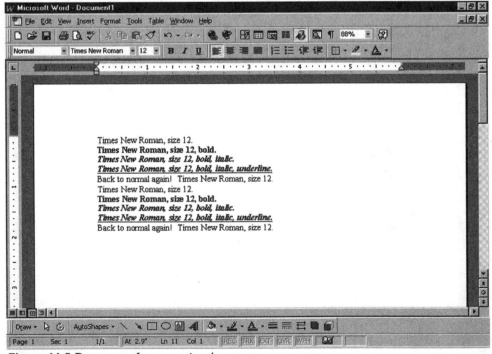

**Figure 11.5** Document after executing the macro

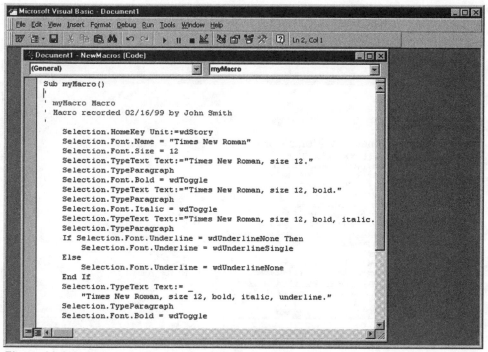

**Figure 11.6** Visual Basic for Applications (Microsoft Word)

## AN EXAMPLE MACRO IN MICROSOFT EXCEL

**1.** Open Microsoft Excel and select Tools/Macro/Record New Macro from the menu. The window shown in Figure 11.9 appears on your screen.

**2.** Change the macro name to `myExcelMacro` and change the storage location to This Workbook. Click the OK button. Your screen should now look similar to Figure 11.10.

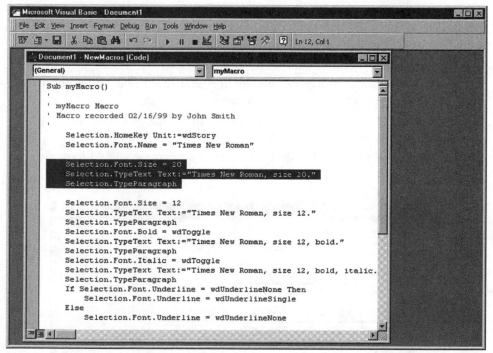

**Figure 11.7** Modify the VBA code

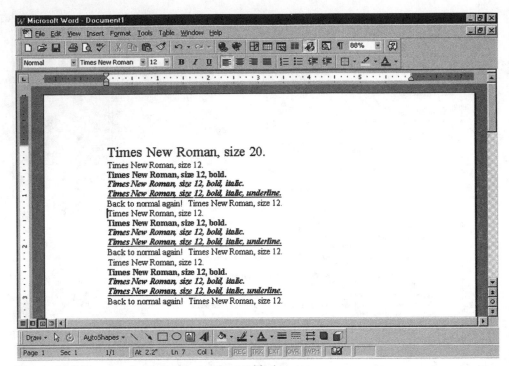

**Figure 11.8** Document after executing the modified macro

3. Notice the Stop Recording toolbar that appears on your screen. This toolbar has a button to stop recording and a toggle button to create a relative cell reference. If this toolbar does not appear on your screen, select View/Toolbars/Stop Recording from the menu.

4. Hold down CTRL and press the HOME key (CTRL+HOME). This places the cursor in cell A1. Now, type in the data exactly as shown in Figure 11.11.

5. Select Data/Sort from the menu. Cells A1 through A10 are automatically highlighted, and the Sort window shown in Figure 11.12 appears on the screen. Click the OK button in the Sort window.

6. Click the Stop Recording button on the Stop Recording toolbar.

7. Next, click on the A at the top of column A and select Edit/Delete from the menu. The contents of column A are now deleted.

8. Select Tools/Macro/Macros from the menu. The Macro window shown in Figure 11.13 appears on the screen.

9. Click the Run button in the Macro window. Your screen should look like Figure 11.14.

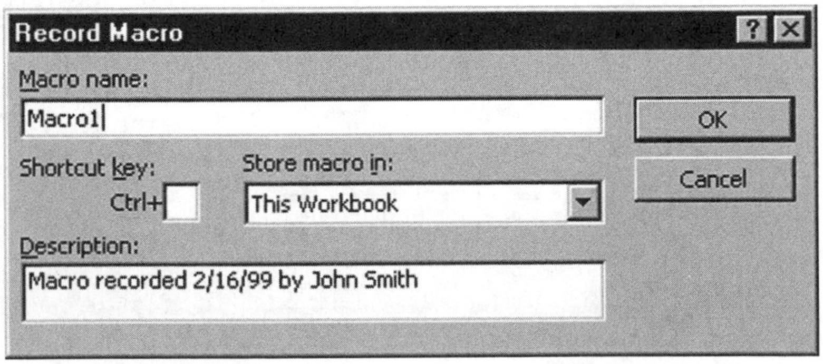

**Figure 11.9** Record Macro window

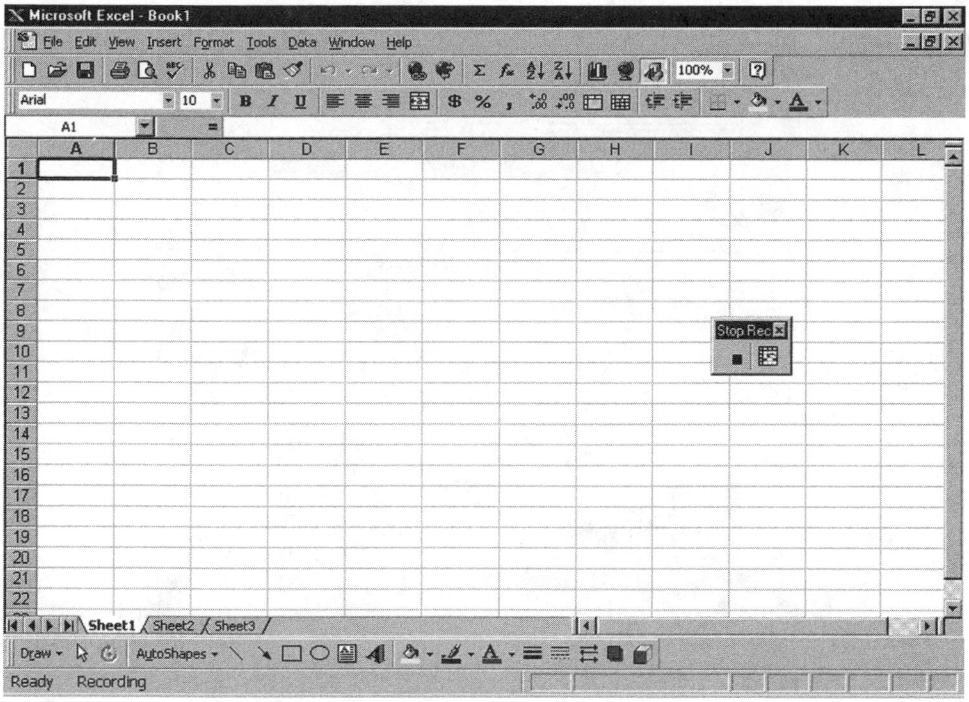

**Figure 11.10** Start recording a macro

**10.** Again, select Tools/Macro/Macros from the menu. The Macro window shown in Figure 11.13 appears on the screen.

**11.** Click on the Edit button. The Microsoft Visual Basic for Applications window opens and the code for the macro appears in a code window. These windows are shown in Figure 11.15.

**12.** Now, let's modify the macro. Change the line of code shown in Figure 11.16 and then exit the VBA window by clicking the close button (the X button) in the upper right-hand corner.

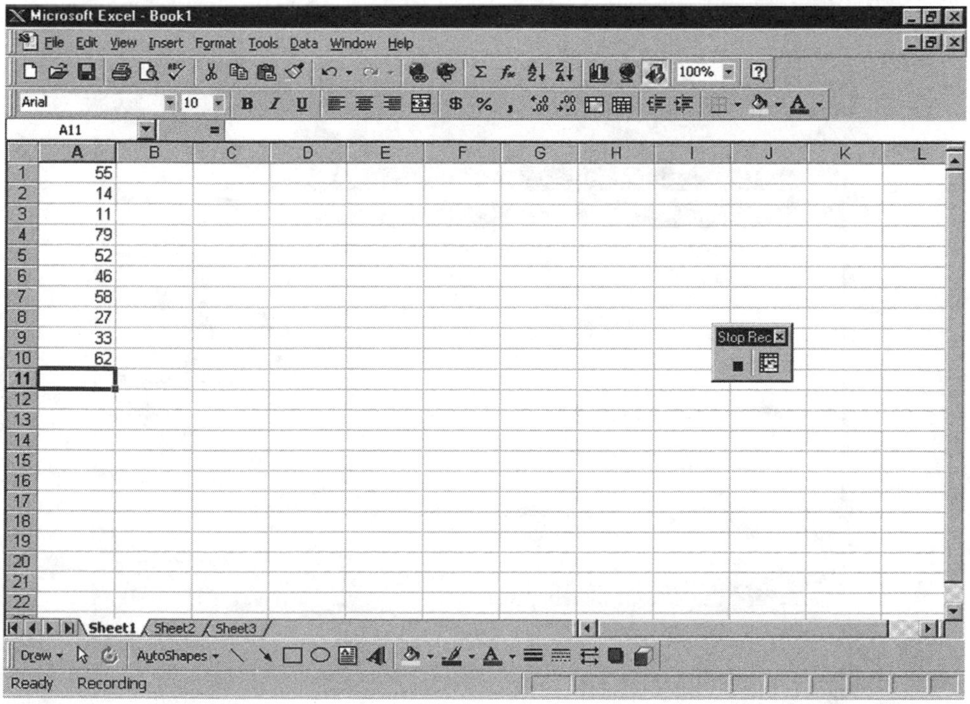

**Figure 11.11** Type in data

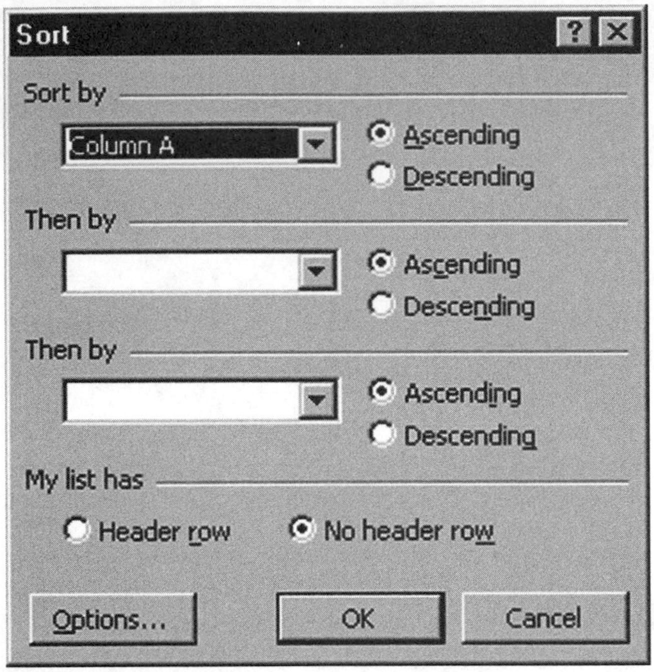

**Figure 11.12** Sort window

**13.** Run the macro again by repeating steps 8 and 9 above. Your screen should now look like Figure 11.17.

**14.** Exit Microsoft Excel by clicking the close button in the upper right-hand corner or by selecting File/Exit from the menu.

## USING MACRO SHORTCUTS

Selecting a macro from the Macro window is time consuming. Fortunately, Microsoft Office provides a means of creating **shortcuts** that make it easier to execute macro

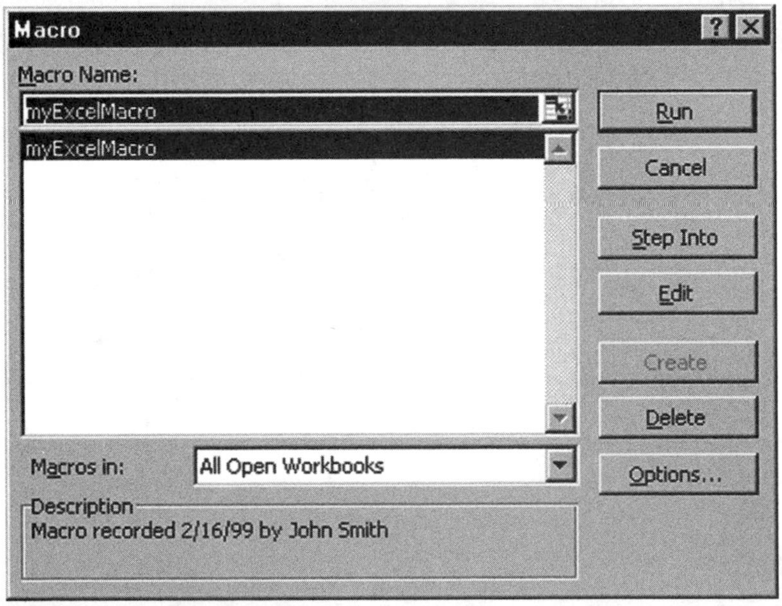

**Figure 11.13** Macro window

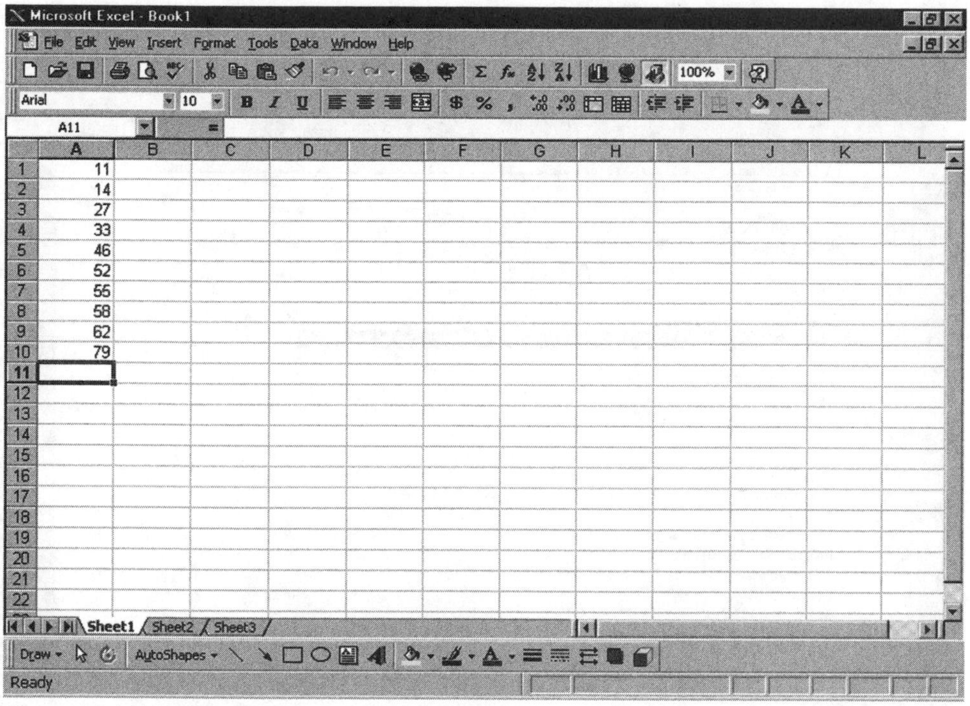

**Figure 11.14** Worksheet after executing the macro

commands. The shortcut feature allows the user to define a shortcut key combination for the macro or place an icon for the macro on the toolbar. An example of this feature in Microsoft Word is outlined below.

1. Open Microsoft Word and select Tools/Macro/Record New Macro from the menu. A window similar to the one shown in Figure 11.1 appears on your screen.

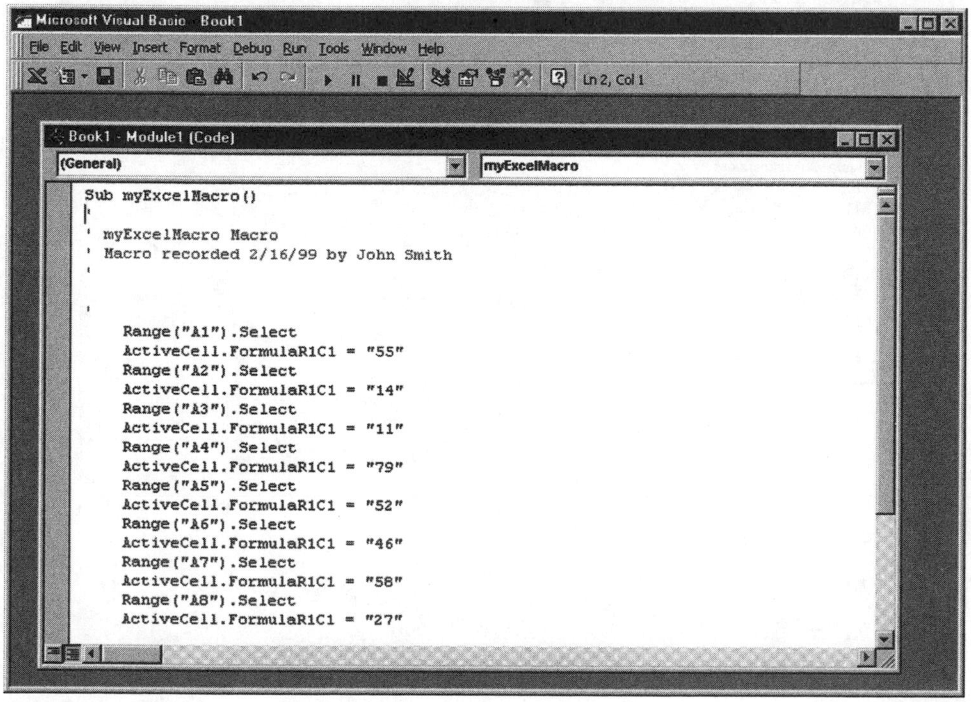

**Figure 11.15** Visual Basic for Applications (Microsoft Excel)

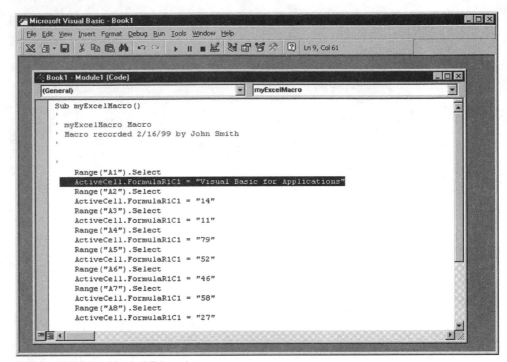

**Figure 11.16** Modify the VBA code

**2.** Change the macro name to `Smiley` and change the storage location to Document1.

**3.** Click the Toolbars button in the "Assign macro to" frame. The Customize window shown in Figure 11.18 appears on the screen.

**4.** Change the storage location ("Save in") to Document1.

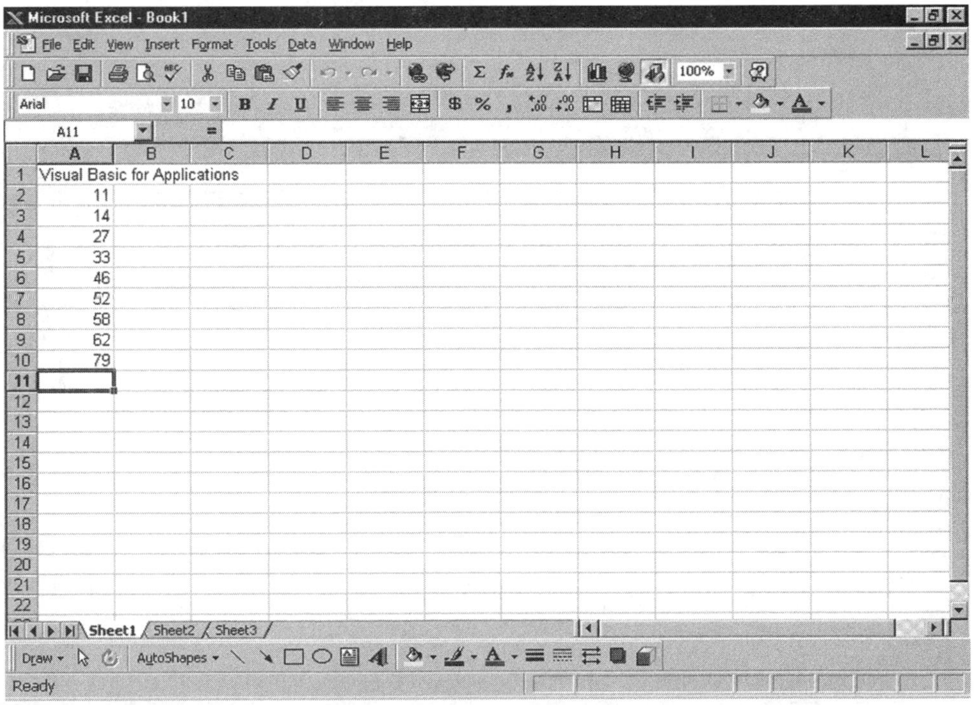

**Figure 11.17** Worksheet after executing the modified macro

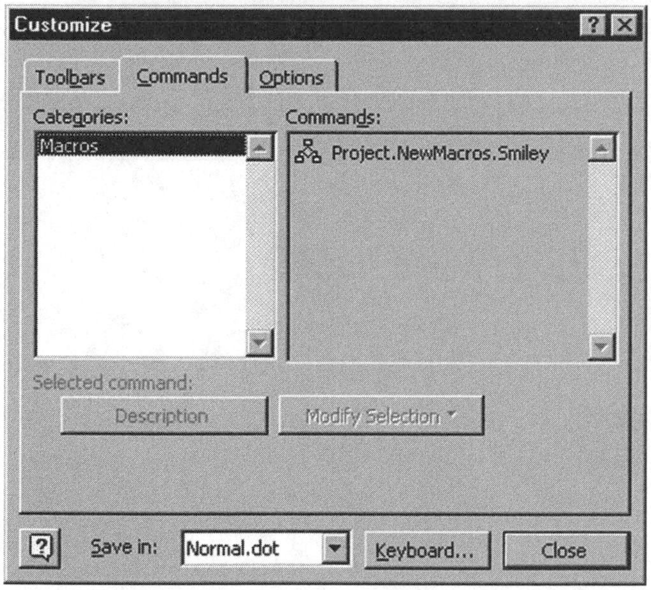

**Figure 11.18** Customize window

5. Click the Keyboard button and the Customize Keyboard window shown in Figure 11.19 appears on the screen.

6. Click on the "Press new shortcut key" text box. Now, hold down the ALT key and press the S key (ALT+S) and "ALT+S" appears in the text box.

7. Click on the Assign button to assign this shortcut key to the Smiley macro. Next, click on the Close button to close the Customize Keyboard window.

8. Now, from the Commands list in the Customize window, click and drag Project.NewMacros.Smiley to the Microsoft Word toolbar.

9. Click the Modify Selection button. Select Change Button Image and select the smiley face from the pop-up menu.

10. Again, click the Modify Selection button and select Default Style. The button on the toolbar now displays only the smiley face rather than the smiley face and macro name.

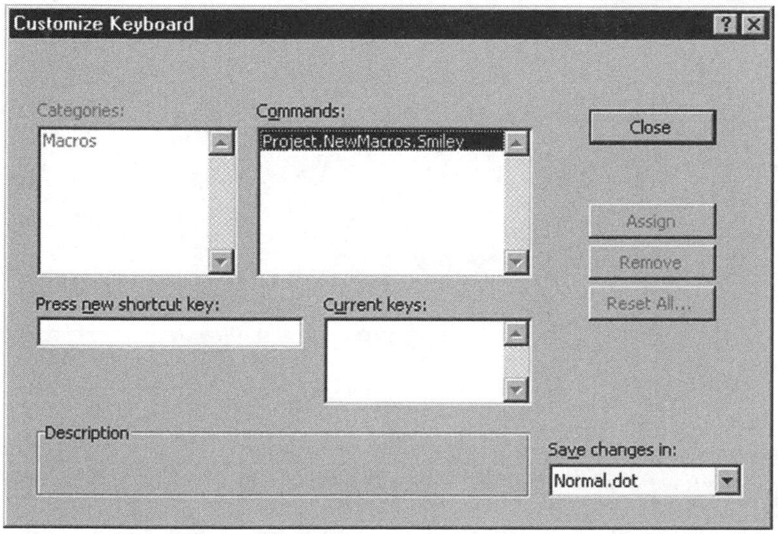

**Figure 11.19** Customize Keyboard window

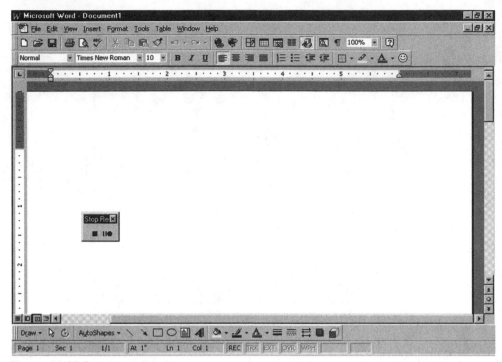

**Figure 11.20** Start recording the macro

11. Click the Close button in the Customize window. You are now ready to start recording the macro. The screen should look similar to Figure 11.20.

12. Type ":-)" and press the ENTER key. This draws a sideways smiley face in your document (a text-based smiley).

13. Click the Stop Recording button on the Stop Recording toolbar.

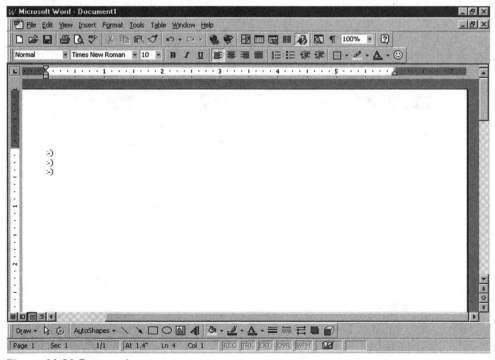

**Figure 11.21** Execute the macro

**14.** Run the macro by pressing ALT+S. Run the macro again by clicking the smiley face button on the toolbar. The screen should now look similar to Figure 11.21.

**15.** Exit Microsoft Word by clicking the close button in the upper right-hand corner or by selecting File/Exit from the menu.

# USING VISUAL BASIC CONTROL OBJECTS IN MICROSOFT OFFICE APPLICATIONS

Microsoft Office also allows you to use various VB controls in your VBA programs. We provide an example of using a command button in Microsoft Excel:

**1.** Open Microsoft Excel and select View/Toolbars/Visual Basic from the menu to open the Visual Basic toolbar. The screen appears in Figure 11.22.

**2.** Click the Control Toolbox icon on the Visual Basic toolbar. This opens the Visual Basic Control Toolbox as shown in Figure 11.23.

**3.** Select the command button control from the toolbox. Notice that the Design Mode icon (the icon on the far right) is activated on the Visual Basic toolbar and the Exit Design Mode toolbar opens. **Design mode** allows you to place Visual Basic control objects in the application and write the corresponding VBA code. The screen should now look similar to Figure 11.24.

**4.** Place a command button in your spreadsheet by clicking-and-dragging the mouse. The screen should now look like Figure 11.25.

**5.** Right-click on the command button and select Properties from the pop-up menu or click the Properties icon in the Control Toolbox. The Properties

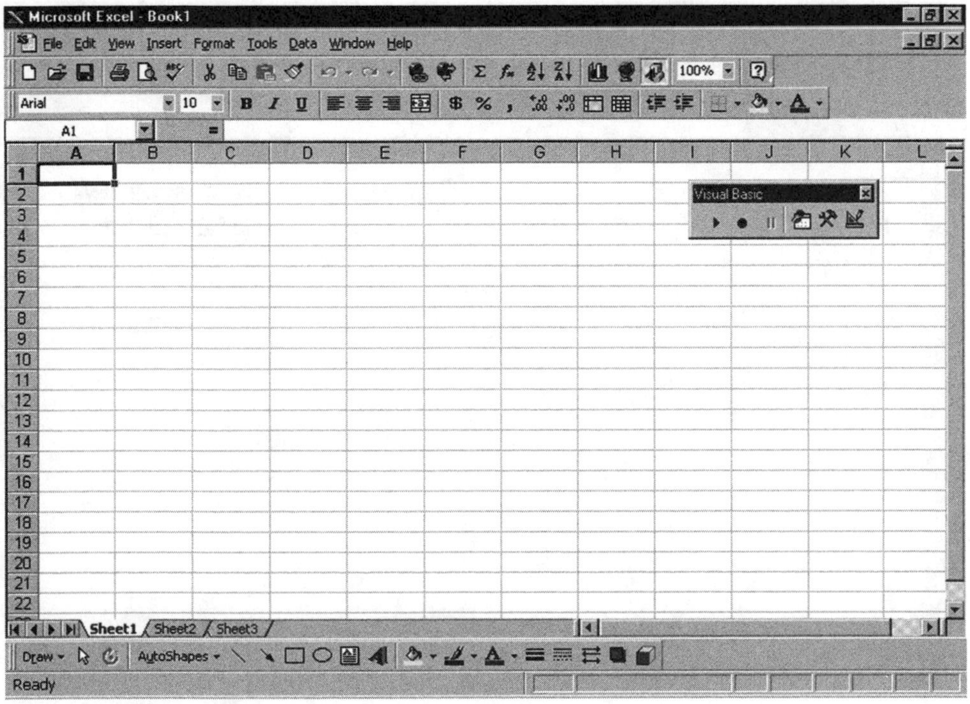

**Figure 11.22** Microsoft Excel with Visual Basic toolbar

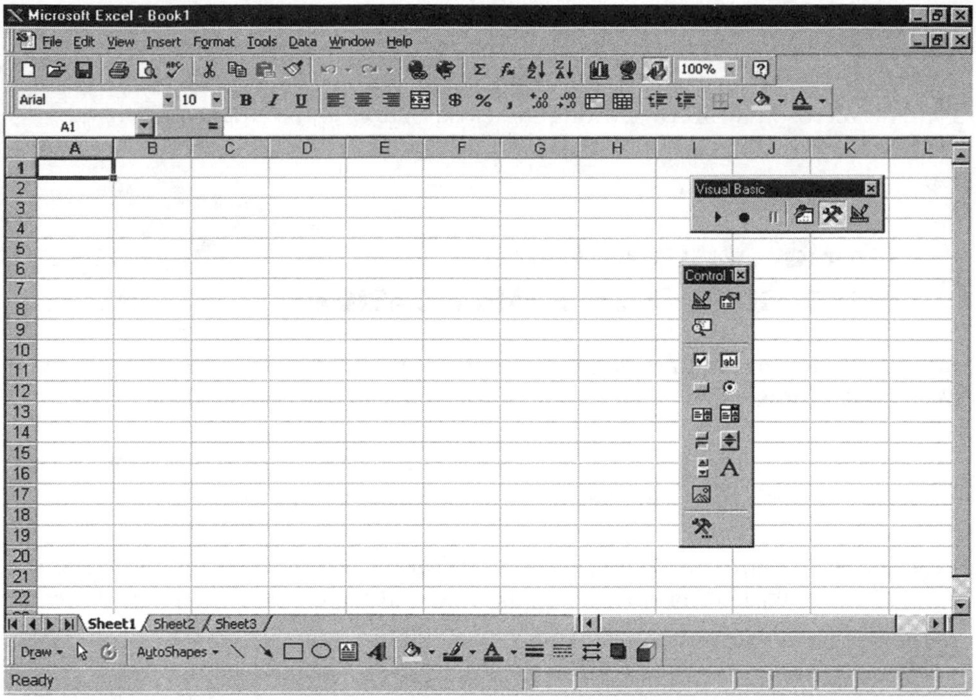

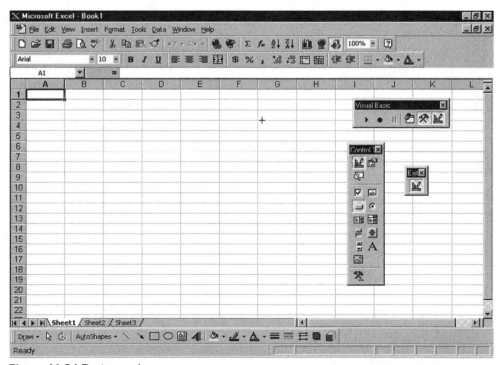

**Figure 11.23** Visual Basic toolbar and control toolbox

window now appears on the screen. Change the (Name) property to cmdActivate and the Caption property to Activate. The screen appears in Figure 11.26.

6. Double-click on the command button to open the Visual Basic editor. Type in the VBA code exactly as shown in Figure 11.27.

7. Close the Visual Basic editor window.

**Figure 11.24** Design mode

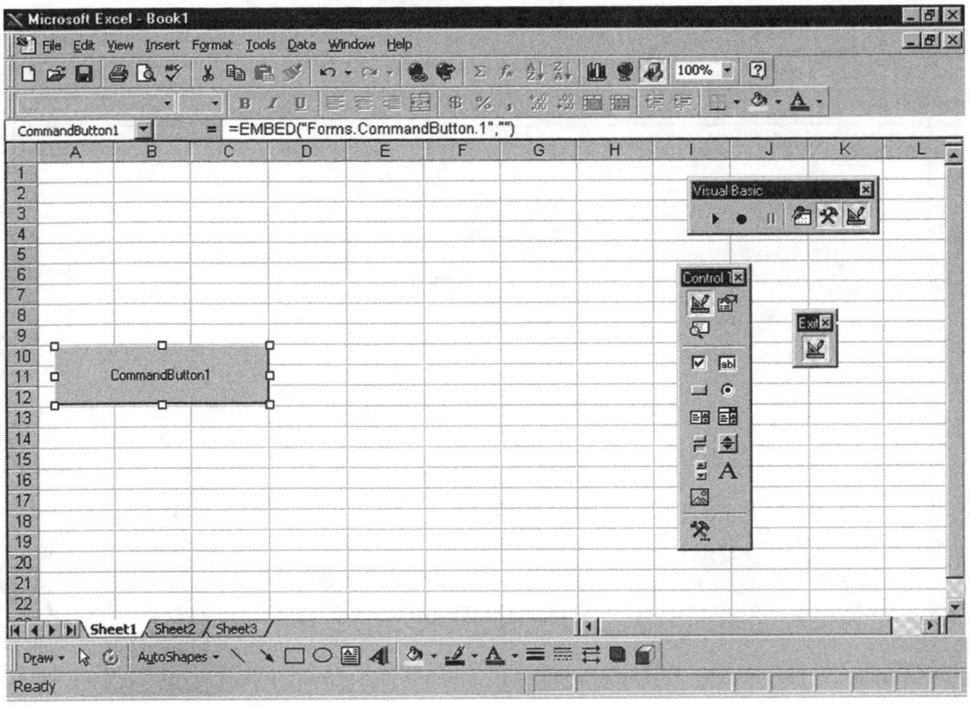

**Figure 11.25** Place a command button in the spreadsheet

8. Close the Control Toolbox and Properties window.

9. Click the Exit Design Mode button in the Exit Design Mode toolbar. Now that we are no longer in design mode, we can activate the command button or any other control objects.

10. Close the Visual Basic toolbar.

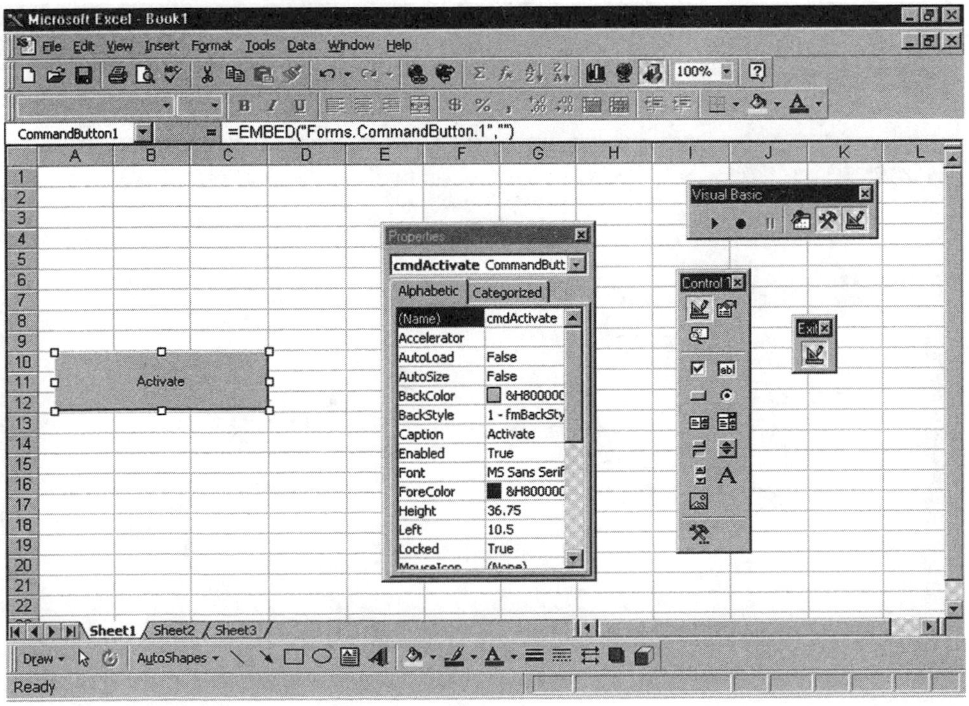

**Figure 11.26** Change command button properties

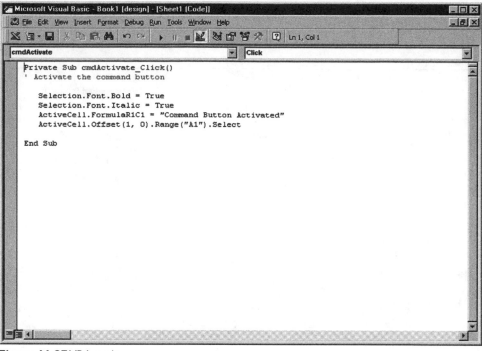

**Figure 11.27** VBA code

11. Select cell A1 in the spreadsheet by clicking in that cell.

12. Click the Activate command button. The screen should now appear as in Figure 11.28.

13. Exit Microsoft Excel by clicking the close button in the upper right-hand corner or by selecting File/Exit from the menu.

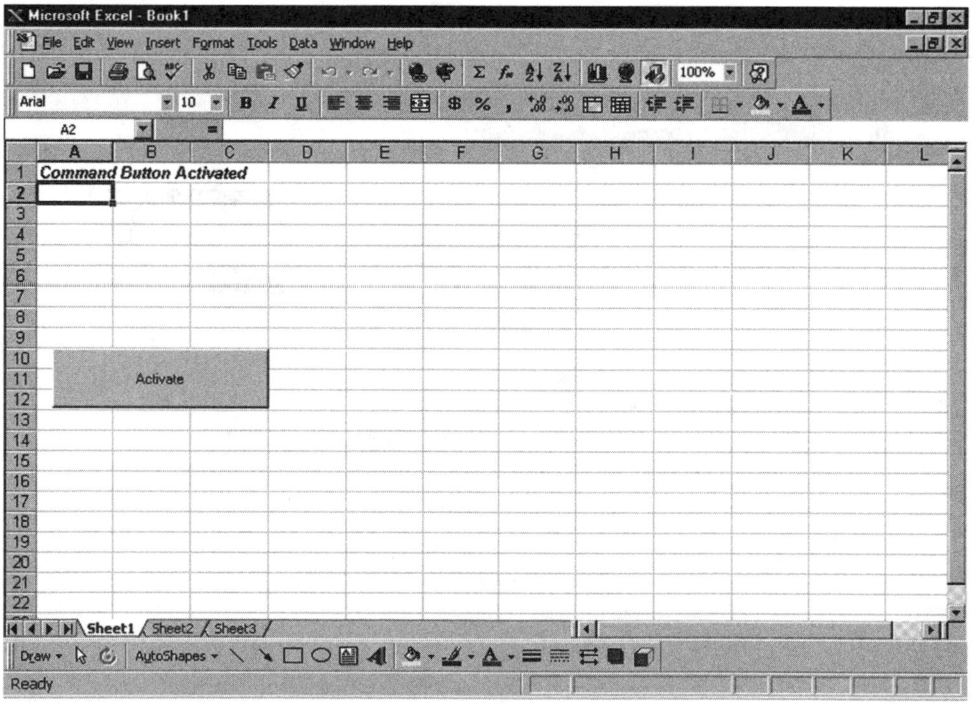

**Figure 11.28** Click the command button

# DIFFERENCES BETWEEN VISUAL BASIC AND VBA

As previously discussed, VBA is the macro language for Microsoft Office applications. VBA provides the same functionality as VB and offers application-specific objects. Therefore, everything that you learned in previous chapters of this text (constants, variables, decisions, loops, subprograms, OOP, and so forth) can (and should) be used in your VBA programs. In other words, since you already learned VB, you also know how to program in VBA. The challenge will be learning to use the methods and properties associated with application-specific objects. These details are described in the VBA help files, and many lengthy trade books are available on the topic of VBA programming. If you plan to do extensive VBA programming, we highly recommend that you purchase one of these texts as a handy reference.

We now close this topic with a simple example in Microsoft Excel. Repeat the instructions in the previous section and place a command button named cmdMyFunction in an Excel spreadsheet. Then, type the following code in the Visual Basic editor:

```
Private Sub cmdMyFunction_Click()

    Dim x As Double

    Range("A1").Select
    For x = -10 To 10 Step 0.5
        ActiveCell.FormulaR1C1 = x
        ActiveCell.Offset(0, 1).Range("A1").Select
        ActiveCell.FormulaR1C1 = MyFunction(x)
        ActiveCell.Offset(1, -1).Range("A1").Select
    Next x
```

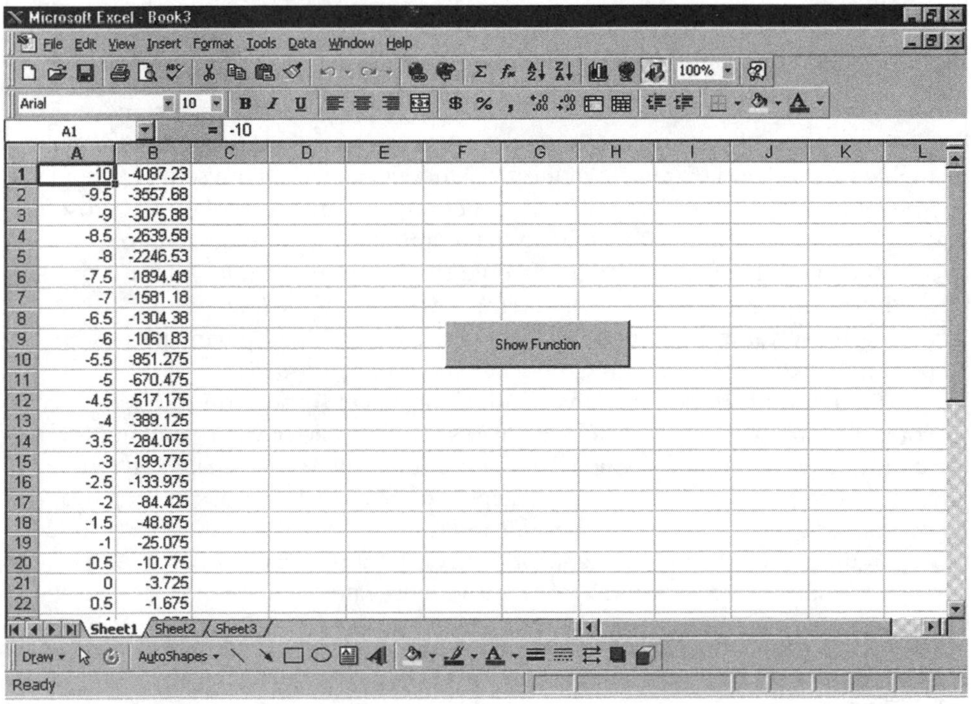

**Figure 11.29** Output of VBA code

```
        Range("A1").Select

    End Sub

    Private Function MyFunction(x As Double) As Double

        MyFunction = (3# * x ^ 3) - (10# * x ^ 2) + (8.35 * x)
        ➡ - 3.725

    End Function
```

Next, exit design mode and click the command button. The VBA code executes and the screen should appear as in Figure 11.29 shown on the previous page.

## PROGRAMMING KEY: TIPS

In both VB and VBA, you can access useful functions, procedures, and methods of other components by referencing them. Select Tools/References from the VBA editor menu or Project/References from the VB menu. Then, simply select the components that you want your program to reference and click the OK button.

Additionally, Microsoft Office applications, such as Microsoft Word and Microsoft Excel, have two toolbars that contain control objects. The Forms toolbar and the Visual Basic toolbar both provide access to controls, such as command buttons and text boxes, but the controls on the Forms toolbar are more limited in terms of properties and functionality.

## CASE STUDY
### A Loan Amortization Table

Brenda was just hired as a loan counselor by the Student Financial Aid Department of the Pacific Institute of Technology, one of the finest and most expensive academic institutions on the west coast of the United States. With highly talented and extremely inquisitive students attending the school, Brenda knows that she has to keep ahead of them. She wants to design a Microsoft Excel spreadsheet and VBA program that computes the monthly loan payment and produces the loan payment schedule (loan amortization table) for a specified loan amount, interest rate, and term (or length) of the loan. Equipped with such a powerful tool, Brenda can answer a student's loan payment questions before the student answers them for her (how embarrassing!).

Brenda finds three functions in Microsoft Excel to perform the necessary computations. The PMT function calculates the periodic payment amount for a loan based on constant payments and a constant interest rate. The PPMT function returns the payment on the principal balance of a loan based on periodic, constant payments and a constant interest rate. Similarly, the IPMT function returns the interest payment for a given period of a loan based on periodic, constant payments and a constant interest rate. Help Brenda design her spreadsheet and VBA program.

Brenda's spreadsheet is shown in Figure 11.30 and her VBA program appears as follows:

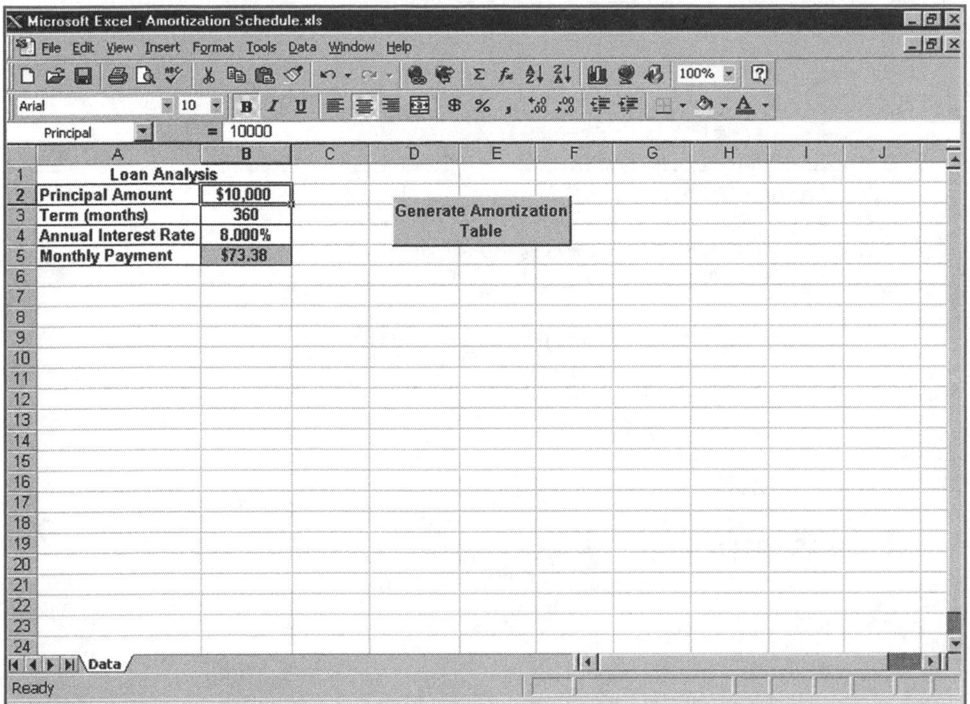

**Figure 11.30** Loan amortization spreadsheet

```vba
' Amortization Table Generation Macro
Option Explicit

Sub GenerateTable()
' Dimension variables
    Dim principal As Double, term As Integer, rate As
    ➡ Double
    Dim startTime As Double, payDate As String, i As
    ➡ Integer
    Dim tempPrincipal As Double, tempInterest As Double
    Dim tempArray() As Double, TableInfo As Range
    Dim SourceRange As Range, FillRange As Range

    principal = Range("principal")
    term = Range("term")
    rate = Range("APR") / 12

' Delete the worksheet named "Amortization Schedule", if
➡ it exists
    Application.DisplayAlerts = False
    If SheetExists("Amortization Schedule") Then
        Sheets("Amortization Schedule").Delete
    End If
    Application.DisplayAlerts = True

' Add a worksheet named "Amortization Schedule"
    Sheets.Add
    ActiveSheet.Name = "Amortization Schedule"

' Assign column headers to worksheet
    Range("A1").Select
```

```vba
        ActiveCell.FormulaR1C1 = "Month of Payment"
        Range("B1").Select
        ActiveCell.FormulaR1C1 = "Payment on Principal"
        Range("C1").Select
        ActiveCell.FormulaR1C1 = "Remaining Balance"
        Range("D1").Select
        ActiveCell.FormulaR1C1 = "Interest Paid"
        Range("E1").Select
        ActiveCell.FormulaR1C1 = "Cumulative Interest"

' Format columns and set the column widths
        Range("A1:E1").Select
        With Selection.Font
            .Name = "Arial"
            .FontStyle = "Bold"
            .Size = 10
            .ColorIndex = 11
        End With
        With Selection.Interior
            .ColorIndex = 15
            .Pattern = xlSolid
        End With
        Columns("A:E").Select
        With Selection
            .HorizontalAlignment = xlCenter
            .VerticalAlignment = xlBottom
        End With
        Columns("A:E").EntireColumn.AutoFit
        Columns("A:A").Select
        Selection.NumberFormat = "mmm-yy"

' Determine the date of first payment and assign it to
➡ cell A2
        payDate = Application.InputBox(prompt:="Enter month and
        ➡ year" & " of first payment (MMM-YYYY):", _
                Title:="Payment Start Date", Type:=1)
        Sheets("Amortization Schedule").Select
        Cells(2, 1) = payDate

' Record starting time
        startTime = Timer

' Fill in remaining payment months
        Set SourceRange = Worksheets("Amortization
        ➡ Schedule").Range("A2")
        Set FillRange = Worksheets("Amortization
        ➡ Schedule").Range(Cells(2, 1), _
                    Cells(term + 1, 1))
        SourceRange.AutoFill Destination:=FillRange

' Redimension tempArray
        ReDim tempArray(1 To term, 1 To 4)

' Calculate values and store results in tempArray
        tempPrincipal = principal
        tempInterest = 0#
```

```
      For i = 1 To term
          tempArray(i, 1) = Application.PPmt(rate, i, term,
          ➥ -principal, 0)
          tempPrincipal = tempPrincipal - tempArray(i, 1)
          tempArray(i, 2) = tempPrincipal
          tempArray(i, 3) = Application.IPmt(rate, i, term,
          ➥ -principal, 0)
          tempInterest = tempInterest + tempArray(i, 3)
          tempArray(i, 4) = tempInterest
      Next i

' Set table range
      Set TableInfo = ActiveSheet.Range(Cells(2, 2),
      ➥ Cells(term + 1, 5))

' Transfer tempArray to worksheet
      TableInfo.Value = tempArray

' Format the worksheet using two decimal currency format
➥ and insert borders
      Range(Cells(2, 2), Cells(2, 5).End(xlDown)).Select
      Selection.NumberFormat = "$#,##0.00"
      Range(Cells(1, 1), Cells(1, 5).End(xlDown)).Select
      With Selection.Borders(xlEdgeLeft)
          .LineStyle = xlContinuous
          .Weight = xlThin
      End With
      With Selection.Borders(xlEdgeTop)
          .LineStyle = xlContinuous
          .Weight = xlThin
      End With
      With Selection.Borders(xlEdgeBottom)
          .LineStyle = xlContinuous
          .Weight = xlThin
      End With
      With Selection.Borders(xlEdgeRight)
          .LineStyle = xlContinuous
          .Weight = xlThin
      End With
      With Selection.Borders(xlInsideVertical)
          .LineStyle = xlContinuous
          .Weight = xlThin
      End With
      With Selection.Borders(xlInsideHorizontal)
          .LineStyle = xlContinuous
          .Weight = xlThin
      End With
      With ActiveSheet.PageSetup
          .PrintTitleRows = "$1:$1"
          .PrintTitleColumns = ""
      End With

'Make top left corner of worksheet the active cell
Cells(1, 1).Select
```

➥

```
' Display table generation time
    Application.ScreenUpdating = True
    MsgBox Format(Timer - startTime, "##0.00") &
    ➥ " seconds", , "Generation Time"
End Sub

Function SheetExists(sName As String) As Boolean
' Cycle through all sheets in the active workbook,
' comparing each sheet's name to sName (as a text
➥ comparison)
    Dim aSheet As Object
    SheetExists = False 'Assume worksheet does not exist
    For Each aSheet In ActiveWorkbook.Sheets
        If (StrComp(aSheet.Name, sName, 1) = 0) Then
            SheetExists = True ' Worksheet names match,
            ➥ so return True
        End If
    Next aSheet
End Function
```

Brenda's VBA program creates the loan amortization table in a worksheet named "Amortization Schedule." A sample output of Brenda's program appears in Figure 11.31.

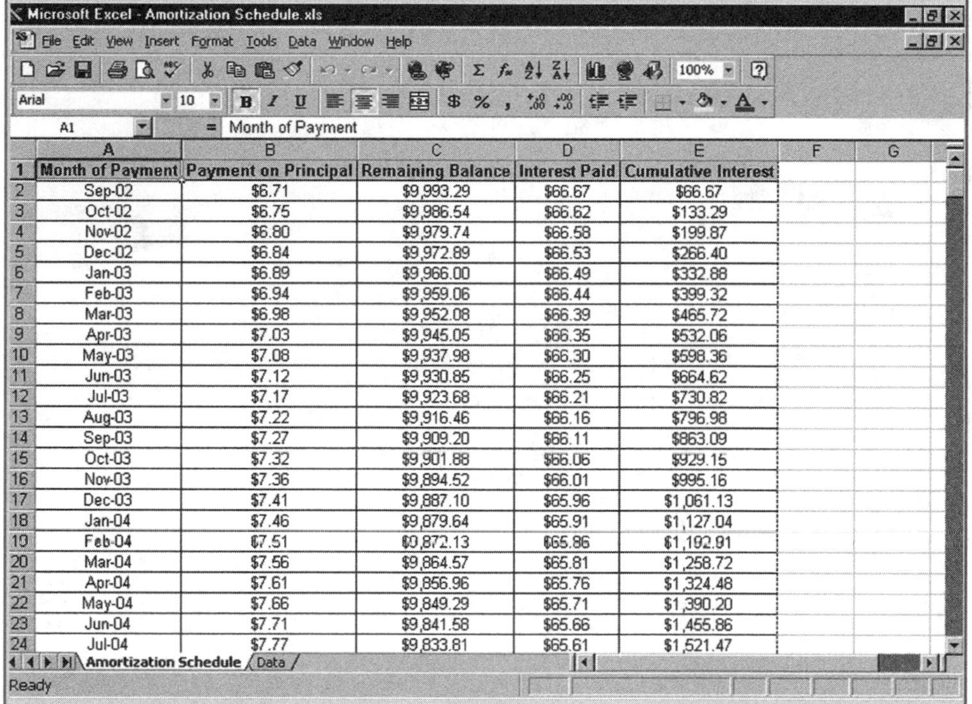


| | A | B | C | D | E |
|---|---|---|---|---|---|
| 1 | Month of Payment | Payment on Principal | Remaining Balance | Interest Paid | Cumulative Interest |
| 2 | Sep-02 | $6.71 | $9,993.29 | $66.67 | $66.67 |
| 3 | Oct-02 | $6.75 | $9,986.54 | $66.62 | $133.29 |
| 4 | Nov-02 | $6.80 | $9,979.74 | $66.58 | $199.87 |
| 5 | Dec-02 | $6.84 | $9,972.89 | $66.53 | $266.40 |
| 6 | Jan-03 | $6.89 | $9,966.00 | $66.49 | $332.88 |
| 7 | Feb-03 | $6.94 | $9,959.06 | $66.44 | $399.32 |
| 8 | Mar-03 | $6.98 | $9,952.08 | $66.39 | $465.72 |
| 9 | Apr-03 | $7.03 | $9,945.05 | $66.35 | $532.06 |
| 10 | May-03 | $7.08 | $9,937.98 | $66.30 | $598.36 |
| 11 | Jun-03 | $7.12 | $9,930.85 | $66.25 | $664.62 |
| 12 | Jul-03 | $7.17 | $9,923.68 | $66.21 | $730.82 |
| 13 | Aug-03 | $7.22 | $9,916.46 | $66.16 | $796.98 |
| 14 | Sep-03 | $7.27 | $9,909.20 | $66.11 | $863.09 |
| 15 | Oct-03 | $7.32 | $9,901.88 | $66.06 | $929.15 |
| 16 | Nov-03 | $7.36 | $9,894.52 | $66.01 | $995.16 |
| 17 | Dec-03 | $7.41 | $9,887.10 | $65.96 | $1,061.13 |
| 18 | Jan-04 | $7.46 | $9,879.64 | $65.91 | $1,127.04 |
| 19 | Feb-04 | $7.51 | $9,872.13 | $65.86 | $1,192.91 |
| 20 | Mar-04 | $7.56 | $9,864.57 | $65.81 | $1,258.72 |
| 21 | Apr-04 | $7.61 | $9,856.96 | $65.76 | $1,324.48 |
| 22 | May-04 | $7.66 | $9,849.29 | $65.71 | $1,390.20 |
| 23 | Jun-04 | $7.71 | $9,841.58 | $65.66 | $1,455.86 |
| 24 | Jul-04 | $7.77 | $9,833.81 | $65.61 | $1,521.47 |

**Figure 11.31** Amortization Schedule

# Summary

## Key Terms

**design mode**—the operating mode in Visual Basic for Applications that allows the user to add control objects and write code

**macro**—a set of actions or commands in an applications program

**shortcut**—a quick method of performing a task, specifically using key combinations or toolbar buttons

**Visual Basic for Applications (VBA)**—a specialized version of Visual Basic built into Microsoft Office applications

## Key Concepts

- Macros are used to simplify common or repetitive operations.

- Microsoft Office applications provide a cassette recorder-type interface for recording macros.

- Visual Basic for Applications (VBA) is a specialized version of VB that is the underlying macro language for all Microsoft Office applications. Thus, recording a macro actually generates VBA code.

- VBA contains application-specific objects. For instance, VBA for Microsoft Excel has objects referring to cells and sheets.

- An easy way to learn about VBA and application-specific objects is to record a macro and then view or modify the macro code.

- Shortcut key combinations and toolbar icons can be assigned as macro shortcuts. This allows the macro to be executed without having to select it through the application menu.

- VBA provides several control objects, such as text boxes and command buttons. These objects can be added to your VBA programs in design mode.

- VBA offers the same functionality as VB. All of the programming structures and techniques that you learned previously should be applied to your VBA programs.

## Review Questions

1. What is a macro? How do you create one? How do you execute one?
2. What is a shortcut? What types of shortcuts are available?
3. How do you assign a shortcut to a macro?
4. What is Visual Basic for Applications (VBA)? Are all versions of VBA the same?
5. How do you modify the code for a macro?
6. How and when (in what mode) can you add a control object to a VBA program?
7. Describe the differences between VB and VBA.

## Chapter 11 Problems

1. Write a macro in Microsoft Word that automatically types the following form letter:

Dear Sir or Madam:

   Please send me a catalog of your fine products. Thank you for your cooperation.

Sincerely,

<Your Name>

2. Repeat Problem 1 and assign the shortcut ALT+L to the macro.

3. Repeat Problem 2 and assign both the shortcut ALT+L and a toolbar icon to the macro.

4. Write a VBA program in Microsoft Word that contains a text box and a command button. The program transfers the text in the text box to the document when the command button is clicked.

5. Repeat Problem 4 in Microsoft Excel. The program transfers the contents of the text box to the next empty cell in column A when the command button is clicked.

## Programming Projects

1. A comma-separated data file contains student first names and quiz scores. Write a VBA program in Microsoft Excel that reads the data file and creates a spreadsheet with columns containing the student name, number of quizzes taken, and average quiz score. Your program should interactively request the name of the input file from the user. A sample input file follows:

```
Beth, 9, 8.5, 9, 7
Bill, 7, 5, 8, 8, 9
Chris, 9, 8
Dave, 6, 8, 7.5, 4, 8
Joan, 8.5, 7, 8
Paul, 9, 9, 8.5
```

2. Write a VBA program in Microsoft Word that counts the frequency of each word in a document. Your program should provide options to save this information in either a text file or another document.

# Databases

**12**

## Chapter Objectives

In this chapter, you will:

- Be introduced to database terminology and concepts

- Gain an understanding of how to efficiently design a database

- Learn how to create a database using the Visual Data Manager

- Learn how to access a database using data controls and data-aware controls

- Use the Structured Query Language (SQL) to perform data queries

- Learn how to create a database through Visual Basic code

- Learn about the three different database object types: data access objects (DAO), remote data objects (RDO), and ActiveX data objects (ADO)

hapter 11 described how to use macros and create VBA programs in Microsoft Word and Excel. This chapter centers around another Microsoft Office application, Microsoft Access, which is a relational database program. A **database program** is designed to provide easy storage, access, and retrieval of data. This chapter describes how to create database files and use these files in your VB programs. Additionally, we introduce the **Structured Query Language (SQL)** and show how VB can harness the power of this language.

## DATABASE FUNDAMENTALS

A **database file** (or **database**) consists of a set of related information. A school, for example, may use a database to record enrollment information, student transcripts, and financial data. Businesses commonly use databases to record product inventory, supplier information, customer data, transactions, and personnel data. There are several commercial database programs available, including Microsoft Access,

### Key Terms

**database**—consists of one or more data files that contains a set of related information specifically for use by a database program
**table**—the primary data structure in a database; a table organizes data into rows and columns, where the rows are records and the columns are fields
**record**—a row in a table that encapsulates a group of related data from several fields
**field**—a column in a table that contains a specific piece of information from each record

Microsoft FoxPro™, Corel Paradox™, Borland dBASE™, and FileMaker's FileMaker Pro™. The word "database" can be used to refer to either the database files or the database program itself, but we adopt the convention of using "database" to refer to a data file and "database program" to refer to the software package.

A database consists of one or more tables. A **table** is organized in rows and columns and looks very similar to a spreadsheet. The rows of the table coincide with database records, where a **record** is a group of related data. Each unique piece of information in a record is called a **field**. The table's columns contain information from the same field of each database record. These terms parallel those used in discussing user-defined data types and records in Chapter 8. Chapter 8 also shows example programs that implement "simple" database programs in VB using arrays, user-defined data types, and objects. Figure 12.1 is an example database table created in Microsoft Access. In this table, the three fields include `LastName`, `FirstName`, and `PhoneNumber`. A record consists of a row of data containing information from each database field. For example, the `LastName` field of the first record contains "Andrews," the `FirstName` field contains "Lisa," and the `PhoneNumber` field has "670-7898." These three pieces of data comprise the first record.

## RELATIONAL DATABASE DESIGN

### Key Terms

**primary key**—a field or set of fields that uniquely identify each record in a table
**foreign key**—a field or set of fields that references the primary key of another table and links the two tables together

A well-designed table should contain a field or set of fields that uniquely identify each record. This field or set of fields is called a **primary key**. When a database consists of more than one table, the tables are usually related and the database is called a **relational database**. In a relational database, a **foreign key** links data from one table to another. Maintaining the **integrity**, or consistency, of data in a database is of primary concern to programmers and database designers. In order to maintain the integrity of the database, it is apparent that the foreign key of one table must appear as the primary key of another table; this is the **rule of referential integrity**. Similarly, it makes sense that no record may have an empty primary key. This is called the **rule of entity integrity**. Figure 12.2 shows an example relational database. In this database, the `Orders` table uses the `Customer#` field as the foreign key that relates to the primary key of the `Customer#` field in the `Customers` table.

There is no single algorithm that can be used to create a relational database design that's suitable for every problem. Much like a well-designed program, a well-designed relational database is a work of art and relies solely upon the logic and creativity of its designer. However, there are certain guidelines that should be followed in order to design the best possible database for any particular problem:

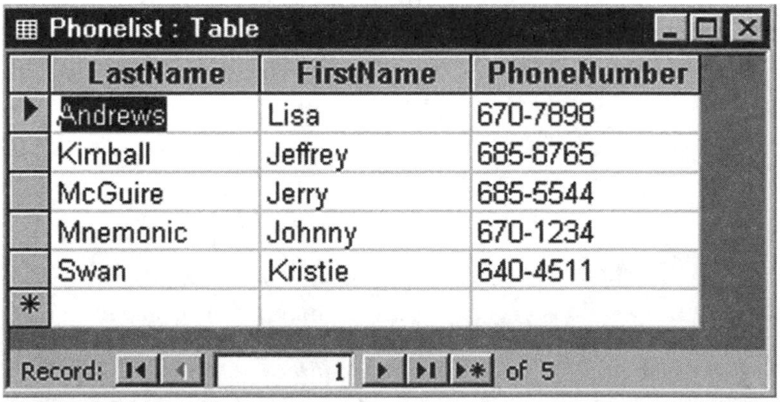

Phonelist : Table

| LastName | FirstName | PhoneNumber |
|---|---|---|
| Andrews | Lisa | 670-7898 |
| Kimball | Jeffrey | 685-8765 |
| McGuire | Jerry | 685-5544 |
| Mnemonic | Johnny | 670-1234 |
| Swan | Kristie | 640-4511 |
| * | | |

Record: 1 of 5

**Figure 12.1** A database table

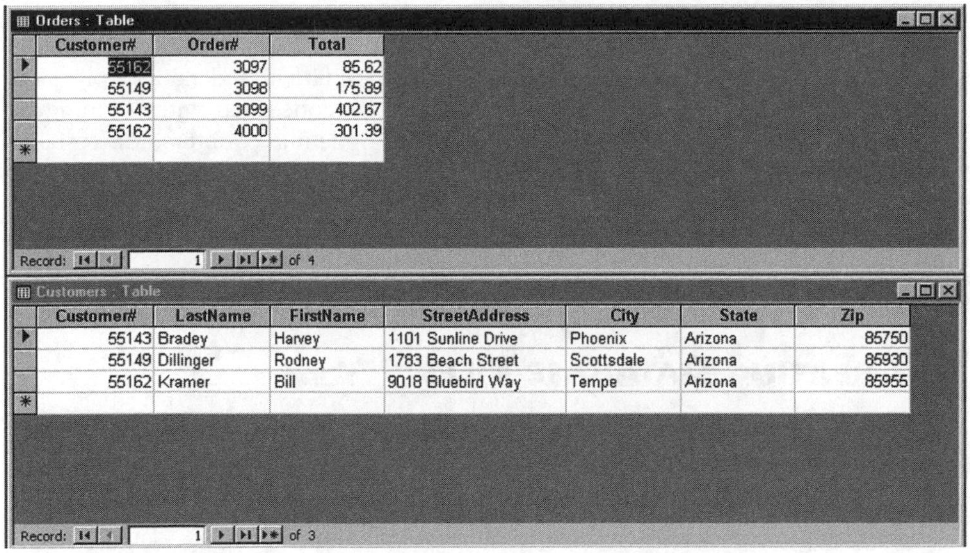

| Orders : Table | | | |
|---|---|---|---|
| | Customer# | Order# | Total |
| ▶ | 55162 | 3097 | 85.62 |
| | 55149 | 3098 | 175.89 |
| | 55143 | 3099 | 402.67 |
| | 55162 | 4000 | 301.39 |
| * | | | |

Record: ◄◄ ◄ [ 1 ] ► ►► ►* of 4

| Customers : Table | | | | | | | |
|---|---|---|---|---|---|---|---|
| | Customer# | LastName | FirstName | StreetAddress | City | State | Zip |
| ▶ | 55143 | Bradey | Harvey | 1101 Sunline Drive | Phoenix | Arizona | 85750 |
| | 55149 | Dillinger | Rodney | 1783 Beach Street | Scottsdale | Arizona | 85930 |
| | 55162 | Kramer | Bill | 9018 Bluebird Way | Tempe | Arizona | 85955 |
| * | | | | | | | |

Record: ◄◄ ◄ [ 1 ] ► ►► ►* of 3

**Figure 12.2** A relational database

1. **Understand the problem and the customer's needs.** What reports does the customer want generated? What data is available? What are the relationships between the different pieces of data? Does it make sense to logically split the data into more than one table? After answering these questions, designing the database is relatively straightforward.

2. **Data should generally be stored in the smallest units possible.** In a customer database, you may be tempted to place the city, state, and zip code all in one field rather than three separate fields. It is relatively difficult to sort the data when all this information is combined into a single field, but it is a trivial problem when separate fields are used.

3. **Avoid redundant, blank, and calculated fields.** Redundant and blank fields waste valuable file space and increase the amount of time required to perform operations on the data. Design your database with enough tables and proper primary and foreign keys to avoid these types of fields. Additionally, calculated fields should be avoided since the values in these fields can be obtained through operations on data in other fields of the database.

4. **Avoid using spaces in field names.** Although Microsoft Access allows spaces in field names, their use should be avoided. Both VB and VBA have difficulty performing queries on databases whose field names contain spaces. If you desire to separate words in a field name, use the underscore character ("_") rather than a space.

5. **Avoid large tables.** Data tables should be "cleaned up" so as not to become unnecessarily large. In other words, records marked for deletion should be deleted. Additionally, tables should be designed with a size limit in mind since large tables require longer search times.

## DATABASE ENGINE

A **database engine** is a set of routines that perform the operations normally associated with a database, such as adding, deleting, sorting, and searching records. VB comes equipped with the Microsoft Access database engine. Consequently, a programmer using VB has the ability to manipulate Microsoft Access database files (as well as database files in several other formats). VB's ability to perform database operations makes it an extremely powerful tool. Unlike the database program examples in Chapter 8, the programmer need not be concerned with opening or closing files, using loops to search for records, updating counters, or resizing dynamic arrays (just to name a few items). All of the file handling and data functions are handled automatically by the built-in database engine. For these reasons, VB is very frequently used by professional programmers to develop database and data-aware applications.

## CREATING DATABASE FILES

Database files are easily created in VB by using the Microsoft Access database engine. There are two methods for creating a database file in VB: using the VB Visual Data Manager or using VB code. It should be noted that VB can also be used to access database files previously created using a database program. Since your database software documentation describes how to create a database file, our discussion focuses on the two VB methods. We begin by introducing the Visual Data Manager and defer discussion of databases created using VB code until the end of the chapter.

## VB VISUAL DATA MANAGER

Even if you do not own database software, the VB Visual Data Manager can be used to create database files in a variety of formats. However, it is available only in the professional and enterprise editions of VB and not in the student edition (Working Model) included with this text. A step-by-step example of creating a database file using the VB Visual Data Manager is provided on the following pages.

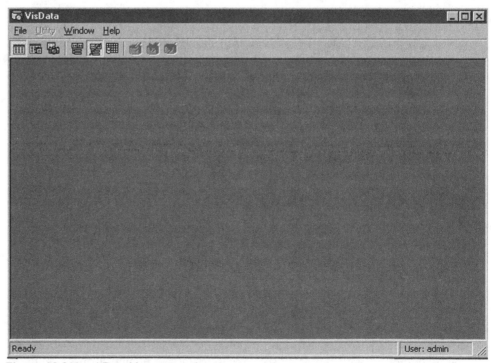

**Figure 12.3** Visual Data Manager window

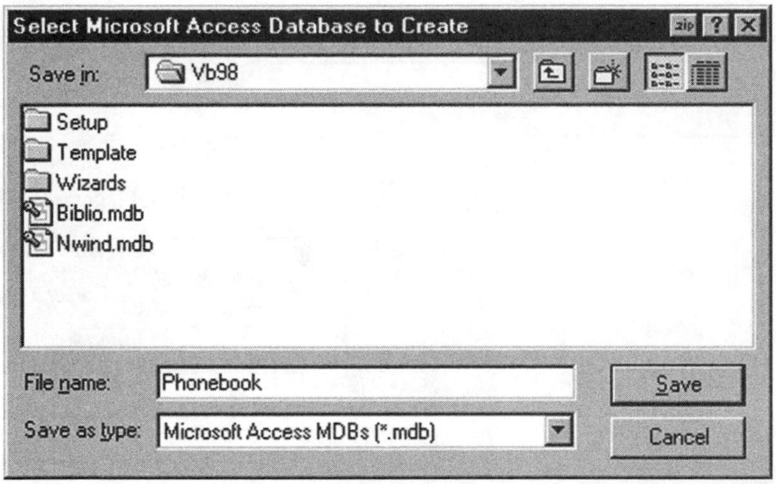

**Figure 12.4** Create a new database

1. In VB, select Add-Ins/Visual Data Manager to start the VB Visual Data Manager. The Visual Data Manager window shown in Figure 12.3 opens on your screen.

2. Select File/New/Microsoft Access/Version 7.0 MDB to create a new Microsoft Access-compatible database file. The Select Microsoft Access Database to Create window shown in Figure 12.4 appears on the screen.

3. Select a location for saving your database file and name the file Phonebook. Click the Save button. The Visual Data Manager window now appears as in Figure 12.5.

4. Right-click on Properties in the Database window and select New Table. The Table Structure window in Figure 12.6 opens on the screen.

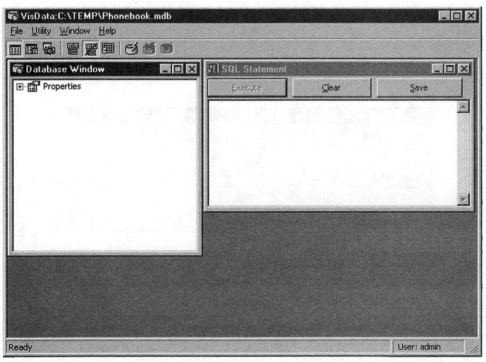

**Figure 12.5** Create the Phonebook database

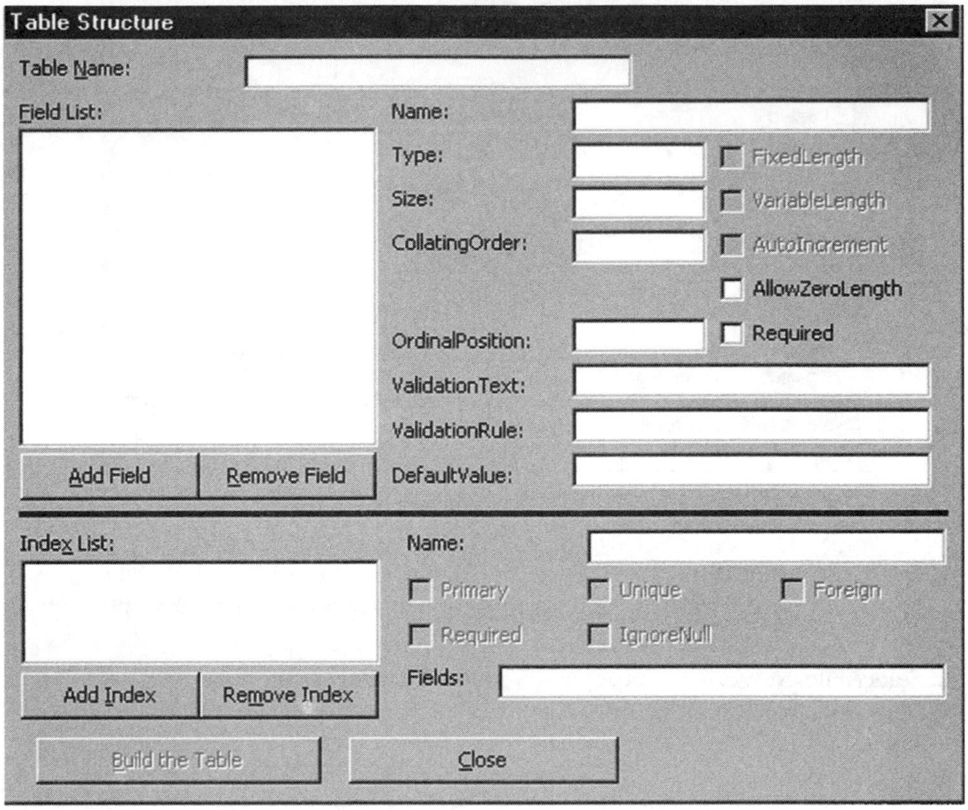

**Table Structure**

Table Name:

Field List:

Name:

Type: ☐ FixedLength

Size: ☐ VariableLength

CollatingOrder: ☐ AutoIncrement

☐ AllowZeroLength

OrdinalPosition: ☐ Required

ValidationText:

ValidationRule:

[Add Field] [Remove Field] DefaultValue:

Index List:

Name:

☐ Primary ☐ Unique ☐ Foreign

☐ Required ☐ IgnoreNull

Fields:

[Add Index] [Remove Index]

[Build the Table] [Close]

**Figure 12.6** Table Structure window

5. Enter `Phonelist` in the Table Name text box.

6. Click the Add Field button to add a new field to the table. The Add Field window in Figure 12.7 appears on the screen.

7. Name the field `LastName` and change the field size to 25 characters. Click the OK button.

8. Add two more fields by using the same method described in steps 6 and 7. Add a `FirstName` field of size 25 characters and a `PhoneNumber` field of size 15 characters. Then, click the Close button in the Add Field window.

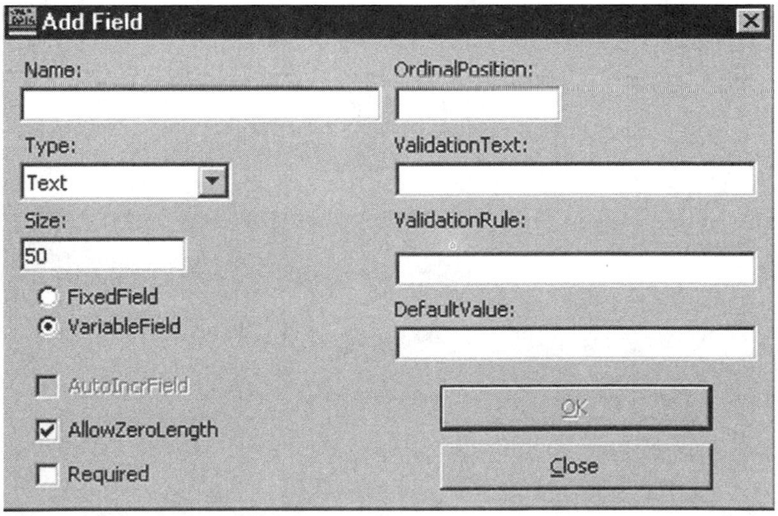

**Add Field**

Name: OrdinalPosition:

Type: ValidationText:

Text

Size: ValidationRule:

50

○ FixedField

◉ VariableField DefaultValue:

☐ AutoIncrField [OK]

☑ AllowZeroLength

☐ Required [Close]

**Figure 12.7** Add Field window

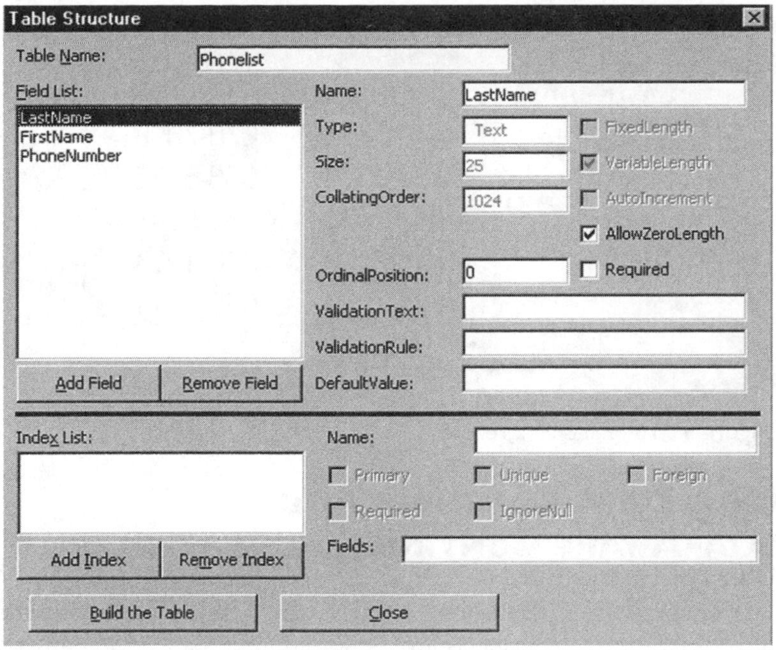

**Figure 12.8** Completed Table Structure window

9. Your Table Structure window now appears as in Figure 12.8.

10. Click the Build the Table button. The `Phonelist` table now appears in the Database window.

11. Double-click on Phonelist to open the table as shown in Figure 12.9.

12. Type in the last name, first name, and phone number from the first row of data shown in Figure 12.10 and click the Update button. A message box will appear asking if you want to "Save the new record?". Click the Yes button. Additional records can now be added by clicking on the Add button.

13. Repeat step 12 for the remaining rows of data shown in Figure 12.10.

14. Click the Close button.

15. Your data is now entered in the Phonelist table in the Phonebook database.

16. Close the Visual Data Manager by selecting File/Exit or clicking the X button in the upper right-hand corner of the window.

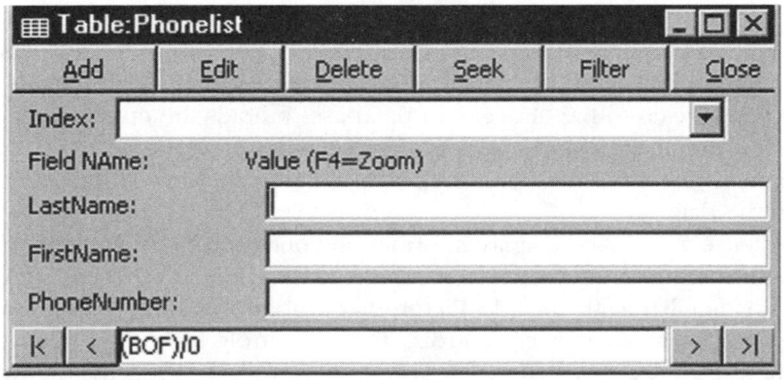

**Figure 12.9** Add a record

Phonelist : Table

| LastName | FirstName | PhoneNumber |
|---|---|---|
| Andrews | Lisa | 670-7898 |
| Kimball | Jeffrey | 685-8765 |
| McGuire | Jerry | 685-5544 |
| Mnemonic | Johnny | 670-1234 |
| Swan | Kristie | 640-4511 |

Record: 1 of 5

**Figure 12.10** `Phonebook` records

## USING DATA CONTROLS AND DATA-AWARE CONTROLS

Adding a Data control to a form allows VB to access a database file and move from record to record. Adding the Data control is no different than adding any other control: simply double-click the Data control icon that appears in the VB toolbox. Once the control has been added to the form, it must be *connected* to a database. This is accomplished by modifying the `DatabaseName` property to indicate the path and file name of the desired database file. If you haven't done so already, add a Data control to your form, changing its `(Name)` property to `datPhonebook` and its `DatabaseName` property to coincide with the previously created phonebook database (e.g., `C:\VBExamples\Phonebook.mdb`). The `Connect` property should also be changed to specify the type of database file being used. The last step in connecting the Data control to a database is to specify the database table from which records will be accessed by the Data control. This is done by changing the `RecordSource` property to specify the name of the table. The `RecordSource` property may contain either the name of a database or an SQL statement that creates a **recordset**. A recordset is similar to a table, but it can also consist of records from multiple tables or portions of multiple tables (i.e., selected rows or columns) that are known as **views**. Thus, when using the SQL statement, the actual data or records in the recordset are first selected at run-time and then assigned to the Data control using the `RecordSource` property. In other words, the `Recordset` property is automatically initialized by the `RecordSource`. The `ReadOnly` property of the Data control indicates whether or not the user can change the record data. Finally, the `BOFAction` and `EOFAction` properties specify the actions to be taken when the first record and last record in the database file are reached, respectively.

If the database was properly connected to the Data control, clicking on the `RecordSource` property will reveal a drop-down menu listing the available tables. For our example database, the only available table is `Phonelist`. Once the Data control is connected to the `Phonebook` database, it holds the **current record** (i.e., the record currently being accessed by the Data control) from the `Phonelist` table at run time. The Data control can thus be used to move through the records contained in the database.

In order to access and display information contained in the database file, **data-aware controls** must be *bound* to the Data control. Data-aware controls that you are already familiar with include PictureBox, Label, TextBox, CheckBox, Image, OLE, ListBox, and ComboBox controls. These controls have the ability to access information from databases. More advanced data-aware controls that allow simultaneous display and manipulation of multiple records include DBList, DBCombo,

DBGrid, and MSFlexGrid controls. To bind a data-aware control to a Data control, set the `DataSource` property of the data-aware control to the name of the Data control. Continuing with our `Phonebook` database example, add a text box to your form, specifying `datPhonebook` in the `DataSource` property. Next, you must specify the name of a field accessed by the Data control for the `DataField` property. For purposes of our `Phonebook` example, choose LastName from the list of available options that appears when you click on the `DataField` property of the text box. We have now bound the TextBox control to the `Phonebook` database. At run time, clicking the arrows on the Data control moves the user forward or backward through the various records in the `Phonelist` table and the TextBox displays the information contained in the `LastName` field associated with the current record.

Now that we've learned how to move through a database using a Data control, how can we edit existing records or add new records? These and other routine database tasks can be performed using the Data control's `Recordset` property. Using a statement of the following general syntax, this property provides several methods for accessing and manipulating data:

```
DataControl.Recordset.Method
```

In this syntax, *DataControl* is the name of the Data control and *Method* is the method to be executed. The `MoveNext` method, for instance, makes the next record in the table (the one following the current record) the current record. Conversely, the `MovePrevious` method makes the previous record in the table the current record. Finally, the `MoveLast` method makes the last record in the table the current record, and the `MoveFirst` method makes the first record in the table the current record. For example, consider the VB statement `datPhonebook.Recordset.MoveFirst`, which designates the first record of the table accessed by Data control `datPhonebook` as the current record. This is similar to moving the file pointer to the first record in a random-access file.

To access the fields of the current record, use the following general syntax:

```
DataControl.Recordset.Fields("FieldName").Value
```

For example, the following VB statements store the data contained in the `LastName` field of the current record in a string variable named `lastName`:

```
Dim lastName As String
lastName = datPhonebook.Recordset.Fields("LastName").Value
```

The `AddNew` method creates a blank record in the `Recordset` and makes this record the current record. The fields of this blank record (the current record) may then be assigned values using the following general form:

```
DataControl.Recordset.Fields("FieldName").Value = fieldValue
```

*DataControl* is the name of the Data control and *fieldValue* is the value to assign to the field *FieldName*. Once the field values are set, the `Update` method should be executed to clear the file buffer and ensure that all changes are incorporated in the database file.

The `Edit` method makes a copy of the current record for editing. Field values of this copy are altered using the same general form as shown above. Again, once the field values are set, the `Update` method should be executed to replace the old record in the database file with the new version.

The Delete method marks a record for removal or deletion from the database file. The record is physically deleted when a data navigation control arrow is clicked or a Move method is executed.

The RecordCount property indicates the total number of previously accessed records in the table or the total number of records in a table-type recordset. The BOF (Beginning of File) and EOF (End of File) properties indicate whether the beginning or end of the database file has been reached, respectively.

**Validation** is the process of preventing invalid data from being entered into the database. In VB, the Validate event provides a means of data validation. This event occurs before a different record becomes the current record and before the Update method is executed. The general syntax of the Validate event handler is as follows:

```
Private Sub DataControl_Validate(Action As Integer,
➡ Save As Integer)
   statement(s)
End Sub
```

The value of Action identifies the operation that causes the Validate event to occur, as described in Figure 12.11. If Action is set to 0 within the Validate event handler, then the operation is cancelled and no action takes place. The value of Save indicates whether data bound to the control has changed: Save is –1 (True) if any data has changed, and its value is 0 (False) otherwise. If Save is set to 0 within the Validate event handler, then any changes made to the database are not saved. The following example illustrates these points:

```
Private Sub datPhonebook_Validate(Action As Integer, Save
➡ As Integer)
   Select Case Action
      Case 5, 6, 7        ' Prevent Add, Update, and Delete
      ➡ operations
         Action = 0
   End Select

   Save = 0             ' Prevent the user from changing
   ➡ data
End Sub
```

This code prevents any changes ➡ to the Phonebook database.

| Action Value | Constant | Description |
|---|---|---|
| 0 | vbDataActionCancel | Cancel operation |
| 1 | vbDataActionMoveFirst | MoveFirst method |
| 2 | vbDataActionMovePrevious | MovePrevious method |
| 3 | vbDataActionMoveNext | MoveNext method |
| 4 | vbDataActionMoveLast | MoveLast method |
| 5 | vbDataActionAddNew | AddNew method |
| 6 | vbDataActionUpdate | Update operation (not UpdateRecord) |
| 7 | vbDataActionDelete | Delete method |
| 8 | vbDataActionFind | Find method |
| 9 | vbDataActionBookmark | Bookmark property set |
| 10 | vbDataActionClose | Close method |
| 11 | vbDataActionUnload | Unload form |

**Figure 12.11** Action parameter values

We now show a full example program in VB that uses our Phonebook database.
Figure 12.12 displays a sample form for the code below:

| Object | Property | Setting |
|--------|----------|---------|
| Form | Name | frmPhonebook |
| | Caption | Phonebook |
| CommandButton | Name | cmdAdd |
| | Caption | Add |
| CommandButton | Name | cmdDelete |
| | Caption | Delete |
| CommandButton | Name | cmdFind |
| | Caption | Find |
| CommandButton | Name | cmdQuit |
| | Caption | Quit |
| Label | Name | lblFirst |
| | AutoSize | True |
| | Caption | First Name |
| Label | Name | lblLast |
| | AutoSize | True |
| | Caption | Last Name |
| Label | Name | lblPhone |
| | AutoSize | True |
| | Caption | Phone Number |
| TextBox | Name | txtFirst |
| | DataField | FirstName |
| | DataSource | datPhonebook |
| | Text | (*Empty*) |
| TextBox | Name | txtLast |
| | DataField | LastName |
| | DataSource | datPhonebook |
| | Text | (*Empty*) |
| TextBox | Name | txtPhone |
| | DataField | PhoneNumber |
| | DataSource | datPhonebook |
| | Text | (*Empty*) |
| Data | Name | datPhonebook |
| | Caption | Phonebook |
| | Connect | Access |
| | DatabaseName | C:\VBExamples\Phonebook.mdb |
| | RecordSource | Phonelist |

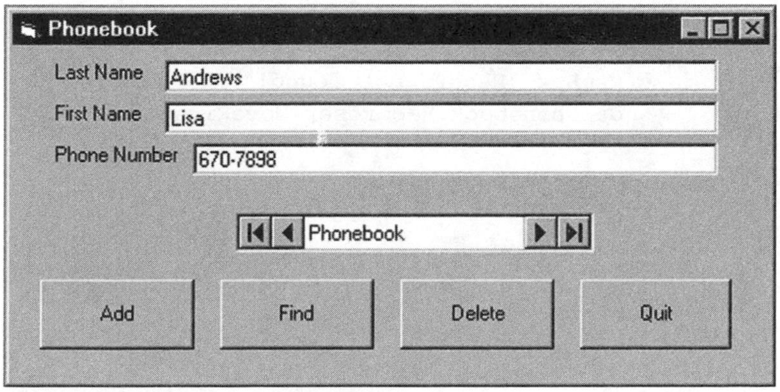

**Figure 12.12** Phonebook program

```vb
' Phonebook Program
Option Explicit

Private Sub cmdAdd_Click()
' Add a new record
    datPhonebook.Recordset.AddNew
    txtLast.SetFocus
End Sub

Private Sub cmdDelete_Click()
' Delete the current record
    If (datPhonebook.Recordset.BOF And
datPhonebook.Recordset.EOF) Then
        MsgBox "No records in the phonebook.
        ➥ ", , "Can't Delete"
    Else
        datPhonebook.Recordset.Delete
        datPhonebook.Recordset.MoveNext
        If datPhonebook.Recordset.EOF Then
            datPhonebook.Recordset.MovePrevious
        End If
    End If
End Sub

Private Sub cmdFind_Click()
' Find a record
    Dim last As String, temp As String, found As Boolean

    last = InputBox("Enter the Last Name", "Find...")
    found = False
    If Len(last) > 0 Then
        datPhonebook.Recordset.MoveFirst
        Do While Not (datPhonebook.Recordset.EOF Or found)
            temp = datPhonebook.Recordset.Fields
            ➥ ("LastName").Value
            If Trim(temp) = Trim(last) Then
                found = True
            Else
                datPhonebook.Recordset.MoveNext
            End If
        Loop

        If Not (found) Then
            MsgBox "Record not found!", , "Find..."
            datPhonebook.Recordset.MoveFirst
        End If

    End If
End Sub

Private Sub cmdQuit_Click()
' Exit the program
    End
End Sub
```

If you prefer that the user sees more than one record at a time, you can use the Data Bound Grid control (DBGrid). This control is not in the Toolbox by default, but it can be added by right-clicking in an empty area of the Toolbox and selecting Components from the pop-up menu. The procedure for adding VB controls to the Toolbox is outlined in Chapter 10 (see the Common Dialog Control section).

We now show a simple example program that uses the DBGrid control. Figure 12.13 shows a sample form for this program.

| Object | Property | Setting |
|---|---|---|
| Form | Name | frmPhonebook |
| | Caption | Phonebook |
| CommandButton | Name | cmdAdd |
| | Caption | Add |
| CommandButton | Name | cmdDelete |
| | Caption | Delete |
| CommandButton | Name | cmdQuit |
| | Caption | Quit |
| Data | Name | datPhonebook |
| | Caption | Phonebook |
| | Connect | Access |
| | DatabaseName | C:\VBExamples\ Phonebook.mdb |
| | RecordSource | Phonelist |
| DBGrid | Name | dbgrdPhonebook |
| | AllowAddNew | True |
| | AllowDelete | True |
| | Caption | Phone Book |
| | DataSource | datPhonebook |

```
' Phonebook Program using the DBGrid control
Option Explicit

Private Sub cmdAdd_Click()
' Add a new record
    datPhonebook.Recordset.AddNew
End Sub

Private Sub cmdDelete_Click()
' Delete the current record
    If (datPhonebook.Recordset.BOF And
    ➥ datPhonebook.Recordset.EOF) Then
```

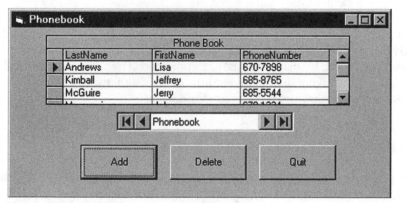

**Figure 12.13** Modified Phonebook program

```
            MsgBox "No records in the phonebook.", ,
        ➥ "Can't Delete"
    Else
        datPhonebook.Recordset.Delete
        datPhonebook.Recordset.MoveNext
        If datPhonebook.Recordset.EOF Then
            datPhonebook.Recordset.MovePrevious
        End If
    End If
End Sub


Private Sub cmdQuit_Click()
' Exit the program
    End
End Sub
```

## STRUCTURED QUERY LANGUAGE (SQL)

The phonebook example in the previous section uses a loop to perform the find operation. There is actually an easier way to search for specific records in a database. The method involves using the **Structured Query Language (SQL)**.

### SQL OVERVIEW

SQL was developed by International Business Machines (IBM) Corporation in the early 1970s as a relational database language. The language allows a user to request specific information from the database or reorganize information in the database. SQL was standardized by ANSI in 1986, and VB uses a version of SQL that complies with the ANSI-89 SQL standards.

SQL provides both **Data Definition Language (DDL)** and **Data Manipulation Language (DML)** commands. There is some overlap of function in each language's commands, but, in general, DDL commands are used to create new databases, tables, fields, and indexes, while DML commands are used to create queries that sort, filter, and extract data from the database.

DDL statements in SQL center around three different commands: CREATE, DROP, and ALTER. The CREATE command is used to create new tables, fields, and indexes, whereas the DROP command is used to delete tables and indexes from the database. Finally, the ALTER command is used to modify tables by adding fields or changing field definitions.

DML statements are built around four different commands: SELECT, INSERT, UPDATE, and DELETE. The SELECT statement is used to query the database for records that meet specific criteria. Batches of data may be loaded into the database in a single operation by using the INSERT command. The UPDATE command records modifications that were made to records or fields in the database. Finally, the DELETE command removes records from a database.

### USING THE SELECT COMMAND IN SQL

SQL is a language in itself that requires a complete textbook to describe in detail. We focus our attention on a single SQL command (SELECT) and describe how to create SQL expressions using this command in VB.

The general form of the SQL SELECT statement is as follows:

```
SELECT fieldList1 FROM tableExp [WHERE criteria]
➤ [ORDER BY fieldList2 {ASC | DESC}]
```

Statements inside the square brackets [ ] are optional and statements separated by a bar | inside braces { } indicate that one of the statements must be selected. For example, if the optional ORDER BY statement is used in the SELECT statement, either the ASC statement or the DESC statement, but not both, must be used. *fieldList1* is a field or set of fields to be selected from *tableExp*, where *tableExp* is any expression that evaluates to a table. The asterisk (*) is a **wildcard character** that indicates all fields. Replacing *fieldList1* with an asterisk indicates that all fields in *tableExp* should be selected. *criteria* is any logical expression and generally involves the fields of the table. The standard VB logical and comparison operators can be used in *criteria*. Additional comparison operators include BETWEEN, which is used to specify a range of values, LIKE, which is used for pattern matching, and IN, which is used to specify records in a database. *fieldList2* specifies the field or set of fields by which the resulting records are ordered.

In the SELECT syntax, *tableExp* is any expression that evaluates to a table. Thus, *tableExp* can be a combination of tables created by joining tables together. The INNER JOIN operation combines records from both tables only when the specified field from the first table matches the specified field from the second table. LEFT JOIN (or left outer join) combines all records from the first (left) table with records from the second table whose specified fields match certain conditions. Conversely, RIGHT JOIN (right outer join) combines all records from the second (right) table with records from the first table whose specified fields match certain conditions. The general syntax for the JOIN statement follows:

```
table1 joinType JOIN table2 ON table1Field = table2Field
```

In this syntax, *table1* and *table2* are the two tables to be joined, *table1Field* is a field from *table1*, *table2Field* is a field from *table2* (specifying the primary and foreign keys), and *joinType* specifies the type of join: INNER, LEFT, or RIGHT.

We now present a simple example program that uses an SQL statement. Figure 12.14 displays the form corresponding to the code listed below:

| Object | Property | Setting |
|---|---|---|
| Form | Name | frmSQLExample |
| | Caption | SQL Example |
| Data | Name | datPhonebook |
| | Caption | Phonebook |
| | Connect | Access |
| | DatabaseName | C:\VBExamples\Phonebook.mdb |
| DBGrid | Name | dbgrdPhonebook |
| | DataSource | datPhonebook |

```
' SQL Example
Option Explicit

Private Sub Form_Load()
    Dim query As String
    query = "SELECT * FROM Phonelist WHERE LastName
➤ LIKE 'M*' " _
```
➤

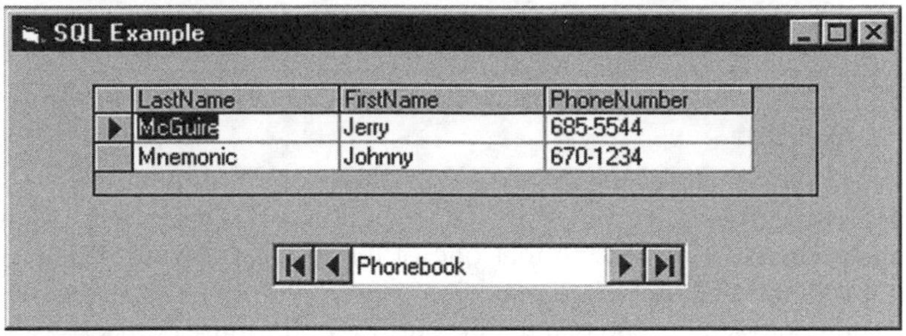

**Figure 12.14** SQL example

```
            & "ORDER BY LastName ASC"
    datPhonebook.RecordSource = query
    datPhonebook.Refresh
End Sub
```

The designers of VB have provided an alternative to SQL statements that allows you to easily find specific records. The `FindFirst`, `FindLast`, `FindNext`, and `FindPrevious` methods of a recordset find the first, last, next, and previous record matching a specific criteria, respectively. The general syntax for the `Find` method is as follows:

```
DataControl.Recordset.{FindFirst | FindLast |
 ➡ FindNext | FindPrevious} criteria
```

`DataControl` is the name of the Data control, and `criteria` specifies the search conditions. The `NoMatch` property indicates whether or not the `Find` operation succeeded. If no record satisfies the conditions specified by the search criteria, the `NoMatch` property will be True, indicating that the search failed and the current record is not defined. The programmer must allow for this condition by including code that repositions the current record pointer back to a valid record. If the search was successful, the `NoMatch` property will be False.

We now modify the `Find` operation of the `Phonebook` program presented in the previous section. The new `Find` procedure uses the `FindFirst` method and significantly reduces the amount of code. The modified procedure appears below:

```
Private Sub cmdFind_Click()
' Find a record
    Dim last As String, search As String

    last = InputBox("Enter the Last Name", "Find...")
    If last <> "" Then
        search = "LastName = '" & last & "'"
        datPhonebook.Recordset.FindFirst search
        If datPhonebook.Recordset.NoMatch Then
            MsgBox "Record not found!", , "Find..."
            datPhonebook.Recordset.MoveFirst
        End If
    End If
End Sub
```

## CREATING A DATABASE THROUGH VISUAL BASIC CODE

Creating a database by using VB code is not complex, but it is a lengthy task. The example program that follows provides a template. The `Phone` database contains two tables, `Phonelist` and `Addresslist`. The `Phone#` field is the primary key of `Addresslist`, and the `PhoneNumber` field is the foreign key of `Phonelist`. This database exhibits a **one-to-many relationship**; that is, one phone number in `Addresslist` may belong to many individuals in `Phonelist` (all living at the same address). In contrast, a **one-to-one relationship** would exist if each phone number in `Addresslist` corresponds to only one record in `Phonelist`. Figure 12.15 displays the results of executing this program.

| Object | Property | Setting |
|--------|----------|---------|
| Form | Name | frmDBExample |
| | Caption | Database Creation Example |
| Data | Name | datAddressList |
| | Caption | AddressList |
| | Connect | Access |
| | DatabaseName | C:\Phone.mdb |
| | RecordSource | Addresslist |
| Data | Name | datPhoneList |
| | Caption | PhoneList |
| | Connect | Access |
| | DatabaseName | C:\Phone.mdb |
| | RecordSource | Phonelist |
| DBGrid | Name | dbgrdAddress |
| | DataSource | datAddressList |
| DBGrid | Name | dbgrdPhone |
| | DataSource | datPhoneList |

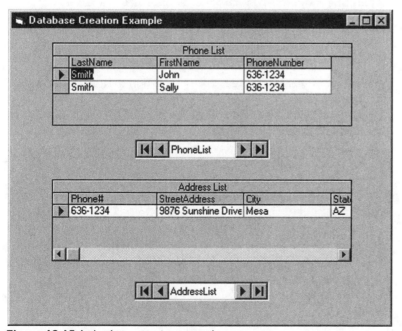

**Figure 12.15** A database creation example

```
' Database Creation Example
Option Explicit

Private Sub Form_Load()
' Create a Database File from VB code

' Define necessary variables
    Dim dbFile As Database, dbWS As Workspace
    Dim PhoneList As TableDef, AddressList As TableDef
    Dim plFields(1 To 3) As Field, alFields(1 To 5) As Field
    Dim plIndex As Index, alIndex As Index
    Dim relate As Relation
    Dim myRec As Recordset
    Dim count As Integer

' Create the Database
    Set dbWS = DBEngine.Workspaces(0)
    If Dir("C:\Phone.mdb") <> "" Then
        Kill ("C:\Phone.mdb") ' Delete previous version of the
                              ' database file
    End If
    Set dbFile = dbWS.CreateDatabase("C:\Phone.mdb",
➡ dbLangGeneral)

' Create the PhoneList Table
    Set PhoneList = dbFile.CreateTableDef("Phonelist")
    Set plFields(1) = PhoneList.CreateField("LastName",
➡ dbText, 50)
    Set plFields(2) = PhoneList.CreateField("FirstName",
➡ dbText, 50)
    Set plFields(3) = PhoneList.CreateField("PhoneNumber",
➡ dbText, 20)

' Add the new fields to the PhoneList Table
    For count = 1 To 3
        PhoneList.Fields.Append plFields(count)
    Next count

' Specify a primary key for the PhoneList Table
    Set plIndex = PhoneList.CreateIndex("PhoneNumber")
    plIndex.Primary = True
    plIndex.Unique = False
    plIndex.Required = True
    Set plFields(3) = plIndex.CreateField("PhoneNumber")

' Add the primary key field to the field list of the index
    plIndex.Fields.Append plFields(3)

' Add this index to the index list of the table
    PhoneList.Indexes.Append plIndex

' Add the table to the database
    dbFile.TableDefs.Append PhoneList

' Create the AddressList Table
```

```
    Set AddressList = dbFile.CreateTableDef("Addresslist")
    Set alFields(1) = AddressList.CreateField("Phone#",
➥ dbText, 20)
    Set alFields(2) = AddressList.CreateField
➥ ("StreetAddress", dbText, _
      50)
    Set alFields(3) = AddressList.CreateField("City",
➥ dbText, 50)
    Set alFields(4) = AddressList.CreateField("State",
➥ dbText, 25)
    Set alFields(5) = AddressList.CreateField("ZipCode",
➥ dbText, 10)

' Add the new fields to the AddressList Table
    For count = 1 To 5
        AddressList.Fields.Append alFields(count)
    Next count

' Specify a primary key for the AddressList Table
    Set alIndex = AddressList.CreateIndex("Phone#")
    alIndex.Primary = True
    alIndex.Unique = True
    alIndex.Required = True
    Set alFields(1) = alIndex.CreateField("Phone#")

' Add the primary key field to the field list of the index
    alIndex.Fields.Append alFields(1)

' Add this index to the index list of the table
    AddressList.Indexes.Append alIndex

' Add the table to the database
    dbFile.TableDefs.Append AddressList

' Set up the relation between the tables
    Set relate = dbFile.CreateRelation("foreign",
➥ "AddressList", _
      "PhoneList")
    relate.Attributes = 0

' Mark the primary field in AddressList
    Set plFields(3) = relate.CreateField("Phone#")

' Mark the foreign key in PhoneList
    plFields(3).ForeignName = "PhoneNumber"

' Add the field to the field list of the relation
    relate.Fields.Append plFields(3)

' Add the relation to the database
    dbFile.Relations.Append relate

' Open a Recordset referring to AddressList
    Set myRec = AddressList.OpenRecordset              ➥
```

```
    ' Create new records in AddressList
      myRec.AddNew
      myRec("Phone#") = "636-1234"
      myRec("StreetAddress") = "9876 Sunshine Drive"
      myRec("City") = "Mesa"
      myRec("State") = "AZ"
      myRec("ZipCode") = "83781"
      myRec.Update

    ' Close the Recordset
      myRec.Close

    ' Open a Recordset referring to PhoneList
      Set myRec = PhoneList.OpenRecordset

    ' Create new records in PhoneList
      myRec.AddNew
      myRec("LastName") = "Smith"
      myRec("FirstName") = "John"
      myRec("PhoneNumber") = "636-1234"
      myRec.Update

      myRec.AddNew
      myRec("LastName") = "Smith"
      myRec("FirstName") = "Sally"
      myRec("PhoneNumber") = "636-1234"
      myRec.Update

    ' Close the Recordset
      myRec.Close

    ' Close the database
      dbFile.Close
    End Sub
```

## PROGRAMMING KEY: VB 6.0 FEATURES

VB 6.0 contains three different database object types. **Data access objects** (**DAO**), the first data objects supported by VB, connect to only the Microsoft Jet™ database engine (the database engine in Microsoft Access). **Remote data objects** (**RDO**) are supported under Microsoft's open database connectivity (ODBC) standard and allow VB to access databases created under applications other than Microsoft Access. Finally, **ActiveX data objects** (**ADO**) are new to VB 6.0. These are the most flexible of the data objects and allow a database to be accessed on a local computer system, through a network, or over the Internet. ADOs also provide a means of accessing **OLE DB**, a set of Microsoft's Component Object Model (COM) interfaces that provides uniform access to data from a variety of information sources.

Microsoft added several new ADO and OLE DB-capable controls to VB 6.0. All editions of VB 6.0 include the DataGrid, DataList, DataCombo, Hierarchical FlexGrid, and ADO Data controls. Furthermore, the professional and enterprise editions of VB 6.0 allow the programmer to browse databases through a Data View window, and the enterprise edition contains an SQL editor.

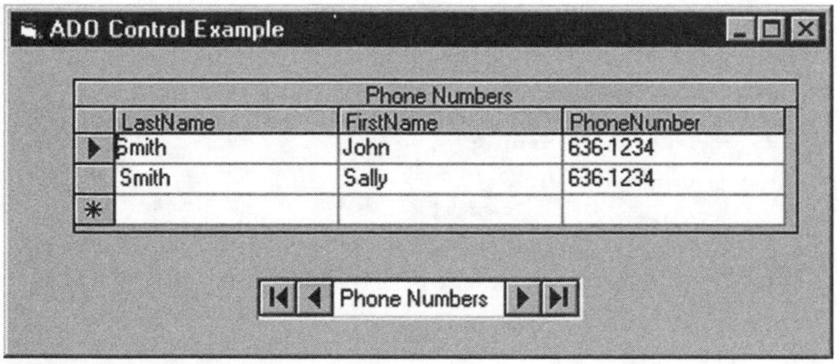

**Figure 12.16** An ADO control example

## USING ADO CONTROLS

We now use the `Phone` database created in the previous program to show an example use of ADO controls. The following program uses both the ADO Data control (Adodc) and the ADO Data Grid control (DataGrid). These controls must be added to your Toolbox by selecting them from the Components window. A sample execution of this code appears in Figure 12.16.

| Object | Property | Setting |
|--------|----------|---------|
| Form | Name | frmADOExample |
| | Caption | ADO Control Example |
| Adodc | Name | adoPhone |
| | Caption | Phone Numbers |
| DataGrid | Name | dgdPhone |
| | Caption | Phone Numbers |
| | DataSource | adoPhone |

```
' ADO Control Example
Option Explicit

Private Sub Form_Initialize()
' Initialize the ADO data control

    adoPhone.ConnectionString = "Provider=Microsoft.Jet.
    ➥ OLEDB.3.51;" & "Data Source=C:\Phone.mdb;"
    adoPhone.RecordSource = "Phonelist"
    adoPhone.Refresh
End Sub
```

---

···········································
C A S E    S T U D Y
### Designing a Relational Database

Jim wants to create a database of his personal contacts. He wants to keep important dates, such as birthdays and anniversaries, as well as address and phone number information in this database. After a little thought, Jim writes the following list of the information he desires to maintain:

Contact's first and last names

Contact's address (including street address, city, state, and zip code)

Contact's phone number

Contact's birth date

Spouse's first and last names

Anniversary date

Spouse's birth date

Children's first and last names

Children's birth dates

Fortunately, Jim just completed a database course using Microsoft Access. He designs his database using three tables: one for the contact's information, another for the spouse's information, and a third for children's information. Now, Jim has to figure out how to relate the information in these three tables. Since more than one person can have the same last name, Jim cannot use the last name as the primary key for his database. (Remember, a primary key must be unique.) Jim decides to use the phone number as the primary key in his design for two reasons:

1. Phone numbers are unique: each address has a different phone number.

2. Jim's database maintains only one phone number per address. Therefore, everyone living at the same address has the same phone number.

Jim now designs the tables and relationships in his database as shown in Figure 12.17. There is a one-to-one relationship between the Contacts table

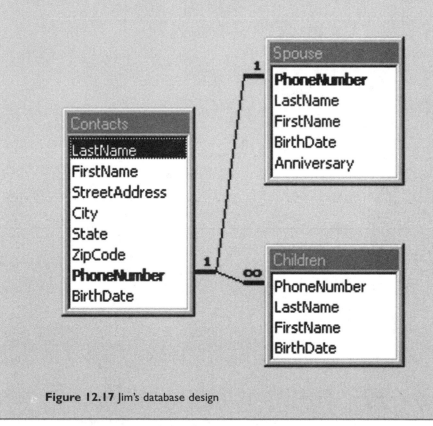

**Figure 12.17** Jim's database design

Contacts : Table

| LastName | FirstName | StreetAddress | City | State | ZipCode | PhoneNumber | BirthDate |
|---|---|---|---|---|---|---|---|
| Penner | Richard | 696 Addler Road | Syracuse | NY | 13205 | (315) 961-1545 | 11/4/69 |
| Patterson | Andrew | 1541 Windmill Lane | San Jose | CA | 95121 | (408) 451-1234 | 9/15/63 |
| Fillmore | Linda | 854 River Park Place | Richmond | VA | 23219 | (804) 531-6672 | 1/11/70 |
| Williams | Judy | 7685 Hope Blvd. | Memphis | TN | 38105 | (901) 876-5199 | 3/15/66 |

Record: 1 of 4

Spouse : Table

| PhoneNumber | LastName | FirstName | BirthDate | Anniversary |
|---|---|---|---|---|
| (315) 961-1545 | Penner | Jennifer | 8/15/71 | 6/15/92 |
| (804) 531-6672 | Fillmore | Bruce | 2/5/70 | 8/3/94 |

Record: 1 of 2

Children : Table

| PhoneNumber | LastName | FirstName | BirthDate |
|---|---|---|---|
| (315) 961-1545 | Penner | Lisa | 9/18/93 |
| (315) 961-1545 | Penner | David | 4/6/95 |
| (315) 961-1545 | Penner | Mary | 7/12/97 |
| (804) 531-6672 | Fillmore | Michael | 12/1/96 |
| (804) 531-6672 | Fillmore | Alexandra | 1/12/99 |

Record: 1 of 5

**Figure 12.18** Sample data from Jim's database

and the `Spouse` table since each contact can have at most one spouse. However, there is a one-to-many relationship between the `Contacts` table and the `Children` table since a contact can have any number of children.

Although it may seem that the use of the `LastName` fields in both the `Spouse` and `Children` tables is redundant and unnecessary, Jim knows that this design gives him the flexibility to account for step-children and spouses who keep their last names. Sample data from Jim's database appears in Figure 12.18.

# Summary

## Key Terms

**ActiveX data object (ADO)**—a data object that can access a database on a local computer, through a network, or over the Internet

**current record**—the record currently being accessed

**data access object (DAO)**—a data object that can connect to a Microsoft Access database

**Data Definition Language (DDL)**—a set of commands used to create new databases, tables, fields, and indexes

**data-aware control**—a control object that can access information from a database

**Data Manipulation Language (DML)**—a set of commands used to create queries that sort, filter, and extract data from the database

**database (or database file)**—a data file consisting of a set of related information specifically for use by a database program

**database engine**—a set of routines that perform the operations associated with a database, such as adding, deleting, sorting, and searching records

**database program**—a program that maintains a database and allows for easy storage, access, and retrieval of data

**field**—a column in a table. A field is a specific piece of information from a record.

**foreign key**—a field or set of fields that references the primary key of another table and links the two tables together

**integrity**—consistency of data

**one-to-many relationship**—an association between two tables where the primary key of one table may match the foreign key of any number of records in a second table

**one-to-one relationship**—an association between two tables where the primary key of one table may match the foreign key of only one record in a second table

**primary key**—a field or set of fields that uniquely identify each record in a table

**record**—a row in a table. A record encapsulates a group of related data and consists of a piece of data from each field.

**recordset (or view)**—a meta-table that may consist of the records from one table, multiple tables, or portions of multiple tables

**relational database**—a database consisting of two or more related tables

**remote data object (RDO)**—a data object that can connect to a database supported by Microsoft's ODBC standard

**rule of entity integrity**—no record may have an empty primary key

**rule of referential integrity**—the foreign key of one table must appear as the primary key of another table

**Structured Query Language (SQL)**—a language developed by IBM for managing, updating, and querying relational databases

**table**—a structure that stores data in rows and columns, where the rows are records and the columns are fields

**validation**—the process of preventing invalid data from being entered into the database

**wildcard character**—a single character used to represent any string of characters

## Keywords

| *Events:* | MoveFirst | DataField |
|---|---|---|
| Validate | MoveLast | EOF |
| | MoveNext | EOFAction |
| *Methods:* | MovePrevious | NoMatch |
| AddNew | Update | ReadOnly |
| Delete | | RecordCount |
| Edit | *Properties:* | Recordset |
| FindFirst | BOF | RecordSource |
| FindLast | BOFAction | Value |
| FindNext | Connect | |
| FindPrevious | DatabaseName | |

## SQL Keywords

| | | |
|---|---|---|
| * (wildcard character) | DROP | ORDER BY |
| ALTER | FROM | RIGHT JOIN |
| ASC | IN | SELECT |
| BETWEEN | INNER JOIN | UPDATE |
| CREATE | INSERT | WHERE |
| DELETE | LEFT JOIN | |
| DESC | LIKE | |

## Key Concepts

- A database program allows access to database files and provides for easy access, storage, and retrieval of data.

- A database file (or database) contains a set of related information. A database consists of one or more tables; each table contains a set of records; each record contains one or more fields; information is stored in each field.

- A database consisting of two or more related tables is called a relational database. In a relational database, the primary key and foreign key link data from one table to another.

- Maintaining the integrity, or consistency, of data in a relational database is of primary concern to programmers and database designers. The rule of entity integrity says that no record may have an empty primary key. The rule of referential integrity says that a foreign key must have an associated primary key.

- A database can be created using the VB Visual Data Manager, directly through VB code, or by using a database program, such as Microsoft Access.

- Data controls and data-aware controls allow VB to access database files. A data-aware control must be bound to a Data control to display specific information contained in the database.

- The `Recordset` property of a Data control specifies the records accessed by the control. The general syntax for accessing the methods and fields associated with a recordset follows:

  ```
  DataControl.Recordset.Method

  DataControl.Recordset.Fields("FieldName").Value
  ```

- The `Find` method quickly locates a record matching a certain criteria. The syntax follows:

  ```
  DataControl.Recordset.{FindFirst | FindLast | FindNext |
  ➡ FindPrevious} criteria
  ```

- The `Validate` event provides a means of preventing invalid data from being entered into the database. The general syntax for this event is:

  ```
  Private Sub DataControl_Validate(Action As Integer,
  ➡ Save As Integer)
     statement(s)
  End Sub
  ```

- The Structured Query Language (SQL) is a relational database language that provides both Data Definition Language (DDL) and Data Manipulation

Language (DML) commands. DDL commands include CREATE, DROP, and ALTER. DML commands are SELECT, INSERT, UPDATE, and DELETE.

● The SQL SELECT statement may be used to set the Recordset property of a Data control. The general syntax of the SELECT statement is:

SELECT *fieldList1* FROM *tableExp* [WHERE *criteria*]
➥ [ORDER BY *fieldList2* {ASC | DESC}]

● An asterisk (*) is the SQL wildcard character that is used to designate all fields of a table.

● In SQL, tables are combined using the JOIN statement. The general syntax follows:

*table1 joinType* JOIN *table2* ON *table1Field* = *table2Field*

● VB 6.0 contains three different data object types: data access objects (DAO), remote data objects (RDO), and ActiveX data objects (ADO). ActiveX data objects (ADO) are new to VB 6.0 and allow a database to be accessed on a local computer system, through a network, or over the Internet.

## Review Questions

1. Describe the organization of a typical database in terms of tables, records, and fields.
2. What is a relational database?
3. How can you create a database without using VB? using VB?
4. State the rule of entity integrity and the rule of referential integrity.
5. Summarize the five guidelines for designing an efficient database.
6. What is the difference between a Data control and a data-aware control? How do you access a database using these VB controls?
7. What is a recordset?
8. What is the purpose of validation and how is it accomplished in VB?
9. What is SQL? Describe the two different types of SQL commands.
10. Name the three different VB database object types.

## Chapter 12 Problems

1. Honest Joe's Used Cars has a current inventory of nine cars listed in the table below. Use Microsoft Access or the VB Visual Data Manager to create a database and enter this data.

| Make | Model | Year | Mileage | Color | Condition | Vehicle ID |
|------|-------|------|---------|-------|-----------|------------|
| Chevrolet | Camaro | 1994 | 89546 | Black | Fair | IZ90763 |
| Dodge | Stratus | 1996 | 43128 | Black | Good | YL65428 |
| Ford | Escort | 1997 | 27021 | Red | Excellent | IP87654 |
| Ford | Taurus | 1993 | 63827 | Maroon | Good | WB15036 |
| Honda | Accord | 1994 | 87543 | Silver | Fair | VB83921 |
| Honda | Accord | 1996 | 52371 | Blue | Good | ZX58723 |
| Mazda | 626 | 1994 | 64180 | Yellow | Excellent | PY89045 |
| Toyota | Camry | 1991 | 109546 | Red | Fair | LX45687 |
| Toyota | Celica | 1992 | 101003 | Silver | Good | TV99325 |

2. Write a VB program that is a "front-end" to Honest Joe's database in Problem 1. The interface should contain command buttons to add, edit, remove, and search records in the database. Do not use SQL commands in your program.

3. Modify your program from Problem 2 to use SQL commands.

4. The current semester course listings for the Computer Science Department at Western State University appear in the table below. Create a relational database using Microsoft Access or the VB Visual Data Manager and enter this data.

| Course number | Course title | Instructor | Number of students |
|---|---|---|---|
| CS100 | Introductory Programming | Kerman | 29 |
| CS100 | Introductory Programming | Brown | 28 |
| CS100 | Introductory Programming | Perkins | 21 |
| CS101 | Advanced Programming | Brown | 17 |
| CS201 | Assembly Language Programming | Perkins | 19 |
| CS210 | Object-Oriented Programming | Smith | 18 |
| CS210 | Object-Oriented Programming | Wesson | 15 |
| CS220 | Data Structures | Finney | 11 |
| CS220 | Data Structures | Jackson | 13 |
| CS300 | Computer Architecture | Kerman | 14 |

5. Write a VB program that is a "front-end" to the database in Problem 4. The interface should contain command buttons to add, edit, remove, and search records in the database. Do not use SQL commands in your program.

6. Modify your program from Problem 5 to use SQL commands.

## Programming Projects

1. Create a checkbook register database through VB code. The database should contain fields for the check number, date, payee, check amount, and notes.

2. Extend your program from Project 1 to include a graphical "front-end" to your database. The interface should contain command buttons to add, edit, remove, and search records in the database. Additionally, your database should contain a second table that tracks the current checking account balance, and this information should be displayed in the interface.

# ASCII (ANSI) Character Values

In the following list, blanks indicate characters that are not supported by Microsoft Windows.

| | | | | | | | |
|---|---|---|---|---|---|---|---|
| 0 | | 32 | [space] | 64 | @ | 96 | ' |
| 1 | | 33 | ! | 65 | A | 97 | a |
| 2 | | 34 | " | 66 | B | 98 | b |
| 3 | | 35 | # | 67 | C | 99 | c |
| 4 | | 36 | $ | 68 | D | 100 | d |
| 5 | | 37 | % | 69 | E | 101 | e |
| 6 | | 38 | & | 70 | F | 102 | f |
| 7 | | 39 | ' | 71 | G | 103 | g |
| 8 | BS | 40 | ( | 72 | H | 104 | h |
| 9 | TAB | 41 | ) | 73 | I | 105 | i |
| 10 | LF | 42 | * | 74 | J | 106 | j |
| 11 | | 43 | + | 75 | K | 107 | k |
| 12 | | 44 | , | 76 | L | 108 | l |
| 13 | CR | 45 | - | 77 | M | 109 | m |
| 14 | | 46 | . | 78 | N | 110 | n |
| 15 | | 47 | / | 79 | O | 111 | o |
| 16 | | 48 | 0 | 80 | P | 112 | p |
| 17 | | 49 | 1 | 81 | Q | 113 | q |
| 18 | | 50 | 2 | 82 | R | 114 | r |
| 19 | | 51 | 3 | 83 | S | 115 | s |
| 20 | | 52 | 4 | 84 | T | 116 | t |
| 21 | | 53 | 5 | 85 | U | 117 | u |
| 22 | | 54 | 6 | 86 | V | 118 | v |
| 23 | | 55 | 7 | 87 | W | 119 | w |
| 24 | | 56 | 8 | 88 | X | 120 | x |
| 25 | | 57 | 9 | 89 | Y | 121 | y |
| 26 | | 58 | : | 90 | Z | 122 | z |
| 27 | | 59 | ; | 91 | [ | 123 | { |
| 28 | | 61 | < | 92 | \ | 124 | | |
| 29 | | 61 | = | 93 | ] | 125 | } |
| 30 | | 62 | > | 94 | ^ | 126 | ~ |
| 31 | | 63 | ? | 95 | _ | 127 | |

| | | | | | | |
|---|---|---|---|---|---|---|
| 128 | 160 | [space] | 192 | À | 224 | à |
| 129 | 161 | ¡ | 193 | Á | 225 | á |
| 130 | 162 | ¢ | 194 | Â | 226 | â |
| 131 | 163 | £ | 195 | Ã | 227 | ã |
| 132 | 164 | ¤ | 196 | Ä | 228 | ä |
| 133 | 165 | ¥ | 197 | Å | 229 | å |
| 134 | 166 | ¦ | 198 | Æ | 230 | æ |
| 135 | 167 | § | 199 | Ç | 231 | ç |
| 136 | 168 | ¨ | 200 | È | 232 | è |
| 137 | 169 | © | 201 | É | 233 | é |
| 138 | 170 | ª | 202 | Ê | 234 | ê |
| 139 | 171 | « | 203 | Ë | 235 | ë |
| 140 | 172 | ¬ | 204 | Ì | 236 | ì |
| 141 | 173 | – | 205 | Í | 237 | í |
| 142 | 174 | ® | 206 | Î | 238 | î |
| 143 | 175 | ¯ | 207 | Ï | 239 | ï |
| 144 | 176 | ° | 208 | Ð | 240 | ∂ |
| 145 | ' | 177 | ± | 209 | Ñ | 241 | ñ |
| 146 | ' | 178 | ² | 210 | Ò | 242 | ò |
| 147 | 179 | ³ | 211 | Ó | 243 | ó |
| 148 | 180 | ´ | 212 | Ô | 244 | ô |
| 149 | 181 | µ | 213 | Õ | 245 | õ |
| 150 | 182 | ¶ | 214 | Ö | 246 | ö |
| 151 | 183 | · | 215 | x | 247 | ÷ |
| 152 | 184 | ¸ | 216 | Ø | 248 | ø |
| 153 | 185 | ¹ | 217 | Ù | 249 | ù |
| 154 | 186 | º | 218 | Ú | 250 | ú |
| 155 | 187 | » | 219 | Û | 251 | û |
| 156 | 188 | 1/4 | 220 | Ü | 252 | ü |
| 157 | 189 | 1/2 | 221 | Ý | 253 | ý |
| 158 | 190 | 3/4 | 222 | ρ | 254 | þ |
| 159 | 191 | ¿ | 223 | ß | 255 | ÿ |

# Visual Basic Programming Standards

The *Visual Basic Programming Standards* from the Operations Research Department at Naval Postgraduate School (NPS) are presented here as an example.

## NPS OPERATIONS RESEARCH DEPARTMENT VISUAL BASIC PROGRAMMING STANDARDS

### DOCUMENTATION IN THE SOURCE CODE

D1. Each program must begin with comments that include your name, course and segment number, and the date.

D2. Each subprogram must have brief comments at the beginning that describe what the subprogram does. Studies have shown that general descriptions at the beginning of each subprogram are more valuable than comments distributed throughout the code. The comments should cover what the code does rather than how the code does it. (You can trace the code to see how it works.)

D3. Comments and blank lines that indicate the major sections of the program are useful.

D4. If (and only if) the meaning of a statement or group of statements is not clear from reading the code, brief comments may be included in the body of the program. In general, these comments are not useful. If they merely state what is obvious from reading the code, they detract. If these comments are necessary, place them at the beginning of the block of code. This will reduce their disruption to the structure of the program.

D5. Variable and subprogram names should be chosen to help describe their meaning. A poorly chosen name that misleads the reader is worse than a nondescript name like X or A. Variable names must be written with lowercase letters, except for the first letter of embedded words which are written in uppercase, such as `taxRate`, `numberOfCars`, and so on.

D6. Object classes and variables begin with an uppercase letter. Method names begin with an uppercase letter.

D7. Each control object name begins with a lowercase, three-letter prefix that indicates the type of control object. For instance, a form begins with frm, a text box with txt, and a command button with cmd. The remainder of the name describes the control's purpose or contents. For example, txtLastName is a text box containing the last name.

## SOFTWARE ENGINEERING STANDARDS

S1. All real and double constants must have a decimal point with a digit on each side.

S2. Mixed-mode arithmetic is arithmetic containing variables of different data types. When possible, avoid mixed-mode arithmetic expressions and mixed-mode variable assignments. Use the data type conversion functions as necessary.

S3. When converting a string to an equivalent numeric value, use the VAL function. When converting a numeric value to a string, use the STR function.

S4. Expressions containing multiple operators and operators of different types must have parentheses for clarity and to indicate precedence.

S5. All variables must be declared. The compiler option that requires explicit declaration of variables must be set. Variable declarations must appear at the beginning of their subprogram.

S6. Unnecessary code should be removed. This is particularly important when the code is inside of a loop that will be executed numerous times. It is not necessary to assign the value zero to a variable or array element before it is assigned a value by another statement. Any such assignment is unnecessary and will be viewed as a violation of this standard.

S7. Avoid global variables. There are potential problems when more than one function or subprogram uses the same variable; one may change the value of a global variable that would then have an impact on another's use of the variable. Sharing variables by passing them as parameters is preferred because it makes the shared use explicit.

## USER INTERFACE

U1. Visual Basic has many different user controls: command buttons, option buttons, drop-down menus, and so on. The user interface that you select should reflect the best user control for the task at hand. For example, if the user must select from several mutually exclusive options, the best choice would be option buttons.

U2. Consistency is a key factor for usability. Use standard dialog boxes whenever possible. For example, there is little benefit in inventing your own dialog box to open a file. Use the common dialog control.

U3. Plan multiple form interfaces carefully. Be sure that you group items in a form in a logical and consistent manner. Avoid the extremes of too many forms or a form that is so overpowering that it is difficult to comprehend.

## ERROR PREVENTION

E1. For each division operation, there should be either a test to determine that the divisor is not equal to zero or a comment that explains why it can never be equal to zero.

## INDENTATION AND BLOCKS

I1. Indentation is an extremely important element of readability. Statements within a subprogram should be indented three spaces. The body of the loop should be indented three more spaces. An example follows:

```
Private Sub cmdLoop_Click()
   Dim outer As Integer

   Rem Subprogram code goes here

   For outer = 1 To 16
      Rem The body of the loop goes here
   Next outer
End Sub
```

Nested loops follow the same pattern, as in the following example:

```
Private Sub cmdNestedLoop_Click()
   Dim outer As Integer
   Dim inner As Integer

   Rem Subprogram code goes here

   For outer = 1 To 16
      Rem The outer loop body goes here
      For inner = 1 To 100
         Rem The inner loop body goes here
      Next inner
      Rem Other outer loop statements go here
   Next outer
End Sub
```

I2. Statements within a decision structure should be indented three spaces, as shown in the following example:

```
Private Sub cmdDecision_Click()
   Dim number As Integer
   number = CInt(Val(txtInput.Text))

   If number > 0 Then
      Rem "If True" statements go here
   Else
      Rem "If False" statements go here
```

```
      End If
End Sub
```

Nested If statements follow the same pattern, as shown below:

```
Private Sub cmdNestedDecision_Click()
    Dim left As Integer
    Dim right As Integer

    Rem Subprogram code goes here

    If left > 0 Then
       Rem "If True" statements go here
    Else
       If right > 0 Then
          Rem Nested "If True" statements go here
       Else
          Rem Nested "If False" statements go here
       End If
    End If
End Sub
```

## REPETITION

R1. Visual Basic has three repetition constructs: the Do While-Loop, the Do-Loop Until, and the For-Next loop. For some repetition situations in a program, there is only one possible repetition construct that can be used. In most situations there is a choice. Each repetition construct was designed for a specific situation; therefore, it is possible to develop standards that will dictate the appropriate repetition to use in most programming situations. The following guidelines almost always dictate the appropriate choice:

a. The Do While-Loop and Do-Loop Until constructs are called indefinite (or indeterminate) repetition structures because the number of times that the loop is executed depends upon calculations within the loop. In contrast, the For-Next construct is called a definite (or determinate) repetition structure because the number of executions of the loop (if any) is determined before any execution of the loop. When possible, use a definite repetition structure (that is, a For-Next) rather than an indefinite one.

b. In choosing between the Do While-Loop and Do-Loop Until constructs, if the loop must be executed at least once, then the Do-Loop Until is the appropriate choice because its selection clearly shows that the loop will be executed at least once. Thus, the Do While-Loop is used exclusively in situations where the loop may not be executed at all depending on the value of the logical expression.

# Visual Basic Trappable Errors

| Code | Message | Code | Message |
|---|---|---|---|
| 3 | Return without GoSub | 61 | Disk full |
| 5 | Invalid procedure call | 62 | Input past end of file |
| 6 | Overflow | 63 | Bad record number |
| 7 | Out of memory | 67 | Too many files |
| 9 | Subscript out of range | 68 | Device unavailable |
| 10 | This array is fixed or temporarily locked | 70 | Permission denied |
| | | 71 | Disk not ready |
| 11 | Division by zero | 74 | Can't rename with different drive |
| 13 | Type mismatch | | |
| 14 | Out of string space | 75 | Path/File access error |
| 16 | Expression too complex | 76 | Path not found |
| 17 | Can't perform requested operation | 91 | Object variable or With block variable not set |
| 18 | User interrupt occurred | 92 | For loop not initialized |
| 20 | Resume without error | 93 | Invalid pattern string |
| 28 | Out of stack space | 94 | Invalid use of Null |
| 35 | Sub, Function, or Property not defined | 97 | Can't call Friend procedure on an object that is not an instance of the defining class |
| 47 | Too many DLL application clients | 98 | A property or method call cannot include a reference to a private object, either as an argument or as a return value |
| 48 | Error in loading DLL | | |
| 49 | Bad DLL calling convention | | |
| 51 | Internal error | | |
| 52 | Bad file name or number | 298 | System DLL could not be loaded |
| 53 | File not found | | |
| 54 | Bad file mode | 320 | Can't use character device names in specified file names |
| 55 | File already open | | |
| 57 | Device I/O error | | |
| 58 | File already exists | 321 | Invalid file format |
| 59 | Bad record length | 322 | Can't create necessary temporary file |

| Code | Message | Code | Message |
|------|---------|------|---------|
| 325 | Invalid format in resource file | 402 | Code must close topmost modal form first |
| 327 | Data value named not found | 419 | Permission to use object denied |
| 328 | Illegal parameter; can't write arrays | 422 | Property not found |
| 335 | Could not access system registry | 423 | Property or method not found |
| 336 | ActiveX component not correctly registered | 424 | Object required |
| | | 425 | Invalid object use |
| 337 | ActiveX component not found | 429 | ActiveX component can't create object or return reference to this object |
| 338 | ActiveX component did not run correctly | 430 | Class doesn't support Automation |
| 360 | Object already loaded | 432 | File name or class name not found during Automation operation |
| 361 | Can't load or unload this object | | |
| 363 | ActiveX control specified not found | 438 | Object doesn't support this property or method |
| 364 | Object was unloaded | 440 | Automation error |
| 365 | Unable to unload within this context | 442 | Connection to type library or object library for remote process has been lost |
| 368 | The specified file is out of date. This program requires a later version | 443 | Automation object doesn't have a default value |
| | | 445 | Object doesn't support this action |
| 371 | The specified object can't be used as an owner form for Show | 446 | Object doesn't support named arguments |
| 380 | Invalid property value | 447 | Object doesn't support current locale setting |
| 381 | Invalid property-array index | 448 | Named argument not found |
| 382 | Property Set can't be executed at run time | 449 | Argument not optional or invalid property assignment |
| 383 | Property Set can't be used with a read-only property | 450 | Wrong number of arguments or invalid property assignment |
| 385 | Need property-array index | 451 | Object not a collection |
| 387 | Property Set not permitted | 452 | Invalid ordinal |
| 393 | Property Get can't be executed at run time | 453 | Specified DLL function not found |
| 394 | Property Get can't be executed on write-only property | 454 | Code resource not found |
| | | 455 | Code resource lock error |
| 400 | Form already displayed; can't show modally | 457 | This key is already associated with an element of this collection |

| Code | Message | Code | Message |
|---|---|---|---|
| 458 | Variable uses a type not supported in Visual Basic | 486 | Can't print form image to this type of printer |
| 459 | This component doesn't support the set of events | 520 | Can't empty Clipboard |
| 460 | Invalid Clipboard format | 521 | Can't open Clipboard |
| 461 | Specified format doesn't match format of data | 735 | Can't save file to TEMP directory |
| 480 | Can't create AutoRedraw image | 744 | Search text not found |
| 481 | Invalid picture | 746 | Replacements too long |
| 482 | Printer error | 31001 | Out of memory |
| 483 | Printer driver does not support specified property | 31004 | No object |
|  |  | 31018 | Class is not set |
| 484 | Problem getting printer information from the system. Make sure the printer is set up correctly | 31027 | Unable to activate object |
|  |  | 31032 | Unable to create embedded object |
| 485 | Invalid picture type | 31036 | Error saving to file |
|  |  | 31037 | Error loading from file |

# Visual Basic Keyword Summary

## VARIABLES AND CONSTANTS

| | |
|---|---|
| Assignment | Let |
| Declaration | Const, Dim, Private, Public, New, Static |
| Check data type | IsArray, IsDate, IsEmpty, IsError, IsMissing, IsNull, IsNumeric, IsObject, TypeName, VarType |
| Refer to current object | Me |
| Require explicit variable declarations | Option Explicit |
| Set default data type | Deftype |

## OPERATORS

| | |
|---|---|
| Arithmetic | ^, - , *, /, \, Mod, +, & |
| Comparison | =, <>, <, >, <=, >=, Like, Is |
| Logical | Not, And, Or, Xor, Eqv, Imp |

## DATA TYPES

| | |
|---|---|
| Convert data type | CBool, CByte, CCur, CDate, CDbl, CDec, CInt, CLng, CSng, CStr, CVar, CVErr, Fix, Int |
| Intrinsic data types | Boolean, Byte, Currency, Date, Double, Integer, Long, Object, Single, String, Variant (default) |
| Verify data types | IsArray, IsDate, IsEmpty, IsError, IsMissing, IsNull, IsNumeric, IsObject |

## MATH

| | |
|---|---|
| Trigonometric functions | Atn, Cos, Sin, Tan |
| General calculations | Exp, Log, Sqr |
| Generate random numbers | Randomize, Rnd |
| Get absolute value | Abs |
| Get the sign of an expression | Sgn |
| Perform numeric conversions | Fix, Int |

## STRINGS

| | |
|---|---|
| Compare two strings | StrComp |
| Convert strings | StrConv |
| Convert case | LCase, UCase |

| | |
|---|---|
| Create a string of a repeating character | Space, String |
| Find length of a string | Len |
| Format a string | Format |
| Justify a string | LSet, RSet |
| Manipulate strings | InStr, Left, LTrim, Mid, Right, RTrim, Trim |
| Set string comparison rules | Option Compare |
| Work with ASCII (or ANSI) values | Asc, Chr |

## CONVERSIONS

| | |
|---|---|
| ASCII value to a character | Chr |
| Convert case | LCase, UCase |
| Date to serial number | DateSerial, DateValue |
| Decimal to other bases | Hex, Oct |
| Number to a string | Format, Str |
| Convert data type | CBool, CByte, CCur, CDate, CDbl, CDec, CInt, CLng, CSng, CStr, CVar, CVErr, Fix, Int |
| Date to day, month, weekday, or year | Day, Month, Weekday, Year |
| Time to hour, minute, or second | Hour, Minute, Second |
| Character to ASCII value | Asc |
| String to a number | Val |
| Time to serial number | TimeSerial, TimeValue |

## DATES AND TIMES

| | |
|---|---|
| Get the current date or time | Date, Now, Time |
| Perform date calculations | DateAdd, DateDiff, DatePart |
| Return a date | DateSerial, DateValue |
| Return a time | TimeSerial, TimeValue |
| Set the date or time | Date, Time |
| Time a process | Timer |

## FINANCIAL

| | |
|---|---|
| Calculate depreciation | DDB, SLN, SYD |
| Calculate future value | FV |
| Calculate interest rate | Rate |
| Calculate internal rate of return | IRR, MIRR |
| Calculate number of periods | NPer |
| Calculate payments | IPmt, Pmt, PPmt |
| Calculate present value | NPV, PV |

## CONTROL FLOW

| | |
|---|---|
| Branch | GoSub...Return, GoTo, On Error, On...GoSub, On...GoTo |
| Exit or halt a program | DoEvents, End, Exit, Stop |
| Loops | Do...Loop, For...Next, For Each...Next, While...Wend, With |
| Decisions | Choose, If...Then...Else, Select Case, Switch |
| Procedures | Call, Function, Property Get, Property Let, Property Set, Sub |

## INPUT AND OUTPUT

| | |
|---|---|
| Access or create a file | `Open` |
| Close files | `Close, Reset` |
| Control output appearance | `Format, Print, Print #, Spc, Tab, Width #` |
| Copy a file | `FileCopy` |
| Get file information | `EOF, FileAttr, FileDateTime, FileLen, FreeFile, GetAttr, Loc, LOF, Seek` |
| File management | `Dir, Kill, Lock, Unlock, Name` |
| Read from a file | `Get, Input, Input #, Line Input #` |
| Length of a file | `FileLen` |
| File attributes | `FileAttr, GetAttr, SetAttr` |
| Set read-write position in a file | `Seek` |
| Write to a file | `Print #, Put, Write #` |

## ARRAYS

| | |
|---|---|
| Verify an array | `IsArray` |
| Create an array | `Array` |
| Change default lower limit | `Option Base` |
| Declare and initialize an array | `Dim, Private, Public, ReDim, Static` |
| Find the limits of an array | `LBound, UBound` |
| Reinitialize an array | `Erase, ReDim` |

## COLLECTIONS

| | |
|---|---|
| Create a collection object | `Collection` |
| Add an object to a collection | `Add` |
| Remove an object from a collection | `Remove` |
| Reference an item in a collection | `Item` |

## COMPILER DIRECTIVES

| | |
|---|---|
| Define compiler constant | `#Const` |
| Compile selected blocks of code | `#If...Then...#Else` |

## DIRECTORIES AND FILES

| | |
|---|---|
| Change directory or folder | `ChDir` |
| Change the drive | `ChDrive` |
| Copy a file | `FileCopy` |
| Make directory or folder | `MkDir` |
| Remove directory or folder | `RmDir` |
| Rename a file, directory, or folder | `Name` |
| Return current path | `CurDir` |
| Return file date/time stamp | `FileDateTime` |
| Return file, directory, label attributes | `GetAttr` |
| Return file length | `FileLen` |
| Return file name or volume label | `Dir` |
| Set attribute information for a file | `SetAttr` |

## ERRORS

| | |
|---|---|
| Generate run-time errors | `Clear, Error, Raise` |
| Get error messages | `Error` |
| Provide error information | `Err` |
| Return error variant | `CVErr` |
| Trap errors during run time | `On Error, Resume` |
| Error type verification | `IsError` |

## MISCELLANEOUS

| | |
|---|---|
| Process pending events | `DoEvents` |
| Run other programs | `AppActivate, Shell` |
| Send keystrokes to an application | `SendKeys` |
| Sound a beep from computer | `Beep` |
| System | `Environ` |
| Provide a command-line string | `Command` |
| Automation | `CreateObject, GetObject` |
| Color | `QBColor, RGB` |

# Index